✓ KU-172-450

'Lepers outside the gate'

Excavations at the cemetery of the Hospital of St James and St Mary Magdalene, Chichester, 1986–87 and 1993

Edited by John Magilton, Frances Lee and Anthea Boylston

With contributions by

Margaret Judd, James Kenny, Mary Lewis,
Keith Manchester, Alan Ogden, Donald Ortner,
Rebecca Storm, Judi Sture

Chichester Excavations 10
CBA Research Report 158
Council for British Archaeology
2008

UNIVERSITY OF WINCHESTER
LIBRARY

Published in 2008 by the Council for British Archaeology
St Mary's House, 66 Bootham, York YO30 7BZ

Copyright © 2008 Authors and Council for British Archaeology

British Library Cataloguing in Publication Data
A catalogue record for this book is available from the British Library

ISBN 978-1-902771-74-8

Cover designed by BP Design, York
Typeset by Archétype Informatique SARL, 11200 Camplong d'Aude, France, www.archetype-it.com
Printed and bound in the UK by Henry Ling Ltd, Dorchester

UNIVERSITY OF WINCHESTER

03071634   94e. e
          MAG

Front cover: A leper woman with a bell, from the Exeter Pontifical, *c* 1400 (BL Lansdowne Ms 451, f 127, © The British Library)
Back cover: (top to bottom) Damage to the feet of adult male burial 21, caused by leprosy; rear of the 'leper cottage', showing the two major building phases; mature male 368 with nodular clumps of calculus, resulting from severe rhinomaxillary syndrome; part of the cemetery during excavation, December 1993

'Lepers outside the gate'

Excavations at the cemetery
of the Hospital of St James and St Mary Magdalene,
Chichester, 1986–87 and 1993

KA 0307163 4

WITHDRAWN FROM THE LIBRARY UNIVERSITY OF WINCHESTER

Contents

Part 4   Discussion

Contents of CD

Appendices for Part 3

List of figures

Picture credits

The photographs for the osteology chapters were taken by Alan Ogden and Rebecca Storm, apart from those in Chapter 14 which were the work of Donald Ortner. The exceptions are either noted in the caption to individual illustrations or listed below.

Figure 10.6 is published by permission of the British Library. The item is *'The forme and shape of a monstrous child, borne at Maydstone in Kent, the xxxiij of October 1568*. Huth. 50, f. 38. Iohn Awdeley, London 1568.

Figure 11.1 is published by permission of the British Library and is entitled *'A description of a monstrous Chylde, borne at Chychester in Sussex, the xxiii daye of May.'* Produced by Leonard Askel for Fraunces Godlyf: London, 1562.

Figure 12.1 is published by permission of the British Library. It comes from the manuscript entitled *'History of the Crusades'* by William of Tyre, Yates Thompson 12, f. 152v. French, between 1250 and 1259.

The photographs comprising Figure 12.10 are from the research slide collection of Donald J Ortner, Department of Anthropology, Smithsonian Institution, Washington, DC, digitised and made available through funds supporting NSF grant SES-0138129 by Richard H Steckel, Clark Spencer Larsen, Paul W Sciulli and Phiilip L Walker, *A History of Health in Europe from the Late Paleolithic Era to the Present* (Mimeo, Columbus, Ohio, 2002).

Figure 16.1 is published by permission of the British Library from manuscript 1187.a.8(1), f. opposite 96, entitled *'Charisma Basilicon, or, the Royal Gift of Healing Strumaes, or Kings-Evil, Swellings by Contact, or Imposition of the Sacred Hands of our Kings of England, etc.'* Author John Brown. London, 1684.

Figure 18.11 is published by permission of the British Library from manuscript Sloane 2345, f. 44v entitled *'Li Livres dou Santé'* by Aldobrandino of Siena. French, late 13th century.

The anatomical diagrams in the Glossary of medical terms are by Caroline Needham.

List of tables

List of tables on CD

Appendix 7: Data to support Chapter 9

Appendix 11: Data to support Chapter 18

Affiliations of contributors

Anthea Boylston MSc, Honorary Research Fellow, Biological Anthropology Research Centre, Division of Archaeological, Geographical and Environmental Sciences, University of Bradford, Bradford, BD7 1DP

Rob Janaway BSc, Lecturer in Archaeological Sciences, University of Bradford, Bradford, BD7 1DP

Margaret Judd BA MSc PhD, Assistant Professor of Anthropology, 3302 WWPH, University of Pittsburgh, Pittsburgh, Pennsylvania, 15260, USA

James Kenny BA, Archaeology Officer, Chichester District Council, East Pallant House, Chichester, West Sussex, PO19 1TY

Frances Lee BA MSc, freelance human osteologist, Church Farm House, Hughley, Shrewsbury, SY5 6ND

Mary Lewis BA MSc PhD, Lecturer in Palaeohealth, Department of Archaeology, University of Reading, Whiteknights, PO Box 217, Reading, Berkshire, RG6 6AH

John Magilton BA MPhil FSA MIFA, archaeological consultant, The Old Cottage, North End Road, Yapton, Arundel, West Sussex, BN18 0DS

Keith Manchester, MB BS BSc DSc(Hon), Honorary Visiting Lecturer and Research Fellow in Palaeopathology at the University of Bradford (retired). Locum General Practitioner in Bradford.

Alan R Ogden BDS BA MSc DDSc DRDRCS, Honorary Research Fellow, Biological Anthropology Research Centre, Division of Archaeological, Geographical and Environmental Sciences, University of Bradford, Bradford, BD7 1DP

Donald Ortner, BA MA PhD, Professor of Anthropology, National Museum of Natural History, Smithsonian Institution, Washington DC, 20560, USA

Rebecca Storm BA MSc, PhD student, Biological Anthropology Research Centre, Division of Archaeological, Geographical and Environmental Sciences, University of Bradford, Bradford, BD7 1DP

Judi Sture BSc PhD, Director of Postgraduate Research Training Programmes, Graduate School, University of Bradford, Bradford, BD7 1DP

Acknowledgments

John Magilton writes:

My first thanks go to those members of Chichester District Archaeological Unit who dug the site in the very cold winter of 1986–87 and the wet December of 1993. Without their work there would be no report, and without their diligent recording of what at times was a tedious site, the report would be poorer. Thanks are also due to Chichester District Council, in particular its Archaeological Advisory Committee, for backing the project despite, I suspect, some personal reservations.

Bradford University's involvement began with a phone call from Dr Keith Manchester on behalf of the Calvin Wells Laboratory, and through him began a happy twenty-year association with my co-author Frances Lee, at that time research assistant at the laboratory, who carried out the initial analysis of all the skeletal remains. By 1993 Frances was working freelance but the earlier bone assemblage was still at Bradford where several generations of students had studied and in some cases published reports on various aspects of the skeletons. When eventually I was able to write up the site, we turned again to the Calvin Wells Laboratory, initially for help with updating the report by incorporating references to the best papers, published or not, by their students, and we were lucky enough to gain the support, co-operation and active assistance of Anthea Boylston who, through her own contributions and soliciting work from others, has ensured that the bone report is as complete and comprehensive as it can be.

Because the report will be both volume 10 in the *Chichester Excavations* series and a CBA research report it contains perhaps rather more background on the history and archaeology of leper houses and their cemeteries than might be expected from the latter. The former has a local readership interested primarily in Chichester and its environs that may be unfamiliar with the wider context. The historical sections of the report have been looked at and commented on in much detail by Prof Carole Rawcliffe (University of East Anglia), to whom I am greatly indebted, and by Tim and Alison McCann of the West Sussex Record Office. The report in general, but the archaeological parts specifically, has been much improved following suggestions by Barney Sloane (English Heritage), and Elizabeth Popescu (Cambridge Archaeology) has also kindly commented on the archaeological aspects and supplied details of her own work in advance of publication. Some initial analysis of the site was carried out by Robbie Browse, James Kenny and other colleagues in Southern Archaeology. James Kenny, now of Chichester District Council, has also assisted in the production of many computer-generated distribution plots in the first part of the report. Most of the final text was compiled at the writer's home and my wife Eleanor deserves thanks for many tedious hours helping to check and recheck the statistics behind the distribution diagrams.

In 2005 Chichester District Council cut its budget for post-excavation studies and it looked as if the report might never be published. However, a phone call to Jane Thorniley-Walker, then editor of CBA Research Reports, met with a positive response, later endorsed by the editorial committee, and her successor Catrina Appleby has been equally helpful in steering the project towards a successful conclusion. Particular thanks are due to Frances Mee for her meticulousness as a copy editor, and for her patience with an author suffering from a spell of ill-health at the critical time.

Frances Lee and Anthea Boylston write:

As far as the post-excavation analysis is concerned, the curation of the human bone, which enabled researchers and academics to have access to the collection, was made possible through Charlotte Roberts, Zoë Chundun and Darlene Weston. Various heads of the Department of Archaeological Sciences at the University of Bradford are thanked for providing facilities for storage of the human remains and for their study both in the laboratory and by X-ray analysis. These include Arnold Aspinall, Mark Pollard, Randy Donahue, Robin Coningham and currently Holger Schutkowski, who is Head of Division in the School of Life Sciences. Charlotte Roberts and Christopher Knüsel have been instrumental in encouraging students to take a fresh look at the Chichester material and undertake original pieces of research. Dr Simon Mays, who reviewed the osteology chapters, did a very thorough job and his comments were most useful.

Donald Ortner wishes to record his debt of gratitude to the pioneer research done on the subject by the late Professor Vilhelm Møller-Christensen. He has also benefited from conversations with Dr Johs Andersen who shared his knowledge of modern-day leprosy as well as his own experience in the analysis of Danish medieval evidence of this disease. His colleagues at the University of Bradford provided advice, assistance and extraordinary hospitality during his many extended visits to the University. His greatest debt is to his friend and colleague Dr Keith Manchester who first invited him to conduct research on the osteology collections curated at the University of Bradford, including the remarkable skeletal sample excavated from the medieval cemetery associated with the hospital of St James and St Mary Magdalene in Chichester.

Other researchers who have contributed to this volume are thanked and acknowledged in the foreword to Part 3. Finally we would like to acknowledge the patience and support of our partners, in particular Ann Manchester and Ian Yarroll, who have lived with this project for over twenty years.

The Council for British Archaelogy would like to thank Chichester District Council for their generous contribution towards the production costs of this volume.

Summary

This report, number 10 in the *Chichester Excavations* series, describes and discusses the excavation of nearly 400 skeletons of men, women and children from the cemetery of the medieval and later Hospital of St James and St Mary Magdalene, originally for leper men, just outside Chichester, West Sussex, UK. This is by far the largest sample of skeletons from an English medieval hospital to be excavated and published to date, and the first sizeable group of European leper graves to be excavated and studied for a generation. Two adjacent parts of the cemetery, an unknown percentage of the whole, were excavated in 1986–87 and 1993, both in advance of development, and both the fieldwork and post-excavation analysis of the archaeology were funded by Chichester District Council. The fieldwork was directed by John Magilton, at the time Chichester District Archaeologist, and carried out by members of Chichester District Archaeological Unit. The skeletal remains form part of the teaching collection at the Biological Anthropology Research Centre, University of Bradford, where most of the palaeopathology was done, and Chichester District Council holds the finds and primary written records.

The report is divided into four parts. The first two are written by John Magilton, the excavator of the site. Part 1 begins with the background to the fieldwork. The Chichester hospital was originally founded as a leprosarium for men in the 12th century, so the nature of the disease and contemporary attitudes and responses to it are discussed in Chapter 2. Medieval hospitals in general, leper hospitals in particular, and their aims and regimes, are also examined, as is their survival of the Reformation. Chapter 3 is an introduction to medieval and early modern cemeteries in England and various other topics related to death and dying, including funerals and status, are discussed. Chapter 4 then summarises the provision of charitable care in Chichester in the Middle Ages.

Part 2 focuses specifically on St James' Hospital and the archaeology of its cemetery. The history of the hospital is recounted in Chapter 5, where the constitution and economy are outlined and hospital dedications discussed. At some stage before the Reformation the hospital began to admit women and (as revealed by the archaeology, although not the written record) children, and by Elizabethan times it was an almshouse for the sick poor. Chapter 6 is concerned with the hospital's physical setting, the analysis of one small fragment of the hospital buildings, and describes excavated features other than graves found within the cemetery, amongst which was a medieval lime kiln pre-dating some of the graves. Chapter 7 deals with the burials.

Amongst the topics covered are the dating and layout of the cemetery and the distribution of individuals according to their ages at death, sex, diseases and similar criteria. There is then a discussion of what can be deduced about burial practice and beliefs, and whether the religious changes of the Reformation are reflected in changing burial practice. Specialist find reports contained in Chapter 8 include a note on textile remains. Appendices containing some of the written sources, including a list of inmates and afflictions in 1594, as well as a catalogue that includes some basic archaeological and pathological data, are published on an accompanying CD.

Part 3, by Frances Lee, Anthea Boylston and other contributors, examines the physical anthropology and palaeopathology of this unique assemblage. (A full skeleton catalogue is included on the CD.) Chapter 9 deals with the demographic composition of the cemetery. The site can clearly be divided into two areas, the burial ground of the leper hospital with predominantly adult male burials and the almshouse phase which has a more normal population structure with men, women and children present. Chapters 10 to 19 discuss particular aspects of disease, including infection, congenital disease, dental health, trauma and osteoarthritis. There are two chapters devoted to the palaeopathology of leprosy in the Chichester skeletons. The first, by Donald Ortner, Professor of Anthropology at the Smithsonian Institution in Washington, examines the specific bone changes of this disease as identified on the inmates of St James' Hospital. He presents a clear photographic record of the evidence of leprosy found on the facial, hand, foot and lower limb bones, which provides a useful guide to those attempting to identify the disease on the skeleton in other populations. The second, by Frances Lee and Keith Manchester, draws together all the evidence for leprosy on the Chichester skeletons and places these individuals in their historical, medical and archaeological context. Frances Lee wrote the original report on the Chichester skeletons with Keith Manchester, who is a world-renowned authority on the study of the skeletal manifestations of leprosy.

Other chapters are written by scholars who have worked on the Chichester skeletons as part of their research. Mary Lewis, a specialist in the palaeopathology of childhood, describes the range of diseases found in the Chichester children. In Chapter 13, Alan Ogden analyses the problems which beset this very particular subset of the medieval population in relation to their dental health. The chapter on trauma is written by Margaret Judd, who is studying this subject in modern populations.

Part 4 contains the discussion and interpretation of the site by Frances Lee and John Magilton. There appears to be a significant change in the pattern of disease through the period of occupation, from the early 12th to the mid-17th century, which reflects both the decline in leprosy in England and changes in the institution. In the later period, after the hospital was refounded as an almshouse, a much broader range of conditions appears including tuberculosis, rare in the earlier period, congenital abnormalities, fractures and metabolic conditions such as scurvy and rickets. There is very little evidence for treatment apart from possible reduction and splinting of fractures. The function of the almshouse can therefore be seen as providing sheltered accommodation for the infirm rather than treatment for the infirmity.

Résumé

Ce rapport, le dixième dans la série de volumes dédiés aux fouilles de Chichester, décrit et met en valeur un groupe de près de 400 squelettes d'hommes, de femmes et d'enfants exhumés au cours des fouilles de l'hôpital St James et St Mary Magdalene; cet hôpital, à l'origine un hôpital de lépreux, date d'époques médiévales et plus récentes et se situe juste en dehors de Chichester dans le West Sussex au Royaume-Uni. Cet échantillon est, à ce jour, de loin le plus considérable provenant d'un hôpital médiéval anglais; la fouille et la publication de ce groupe constitue le premier ensemble important de sépultures de lépreux qui ait été étudié depuis une génération. Le cimetière fit l'objet de fouilles en 1986–77 et en 1993 sur deux zones adjacentes qui représentent un pourcentage inconnu de l'ensemble. Ces deux zones furent explorées dans le cadre de missions d'archéologie préventive; les travaux et les analyses en découlant furent financés par le Conseil du District de Chichester. Les campagnes de fouilles furent dirigées par l'archéologue municipal John Magilton et exécutées par l'équipe de l'Unité Archéologique du District de Chichester. Les restes humains ont étés incorporés à la collection didactique du Centre de Recherches en Anthropologie biologique de l'Université de Bradford; c'est là que la plupart des analyses paléopathologiques ont été faites. Le District de Chichester est le dépositaire du mobilier et de la documentation de base.

Le rapport comprend quatre parties, dont les deux premières sont rédigées par le responsable des fouilles, John Magilton. La première partie décrit le contexte dans lesquelles les fouilles s'inscrivent. L'hôpital de Chichester a été fondé au 12ème siècle pour secourir des hommes souffrant de lèpre; la nature de cette maladie, les attitudes envers elle à l'époque médiévale, les hôpitaux médiévaux en général et les hôpitaux de lépreux en particulier, leurs buts et régimes, ainsi que leur survie au-delà de la Réforme forment les sujets explorés au chapitre 2. Le chapitre 3 sert d'introduction aux cimetières d'époque médiévale et du début de l'époque moderne en Angleterre; la mort, les funérailles et le statut du défunt font également partie des thèmes traités. On trouvera au chapitre 4 un résumé de la charité sur laquelle les habitants de Chichester pouvaient compter au Moyen-âge.

L'hôpital St James ainsi que l'archéologie de son cimetière forment le sujet de la seconde partie. Son histoire, y compris sa constitution, son économie est ses dédicaces, figurent au Chapitre 5. Les femmes et les enfants furent admis avant la Réforme (d'après les données archéologiques, en l'absence de documents historiques) et à partir du règne d'Elizabeth I l'hôpital devint un hospice pour les malades pauvres. On trouvera la description de la configuration de l'hôpital, ainsi qu'une analyse d'une petite partie de ses bâtiments au Chapitre 6; ce chapitre contient aussi la description des structures fouillées, y compris un four à chaux médiéval datant d'avant la construction de l'hôpital. Les sépultures du cimetière sont traitées au chapitre 7. Dates et plan du cimetière ainsi que la répartition des individus suivant leur âge, sexe, maladie ou autres critères y sont examinés. Suit une discussion sur les pratiques mortuaires et les croyances représentées, ainsi qu'une réflexion sur l'impact de la Réforme, en particulier si elle se reflète dans le mode de sépulture. Les vestiges en textile figurent parmi les rapports de spécialistes au chapitre 8. Un CD accompagnant le rapport contient une série d'appendices illustrant certains documents, tels une liste des pensionnaires et de leurs maladies datant de 1594, ainsi qu'un catalogue des données archéologiques et pathologiques.

La troisième partie contient les rapports de Frances Lee, Anthea Boylston et autres collaborateurs sur l'anthropologie physique et la paléopathologie de cet ensemble unique. (On trouvera également un catalogue complet des squelettes sur le CD). La composition démographique du cimetière occupe le chapitre 9. On distingue deux zones dans le cimetière: celle de l'hôpital des lépreux, avec une majorité de sépultures d'adultes males, et celle correspondant à la phase de l'hospice, avec une distribution démographique normale, comprenant des hommes, des femmes et des enfants. Quant aux chapitres 9 et 10, ils traitent de certains aspects de la maladie, comme les infections, les maladies héréditaires, la santé dentaire, les lésions traumatiques et l'ostéoarthrite. La paléopathologie de la lèpre, sur les données des squelettes de Chichester, fait l'objet de deux chapitres de spécialistes. Le premier, de Donald Ortner, Professeur d'anthropologie à la Smithsonian Institution à Washington, examine les changements que cette maladie produit dans les ossements, à la lumière des squelettes de l'hôpital St James. Les indices de lèpre sur le visage, les mains, les pieds et les membres inférieurs font l'objet d'un relevé photographique précis; son utilité devrait s'étendre à l'identification de cette maladie dans d'autres ensembles de squelettes. Le second chapitre, de Frances Lee et Keith Manchester, résume toutes les données concernant la lèpre sur les squelettes de Chichester et les replace dans leur contexte historique, médical et archéologique. Frances Lee est l'auteur de l'analyse ostéologique des squelettes de Chichester, tandis que Keith Manchester est un expert de renommée internationale sur les signes de lèpre sur le squelette humain.

Les squelettes de Chichester alimentent encore d'autres chapitres spécialisés. Mary Lewis, spécialiste en paléopathologie de l'enfance, décrit les maladies observées sur les enfants de Chichester, tandis qu'Alan Ogden analyse les problèmes de santé dentaire qui affligent cette portion de la population médiévale au chapitre 13. Enfin Margaret Judd, spécialiste de ce sujet dans les populations modernes, se penche sur la traumatologie.

Frances Lee et John Magilton dédient la quatrième partie du rapport à la discussion et à l'interprétation du site. Ils observent un changement important dans le comportement de la maladie au cours des périodes d'occupation qui s'étendent du 12ème au milieu du 17ème siècle: ces changements reflètent d'une part le déclin de la lèpre en Angleterre et d'autre part les transformations subies par les institutions. On observe un éventail bien plus étendu de maladies telles que la tuberculose (rare aux époques antérieures), les malformations congénitales, les fractures, ainsi que les maladies du métabolisme comme le scorbut et le rachitisme à une époque tardive, datant d'après la fondation de l'hospice. Les données concernant le traitement des malades sont rares, mis à part quelques réductions de fractures ou la pose d'attelles. L'hospice a donc rempli une fonction d'accueil aux malades et infirmes, plutôt que celle d'un centre de traitement.

Zusammenfassung

Dieser Bericht, der 10. aus der Serie *Chichester Excavations*, beschreibt und diskutiert eine Ausgrabung, bei der fast 400 Skelette von Männern, Frauen und Kindern geborgen wurden. Sie waren auf einem ursprünglich für Leprakranke eingerichteten Friedhof bestattet, der zum mittelalterlichen Krankenhaus St James und St Mary Magdalene gehörte und sich direkt ausserhalb der Stadtgrenze von Chichester in der Grafschaft Sussex im Vereinigten Königreich befand. Die Skelettsammlung ist die bisher Größte aus einem mittelalterlichen Krankenhaus in England und die erste große Europäische Sammlung von Gräbern von Leprakranken, die in dieser Generation ausgegraben und untersucht wurde. Zwei nebeneinanderliegende Teile des Friedhofes wurden 1986–87 und 1993 im Ramen von Bebauungmaßnamen ausgegraben, der Gesamtumfang des Friedhofbereiches ist nicht bekannt. Die Geländearbeit und archäologische Fundanalyse wurde vom Chichester District Council (der Gemeinde) bezahlt. Die Geländearbeit wurde von John Magilton, dem Gemeindearchäologen von Chichester geleitet und von Mitgliedern der Chichester District Archaeological Unit ausgeführt. Ein Teil der Knochenüberreste sind jetzt Bestandteil der Lehrkollektion im Forschungszentrum für Biologische Anthropologie der Universität Bradford, in der die paläopathologischen Untersuchungen durchgeführt wurden, andere befinden sich in der Obhut des Chichester District Council (die Gemeinde Chichester) wo die Funde und Ausgrabungsberichte archiviert wurden.

Der Bericht besteht aus vier Teilen, die ersten beiden sind von dem Ausgrabungsleiter John Magilton geschrieben. Teil 1 beschreibt den Hintergrund der Geländearbeit. Das Krankenhaus in Chichester wurde ursprünglich als ein Leprosorium für Männer und Frauen im 12. Jahrhundert eingerichtet. Das Krankheitsbild, Vorurteile und Reaktionen der Gesellschaft auf diese Krankheit werden im 2. Kapitel diskutiert. Mittelalterliche Krankenhäuser im allgemeinen und Leprosoriua besonderen werden untersucht, im Hinblick auf deren Ziele und Regime, als auch deren Fortbestand im Zuge der Reformation. Das 3. Kapitel stellt Friedhöfe aus dem Mittelalter und der frühen Neuzeit in England vor. Auch verschiedene andere Themen, die den Tod und das Sterben betreffen, under anderem Begraäbnisriten und Status, werden diskutiert. Im 4. Kapitel wird die Bereitstellung wohltätiger Pflege im mittelalterlichen Chichester zusammengefasst.

Teil zwei befasst sich insbesondere mit dem Krankenhaus St James und dem dazugehörigen Friedhof. Die Geschichte des Krankenhauses wird im 5. Kapitel berichtet, hier wird unter anderem die Satzung und Kostenwirtschaft des Krankenhauses dargestellt Widmungen diskutiert. Zu irgendeinem Zeitpunkt vor der Reformation wurden auch Frauen (was aus dem archäologischen Funden hervorgeht, aber nicht aus den geschriebenen Quellen) und Kinder zugelassen, und in der Elizabethanischen Zeit wurde es ein Armenhaus für die Kranken. Das

6. Kapitel beschreibt die räumliche Gliederung des Krankenhauses, ein Bruchstück des Krankenhausgebäudes wird analysiert und beschrieben, und andere Ausgrabungsfunde werden beschrieben, wie zum Beispiel ein Kalkofen, der zeitlich früher eingeordnent wird, als einige der Gräber. Kapitel 7 beschäftigt sich mit den Begräbnisriten. Es werden Themen behandelt wie die Datierung und Anordnung der Gräber, die Aufgliederung der individuellen Gräber nach Alter, Geschlecht, Krankheitsbild und ähnlichen Kriterien. Es folgt eine Diskussion der Begräbnisrituale, und welche Schlußfolgerungen gezogen werden können was Rituale und Glauben betrifft, und inwiefern sich die religiösen Veränderungen während der Reformation auf die Begrägnisrituale auswirkten. Fundberichte von Spezialisten in Kapitel 8 beinhalten unter anderem einen Bericht über Textilien. Der Anhang ist als CD veröffentlicht und hier werden einige der Quellen aufgezeigt, unter anderem eine Liste von Patienten und deren Krankheiten aus dem Jahr 1594, sowie ein Katalog in dem einige der archäologischen und pathologischen Untersuchungsergebnisse aufgelistet sind.

Im dritten Teil, untersuchen die Autoren Frances Lee, Anthea Boylston und andere, die Anthropologie und Paläoepathologie dieses einzigartigen Fundsatzes. (Ein umfassender Katalog der Skelette ist auf der CD veröffentlicht.) Das 9. Kapitel beschäftigt sich mit den demographischen Faktoren dieses Friedhofs. Das Gelände kann deutlich in zwei Areale aufgeteilt werden: der Friedhof für Leprakranke, der haupsächlich aus Männern besteht und ein Teil aus der Armenhaus Phase, mit einer eher typischen Bevölkerungsstruktur von Männern, Frauen und Kindern. In Kapiteln 10 bis 19 werden die speziellen Krankheitsbilder behandelt, wie zum Beispiel Infektionen, Erbkrankheiten, Zahnmedizin, Trauma und Osteoarthrose. Zwei Kapitel widmen sich der Paläopathologie der Lepra in den Skeletten aus Chichester.

In einem Kapitel von Donald Ortner, Professor für Anthropologie des Smithonian Institut in Washington werden die speziellen Knochenveränderungen untersucht, die diese Krankheit an den Patienten des St James Krankenhaus verursachte. Er kollationierte ein überschaubares photographisches Register des Krankheitsbilds an Gesichts-, Hand-, Fuß- und Beinknochen von Lepra. Dieses Register liefert ein wichtigen Datensatz, der anderen Forschern bei der Identifizierung dieser Krankheit in anderen Bevölkerungsgruppen assistieren kann.

Im nächsten Kapitel von Frances Lee und Keith Manchester, werden die allgemeinen Ergebnisse der Lepraforschung an den individuellen Skeletten von Chichester in ihren historischen, medizinischen und archäologischen Rahmen gesetzt. Frances Lee schrieb den ursprüngliche Bericht über die Skelette der Chichester Ausgrabung zusammen mit Keith Manchester, einem weltweit renommierten Fachexperten der Studie von skeletalen Erscheinungsformen der Lepra.

Andere Kapitel sind von Wissenschaftlern geschrieben, die an den Chichester Skeletten als Teil ihrer Forschung gearbeitet haben. Mary Lewis, eine Spezialistin in der Paläopathologie von Kindern, beschreibt die Vielfältigkeit der Kinderkrankheiten in Chichester. Im 13. Kapitel analysiert Alan Ogden die zahnmedizinischen Probleme, von denen diese bestimmte Bevölkerungsgruppe befallen war. Das Kapitel über Trauma wurde von Margaret Judd geschrieben, die dieses Gebiet an der modernen Bevölkerung erforscht.

Der vierte Teil beinhaltet die Diskussion und Interpretation dieses Fundorts durch Frances Lee und John Magilton. Strukturveränderungen. Das Schema des Krankheitsbildes verändert in der Zeit zwischen dem frühen 12. Jahrhundert bis in das mittlere 17. Jahrhundert maßgeblich. Das spiegelt zum einen den Rückgang von Lepra in England allgemein wieder und andererseits den Wandel dieser bestimmten Institution. In der späteren Phase, nachdem aus dem Krankenhaus ein Armenhaus wurde, trat ein breiteres Spektrum von Krankheiten auf, dazu gehörten Tuberkulose, welche in der früheren Periode sehr selten war, erbliche Mißbildungen, Knochenbrüche und Krankheiten, die durch Stoffwechselstörungen ausgelöst wurden, wie zum Beispiel Skorbut und Rachitis. Es gibt nur wenige Beweise für Behandlungen, mit Ausnahme von Reposition oder Schienung von Frakturen. Es wird davon ausgegangen, daß das Armenhaus lediglich zur Beherbergung von Kranken diente, und nicht als Behandlungsort für Krankheiten.

Part 1

Introduction

1 Background *by John Magilton*

1.1 The hospital site (Fig 1.1)

The site of the medieval hospital, originally for lepers, of St James and St Mary Magdalene at Chichester has never been forgotten. The knowledgeable 21st-

century motorist, driving down Spitalfield Lane, will be able to deduce from the street name, first recorded in 1535 (Mawer and Stenton 1929, 14), that there was once a medieval hospital in the locality; both the name and the lane considerably pre-date their first

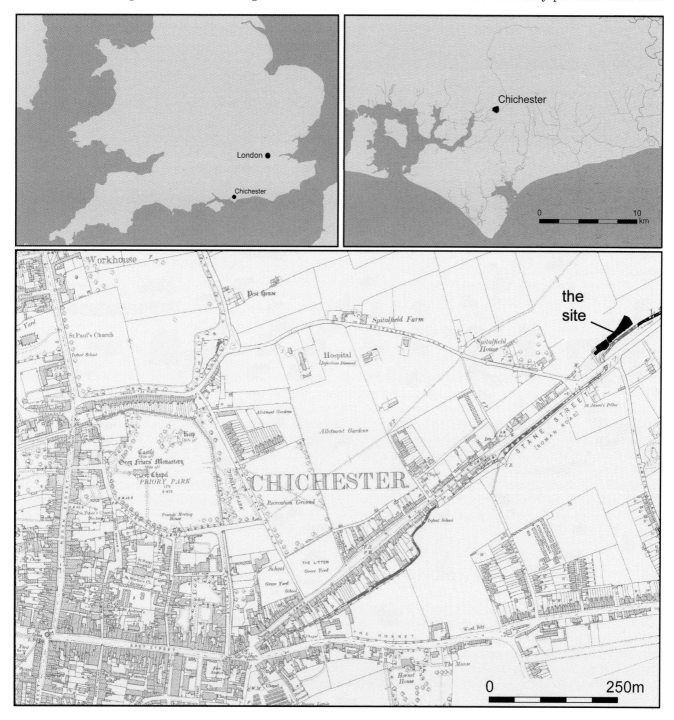

Figure 1.1 Location maps. The large map is the Ordnance Survey 25 inch map of 1898 reproduced at a reduced scale. It shows the hospital's position relative to the walled city. St James' Hospital ('the site') is 1km from the east gate

3

Figure 1.2 The 'leper cottage', 3 Westhampnett Road, showing the first-floor commemorative plaque on its front wall, photographed in autumn 1986. For a transcription of the plaque, see Chapter 6, fn 15

Figure 1.3 The concrete memorial slab in The Litten cemetery, Chichester, marking the reinterment of human remains exhumed when part of the hospital site became the Swanfield Drive housing estate in 1947

documentary appearance.[1] A pedestrian, curious to see more of the thatched cottage (3 Westhampnett Road) near the junction of Spitalfield Lane and St Pancras, the main road north-east from Chichester, will be able to discern on the front of the building a plaque erected by the Revd William Walker, rector of St Pancras for 50 years until his death in 1827, recording its construction from remains of the leper hospital (Fig 1.2). The cottage itself contains medieval architectural fragments in its north-west wall although most of the building post-dates a fire of 1781 (Steer 1962b, 23). Before then, some at least of the medieval hospital stood. Yeakell and Gardner's map of Chichester (1769) shows one surviving building (not on the cottage site) with foundations to the north-east labelled 'St James' ruins', and the last known reference to the building as inhabitable is in 1755 when a Mr Newland sought to have use of St James' House 'to air his relations' who were recovering from smallpox (Dangerfield 1938, 147). As a functioning institution, the hospital had effectively come to an end at the start of that century (McCann 1987, 254).

1.2   The rediscovery of the cemetery

The hospital was sufficiently peripheral to Chichester to escape redevelopment until 1947 when the City Council erected an estate of prefabricated semi-detached houses. During construction, burials from the hospital cemetery were encountered, removed and sent for examination. A florid account of their discovery was given in the *Sussex County Magazine* for 1947 (**21**, 173) where specialists are quoted as saying, in quaint language more appropriate to an earlier century, 'We have had nothing like this before, neither have bones of such antiquity been

available to scientists'. Also reported was 'a tangled mass of human remains'. A former City Engineer, Mr R A J Cork, gave a more factual and prosaic account to the writer in 1986. He had been in charge of the project, and recalled that the burials had been found north of the cottage, laid out in ranks, about 18ins (0.5m) below ground when the new access road for the estate, Swanfield Drive, was laid out. The fingertips of the skeletons were examined by leprosy specialists, but no trace of the disease was found. The remains were reinterred in The Litten cemetery where they are commemorated by a slab (Fig 1.3).

1.3   Archaeological excavation (Fig 1.4)

Despite rumours of subsequent discoveries of burials (for example, when police houses were built at the junction of Swanfield Drive and Spitalfield Lane) there are no confirmed reports until 1986. Early in that year, electricity board workers disturbed the remains of two burials in a service trench close to the thatched cottage, 3 Westhampnett Road, and in the summer burials were noted during archaeological monitoring of the first few foundation trenches for a series of old persons' bungalows being constructed south of Swanfield

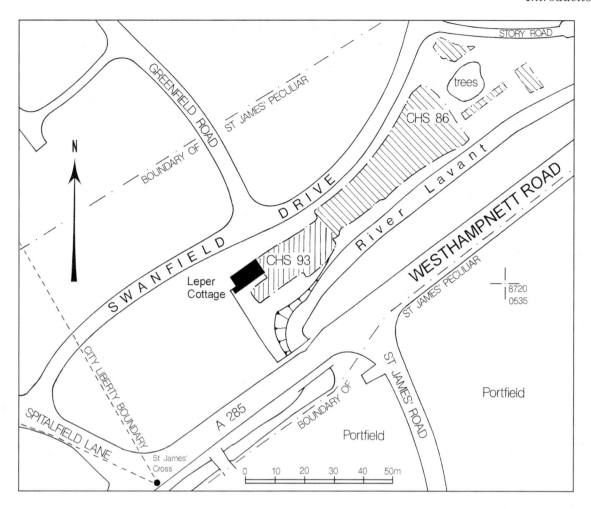

Figure 1.4   Map of the 1986–87 and 1993 excavated areas and location of the 'leper cottage'. Scale 1:1250

Drive and north-east of the cottage. The development, by Chichester District Council, was stopped to allow for excavation of the affected part of the cemetery. Chichester District Archaeological Unit, directed by the writer, carried this out between July 1986 and February 1987 (Fig 1.5). A Community Programme Agency environmental improvement squad also took part in the excavation, assisting with topsoil stripping.

The skeletons, confined to the western part of the development area, numbered over 330. This was the first European leper cemetery to be investigated on any meaningful scale since work in Denmark in the 1950s and the first large-scale investigation of a medieval hospital cemetery in Britain. At the time, the Calvin Wells Laboratory for Burial Archaeology in the School of Archaeological Science at Bradford university was undertaking a study of leprosy, and the skeletons were sent there and analysed by Frances Lee, initially as a research student of the university and later as a freelance consultant. Because of interest in the burials, interim reports were published as soon as an initial analysis of the skeletal material was complete (Lee and Magilton 1989; Magilton and Lee 1989), and students of the university and others subsequently published

numerous research papers on specific aspects of the palaeopathology (see Bibliography).

Further excavations were undertaken in 1993 when Chichester District Council, which then owned the thatched cottage, decided to sell the house and, separately, the greater part of its garden, the latter for housing development. It was felt that a satisfactory sale of the garden could more readily be achieved if it were cleared of burials, and the District Archaeological Unit carried out the work at the local authority's expense late in 1993, uncovering a further 44 burials (Fig 1.6), a lime kiln and some linear features. A brief note on the results was published with a plan (Magilton 1993) but full publication was delayed, partly by the privatisation of the District Archaeological Unit in June 1994 and the winding up of its successor in December 1998. Frances Lee carried out analysis of the additional skeletons, which have now been added to the original assemblage at Bradford University.

By 1999 the prefabricated council houses erected in 1947, some of which had subsequently been sold to their tenants, were beyond economic repair and the District Council began to implement a comprehensive redevelopment programme. This had been discussed and planned for several years, and was

Figure 1.5 General view of the north-east part of the 1986–87 site showing the orderly columns of graves and in the centre of the site a prehistoric ditch in the course of excavation

another factor in delaying publication of the earlier excavation results, since it was thought that a third investigation might be needed. Fortunately, the most sensitive area, north of the cottage and cemetery on the north side of Swanfield Drive, has been left a public open space in the new scheme and neither graves nor the buried remains of hospital buildings are likely to have been affected.[2]

1.4   The aims and layout of this report

This report was originally intended as a further volume in the long-established *Chichester Excavations* series funded mostly by Chichester District Council, but a shortfall in the council's budget in 2005 led us to seek an alternative publisher and we were pleased and gratified that the CBA agreed to take over publication. This is therefore both volume 10 in the *Chichester Excavations* series and a CBA Research Report. Because the former has always had a local readership of historians and others interested specifically in Chichester and its hinterland, we have attempted to give rather more in the way of background than would have been the case had we been writing for an audience of professional medieval archaeologists and historians. It was also our hope that the book would appeal to those with

an interest in osteoarchaeology whose expertise lay with bones rather than dirt or documents, and that they too might find the background commentary of value. For those wanting to know more, ideas for further reading have also been included, although research for this volume effectively stopped in October 2005 with the publication of *Requiem* (Gilchrist and Sloane 2005), and no more recent publications have generally been noted.

For the reader's convenience this report has been split between the palaeopathology (Part 3), the history and archaeology of the site (Part 2), and introductory chapters on lepers, leprosy and hospitals (Part 1). Part 4 gives an overview. This is wholly artificial and somewhat arbitrary since any discussion of, say, cemetery organisation would be meaningless unless we knew, where it could be determined, the sex of the deceased. Similarly, the palaeopathology, although of intrinsic interest to specialists, is significant often because of its archaeological and/or historical context. Deciding where to present conclusions has not always been straightforward, and some repetition has been unavoidable. A distinction has been made, for example, between the Grave Catalogue (on CD), listing mainly archaeological concerns, and the Catalogue of Skeletons (on CD), concerned with palaeopathology; both give the sex and age of the deceased and whether or not

Figure 1.6 Part of the graveyard during excavation, December 1993. The main area was protected by a polytunnel that allowed work to continue despite the very wet weather

diseases were present, but for details the latter must be consulted.

1.5 Archaeological recording

The site lies a little under 1km north-east of the east gate of Chichester on the north side of Stane Street, the London–Chichester Roman road,[3] on alluvial fan deposits of the ancient River Lavant at about 16.5m OD. The river now runs in a culvert between the excavations and the road but has done so only since an 18th-century diversion from the opposite side of Stane Street, although that course too was canalised. In the Middle Ages the Portfield, the larger of the town fields, was on this side of the road and extended as far south as a road called The Hornet, the other main highway to emanate from Chichester's east gate. The area is now thoroughly suburban but before the middle of the last century it must have marked the beginning of the countryside, albeit one scarred by brickworks and gravel pits, where the supermarkets now loom.

The first skeletons, at the south-western end of the cemetery, were discovered in 1986 in the foundation trenches dug for sheltered homes. Although archaeological monitoring was taking place, some were badly damaged before construction could be halted. Trial trenches were then machine-dug to determine the north-eastern limits of the cemetery but, thereafter, archaeological excavation was by hand, beginning with the known burials at the south-west and extending north-eastwards until boundary ditches were found and the graves ran out. Excavation continued for some distance beyond the north-easternmost graves and by early 1987 we were confident that the eastern and southern limits of the cemetery had been located. The 1993 site was a straightforward area excavation in which the topsoil was stripped by machine. Hand-dug trial trenches were used to determine how much topsoil could be mechanically removed without disturbing graves and to ascertain the course of some linear features that were sampled, not fully excavated.

Methodology

The excavation and recording methods for skeletons were common to both seasons. Once identified, usually from their skulls, the uppermost part of the skeletons, the bones were quickly exposed, cleaned, photographed using monochrome negatives and colour slides, drawn at a scale of 1:20 and lifted. Any apparent abnormalities were photographed in detail whilst the skeleton was in situ. It was usually impossible to determine the edges of the grave pit since the grave filling was identical, in all but compactness, to the 'natural' through which the grave had been cut. Plans were drawn in pencil on plastic drawing film with a graph paper backing, and field drawings were made with a planning frame with 100mm or 200mm divisions depending on the planner's preference. Where there were many burials overlying each other, a plan had to be drawn for each level but these were not 'phase' plans as such. Coffin nails and other finds from graves were recorded on the plans, given a reference to the site grid and a level was taken, following normal practice. Wherever possible, especially in 1986–87, the whole operation was done in a day so that exposed skeletons were not left in situ overnight and vandalised.[4]

The written record was made on standard A4 record cards using a single context system in which a grave cut was given a separate number from its filling. Although similar cards had been used elsewhere for many years, this was the first major site in Chichester not to employ the 'laboratory notebook' with alternate pages of lined and graph paper. Also used for the first time locally were A5 skeleton record cards where the presence or absence of parts of the skeleton could be indicated by ringing the missing bones on a labeled schematic sketch. Simple numerical lists were kept for small finds, photographs etc. The site code CHS, the year of excavation (86, 87, 93) and the context number were marked on pottery with Indian ink. In this report the skeleton number alone is usually used to designate a grave and its contents. For example, skeleton 320 occupied grave pit 672, the filling of which was 673, but it is perhaps more helpful to the reader to know that three fragments of iron nails were found with skeleton 320 than in context 673.

After excavation in 1987 the skeletons and other finds were taken to a nearby warehouse leased, appropriately, on St James' Industrial Estate (the archaeological unit did not then have its own store) and washed before being taken to Bradford University for study. Records were photocopied for security and fair copies in ink on plastic film were made of field drawings.

In retrospect, the methodology could have been improved, and having a human bone specialist on site would have been a major asset. The main excavation was, however, some years before Planning Policy Guidance note 16, when many planning authorities had yet to accept the 'polluter pays' principle and funds were limited. One criterion for funding the excavation had been that the archaeological unit was cheaper than commercial organisations specialising in graveyard clearance.

Records and finds deposition

The skeletons are all still at Bradford University, where it is hoped that they will continue to be a valuable teaching resource for years to come, the outcome of further research informing us better about the lives and deaths of some of the city's most disadvantaged individuals. The licence under which they were exhumed allows for their retention for a period of study (length unspecified) before reburial. The written and drawn archive will be deposited at the County Record Office following normal local practice. The finds will be stored at the Collections Discovery Centre at Fishbourne. As both parts of the site were dug whilst the landowner was Chichester District Council, they remain the property of the local authority.

Notes

1. As the boundary of the Liberty of Chichester followed the centre line of part of Spitalfield Lane in the late 13th century, this gives a reasonable *terminus ante quem* for the road. See Salzman 1935, 71.
2. A watching brief of sensitive areas, commissioned by Chichester District Council, revealed nothing noteworthy.
3. This has a series of local names. The stretch past the hospital site is called Westhampnett Road after the adjoining parish to the north-east and the stretch heading towards Chichester is called simply St Pancras after the parish through which it runs. This occasionally leads to confusion as to whether the parish or road is meant, and in this report St Pancras alone means the road and St Pancras parish designates the civil/ecclesiastical unit.
4. There are references in the osteological report to the 'weathering' of bones, from which it might be assumed that skeletons, once exposed, were left in situ for some time before lifting, but this was rarely so and the phenomenon must have another cause.

2   Leprosy, lepers and their hospitals

by John Magilton

Had this chapter been written 30 years ago it would have required little explanation or justification since the standard general work on the subject then was still *The Mediaeval Hospitals of England*, first published in 1909 and reprinted in 1966. It is a tribute to the scholarship of the author, clergyman's daughter Mary Rotha Clay, that her work dominated medieval hospital studies for so much of the 20th century,[1] but a sad reflection of the lack of scholarly interest in hospitals collectively that little to supplement it and nothing to supersede it had appeared by the 1960s. The last quarter of the century, however, saw the publication of a series of studies, mostly cited in the bibliography of this report, to make good that deficiency, starting with *The Medieval Leper and his Northern Heirs* by Peter Richards (1977, reprinted Woodbridge 2000). Hospitals, including leper hospitals and the disease which gave rise to them, are nevertheless amongst the lesser-known institutions of the Middle Ages when contrasted with, say, castles, which have a vast bibliography for individual sites and have been the subject of numerous regional and national studies.

This chapter is not a comprehensive guide to the subject matter indicated in its title, nor an original contribution to leper studies. It is a selective compilation, mainly from secondary sources, which will, it is hoped, enable the reader to put into context the more specific history and archaeology of St James' Chichester related in Part 2, and the detailed results from palaeopathological examination of the skeletons from its cemetery reported in Part 3. The best published modern national survey of medieval hospitals is Part 1 of Orme and Webster's *The English Medieval Hospital 1070–1570* (1995), whilst the work by P Richards (1977), already cited, is a readable account dealing specifically with lepers and leper hospitals. Both are superseded by A E M Satchell (1998), The Emergence of Leper-Houses in Medieval England (unpubl Oxford DPhil).

2.1   Leprosy

How and when the infection now sometimes known as Hansen's disease[2] arrived in Europe and spread to Britain is still uncertain. The first written records of a disease known as *lepra* in Britain are 10th-century (Richards 1977, 4) but it was not necessarily the same as Hansen's disease. True leprosy, Hansen's disease, seems not to have become a significant social problem until the 11th century and was dying out by the 14th century. To the medieval mind, the symptoms of leprosy were manifestations of a diseased soul and it would be anachronistic to

ask whether physicians and others were able to distinguish between Hansen's disease and other skin complaints; if it looked like lepra, then it was lepra, and as excavations of hospital cemeteries in Chichester and elsewhere have shown, the inmates were commonly but not necessarily exclusively sufferers from Hansen's disease.

Leprosy is a chronic infectious disease that, fortunately for the archaeologist, commonly leads to bone changes and can be identified from skeletal remains (see Chapters 13 and 14). In the English archaeological record,[3] Hansen's disease has been identified at Roman Cirencester (Manchester and Roberts 1986) and in the feet and lower legs of several skeletons from the late Roman cemetery[4] at Poundbury, Dorchester, Dorset (Reader 1974). Although the diagnosis has been questioned, a consensus of opinion is that the skeletal changes are compatible with a diagnosis of leprosy (Manchester and Hart, pers comm). A possible example of 6th-century date from the Saxon cemetery at Beckford (Gloucestershire) is known (Wells 1962). Eccles (Kent) has yielded an example from the 7th century (Manchester 1981); another of similar date comes from Burwell (Cambridgeshire) where cranial and post-cranial features of leprosy were recognised on a male skeleton (Møller-Christensen and Hughes 1962), and a third, a bed burial, from Edix Hill, Barrington (Malim and Hines 1998, 176–7).[5] Also of 7th- to 8th-century date is a case from Tean on Scilly (Thomas 1985, 183–4). A more significant site of the period is Cannington (Somerset) where there is good evidence for at least three and perhaps more cases in the community (Rahtz *et al* 2000). Given that others will have had the disease without suffering skeletal changes, this is the earliest British community where leprosy emerges as a noticeable health threat. A Saxo-Norman group comes from the church of St John Timberhill, Norwich, where a possible 35 lepers (24 fairly certain) were present amongst the 180 assessable skeletons (Anderson 1998; Popescu forthcoming).[6]

The disease was no respecter of rank. Many prominent medieval persons were deemed leprous. King Baldwin IV of Jerusalem (1160–85) (Hamilton 2000) and early members of the crusading Order of St Lazarus,[7] the living dead mobilised to fight the Infidel, were amongst those who had the disease (Marcombe 2003). Louis the Great (died 1382), Hungary's greatest medieval king, is said to have died from longstanding leprosy (Pálfi *et al* 2002, 206). Other European monarchs allegedly afflicted included Robert the Bruce of Scotland (died 1329) and Magnus II of Norway; nobles included Count Thibaut VI of Chartres and Count Raoul of Vermandois, and

Figure 2.1   Two human heads from the vaulting of the Angel Choir at Lincoln Cathedral, one with gaping mouth showing rhinomaxillary changes characteristic of the facies leprosa. Both may be portrayals of the same individual (possibly Robert FitzPernel, Earl of Leicester) and constitute a 'before' and 'after' pair. Photos: Jo Buckberry

prominent churchmen Abbot Richard Wallingford of St Albans (Richards 1991, 152). Robert FitzPernel, Earl of Leicester (died 1204), allegedly infected for unjustly obtaining one of Lincoln's episcopal estates, and his son William the Leper were both patrons of leper hospitals (Marcombe 2003, 138–9).

Leprosy is a chronic infective disease caused by the *Mycobacterium leprae*. The symptoms seen in individuals can vary considerably, depending on the general health and resistance to infection of the sufferer. In the more severe cases (lepromatous leprosy), the face becomes blotchy and lumpy, the bridge of the nose collapses and has a persistent discharge, the eyes become inflamed and, in extreme cases, blindness ensues. The face can become an almost shapeless mass (Fig 2.1). A hoarseness of the voice is characteristic of the advanced stage of the disease. Even in less severe cases (tuberculoid leprosy) infection can destroy bones, leaving a useless, deformed hand or foot. Gangrenous parts emit a foul smell and the debilitated victim is rendered vulnerable to other ailments.

The accuracy with which the disease could be diagnosed by medieval physicians and others has been, and continues to be, a matter for debate. Amongst the complaints with which it might be confused were impetigo, psoriasis, dermatitis, Raynaud's disease, and fungal infection (Richards 1991, 151). Gilchrist (1992, 112) considered that the chance of a correct early diagnosis was slight and Brody (1974, 41) has questioned whether medieval doctors could tell it apart from other diseases. However, the same writer has suggested that, in societies where leprosy is endemic, primitive peoples

are able to diagnose its early stages precisely (Brody 1974, 32) and, by the 12th century at least, the disease must be considered endemic in Europe and the Latin states of the Holy Land. In the specific case of Baldwin IV (Fig 12.1), the worst seems to have been feared as soon as anaesthesia, an early symptom, was noticed in the boy's right arm (Hamilton 2000, 27), although no visible changes had taken place, but with persons of rank physicians must have been tempted to defer diagnosis until incontrovertible symptoms appeared.

The 13th-century English lawyer Bracton laid emphasis on deformity as the criterion for segregating lepers (Clay 1909, 57) and those who sought and gained admission to hospitals almost certainly had the disease in an advanced and disfiguring form. Contemporary medical opinion was also to the effect that isolation should depend on the severity of the symptoms (Richards 1977, 98); two early authorities, Bernard of Gordon and John of Gaddesden, Edward II's physician, exhorted their fellow doctors to defer seclusion until leprous distortion of the limbs was indisputable (Richards 1991, 151–2). It would thus be unsurprising to find a high percentage of skeletons in a leper hospital cemetery that exhibited changes due to leprosy, and just under 70% of the skeletons from a hospital at Naestved, Denmark, evinced such changes (Møller-Christensen 1978). It is more difficult to account for the remainder. Some may have been lepers with the disease in its early stages but who had died of some other cause before skeletal changes had taken place. Others were perhaps the staff, benefactors and others connected with the hospital who had sought burial there.[8] In its more advanced forms, leprosy was recognisable from a range of symptoms specified in medical textbooks but, as Margery Kempe's son was to find out to his cost (see below), mistakes were still possible, particularly as diagnosis was far from being a medical monopoly.

The decline in leprosy is seen both at existing leper hospitals, which by the early 14th century had fewer inmates than they could support, and by the declining number of new leper houses from this period onwards. In 1341 a summary of the history of St Nicholas' Carlisle says: '... by lapse of time the greater part of the lepers died, when ... their places were filled by poor impotent folk' (Clay 1909, 38). It is clear from this and other more circumstantial evidence that what took place was a real decline in the disease, not, for example, an increasing antipathy by lepers to enter hospitals or an increasing reluctance by the hospital authorities to admit them. The leprosarium at Sherburn, Co. Durham, once England's largest, held only two lepers under a revised constitution of 1434 and was taking in 'poor men' (Richards 1977, 83). New houses founded in the later Middle Ages tended to be small, typically having three beds, and raw statistics showing a decline in the numbers of new hospitals after *c* 1300 (Orme and Webster 1995, 11) are perhaps masking a more dramatic picture that would have emerged if bed-numbers had been taken as the unit for statistical purposes. It must, however, be remembered that the population as a whole diminished rapidly after the Black Death and subsequent epidemics, and that hospitals for the sick poor also declined.

From having been a universal scourge, leprosy in Britain began to be found only in increasingly remote rural areas and by the 18th and 19th centuries was confined to the Scottish islands. The reasons for the decline in leprosy are likely to be complex, involving social, demographic and environmental as well as bacteriological factors.[9] The only certainty is that segregating lepers had a minimal effect. The decline of leprosy in Europe was paralleled in the Latin Kingdom of Jerusalem, where the Order of St Lazarus, formed specifically for knights and sergeants who contracted the disease,[10] was admitting the healthy by the 13th century (Mitchell 2000, 257). Hansen's disease is often associated with poverty, and rising standards of living for survivors of the Black Death and its successors in Europe may be another factor in its retreat.[11]

From a medical and demographic, as opposed to social, point of view, leprosy was relatively unimportant. In its epidemic phase, when newly introduced to a susceptible community, it is said to affect up to 30% of the population in all age groups (Mitchell 2000, 249). In areas where leprosy is endemic today, the number of sufferers is variously put at fewer than one in a hundred (Rawcliffe 2000b, 233) or around 1–5%, typically appearing in children or young adults with peak presentation between 10 and 20 years (Mitchell 2000, 249). Before the Black Death, smallpox and measles, both then diseases

of childhood, would have been a greater check on population growth and even malaria, endemic in some parts of England, was perhaps responsible for more premature deaths than leprosy. Leprosy is not particularly easily caught, but its horrible effects coupled with the biblical, especially Old Testament, injunctions on how supposed sufferers should be treated, gave it a special status. Its impact was quite disproportionate to the number of sufferers.

2.2 Medieval attitudes to leprosy and lepers

As in many other spheres, medieval attitudes towards leprosy and its victims were varied, ambivalent and frequently contradictory, the disease eliciting both sympathy and horror.[12] Whilst there is some evidence that attitudes had changed by the end of the Middle Ages, they will also have depended on the social position of both the sufferer and the observer.

The Church

The earliest noteworthy English leper[13] was Aelfweard, bishop of London, who had to resign in 1044 because of the disease. When he sought to return to his home abbey of Evesham, Worcestershire, the monks would not admit him. In retaliation, he took back books and relics he had given them and migrated to Ramsey, Huntingdonshire (Orme and Webster 1995, 24). It was not possible to be a confirmed leper and to carry on as normal; 11th-century society required the leper to withdraw from the world, and even the monks of Evesham could not summon up sufficient Christian faith or charity to receive a sufferer. A Norman successor, Hugh of Orival (bishop 1075–85), who also suffered from leprosy, underwent castration in the hope of a cure and so earned the derision of the chronicler William of Malmesbury (Rawcliffe 2000b, 236). Although poor lepers remained unwelcome in most religious houses, high-status lepers would be admitted for a fee. Nostell Priory (Yorks) for one was prepared to admit a leper as a full brother (*in plenarium fratrem*: Farrer 1914–16, **3**, 275–6, no. 1610) in return for a consideration.

The theological response to leprosy is one area where changes can be seen as the doctrine of purgatory was developed in the later Middle Ages. Theologians sometimes took a harsh view, seeing the disease as a symbol of deep-seated moral decay or as a physical manifestation of the wickedness of the sufferer or his parents. The condition itself was thought to be sexually transmitted (Rawcliffe 1995, 14–15) and to make sufferers lustful (Orme and Webster 1995, 26). Prostitutes, it was believed, could pass on the disease without themselves succumbing (Richards 1991, 160). As the leper was stricken as a punishment for sin, he was expected

Fig. 2.2 Dives and Lazarus, from the 12th-century Cistercian Abbaye de Cadouin, Dordogne, France. Lazarus is here shown as a leper with a clapper in his right hand. Although in the Bible Lazarus is not said to have been a leper, he was firmly believed to have been one by the Middle Ages – hence the Order of St Lazarus and the term lazar house for a leper hospital. Dives has set his dogs on Lazarus in an attempt to drive him away. Photo: Keith Manchester

to fulfil the role of penitent (Gilchrist 1992, 114); at the St Alban's leper house 'those who are smitten … ought to bear themselves as more to be despised and as more humble than all other men' (Brody 1974, 78). Yet, from the 11th century onwards, the leper might be seen also (or instead) as one of the elect, allowed by God to endure purgatory on earth and thus pass directly to heaven (Rawcliffe 1995, 16). As early as 1239 the bishop of Tournai had argued that leprosy was a gift from God (Brody 1974, 101), and the parson in the *Canterbury Tales* expressed a similar idea. As Christ came to assume a greater degree of humanity and emphasis was placed upon his suffering, he was often described as being *quasi leprosus*.

The concept of purgatory, still a doctrine of the Roman Catholic Church, is so central to understanding late medieval Christianity that it merits a brief explanation. Up to the later 12th century it seems to have been believed that the soul slept

or hovered around aimlessly waiting for the Last Judgement, when it would be weighed, as would all other souls, and despatched to an appropriate destination. The invention of purgatory as a kind of anteroom is ascribed to the 'school' of Notre Dame, Paris, between 1170 and 1180 and it was conceived as somewhere where the souls of those who in life had been prevented from repenting or completing their penance could do so (Daniell 1998, 88). Pope Innocent IV gave the first formal definition, which still applies, in 1254. The prayers of the living, it was believed, could intercede on behalf of the dead and shorten the time they spent in purgatory. Specific acts of piety and, particularly in the later Middle Ages, substantial cash donations to the Church, could win the benefactor a considerably shortened sentence, and disgust over the sale of 'indulgences', as they were termed, was an important inspiration for the Reformation.

This new doctrine was hard to reconcile with the older idea of sleep until the Last Judgement. One way round was to reserve purgatory, which some at least saw as a temporary stay in hell, for the soul alone (the physical resurrection of the body, although not Church doctrine, was a widespread folk belief), whilst a kind of parallel institution known as Abraham's Bosom was invented for those of a saintly disposition (Horrox 1999, 111). The biblical Abraham's Bosom (Luke **16**, 22) is the place to which the angels bear off Lazarus, the beggar covered in sores who was believed to be a leper, and thus lepers in general were thought to occupy what some would have seen as a staging-post to heaven (Fig 2.2). From being sinful penitents who had brought the suffering on themselves, sometimes through sexual excess, lepers were suddenly elevated in status. Enduring purgatory on earth, for all its unpleasantness, was preferable to the 'real' purgatory where the ingenuity of the tormentors was best not imagined.

A specific event that benefited lepers and others in receipt of charity was the promulgation by the 4th Lateran Council (1215) of the idea of the 'holy poor', amongst whom lepers, or at least those in hospitals, were numbered. Christ's sermon on the Last Judgment (Matthew **25**, 32–6) warned that those who failed to perform six specific acts of charity – feeding the hungry, clothing the naked, visiting prisoners and the sick, giving drink to the thirsty and receiving poor strangers – were destined for the flames. The requirement to visit the sick and feed strangers seems commonly to have been met by bequests to hospitals and maisons dieu (Hadley 2001, 170). Charitable acts could be used to counterbalance spiritual contagion. Louis IX of France (1226–70) and Henry III of England (1216–72) were rivals in charity (Rawcliffe 2000a, 4), carrying on the tradition of their predecessors. In 1177, for example, Henry II had given 500 marks in alms to the Hospital of Jerusalem (Hamilton 2000, 121). Louis VIII of France, who had died in 1226, had contributed to the competition by leaving 100 *solidi* to each of the 2000 leper houses in his realm (Richards 1991, 156).[14]

The first chantry chapels in England anticipate Innocent IV by a decade or more, and in the later Middle Ages those who could afford it were increasingly endowing masses with the aim of shortening their stay in purgatory. If the prayers of the living could reduce the term of suffering for the dead, it followed that those who had died and achieved salvation could intercede for the living (Horrox 1999, 111). Lepers, in one sense the walking dead but heading for salvation, were an important source for prayers and indulgences. For those who could afford it, founding leper hospitals or endowing existing ones were good investments. As a by-product of the new doctrine, lepers in hospitals had to lead increasingly disciplined lives – a leper purged of sin was a more effective intercessor than a sinful one – and the daily burden of prayer increased as benefactors expected a spiritual return for gifts in cash or kind. Lepers at the house of St Margaret and St Sepulchre, Gloucester, had to say 200 *Aves* and 200 *Pater nosters* a day as part of the normal round and donations to the hospital, however welcome, meant extra prayers (Rawcliffe 2000b, 244). Ironically, the disease was in decline by the time these doctrines were fully formulated.

Less good news for lepers in hospitals was elaboration in the liturgy in which the sick poor had to play their part. The moribund or those crippled by whatever cause became increasingly unwelcome, as followers of John Wycliffe noted (Rawcliffe 2000a, 107), and the transformation of many hospitals to chantry chapels pure and simple was complete.[15] They may, in Carole Rawcliffe's memorable phrase (Rawcliffe 2000a, 105), have offered the spiritual equivalent of intensive care, but treatment for ills of the flesh became harder to find for the poor. By Henry VII's time even the Crown had become alerted to this lack of provision: 'there be fewe or noon commune Hospitallis within this our Reame, and ... for lack of them infinite nombre of power people miserably daily die, no man putting hand of help or remedy' (Rawcliffe 2000a, 194). Early in Henry VIII's reign the corruption of hospitals was attacked in *A Supplicacyon for the Beggers* by one Simon Fish in which it was alleged 'the fat of the whole foundation hangeth on the priests' beards', and later still in the *Complaynt of Roderyck Mors* (1642) that 'the masters of your hospitals be so fat that the poor be kept lean and bare enough' (Marcombe 2003, 172–3).

To a pious minority, purgation before death (which was how leprosy came to be seen) was a privilege rather than a curse and, like those Early Christians who actively courted martyrdom, they sought to infect themselves. The 'logic' was that lepers who suffered with humility were assured of salvation and, as long as it could be endured with appropriate Christian fortitude, the disease guaranteed a passport to paradise (Rawcliffe 2000b, 241–2). Holy men and women, according to their hagiographers, begged God to afflict them and an Irish saint, Finian Lobhar (Finian the Leper), cured others by assuming the disease himself.

The law

By a decree of Pope Alexander III (the canon *de Leprosis* of 1179), confirmed at Westminster by a synod of the English Church in 1200, those lepers who were already living apart were allowed to have their own cemeteries and chapels. Under ecclesiastical law, lepers were not bound to enter hospitals, but few could afford to isolate themselves at home. Leprous priests fared better than many as they continued to enjoy the income from a living, appointing a curate to do their duties (Richards 1977, 48–9). The canon says that lepers cannot dwell among the healthy or attend church with others, but as no mechanism is set up to enforce their separation, it may simply be confirming existing practice (Satchell 1998, 30).

The status of lepers in English secular law was variable. Bracton, in the mid-13th century, claimed that a leper could neither plead a case nor inherit or bequeath property (Clay 1909, 57; Orme and Webster 1995, 25); in 1227 Agnes, the leper wife of John of Westwick, sued for dower – unsuccessfully (Brody 1974, 82–3), but others were able to exploit various mechanisms for passing on property to their heirs whilst retaining adequate resources for personal use (Satchell 1998, 36). Those accused in London of being lepers could be required under a mandate of Edward III in 1346 to be assessed by medical and by lay persons and, if found leprous, could be exiled from the community (Richards 1977, 40). Lepers could be expelled and excluded from towns and cities by local by-laws, and the right to expel lepers was acknowledged before it was legally enforced. In Sussex, for example, a certain William son of Nicholas Malesmeins was consigned to the leper hospital at Bramber with the assent of his friends in 1220 (Clay 1909, 52–3).

The dates at which lepers were barred from urban centres varied from place to place (Fig 2.3). They may have been excluded before the first by-laws to survive were written down, and by custom even earlier than the first specific legislation. In Exeter there were apparently no restrictions until 1244 (Richards 1977, 50). In London lepers were excluded only from 1276 (Clay 1909, 53) but legislation was one thing, enforcement another. The ban on lepers in London was reinforced by the 1346 mandate but even so, in 1372, the mayor and aldermen had to threaten a leprous London baker named John Mayn with the pillory if he returned (Brody 1974, 94). More legislation, again by Edward III, in 1375 by which the porters at the London gates were sworn to bar lepers, is testimony to the ineffectualness of earlier measures. At Berwick-upon-Tweed lepers might have their clothes burnt and be ejected naked if they were caught in the town (Clay 1909, 54) but a hospital was provided for them on the periphery. In practice there was probably more social interaction between lepers and the healthy than lawyers and civic authorities chose to acknowledge. The inmates of some leper houses, amongst them Exeter and

Figure 2.3   The procession of lepers on 'koppermaandag' at Amsterdam in 1604 by Adriaan van Nieulandt (1587–1658). Lepers, normally barred from the city, were admitted for the festival on the first Monday after Epiphany to collect money for their house and enjoy a meal. © Amsterdams Historisch Museum

Reading, were allowed by their hospitals to travel as long as they observed the customary rules (Rawcliffe 2000b, 237).[16]

The medical profession

Physicians and surgeons were less inclined than clergy to moralise about leprosy (Rawcliffe 1995, 17), perhaps because by trying to banish pain and prolong life they themselves were seen by the pious as seeking to defy God's will.[17] The medieval physician's primary aim was not to cure disease but to alleviate its symptoms (Horrox 1999, 91). He was exhorted to treat the poor as an act of charity and may have done so, but his powers were strictly limited (Rawcliffe 2000a, 11). The 4th Lateran Council (1215) re-emphasised the spiritual aspect of earthly disease and threatened doctors with excommunication if their patients had not made, or promised to make, a full confession before treatment (Rawcliffe 2000a, 103). Most lepers, especially those in hospitals, will have had little contact with physicians, who tended the well-to-do in their own homes; what the hospitals could offer was a sufficient diet,[18] clean surroundings, warmth and bed-rest for those who needed it. The hospital of the Order

of St Lazarus at Jerusalem, arguably the premier leper house of western Christendom, seems to have offered no more by way of treatment than a chance to relieve suffering through a dip in the Jordan (Marcombe 2003, 9).[19]

Both legal and medical definitions of leprosy laid stress upon facial disfigurement as the critical diagnostic factor. John of Gaddesden, physician to Edward II, declared 'no-one is to be adjudged a leper, and separated from intercourse of mankind, until the figure and form of the face is actually changed' (Clay 1909, 60). Restrictions on lepers, such as those that forbade them to walk unshod (*ibid*, 175) or to touch articles which they wished to buy (Richards 1977, 50), seem initially to have been inspired by fear of ritual defilement rather than contagion. The idea that infection was misunderstood in the Middle Ages has been challenged (Richards 1991, 153), but miasmas were commonly blamed for the spread of disease after the Black Death.

By the 14th century, standard medical books contained descriptions of leprosy that would allow its diagnosis in advanced stages. One of many guides was by Guy de Chauliac (died 1363), which advocated that isolation should depend on the severity of symptoms (Richards 1977, 98) – but determining whether or not an individual was leprous was not

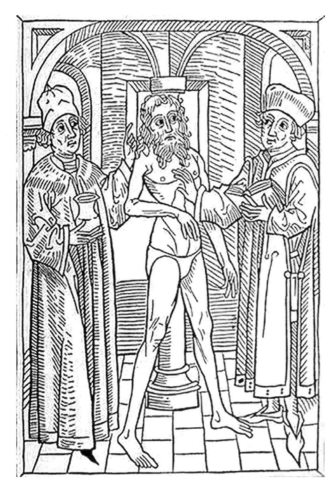

Fig. 2.4 *Two 15th-century physicians examine a patient with leprosy. From Dickmut* Regimen sanitatis, *reproduced in* Grand-Carteret L'Histoire, *vol I, p 389.* © *Mary Evans Picture Library*

Figure 2.5 Two comprehensively spotty naked men are guided by an angel to the herb fumitory, used against leprosy. From an Italian herbal of c 1500. University of Vermont MS 2

Baldwin IV (Fig 12.1), according to the chronicler William of Tyre, was treated with 'repeated fomentations, oil rubs and even poisonous remedies'; other approaches included dietary modifications, bathing in hot springs and bloodletting (Hamilton 2000, 250, 254).

Society in general

The attitudes of society to lepers can be judged only indirectly. For example, by-laws excluding lepers from towns are essentially the laws of an urban elite – the burgesses – and not those of the townspeople at large, who may not have shared the burgesses' concerns; alternatively, the by-laws may be a belated response by what was essentially the mercantile class, willing to trade even with lepers, to the fears of the whole urban community.

When the disease was at its height in England, in the 12th and 13th centuries, it must be suspected that the general public reaction was one of dread, any natural sympathy for the sufferer being overcome by loathing for the disease and its symptoms. For example, Bishop Hugh of Lincoln (died in 1200, canonised 1220) horrified contemporaries by kissing the sores of lepers (Gilchrist 1992, 115). His justification was that lepers were 'beloved by God, as was Lazarus' (Clay 1909, 66) and his intention may have been partly to allay public fears and soften attitudes. A Sussex contemporary, Abbot Walter de Lucy of Battle (died 1171), also waited on lepers (Clay 1909, 49); he would wash their hands and feet and kiss them, according to the Chronicle of Battle Abbey (Rawcliffe 2000b, 231). A third prominent 12th-century person to minister to lepers as representatives of Christ was Queen Matilda (Maud), first wife of Henry I and daughter of St Margaret of Scotland, who would wash their feet and kiss their hands (Orme and Webster 1995,

a medical monopoly. As well as physicians (Fig 2.4), clergy, civil officers or a jury could be called upon to make the decision (Clay 1909, 59), the clergy because of Levitical precepts that still apparently applied in New Testament times (Luke **17**, 14; Brody 1974, 62–3).[20] In London, the barbers diagnosed the disease (Cullum 1991, 39). In 12th-century Cologne three inmates diagnosed new arrivals at a leprosarium (Brody 1974, 63). In 16th-century Glasgow the magistrates had this responsibility, in 17th-century England one of the last suspected lepers was given a clean bill of health by the Royal College of Physicians and in 18th-century Shetland the Kirk, at a meeting of the parish council, had the task of diagnosis (Richards 1977, 40–1).

Some medieval 'cures' for leprosy were by modern standards bizarre, quite ineffectual (Fig 2.5) and unlikely to command Church support. Alchemist's gold could purify the leper, as could the earth from an anthill or the perfumed water in which the Christ child had been washed. Turtle blood might be tried, or the blood of an infant. There are nevertheless occasional records of 'lepers' recovering and being discharged (Brody 1974, 71–2). In the Crusader east,

24). As well as St James' Chichester, she is credited with establishing a leper hospital near London; to Henry I are attributed St Bartholomew's (Oxford) and Colchester, and endowments to existing hospitals. Although Henry's second wife Adeliza of Louvain, when widowed, married William d'Albini, Earl of Arundel, she has no known connection with the hospital for female lepers, dedicated to St James, which had been founded outside that town by 1182 (Hudson 1997, 31–2), nor with St James' Chichester.

The brief but heroic career of Baldwin IV of Jerusalem may also have contributed to a softening of attitudes. His victory at the battle of Mont Gisard in 1177 against the infamous Saladin, in which St George was seen fighting with the Christian host,[21] and subsequent successes, although militarily insignificant, were a sure sign that God was with the leper king. Unfortunately, God's representative on earth, Pope Alexander III, was less impressed. In his encyclical calling for a third crusade in 1181 he referred to 'Baldwin ... so severely afflicted by the just judgement of God ... that he is scarcely able to bear the continual torments of his body' and said he was unfit to rule (Hamilton 2000, 164).

In the later Middle Ages Margery Kempe, the 15th-century mystic, believed she was commanded by Jesus to kiss lepers, an activity her long-suffering confessor allowed if the lepers were female (Morgan 1999, 129–30). She herself had earlier loathed lepers and her son had lost his job because of a skin infection resembling leprosy that she believed was a punishment for sin (Orme and Webster 1995, 24).

Public reaction to those of noble birth or potentially heading for canonisation who chose symbolically to administer to lepers was one thing,[22] lesser mortals who cared for lepers on a daily basis did not fare as well. Clarice, the novice mistress at Sempringham, who nursed one of Gilbert's own protégées in the late 12th century, was shunned by the other sisters for fear of infection (Rawcliffe 2000b, 240). Her experience, it must be suspected, was the more usual. Contemporary with Clarice's rejection was the *Revelation of the Monk of Evesham*, again perhaps composed to allay public fears. In brief, a 'worshipful abbess' who tended two leprous young sisters shunned by the rest of the community went rapidly to paradise as a reward (Rawcliffe 2000b, 244).

The general conclusion that lepers were feared, despised and shunned by most of the population throughout the Middle Ages is seemingly contradicted by individuals who may have been elderly or infirm, but were not leprous, seeking admission into leper hospitals. Most hospitals had originally been founded to provide free services to the needy *pro Deo*, but the practice had grown up of making a gift on entry that, in time, had become in essence an admission fee or corrody. It thus became possible to purchase what, in the 21st century, might be termed 'sheltered accommodation', and individuals did so from an early date. The leper hospital at Whitby admitted non-lepers soon after its foundation in 1109, and in St Mary Magdalene's, King's Lynn, ten of the thirteen inmates were non-lepers by 1174 (Orme and Webster 1995, 29). In the same year Robert de Torpel, having developed leprosy, entered Peterborough Abbey as a monk-corrodian with his servants, ending his days in the monastic leprosarium (Rawcliffe 2000b, 234); those of his social class normally took orders or endured the disease in isolation at home. There were occasional attempts at segregation between lepers and non-lepers within most hospitals that encouraged non-lepers to seek admission from an early date, and by the time leprosy was in decline in England the presence of non-leprous inmates was a justification for the hospital's continued existence, albeit as an almshouse. Rich lepers could build their own houses within the hospital grounds and the hospitals were themselves no doubt class-conscious institutions. In Dauphigne, for example, there was one leper house for the commons, another for the nobles and a third for the ladies of the court (Brody 1974, 70), and Noyon and Walsingham were similarly reserved for lepers of good families (Richards 1991, 157).

Lepers in literature and art

Literary references to lepers may mostly be divided into Biblical and medieval. Leviticus is the main Old Testament book for understanding what, in the Middle Ages, was thought to be leprosy, but the two relevant chapters are not concerned with judging the leper; he is merely one of a group of ritually impure persons, and it is necessary to turn to other Old Testament allusions to the disease to understand fully how the Bible influenced medieval thinking.[23] Another major factor influencing medieval attitudes and understanding was the arrival of Arabic/Greek works on *lepra/elephantiasis* from the late 11th century.

Lepers are explicitly mentioned in Exodus, Numbers, Deuteronomy, II Samuel, II Kings and II Chronicles. One case is that of Miriam, whom God made leprous for criticism of Moses' marriage to 'the Cushite woman'. She was duly shut up 'without the camp' for a week until God cured her (Numbers **12**) and is a clear example of leprosy as divine punishment. Another is that of King Uzziah, who was made leprous for usurping a priestly prerogative by himself burning incense: 'and Uzziah the king was a leper unto the day of his death, and dwelt in a several house, being a leper; for he was cut off from the house of the Lord: and Jotham his son was over the king's house, judging the people of the land' (II Chronicles **26**, 21). To the medieval mind, the clear message was that persons punished with leprosy were no longer fit to rule and ought to live out their days in isolation. Interestingly, in death Uzziah was rehabilitated for 'they buried him with his fathers in the field of burial which belonged to the kings' (II Chronicles **26**, 23). One of the punishments with which the Jews were threatened if they ignored the

Mosaic covenant was being smitten 'in the knees, and in the legs, with a sore boil (*ulcus pessimus*), whereof thou canst not be healed, from the sole of thy foot to the crown of thy head' (Deuteronomy **28**, 35).

Brody (1974) has comprehensively studied leprosy in medieval literature. In the story *Der Arme Heinreich* of *c* 1195 an apparently otherwise blameless knight is stricken with leprosy for his vainglory. His physician tells him that he can be cured only by the sacrifice of a young girl. Having disposed of his wealth, Heinreich retires to a farm where the daughter of the peasant who runs it offers herself as a sacrifice, leading to Heinreich's acceptance of God's omnipotence with humility. The German version of a European folk-tale called *Constantine and Silvester* is another example of leprosy as divine punishment. The (utterly unhistorical) story in brief is that the Emperor Constantine had been persecuting and killing Christians. As a punishment, an angel throws water over him whilst he is in bed and he becomes leprous, subsequently seeking a cure from Pope Silvester.[24] According to the legend, he discovers he can recover by bathing in children's blood but at the last minute takes pity on them. As a reward, God tells Constantine that Silvester can cure him, which he does by converting the emperor to Christianity. These and similar tales are not, of course, a reflection of quotidian responses but have a symbolic nature.

Amis and Amiloun is a French romance in which leprosy again figures as a divine visitation. Amis has (rightly) been accused of making love to his overlord's daughter. Because he protests his innocence, he is given the chance of trial by battle, but he will necessarily be killed, as he is guilty. His friend Amiloun offers to switch identity and Amis agrees to live chastely with Amiloun's wife. Amiloun fights, wins and, still posing as Amis, bigamously marries the girl. His behaviour is punished by leprosy and a cure is brought about only when Amis kills his two children so that Amiloun can bathe in their blood. In an English version, the leprosy is a visitation of divine grace according to one commentator; it is also obviously a test of loyalty as well as a punishment:

> *Fouler mesel was never non*
> *In the world than thou schal be!* (1259–60)
> (Brody 1974, 165).

A further example is *The Testament of Cresseid* by Robert Henryson (died before 1508), written as a sequel to Chaucer's *Troilus and Criseyde* at a time when leprosy in England was becoming rare. In it, Cresseid has left Troilus for Diomed, who has deserted her. She becomes a whore and then a leper. The link between lust and leprosy is even more explicit in the earlier version of *Tristan and Isolde* by Eilhart von Oberge. In some versions the lovers are sentenced to burn, but in Eilhart's variant Isolde is given to the lepers so that she will come to acknowl-

edge the illicit nature of her own lust (Brody 1974, 180).

Leprosy in art can be as symbolic as in literature. Earlier medieval illustrations generally show lepers as comprehensively spotty, paying little attention to anatomical accuracy.[25] The viewer, it is assumed, is as familiar with spottiness as the Levitical symbol of leprosy as he is with a crown as the symbol of kingliness. To make the point superabundantly clear, the leper is invariably depicted with the rattle, bell[26] or horn that he was obliged to sound as he moved amongst the healthy, and carrying a dish in which purchases and donations might be placed without direct contact with the sufferer (Fig 2.6).[27] Stained glass is a medium in which lepers may have figured, but the only example known to the writer is at Canterbury where a depiction of the cure of the leper monk Elias occurs as a piece of propaganda to reinforce Canterbury's miracle-working credentials over its rival, Reading Abbey.[28] The north aisle of the Angel Choir of Lincoln Cathedral incorporates the 13th-century head of a leper, possibly meant for Robert FitzPernel, Earl of Leicester (Fig 2.1), with a squashed nose, toothless gaping smile and

Figure 2.6 A leper woman with a bell from the margin of the Exeter Pontifical, c 1400. The bell to warn of her presence is less usual than a wooden clapper. Her face is comprehensively, if unconvincingly, spotty to make it clear that leprosy accounts for her missing left hand and right (?) foot. As she is gathering alms for herself, she may not have been part of a hospital community. BL Lansdowne MS 451, f 127, © The British Library

bulbous eyes (Marcombe 2003, 139) and other grotesques may, on detailed inspection, betray similar characteristics of lepromatous leprosy. Not surprisingly, the English headquarters of the Knights of St Lazarus at Burton Lazars has yielded a stone corbel with a shrouded leper's head (Marcombe and Manchester 1990).

The later Middle Ages yield a few examples of anatomically correct paintings taken from life, the artists showing complete familiarity with the classic symptoms of the disease. One such is *Doomsday* by Barend van Orley (1492–1542) where the upturned nose and twisted limbs of the leper beggar are gruesomely convincing. Another, of the Cologne School of the 15th century, shows St Elisabeth of Hungary (1207–31) ministering to an equally realistic leper. A founder of leprosaria, she also treated lepers herself and is often portrayed bathing them. Another 15th-century painting of her ministry (Pálfi *et al* 2002, 210, fig 3) shows a patient with impressive blotches on his back, leaving the viewer in no doubt about his complaint. A contemporary English depiction, somewhere between art and symbol, is the well-known seated spotty leper woman, her nose damaged and face disfigured, begging with a bell, a marginal sketch from the Exeter Pontifical, below the banner reading 'Sum good my gentyll mayster for God sake' (Fig 2.6). She is missing her left hand and right foot and the visible parts of the respective limbs are bandaged. By the end of the Middle Ages and certainly by the 16th century syphilis had taken over from leprosy as the spotty disease in art and the two were sometimes equated (Brody 1974, 56), doubtless because it was still popularly believed that leprosy was sexually transmitted.

A factor behind the transition to realism is likely to have been the Greek/Arabic medical works that were by then circulating widely. Their illustrations reveal a keen understanding of the symptoms of Hansen's disease and its diagnosis.

2.3 Hospitals and their origins

Medieval England and Wales had over 1100 quasi-independent institutions that contemporaries would have called hospitals (Knowles and Hadcock 1971), and there were many more attached to monastic houses. All were essentially religious institutions that sought to heal the souls of sinners, although some came to specialise in the care of the sick poor. Medical care, as understood in the 21st century, seems to have been offered by a very few hospitals late in their history.

'Hospital' is from Latin *hospes,* 'host' or 'guest', which is also the root of the words hospice and hospitality, and this gives a clue to the origins of some hospitals, for the first seem to have been to accommodate poor travellers, particularly pilgrims, especially in remote areas.[29] In England, most were established in the 12th and 13th centuries. It has been claimed that the great period of hospital foundation was the early 12th century (Palliser 1993, 3; Satchell 1998, 102) but others (eg Orme and Webster 1995, 11) would put it slightly later. The problem is partly one of dating such institutions from documentary sources, for some of the smaller houses in particular may have been founded long before their first appearance in the written record and others which seem to be new foundations of the later Middle Ages may be unrecorded older hospitals with a revised constitution.

Soon after foundation, certain hospitals gained a reputation for looking after sick travellers. Some pilgrims were of course sick before they set out and were undertaking the journey in search of a cure, whilst others fell ill along the way. Such hospitals, amongst them St Bartholomew's Smithfield, are the real ancestors of today's hospitals. Although the reception of casualties was not entirely unknown,[30] professional medical treatment seems rarely to have been available;[31] what hospitals could offer 'patients' were spiritual exercises to purge the soul of sin in an era when any distinction between physical and spiritual would, if imaginable, have been thought at best perverse. In return, founders and benefactors received the intercessory prayers of the inmates to speed their souls, and those of their ancestors, through purgatory.

Some hospitals continued to have a dual role. The statutes of St Mary's Chichester state:

If anyone in infirm health and destitute of friends should seek admission ... let him be gladly received and assigned a bed ...

In regard to the poor people who are received late at night, and go forth early in the morning, let the Warden take care that their feet are washed, and, as far as possible, their necessities attended to. Care must be taken that they do not annoy the sick, that they do not pilfer, that they behave respectfully in word and deed.
(Cavis-Brown 1905, 8).

From around 1170 to about 1270 was the great age of pilgrimage to, from and within England. Such destinations as Canterbury and Walsingham needed to provide accommodation for pilgrims to their respective shrines, and the country's southern ports had to house pilgrims to continental destinations as well as any from abroad newly arrived in England. The ultimate destination for pilgrims, when political circumstances allowed, was Jerusalem itself, where the Order of St John had a hospital with over 750 beds, the largest in Christendom. Its statutes are a model of Christian concern, requiring the brethren to serve the sick poor 'with zeal and devotion as if they were their lords' (Hamilton 2000, 56, 237). By the 14th century there were still many pilgrims, including professional 'palmers' and hirelings fulfilling vows by proxy, as well as vagrants who were causing concern to a government troubled by labour shortages and vagabondage. Hospitals began to reflect changed circumstances by favouring the chronically ill or simply the poor rather than itinerants. When renewing statutes in 1342, St Thomas' Hospital, Canterbury, elected to entertain poor pilgrims in good health for one night only. The able-bodied and well-to-do were expected to find lodgings or to use inns. Some hospitals, amongst them St Giles', Norwich, actually owned inns for the accommodation of pilgrims (Rawcliffe 2000a, 60). There were a few new foundations for wayfarers, and the century also saw the first maternity hospitals.[32] A very few hospitals, best known of which was St Mary Bethlehem (Bedlam) in London, catered for the insane.

By the 15th century many pious travellers lodged in inns – at Glastonbury, for example, Abbot Selwood built the George and Pilgrim Inn *c* 1475, the monks of Gloucester built the New Inn *c* 1457 and in the reign of Henry VII the George was built at Winchcombe for visitors to St Kenelm (Webb 2000, 225–6) – but provision continued to be made for poor travellers. In northern England, where towns were fewer, the need was often supplied by hospitals attached to monasteries, and in the south the seaports still provided for travellers. God's House (St Julian's) Southampton spent £28 on 'daily hospitality to wayfarers and strangers from beyond the sea' out of a total annual income of over £140 in 1535 (Knowles and Hadcock 1953, 307).

A curious and, by modern standards, indefensible trend amongst hospitals that had once catered for the sick poor was to refuse admission to the seriously crippled and acutely ill. As noted, cripples could not play a full part in the increasingly elaborate rituals that late medieval benefactors expected in return for their patronage, and the sick were more expensive for cash-strapped hospitals to look after than the poor but able-bodied.[33] According to one estimate, there were as few as 39 institutions open to the sick poor in 1535 (Carlin 1989, 36). The poor but able-bodied were themselves under suspicion following the demographic changes of the 14th century and hospitals were seen in some cases as assisting lazy shirkers (Rubin 1989, 52–3). Some hospitals gave up all pretence of charitable work and became chantry chapels pure and simple, staffed by regular clergy charged with praying for the souls of patrons and benefactors. A significant number developed educational functions but more went out of business.

2.4 Leper hospitals – their origins, purpose and decline

Of the medieval hospitals listed for England and Wales by Knowles and Hadcock (2nd edn, 1971) leper hospitals account for 25.8%, almshouses 55.6%, hospices 10.2% and institutions for the sick poor 8.4% (Gilchrist 1992, 102),[34] and leper houses were the largest group by far of hospitals founded for a specific purpose. In the 13th century Britain had a minimum of around 200 leper hospitals each with, on average, about ten beds,[35] so approximately 2000 lepers could, in theory, be accommodated (Richards 1977, 11).[36] Others have suggested a higher total of around 300 hospitals or more established before the Dissolution (Rawcliffe 2000b, 231; Satchell 1998, 81) but not all would have existed simultaneously. The total population at the time may have been about 3 million, but it would be wrong to use these rough figures to calculate the incidence of leprosy. There can be few who voluntarily admitted to having the disease (denunciation by neighbours, followed by an investigation, usually preceded diagnosis), and many with mild forms will have escaped detection. The afflicted but wealthy will often have chosen to be confined within their own homes. Some, perhaps a majority, with the disease will have become pilgrims or vagrants rather than consenting to endure the quasi-monastic life of a hospital, although they may have taken advantage of the doles that some hospitals provided.[37] Some may have been expelled from such institutions. Inmates of some leper hospitals were non-lepers, an unknown percentage of beds may have been unfilled at others and a few hospitals may have supported more people than their endowments were intended to do.

Hospitals would often give preference to the founder's kin, those who occupied the lands of the endowment or the immediate neighbourhood (Orme and Webster 1995, 117–18) and those who founded hospitals, even the Crown, expected family and servants to receive preferential treatment.[38] For example, the hospital of the Holy Trinity founded at Arundel by the earl in 1395 gave preference to the earl's servants (Hudson 1997, 31–2; Orme and Webster 1995, 117). Admission fees were often considerable, the corrody at both Dover and London being 100s, and inmates were additionally required to bring with them such everyday possessions as they had: the 'pottis, pannys, pewter vessel, beddyng and other necessaries' specified in the constitution of St John's, Heytesbury, Wiltshire (Richards 1977, 33–4).

Chantry chapels, normally either reserved areas within churches, extensions to them or, rarely, free-standing structures, were founded by the wealthy in the belief that prayers of the living could shorten time that the souls of the deceased would have to spend in purgatory, and chantry priests, supported by endowments, would offer up a weekly, or even daily, mass for the repose of specific souls. It may be no more than coincidence that, according to Orme and Webster (1995, 11), there is a slight decline in the foundation of new hospitals from a peak in 1151–1200, but some endowments that would once have gone to hospitals undoubtedly went to chantries instead. Whatever the theological niceties, some may have thought that the prayers of a professional chantry priest were more efficacious than the mumblings of the sick poor, and chantries were, on the whole, cheaper to establish and maintain than hospitals. However, chantries could be, and were, founded within hospital chapels and, as charitable acts, hospital maintenance and care of the sick poor were by no means mutually exclusive.

The purpose of hospitals in general is made plain by the constitutions of such places as St Giles' Norwich (not a leper hospital), founded in 1249, which by 1420 boasted a master, eight chaplains, two clerks, seven choristers, two sisters ... and eight inmates (Richards 1977, 11). The intercessory prayers of the grateful inmates offered a hope of redemption to those who feared outright damnation or at best a painful spell in purgatory, and charity was an infallible cure for diseases of the soul. Some hospitals were at times difficult to distinguish from churches. Friarside, Co. Durham, for example, a probable hospice for wayfarers, was sometimes spoken of as a chapel or chantry (Knowles and Hadcock 1953, 272), and within the walls of Chichester, St Mary's Hospital may have evolved from a small parish church of the same dedication originally sited at the carfax.

There were no restrictions, other than financial, on who could set up hospitals, and amongst those who did were the crown, the aristocracy, bishops and religious orders. Some were no doubt founded as a matter of peer group display, but the greater number were a result of piety or charitable impulses coupled with an increasing concern for the welfare of the soul as the doctrine of purgatory evolved. A few may have coalesced around a hermit or other holy individual,[39] and others perhaps grew from informal communities of sufferers. It is not always easy to identify hospital founders, and there were no doubt spurious attempts to claim that privilege when original charters had gone astray and institutional memories grown dim. For example, some town corporations came to possess leper hospitals, but it has been suggested that these were by acquisition rather than through foundation. There is a chronology of foundation in which the Crown, Church and aristocracy are responsible for many leper hospitals before the mid-12th century, and lesser lords and lay folk thereafter (Satchell 1998, 126).

Some large hospitals were adequately endowed, but many were under-resourced from the start and others impoverished by unscrupulous clergy 'diverting' funds (Prescott 1992, 24). The richer foundations tended to admit the better-off, many by imposing an admission payment or selling corrodies beyond the means of the poor and against their founder's intention. The main potential area of conflict was where hospitals possessed a chapel and graveyard. This was addressed by the 3rd Lateran Council (1179), which allowed these amenities to leper hospitals as long as they were not to the detriment of the local parish church (Orme and Webster 1995, 37). Other privileges included an exemption from paying tithes on their produce and animals (Richards 1991, 154). Many founders and benefactors associated themselves so closely with their hospitals that they sought burial there (Clay 1909, 83; Rawcliffe 2000b, 245). Not all with an interest in hospitals founded new institutions, and some at least who could have afforded to do so endowed existing institutions, with the result that,

in their heyday, some hospitals tended to increase in size as well as in number.

Given the dread in which leprosy was often held, it might be assumed that leper hospitals were, in the words of one writer, 'isolation hospitals which provided permanent accommodation and fulfilled a general social purpose by segregating a stigmatised group' (Gilchrist 1992, 103). This cannot have been so. Entry into the many monastic-run leprosaria was voluntary and vocational, with men and women swearing an oath of poverty, chastity and obedience. The constitutions of leper hospitals such as Dudston, Gloucester, in the 1150s included expulsion amongst the disciplinary measures at their disposal. There is admittedly only one account, from Ilford, of the actual expulsion of a leper (for sexual misconduct: Richards 1977, 53; Clay 1909, 141) but the punishment may have been more common than records suggest, and the fact that it was available as the ultimate punishment undermines the 'isolation hospital' hypothesis. In 1442 most of the inmates of St James' Chichester were expelled but it is not known how many, if any, were lepers (McCann 1987, 253). One leper to leave his hospital was William Malesmeins, who had been confined at Bidlington since he was a minor, who emerged on his majority to do homage for estates at Lancing.[40]

The decline of leper hospitals

The peak period for the founding of all hospitals was from *c* 1150 to 1300, by which date there were at least 496. This was also more or less the period when leprosy was most widespread, but it would be wrong to assume that either containment or treatment of the disease was the spur. In the next 50 years, although a further 101 hospitals were established, the total number of hospitals increased by only 45 as some of the older hospitals ceased to function (Orme and Webster 1995, 11). Almost all 'hospitals' founded after the mid-14th century were maisons dieu, many under secular control, which offered the obedient and compliant pauper a secure old age in return for prayers (Rawcliffe 2000a, 192). A steep decline in the incidence of leprosy in England, beginning as early as the mid-13th century according to one view (Rubin 1989, 45), was more or less contemporary with the end of some hospitals and, whilst cause and effect cannot at present be demonstrated, the argument is not necessarily a circular one. Although references in the later Middle Ages suggest that presumed victims of the disease could still readily be found, amendments to hospital constitutions confirm that they were fewer. For example, Holy Innocents' Hospital, Lincoln, in a royal grant of 1457, is required to take three lepers from the royal household, or if three cannot be found, three leprous tenants from royal estates (Marcombe 2003, 166).

The smaller and less well-endowed hospitals were usually the first to go. Hospitals founded originally for lepers were taking in others, and in some cases amending their constitutions to reflect changed circumstances. Even England's largest leper hospital, Sherburn, founded originally by the bishop of Durham in 1181 for 65 lepers, male and female (Richards 1991, 157), had places for only two lepers 'if so many could be found' under a revised constitution of 1434 but also had room for thirteen 'poor brothers' (Carlin 1989, 23). By the reign of Henry VIII none could recall why the Shrewsbury leper house had been founded (Richards 1977, 83). At Norwich, the five extramural leper houses began to cater for the sick poor during the 15th century although they were still receiving lepers in the later part of that century (Rawcliffe 2000a, 193, 203). In 1342 Ripon was diverting funds to succour the general poor; in 1348 the large house at St Albans had only three inmates and the lazar houses of St John and St Leonard at Aylesbury were in ruins (Richards 1991, 161).[41]

The decline in the total number of hospitals, including leper houses, has been linked with the Black Death. Orme and Webster (1995, 11) put the total number of hospitals at 541 in 1350, with a decline thereafter in both new foundations and in totals until 1451, when the total rises to 552. However, a decline in the number of new foundations is perceptible in the period 1301–50 and, whilst the economic dislocation following the Black Death cannot have benefited hospitals, it may have done no more than hasten a process that had already begun. In Bristol it has been noted that from the early to mid-14th century onwards wealthy patrons were less willing to make large donations of land to local hospitals, perhaps because of concerns about mismanagement or fraud (Price 1998, 210).

An alternative to letting a hospital die was to annexe it to another institution, either a hospital or religious house. St James' Arundel, originally for female lepers, was annexed to a collegiate church in 1383 (Orme and Webster 1995, 131). Others carried on in theory alone, their incomes being devoted solely to the upkeep of clergy. This was the fate of Windham, Sussex, in c 1520 when Bishop Sherborne of Chichester used the endowment to fund a new cathedral prebend (*op cit*). Post-Reformation, a similar fate nearly befell St James' Chichester.

Very many hospitals disappeared under the parliamentary statute of 1536 abolishing religious houses with an annual income of less than £200. Others lasted a few years longer, with Arundel, for example, disappearing in 1546 with the dissolution of the collegiate church (Hudson 1997). Amongst the few survivors were such hospitals as St James' Chichester, linked to a now-Protestant cathedral, that were able to convince the authorities that intercessory prayers, now illegal, were no longer part of their daily lives.

2.5 Life and death in leper hospitals

All but the smallest hospitals will have had a constitution, perhaps modelled on that of one of the monastic orders, and their own customs that developed over time, perhaps eventually being written down and incorporated in the statutes if the constitution needed to be amended. The rule was commonly based on that of the Augustinians, modified to suit local circumstances, which was less rigorous than that of the Benedictines but nevertheless encouraged a way of life for priests in proximity to lay society, allowing them time for teaching, pastoral care and charity as well as a full liturgical life (Rubin 1989, 48). The rule, introduced in England by Henry I, had its origin in a letter by Augustine of Hippo advising a way of life for women in a community, and each house made its own interpretation of its meaning (Cullum 1993, 13). In leprosaria it may have been more common to expect the inmates to abide by the rule of the house than in other hospitals (Cullum 1993, 11). Confession and absolution were a condition of entry into some leper houses and general hospitals even before the 4th Lateran Council (1215) insisted on them at the onset of medical treatment (Rawcliffe 2000b, 249).

The general rules of hospitals following a strict regime were those of poverty (although this was relaxed as time progressed: Clay 1909, 134–5), obedience and chastity, and in the case of a husband and wife both afflicted and admitted to the same leprosarium, living apart was initially required (Richards 1977, 64). As noted, the original intention seems usually to have been to offer free admission *pro Deo* to those who needed it, but the practice of charging fees had become widespread. In some hospitals, amongst them St James' Chichester, existing inmates had a veto over new admissions, and patrons or donors sometimes kept the nomination of one or more beds (Clay 1909, 130). Hospitals often gave preference to people connected with the founder, the lands of the endowment or the immediate neighbourhood (Orme and Webster 1995, 118). To enter a hospital, particularly one of early foundation, practically involved the life of a religious although the religious orders themselves would not usually admit lepers. Some hospitals – mainly the larger foundations – required the staff and inmates to wear a distinctive quasi-clerical garb. Many, less well endowed, will have been unable to afford such a luxury but will have received suitable clothes as gifts, perhaps often as bequests, to the inmates. At St James' Chichester the inmates had no specific uniform but were required to wear shabby clothing, either white or black, as a sign of humility and to donate their best garment to the brotherhood when they died (Appendix 2).

Whatever the rite on admission, an oath of obedience to the hospital constitution will have been required as a condition of acceptance, after which the new inmate joined a group which, in one of the stricter, quasi-monastic houses would, like other religious, be said to be dead to the world. When admitted, the new inmate bequeathed all or part of his possessions to the institution.[42] In return, he received care for life as long as he obeyed the statutes. At St James' Chichester fines were exacted for minor offences but sexual incontinence could lead to expulsion (Appendix 2). Assurances might be offered to the recently admitted leper as a comfort after diagnosis, especially Isaiah **53**, 3–4, verses that in Jerome's Vulgate translation, describe Christ as a leper.[43] As Brody (1974, 103) has remarked, soldiers returning from the First Crusade with the disease could hardly be treated as sinners; a sacred malady, no matter how unpleasant, was preferable to all.

The daily life for inmates was one of prayer, centred round the chapel. At Sherburn, Co. Durham, 161 *pater nosters* a day were required (Richards 1977, 53). At St James' Chichester inmates would be admitted only if they knew the Lord's Prayer and Creed 'at least generally in the manner of the laity' and there were daily and nightly rounds of prayers for benefactors and the Church (Appendix 2). As has been suggested, very many leper hospitals were founded for spiritual profit rather than in the cause of public health, and the founder and other benefactors will have expected prayers to help their souls in the world to come (Clay 1909, 88). Founders' days or festivals might be marked by special gifts or food. In most leper hospitals the inmates would have heard mass daily and kept canonical hours unless they were too ill to do so. When they were not engaged in spiritual exercises, able-bodied lepers will have been expected to undertake physical work which might include labour in the hospital gardens, in the same manner as their counterparts in the religious orders.

A Master or Prior, who might himself be a leper, often nominated by the patron but occasionally elected by the inmates, headed the leper household. Ilford provided for a healthy and a leper master, and Dover said that the master might be a leper (Clay 1909, 143–4). At Chichester the appointment was made by the bishop, the master being a clerk in holy orders until the Reformation, when lay masters were appointed. The most important member of staff was the chaplain,[44] and there might be additional healthy brethren to undertake various practical and administrative duties. The healthy and leprous seem normally to have lived apart, and in the few houses where both sexes were admitted, they too were segregated. There would not normally have been a physician, either resident or visiting (Clay 1909, 63–5). At Sherburn there were two baths, the hair was washed weekly and laundry done twice a week, and at Higham Ferrers the barber visited (Clay 1909, 173).

Periodic visitations, usually by the bishop or some other ecclesiastical dignitary, were made to ensure that hospitals obeyed their statutes. Discipline within the hospital was usually a matter for a weekly chapter meeting. Flogging, fasting and fines were the common punishments but expulsion was the ultimate sanction. The only description of an expulsion is the one at Ilford, where a leper 'having brought into his chamber a drab, and sayd she was his sister' was, after mass, ritually ejected from the church and put in a cart which was pursued by the mob (Richards 1977, 53). Although the date of this event is not known, it may well be earlier than 1346, in which year the danger of infection from lepers was acknowledged in a letter to the rulers of London by Edward III. At St Julian's hospital near St Albans the constitution was revised at about this time to require the leper inmates to live apart, and restrictions on visitors to leper hospitals were occasionally being imposed in Scotland by the end of the Middle Ages (Richards 1977, 56–9).

The physical treatment of leprosy (the spiritual side of the disease was catered for by the daily round of prayers) is a subject about which little is known, and the medieval mind would have had as great a difficulty with separating the two aspects as the 21st-century mind has with accommodating a spiritual dimension to disease. The only biblical help came from II Kings **5** where Naaman the Syrian general was cured after bathing in the Jordan seven times on Elisha's advice. A leper called Ramp, the supposed founder of a leper hospital at Beccles (Suffolk), is said to have overcome the disease by bathing in a sacred spring and allegedly established the hospital in gratitude (Rawcliffe 2000a, 37). He may have been re-enacting Naaman's treatment at a more convenient water source, although some did make the pilgrimage to the Jordan itself hoping to be cured (Marcombe 2003, 9).

Bathing as a cure is also described in the story of Elias the Leper. Elias, a Reading Abbey monk, wanted to make a pilgrimage to St Thomas' shrine at Canterbury in the hope of a cure. However, he despaired of gaining his abbot's permission as Reading and Canterbury were rivals in the pilgrim trade. He instead asked and received permission to try the hot springs at Bath,[45] and doubled back to Canterbury. On the way he met a knight who produced a phial of the martyr's water that Elias tasted and then used to wash his face. He then went to Bury St Edmunds, obtained a cloth tinged with Thomas' blood and washed away the leprosy (Webb 2000, 48 and 57).

Elias was one of many lepers allegedly cured by St Thomas, either through drinking holy water containing the tiniest droplets of his blood or through bathing in it. Another was a nobleman, 'despised and deserted even by his own men' despite the dignity of his birth, who found relief at the tomb. The shrine itself, given the ills of some of its visitors, must have been a potential source of infection; perhaps it was believed that the sanctity of the place was sufficient to protect pilgrims. Nor was Thomas the only native saint able to dispel the disease; a destitute Kentish leper was cleansed through contact with the water in which St Wulfstan had washed his hands after celebrating divine office (Rawcliffe 2000b, 238).

Hospital endowments had usually to be augmented by what the institution itself could raise. Few hospitals can have aimed at self-sufficiency in food production, and alms gathering was important. As lepers themselves had limited access to places where people gathered, the hospital commonly appointed a proctor, a healthy individual with a portable money-box who in time evolved from itinerant alms gatherer to resident administrator. The post of master often became a sinecure and it was effectively the proctor who ran the institution. Another official of increasing importance in the later Middle Ages was the pardoner, who granted indulgences for alms or to people attending the chapel. The roles of proctor and pardoner, insofar as both involved fundraising, overlapped. Curiously, the term 'pardoner' for a hospital officer survived the Reformation (Clay 1909, 189).

As noted, the 3rd Lateran Council in 1179 confirmed, despite clerical opposition, a leper house's rights to its own chapel and graveyard, the latter with the usual stipulation that only lepers and their carers should be interred therein. In practice, only the larger institutions availed themselves of these privileges, and some already had their own cemeteries through local negotiation. For example, the bishop of Gloucester gave approval to the abbot for a cemetery at St Margaret's leper house, Gloucester, 45 years before the Council met (Rawcliffe 2000b, 248). Hospitals that were no more than cottages with beds for two or three lepers presumably buried their dead in the local parish church. Yet the cemetery of St Helen-on-the-Walls, a poor intramural York parish, contained not one identifiable leper amongst more than 1000 skeletons (Dawes and Magilton 1980). The same was true at the church (later Gilbertine priory) of St Andrew's Fishergate outside the walls of York, where over 400 skeletons were examined (Stroud and Kemp 1993). The 45 skeletons from St Bartholomew's Hospital, Bristol, which was not a leper hospital, were similarly without the disease (Price 1998). Our sample of medieval graveyards is still tiny, but the absence of lepers from 'normal' cemeteries leads one to ask if a custom had emerged of burying all lepers, whether inmates or not, in the local leprosarium graveyard.

On his death, the personal possessions of a leper usually reverted to the hospital. In Chichester he was required to leave his best daily habit to the brethren jointly and to leave money for a feast for the surviving brethren on the day of his burial (Appendix 2). If he had his own clothing and furniture the hospital might, on the precedent of the heriot of manorial custom, appropriate the bed in which he died, his chest, his best robe and hood, as at Lynn, whereas the Heytesbury statutes allowed the leper to keep half of any money acquired during residence. The goods of a deceased resident, whether 'gownes, hodys, cotys, skertys, hosyn or shone', were to be distributed amongst the living (Clay 1909, 134–5).

There is no evidence that in death the leper was treated very differently from any ordinary parishioner (see Chapter 6 below). The funeral would normally have been soon after death, sometimes on the day of death. The grave would be dug after mass, in the presence of the cortège, and any other bones disturbed would have been sent to the charnel (Horrox 1999, 101–4). Where hospitals had their own cemeteries it may have been normal practice to inter leper inmates in coffins rather than just shrouds, but there is insufficient evidence to substantiate this. Funerals were, however, a priority in the later Middle Ages, with many joining the socio-religious guilds in order to ensure a good send-off, and funerary prayers, candles, bells and masses were all believed to relieve the pains of purgatory (Rawcliffe 2000a, 5).

One of the dangers for lepers in hospitals was that they ceased to be individuals or indeed human beings at all, becoming little more than symbols on which the charity of benefactors could be lavished, for it was the charitable act itself, not its consequences, that came to be all-important. The inmates' prayers, which could be bought – Henry II paid the lepers of Harbledown just outside Canterbury 20 marks to pray for his murdered archbishop – were their greatest asset. Even before the doctrine of purgatory was formalised, the chosen were in a good position to, as it were, bend God's ear, and the purpose of benefactions changed from a vague charitable urge to the specific task of saving souls through intercessory prayers. From having been a straightforward scourge, albeit one with a pronounced spiritual dimension, leprosy ended up as a state of grace. At its most extreme, the idea manifested itself through the concept of Christ as leper, an idea that had been developed by St Jerome and then Gregory the Great (died 604).[46] This is all far removed from the reality of caring for those with a hideously disfiguring disease. The case of Richard Sunieve of Edgeworth brings us back with a jolt; even his mother, who devotedly nursed him for eight years, was so overcome by the stench that she had reputedly to feed him at the end of a long stick (Rawcliffe 2000b, 240, n60).

Notes

1. Not all subsequent scholars have been enthusiastic. Carlin (1989, 21) accuses the book of being seriously flawed by meagre documentation and the author's essentially romantic and unscholarly treatment of the subject.
2. The older term 'leprosy' is, however, used in this report because it has social as well as medical implications. As will be seen, sufferers from this disease were, uniquely, legally disadvantaged as well as being treated as outcasts on the fringe of society, somewhere between the living and the dead. For an alternative view on nomenclature, see Norway (Richards 1977, 93).
3. For a recent summary of the evidence, see Roberts *et al* (2002), 213–21.
4. Early Roman cemeteries in Britain (up to *c* AD 200) were mostly cremation cemeteries where evidence for leprosy would very rarely survive, so it cannot be assumed that the disease necessarily arrived late in the Roman period. Late Iron Age burials are very uncommon. Some at least were normally cremations, although

regional traditions can be identified that included inhumations.

5. I am grateful to Elizabeth Popescu for pointing out this reference to me.

6. The articulated remains represented a minimum of 149 adults, 59 males, 76 females, 14 unsexed, and 35 children. Leprosy apart, other interesting pathologies included a good example of Perthes disease, a fractured elbow with pseudoarthrosis and a possible case of poliomyelitis. I am most grateful to Elizabeth Popescu for this information in advance of her own publication.

7. Their original headquarters was the Hospital of St Lazarus at Jerusalem, where a leprous pilgrim could receive comfortable sleeping quarters, good food and a chance to bathe in the Jordan. As a fighting force, they were undistinguished but their presence on a battlefield must have been akin to that of holy relics. The medieval order survived in a much altered form until 1946, and has since been revived (Marcombe 2003).

8. Current research is succeeding in extracting DNA material from M. leprae cells in ancient bone. Some bones with no sign of leprosy can show a positive DNA result, but others where leprous changes have taken place can test negative. I am most grateful to Claire Watson for a summary of her research. Although exciting, these results are perhaps less illuminating for the historian than they first appear, for an important question is not who had the disease, but who was thought to have the disease. Any non-lepers who have been misdiagnosed will nevertheless have been treated as lepers, whilst those who had the disease in its early stages (and who themselves were perhaps unaware of it) will have been treated as healthy.

9. It has even been suggested that the medical profession had, by the 14th century, become better at recognising leprosy so that, whereas earlier anything from acne through to measles and smallpox might have been mistaken for Hansen's disease, their diagnosis was increasingly accurate (Gottfried 1983, 14). Amongst a number of objections to the idea is that diagnosis was by no means a medical monopoly.

10. Knights and sergeants who contracted the disease had to join the Order and fight as long as they could.

11. Carole Rawcliffe, pers comm.

12. Like all minority groups, lepers were potential scapegoats. The secular authorities in southern France and the Crown of Aragon persecuted Jews and lepers in 1321 after an alleged plot to poison wells was discovered (Richards 1991, 161–2; Rawcliffe 2000b, 235) and, although there was no comparable event in England, individuals and groups of lepers doubtless suffered unjustly from time to time.

13. Or alleged leper. This diagnosis is not confirmed in medieval chronicles (Rawcliffe 2000b, 230).

14. The number of leprosaria may be exaggerated, but as the population of France was four times that of England it is not impossible.

15. Butler (1993, 79) appears to express a minority view in claiming that after the Black Death the liturgy was no longer an end in itself except for vicars choral or chantry priests, and that good works replaced efficacious prayers, especially in towns where the performance of such works was more necessary and more beneficially visible. There may be a valid distinction to be made between the hospitals surviving from before the Black Death, which tended to follow the chantry chapel route, and the newer foundations, almshouses founded in the name of Christian charity and often the urban elite's response to the threat of social unrest, although it has been claimed that prayer was equally central to these.

16. In the Latin Kingdom of Jerusalem lepers were more generously treated and knights afflicted with the disease could continue to hold their fiefs if they arranged a substitute to undertake their military duties. Even so, Baldwin IV could not marry and beget a legitimate heir because leprosy was thought to be sexually transmitted (Hamilton 2000, 29, 109).

17. A number were Jewish and therefore untroubled by this specifically Christian doctrine. At a humbler level, the village 'wise woman' with her herbal remedies was routinely suspected of collusion with diabolic powers.

18. The diet at hospitals will become better understood as more are excavated. Animal bones and an inventory of 1303 from St Bartholomew's Bristol (not a leper hospital) indicate a fairly good diet of young sheep/goats and cattle, some young pigs and poultry including chicken and goose. Brawn may have been prepared from sheep's heads. Mutton became more common in the diet after c 1400. Stewing and boiling seem to have been the usual method of cooking, judging from cut marks on the bones (Price 1998, 92, 223–4). The diet at St Mary Spital London can be partly reconstructed from animal bone remains, and exhibits some changes over time (Thomas et al 1997, 113–14). As Fridays and fast days in Lent would have been strictly observed, fish would have been an essential dietary component. Meat was not necessarily part of the diet on non-fast days. The hospital of St John at Ely allowed meat to the chaplains only twice a week (Rubin 1989, 49–50) and for most medieval people cereals, in the form of bread, pottage and ale, were the main foodstuffs.

19. In England, London's Savoy hospital under its statutes of 1505 is the first where the permanent attendance of a physician and surgeon was provided (Thomas et al 1997, 107).

20. 'It belongs to the office of a priest to distinguish between one form of leprosy and another' according to Bishop Bronescombe of Exeter (1258–80), quoted in Cullum 1991, 39, n7.

21. His shrine at Lydda was under Muslim siege.

22. Kings and nobles ministering to lepers were not an exclusively insular phenomenon. Examples from the European continent include the French king Robert the Pious (died 1031) and Theobald the Great, count of Blois and Champagne (died 1152). Noble women included Radegund, Queen of the Franks (died AD 587), and Elisabeth of Hungary. Amongst the saintly, Francis of Assisi lived with lepers (Rawcliffe 2000b, 239).

23. Not just Christian thinking. Attitudes in medieval Judaism mirror those in Christianity, not because of any direct contact between Jewish and Christian scholars but because both had a common source (Brody 1974, 119–21).

24. A variation in Dante's *Inferno* suggests that pride, not persecution, was the cause of Constantine's downfall.

25. One such is redrawn in Clay 1909, 59, fig 7.

26. Bells might be attached to his shoes.

27. Clay (1909, 177, fig 26) has a redrawing of a leper with a rattle in the right hand and a bowl in the left.

28. Clay 1909, 64, fig 8.

29. Medieval Latin *hospitium*, the usual word for a hospital, could also mean an inn. Conversely, the word *spittle* (now usually spelled *spital*), the usual form of the word in English, can also mean a shelter for travellers. Another word found, although less commonly, is *xenodochium* from Greek *xenos*, a stranger. It occurs as a synonym for hospitium but is commonly used for pilgrims' lodgings and monastic guesthouses, contexts where no treatment of the sick is implied.

30. In 1305 the hospital of St John the Baptist, Oxford, treated one Robert Attwyndyate who had broken his finger (Carlin 1989, 24).

31. St Bartholomew's Bristol, one of the few English hospitals to have been excavated on a reasonable scale (in 1976–78), produced no artefacts of any period that could be considered intrinsically medical (Price 1998, 79). In the 16th century two of the London hospitals retained their own professional practitioners and in the late 15th century a London mercer left money to fund a peripatetic surgeon for a number of London hospitals (Carlin 1989, 29–31). In the *Valor Ecclesiasticus* the Savoy hospital, London, is the only one to record payments to apothecaries for medicine.

32. The only one outside London was the former leper hospital of St John the Evangelist, Blyth, Notts, refounded in 1446 for poor strangers and pregnant women. The London hospitals were St Bartholomew's Smithfield, St Thomas' Southwark and St Mary without Bishopsgate. Dick Whittington (died 1423) is said to have founded the ward for unmarried mothers at St Thomas' (Carlin 1989, 33). Some hospitals had provided for expectant mothers amongst others at an earlier date. In 1240 Henry III gave money to St John's Oxford for a maternity ward and St Paul's Norwich *c* 1200–50 housed poor child-

bearing women. Others specifically excluded them (Orme 2001, 86). In *The Highway to the Spitalhouse* (*c* 1536) it is said that 'Poor women in childbed have here easement', as if this was a facility that hospitals ought to offer (see Appendix 5).

33. Nearly all hospitals were in or near towns and would normally have looked to the wealthier burgesses for financial support. By the early to mid-14th century rural wages were rising but the goods and services provided by towns were in less demand and the burgesses consequently less well off. More to the point, they were inclined to divert their declining charitable funds to institutions other than hospitals (Rubin 1989, 52).

34. Carlin (1989) proposes different figures based on the same data, putting leper houses at 31% (345 examples) and almshouses at 67% (742 examples). Hospitals could and did change functions over time and the discrepancies may in part be explained by the respective (unstated) horizons of the authors.

35. The largest, at Sherburn, Co. Durham, was founded in *c* 1181 for 65 monks, nuns and other leprous religious in the north of England (Carlin 1989, 23).

36. For Europe as a whole, a figure of 19,000 lepers out of a total population of 60–70 million has been proposed (Richards 1991, 153).

37. St Mary Magdalene's Ripon (Yorks) may have provided clothing as well as food (Cullum 1991, 45–6).

38. Some hospitals were no doubt founded by wealthy families already afflicted with leprosy for the reception of their unfortunate kin.

39. And of course some pious individuals may have been inspired to take up residence in existing hospitals.

40. *Curia Rolls 1219–20*, 308–10.

41. The decline in leprosy was not an insular phenomenon. At Rheims, for example, the hospital of St Lazarus had beds for eight lepers but only one was occupied in 1336 and it was often completely empty in the 15th and 16th centuries. In 1351 the number of lepers in the 59 leprosaria of Paris was only 35. From the early 15th century to the mid-16th century the leper house at Namur had an average of only four or five inmates, and by the 17th century the disease was more or less extinct in Western Europe (Richards 1991, 161), although it lingered in the north.

42. At St Mary's Chichester the formula was as follows: *I, N, promise to God and to the Blessed Mary that hereafter, with their assistance, I will observe towards myself chastity, towards my superiors obedience, and that I will hold no property of my own without the license and consent of the Warden* (Cavis-Brown 1905, 6–7).

43. 'He is despised and rejected of men; a man of sorrows and acquainted with grief; and we

UNIVERSITY OF WINCHESTER
LIBRARY

hid as it were our faces from him; for he was despised and we esteemed him not. Surely he hath borne our griefs and carried our sorrows; yet we did esteem him stricken, smitten of God and afflicted.' Jerome's version ends *'et nos putavimus eum quasi leprosum et percussum a Deo et humiliatum'*.

44. The terminology can be confusing. It seems that at St James' Chichester in the Middle Ages the head of the hospital was in holy orders and called the master. He was sometimes referred to as the chaplain. The senior leper inmate was called the prior. It was not unknown for the head of a hospital to be a secular, and at St Leonard's, York, in 1245 this is explicitly stated to have been the case (Cullum 1993, 11).

45. The hospital of St John the Baptist had been founded at Bath to allow the sick poor to bathe in medicinal waters. St Michael's, Welton, Northumberland, was another spa hospital (Carlin 1989, 33).

46. In one of his most famous homilies, a monk called Martyrius carries an exhausted leper to the gates of a monastery. The leper changes into Christ and, ascending to heaven, assures the astonished monk that he will be rewarded in the next world (Rawcliffe 2000b, 246).

3 Medieval and early modern cemeteries in England: an introduction *by John Magilton*

The dying leper, having made his last confession in the infirmary in front of the chaplain and his fellow brethren, would receive extreme unction. Whilst he received communion, psalms were recited and a cross and lighted candles were placed at the head of the bed. After various services for the dead had been sung, the body was washed, wrapped by and sewn into a winding sheet and placed on a bier (in medieval times, a kind of stretcher with short legs: Fig 3.1). From now until burial the body lay in the chapel, and throughout the night psalms were recited. In the morning, after a funeral mass, the body was carried in procession for the short distance from the chapel to consecrated ground where burial was to take place. Over the bier was set a frame (the hearse) covered by a cloth (the pall)[1] that hid the body from view. At the grave the body was censed and sprinkled with holy water, had earth cast on it and was buried.[2]

Each parish had its own hearse and pall to be loaned or rented out for funerals (Horrox 1999, 102); so, presumably, did all hospitals that possessed their own graveyards, and perhaps some that used the local parish churchyard. The obligation to bury those who died in their care was explicit in the charters of some hospitals,[3] and hospital inmates, including corrodians, would have enjoyed free burial but others, even benefactors, may have paid significant sums for the privilege.[4] For those who sought burial other than at their own parish church, hospitals did not enjoy anything like the popularity of friaries, for example, and there is not a single case from surviving wills of Chichester citizens seeking

Figure 3.1 The parish bier from St Mary's Church, Debenham, Suffolk. Photo: Jo Buckberry

burial with the lepers (see Appendix 4), although a cathedral prebend, John Wytcliff, rector of Horsted Keynes (E Sussex) willed in 1383 to be buried in the hospital chapel of SS Peter and Paul at Maidstone (Kent).[5] Too few hospital cemeteries have been investigated and published on a scale adequate to determine whether there was any segregation (eg between staff and inmates) within the graveyard. Monks and canons usually had discrete cemeteries at the east end of the church in religious houses but Cistercians were allowed to bury two lay 'friends' in the monastic cemetery (Daniell 1998, 96). Segregation by age seems to have been practised by the Black Friars of Oxford where the bodies of children under fifteen were mostly confined to the chapter house (Harman 1985).

The place of burial reflected the status of the deceased, the élite generally expecting burial in church or chapel but most making do with an 'ordinary' grave in the cemetery. Excavated cemeteries reveal that there were favoured locations within the graveyard, as there were within the church, but the few surviving late medieval parish accounts imply a standard charge for all outside burials (Daniell 1998, 58–9). Many churches had a south door approached by a path from which the more elaborate funerary monuments could be viewed, and opportunities for display may explain the alleged popularity of burial on this side (Hadley 2001, 47). It has been suggested that in Ireland burial at an entryway, threshold or boundary was reserved for those of high status (Fry 1999, 170), perhaps because a liminal body, neither within nor without, was, with typical Celtic love of ambiguity, not quite either dead or alive.

The site of the grave would have been marked before ceremonies began by the priest, who would have sprinkled it with holy water and marked it with a cross. The pit was usually dug in the presence of the cortège and tended to be shallow[6] – hence an insistence on walling or fencing graveyards to exclude pigs and other rooting animals (Horrox 1999, 104). There must, however, have been times when the pit was dug in advance of burial since the mismatch between the size of the pit and that of the corpse seen in some archaeological excavations is otherwise inexplicable. Odd bones from earlier burials would have been kept for the charnel pit or house; and at urban cemeteries, whether of hospitals or churches, on restricted sites, intersections between graves will have become common before the end of the Middle Ages, providing another incentive to make new graves shallow. Theologically there was no objection to disturbing older graves as the soul was deemed to be elsewhere, especially once the doctrine of purgatory had been fully formulated, but it must have been inconvenient to have to gather up at least the larger bones for the charnel.

Putting a shrouded corpse into a grave cannot have been easy and would have become increasingly difficult with deeper graves. The act of burial is rarely depicted in English art and a stained glass roundel from Leicester is one of only a few examples (Clarke 1962). The grave has been newly dug and has a spread of disinterred bones beside it. The priest sprinkles the body with holy water from a sprig of hyssop (Psalm **51**, 7) and touches it with a processional cross as it enters the grave. In the Bedford Book of Hours[7] a man standing in the grave is receiving the corpse head-first. Another drawing, by Simon Marmion, shows the body being lowered by a rope round the shoulders (Daniell 1998, 50).

Once interred, the body was generally unlikely to be disturbed by anything other than the intersection of a later grave. Archaeology has revealed a few examples where an earlier grave was deliberately reopened to take a second body, and these imply some type of grave-marker. Where one burial followed another in relatively quick succession, the mound over the earlier grave may have sufficed to indicate its location. Burials in church or chapel could be marked in a variety of ways, determined by the wealth of the deceased and the fashions of the era. Outside burials seem rarely to have had any permanent markers and churchyard gravestones do not become common until the 18th century.

What follows was largely written before the publication of *Requiem. The Medieval Monastic Cemetery in England* (Gilchrist and Sloane 2005). As this is likely to remain the standard work on the subject for some years, it would have been possible to refer readers to the new book for all they needed to know on the subject and simply delete everything below. However, the original intention of providing the reader with enough background to see the Chichester cemetery in context has been retained and, as with the history in Chapter 2, the aim has been to present a selective account that is pertinent to the Chichester cemetery.

3.1   Death in history

Death defined

The Middle Ages was a period that, if not generally characterised by radical changes in lifestyle or thought, at least saw perceptions alter over time; one relevant example, discussed in the previous chapter, was the formulation and elaboration of the doctrine of purgatory. Attitudes to, and even definitions of, death will not have been the same in 1050 as they were in 1550 but it is for the later period, and for the wealthier, that most historical information survives. Attitudes will not only have been affected by chronological factors but by the status, occupation and place of residence of an indi-

vidual, for it is doubtful if a 14th-century serf in Cornwall held many folk-beliefs in common with his Yorkshire contemporary. The better-off members of society are, after the clergy themselves, most likely to have subscribed to the orthodox theology of the day, insofar as it can be determined. Despite its claim to be Catholic (meaning 'universal'), there was often a wide divergence of interpretation of doctrine between dioceses of the Church. To take again the example of purgatory, in England this was universally portrayed as a simulacrum of hell, albeit of finite duration, whereas in Italy, if Dante is to be believed, it was seen more as an anteroom of heaven where souls were healed (Daniell 1998, 11).

Death, for the Church, occurred when the immortal soul left the mortal body and joined with an immortal body. It was often difficult to tell when a person was dead, the traditional means of a feather, straw or mirror to the nostrils or of listening for the heartbeat being notoriously unreliable. Having taken up the crown, Henry V was embarrassed by the revival of the supposedly deceased Henry IV, an event dramatised by William Shakespeare (*Henry IV* part 2, iv, 20–90). The soul was untroubled by bodily illnesses but the converse did not apply. A sick soul could and often did manifest itself in such earthly diseases as leprosy. The Church's role was primarily to look after the immortal soul through such spiritual exercises as confession. This was intended to lead to repentance, which might in turn inspire almsgiving to the sick or poor. When a choice had to be made, the soul took precedence in the Church's eyes: an unrepentant heretic might, in an extreme case, lose his life in order that his soul might be saved. This was the justification for the Inquisition.

The deathbed

In the 21st century death is a terminal event, but in the Middle Ages it was more commonly regarded as a transition from one form of existence to another, from association with the living to a spirit world, both of which, however, formed a single 'communion of saints'. The transition might well be protracted and for certain groups, including monks and lepers, it began long before bodily death was expected.

The deathbed was a busy place where both the dying and onlookers had roles to play. It was important to make a 'good death' and in the later Middle Ages the literate had access to treatises on the *Ars Moriendi* to ensure that they knew their part. Such works as *Arte and Crafte to know well to dye* (1490) have been described as distance learning packs not only for the dying but also for those who might have to organise the deathbeds of family and neighbours (Morgan 1999, 128). Such treatises were, however, a feature of the late Middle Ages and may reflect a society which, thanks to the Black Death and successive waves of plague, had become over-familiar with dying. Whether the 15th-century townsfolk of King's Lynn would have welcomed

Margery Kempe's keening at their deathbeds in earlier centuries is a moot point – it might well have been considered so excessive as to challenge divine will, or at least to imply a lack of faith in the salvation of the deceased.

3.2   Funerals and status

Dread of a pauper's burial seems to have been as keenly felt in the Middle Ages as later, and is reflected in at least one late medieval will, that of John Lounesdale (died 1495), in which money was left for those who did not have the means to be buried (Hadley 2001, 171). Burying the dead is one of the Seven Comfortable Works, and thus as vital as giving food and drink to the poor. In the later medieval period the various socio-religious guilds such as, in Chichester, the Guild of St George, were as much burial clubs as mutual assistance societies or religious confraternities. They have been described as 'co-operative chantries' and some were actually founded to take over chantry chapels for which funding had ceased (Hadley 2001, 81–3). In general, the elaboration of a funeral reflected the wealth and status of the deceased – there was scope for improvisation within accepted funerary practice – although a very few opted for a simple funeral as a sign of humility. At the small intramural church of St Helen-on-the-Walls, York, rector John de Burton (1407) enjoined his executors to bury him in a simple shroud, not in a wooden coffin (Magilton 1980, 9), and it is thus valid to infer that a coffin was regarded as a priest's right in 15th-century York.[8] Much higher up the ecclesiastical ladder, Archbishop Warham of Canterbury expressed a similar antipathy to extravagant outlay in 1530 (Hazlitt 1905, 252).[9] Occasionally individuals would express their humility through their preferred place of burial rather than through the nature of the obsequies. When John Shillingford, canon of Exeter Cathedral, made his will in 1388 he asked to be buried next to his mother at Widecombe on remote Dartmoor rather than to exercise his right to a cathedral burial (Orme 2001, 341). However, because the Lollards criticised lavish funerals and favoured very simple burials, those who opted for too plain a ceremony might be suspected of heretical leanings.

One of the attractions of life in a hospital or almshouse was almost certainly the guarantee of a good send-off. Institutional burials in general are likely to have been conservative when compared with changing practices in the secular world, although they will doubtless have developed their own quirks and usages, and were perhaps more immune to the folk customs which, it must be suspected, were an important element in many lay burials. Inevitably, more is known about the customs and practices of the monastic orders and similar institutions than those of lay society, but as hospitals such as St James' were essentially religious houses the monastic evidence is the more pertinent.

Life beyond the grave mirrored life on earth. The deceased maintained his or her gender, occupation and rank and the dead in general formed a distinct social group that continued to influence the living (Gilchrist and Sloane 2005, 6).

The origins of Christian burial practice

Caves might be thought to be the natural place of burial for Christians, in imitation of Christ. Despite a common assumption that catacomb burials were surreptitious events forced upon a persecuted minority, they could represent the preference of the earliest Christian communities to follow their leader's example. By the time that Constantine permitted, and finally encouraged, Christianity in the 4th century, the normal method of burial in the Roman world was inhumation with few or no grave goods, and civic cemeteries were subdivided into inhumation-sized plots. The earlier custom had been to cremate the dead, but for reasons that are not understood, inhumation became near-universal.[10] In Britain this had generally occurred by around AD 200 but a few later cremations are found that have sometimes been ascribed to conservative pagans, perhaps priests, clinging resolutely to the older tradition.

Roman paganism was not static. The 3rd century AD had seen moves towards monotheism (thereby paving the way for Christianity?) through the zealous promotion of the Unconquered Sun as supreme deity by some emperors. The 4th-century custom of interring bodies with their heads to the west (sunset) may reflect this enthusiasm for solar deities. Whatever the reason, it had become the commonest alignment and, perhaps simply because there was nothing overtly pagan about it, the new Christians of the 4th century continued the tradition. By the Middle Ages, attempts had been made to 'explain' the custom but these, including the still-current one that Christians were so laid out that they would face their Maker when reanimated on Judgement Day, seem not to occur before the 9th century.

Burial rituals: historical sources

As the rituals of the deathbed mostly leave no archaeological trace they need not be described in any detail; for the end of the Middle Ages they are conveniently summarised in Duffy (1992). More relevant is what happened to the body after death. No record survives of what took place in an English hospital but we do have details of Cluniac practice (Rowell 1977, 64–5), which in broad outline is likely to mirror customs in other religious houses including all but the smallest hospitals.

There were reasons of hygiene for burial to follow death as soon as practicable. One of the more repulsive features (to us) of the aftermath of Becket's martyrdom was an army of lice bubbling up like a liquid from his haircloth undergarments as the body cooled (Urry 1999, 142). Onlookers, seeing that he

Figure 3.2 The funeral procession of Edward the Confessor as depicted in the Bayeux Tapestry. The corpse is tightly bound in a winding sheet that reflects the contours of the body

had mortified his flesh in penance, took this as a sign of sanctity. Whilst the burial of a monk might take place on the day of his death, or at worst the day after, élite burials were not so swift. This was partly a practical consequence, since only the better-off are likely to have travelled any distance beyond their parish church, the normal place for burial, and died away from home. Where the journey back was a long one, the body might be embalmed or, in *mos teutonicus,* boiled up in wine and vinegar and the skeleton alone sent home (Fry 1999, 120).

There is a hint from the customs of the Knights Hospitallers that there was normally a specific hour for burials since they were laid out for a varying length of time before burial depending on the hour at which they had died (Gilchrist and Sloane 2005, 26)

3.3 Dressing for death

Shrouds,[11] winding sheets and cerecloths

Laypersons and others without a distinctive uniform (a category which probably included the inmates of all but the largest hospitals) were wrapped in a cloth, usually of linen,[12] for burial. Ecclesiastics and the very wealthy might be permitted burial in their robes of office or embalmed, and exceptionally the privilege might be accorded to such members of the middling orders as the Worcester pilgrim (Webb 2000, 210–13). It has been estimated that perhaps 2–3% were buried in some sort of clothing (Gilchrist and Sloane 2005, 80). The poet John Donne, in the process of preparing for death, put on his winding sheet whilst still alive 'so tied with knots at his head and feet, and his hands so placed as dead bodies are usually fitted to be shrouded and put in the grave' (Gittings 1999, 168). He then had a painting made and, although it does not survive, a marble effigy of *c* 1631 in St Paul's Cathedral, London, based on the painting, is extant. The face is exposed but otherwise the body is shown as prepared for burial. The outline of the arms can be seen, with the wrists crossed over the stomach, and the shroud is ruched at head and feet as if he had been rolled in it and a short cord used to tie each end. There is no trace of shroud pins or other fastenings.

Medieval examples can be seen in the 'shroud' brasses of the 15th and early 16th centuries (Norris 1992), in cadaver sculptures such as that of Sir John

Golafre (d.1442) at Fyfield church (Platt 1997, 158, fig 67) and in a 19th-century drawing of stained glass at Thornhill, Yorkshire (Hadley 2001, 156, fig 71). The method of shrouding used by Donne is said to have come into use in the 14th century (Horrox 1999, 99). A variant was to use a large single sheet of cloth which went over the head and was tied at the feet only, as depicted in the stained glass burial scene from Leicester (Daniell 1998, 43; Clarke 1962).

The earlier practice seems to have been to tuck in the shroud at the head and feet to give a smooth outline revealing the contours of the corpse, and the corpses shown in the Bayeux Tapestry where the death of Edward the Confessor is represented are closely swathed (Fig 3.2). Some illustrations show the body hugged so tightly by the shroud that it must have been sewn, pinned or taped in place. The first practice is attested at Bury St Edmunds in 1514, when a certain Alice Bumpsted left 2d apiece to 'the two women that shall sew my winding sheet' (Dinn 1992, 154); shrouding seems normally to have been a woman's task (Daniell 1998, 43) not infrequently, and with unmistakable symbolism, carried out by the local midwife (Richardson 1988, 19).[13] It must have been both physically and emotionally demanding. An uncoffined corpse must have been difficult to handle and tight shrouding may have made the task easier (Fig 3.3). The position of the arms and hands in illustrations varies from that adopted by Donne and appears to have no chronological significance.[14] The de Lisle Psalter of *c* 1300 showing the Three Living and the Three Dead Princes (Fig 3.4) has the latter in two different poses. The one on the left has wrists crossed over the chest with hands pointing to the shoulders.[15] The one in the middle may have been interred in similar fashion but has one hand on his neighbour's shoulder, as if to attract his attention. The one on the right has arms straight by his sides. The legs are all simply extended (Horrox 1999, pl 7).[16] All three are shown on a green background with stylised white flowers at regular intervals; are they meant, at this early date, to be 'pushing up daisies'?

Children are rarely depicted in funerary art and the earliest known portrayal of a child in a shroud is a monumental brass of 1467 (Daniell 1998, 43). The practice is certain to be much earlier since the only real alternatives for someone other than an infant were to use a coffin and/or everyday clothes: the former, we have seen, was regarded as prestigious and the latter a privilege.[17] Babies under four weeks old might be buried with a chrisom, the piece of cloth tied round the forehead after baptism to stop the baptismal oil applied after immersion from dripping onto the swaddling clothes.

Cerecloths were a form of winding sheet impregnated with beeswax used in important lay and ecclesiastical burials as part of an embalming process. Although reasonably well attested in the written record, the only recent archaeological discovery is from St Bees Priory (Cumbria) where the body had been preserved through encasement

Figure 3.3   Miniature of a priest and mourners at the burial of a shrouded corpse. From a French illuminated manuscript. © The British Library

in a lead-lined coffin (Gilchrist and Sloane 2005, 108–10).

Hides with the hair left on as post-mortem penitential shirts are also recorded but rarely survive in the archaeological record (Gilchrist and Sloane 2005, 107).

Coffins

Despite a confident assertion that 'no fifteenth-century peasant or artisan expected to be buried in a coffin; by contrast, no nobleman would have been subjected to shroud burial in the churchyard' (Litten 1991, 86), coffins were probably used increasingly as the Middle Ages progressed although the evidence to date is ambiguous.[18] During the Black Death some continental cities insisted on coffined burials to prevent supposedly pathogenic miasmas from decaying bodies escaping into the air (Horrox 1999, 104) and this may have encouraged their use in England. The problem is partly an archaeological one of determining valid criteria for the presence or absence of a coffin when, as is usual, no physical remains of the wooden part of the coffin survive. Some burials were part-coffined in that they were covered in planks propped on earth or stones before backfilling (eg at St Andrew Fishergate, York: Stroud and Kemp 1993, 158).

Figure 3.4   The Three Living and the Three Dead Princes. This illustration is from the de Lisle Psalter of c 1300 but the motif, with its grim warning of the transience of earthly life, is not uncommon. For the student of burial archaeology the alternate ways of laying out the corpse before enshrouding it are a point of interest, since the illustration seems to demonstrate that contemporaries of equal rank might nevertheless be prepared for death in different ways. For Chichester examples see Figs 7.29 and 7.30. © The British Library

Daniell (1998, 163) has claimed that 'the role of the coffin is more or less defined by its function as something to bury the body in', but this definition, valid for modern times, does not cover medieval usage. Like the bier, hearse and pall, a coffin might be parish property, loaned out or leased to transport the body to the grave and reused when next required.[19] From the occasional 'back to front' interment (there were two at St Helen-on-the-Walls, York: Dawes and Magilton 1980) it can be deduced that some coffins were simple boxes with the head and foot ends undifferentiated.[20] Others were in some way shaped. In mid-14th-century Flanders, coffins had 'gable ends' and a pitched top (Platt 1997, 4, fig 3) reminiscent of the hogback tombstones of Viking England. Two pairs of mourners carry one in procession by means of two short staves beneath it. Others tapered from head to foot, as shown in the Holkham Bible Picture Book of about the same date (Horrox 1999, 99, fig 38). A wall painting at Blyth, Notts, depicting the Last Judgment, shows a variety of plank-made coffins, amongst them a seeming skeuomorph of a stone tomb chest with the lid and base projecting beyond the sides, two with decorated sides, at least one with a shaped lid and another with a prow at each end rather like a punt[21] (Hadley 2001, pl 11).

3.4   Cemeteries

The first explicit mention of consecrating a cemetery is by Gregory of Tours *c* AD 581, and interment around churches became the norm in Carolingian France in the 8th century or later (Fry 1999, 42). The idea of consecrated ground seems in England to date to the late 10th century, as do regulations about who could be buried there. Those not permitted churchyard burial included usurers, excommunicates, the indicted, strangers to the parish, concubines of clergy and those married without banns.[22] Suicides, barred in Anglo-Saxon times, were not mentioned in the later Middle Ages, probably because juries rarely convicted people of the offence (Hadley 2001, 35–6, 51).[23] The canon law adopted for cemeteries (1205–14) did not require Christians to be buried in a consecrated cemetery but each grave had to be blessed at burial; those who could not receive Christian burial were to be laid in a place set apart (Fry 1999, 180–1). If a mistake was made, the body could be exhumed and removed. The bones of John Wycliffe (died 1384) were supposedly dug up, burned and thrown in a stream in 1424 (Fry 1999, 181). Probably the largest category denied burial in a formal cemetery were soldiers killed in battle who, unless nobles, were interred in mass graves at or near the field of conflict (Fiorato *et al* 2000).

Medieval cemeteries, places of sanctity that might be so defiled by bloodshed or other improper behaviour as to need reconsecration, were in general well defined[24] and, at least in theory, secure from the predations of pigs and other rooting animals.[25] They would normally have contained nothing except burials and a churchyard cross, but the existence of legislation forbidding, for example, the erection of buildings on cemeteries is evidence that abuses took place.[26] They could, on occasion, host plays, festivals and markets, and were often used for sports (Hadley 2001, 175–6), but these activities leave no archaeological trace. Perhaps the most important potential use was for markets and fairs. As part of the sanctuary lands of the Church, they were beyond what has been called 'the long and taxing arm of the law' although English statutes from the mid-13th century forbid markets in sacred places (Fry 1999, 50–1). Leper hospital cemeteries in particular were very often sited next to a highway, but whether this was to emphasise the liminal position of the leper (Gilchrist and Sloane 2005, 33) or simply to remind the passer-by of his own mortality in the hope that his alms-giving would be all the more generous is debatable. The actual or potential use of the space for trading purposes was perhaps the most important factor.

Medieval graveyards were often gruesome places, overcrowded with human remains that, once interred, were perhaps treated with scant respect. The following description, although from 19th-century rural Ireland, accords with the picture derived from excavated sites in medieval and early modern England:

> *The horrible habit of digging out all the contents of the grave is usual; the older coffin planks are thrown away, and the human remains placed on the new coffin. Where burials take place at short intervals the results are best left untold, but such cases are rare. A consequence of this fearful overcrowding is that no old graveyard is free from coffin planks and plates, bones, and fragmentary or whole skulls*
> (Westropp 2000, 77).[27]

Any reader inclined to doubt the validity of this picture for earlier periods is invited to recall Shakespeare's *Hamlet,* with its graveyard littered with bones and skulls.

The Reformation seems to have had little impact on the improper uses to which cemeteries might be put.[28] Edmund Grindal, archbishop of York 1570–76, issued a visitation article banning amongst others those such as morris dancers who irreverently came into churchyards 'there to dance, or play any unseemly parts with scoffs, jests, wanton gestures or ribald talk'. This text, modified to suit local purposes, was used within and outside the Province of York in Elizabeth's reign and later. For example, a Canterbury variant in 1577 omits any reference to rush-bearings as occasions when unseemly behaviour might occur, presumably because the custom was unknown there. The Visitation Articles of the Diocese of Lincoln in 1604 ask whether the churchyard was well fenced and clean, specifying (amongst others) bowlers and bear-wards as potential profaners of the cemetery. Such injunctions persisted down to the Interregnum (1649–60), when the episcopacy was abolished (Forrest 1999).

Hospital cemeteries

In 1179 the 3rd Lateran Council at Rome had decreed that leper communities could have their own churches, priests and cemeteries subject to regulations protecting the rights of churches within whose parishes they fell. St James' Chichester considerably pre-dates the Council and so, it must be suspected, do its burials, although this cannot at present be demonstrated either by documents or excavation. As noted (Chapter 2), St Margaret's leprosarium, Gloucester, had obtained burial rights with the bishop's consent early in the 12th century and St James' may have acted similarly.

Hospitals often had separate burial places for inmates and the religious (Hadley 2001, 50). However, there is no evidence from St James' for segregation (see Chapter 7), no priestly graves marked by chalice and paten were found within the areas examined and the healthy brethren may have been buried apart from the sick, perhaps even at the cathedral. Leper hospitals, catering as they did for social outcasts, occasionally undertook the burial of other ostracised groups such as executed criminals. At Lincoln, the brethren of St Katherine's Priory were paid by the Master of the Hospitaller Preceptory of Maltby to inter the executed on the common near the gallows (Hadley 2001, 51). However, the Chichester gallows were, at least in post-medieval times, north of the city alongside the then preferred route to London and there is no reason to suspect intrusive burials of this nature at St James'.

There is a theoretical distinction to be made between the cemeteries of hospitals catering mostly for travellers and pilgrims and those for the sick, whether lepers or not, where the patient, once admitted, was likely to spend the rest of his days. A cemetery attached to what was mostly a travellers' hostel would be expected to contain a small number of predominantly young adults, whereas an infirmary would exhibit more individuals, a wider age range and include persons suffering from chronic conditions. Such a distinction is apparently visible at St Mary Spital, London, where parts of three cemeteries are known, the first belonging to the priory and the other two to the hospital that it came to administer (Thomas *et al* 1997).

3.5 Historical events and their impact

Two national events, at least in theory, should have influenced burial in the Middle Ages. The first, an interdict of Innocent III in force from 1208 to 1214, was in effect a call for a strike by clergy that should have prevented burials in consecrated ground. The lesser clergy, who perhaps needed mortuary fees to survive, may have ignored it, and there is as yet little confirmation from archaeology of short-lived secular graveyards of the period (Gilchrist and Sloane 2005, 46–7). Historical sources are also scanty. One of the more interesting cases was at Basingstoke (Hants) where, apparently, interdict burials on a hill north of the town were later sanctified by the construction of a chapel to the Holy Ghost (Cox 1903, 214). When the interdict was lifted, the alternative to consecrating secular graveyards was to reinter the deceased in ground that had already been sanctified, and a plaque of 1215 from Lindisfarne (Northumbria) seems to attest just this, recording the removal of monks' remains from the priory garden to its cemetery (Salvin 1857, 286).

The other was the Black Death of 1349, not so much an event but the first of a series of epidemics that finally ended in 1665. Its recurrence in 1361 hit in particular the children of those who had survived its first appearance. Some chapels were given burial rights for the initial emergency and sought to retain them afterwards. Existing churches applied successfully to open new cemeteries to cope with the crisis; one such was Newark (Notts) in 1349. In some other towns, where churchyards were perhaps already uncomfortably full and open areas few, mass burials were made in pits and trenches (Hadley 2001, 49). Efforts to maintain a decent, orderly standard of burial seem to have been made whether burials took place in rows/columns or in pits. The impact of the plague on religious communities was uneven, but one estimate of monastic mortality puts the reduction in the religious communities to around 45% between 1348 and the 1360s (Hatcher 1986). Mortality rates will have varied according to the general health of individuals contracting the disease, and its impact will potentially have been highest amongst the chronically ill. St James' leper hospital, Westminster, lost all but one of its community (Rosser 1989, 306).

3.6 Attitudes and rituals: the post-Reformation traditions

With historical hindsight it is possible to see the Reformation as a sequence of inevitable and more or less irreversible events, but those alive at the time, whether sympathetic to or opposed to reform (or indeed indifferent to religious debate, as many must have been), would have been very unsure as to what the current orthodoxy had become and, equally to the point, whether the next in line for the throne was likely to endorse it. In such circumstances, zealous Protestants excepted, the temptation must have been to cling to what could be retained from the past until it became specifically forbidden. Wills down to the 1570s still refer to obits, months' minds

and prayers for the dead (Roffey 2003, 349). The use of lights at funerals, an inseparable part of Catholic ritual, barred by Edward VI, revived under Mary and banned again under Elizabeth, survived by the simple expedient of burying people after dark, when formerly symbolic lights became a necessity (Harding 2003, 391–2). Almost equally suspicious to Protestant minds was bell-ringing, but that too survived.

The most significant institutional change brought about by the Reformation was the eradication of what has been termed 'the industry of prayers for the dead'. The last visible monuments were chantry chapels, condemned as the product of 'devising and phantising vain opinions of Purgatury' (Morgan 1999, 142), their end postponed until 1547 by the death of Henry VIII. The new prayer book of 1552, with its drastically shortened funeral service, omitted all prayers of commendation to the soul. That of the Elizabethan restoration (*The Book of Common Prayer*, 1559) at least included prayers for the repose of the souls of the dead. The logical outcome of the new Protestant theology was seen finally in the Interregnum with the formulation of *A Directory for the Publique Worship of God* (1644) with its all but secular burial rites. A 'good death' now involved putting one's earthly affairs in order and making peace with God and mankind. The prayers of the faithful, godly lay folk as well as ministers, sustained the dying Christian and he reciprocated with words of comfort for the onlookers before willingly surrendering his soul.

The 'abolition' of purgatory (belief in it was forbidden by the King's Book, 1543: Gilchrist 2003, 399) left a gap that was hard to fill. Where exactly was the soul to go after death? One answer was to revert to the older belief that it slept in the grave until Doomsday, when it was reunited with the body and arose for judgement. For those who believed this, it must have become increasingly important to avoid disturbing the grave and this could be reflected archaeologically in the better management of cemeteries so that intersections between graves were avoided. One former practice, the use of charnel pits and houses to accommodate disturbed burials, seems to have ceased at the Reformation (Harding 2003, 390). Others brought forward the Day of Judgement to the moment of death, assuming that the soul went straight to its final destination. Calvinists retained the concept of Abraham's Bosom as a resting place for the righteous (ie themselves), leaving the wicked less comfortable accommodation in which to await the Last Trump. An even more radical view suggested that the soul slept or even died temporarily (Gittings 1999, 152). About the only point of agreement between all Protestants was that the fate of the soul was sealed at the moment of death; the prayers of the living could have no effect on the final outcome. Individual Protestants, however devout, were expected to profess their own unworthiness for salvation; death thus became a more decisive moment than in the Middle Ages for the dying, and a more hopeless one for the mourners whose intercessory role had been taken from them.

Parallel with developing Puritan theology was the sacramental tradition lingering amongst conservative clergy of the Church of England, which continued to emphasise the old Catholic virtues of confession and absolution and the comfort of the viaticum for the final journey (Houlbrooke 1999, 180). New manuals on the *Ars Moriendi* were published, most famously Jeremy Taylor's *The Rule and Exercise of Holy Dying* (1651) (Gittings 1999, 156), which drew on medieval Catholic traditions. The proscribed English Catholic communities maintained late medieval practices as far as possible, including prayers for the dead, and Catholic usages persisted in certain English regions to become the folk customs of the early modern period. One belief of probable medieval origin was that the corpse was not properly dead until buried. In Yorkshire, food and drink was provided for the corpse in case it woke (Addy 1895, 123), it was believed that a signature or mark made by a corpse whilst it was still warm was valid in law, that a corpse could indicate its displeasure if a will read in its presence were false[29] and that a murdered body would bleed in the presence of its assassin (Richardson 1988, 15).[30]

One inevitable consequence of the Reformation was to restrict the scope for burial outside one's parish church and churchyard. In medieval Chichester, some of the will-making classes (Peckham 1948; 1950) had sought burial with the Friars but, as those whose wills were written down and survive are an unknown percentage of the total population, we cannot be sure how common this had been. The closure of conventual cemeteries put increasing pressure on those, perhaps already overcrowded, that survived. In post-Reformation London parishes developed new, peripheral graveyards but the old ones were still greatly preferred (Harding 2003, 389).

For the archaeologist, the question is what impact, if any, the new Protestant theology had on burial rites, insofar as they are recoverable by archaeological means. In the short term it must be suspected that practices carried on as before, even if old customs had to be invested with a new symbolism to placate the more zealous reformers. The secularisation of the disposal of the dead was accompanied by continuing concerns about public health, a cause of great anxiety in the later Middle Ages too when 'miasmas' were blamed for the spread of disease. In 1583 the bishop of St David's ordered corpses not to be interred in churches 'for that by their general burying there great infection doth ensue' but made an exception for 'the best sort of the parish' (Gittings 1999, 157).[31] There may have been a folk belief that the presence of remains of local notables in some way protected the building. Coffins were more commonly used (Gittings 1984, 61 and 114), perhaps again reflecting a new concern for hygiene, and by the 18th century were thought of as essential for a decent burial, even of the poor (Houlbrooke 1999,

193). Those who achieved burial within a church (now perhaps representing a greater proportion of the population: Harding 2003, 388–9) were more likely to mark the fact with a monument (perhaps recycled from a suppressed religious house: Hutchinson 2003) and may betray an increasing uncertainty about immortality in their desire for worldly commemoration. In an age of intercessory prayers, death had been a process of transition from one existence to the next. With the new theology, which cut off communication between the living and the dead, death was much more of an event. Perhaps the only bonus was a reduction in funeral expenses as extra masses no longer had to be funded, leaving more to be spent on physical memorials. One can sympathise with Sir James Taylor, a priest in 1519, who asked for 'a lowe dirige and masse of requiem because I have but smalle goodes' (Harding 2003, 391) but less so with William Swetman, a Norwich mercer and former mayor, who commissioned 4000 masses (Finch 2003, 440).

One economics-driven change in burial practice arose from the parliamentary Acts for Burial in Woollen passed from 1666 onwards, designed to boost a home industry. They could be ignored by those few who were affluent enough to afford a £5 fine, and gave rise to a folk belief that it was lucky to be buried in linen (Richardson 1988, 21). The poor of such almshouses as St James' Chichester will have had no such choice by this date, and the devout may well have been distressed by their inability to follow Christ's example in having a linen shroud. St Mary Spital, London, has yielded a fragment of such a linen shroud from a waterlogged medieval context (Thomas *et al* 1997, 121, fig 81).

3.7   The archaeology of hospital cemeteries

Inhumation cemeteries with few or no grave goods have, historically, had little appeal for archaeologists despite such pioneering work as that at St Helen-on-the-Walls, York, which, with all its flaws, revealed something of their potential for study (Dawes and Magilton 1980; Magilton 1980), and subsequent advances in forensic archaeology in particular. An additional problem has been the occasional disregard by developers of planning requirements and the removal of ancient cemeteries without record, although public aversion to the bulldozing of graves is such that the resultant public relations disaster must make it rarely worthwhile.[32] An estimate made in 1998 (Daniell 1998, 143) puts the total number of excavated medieval cemeteries at around 30, of which only ten had more than 100 bodies and not all of which have been published in any detail. Whilst this must now be considered an underestimate (Gilchrist and Sloane 2005), the total remains unimpressive.

This section would ideally review burials at other English leper hospitals alone to provide contrasts and parallels with Chichester, but the data are so small that little could be written. It has therefore been broadened to include all hospitals that were not physically part of monastic establishments. Many houses, initially for lepers, later amended their constitutions to take in the sick poor, and at least one hospital, St Leonard's at Grantham, was seemingly for the sick poor but had lepers buried in its cemetery, so a hard and fast distinction between leprosaria and the rest may not be justified. Many hospitals had no cemeteries and the smallest were simply cottages. Hospitals attached to monastic communities would have used the community's graveyard, where a distinction may have been made between lay and religious interments but those who died in the infirmary would be inseparable from their peers. Numerically, more burials have been excavated and analysed from St James' than from all other English hospitals combined, although this will change with the full publication of skeletons from St Mary's Hospital, Bishopsgate, London, where over 10,500 burials have been examined.

As there may be regional variations in burial practice, the hospitals have been assigned to three groups, south-eastern (here meaning Sussex, Kent, Surrey and Hampshire), London and Middlesex, and the rest of England. Only hospitals where at least one burial has been found are included. In many cases, detailed reports on the pathology and of individual interments have yet to be published, and the only published source is a note in *Medieval Archaeology*. Some of the burials were disturbed during road works, reflecting the positions of many hospitals on major routes.

Hospital cemeteries in the south-east

One of the larger groups of burials came from St Mary Magdalene's, Bidlington, East Sussex, originally founded for leper men but by 1366 re-established as an almshouse. Its cemetery was first mentioned in 1269 and the hospital survived the early years of the Reformation, closing some time after 1553. Most of the excavated burials were found during the development in 1959–60 of Maudlyn Park, under 23 and 24 Maudlyn Parkway (Lewis 1964). Forty-six burials were located, mostly cut into the chalk about 2ft 6in (0.75m) below the ground surface but two were about 2ft (0.6m) deeper. All were aligned with heads to the west but some at the west end of the site were approaching south-west/north-east in orientation. There was some indication, particularly at the east end of the site, that the cemetery had been planned so that the graves lay in columns. One grave had a nail in it. Another had three chalk blocks arranged around the skull, a third skull rested on a chalk 'pillow' with chalk blocks on both sides, and a fourth had a large flint nodule under the skull. One of the deep graves had been backfilled with chalk blocks 'of some size'. A young adult male and young adult female occupied the same grave pit. At least two burials were of the type with the

hands laid across the pelvis. Two of the skeletons were female and five male but the remainder were mainly unexamined. Six skeletons, all but one male, had changes associated with leprosy according to Møller-Christensen, who was sent colour photographs. The arrangements of stones beneath and around the skull are reminiscent of those seen at St James' Chichester (see below).

The hospital of St Mary the Virgin,[33] Strood, Kent, was founded in 1193 just north of Watling Street, the London–Canterbury road, by Bishop Gilbert de Glanville of Rochester for the poor, and one of its duties was the repair of part of Rochester Bridge. It closed in 1540. The site was investigated in 1966 (Harrison 1969). The structural remains consisted of a rectangular chapel attributed to the 13th century and an adjoining hall range, aligned north–south, of the same period but subsequently subdivided. A double burial came from a single grave in the hall, at the centre of an archway leading to the chapel. The grave was 'shaped', with a round hole for the skull and tapering body, and was made mostly of yellow bricks facing rubble. Both skeletons were robust males aged over 40 with slight arthritic changes and badly worn teeth. A copper buckle was found with one of the skeletons, but no other artefacts, and, given the shape of the grave, at least the earlier corpse must have been in a shroud alone. The bones of the later burial were much disturbed and looked as if they might have been tipped out of a coffin.[34] A third burial, found west of the hall where the cemetery may lie, was of a young adult male with little dental attrition.

Another Kentish hospital dedicated to St Mary the Virgin[35] lay at Ospringe, again on Watling Street (now the A2) west of Canterbury (Rigold 1964; Smith 1979). Initially for the poor and travellers, it received its first grant in 1234, was refounded in 1470 and closed in 1516. Its archaeology is known mainly from excavations in 1977 and 1989, and it was a major building complex, of which the walls of two undercrofts survive. Fragments of human bone were recovered from a number of contexts but only two burials out of six identified in the hospital cemetery in the north-west corner of the site were excavated deliberately. Both were west–east inhumations in coffins, of which the nails survived, and the bases of the grave pits were about 1.15m below the modern ground surface. Both were adult males, aged 25–35 and 35–45, the older having so many abnormalities, including ossification and degeneration of the joints and bone changes of traumatic origin, that his 'rest' position must have been sitting. Taking the fragments into account, one female and six possible/probable/certain males were represented, and eighteen burials were adult as opposed to five juveniles aged 6–17. These last, if they were inmates, demonstrate that the institution was not merely a home for the elderly.

At New Romney (Kent), on the borough boundary, lay the hospital of SS Stephen and Thomas. It was founded as a leper hospital around 1185[36] and refounded in 1363 by John Fraunceys for the deserving poor at a time when the buildings were derelict and no lepers remained. It closed in 1481. The site is known from a small-scale research excavation in 1935 (Murray 1935) and work in advance of development in 1959 (Rigold 1964). One of the features found in 1935 was a tomb that tapered towards the feet made of, *inter alia*, poorly baked yellow bricks. The tomb appeared to be stratigraphically late, perhaps even post-dating the closure of the hospital. Although the site was planned, the plan was not published with the original account and was lost during World War Two. The 1959 excavation located burials north and south of the main building but these were not further investigated. Within the chapel a grave with a lining of irregular yellow bricks was found in front of the altar. It was not the same as the one discovered in 1935 and may have housed the refounder of the institution. No bone report was published. The use of yellow bricks in both tombs is reminiscent of Strood Hospital near Rochester. The bricks may all be 14th-century imports.

The leper hospital at Winchester (Hants) was the subject of a brief television-sponsored research excavation in 2001. St Mary Magdalene's hospital, just beyond the city limits, thought to have been founded in the 1130s, was first recorded in 1148. Two late 17th-century graves were found in the chapel and to its south was a male burial betraying some early signs of leprosy.

Lewes (Sussex) had two hospitals, one centred on the original Cluniac priory church and later infirmary chapel of St Pancras (Lyne 1997) north of the infirmary hall from which 27 burials are known, and the hospital of St Nicholas, a foundation perhaps as early as the late 11th century that in almshouse guise lasted until 1810 (Barber and Sibun 1998). St Nicholas' lies *c* 700m outside the town on the west side, its cemetery facing onto Spital Road. It is said to have been founded by William de Warenne and in an account of the Battle of Lewes (1264/65) it is described as a leper house. During excavations in 1994, 102 burials were lifted and have been analysed. Most of the graves were quite shallow. There were three 'anthropomorphic' grave pits where a space for the head was defined in imitation of stone tombs, and at least nineteen burials were in coffins. At least seven burials had 'ear muffs', chalk blocks on either side of the skull, a practice dated by the excavators to the late 12th/13th centuries. Individual burials of interest included one with an iron manacle perhaps, as the authors suggest, for restraining a criminal or lunatic, although a penitential use cannot be excluded. Two individuals were buried apparently with their hands tied behind their backs, and one of these had a displaced cervical vertebra suggesting he had been hanged. This recalls St Katherine's Lincoln, which offered Christian burial to executed criminals (see above). The cemetery organisation, if any, could not be understood, so changes over time cannot be studied. There was no spatial patterning with regard to age, sex or pathological condition. Only two lepers could be identified from the palaeopathological study, but this does not invalidate the identification of the institution as a leper hospital as the earliest graves may lie elsewhere.

Hospital cemeteries in London and Middlesex

The hospital most extensively excavated is St Mary's Spitalfield without Bishopsgate north of the walled city, founded in 1197 as a priory and refounded as a hospital in 1235, closing in 1538–40.[37] Excavations since the early 1980s have revealed numerous graves, some belonging to the priory but more to the hospital (Thomas *et al* 1997). The skeletal evidence and a detailed analysis of the cemeteries await full publication. The areas of cemetery (excluding burials within buildings) comprise Open Area 2, south of the hospital church, which seems to have housed the inmates of the first priory up to 1235; Open Area 5, the infirmary cemetery from 1235 to 1280; and Open Area 11 south of the Lady Chapel belonging to the period of the new infirmary and cloister, 1280–1320. The total area set aside for cemeteries has been calculated at 29% of the area available (Thomas *et al* 1997, 116).

The existence of three cemeteries that are physically and temporally discrete allows parallels to be drawn and contrasts to be made with regard to both cemetery organisation and the characteristics of individual burials. The earliest cemetery was apparently planned as six columns with eighteen burials in each and measured 221m^2 (St James' Chichester cemetery was probably eventually around ten times that size). The early infirmary cemetery was planned as nine grave columns with 25 burials in each although it did not seem to have any formal physical boundary. The latest cemetery examined consisted of an orderly northern part and a chaotic southern part. The two early cemeteries contained abnormally high numbers of young people, perhaps migrant workers, servants or pilgrims. Occupants of the latest cemetery seem to have enjoyed less good health than their predecessors. Individual graves varied from 0.5 to 0.6m deep in the open cemeteries and deeper within buildings.

Most individuals were buried in winding sheets, coffins or a combination of the two, and a linen fragment of the first was recovered from Open Area 5. Graves that were in some way distinctive included two with chalk pillows (the provision of which may have been a graveside ritual) and another (from the chapel) containing a papal bulla that would originally have been attached to an indulgence promising the deceased a shortened spell in purgatory.[38] Waterlogging in part of the cemetery led to the preservation of an oak plank coffin with pegged sides and base and a top of nailed planks.

From Open Area 5, the short-lived cemetery of the first infirmary, 101 skeletons were examined. The ratio of males to females was 2.4:1 and the population was young, with 54% dead by the age of 25. The physical afflictions of the deceased reflected their relative youth, with tooth wear considerable, caries rare, but enamel hypoplasia indicative of an inadequate early diet or spells of serious childhood illness common. Amongst the patients were women in childbirth, and the report suggests that the institution may have looked after the children of mothers who died until they reached seven. The cemetery of the new infirmary, Open Area 11, had a male to female ratio of 1.15:1 and contained few pre-adults and few elderly adults. The dental health pattern was much the same as in Open Area 5 but in general the deceased had enjoyed less good health. The dental pathology of burials from within the buildings showed a very high caries rate, presumably due to honey or other natural sugars as significant elements in the diets of those individuals. There was no real evidence from the skeletal remains for care and treatment and it is by no means certain that, for example, fractures that had been successfully set and healed were the work of the hospital staff.

Also known through recent excavations is St Thomas' London Bridge, founded in 1215 and surviving until 1862. Amongst the finds relating to its cemetery are two grave slabs, one for an adult and the other for a child, reused in a cess pit. A probable undercroft of the hospital was found in 1982 and wall foundations and a floor in 1988.

Hospital cemeteries in the rest of England

One of the better-explored hospitals, catering for the poor, was St Bartholomew's, Bristol (Price 1998). Founded in 1232–34, it survived until 1532. The cemetery was first mentioned in 1340 and 45 burials assigned to the period 1400–1532 were excavated during fieldwork in 1976–78. As all were in the church they were more likely to be staff and patrons than bedesmen. Nails and staining indicate that some at least were coffined. A bronze buckle and part of a leather belt were found with one burial but there were no other 'grave goods'. Eight were certainly, and four probably, male, four were female and seven probably female, and three adults and four subadults were of uncertain sex. The deceased were generally elderly although some had died in childhood or early adulthood. Dentition was mostly poor and some showed signs of dietary insufficiency or stress in early life. Amongst the conditions affecting the bones, osteoarthritis was by far the commonest and there were no signs of TB or leprosy.

Another hospital with the same dedication was South Acre (alias Racheness), Norfolk, a leper house founded 'about the time of Henry II' and dependent on Castle Acre Priory that closed perhaps c 1350. A dozen burials, four of them very fragmentary, were salvaged during roadworks in 1967 and reported on by Calvin Wells (Wells 1967). They occurred at a depth of 0.9–1.2m (3–4ft) but are otherwise not described. Three were certain or probable males,

seven female and two unsexed. All were adult and had poor dentition but less attrition than usual, perhaps because the hospital served a softer than average diet. There were two cases of osteoarthritis. Three were almost certainly lepers, three probable and one possible. With one exception, all these were female. Was this a leper house for females, one of whom was wrongly sexed?

The ten or a dozen burials from St Margaret's, High Wycombe (Bucks), a leper house founded by 1229, were also salvaged during roadworks (Farley and Manchester 1989). They lay at between 0.54 and 0.75m below ground level. One was flexed at the knees and lay on its left side but the others were all extended inhumations. The gravel subsoil prevented the survival of evidence for coffins and fittings. Three graves contained peg-hole roof tiles but there were no other 'grave goods'. Two of the skeletons were female and three male, and all were adult, mainly in their 20s, based on dental attrition. Dental hygiene was poor. Only one skull exhibited rhinomaxillary changes pathognomonic of lepromatous leprosy and by far the commonest infective change was to the tibiofibular bones, occurring in all but three skeletons.

Burials at West Street, Doncaster (S Yorks), were recovered through a salvage operation in 1957 (Buckland et al 1989). The cemetery is thought to be part of St Nicholas' Hospital for the sick poor, founded late in the 12th century and dependent on the house of Premonstratensian canons at Bayham, East Sussex. The site, just outside a town gate in the angle between two streets linked by West Street, is a classic one for a hospital and it is unfortunate that the institution cannot yet be positively identified. Six burials plus fragments of perhaps another six were recovered and photographed but no other adequate records survive. The only detail we have of the graves is a comment that they were shallow. All the skeletons for which an age could be determined were adult, consisting of one adult male and four probable males, three adult females, three probable adult females and one young adult (under 25) of undetermined sex. The only noteworthy skeletal change was tuberculous infection of the spine (Pott's Disease) in one adult, probably male, who had, not surprisingly, been buried on his side.

Skeletons thought to be from one of Doncaster's other hospitals, the leper house of St James at Shakespeare Dock, were found during building works in 1961. St James' was founded in 1222–23 and may have lasted until 1548, having been refounded to look after the deserving poor. Of the probable nine skeletons, that of a young adult female exhibited changes possibly compatible with leprosy but a re-examination of the bones could not confirm the diagnosis (Buckland et al 1989). The burials could conceivably belong with the ill-recorded hospital of St Leonard's and are not very distant from the supposed site of St Nicholas'.

St Leonard's at Newark (Notts) was founded on the Fosse Way by the bishop of Lincoln, perhaps in

1133–34, and moved to a new site in 1642. Its foundation charter speaks of the 'poor and sick' but one clause mentions lepers. Burials from its cemetery were found in 1979 during repairs to the Lincoln Road viaduct (Bishop 1983). The sex of the deceased could be determined in 77 cases, and 85% were male and 11% female. The age at death range, determined in 54 cases, was from young adult to elderly; there were no children. An interesting feature was calculus on the occlusal surfaces of teeth from nine individuals, indicating a period of sickness before death. In all, 46% of burials were sick and/or suffering degenerative changes due to old age. Only one leper was positively identified (from gross periostitis of the tibiae and fibulae) but there were five cases of cribra orbitalia, here attributed to an inadequate diet. There was one priest burial with pewter chalice and paten in a 2ft (0.6m) deep stone-lined grave, head to the east. The graves in general were no larger than necessary and a single example of one grave on top of another implies a grave marker. One burial was 'special' in that a number of thin lias stones had been thrown in above the chest. A few sherds and a few shells were noted, but no other grave goods.

Grantham (Lincs) had, from the 13th century, a hospital dedicated to St Leonard on the Great North Road at Spittelgate south of the town, although the exact site of the buildings is unknown.[39] A small excavation in 1991 revealed 49 burials (building contractors had destroyed a further 20 or so), several of which had signs of leprosy. Others had been discovered in the vicinity in the 19th century (Hadley 2001, 50–2), and the extent of the graveyard is undetermined. The 1991 site included burials of both sexes and children as well as adults. The lepers, male and female, lay at the western end of the excavated area and had perhaps been segregated from the other burials. The hospital is not known to have catered for lepers, and few hospitals took in lepers of both sexes. Perhaps it was a hospital for the sick poor that from time to time took in the occasional leper; alternatively its history may have mirrored that of St James' Chichester, having been founded for lepers but refounded to look after the sick poor.

Yet another hospital dedicated to St Leonard is known at Chesterfield (Derbys) and he was the second most popular saint in later medieval England for leper houses (Hadley 2001, 50). It lay on the south-east side of the borough at a place called Spital Bridge on the Rother. John originally endowed it in 1195, when he was count of Mortain, with dues from markets and fairs, but the payment was later commuted to cash. The inmates were still referred to as leprous men in a royal grant of 1334. One of the burials in a stone-lined grave from recent excavations was apparently that of a priest, since it contained a lead[40] paten and a chalice that had disintegrated to dust. A radiocarbon date suggested late 11th to early 12th century for the burial (Hadley 2001, 113–14 and pl 35).

The York hospital known as St Mary in the Horsefair

lay in the northern suburbs at Union Terrace. It was excavated in response to the threat from a ring road in 1972 (Richards *et al* 1989) but the burials have yet to be published in detail. The hospital was founded in 1314 for six aged and infirm chaplains and was said to be empty and ruinous by 1557. Over 30 burials were recovered from the chapel. The fragmentary skeletons, largely of elderly individuals, included women as well as men although where sex could be determined, women were outnumbered three to one. Most pathological changes were arthritic, as might be expected in an elderly population. Amongst the latest graves was one with a pewter chalice and another with a copper-alloy buckle. There were earlier burials relating to the original use of the site as a Carmelite friary. A York hospital, inferred from its cemetery, was perhaps attached to the Gilbertine Priory in Fishergate. This was originally the church of St Andrew, and amongst the burials of that period were twelve men with weapons injuries, perhaps the victims of a single event. Amongst the later burials there were at least seventeen others ranging in date from the 12th to 14th century which, it is suggested, were the victims of trial by battle who had come to the Gilbertines because their infirmary specialised in weapon injuries (Daniell 2001). The hospital is otherwise unattested.

In North Yorkshire the secular hospital of St Giles at Brough Bridge, founded in 1166 beside a medieval bridge over the River Swale, was investigated because of erosion from the river.[41] Forty-two burials were recovered from within and around the chapel, which was rebuilt on a larger scale on the same site in the late 13th century. No details of the graves are known.

The leper hospital (later almshouse) of St Mary Magadalene in Brook Street, Colchester, was founded in the 12th century and refounded in 1610.[42] Excavations in 1989 located the chapel and accommodation block of the original hospital. By the mid-13th century the chapel had been extended and converted to a parish church and the accommodation block was incorporated into the graveyard. Further excavations in 1995 showed that the hospital moved north to a new site. The buildings included a new, larger chapel (the Maudlin Chapel) and separate living quarters to the east. These were retained after 1610 when the hospital became an almshouse, and demolished early in the 19th century.

Ilford (Essex) had a leper hospital founded in c 1140 dedicated to SS Mary and Thomas the Martyr that later became an almshouse, finally closing in the mid-16th century. Nine burials, two of them leprous, are known from north of the chapel; two were male, four female and two subadult (Gilchrist and Sloane 2005, 240). The house is well known for its expulsion of a leper for unchastity, as recorded in a ledger of Barking Abbey (see Chapter 2).

Medieval Huntingdon had a leper house of 12th-century foundation dedicated to St Margaret.[43] Some 55–60 burials were found during road widening of the A1126 at Spittal's Link in service trenches on a roundabout, many from two charnel pits over 100m apart. Those under threat were removed. Analysis detected a 28% incidence of leprosy. The ratio of males to females was 1.1:1, with 25% subadults (Popescu and Mitchell in prep).

A hospital attached to Gloucester Blackfriars has been deduced from a trench in Ladybellegate car park that yielded 140 burials, amongst them many women and children.[44] Whilst they may have been the families of benefactors or others who sought burial with the friars, a preliminary examination of the bodies revealed a high degree of pathology. Most notable was a young female aged 17–25, attributable to the early 15th century on stratigraphic grounds, who died of advanced syphilis. If both the interpretation of the stratification and diagnosis are correct, the burial is of major importance in confirming the pre-Columbian (earlier than 1493) presence of the disease in Europe. Of the remaining burials, one with a pewter chalice and paten was presumably that of a priest. Gloucester had a leper house, St Margaret's, on the London Road, founded after 1150 and refounded as a almshouse at some later date. In 1991 the western boundary ditch of the hospital, backfilled in the 14th century, was found with four burials aligned north-east/south-west cut through it.[45] On the same road, of mid-12th-century foundation, was St Mary Magdalene's for leper women. It too later became an almshouse.[46]

At Ipswich, one of the Greyfriars buildings may have been used as a hospital after the Dissolution. During redevelopment in 1990 56 burials were excavated. Most were said to have been interred in a casual way, as if paupers or plague victims, and most were post-medieval in date.[47] Also in Suffolk, six burials have been recovered from the hospital chapel of St Saviour's, Bury St Edmunds, an Augustinian institution founded in 1184 and dissolved in 1538. All were male and half over 45 years old. All but one were considered 15th-/16th-century in date (Caruth and Anderson 1997). Half the sample had DISH.

Hospitals that will add to our future knowledge include St John the Baptist's Lutterworth, Leics, founded before 1218 for the poor, aged and sick, and still functioning in 1577, where an evaluation and excavation revealed 22 graves from its cemetery.[48] All were seemingly of mature adult males apart from one juvenile buried with his head to the east, and one female. Eleven were elderly. There was one instance of a burial deliberately on top of another. The lower grave was the only one to contain coffin nails. The one above had in its fill six 14th-century floor tiles decorated with the arms of Beauchamps. The only other grave good was a simple penannular brooch. Burials and rubble had been noted in the 1890s when the adjacent A426 road was built. Another recent excavation with much potential for understanding rural hospitals is at Partney (Lincs), a cell of Bardney Abbey investigated during the construction of a bypass (Atkins and Popescu 2005; Atkins and Popescu in prep).

Conclusions

Despite their monastic or quasi-monastic rule, hospitals, particularly those physically detached from the parent abbey, in the care of the bishop or simply 'private' institutions with lay founders and patrons, seem to have been much more part of their local community than the larger religious houses, which were simply branches of an institution with, very often, the 'head office' abroad (the friaries, particularly early on, were exceptions to this generalisation). A greater variation would be expected between the burial practice at hospitals at opposite ends of England than between, say, Benedictine houses similarly situated where conformity in life may well have been reflected by uniformity in death. It is too early yet to speak of regional burial practices in England beyond voicing a suspicion that they exist, but future mapping of the distribution of 'ear muffs', for example, may define a southern or south-eastern burial province whilst the use of planks to line or protect graves (see below) may turn out to be a Yorkshire phenomenon. The organisation of cemeteries is another area in which local variants may become apparent but the data are at present so small that we cannot guess where the differences may lie. The demographic profiles of institutions too may be critical for understanding their functions (what they actually did, rather than what their charters specified), but to be valid these depend on a large enough sample and an appreciation that functions changed through time.

3.8   English medieval cemeteries: some observations

Although they are not numerous, it is beyond the scope of this section to catalogue the remaining English medieval cemeteries. Instead, it looks at some results from their excavation and makes some observations about burial practices in the Middle Ages as a background for what will be outlined at St James' Chichester in subsequent chapters. A much more comprehensive guide to the variations found in medieval cemeteries can now be found in Gilchrist and Sloane (2005).

Density and distribution of burials

The organisation of cemeteries can assume a variety of forms, some of which are illustrated in Figure 3.5. The type of organisation can affect the overall plan of the cemetery, those with a single focus (type D), whether oriented or not, tending towards a circular plan,[49] those in columns (types A and B) tending towards a rectangular plan and polyfocal examples (types E and F) tending towards an irregular plan. The linear or string-grave pattern (type C), with the son buried at his father's feet, is found in Anglo-Saxon England and perhaps Ireland (Fry 1999,

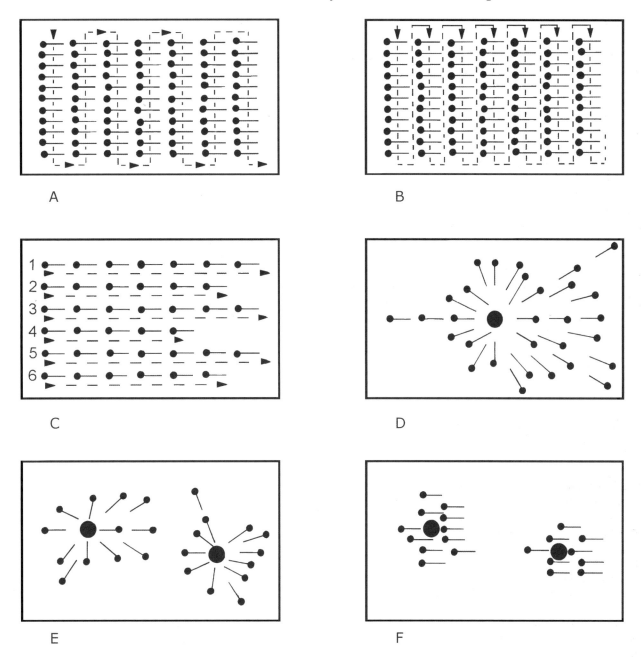

Figure 3.5 Theoretical cemetery development plans: (A) boustrophedon, (B) columnar, (C) linear, (D) monofocal, (E) polyfocal and (F) polyfocal oriented. Examples of each are attested, as are sites combining two or more patterns. St James' Chichester is essentially A or B with an overlay of F, for example

168). If the desired result is an orderly cemetery of west–east inhumations there is more than one way to achieve it but the usual practice, in Roman and medieval times, was to bury shoulder-to-shoulder in columns (types A and B). Type A is boustrophedon, the new column starting level with the last burial of the old,[50] and type B is what may be termed columnar, with each new column starting at the 'top'. Archaeologically they may be difficult to tell apart, and it may be equally difficult to determine whether expansion was, as at Chichester, from west to east or, as at the London hospital of St Mary Spital, Bishopsgate, the opposite (Gilchrist and Sloane 2005, 47). In some medieval cemeteries, often on restricted sites, the apparently chaotic situation with numerous intersections between burials can be resolved into a series of superimposed columns resulting from different phases of cemetery organisation. One such excavated example is Whithorn, Galloway (Hill 1997).[51]

The system could break down because there were favoured spots within the cemetery[52] and others that were less desirable. In both English and European folklore, the north side of any church is allegedly reserved for suicides and other offenders against church law (Harland and Wilkinson 1867, 275; Nörlund 1928, 408), but in practice there seems to have been little difference in burial density (see, for an urban example, St Helen-on-the-Walls, York: Magilton 1980).[53] At Raunds in rural Northamptonshire, however, there were more adult females on the north side than the south, perhaps because adult males were more likely to be buried in prestigious places within view of the path to the south door of the church (Hadley 2001, 47). Another exception is the Dominican church at Oxford, where excavation revealed a clustering of burials in the south aisle (Lambrick 1985, 143). A favoured position is said to have been beneath the eaves-drip of a church where the corpse would be sprinkled with 'holy' water from the roof, but this seems to have been an Anglo-Saxon custom and restricted to children (Crawford 1993; Taylor 2001, 176). In later medieval cemeteries, clusters of children have been observed at the west and east ends of churches (Daniell 1998, 128). At Bolsover, for example, there was a cluster of infants on the north side of the tower (Hadley 2001, 48). At St Helen-on-the-Walls, York, there was slight evidence for a clustering of children and young adults in the south corner of the graveyard, but no specific area had been reserved for neonates and infants up to a year old were poorly represented. Segregation between the sexes did not occur.

Orientation of burials

Orientation was liturgical rather than geographical, and a tendency in inhumation cemeteries of all periods has been for burials to lie parallel to the nearest straight line where it approximates to the correct alignment (see, for example, St Andrew Fishergate, York: Stroud and Kemp 1993, 145; or the York Minster excavations: Hadley 2001, 106). It would, however, be wrong to conclude that orientation did not matter. Even in a London plague pit the bodies were properly placed with heads to the west (Hawkins 1990). In Ireland similar care was taken to orientate the grave. A poem *The Battle of the Sheaves* dated to *c* 1200 has the lines: *Rise up, my friend, without fault, fix the coffin without stain, straighten its front to the wall* ... (Fry 1999, 67). At Norwich in the churchyard of St Margaret in Combusto *ubi sepeliuntur suspensi* ('where are buried the hanged') some bodies were reversed, others lay north–south or south–north and a few were prone, presumably to express society's disgust at whatever deeds had led to their execution (Ayers 1990; Bown and Stirland forthcoming), but they nevertheless occupied consecrated ground. It is only with some of the landscaped municipal cemeteries of Victorian England that orientation finally ends.

The one alleged exception to the rule is that of priestly burials. According to still-current tradition, they were buried with heads to the east so that they faced their congregation on Judgement Day, but the practice is, archaeologically speaking, elusive. Daniell (1998, 149) and Hadley (2001, 113, 118) have suggested that it may be a post-medieval practice, the former citing the examples of medieval priestly graves at Deerhurst and St Andrew Fishergate,

York, so identified because they contained a chalice and/or paten, which nevertheless face the same way as the rest of their flock, and the latter proposing that the custom of putting chalice and paten in the grave may be a 13th-century and later usage. There is a credible record of a west–east priestly burial with both a chalice and paten in pewter from the Newark (Notts) hospital cemetery that closed in 1642 (Bishop 1983), but although it is likely,[54] it is not certain that the burial was pre-Reformation.[55] There were several examples of priests' and monks' graves at Partney, Lincolnshire, that were in a separate area of the cemetery but they share the usual orientation.[56]

West–east burials are recorded in York at both St Andrew Fishergate (one example) and St Helen-on-the-Walls (two examples). At the latter the reversals are most probably accidental, but at St Andrew's the body had been decapitated and, as at St Mary in Combusto, a ritual explanation is most likely.

Grave pits

The grave pit in a churchyard was normally of a size and shape appropriate for the body, whether or not it was in a coffin, because it was dug in the presence of the cortège. At St Helen-on-the-Walls, York, it was noted that the pits within the church were frequently narrow, straight-sided and flat-bottomed, and the same was true for pits in the cemetery where they could be satisfactorily defined. The depths of graves within buildings were commonly greater, presumably to ensure that any noxious miasmas from decomposition were unable to escape.[57]

At St Helen-on-the-Walls, the vast majority of grave pits were featureless. 'Special' graves included a few with irregular limestone blocks around the skull, one with a mortar base lined with ashlar blocks, another with a mortar lining and a charcoal burial, of which only the feet survived (Dawes and Magilton 1980, 15–16). At St Andrew Fishergate there were two graves lined with unused ceramic roof-tiles, one had a cradle of cobbles around the skull, two had upright uninscribed stone slabs at the head, two child burials were in graves lined with stones and one was in a grave with a deposit of lime (Stroud and Kemp 1993, 156–7). Graves tended to be shallow, and were perhaps deliberately so in densely packed urban graveyards of the later Middle Ages where any deep excavation was certain to disturb earlier remains. It has been suggested (Hadley 2001, 65) that narrow graves are an indicator of a clothed or shrouded burial as opposed to a coffined one, but it is not always possible to define the grave cut, especially in town cemeteries used over long periods.

Examples of graves dug to contain more than one body are occasionally found. Both St Andrew Fishergate and St Helen-on-the-Walls in York yielded examples, and at Pontefract (Yorks) the bones from an earlier burial were carefully stacked around the coffin of a later one (see Hadley 2001, 66, pl 22).

Burial positions

In York at St Andrew Fishergate as many as nine burial positions were identified. Most (142 in total) were with legs extended and arms on the body. The next most common position was with legs extended and arms at the side (83 in all). Burials with one or other arm on the body and legs extended were found in 35 graves. The remaining positions each accounted for four or fewer burials each (Stroud and Kemp 1993, 145–51). The picture was broadly mirrored at St Helen-on-the-Walls, where over half were with legs extended and arms on the body and most of the remainder had arms at the side. There seemed to be no correlation between the two main types of burial and either the sex or age of the deceased; both occurred throughout the 500 or more years that the cemetery was in use and were found in burials thought to have been coffined as well as those apparently interred in shrouds alone (Dawes and Magilton 1980, 13–14). A much smaller sample from Chester Black Friars revealed 23 with arms on the body and only six with arms at the side (Ward 1990, 124). The burial position most often represented in sculpture and on brasses is with arms on the body, usually with hands in the attitude of prayer, sometimes with the arms crossed on the chest and least frequently with the hands over the groin (Daniell 1998, 118). Future statistical analysis when a bigger sample is available may reveal regional or chronological trends.

Some seemingly odd burial positions will have physical causes that may sometimes be reflected in the skeletal remains. One such from St Helen-on-the-Walls, York, skeleton 5772, had possibly suffered super hyperparathyroidism. One from St Andrew Fishergate, York, skeleton 1847, had been badly decomposed before being tightly wrapped in a shroud and may have been exhumed for reburial. There were also a number of double graves. Those containing both male and female skeletons were presumably family graves and reflect the wish expressed in some medieval wills that the testator is to be buried with his or her spouse, but there were examples of double burials of individuals who had suffered blade injuries (Stroud and Kemp 1993, 157–8). At St Mary Spitalfield, London, a neonate was buried prone (Thomas *et al* 1997, 38) and this is said to be normal practice for the unbaptised.

Grave markers

An Anglo-Saxon cemetery at Thwing, Yorkshire, not apparently associated with any church, has produced evidence for wooden grave markers in the 8th or 9th century, as has St Mark's Lincoln (Hadley 2001, 64 and 133). In a churchyard, the inevitable shallow mound over a grave may often have been a sufficient marker, especially in rural communities where folk memories may have identified family plots. At Addingham (Yorks) empty graves, the result of moving the body to a new place of interment, have been found, and these imply a high degree of cemetery organisation (Hadley 2001, 66). Grave markers within churches in the form of slabs and brasses would have been fairly common by the end of the Middle Ages, and necessary if the requests to be buried with one's spouse commonly found in wills were to be carried out.

Grave goods

There are virtually no medieval English examples of grave goods in the accepted sense of the term and anything deliberately put in the grave must usually have been of a perishable nature. Hadley (2001) and Daniell (1998) have argued that this is an over-simplification, but many of the examples that the latter lists in support of his argument are either symbols of office such as chalices and patens[58] or items of jewellery that happened to have been worn at the time of burial. They are neither gifts for the deity nor intended for the use of the deceased within or beyond the grave. The very few exceptions at St Helen-on-the-Walls were mainly with juveniles and probably signify nothing more than might the inclusion of a favourite toy in a modern child's grave. At St Mary Spitalfield and some other London cemeteries a few individuals seem to have been buried with indulgences, of which the seals survive, but given the alleged widespread sale of indulgences, the custom of burying them seems rare.

The only items made specifically for burying seem to have been lead mortuary crosses, examples of which were found at St Edmund's Abbey, Bury St Edmunds, and elsewhere (Sloane and Gilchrist 2005, 91–2) which were perhaps either to identify the grave as Christian or to ward off malicious spirits. The choice of metal is interesting; its association with death may have come about through its occasional use for lining coffins; alternatively Saturn, the planet of death and old age, is associated with lead.

Shroud pins, usually of copper alloy, are found with some burials, including those in coffins, for coffins were an addition to, not a replacement for, shrouds. They may occur singly but two or more were occasionally found with a single burial. Also from St Helen-on-the-Walls, although their significance was not recognised when the report was published, were numerous bronze items referred to as 'bootlace tags' at the time of excavation and later thought to be lace-tags from clothing. They may have been the ends of cords securing the tops and bottoms of winding sheets.

Coffins and other containers

Coffins themselves rarely survive and their former existence is usually inferred from nails and perhaps distinctive fittings. Professional undertakers are unknown before the later 17th century (Houlbrooke 1999, 190) but there were undoubtedly specialist coffin-makers before that date even if they were general carpenters too when the opportunity arose. In some cases coffins were literally boxes and a few of the 8th- to 9th-century burials at Whithorn were in what seem to have been domestic chests (Hill 1997). Barton-on-Humber has produced a variety of coffins, including an oak dugout example, one made from recycled timber, perhaps originally a bed, one formed of loose planks and five seemingly clinker-built, perhaps from bark (Hadley 2001, 103–4). Amongst the more unusual coffins recorded in western Europe are wickerwork examples from the treeless Irish midlands and children's coffins of chestnut bark bound with broom from pre-Revolutionary France (Fry 1999, 126 and 129), neither of which would normally be detectable archaeologically. Coffins of conventional plank construction may commonly have been fastened together with wooden dowels rather than nails (this was the case at the 11th- to 12th-century church of St Benet, York: Stroud and Kemp 1993, 153) and these too would have perished without trace in normal conditions. Others were composite, with the box dowelled and the lid nailed, as at St Mary Spitalfield, London (Thomas et al 1997, 118, fig 78).

Iron nails and other fittings survive in some cemeteries but it is hard to know how many nails would be needed to make a coffin. It may, for example, have been normal practice to make the 'box' using dowels but to nail the lid. Only when the wood itself survives can we be certain of the presence and shape of the coffin. At St Helen-on-the-Walls, York, there were only five examples of the survival of wooden coffins and only two complete coffin outlines were recorded. One was a simple box with rounded corners and the other was also a box but with a hint of cross-braces at the corners (Dawes and Magilton 1980, 14). In exceptional circumstances the wood can survive well enough to permit identification. Oak and pine are found as well as elm (Daniell 1998, 164), which was traditionally used. At the Austin Friars cemetery, Hull, 39 later medieval coffins survived from over 240 burials. Three were decorated and all but one were fashioned from Baltic oak, reflecting the port's trading connections (Hadley 2001, 115).

As well as wooden coffins, there were occasional sarcophagi of stone. These were sometimes monolithic but could be constructed from slabs, rubble or even brick. They must generally represent high-status burials and when more data have been gathered it would not be surprising to find that they are commonest in areas with suitable local materials. They occur mainly in churches rather than outside in the cemetery. Mortared stone cists occur in cemeteries of the 11th and 12th centuries but thereafter are allegedly to be found only within buildings (White 1988).

Cemetery boundaries

In view of concerns in written sources (see Daniell 1998, 110–15) about the exclusion of animals from cemeteries, it might be expected that they would be very securely protected. The graveyards of urban churches in particular might be encroached upon piecemeal, whereas the main threat in the villages was perhaps from inappropriate uses, agricultural, commercial or social. The incumbent bore the responsibility for maintaining the churchyard wall, and current canon law requires, as it is said to have done from the 13th century, that every graveyard should have its 'keeper' (Fry 1999, 72).

Of the two York churches discussed above, St Helen's churchyard was bounded to the east by the medieval rampart of the city walls, on the west by a deep ditch of pre-Norman date known as the Werkdyke, to the north by the hall of the Merchant Taylors and its southern boundary was undetermined. Double ditches (reinforcing a hedge?) apparently bounded St Andrew's cemetery on the north and south sides but its other limits were undetermined. Hospitals would have been enclosed in any case, so the graveyard wall, hedge or fence would have been an internal feature unless the cemetery lay on the hospital boundary.

The means of defining its cemetery would have depended on an institution's priorities, resources and the local availability of materials. Chichester lacks good building stone but timber was relatively plentiful, and at St Andrew-in-the-Oxmarket, an intramural city church, fencing panels seem to have been used to delimit the graveyard in the 16th and 17th centuries (McCann 1978). A more durable but still relatively cheap solution would have been to dig a ditch and plant a thorn hedge on the bank formed by the upcast, and this may have been the usual practice in rural areas where resources were scarce. The normal Chichester building stone is flint from the Downs, supplemented by a variety of stone from further afield for quoins, window dressings and the like, and chalk for lime-burning is available from the same source. For St James', the nearest convenient source of both chalk and flint was probably at Halnaker on Stane Street, the old Roman road to London, about 3 miles (5km) distant to the northeast; although the same materials might be found closer to hand due north of the hospital, the roads are unlikely to have been as good. A chance reference to it in a rental (Appendix 6) means that at least part of the St James' cemetery was walled.

3.9   Further reading

The end of the 20th century and the start of the 21st has seen a flood of books and papers relating to death and burial in medieval England, some specific and others covering a wider chronological or geographical canvas. Amongst the earliest was *Death in Towns: Urban responses to the dying and the dead, 100–1600* (1992) edited by Steven Bassett, the product of a conference at Birmingham University in 1991. Another compilation, *Death in England,* edited by Peter Jupp and Clare Gittings (1999), concentrated on the documentary evidence. Christopher Daniell's *Death and Burial in Medieval England 1066–1550* (1998) is mainly archaeological with some use of documentary sources. Paul Binski's *Medieval Death* (1996) is European in scope but almost exclusively historical and art historical in source materials and therefore restricted to the middle and upper echelons of medieval society. *Burial in Early Medieval England and Wales,* edited by Sam Lucy and Andrew Reynolds (2002), and *Burial Practice in Early England* by Alison Taylor (2001) are, because of their chronological range, of marginal interest for present purposes. The same limitation applies to Elizabeth O'Brien's monumental *Post-Roman Britain to Anglo-Saxon England: Burial Practices Reviewed* (1999). The similarly monumental *Cannington Cemetery* (Rahtz *et al* 2000) is equally irrelevant as to date but interesting for its methodology as well as for its early cases of leprosy. Dawn Hadley's *Death in Medieval England: an archaeology* (2001) is, despite the title, a regional study restricted to four Danelaw counties but nevertheless contains much of relevance. Susan Fry's *Burial in Medieval Ireland* (1999), the first ever study of Irish burials in the Middle Ages, is a history that emphasises similarities with Britain and Western Europe. Ruth Richardson's *Death, Dissection and the Destitute* (1988) has a valuable introductory chapter, 'The Corpse and Popular Culture', that highlights the potential contribution of folk-life studies. Complementing these and other works have been new books on palaeopathology, some technical (eg *Counting the Dead. The epidemiology of Skeletal Populations* by Tony Waldron (1994); *A Field Guide to Joint Disease in Archaeology* by Juliet Rogers and Tony Waldron (1995); *Bodies of Evidence* edited by A L Grauer (1995)) and others interpretative, site-specific and aimed at non-specialists (eg *Raising The Dead. The Skeleton Crew of Henry VIII's Great Ship,* The Mary Rose by Ann Stirland (2000) and *Blood Red Roses. The Archaeology of a Mass Grave from the Battle of Towton AD 1461* (2000) edited by Fiorato *et al*). The archaeology of the Reformation, including its cemeteries, is tackled in the first monograph of the Society for Post-Medieval Archaeology (ed Gaimster and Gilchrist 2003). Most comprehensive of all recent publications is Gilchrist and Sloane's *Requiem. The Medieval Monastic Cemetery in Britain* (2005) that appeared as this account was being finalised.

Notes

1. The pall or hearsecloth in the Middle Ages could be vividly decorated with symbols of a guild or fraternity. Only in post-Reformation times did it become a dark enveloping cloth (Harding 2003, 392).

2. This imaginative reconstruction is based on Cluniac practice (Rowell 1977) and may be over-elaborate for all but the largest lazar houses. Benedictine and Augustinian practice in early 14th-century England is attested in a custumal of St Augustine's Abbey, Canterbury (Taunton 1897), and all three have features in common with each other.

3. For examples, see Gilchrist and Sloane 2005, 63–4.

4. Some institutions had 'traditional' benefactors who may have expected the family to be buried together (Gilchrist and Sloane 2005, 61).

5. For reference, Gilchrist and Sloane 2005, 61.

6. One illuminated manuscript shows the grave-digger climbing out of the pit as the coffin is borne from the church. The grave is short, perhaps for a child, and shallow, not reaching the digger's knee (Orme 2001, pl 43).

7. Books of Hours, very popular from the mid-13th century to the 16th, included psalms collectively known as The Office of the Dead that besought the living to intercede for souls in purgatory. Although they can be illustrated with vignettes charting a funeral from sickbed to graveside, these need to be used with caution as a guide to contemporary English practice as the scenes may be copied from earlier books and portray the customs of continental Europe.

8. Hadley (2001, 103) has concluded that it is inappropriate to use the presence or absence of a coffin as indicating status, a view that this writer does not hold whilst recognising that the correlation may not be straightforward.

9. *Non convenit enim eum quem humiliter vivere decet, pompose sepeliri, nisi velit, et id frustra, cadaveri mortuo maiores honores deberi quam corpori vivo.*

10. The abandonment of cremation began in Italy in the 1st century BC, so the phenomenon starts too early to be attributed to Christian beliefs in a physical resurrection. Future historians of the 20th century may be equally at a loss to explain the opposite phenomenon at the end of the 2nd millennium.

11. As with much funerary terminology, the modern use of the word does not convey its older meaning. A shroud is technically a garment made specifically for burial and its first appearance in literature is post-Reformation (OED). Whilst it is convenient to refer to shrouded burials in the Middle Ages, winding-sheeted would be more accurate.

12. In imitation of Christ: Mark **15**, 46. Shrouds allegedly in other materials are probably items of clothing that have been misidentified (Gilchrist and Sloane 2005, 106).

13. The rituals of death were of course a repeat of those of birth, the washing of the corpse being a sort of lay baptism and the winding sheet the equivalent of swaddling bands.

14. The positioning of the body would normally have to be carried out before *rigor mortis* set in. As will be known to all readers of detective stories, the onset generally takes place within three or four hours of death, stiffening is complete after about ten hours and the condition lasts for around 36 hours. The process is delayed if the body is kept warm.

15. Hence the widespread children's saying 'cross my heart and hope to die'? This was current during the writer's childhood in Chester in the 1950s and also in Bristol (K Thompson, pers comm) and West London (Richardson 1988, 303) in the same era.

16. In more recent times the legs were held straight by strips of cloth called foot bands. In some parts of Britain these were left tied to prevent the corpse from walking and in others loosened so as not to restrict the reanimated body when the last trump sounded (Richardson 1988, 20).

17. It was however normal practice in medieval Greenland (Nörlund 1924) and it has been claimed that the phraseology of the Acts for Burial in Woollen imply that ordinary clothes might be used for burial (Richardson 1988, 20). Burial in a shroud without fastenings is said to have been near-universal by late Saxon times (Taylor 2001, 174).

18. The five coffins where traces of wood survived at St Helen-on-the-Walls, York, were all within the confines of the latest church. There were, however, many other coffined burials attested only by nails in the grave pit (Dawes and Magilton 1980, 14).

19. A parish coffin, probably Elizabethan or Jacobean, survives at Easingwold, Yorkshire. It is made of oak with a hinged lid. No tradition of its use survives, and it was regarded as an oddity by the 1820s (Richardson 1988, 303). An illustration in a French Book of Hours of *c* 1470 shows a tapered wooden box with a lid being used to transport the corpse to the grave but the body itself, tightly shrouded, is buried in a shallow unlined pit (Binski 1996, pl V).

20. Back to front burials could also be a sign of censure or disapproval.

21. This may have been a lid.

22. Who could and could not be buried in consecrated ground was outlined by the Austin canon John Mirk in the later 14th century. See Gilchrist and Sloane (2005, 71) for references.

23. According to Gregory of Tours, Palladius count of Javols committed suicide but was accepted for burial at the monastery of Cournon, although he was interred away from the rest of the community. Did this symbolise, or even help to determine, his likely fate in the afterlife (Hadley 2001, 131)?

24. To stop, amongst other things, the illicit burial of unbaptised babies by night, the Hereford cathedral authorities applied to wall in their cemetery (Gilchrist and Sloane 2005, 34).

25. Grazing animals were less of a problem. Tethered goats would have been an effective means of cropping grass and weeds, and were so used in rural Ireland in the recent past.

26. Two different sets of statutes, adopted at Worcester in 1229 and 1240, state that there are not to be any buildings in cemeteries except at times of hostilities. Other dioceses adopted similar statutes at about the same time. Yet at St Paul's London there were over 30 dwellings in the cemetery by 1411 (Fry 1999, 59).

27. Things were no better in the 18th century when Samuel Molyneux visited Aughrim cemetery, Co. Galway, in 1704 and noted 'a few dead men's sckulls scattered in ye fields yet remains of yet battle there fought [in 1691] in ye troubles' but a 14th-century work describing Ennis Abbey, Co. Clare, in 1305 speaks of 'well-kept graves, homes of the noble dead' (Fry 1999, 67–8). Respect for graves seems to have been restricted to the élite class.

28. Boxgrove Priory cemetery, *c* 5km (3 miles) from St James', is famous as the site of a cricket match played during Evensong on 28 April 1622 and again on the following Sunday when the two churchwardens joined in. All were hauled before the Consistory Court at Chichester Cathedral and the punishment included public penance (McCann and Wilkinson 1972).

29. These two obviously testify that deathbed wills were still commonplace.

30. The belief that corpses retained some form of life until the flesh had rotted off the bones is present in medieval literature (Horrox 1999, 95).

31. This was not without many precedents. In 1070 the Legatine Council, which met at Winchester, had decreed that there was to be no burial in churches, and in 1152 the Cistercian general chapter determined to bury only royalty and senior ecclesiastics in their churches (Fry 1999, 158). As early as 1292 the Statutes of Chichester forbade burials in church or chancel other than of manorial lords, patrons and their wives, and priests, and in 1342 the dean of Carlisle issued a similar injunction (Daniell 1998, 96–7). Whether the concern was one of public hygiene, social status or merely another means of raising money by obliging those who felt they should qualify but were now excluded to buy a licence is unclear. In the later Middle Ages the will-making classes certainly expected burial in church (Hadley 2001, 43) and in London a greater proportion of the parishioners seems to have been buried in churches post-Reformation than before (Harding 2003, 389).

32. As at St Andrew-in-the-Oxmarket, Chichester, in 1988 (Kenny 1988).

33. Also known as The New Work.

34. The individuals may have been William of Basing (died 1383) and Thomas Bromelegh (?died 1390), either of whom may be regarded as the second founder of the hospital.

35. But commonly referred to as the Maison Dieu.
36. By Adam of Charing, a lay landowner.
37. The closure must reflect the perceived indivisibility of the priory and hospital. Other London hospitals (St Bartholomew's, St Thomas', St Mary of Bethlehem, St Katherine's) lost their religious function but continued to take care of the sick.
38. Other bullas from London cemeteries include two from St Botoloph's Billingsgate and one from Charterhouse in the tomb of its founder (Thomas *et al* 1997, 123).
39. *Medieval Archaeology* **36** (1992), 251.
40. Hadley (2001, 115) states that priests would often have a duplicate chalice and paten: a silver set for church services and a pewter or lead set to be buried with the body.
41. *Medieval Archaeology* **33** (1989), 220; *Medieval Archaeology* **34** (1990), 217; *Medieval Archaeology* **35** (1991), 196.
42. *Medieval Archaeology* **40** (1996), 253.
43. *Medieval Archaeology* **38** (1994), 194–5; Gilchrist and Sloane 2005, 238.
44. *Medieval Archaeology* **36** (1992), 225–6.
45. *Medieval Archaeology* **35** (1991), 147.
46. *Medieval Archaeology* **35** (1991), 147.
47. *Medieval Archaeology* **35** (1991), 189.
48. *Medieval Archaeology* **44** (2000), 288; *Medieval Archaeology* **46** (2002), 152.
49. More or less circular cemeteries are to be found in Ireland. The Old Irish word for a cemetery is *reilic*, a borrowing from Latin *reliquae* meaning 'the relics (of saints)'. These ought to be monofocal, but too few have been excavated to confirm the point.
50. This practice is historically attested at Wells, where resident canons were to be buried in the cloister to the south of the church, starting at the south door and proceeding southwards, and then back again (Gilchrist and Sloane 2005, 47).
51. The existence of what may be termed 'row cemeteries' has been challenged by Elisabeth Zadora-Rio (2003, 2) who, speaking of early medieval graveyards, has suggested that an impression of regularity is a by-product of grave orientation, actual rows being infrequent and generally restricted to a small number of graves.
52. For example, next to the churchyard cross, which was often more or less central, or a founder's burial if it lay outside the church.
53. One ingenious explanation of the custom is that north was the side of the church from which the Gospel was delivered, whilst the Epistle was read from the south. Therefore those who died outside the grace of God were buried on the north where they could benefit from Gospel teaching (Fry 1999, 163).
54. On the grounds that post-Reformation masters are not known to have been priests.
55. A 17th-century source suggests that their east–west orientation was one element of changes in Catholic ritual in that era (Barney Sloane pers comm). He believes it to be a post-medieval phenomenon.
56. E Popescu, pers comm.
57. At St Mary Spital, London the range was 0.8 to 1.07m for internal burials, contrasted with 0.5 to 0.6m for burials outside (Thomas *et al* 1997, 121).
58. Hadley (20001, 121) has suggested that broken seal matrices were the secular equivalent, citing the example from St Andrew Fishergate, York, symbolising the break up of a noble household.

4 The provision of charitable care in Chichester
by John Magilton

The history and archaeology of St James' Hospital needs to be viewed in the light of provision for the sick poor in Chichester and its immediate environs, since it was but one institution amongst several with similar aims. Most medieval towns of any size supported at least two hospitals, one for the infirm and poor travellers, and the other for lepers. Where more than one hospital of each sort existed, there was necessarily competition between them for alms and gifts and, in the later Middle Ages, when many former leper houses became *de facto* alms-houses, the erstwhile leprosaria were competing with institutions founded for the infirm. National-ly, London and York[1] had each about 35 hospitals catering variously for the poor, the sick poor,

lepers and wayfarers, Norwich and Bristol around nineteen, and Exeter and Canterbury about nine or ten (Price 1998, 198). As the cathedral city of Sussex, Chichester had a number of hospitals with a potential claim on the purses of alms givers, all of them equally dependent on the urban economy for both alms and inmates.

As noted in Chapter 2, hospitals for those thought morally, and later also physically, infec-tious lay outside urban centres, and whilst in places that experienced exceptional growth leper hospitals might as a consequence find themselves in the suburbs, they will have started off as institu-tions of the urban periphery. In the case of walled towns such as Chichester, it is tempting to regard

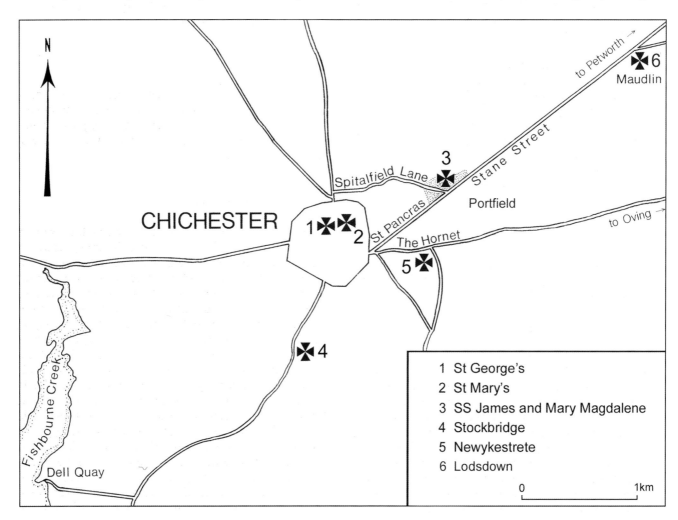

Figure 4.1 Medieval hospitals in and around Chichester. The pattern is the usual one of an intramural institution for the sick poor and travellers and extramural hospitals at nodal points in the road system for lepers. For a relatively small city Chichester was well provided with the latter, perhaps because ports were more vulnerable to infection than inland towns, although the hospitals at Stockbridge and Newykestrete were perhaps small and relatively short-lived. Additionally there were almost certainly places where lepers who eschewed the institutional life would gather to solicit alms

the defended enceinte as the urban core, but some places had extensive suburbs by the time their first hospitals were built and large areas within their walls of little commercial value because they belonged to the church. Chichester's western half was divided into the cathedral precinct (south-west quadrant) and a north-west quadrant that, street frontages excepted, was virtually without buildings in the Middle Ages. Half of the north-east quadrant too had been lost to the castle and, later, the Franciscans, and even the south-east quadrant was sufficiently empty for the Dominicans to acquire a generous precinct that fronted onto East Street. The geographical centre of Chichester was not so much the cross at the carfax but a point somewhere near the East Gate, since Chichester's only significant extramural area was its suburb of St Pancras, beyond which lay St James' Cross marking the city boundary, with the leper house of St James and St Mary Magdalene just outside. Pilgrims and the sick poor were another matter. The former wanted to be close to their destination (at Chichester, the shrine of St Richard of Wych in the cathedral) and, for alms collection purposes, the sick poor needed to be near the commercial centre. Property might be more expensive in the middle of town, but the advantage of a town-centre site to a hospital founder or patron was the greater number of passers-by who might pray for the swift passage of his soul through purgatory.

The history of St James and St Mary Magdalene's leper hospital, or as much as can be recovered, is examined in detail in Chapter 5. This chapter briefly summarises what is known of the other institutions of the city, including leper houses, that in some way catered for the sick poor.

4.1 Hospitals and almshouses before the Reformation (Fig 4.1)

Intramural hospitals

St Mary's Hospital (Fig 4.2)

The earlier of the two hospitals within the walls was St Mary's. Perhaps founded *c* 1158, it originally occupied a site near the intersection of Chichester's four main streets, between South Street and East Street behind the present Punch House. In effect refounded by Thomas of Lichfield, Dean of Chichester 1227–39, it acquired most of its endowments around that time. It moved to its present site, on the east side of St Martin's Lane, in 1269, and work on the main building, a communal hall with attached chapel, is datable on architectural grounds to *c* 1290. It catered both for poor travellers and for the sick (Cavis-Brown 1905, 8). There were up to thirteen inmates, both male and female, some infirm and others healthy, in 1402. By the later 15th century the hospital administration had become lax and corrupt, although it still attracted bequests in

Figure 4.2 St Mary's Hospital, Chichester. The hospital acquired its present site in about 1290 when the Franciscans, former occupiers, moved to new premises within the walls of the now-redundant castle. In outward appearance St Mary's resembles contemporary churches in which the pitched roof embraces both nave and aisles without interruption. Huge brick chimney stacks were inserted into the former infirmary hall and it was divided up into separate apartments in the 17th century. These, appropriately modernised, still provide accommodation for elderly women who fulfil the entrance criteria

local wills. Under Dean Fleshmonger's revised constitution of 1528 it effectively became an almshouse catering for five poor brothers and five poor sisters but no provision was made for wayfarers (Cavis-Brown 1905, 10).

St George's Almshouses

The other intramural hospital lay not far from St Mary's and was also in St Martin's Lane, although on the west side. It is usually called St George's Almshouses and its foundation is attributed to the Guild of St George, a religious body which, by the end of the Middle Ages, was acting as the spiritual arm of the merchant guild (ie the city council) whose mayor, under a reorganisation of 1446, was *ex officio* master of St George's Guild (Salzman 1935, 92). The Guild is recorded in a will of 1418 when William Neel left to it 13s 4d (Godfrey 1935, 364) and, on the basis of other 15th-century wills, the original endowment seems to have been for six poor men. Most hospitals of late foundation were of the almshouse type. In Bristol, for example, Holy Trinity Hospital, founded by John Barnstaple in 1395 and transferred to the mayor and commonalty *c* 1408, had two components, an almshouse and a religious fraternity. In the same city at least two almshouses originated below the halls of craft guilds (Price 1998, 201–2). Although it has been argued that these late foundations by rich citizens and craft guilds were mainly aimed at getting the poor off the streets (Price 1998, 15), it is clear that many were very selective and admitted only the deserving poor, not vagrants. As prayer was still central to their regime, the spiritual side must have remained important (Orme and Webster 1995, 55).

The inmates were called bedemen[2] in 1525 in the will of Richard Barnam of Rumboldswick (Godfrey 1935, 365), but St George's Almshouses seem to have been considered separate from the brotherhood, which was dissolved under the 1547 Chantries Act and its property granted to the city.

Extramural hospitals

In his section on religious houses in the *Victoria County History*, Page (1907) identified four extramural hospitals, at Lodsdown in Westhampnett parish, Stockbridge near Chichester, Rumboldswick alias Newykestrete, thought to lie outside the south gate of the city, and St James and St Mary Magdalene at Spitalfield. As this list has tended to be somewhat uncritically accepted by later writers, the evidence merits a review.

One of the earliest gifts to a Chichester hospital is that of William de St John who between 1173 and 1180 gave eight cartloads of beech from Goodwood to 'the church of St Mary Magdalene of the sick of Chichester' (Peckham 1942–43, 289, no. 918). The problem is identifying the hospital. As it was in Chichester and for the sick, it might be suspected that the intramural St Mary's was meant and that its patron was (mistakenly) thought to be to St Mary Magdalene. On the other hand, the term 'sick' could be used loosely. Gervase of Canterbury, writing *c* 1200, describes St Oswald's, Worcester, as for *'infirmi, item leprosi'* (Clay 1909, 48) so the Chichester hospital mentioned here might have been a leper house. The obvious candidate would then be the Spitalfield hospital, known from Seffrid II's confirmation charter to have been dedicated to St Mary Magdalene and although it was invariably referred to as St James' in the medieval period, both saints were patrons. St Mary Magdalene alone was also patron of a leper house at Lodsdown. Could this have been meant? Both Goodwood and Lodsdown are in the same parish, Westhampnett, but the hospital is rather distant from the city to be described as 'of Chichester'. Is there a fourth possibility?

The will of William de Keynesham, a canon of Chichester, in 1237 or later (Peckham 1942–43, 142, no. 548), leaves 6d to the Hospital of St James, 4d to the lepers of Londesdon (ie Lodsdown), 3d to the lepers of Wikes and 3d to the lepers of Stocbrugg. He obviously had a special concern for lepers since, although the inmates of St James' are not specified in the will, they were certainly lepers at this period and for some time to come if other testators are to be believed. The terminology of the will is interesting because it mentions a *hospital* of St James but otherwise refers to 'the lepers of so-and-so', perhaps suggesting that they lived in less formal communities.[3]

The hospital at Stockbridge

The lepers of Stockbridge, the hundredal meeting place south of Chichester, may have occupied nothing more elaborate than a cottage and are otherwise unrecorded. They were however well placed for alms gathering at the wooden bridge implicit in the place-name.[4] Hospitals were often sited next to bridges (eg St Giles', Brompton Bridge, Yorkshire, and St Nicholas on the Aylewood Bridge, Salisbury) and obligations to maintain them were sometimes imposed on hospitals (Rawcliffe 2000a, 35) but there is nothing to suggest that the Stockbridge lepers had any such responsibility. The lepers of Lodsdown and their hospital at Westhampnett are adequately attested in later documents down to the mid-16th century and do not present any problem of identification, but the lepers of Wikes do not appear elsewhere, at least under that name. They may have formed, as suggested for the lepers of Stockbridge, a small and perhaps short-lived community, or they may recur in later documents under a different name. They were, as noted, tentatively equated by Page (1907, 103) with the 'hospital of Newykestrete' recorded in a will of 1384 by chancellor John Bishopstone (Godfrey 1935, 366) and placed by him outside the south gate of the city, although it is not now clear why he so located it.

The hospital of Wikes (alias Newykestrete?)

If both references are to the same hospital or community, it must have been in Rumboldswick[5] parish and on Newykestrete. The latter is well attested as an old name for the street now called The Hornet (Morgan 1992, 166) outside the east gate which, as an important route to Oving, Aldingbourne (where the bishop had a palace) and other villages of the coastal plain, would have been a good site for a hospital. Both sides of The Hornet just outside the east gate were in St Pancras parish but further east only the northern side fell in St Pancras, the road forming the northern limit of the parish of Rumboldswick as far east as Whyke Road. Beyond here the parish boundary, although parallel with the road, is a little south of its southern edge. The hospital must therefore have been on the south side of The Hornet at least 200m beyond the east gate but west of Whyke Road, and this was the reasoning behind the authors' siting of the hospital in earlier publications (eg Magilton and Lee 1989, fig 1).

As the 1384 will of John Bishopstone specifies a hospital of Newykestrete, it might be supposed that some other record would survive, and there are possible later references to it. The will of Richard Myldewe, proven on 4 September 1487 (Peckham 1950, 142) includes a bequest of 6d to 'the poor of the hospital of St Mary Magdalene in le portefeelde'.[6] This cannot be St James' Hospital under its alternative (and rarely used) name because there is also a bequest of 8d to the Hospital of St James nigh Chichester, nor is it likely to be the same bequest listed twice since the amounts are different, and it cannot be the intramural St Mary's since that is nowhere near the Portfield or any other field and in any case is listed separately, receiving 6d. A near-contemporary will, that of Richard Dorkyng in 1492 (Peckham 1948, 9) also leaves money to 'St Mary Magdalene nigh Chichester' and it is again clear that this is not St James' or St Mary's within the walls or the hospital at Lodsdown, since all three also received small legacies.

There are two 14th-century records that may relate to the hospital. In 1320 Henry de Garlandia, Dean of Chichester, left 3d to the lepers of la Portefelde as well as 3d to the lepers of St James, Chichester (1942–43, 78–9) and there is a will of 1366–67 by Lady Margaret Covert of Sullington which seems to imply a hospital of St Mary Magdalene separate from St James' at Chichester (Godfrey 1935, 366). It is therefore reasonably clear that there was a hospital dedicated to St Mary Magdalene, described as near Chichester in 1492 and in the Portfield in 1487, when it was for 'the poor', and that there were lepers in the Portfield in 1320. These cannot refer to St James' Hospital under its other name, but could refer to the Rumboldswick hospital which, if correctly sited on the south side of The Hornet, may have been in a part of the Portfield which lay in Rumboldswick parish.

St Mary Magdalene in the Portfield

This is possibly the hospital of Wikes under yet another name. Unfortunately there is almost no additional topographical information with which to locate the hospital. An undated medieval document listing tithes in Rumboldswick belonging to the rectory of St Peter the Great and appropriated to the dean and chapter speaks of '24 acres lying on both sides of the king's high way from the House of lepers of St Mary Magdalene to Drayton' (Peckham 1942–43, 204, no. 751). If the highway is what is now called the Bognor road (A259), the house of lepers must lie at or near that road's intersection with The Hornet, roughly opposite where The Four Chesnuts (*sic*) now stands.[7] This is a nodal point in the local road network and would be a good site for a hospital. The hospital in the document cannot be St James' at Spitalfield Lane and the highway St James' Road since that road falls totally in Oving parish, and its southward continuation, Florence Road, can also be ruled out as it is the Rumboldswick parish boundary, its eastern side being in Oving.

The only additional references to the Portfield hospital so far found are equally undated. One occurs in a list of Corporations Secular and Regular where the 'Hospital of St Mary Magdalene, Chichester, of the Bishop's foundation' is listed above St James' Chichester and St Mary Magdalene's Lodsdown next Halnaker. A second probable reference occurs in 'The sum of all synodals of the Archdeaconry', perhaps late 13th century, where it is said, 'Of the Bishop's portion the Precentor has 20s, the Chancellor 20s, the prebend of Middleton 10s, the lepers of St Mary Magdalene 10s ....' (Peckham 1942–43, 178, no. 690), although this could be St James' by its alternative title. Lodsdown is unlikely to be meant, as it has no known cathedral connection.

Little Maudlin at Lodsdown

The real extramural rival to St James' was the hospital at Lodsdown in Westhampnett parish, effectively on the same road as St James' and positioned so that the traveller from Arundel and places east of Chichester, or journeying from the London direction via Petworth down the old Roman road, Stane Street, could be relieved of his alms before getting too close to the city suburbs. From the will of William de Keynesham it is known that there were lepers at Lodsdown by about 1237 and by 1320, if the will of Henry de Garlandia is to be believed, there were two leper houses at Lodsdown. The inmates were still described as lepers in 1373 in the will of William de Lenne, Bishop of Worcester, perhaps anachronistically, but as 'poor people' or 'alms people' thereafter. In *c* 1275 the title of the institution was *Hospitale Sancte Maria Magdalene de Loddesdowne juxta Halnaked* (Mawer and Stenton 1929, 78) and in a will of 1544 it was known as 'Lytill Mawdlyng', possibly in contrast with St James' or more likely with the Portfield hospital, if it still survived (Godfrey 1935, 340). This is the latest record of the Lodsdown hospital as a functioning institution. Its former existence is commemorated today in the minor name Maudlin for a clutch of houses at the road junction, and it is more than likely that the hospital stood at the intersection of the Petworth and Arundel roads since this, according to the Boxgrove Cartulary, is where Lodsdown lay (Fleming 1960, 164, no. 376). It is not known to have had a cemetery.

Boxgrove Priory hospital

Almost nothing is known about the priory hospital. In its final year it seems to have been an almshouse with six poor persons *ibidem inhabitantes* receiving a farthing a day in accordance with the ancient statutes of the house (Page 1907, 59) and it was dissolved with the Benedictine abbey in 1536. The monks seem also to have run a school that had eight pupils in its last year of existence.[8]

4.2 Hospitals and almshouses after the Reformation (Fig 4.3)

One practical side-effect of the Dissolution was the loss of hospitals and almshouses, over 100 of which were catalogued in the *Valor Ecclesiasticus*, formerly

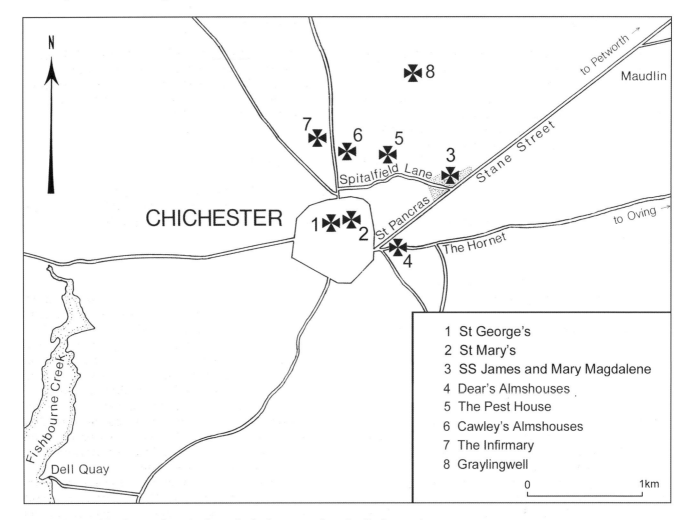

Figure 4.3 Chichester hospitals and almhouses after the Reformation

run by monasteries and collegiate churches, which had provided bed-care and shelter for the aged and infirm. A spiritual side effect of the ongoing process of reformation was the removal of one of the main incentives to found and maintain a hospital; the doctrine of purgatory now no longer applied and the prayers of the 'holy poor' were no longer needed to speed souls on their afterlife journey. National initiatives to found more almshouses came to nothing and it was left to individuals and local communities to respond as best they could (Rawcliffe 2000a, 202–3).

Of the hospitals described above, only St Mary's Hospital and St George's Almshouses within the walls and St James' outside them were still functioning in the later 16th century and there may have been pressure on all to take in more people than their endowments could support or their buildings comfortably accommodate.[9] In Chichester, as elsewhere, new institutions were eventually founded to make good the deficit through a combination of the Christian charity of individuals and a fear of civil unrest by the urban élite. These were mostly on the urban periphery.

The extent of hospital provision in the late 17th century is attested in a list drawn up some time during the episcopacy of John Lake, bishop of

Chichester from 1685 to 1690, perhaps in 1687. The Chichester section begins as follows:

Without the Eastgate of the city is the Hospital of St James and St Mary Magdalene, of very ancient foundation; whereof Mr. Peter Edge, Rector of St Pancras, in the city of Chichester, is Master. It is of small revenue, and hath only one poor person (but she a miserable idiot) in it ...' (Turner 1861, 305–6). Also listed are St Mary's and Cawley's Almshouses.

Intramural hospitals and almshouses

St Mary's Hospital

St Mary's survived the Reformation because, like St James', it was governed by the cathedral (Page 1907, 100–2) and had recently revised its constitution. As most of the hospital building and much of its archive have survived, it has been much studied (eg Wright 1885, Cavis-Brown 1905, Powell 1955, Steer 1962; see Munby 1987 for a comprehensive bibliography) and is one of a very few hospitals of medieval foundation still operating in Europe.

St George's Almshouses

The almshouses in effect the became city poorhouse and the church authorities must have been persuaded that a daily round of prayers for the souls of benefactors was no longer part of its post-Reformation role. The building was auctioned following inspection by the mayor in 1744 which found it 'very ruinous, likely to fall down and dangerous to passengers' (Morgan 1992, 129). Its successor was Cawley's Almshouse (see below).

Extramural hospitals and almshouses

Rumboldswyke

Elizabeth Gubbett in 1617 catered for the poor of Rumboldswick parish just outside Chichester, by leaving them £20 with which her executors bought a house in Tower Street to provide an annuity (Morgan 1992, 16).

Hospital of St Bartholomew

Outside the north gate of Chichester lies the Hospital of St Bartholomew, established in 1625–26 by William Cawley for the maintenance of twelve decayed tradesmen of the city. Although still generally known as Cawley's Almshouses, its trustees, the mayor and corporation, converted it to a workhouse in 1681 (Salzman 1935, 81). In 1753 Cawley's Almshouses were appropriated by Act of Parliament as the poorhouse of the eight united parishes of Chichester (Salzman 1935, 81). As noted above, St George's Almshouses, also known as the poorhouse, in St Martin's Lane had been sold and demolished a few years earlier.

Dear's Almshouses

Dear's Almshouses in The Hornet are of unknown date of foundation. In 1786 the six houses were empty, dilapidated and used as sheds (Morgan 1992, 17). They take their name from Martha Dear, under whose will they were re-endowed about 1806, and they were further endowed in 1870 (Salzman 1935, 167–8).

The Pest House

The now-demolished Pest House in College Lane, built in 1665 if its date-stone is to be believed, but not necessarily as a hospital, was the first post-Reformation charity to offer medical care. It was used until 1920 when superseded by the Infectious Diseases Hospital at the north-west end of Spitalfield Lane (Morgan 1992, 30, 195). Later a nurses' home for St Richard's Hospital, it was developed for housing in the 1990s.

The Infirmary

The eventual successor to St James' Hospital began, for outpatients only, outside the North Gate as the Dispensary for the Sick Poor in 1784, becoming the Infirmary in 1826 and the Royal West Sussex Hospital in 1913 (Steer 1960).

Graylingwell

Graylingwell, north-east of the city, for the mentally ill, was begun in 1897 on lands bought from the Ecclesiastical Commissioners (Morgan 1992, 195–6).

Notes

1. Butler (1987, 175) puts the York total at only 24. His figures for other Yorkshire towns are: Hull 12, Beverley 10, Scarborough 6, Pontefract 5.
2. The term derives from the Anglo-Saxon word for a prayer and is a reminder that, even at this late date, intercessory prayers were sought from inmates on behalf of hospital founders and patrons. The word in its modern sense 'bead' derives from the round perforated elements that make up the rosary. The term 'bedesman' for an almshouse resident survived the Reformation, but intercessory prayers did not.
3. The deed of confirmation for St Lawrence's leprosarium, Bristol (Price 1998, 199), refers to a croft for lepers near the town and could reflect a parallel situation in which the lepers lived in a physically isolated and, as far as possible, self-supporting community – what might have been termed in the recent past a 'leper colony'. There was also a sizeable group of lepers living on the outskirts of Norwich half a century before the first leper hospital was founded (Rawcliffe 2000b, 233).
4. Or so it would normally be assumed. However, a deed dated 1376 grants a piece of land 'in Portfield at Stokkebregg' (Peckham 1950, 126, no. 32) and is a reminder that the term would have been descriptive of many wooden bridges. It is difficult to think of any feature in the Portfield area that would require bridging apart from the River Lavant along its northern edge (in modern terms the north end of St James' Road). However, William de Keynesham can hardly mean the Portfield Stockbridge since he also makes a bequest to St James' and it is very unlikely that a second community of lepers was established across the road from it.
5. Rumboldswick (a variety of spellings is found) seems earlier to have been known simply as Wyke, Whyke etc. The prefix may have been to distinguish it from Shopwyke in Oving parish. The latter seems occasionally to have been referred to as Wikes etc, just to add to the confusion: see *Boxgrove Chartulary* 66 (Fleming 1960).

6. At the time of its enclosure in 1848 the name
    Portfield applied exclusively to land in Oving
    parish (see WSRO QDD/6/W15) but it may once
    have been more extensive; its westernmost part
    was called Guildenfield. A survey of Rumbold-
    swick in 1608 records its open fields as Wick
    Field, Town Field and Port Field (Salzman 1953,
    172). The Rumboldswick Portfield presumably
    lay in its north-east corner; it seems perverse
    to postulate it anywhere else. A 15th-century
    hospital in the Portfield could therefore lie in
    Wick parish.
7. The only other candidate possible would seem
    to be Whyke Road. As this and the Bognor road
    both converge before the junction with Oving
    Road it does not matter, for present purposes,
    which was meant. The 1848 Rumboldswick
    Tithe Award (WSRO TD W103) was examined
    in the hope that field names would help to locate
    the hospital, but to no avail.
8. Anon. 1901. 'Inventories of Goods of the Smaller
    Monasteries and Friaries in Sussex at the time
    of their Dissolution', *Sussex Archaeological Col-
    lections* **44**, 55–72.
9. In 1582 St Mary's had again amended its
    constitution, dropping part of its former role
    as a hostel for poor travellers, confirming its
    commitment to the poor and infirm although
    restricting their number to five (Cavis-Brown
    1905, 10).

Part 2

The hospital of St James and St Mary Magdalene, Chichester

5   A history of the hospital *by John Magilton*

This chapter attempts a chronological account of the institution from its foundation through its transition to an almshouse for 'poor men' and its admission of women. It then looks in more detail at specific aspects of the hospital in the Middle Ages and in the early modern period. As the hospital's original records do not survive, what can be gleaned of its history comes either from chance references in other sources, such as wills, or from transcripts made when its records were extant. The hospital seal was in Lewes Museum at the start of the 20th century (Clay 1909, 324) but cannot now be found.

5.1   History

The 12th century

The little that is known or can be deduced about the origin of the hospital is mostly rehearsed below in discussing its constitution and economy. In essence, the hospital seems to have been founded on Crown land before 1118, administered by the cathedral and originally intended for the accommodation of eight leper brethren. By *c* 1200 the *Mappa Mundi* (a list, not a plan) ascribed to Gervase of Canterbury records St James' Chichester, for lepers, as the only Sussex hospital (Orme and Webster 1995, 1), implying that the county then had no other noteworthy institution.

The appearance of the early hospital must, in the absence of archaeological investigation, remain speculative. Unlike, say, monasteries with their inevitable claustral design, hospitals have no standard plan and probably vary more in size, date, architecture and inmates than any other type of religious house (Cullum 1993, 11). Many seem to have grown organically from small beginnings. Any sizeable 12th-century hospital would have included a chapel, accommodation and a barn,[1] and a perimeter wall to ward off the spiritual contagion of the outside world would have enclosed all but the very smallest; internally it would have been walled off into discrete compartments (Rawcliffe 2000a, 55).

A contemporary description of Lanfranc's foundation, later known as St Nicholas', at Harbledown, Canterbury, talks of wooden houses on the downward slope of a hill assigned for the use of lepers – some for men and separate ones for a community of women (Eadmer's *History of Recent Events in England*, quoted in Orme and Webster 1995, 20–3). In physical appearance, this very early hospital may have had few successors although it is sometimes assumed, presumably on the basis of Eadmer's description, that lepers commonly occupied individual cells

of thatch and timber grouped round a church (eg Godfrey 1955, 17–18; Price 1998, 15 and 217; Cullum 1993, 11).[2] In later hospitals a communal infirmary or dormitory was often attached to a chapel, the two plan-elements forming the equivalent of nave and chancel in a church (Fig 5.1), or the infirmary hall might instead lie at right-angles to the west end of a chapel, making a T-shape in plan. In time, the dormitory could be partitioned off into almshouses, as happened at St Mary's Chichester. A third basic plan type was the collegiate or courtyard design (eg St Cross, Winchester) but small, late medieval almshouses usually aspired to nothing more complex than a rectangular block plan. Guilds might build hospitals in the undercrofts of their halls, and individuals owning several houses might leave one for the use of the sick poor which, given its origins, would be architecturally indistinguishable from its secular neighbours. Hospitals could change through time. Individual leper houses, to permit greater privacy, had replaced the communal facilities at Sherburn (Co. Durham) by the early 14th century (Marcombe 2003, 138).

If St James' had originally housed its lepers in a communal hall, it would have made life less harsh for those summoned to prayer after midnight (see *The constitution*, below and Appendix 2). They would not in practice have had to leave the building and any who, through infirmity, could not rise could still have participated in services in the adjoining

Figure 5.1. The late Norman hospital at Stourbridge, Cambridge. In plan the building is virtually a standard church with 'nave' and 'chancel', although the chancel south door would be an unusual feature, and a similar building must be envisaged at St James' in Chichester. The hospital was supported by a fair on the nearby common from 1211 onwards that allegedly became the largest medieval fair in Europe. © Anthony Eva / Alamy

chapel from their beds. It is, however, clear that by the 18th century the hospital and chapel were two separate buildings, assuming that the building then known as the chapel was correctly identified. In the later Middle Ages it was usual for the master and healthy brethren to live separately from the lepers (Clay 1909, 146), and the master's lodge might be expected to lie close to the chapel (Gilchrist 1992, 104). The 'Spittle House' of St James' Hospital in the 18th century may have been in origin the master's house or some other building constructed or converted for the purpose.

At the very end of the 12th century comes the first record of non-leper burials at St James'. The information is incidental to a dispute between the rector of Itchenor, a parish south-west of Chichester, and his parishioners, in which the rector claims that payments made to him for burial are insufficient. One of the witnesses, Ansela de la Coudre, states that 'Richard son of the clerk rests in the graveyard of the hospital of St James in the suburbs of Chichester, and he left with his body [ie as mortuary dues] one ox which the Dean, Nicholas de Aquila, had. He says that his mother and her husband are buried in the graveyard of the said Hospital ...' (Peckham 1942–43, 7). The clear statement that a woman had been buried at the hospital as early as the century of its foundation is important in the light of the results from the cemetery excavation (see Chapters 7 and 8).

In 1173–80 William of St John gave one beech tree yearly from *Godynewood* (Goodwood) in Boxgrove parish to 'the church of St Mary Magdalene of the sick of Chichester' (Peckham 1942–43, 289, 918). If this means St James', it is the earliest local bequest to the hospital; another possible beneficiary is St Mary-in-foro, the precursor of the intramural hospital, although it is not known to have been dedicated to the Magdalene (see Chapter 4).

The 13th century

Virtually nothing can be said about the hospital in this century. The list of masters begins in 1244 (see Appendix 1) and one of the longest-serving of all the medieval masters (assuming his mastership to have been continuous) was Leger de Hampton, appointed in 1249, noted in 1275 and perhaps not replaced until 1282 on the appointment of Peter de Lewes. Compared to the intramural hospital of St Giles at Norwich, where masters served on average a little over seventeen years for the period up to 1372 and then around eight years up to 1546 (Rawcliffe 2000a, 139), the turnover at Chichester was quite brisk.

The earliest surviving 13th-century bequest is that of William de Keynesham (1237–) who left 6d to the Hospital of St James and lesser sums to the lepers of Londesdon, Wikes and Stocbrugg. The only other will of this period to mention the house is that of Geoffrey de Glovernia, Dean of Chichester, who left 3d to the lepers of St James' Hospital,

contrasted with a total of 19d to St Mary's Hospital and 1d to the recluse of St Cyriac. His predecessor as dean, Thomas of Lichfield, appointed in 1232, had virtually refounded the intramural St Mary's Hospital (Page 1907, 100) and Geoffrey may have felt that St Mary's was a particular responsibility of the dean's. There were also grants of small sums from other cathedral officials (see Appendix 4).

The earliest cash endowments to hospitals were royal alms paid by the county sheriff from the profits of crown lands, and the *infirmi* of Chichester had benefited from such a donation in the period 1158–78 (Clay 1909, 178–9). In 1231 Henry III directed former sheriff John de Gatesdean to give the chaplain whatever remained from the king's alms budget (Page 1907, 99), and later gave 60s 10d per annum (2d a day) for his maintenance.[3]

The latter part of the century may have seen the hospital's endowments under threat if speculation that the tolls from St James' Fair originally went to the hospital is correct (see below). This probable element of the endowment had been challenged by the earl of Arundel, who in 1288 claimed to hold the fair in his own right, and the dispute was resolved in the following year when Edward I proclaimed the fair himself (Salzman 1935, 98).

There seems to be general agreement that the incidence of leprosy was past its peak by the end of the 13th century. This may have engendered a feeling that institutions founded in response to the disease were becoming redundant and their incomes fair game for diversion by the unscrupulous.

The 14th century

Written sources for the hospital become more numerous in the 14th century. Amongst them are wills (Appendix 4), starting with that of Henry de Garlandia, dean of Chichester, made in 1320, in which he leaves 3d to the lepers of St James. Lady Margaret Covert of Sullington's bequest, made in 1367, leaves 2s to the poor of St James' Hospital and is significant because it appears to be the earliest reference to the inmates as poor rather than leprous. Even more interesting is the will of William de Lenne (or Lynn), bishop of Worcester, who in 1373 left 20s to the poor of the hospital of St Mary Magdalene and St James near Chichester and to the lepers of Lodsdown. The bishop had been a local man, formerly bishop of Chichester – hence the bequests – and it must be assumed that the distinction he made between the *poor* at St James' and the *lepers* at Lodsdown (alias Little Maudlin in Westhampnett parish) was, or had been, valid. Later wills in the 14th century give sums either to the institution ('half a mark to the hospital of St James') or refer to its inmates as 'the poor'. Apart from the bishop, who knew and used the correct title for the hospital, all the testators before 1487 refer to the hospital as St James', presumably to avoid any confusion with either St Mary Magdalene's at Lodsdown or the Portfield hospital (for which, see Chapter 4), and it may be imagined that in everyday speech the Spitalfield Lane hospital was invariably 'St James'.

A relatively quick succession of hospital masters occurred in the century. The first to be appointed, in 1309, lasted only two years, the next managed six but the third died in his year of appointment. As we have no idea of the ages of masters at the time of their appointments, it is difficult to make anything of these figures. There was not a particularly quick turnover around the time of the Black Death, but there is no evidence that 'closed' communities such as hospitals and monasteries were any more immune to its ravages than the general populace. Even when the exaggerated and incredible figures are put to one side, there is still an inexplicable difference between the impact of the plague on what appear to have been broadly similar communities (Platt 1997). In the leper hospital of St James at Westminster, for example, all but one of the brothers and sisters died of plague (Rosser 1989, 306). The plague arrived through Southampton[4] in autumn 1348 and its effect on towns in general seems to have been more devastating than in rural areas. Amongst those suffering the highest casualty rates were the parish priests, and the church was reduced to recruiting men from minor orders who were seriously under-qualified.

One problem for St James' and other relatively small hospitals may have been a dearth of qualified candidates for the mastership as more lucrative opportunities arose. Whereas many minor religious houses disappeared as a direct result of plague, others saw a rise in recruitment as recent widowers sought the security of institutional life (Platt 1997) and some hospitals may have seen a growing demand for places. The Black Death was simply the first of a succession of plagues to act as population checks, and one of the demographic consequences in a population greatly reduced overall was an increase, proportionately, in the elderly – those who had gained immunity through surviving earlier outbreaks of the plague.

In 1362 William de Lenne (or Lynn) confirmed the earliest surviving hospital charter, by Bishop Seffrid II. In the following year the Dean and Chapter gave St James' a rent charge of 3s 4d per year.

The 15th century

There was good news and bad news at the start of the 15th century. The good news was a substantial new source of income – the farm of The Broyle – and the bad news, if the motivation behind the 1408 custumal is rightly understood, that the contingency funds had been misappropriated (for both in more detail, see below). Bequests continued: in a will dated 31 May 1414 John Taverner of St Pancras left 2s to the brothers of St James'. It may be inferred that, although perhaps a *de facto* almshouse, the hospital was still a male institution. This is admit-

tedly the only will to speak of the inmates as brothers, but the testator, resident in the adjoining parish, is unlikely to have been mistaken. In 1418 William Neel of Chichester left 6s 8d to the lepers of St James', and this is the latest will (but not the last document) to refer to leper inmates. How many of the residents were victims of the disease at this date is uncertain. In 1493 the will of Walter Maryng of Subdeanery leaves 8d to the poor men *and women* of St Mary Magdalene and St James, and this is the first reference to women in the hospital. The will is carefully worded, and the phrase 'poor men and women' could not be a catch-all to describe the inhabitants of a number of institutions, some of which admitted one sex or the other and some both, which were then listed. Such ambiguity occurs in 1495 in the will of Richard Aspynalgh who leaves '2s to the brethren and sisters of the hospitals of St Mary, St James and St George'.

The date after which women were admitted can be tied down more closely. It was certainly no earlier than 1443 when married men and simoniacs were expelled (see below). No irregularities are reported at the next visitation in 1478, but by 1488 the prior and two colleagues were being warned by the Court of the Dean's Peculiar to observe the customs of the hospital. One of the ways in which they had been broken may have been by admitting women; another is by admitting more corrodians of either sex.

The early 16th century

Bequests continue into and beyond the 16th century. In his will dated 8 December 1502 Bishop Edward Storey left 6s 8d to the hospital and a further 6s 8d to a named inmate, John. In 1527 John Cressweller of Subdeanery left 2d to every brother *and sister* of St James. How the sisters were accommodated is uncertain; they would have been strictly segregated. The general impression of the hospital in the 15th and 16th centuries is not one of a level of prosperity that would enable it to build new quarters, and the assumption must be that an existing building was utilised or converted for the purpose.

In 1535 an exact valuation of church wealth, the *Valor Ecclesiasticus*, was made in connection with a new tax of a tenth of the net income of all ecclesiastical benefices. A local copy of the *Valor*, made by or for Chichester cathedral, gives some insight into the hospital economy at the start of the Dissolution and a 1539 rental (Appendix 6) gives the same in its immediate aftermath, although not all of its entries can be understood.

The later 16th century

St James' Hospital, like St Mary's within the walls, survived the Dissolution because, as part of what was now a Protestant cathedral charged with carrying out charitable work as part of its refoundation, it was able to demonstrate that prayers for the dead no longer formed part of its daily liturgy. What that ritual now comprised is unknown but it will have been stripped of all its pseudo-monastic features, no doubt to the relief of inmates who were perhaps at last allowed to sleep through the night. Its new role was as an almshouse for the mentally and physically handicapped, both men and women.

At least one new post, that of 'singing man', had been created by 1597 and must reflect a change to the constitution of the hospital. It was then held by Richard Woods and was worth 20s per year, not a generous amount but nevertheless a big slice of the hospital's income (Page 1907, 100). Another seemingly new post was that of proctor, first mentioned in 1594 (see Appendix 3), unless this is the prior (ie the senior inmate) under a new title. As the name implies, the main function of a proctor was to gather alms on behalf of the hospital (*sc.* by proxy) and in some institutions he became the *de facto* administrator as the post of master became a sinecure. A chaplain is also mentioned and cannot be the Master in another guise as the latter was now usually a layman.

The names of the master and inmates are known in 1594 (see Appendix 3) and the afflictions of the latter give an idea of those for whom the hospital now catered. No children are recorded, but the female inmates are all just about of child-bearing age although the afflictions of some, unless exaggerated, would seem to rule out motherhood. We have the name of only one other hospital resident in the later 16th century, tailor John Redfern who, in his will of 1589, describes himself as 'of the poorhouse or Hospital of St James near Chichester'. This seems to mean that he was a genuine resident of the institution, not merely an inhabitant of the parish of St James' Hospital, although he may have had a separate house within the hospital grounds. A man of substance, he left the hospital a considerable amount of barley as well as gifts of clothing (McCann 1987, 253).

The 1539 rental (Appendix 6) belongs to the immediate aftermath of the Dissolution. Although not all of its entries can be fully understood, the hospital seems to be doing what it could to maximise income but with limited success. On 11 January 1594 the Sussex Charity Commissioners held an inquisition into the hospital. It was stated by the hospital's master, Charles Lascelles, that Bishop Seffrid II had founded the hospital and that its mastership was in the gift of the bishop of Chichester. This was disputed in a letter to the commissioners, which also accused Lascelles of misusing and retaining hospital revenues. At the time, the revenues amounted to £6 2s 10d, much as they were said to have been in 1539.

The 17th century

In 1609 Charles Lascelles, master of St James' since at least 1594, died and a little can be gleaned from his probate account. John Lambert succeeded him, to whom 10s was paid for dilapidations (ie damage done to the fabric of the hospital and not put right) by the administrator of Lascelles' will. There had also been a dispute over eight quarters of barley stored at the hospital at the time of Lascelles' death that had been listed amongst his assets. This, it was claimed, belonged to the hospital and 'for avoiding further troubles, the accomptant has given John Lambert to the use of the poor there 36s' (McCann 1987).[5]

The next record is in 1618 when master William Lawes petitioned the Justices of the Peace for payment of a yearly sum to be given to the hospital, and this was agreed by the justices on condition that they should have the right to nominate inmates and that their number should be reduced to eight (Salzman 1935, 100), the probable size of the original foundation. It was claimed that the hospital was almost fallen to the ground and that the inmates were badly in need of bedding, apparel and lodgings. The implication is, perhaps, that demand for hospital places had far outstripped its resources. In 1637, when cathedral verger Humfrey Knapp made his will bequeathing 12d 'to the poor of St James' the almshouse must still have been a going concern (McCann 1987). By the end of the century, *c* 1685–89, however, circumstances had changed. 'Without the Eastgate of the city is the Hospital of St James, and St Mary Magdalen, of very ancient foundation; whereof Mr. Peter Edge, Rector of St. Pancras, in the City of Chichester, is Master. It is of small revenue, and hath only one poor person (but she a miserable idiot) in it' (Turner 1861, 305–6).

The 18th century

Seemingly the last recorded resident is William Lawrence 'late of S^t. Jameses Hospitall neere the Citty of Chichester deceased'. A 1701 probate inventory of his estate reveals, as Morgan (1992, 171) puts it, 'comfort and possessions'.[6] How he came to be there is unknown. A person needing medical attention and able to pay for it would normally have received treatment at home in this period and it is hard to imagine someone of Lawrence's economic standing seeking care in an institution which had until recently (and perhaps still had) 'a miserable idiot' as its only inmate. His connection with the hospital may have been indirect; perhaps he lived elsewhere in the Peculiar, 'hospitall' being cited only as part of the name of his home parish by those compiling the inventory. Alternatively, like tailor Redfern in the 16th century, he may have rented a house within the hospital complex quite separate from the almshouse.

If the hospital was moribund at the start of the century it was, in all but legal fiction, extinct at the end of it. A bishop's commission on 1 February 1705 reported that 'the house of the Hospital of St James is in a very ruinous condition for want of repairs and that an ancient piece of building called the Chapel hath been for many years past used as a Barn and is now also become very ruinous being without a roof, and the walls thereof only standing, that the east end of the said house may be conveniently taken down for the repair of the residue of the said house, there being sufficient room in the said house besides the said east end for the poor of the said Hospital and to lay up the corn thereof'. As the £47 needed to put the house into proper repair could not be found from the hospital's own revenues, instructions were duly given for the scheme outlined above to be carried out. The chapel was no longer to be used as a barn but its doorway blocked up and the building abandoned. The rents and profits of the hospital were to fund the work; these had not been paid since the death of Peter Edge, the last master, in 1702 (McCann 1987).

St James' seems to have been sufficiently repaired to be habitable since in April 1755 a Mr Newland requested that he might use the hospital 'to air his relations. Also that Mr Halsted should have the use of St James House to air himself in' (Dangerfield 1938, 147). The intention seems to have been to use St James' as a nursing home to provide an intermediate stage of care between that of the Pest House (for infectious diseases, established after 1665 in what is now College Lane) and home. The Pest House, although not strictly part of it, seems to have been administered by the guardians of the workhouse, and they seem also to have controlled admission to St James' since it was to them that the appeal was made.

According to local diarist James Spershott, in 1721 '(and till some years after) the wall[s] of St James's Chapel were standing showing the form of its windows and door &c., but are since demolished' (Steer 1962b, 16). Yeakell and Gardner's map (1769) apparently shows foundations only of buildings north-east of the one surviving structure,[7] but the chapel, if it is represented, cannot be identified from its ground-plan. On 13 December 1781 'The large old Spittle House belonging to St James' Chapel burnt down' (Steer 1962b, 23) but no casualties are reported.

The existing 'leper cottage' at the site (this is the local appellation for 3 Westhampnett Road) embodies some of the original fabric (see below). Salzman (1935, 82) says 'The north wall of the cottage built some years later incorporates part of the original structure', apparently meaning that there are architectural fragments from older buildings in the wall, and such items as a step from a newel staircase can be made out readily. However, the greater part of the south wall, which is much thicker than the other walls, is potentially of medieval date although no diagnostic features are now visible. The cottage is not on the site of the 'Spittle House' shown on Yeakell and Gardner's map but seems to incorporate the greater part of the ruin depicted next to it.[8]

The 19th century

A Dispensary for Sick Poor, opened on Broyle Road north of Chichester in 1794, later became the West Sussex Infirmary and, after extensive additions, the Royal West Sussex Hospital (Salzmann 1935, 81). Many of the later buildings were demolished in the 1990s, the original building converted to flats and the grounds developed for housing. One of the founders of the Dispensary was Revd William Walker, rector of St Pancras, who had the plaque put on the 'leper cottage', and he is credited with moves to transfer the income from St James' to the Dispensary. The scheme was put to the Charity Commissioners in 1825 and although they considered it would be 'a most useful and appropriate application of the property' (McCann 1987), it was abandoned because an Act of Parliament would have been required.

In 1835 the hospital still had a master with the not inconsiderable annual income of £42 derived from the rents of five tenements in St Pancras, a storehouse in Little London, and the tithes of 75 acres in Colworth. Of the revenues, £5 was distributed annually to the poor. Eventually, under a scheme devised by the Court of Chancery in 1855, the net income was paid to the West Sussex Infirmary (Salzman 1935, 167). A quarter of the net income was applied to the chaplaincy fund of what, by the 1930s, had become the Royal West Sussex Hospital, a decision which would doubtless have been approved by the 12th-century founders of the leper hospital.

5.2. The hospital constitution

The content of the original charter is known only through its confirmation by Church and Crown. Bishop Seffrid II's first ecclesiastical confirmation charter, of 1187, was reconfirmed by Bishop William in 1362 (see Appendix 2). The dean confirmed the customs of the house in 1408. The Reformation brought changes. At some time between 1535 and 1540 a further alteration to the statutes must have been made since by the latter date there was a lay master and sisters as well as brothers in the house, although sisters are attested as early as 1493 in the will of Walter Maryng (see p 59 and Appendix 4). The number of inmates was probably increased to twelve (see below). In 1618, £10 which had been diverted from the hospital's income was restored on condition that its inmates were reduced to eight (Page 1907, 100), and the constitution was presumably amended to reflect this reduction.

The hospital's own copy of its records disappeared long ago. In 1604 a petition was presented to James I asking him to search the royal archive as the hospital had lost all evidence of what revenues were due to it, and records in the Tower of London were duly consulted. When the Charity Commissioners enquired into the hospital in 1835, the master produced a manuscript book of copies of documents, presumably the fruits of research in 1604, but this too has since been lost (McCann 1987). The history of the hospital, including that of its constitution, has therefore to be gleaned from a variety of secondary sources.

From Bishop Seffrid II's confirmation charter it can be deduced that the hospital was a royal foundation earlier than 1118 for eight leper brethren.[9] To the original endowment Bishop Seffrid added a grant of eight linen shirts at Christmas and eight linen coats at Easter, and the number of garments is the basis for deducing the number of inmates of the original foundation. As an incentive to further almsgiving, he also granted fifteen days' relaxation of penance to those who visited and relieved the poor inmates (Appendix 2).

Bishop William inspected and confirmed Bishop Seffrid's confirmation charter in 1362. He represents the hospital as having been founded in honour of St Mary Magdalene and St James, and grants 40 days' indulgence to visitors to the hospital on those saints' days. Both days are in fact close together, respectively 22 July and 25 July in the modern calendar, and the latter was a fair day when more visitors than usual might be expected. The fair itself was a matter of some dispute in the 13th century. In brief, in 1254 a fair was granted to Richard, earl of Cornwall, to be held on the vigil, feast and morrow of St Michael (28–30 September New Style). In 1288, however, Edmund earl of Cornwall proclaimed two fairs in the city. In response Richard Fitz Alan, earl of Arundel, claimed that the Michaelmas Fair was merely an informal gathering, and said that he himself held a fair on the vigil and feast of St James every year near the hospital outside the city. Edward I claimed this fair in 1289 and commanded the sheriff to proclaim it in his name (Salzman 1935, 98). Although the evidence is lacking, it may be suspected that the tolls and dues from the fair were originally part of the hospital endowment. According to Hay (1804, 392–3) a fair was still held on St James' Day in the early 19th century.

Hospital fairs are attested elsewhere (Clay 1909, 182–3) and were usually held annually on the patronal festival. Norwich's first leper hospital, St Mary Magdalene's, which lay in a northern suburb, had an extremely lucrative yearly fair, its rights bitterly contested by the burgesses of Norwich for commercial reasons. In 1441 the mayor was involved in an affray outside the leper house (Rawcliffe 2000a, 40). The leper women of Maiden Bradley had a weekly market as well as an annual fair (Richards 1977, 35). A 'little Pedling FAIR is still kept on St *Bartholomew's* Day' at South Acre, Norfolk, according to an 18th-century county history (Blomefield 1769, III, 419), although the hospital itself may have disappeared around the time of the Black Death (Wells 1967), and St Margaret's at High Wycombe (Bucks), another leper hospital, had enjoyed the profits from an annual fair on the vigil and day of the patronal feast since 1229 (Farley and Manchester 1989, 82).

St James' was administered by a chaplain or master who received 2d a day from royal revenues

in the county. Bishop William's confirmation charter mentions that the senior inmate was known as the 'prior'. Most of what is known of the customs of the hospital comes from the dean's confirmation of 1408 (for the text, see Appendix 2). Admission was by the consent of the chaplain and a majority of the inmates, and individuals could be expelled if they were absent without leave of the prior, if they married or were convicted of sexual misconduct. The prior, the senior inmate, had to take an oath to the chaplain and brethren to be diligent in his responsibilities. The infirm were to be looked after by the fit. Each had a weekly allowance of money but could be fined if he spent it recklessly, relying on his brethren for support. Brothers who were quarrelsome or revealed the secrets of the house to strangers could, after warning, be required to pay a fine to the light of St James in the hospital chapel.

An essential condition of admission was knowledge of the Lord's Prayer and Apostles' Creed 'at least in the manner of the laity'. The sacrist had to rise before one o'clock in the morning and ring a bell to summon all, unless they were too feeble, to prayers. These consisted of memorial prayers for the king and queen, the realm and all benefactors, the creed and the Lord's Prayer, and Salutation of the Blessed Virgin and intercessions for the Catholic Church. If omitted, they had to be said the following day. There was no uniform, but the inmates were to wear shabby clothes, either white or black, as a sign of poverty. As death approached each brother was to give 6d to each of the other brethren for a meal on his day of burial and leave his best daily habit to the community.

Later in the century the management of the hospital became corrupt. All inmates had secured admission by payment to the master, six, including the prior, usually spent the night at home with their wives, and the prior completely neglected his duties, according to a visitation held in 1442 (Page 1907, 99). It is interesting because it confirms that admission by payment was not the custom at Chichester. A marginal note in the bishop's register reads *uxorati et simonaici expelluntur* (McCann 1987, 253), which implies that the hospital was cleared of inmates. It may be asked why most of the 'inmates' had bought admissions in the first place if they normally lived at home with their wives. Presumably the potential value of the pension and perhaps other 'perks' outweighed the initial admission fee (in this instance, bribe) to the chaplain.[10]

Corrody payments were in the nature of an insurance policy, and from a hospital's point of view needed to be set with care since any unexpected longevity by the corrodian would leave it out of pocket. At St Mark's Bristol the practice of establishing long-term corrodies had begun by 1248 when a carpenter granted lands to the hospital in return for a promise of residence when his wife died (Price 1998, 213).[11] At St Leonard's York the most expensive corrody was that paid by John and Beatrice de Cundall of Huby in 1349, amounting to

£81, for which they were to have their own house in the grounds (Cullum 1993, 16). A sum of this magnitude would have kept St James' Chichester in funds for more than a decade.

At the next documented visitation, in 1478, a prior and five brethren are listed, and the prior exhibited the statutes of the hospital. Things appear to have become lax again, however, because by 1488 the prior, John of London, and two other inmates were being summoned before the court of the Dean's Peculiar and warned to observe the hospital's customs. By the 15th century the usual term for the hospital's inhabitants in wills is 'poor men' or 'almsmen'. The last reference to the inhabitants as lepers in wills is in 1418 but it was still officially a house for poor lepers in the 1535 *Valor*. If the hospital in practice was well on the way to becoming an almshouse as leprosy died out, it was still notionally an all-male institution.

In brief, then, the medieval hospital was a royal foundation of the early 12th century for eight leper men, administered by the dean and chapter, and its customs recorded in 1408 detail a quasi-monastic regime that is typical for hospitals of early foundation. By the 15th century it was an almshouse for poor men, and had generally been described as such since the middle of the previous century in wills (see Appendix 4). Women were admitted from late in the 15th century.

The constitution was amended after the Dissolution so that the master became a layman, women were perhaps officially admitted for the first time and the total number of inmates was increased, probably to twelve. The rules must have been changed between 1535 and 1540, since by the latter date the master was a layman and there were sisters as well as brothers in the house. In 1535, according to the *Valor Ecclesiasticus*, the prior had received an annual pension of 4s 4d (Ray 1931, 2). The master seems to have been appointed by the bishop for life, since in 1574 Thomas Ware was so appointed as master or warden on the resignation of his predecessor, Edward Waller (Peckham 1959, 89, no. 783). Although we cannot recover the details, one additional change must have been an increase in the number of inmates. When an inquisition was held in 1594 the master was Charles Lascelles and the inmates, who included a proctor and his wife, numbered thirteen (see Appendix 3). This, the first reference to a proctor, may simply be another term for the senior inmate earlier known as the prior. The proctor in 1594, William Egle, and his wife were about a decade older than the oldest of the other residents. In late 16th-century Chichester any of the inmates could theoretically leave the house to seek alms but physical disabilities may have prevented them from doing so. Three years later William Egle was given a royal license as 'guider of ye said house' to collect money. Other hospital staff at the time included a chaplain and a 'singing-man' in addition to the master (Page 1907, 100) and these apparently new posts may represent

some alteration to the constitution following the 1594 inquisition.

The hospital inhabitants listed in 1594 (Appendix 3), five men and six women, excluding the proctor and his wife, were all in some way crippled, but a few years earlier, in 1589, they had included a married tailor who had two servants and owned the lease of a house in St Pancras, the parish adjoining the hospital. As well as eleven bushels of barley, John Redfern left in his will six shirts and smocks to 'six poor folks' of the house (McCann 1987; Appendix 4). This may mean that the number of inmates had been increased to twelve, assuming the shirts were for the men and the smocks for the women. This would be compatible with the 1594 list if the proctor is listed with the male inmates and his wife omitted, or if both proctor and wife are omitted and the men assumed to be one short of their maximum number.[12] The reduction in hospital numbers insisted upon in 1618 was perhaps from twelve to the eight assumed to have been specified in the foundation charter.

5.3   The hospital economy and landholdings

The hospital economy before 1187 was based mostly on gifts of food, clothing, lands and rents from the church comprising 10s from the Archdeaconry of Lewes, tithes from Colworth Manor in Oving parish and a rent of 4s from the lands of Warin de Preston, as confirmed in Bishop Seffrid II's charter (see Appendix 2).[13] The Crown is assumed to have provided the land on which the hospital was founded, and income from that land, whether it was worked directly by the hospital, let to others or some combination of the two, would have provided additional income. Private individuals supplemented the hospital's income with gifts in cash or in kind.[14] In a grant of 1173–80, for example (Peckham 1942–43, 289, no. 918), William de St John gave annually eight cartloads of beech from Goodwood in perpetuity to 'the church of St Mary Magdalene of the sick of Chichester', which may be St James' by its less familiar name.

Henry II gave a general charter of confirmation at Rouen, promising 'the infirm of Chichester whatever is reasonably due to them' (Peckham 1942–43, 289 no. 917). In 1158–78 the Crown paid subscriptions to, amongst others, the Chichester *infirmi* (Clay 1909, 178–9). The *Mappa Mundi* ascribed to Gervase of Canterbury *c* 1200, listing St James' Chichester for lepers as the only Sussex hospital (Orme and Webster 1995, 1), implies that the others were so small and obscure as to be unknown outside their immediate locality, thus confirming that the Chichester *infirmi* receiving royal alms were most likely the inmates of St James'.

The Crown also, from time to time, made gifts to the hospital and similar charitable institutions from the sheriff's profits on Crown land. In 1231 the former sheriff of Sussex was directed by Henry III to give whatever remained of the king's alms to the chaplain of the lepers. Edward I confirmed a payment from the profits of Crown land in Sussex of 2d per day to the chaplain (Page 1907, 99) and the gift may have dated from the hospital's establishment.[15] Added to these sources were alms and other income generated by the hospital itself, and perhaps (see below) the profits of an annual three-day fair in July on the eve and day of the patronal feast. Certain fees and legacies would also have accrued from the hospital's possession of burial rights. At the time of the Taxation of Pope Nicholas the hospital had a chantry that was tax-exempt (Peckham 1942–43, 306, no. 954) which, in its last years of existence, was worth 3s 2d annually to the hospital (Ray 1931, 14). Boxgrove Priory also made a token contribution of 4d at Michaelmas each year (Fleming 1960, 197).

The cathedral's officers would make occasional grants, usually of modest amounts, to Chichester hospitals. In 1237 William de Keynesham, canon of Chichester, gave the hospital of St James 6d, the lepers of Londesdon 4d, the lepers of Wikes 3d and the lepers of Stockbridge 3d (Peckham 1942–43, 142, no. 548). In 1246 Ernis de Tywa, precentor, gave 2d to the lepers of the hospital of St James and 9d to its chaplain. He had been warned that the lands and rents that were supposed to support these and other grants were insufficient, and in 1252 the dean and chapter had to reapportion the grants, increasing the payment to the lepers of St James' to 3d but omitting the payment to the chaplain (Peckham 1942–43, 147, nos. 566 and 567). In 1246–49 the treasurer, William de Nevill, gave 6d to the chaplain of St Mary's Hospital, 6d to the sick there, 8d to the lepers of St James' Hospital and 2d to the chaplain serving there. In the near-contemporary grant of 1247 Dean Geoffrey de Glovernia gave 7d to the brethren and sisters of St Mary's and 12d for food for the sick, 3d to the lepers of St James' Hospital and 1d to the recluse of St Cyriac (Peckham 1942–43, 142, no. 572 and 154, no. 595; Appendix 4).

On the death in 1253 of the Chichester bishop Richard of Wych, it was discovered that he had worn a hair shirt and iron bands, and miracles were reported at his tomb. Canonisation followed in 1262 and Richard Archbishop of Canterbury awarded an indulgence of 40 days to pilgrims at his tomb (Webb 2000, 68). The cathedral was, he said, noted for its collection of relics and the canons proposed to 'publish' them on the feast of St Denis (9 October). This was good news for the economy of the city and, indirectly, for the hospital. Most pilgrims travelled with money in their pockets and almsgiving was usual, especially by penitential pilgrims and those who carried out pilgrimages on behalf of others (Webb 2000, 216). The enterprising inmates of Holy Trinity Hospital, Dartford, even had a stall in the parish church selling Canterbury pilgrim souvenirs (Webb 2000, 227).

In due course the hospital's income was enhanced by further charitable donations. These included gifts from the cathedral clergy, as before. In 1187, for example, Bishop Seffrid II had made additional annual gifts of clothing and a side of bacon to the inmates. By 1362 it had become the custom to commute the gift of clothing to a cash payment of 20s a year at the bishop's discretion and the communar was supporting the hospital with a gift of 4s 4d from cathedral funds, as he was said to have done time out of mind (Appendix 2). Dean Henry de Garlandia in 1320 gave 6d to the sick poor in St Mary's Hospital, 3d to the lepers of St James', 3d to the lepers of la Portefelde and 3d to the two houses of lepers at Loddesdone (Peckham 1942–43, 78–9, 288; Appendix 4). Unfortunately, funds diverted by unscrupulous clergy to their own ends may have exceeded these additional sources of income. One practical attempt by the Church to improve hospital administration was Canon 17 of the Council of Vienne, which met in 1317, requiring an annual presentation of accounts by all charitable institutions (Rawcliffe 2000a, 68).

By the late 13th century, leper hospitals in general were exempt from royal taxation as long as they had a leper master (Orme and Webster 1995, 96) and although the master of St James' was not a leper, the institution, as a royal foundation, may have enjoyed similar fiscal privileges. Less helpful to all religious institutions was the Statute of Mortmain (1279), which added to existing penalties for transferring land to the Church without the lord's permission, thereby freeing its tenants from paying taxes that would formerly have come to the lord. However, there were ways round it, including creating trusts. Forest Law decreed that the meat from any animal found dead or wounded was to be sent to the local leper house if there was one nearby (Clay 1909, 167–8) and St James' should have benefited from animals found in The Broyle just beyond the north gate of Chichester which was royal forest until granted to the bishop by Henry III in 1229 and cleared for farming (Morgan 1992, 190–1).

England in the 14th century was beset by a series of difficulties to which the hospital would not have been immune, starting with the famines of 1315–22, in the first year of which over 100 hospitals and religious houses were placed under royal protection (Kershaw 1973). Next came the Black Death of 1348–49, a recurrence of plague in 1361 and further attacks until 1665. In the immediate aftermath of the Black Death it has been claimed that about half of England's 300 urban hospitals were lost, although numbers more than recovered in the next two centuries (Butler 1993, 79). Hospitals in general tended not to be over-generously endowed and their incomes declined in relative and absolute terms. England's wealthiest and largest hospital, St Leonard's in York, saw its income fall from £1263 in 1287 to less than £310 in 1533 (Rawcliffe 2000a, 65). Financial corruption is said to have been a particular problem in English hospitals in the 14th century (Price 1998, 15).

The start of the 15th century saw a significant new endowment for St James' with the grant of the farm of The Broyle made by the cathedral (see Appendix 6), a gift worth 36s a year and, apart from the Exchequer's continuing 2d per day for the priest, the hospital's largest single source of income. Not long afterwards there are strong hints from the dean's custumal (1408) that what may be described as the hospital's contingency fund had been misappropriated and it had become necessary to have a special appeal to replace it. The total raised was a modest 13s 4d, 10s of which had come from two otherwise unknown laymen and 40d from Thomas the chaplain. Access to the chest in which the cash and archives were kept was henceforth to be made more secure; two or three locks were to be fitted so that no one keyholder could gain access without the other two.

A surviving local copy of the 1535 *Valor Ecclesiasticus* (Peckham 1954) details the hospital's income on the eve of the Dissolution and may be contrasted with a rental of 1539 that shows both more detail and more income (Appendix 6). The assets of St James' may have been deliberately understated for the *Valor*. A major omission from the 1535 figures is income from the farm of The Broyle, which in the 1539 rental was worth £1 16s (see Appendix 6). By 1539 the hospital seems to have started a number of innovative measures such as leasing the cemetery and taking in corrodians aimed at maximising its income. The dissolution of chantries in 1547 had not been a severe economic blow – it lost only 3s 2d (Ray 1931, 14).

The value of alms cannot be assessed from the records, but it must be suspected that it was on average no more than 25% of total annual expenditure. Accounts survive for the much bigger intramural hospital of St Giles at Norwich for the years 1465–1527 and the income from casual giving shrank over the period, providing only £40 of the £332 spent in 1526–27 but £28 of the £117 spent in 1465–66 (Rawcliffe 2000a, 99, table B). In the late 15th and 16th century sums left in bequests to the hospitals and almshouses then extant in Chichester were generally no more than a few pence, and when it is remembered that those with sufficient assets to make wills were the better-off members of the ecclesiastical and mercantile classes, there must have been very many who left nothing at all.[16] When cathedral verger Humfrey Knapp made his will in 1637, he left 12d 'to the poor of St James his house' (McCann 1987; Appendix 4), again an insignificant amount when contrasted with the total income of the institution, let alone its needs. At the end of the century (c 1685–89) it was said that the hospital was 'of small revenue' (Turner 1861, 305–6). Casual alms in the form of gifts of food, drink and clothing are not recorded in Chichester and rarely listed elsewhere, but they may have been significant.[17]

The value of its garden to the hospital is perhaps easily underestimated. It could have provided herbs and medicinal plants as well as food.[18] Scented candles were used to mask unpleasant smells such as those from unburied bodies, which were considered pathogenic; rosemary was carried at funerals as well as being wrapped round corpses before interment;[19] herbal baths were perhaps used in treatment and aromatic preparations were considered more immediately effective than medicines taken by mouth (Rawcliffe 2000a, 51–2). The sale of any surplus garden produce could have generated a modest profit, and any surplus garden leased to tenants.

As already noted, the assets of St James' may have been deliberately understated for the *Valor*, and by 1539 the hospital seems to have started a number of new measures aimed at increasing its income. By this date the only other local hospitals competing for donations were St Mary's and St George's within the walls, and all may have benefited from a lack of competition with institutions that had been dissolved although they must have attempted to fill the gap left by their erstwhile competitors.

In 1594 the hospital's income had risen to £6 2s 10d, a few pence more than in 1539, assuming the figure to represent gross income. After deductions for repairs, the balance was split between the master, Charles Lascelles, who received half, and proctor William Egle and the inmates. As the latter was soon afterwards given a royal licence to gather alms it was plainly inadequate. In 1597 payments to a chaplain amounted to £1 6s 8d and 20s was paid to another for 'acting as a singing man', and both were in addition to the proctor and master (Page 1907, 99–100). The 1604 petition to James I to try, in effect, to recreate the hospital's lost charters (McCann 1987), was doubtless inspired by inadequate revenue, and a few years later the hospital was still in financial crisis when in 1618 the then master successfully petitioned to have £10 of annual income restored (Page 1907, 100).

A problem was, as noted, misappropriation of funds. Early in the 18th century, when extensive repairs to the fabric were needed, the bishop's commission reported that they could not be funded from the hospital's own revenues, 'the greatest part thereof having been long since concealed and lost'. This was not a new problem. A century earlier, in 1609, there had been a dispute over whether a quantity of barley had belonged to the late master personally or whether to the hospital poor, as was (successfully) claimed (McCann 1987).

Throughout the 18th century, mastership of the hospital became a perquisite of successive members of the cathedral establishment (Salzman 1935, 167). In 1835 the master's income had risen to £42 per annum, derived from five tenements in St Pancras street, a storehouse in Little London and the tithes of 75 acres at Colworth, Oving, presumably part of the original endowment. Leases were still granted in the name of the master, brethren and sisters of the hospital of St Mary Magdalene and St James, and sealed with the hospital seal (McCann 1987). Even in the middle of the 19th century the hospital remained a landowner. When it was proposed to enclose the Portfield and a map of existing owners was drawn up in 1847–48 the prior and brethren of St James' Hospital were found to have the freehold of four strips in that part of the field lying between Church Road and St James' Road.[20]

5.4   The hospital dedications

St James was by far the most popular apostle for hospital dedications and in central Europe more leper hospitals were dedicated to him than to any other saint. Clay (1909, 253) lists 26 partly or wholly dedicated to him in England. His popularity was doubtless due to the renown of the shrine at Compostella as a goal for pilgrims, and hospital seals depict the saint as a pilgrim, with water bottle and scrip (bag for alms), whilst one shows scallop shells. The distribution of such dedications reflects, although it is not confined to, the ports of medieval England. In Sussex, there are dedications at Arundel, Chichester, Lewes, Seaford and Shoreham but no examples from non-coastal sites. The inland county of Shropshire, for example, has only one example of a hospital dedicated to St James, although the total numbers are admittedly fewer than for Sussex.

Dedications to St Mary Magdalene in England were so common that 'Maudlin' became almost synonymous with leper hospital.[21] The reason for the popularity of the dedication is a typical story of medieval confusion and conflation of biblical sources (Richards 1977, 8) and also takes in St Lazarus, whose name means 'God is my help' (Marcombe 2003, 3). One element in the confusion was a medieval belief that leprosy could be transmitted by sexual contact and was associated with sexual sin (Gilchrist 1992, 114). Some lepers were therefore stricken as a punishment for sin, and sufferers were expected to act like penitents. The biblical role model for repentance from sexual sin was, of course, St Mary Magdalene although, inevitably, the matter was not straightforward, the medieval saint being a composite creation embracing the sinner healed of evil spirits and infirmities (Luke **8**, 29; the 'real' Mary Magdalene) and the woman (Mary of Bethany) who both anointed Christ in the house of Simon the Leper (Mark **14**, 3) and, with her sister Martha, tended her sick brother Lazarus (John **11**, 1). Another Lazarus, 'a certain beggar ... full of sores' (Luke **16**, 19) lying at the gate of the 'rich man' (*dives* in Latin, but taken to be a personal name by the unlettered) who sought alms in vain seems to have been a folk-hero of medieval England. He is commemorated in a song that passed into the oral tradition as 'Diverus (*sic*) and Lazarus' in which the unfortunate Dives is condemned 'to sit upon a serpent's knee' in hell for his lack of charity whilst Lazarus goes to heaven for his virtuous acceptance of poverty.

There is no biblical authority for assuming that Lazarus of Bethany, brother of Mary and Martha, was the beggar covered in sores, or that either had leprosy, but the medieval mind equated the two, leading to the terms 'lazar house' and 'lazaretto' for leper hospitals. Hospitals were dedicated to St Lazarus, especially in France (Clay 1909, 252),

perhaps because one legend made Lazarus a bishop of Marseille, martyred by Domitian and buried not too far from St Mary Magdalene/Mary of Bethany (Marcombe 2003, 3–6). There was, as noted in Chapter 2, an Order of St Lazarus of Jerusalem, its main English house, at Burton Lazars, Leicestershire, having been founded by a crusading Mowbray during Stephen's reign (Clay 1909, 251; Richards 1977, 208; Marcombe 2003, *passim*). In Sussex, the leper hospital of St John the Baptist, Harting, was originally connected with this order before being sold to Durford Abbey in about 1248 (Godfrey 1959, 131–2; Marcombe 2003, 156).

As Clay (1909, 252) pointed out, the most popular dedications for hospitals depended on where they were. In England, St Mary Magdalene was patron of nearly twice as many hospitals as her nearest rival, St Leonard. In France, St Lazarus enjoyed a similar popularity, central Europe favoured St James and northern Europe St George, his dragon symbolising disease (Richards 1991, 156). There may be chronological as well as geographical factors at work here. The most favoured dedications in 12th- and 13th-century England were St John the Baptist (for the infirm) and St Mary Magdalene, and Satchell (1998, 106) has used the dedication of the patronal saint to date the foundation of English leper houses in the absence of more conventional sources as many were fashionable for limited periods. Three other common patrons were St Bartholomew (who, as he died by being flayed alive, may have been especially venerated by those with skin complaints), St Giles (an acknowledged patron of cripples and, like St Leonard, nursing mothers) and St Leonard (very popular in France, with a reputation as a healer, and therefore venerated by the Anglo-Norman aristocracy). Others who figure frequently are Anthony, James, Lawrence and Nicholas, each having links with liberality, help to travellers or disease (Orme and Webster 1995, 50). Many saints, especially Giles, Leonard and John the Baptist, were associated with confession, which became mandatory in 1215.

Hospitals with multiple dedications were uncommon but not rare. England's largest leper house, at Sherburn, Co. Durham, was dedicated to Christ, the Blessed Virgin, Saints Lazarus, Mary Magdalene and Martha (Clay 1909, 289). Usually no more than two patrons sufficed. The second confirmation charter for St James' in Chichester in 1362 speaks of 'St Mary Magdalene and St James, to whom the hospital and its chapel are dedicated' (Appendix 2), but the phrase does not seem to imply that the hospital enjoyed the patronage of one saint and the chapel that of the other.

In Chichester, the Spitalfield Lane site was commonly known as St James' in medieval sources that cited only one patron, as most did. However, the hospital at Lodsdown, Westhampnett, is called 'Little Maudlin' in a 16th-century will (Godfrey 1940–41, 340) and this would seem to imply that another site was also commonly known as 'Maudlin', at least in general conversation, since the diminutive is otherwise redundant. In the past it might have been assumed that the contrast was with St James', but a reconsideration of the evidence has identified a third Chichester hospital with this dedication lying somewhere in the Portfield (see Chapter 4).

There may have been a specific reason, stemming from the devotion of its founder, why the Chichester hospital was dedicated to St James. Henry I had not only founded Reading Abbey, which was to become his own burial place, in 1103 but had also endowed it with the hand of St James and it subsequently became a pilgrimage destination of some importance (Webb 2000, 115).

Notes

1. And, amongst the lesser buildings, a brewhouse, kitchen and bakery. Many hospitals had a dovecote and also kept bees. Honey was used internally and externally, as an antiseptic (Rawcliffe 2000a, 52). An inventory in 1303 at St Bartholomew's Bristol lists in the cellar two great barrels, one cask for ale, two old broken barrels, two great vats, four tubs and one box for storing flour. The contents of the bakehouse included a handmill for grinding malt (Price 1998, 58).
2. A picture of Harbledown in 1766 serves to reinforce the written description: see Godfrey 1955, pl 1(b).
3. *CPR* 1247–58, 32.
4. According to the medieval historian Henry Knighton, cited in Platt (1997, 5). It is more commonly said to have arrived through the small Dorset port of Melcombe in June (Daniell 1998, 189).
5. A quarter contained 8 bushels, each of which had a capacity of 8 gallons. A quarter of malted barley might be expected to produce between about 50 and 100 gallons of ale, depending on the desired strength (Rawcliffe 2000a, 183). Wheat was normally used exclusively for bread making, although the poor of St Mark's, Bristol, in *c* 1230 were fed on loaves made of wheat, beans, barley and rye in equal quantities (Price 1998, 224).
6. WSRO EPI/29/42, no.155. He was not quite as well off as Morgan suggests, his pewter vessels numbering 21, not 120.
7. They could be meant as roofless buildings. There are no other structures similarly depicted on the map to make plain what was intended.
8. The few upstanding remains of the hospital are described in Chapter 6.
9. The number of inmates is confirmed indirectly by some gifts and bequests. In the mid-13th century William de Nevill, the treasurer of Chichester, left 8d to the lepers, ie a penny each, as did Richard Myldewe and Walter Maryng at the end of the 15th century (Appendix 4). Bequests of 3s 4d and 6s 8d that appear in the

period are similarly readily divisible by eight but need to be treated with caution as they represent quarter and half marks and be no more than round sums of money.

10. Where it was the custom to charge a corrody or admission fee, it was usually set at the estimated cost of ten years' support. Those who had paid to gain admission did not always mix with the poor. The new inmates at Holy Trinity, Beverley, felt no obligation to spend their days in church with the poor brethren and categorically refused to pray for the founder (Rawcliffe 2000a, 172).
11. Students of medieval demographics will be interested to note his confident expectation of outliving his wife! She may of course have been ill by the time of the agreement.
12. Two wills of 1538 and 1544, both of which leave 12d to the hospital, could be taken as additional confirmation of the number of inmates but they may again be no more than round sums of money.
13. As gifts of land accrued, some hospitals began to be perceived as landlords rather than charities and this was not helpful for their image (Price 1998, 211). Hospitals were not always good landlords and the Peasants' Revolt (1381) targeted at least two unpopular hospitals (Orme and Webster 1995, 103).
14. Hospital founders appear consistently to have underestimated the true cost of endowment. To take a Sussex example, St Richard of Wych's foundation for old and infirm priests at Windham needed more than the £20 he left it in his will and his successor Bishop Climping stepped in to complete the endowment (Rawcliffe 2000a, 70). The sale of indulgences by ecclesiastical patrons was understandable in such circumstances. By the 1320s the penitent visitor to St Mary Magdalene's, Liskeard, Cornwall, could clock up a useful 14 years 400 days' (*sic*) remission from purgatory (Rawcliffe 2000a, 106).
15. The *Valor Ecclesiasticus* describes the 60s 10d a year as *ex antiqua concess'* . The master of the intramural hospital of St Giles at Norwich, for example, had a seemingly more generous annual stipend of £4 (Rawcliffe 2000a, 158) but as it was a mid-13th-century foundation the sum may reflect inflation.
16. Relatively few Chichester wills survive. In Bristol some 300 pre-Reformation wills are known. Most testators left money to the fabric of the church where they were to be buried and to the friars. Most also made provision for the poor (a common bequest was a farthing-loaf to individuals) but did not usually specify any particular hospital or almshouse as the beneficiary (Price 1998, 211).
17. Carole Rawcliffe, pers comm.
18. Several scholars have remarked on the almost complete absence from surviving hospital accounts of sums expended on the purchase of medicines and have concluded from this that

medical treatment was virtually non-existent. The truth may be that most grew their own ingredients and prepared their own potions, needing to purchase only the occasional exotic item.

19. One surly old man from Lincolnshire in the 1870s said of his late wife that he 'never liked her looks since he married her half so well as when he saw her with rosemary under her chin' (Richardson 1988, 22).

20. WSRO QDD/6/W15. The hospital had also held land in the North Field, according to the Boxgrove Chartulary: The Prior of St James holds one acre in the same place [Northfield], paying as above 8d (Fleming 1960, 190).

21. The first two hospitals to be founded in Cambridgeshire were both leper houses dedicated to St Mary Magdalene (Rubin 1989, 44).

6 Geography, architecture and archaeology
by John Magilton

6.1 Precinct and setting

The siting of the hospital

As Gilchrist (1992) remarked, hospitals are primarily urban or suburban. In Yorkshire, 80% of hospitals are in or near towns, and in Norfolk and Suffolk 74%. Satchell (1998, 98) puts the national figure at 85%. In Sussex, the hospital at Harting, founded by the Knights of St Lazarus (Gordon 1877, 28), is one of the few with a rural location. Leper hospitals, however, with a very few exceptions (St Leonard's, Tickhill, South Yorkshire, is one: Magilton 1979) are found beyond the town gates (although sometimes only just beyond them) on the main roads, and there is one example, St John's Thetford, of the suppression of a leper hospital because the town expanded around it (Orme and Webster 1995, 44). Many leper hospitals stood on the town or city boundary which was usually some way beyond the walls (Cullum 1993, 12) and St James' Chichester, with land on both sides of the cross marking the limits of the city liberty, is a prime example.

Several factors explain the peripheral locations of leper hospitals. The biblical authority is from Leviticus **13** and **14**, although the Hebrew term *tsara 'ath* translated as 'leprosy' describes ritual uncleanness, not a specific disease (Manchester 1983, 43). The critical verses (Leviticus **13**, 45 and 46) are:

> *And the leper in whom the plague is, his clothes shall be rent, and the hair of his head shall go loose, and he shall uncover his upper lip, and shall cry, Unclean, Unclean. All the days wherein the plague is in him he shall be unclean: he shall dwell alone; without the camp shall his dwelling be* (Holy Bible, Revised version).

The liminal position of the leper 'without the camp' was, to the medieval mind, reinforced by New Testament teaching about Lazarus (see below) and the lepers themselves were seen as transitional between the living and the dead. Several scholars note the Rite of Sarum, of the 1530s or 1540s, where the order for the seclusion of lepers involved a mock funeral mass before the leper was led outside and earth thrown at his or her feet (eg Morgan 1999, 129–30), but there is no reason to believe that this dramatic ceremony was ever used in England. However, admission to a leper hospital in the earlier Middle Ages did more or less involve taking on the life of a religious (Clay 1909, 131).

There are practical reasons too for siting leper houses on the fringes of towns. There was more room for gardens[1] and orchards through which able-bodied lepers might augment the hospital's income, and the edges were quieter and healthier than the built-up areas (Orme and Webster 1995, 45). If, as has been argued, a hospital was not established primarily in the cause of public health but as a notable act of piety (Richards 1977, 11), this could be achieved at a lesser cost beyond the suburbs where land was cheaper. Alms gathering from passers-by was a potentially important element in a hospital's income, and main roads, especially road junctions and bridges or river crossings, were favoured sites.[2] Although perhaps some distance from centres of population, these were areas where wayfarers would congregate, and the medieval traveller would have known he was approaching a town when roadside hospitals and their importuning inmates or proctors began to appear. It is said that leper hospitals tend to be downstream of water-courses serving towns (Gilchrist 1992, 112) but St James' Chichester is an exception if the River Lavant bounding the hospital was used as a source of drinking water.

Some leper houses may have been founded at sites convenient for begging where lepers had congregated, perhaps on waste ground or at such minor local landmarks as wells or crosses, before the formal establishment of accommodation by civil or ecclesiastical authorities or through their own initiative. Bequests to the lepers of a certain place that do not mention a hospital (see Appendix 4 for Chichester examples) may well have been alms for distribution at a spot where lepers were known to assemble.

In all, St James' Chichester is in a classic location for a medieval leper hospital, on a main road and close to two road junctions, one to the south where the lane now called St James' Road took travellers towards Mundham and the coast (Peckham 1950, 149, AY14) and another (Spitalfield Lane) bypassing Chichester to take travellers north-west beyond its north gate. It was highly visible to travellers heading either for Petworth and London along the old Roman road Stane Street or towards Arundel. Where the roads diverged at Maudlin, Westhampnett, the charitable traveller had a second opportunity to give to a lazar house.

The Liberty of St James

Those lands of St James' Hospital which lay next to the hospital buildings formed a discrete block of land of *c* 4ha (10 acres) known as the Liberty of St James which, in terms of ecclesiastical organisation, was a Peculiar, outside the parochial system and the jurisdiction of the bishop and archdeacon and also mostly outside the city limits until 19th-century boundary changes.[3] Peculiars were, as the word indicates, generally uncommon but an odd administrative arrangement had come about in Chichester whereby most of the small city parishes, including the chapelries (later parishes) of Fishbourne and Rumboldswick, were under the jurisdiction of the dean acting on his own rather than the bishop and regulated through the dean's Peculiar Court. They were in other respects normal parishes, not extra-parochial like St James' Hospital, and it is unfortunate that the same term covers both types of arrangements.

In medieval parochial terms, the abuttals of the Liberty of St James were Subdeanery (ie the cathedral parish, otherwise St Peter the Great) to the north-west, St Pancras in the south-west, Oving to the south-east[4] and Westhampnett to the north-east. There seems subsequently to have been some doubt about the precise boundary with St Pancras, giving rise to the description 'no man's land' to an area thought to lie between the two (Morgan 1992, 171). Physically, the canalised River Lavant marked the south-eastern and, possibly, the north-eastern boundaries of the peculiar. The canalisation of the river has been ascribed to the 10th century (Magilton 1996) but it has followed its present course on the north side of the road only since 1768 (Steer 1962b) and the Peculiar of St James' included the highway in its southern portion.

The hospital seems to have been a joint foundation by Church and monarch, the Church providing income from its estates at Colworth and elsewhere, and the Crown a regular income to support the master or chaplain, and occasional gifts. The hospital liberty was probably former Crown property, either purchased specifically for founding a hospital or, more likely, already owned by the king. There were other crown properties along Stane Street[5] in St Pancras parish at least as early as the 11th century, but how such a concentration occurred is unknown. It must be suspected to have survived from before the Conquest; Domesday Book records land in Stockbridge Hundred held by Ketel [Esterman] for one plough containing a mill, five acres of meadow and a smallholder [*bordar*] valued at 25s which King William had assigned to him (Morris 1976, 11, 42). Ketel exchanged part of the land with the earl of Arundel, and the earl and his brother gave it to Ralph de Luffa, bishop of Chichester. On part of the land previously held by Ketel the king had a garden in 1212 that was granted to the bishop of Chichester in 1227 to become the city's main cemetery, The Litten (Salzman 1935, 82). The Domesday mill was probably on the south side of Stane Street where the River Lavant ceases to follow the roadside but swings southwards to run behind properties fronting the street. Here, in the suburban part of St Pancras parish, stood the city mill (also known as the King's Mill) from at least 1231 until its demolition in the mid-18th century (Morgan 1992, 55 and 172). The parish had, however, a rural part connected to it by a narrow lane (formerly Snag Lane, now part of Market

Road and Caledonian Avenue) which contained Kingsham, glossed in a Latin charter of Henry I as *Orrea Regis*, 'King's Barns' (Salzman 1935, 104). This is another intriguing record of royal interest and agriculture in the neighbourhood, and a further probable pre-Conquest royal holding.[6]

Parishes around the city at least are likely to have acquired fixed bounds by the time of the hospital's foundation[7] and St James' must originally have formed part of one of them. Of the four possibilities, Westhampnett is the least likely. It had, or came to have, its own leper hospital at Maudlin towards its eastern boundary and there are no known connections between St James' hospital and the parish. A connection with Oving is at first sight promising as the hospital held lands at Colworth within that parish. Colworth was a prebendal manor supposedly granted by Aethelred II in AD 988 but the charter is a forgery (Barker 1949, 103–9; Sawyer, 1968, 83, 48), albeit with the pious intention of securing a title rather than attempting to deceive. Colworth is, however, in the south-east part of Oving parish, quite distant from the hospital, and had its own chapel although little seems to be known of it (Salzman 1955, 170). The vast parish of Subdeanery, the cathedral parish, may have lost a roadside strip to the peculiar of St James, and is perhaps the most probable donor; alternatively, St Pancras may have lost its north-east end. St James' is now part of Portfield,[8] a Victorian parish named after the larger town field.

How St James' Hospital came to be outside the parochial system is uncertain. It may have been so established at its foundation, and Clay (1909, 203) cites other examples of hospitals of royal origin that had 'free' chapels. Even more interesting are the few leper houses, including St Leonard's Northampton, St Nicholas' York and the leper house in Lincoln, which acquired full parochial rights, including those of baptism and burial.

As noted, St James' is a classic location for a leper hospital, on the main road out of the city and at the first road junction of any importance. The antiquity of Spitalfield Lane is hinted at by St James' Cross, which stood at its junction with Stane Street marking a limit of the city in the 13th century and perhaps earlier; the city boundary follows the line of the lane for a short way (Morgan 1992, 9–10). The present roadside obelisk dates to 1714, replacing the medieval cross overturned by treasure hunters in 1547 (Salzman 1935, 82). Also within the hospital liberty was the start of a lane, now St James' Road and formerly (Leather) Bottle Lane, going south to Mundham and coastal villages. Why the main highway itself was included in the liberty is uncertain. One of the hospital's duties may have been maintenance of the highway, but there is no record of it. Mending roads, and particularly bridges, was regarded as a charitable act and it would therefore have been regarded as meritorious to support with alms those who did such work. St James' Cross would have been an ideal spot for alms gathering.

6.2   Buildings and structures

The Leper Cottage

What survives of the hospital today is the building known locally as the 'Leper Cottage'. It attained its present form after the fire of 1781 and much of the structure is undoubtedly 18th and 19th century. A small part is, however, in all probability medieval.

Maps

The only known map of the hospital site to pre-date the Ordnance Survey 1:2500 first edition of 1875 (Fig 6.2) is Thomas Yeakell and William Gardner's city map of 1769 (Fig 6.1 inset). It is at a similar nominal scale (1:2449 or a little over 25 ins to the mile) but not entirely accurate, the errors becoming more pronounced towards the map edges. The hospital is shown near the eastern edge. Two buildings (or perhaps one long building) labelled 'St James's Ruins' occupy the middle of a narrow field defined by hedges parallel to Westhampnett Road and are depicted by faint lines. They seem to represent roofless structures, since the outlines of intact buildings elsewhere are infilled with diagonal shading. To the south-west, in the same field but on its boundary with Westhampnett Road, is a standing rectangular building which, it must be assumed, is the 'Spittle House'[9] which burnt down in 1781. Apart from the ruins, the only named feature in the immediate vicinity is the then new bridge over the River Lavant labelled 'Bridge'. Spershott's memoirs date the diversion of the Lavant to the north side of Westhampnett Road and construction of the bridge to 1768, and the existing brickwork on the north side of the road appears consistent with this date.

If both maps are enlarged to a common scale,[10] the approximate position of the Spittle House can be determined (Fig 6.1). In terms of the modern topography, it is partly beneath Swanfield Chapel south-west of no. 3 Westhampnett Road (Leper Cottage), to give it the local designation. The cottage itself appears to be represented by the ruin nearest the Spittle House' since it is the right size, and the other, smaller, part of the ruin lies north-east of it. A noteworthy feature is the width of the road south of the hospital. The Spittle House site is now about 12m from the line of Westhampnett Road but in the 18th century there seems to have been a much wider 'road zone' of 20m or more, marked by the hedge on the hospital side and the headlands of the strip fields of the Portfield on the opposite, through which the actual carriageway meandered. The width is close to that expected for a Roman road, which Westhampnett Road is in origin, and it would be an entirely suitable place for holding an annual fair. The hedgerows shown in 1769 do not seem to reflect the limits of the hospital peculiar, and the field north-east of the one containing the hospital and its ruins is a huge open field with only

the portion next to Westhampnett Road lying within the extra-parochial area.

The 1875 map (Fig 6.2) shows much additional detail, some of it pertaining to features of the landscape post-dating the 1769 map. Unfortunately, most of the field boundaries shown on the earlier map have been altered. The north-west and south-east boundaries of what may be termed the 'hospital field' have disappeared, except where the Lavant perpetuates the latter; the north-east boundary, formerly an edge of the cemetery, has also gone and a new field boundary, the southernmost part of which survived into the 1980s as the Leper Cottage garden fence, has been created about 25m north-east of the cottage. A minor feature not shown in 1769 but which may nevertheless have been extant then is a track that led north-east from the front of the cottage to the new field boundary, where in 1875 it stopped. Its line seems to be reflected in ditches found in the 1993 excavations and it may have demarcated the south-east edge of the cemetery. If projected south-westwards, it follows a line that takes it past the north-west wall of the Spittle House, ie the Leper Cottage and the Spittle House are on opposite sides of the same track or lane. Another feature of the 1875 map is a lane with a bridge (still extant) across the River Lavant just within the north-east boundary of the Peculiar of St James'. Reference to the 1778 Yeakell and Gardner map shows that the lane once extended northwards to Graylingwell Farm. To its east was mostly pasture and to the west arable.

Drawings and paintings

Two engravings in the *Gentleman's Magazine* depict the front (south-east) wall of the Leper Cottage. The earlier, of 1792 (Fig 6.3, also reproduced in McCann 1987), shows a building of at least two phases. The cottage has a chimney in its north-east gable, a single window, perhaps with a central mullion, in the middle of the first floor and at ground level a flat-headed doorway (or possibly a window) close to the gable wall. The roof is thatched and the walls have wavy horizontal lines, perhaps to depict flint rubble. The south-west gable is hipped, and against it is seemingly a lean-to of a different stone (possibly coursed ashlar) to the cottage. In this wall, immediately adjoining the cottage, is a round-arched doorway, apparently with large ashlars above it, and left of it a second round-headed arch, the opening blocked, can be seen near ground level. The 'lean-to' is not obviously thatched; what might at first be taken for thatch is shadow from or the foliage of adjacent trees. It is tempting to assume a roofed structure because the top of the wall seems to have continued the line of the hip-gabled roof, but this is conjecture. Next to it is what appears to be a timber structure, perhaps a gate, and beyond it is a further ruined structure at most perhaps a metre high.[11] Some distance north-east of the cottage is a wall about 2m high, apparently of brick since it is

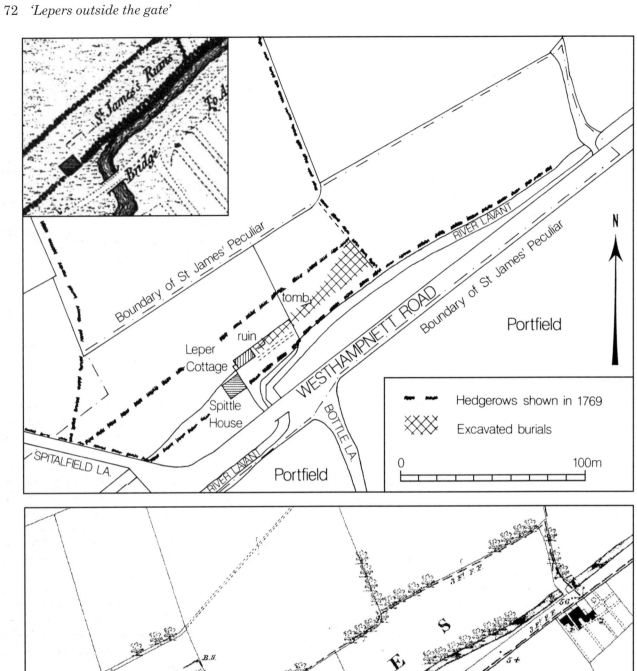

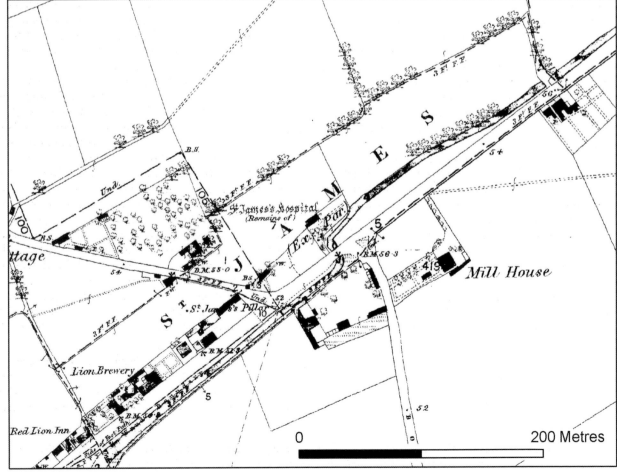

Figure 6.3 *St James' Hospital in 1792. This engraving in the* Gentleman's Magazine *is the earliest picture of the 'leper cottage' and is a fairly convincing representation of its late 18th-century appearance*

Figure 6.4 *Despite the caption, this childish representation of 1804, again from the* Gentleman's Magazine, *is obviously St James' Hospital. The cottage has gained its commemorative plaque and the first-floor window its Y-tracery*

of similar appearance to the bridge built over the Lavant in 1768. On the line of the façade of the cottage, extending to the right, is a hedge, and in front of it a post and rail fence, the two defining a lane or track leading to the cottage door from the north-east. This is presumably the track which survived at least until 1875 to be depicted on the first Ordnance Survey plan (Fig 6.2). In the foreground, what must be intended for the River Lavant is shown as a dark linear feature flowing beneath the brick parapets of the new bridge on the extreme left of the engraving, and the windlass of a well can be seen above the parapet. In the foreground on the right is what must be the former course of the river, the two small arches in the centre of the picture perhaps being a now redundant culvert beneath St James' Road (earlier Bottle Lane).

A second, much more inept, engraving appeared in the same magazine in 1804, wrongly titled 'St George's Hospital, Chichester' (Fig 6.4). The building is unchanged in broad outline but differences make it clear that it is not simply a bad copy of the earlier engraving. The doorway near the north-east gable is shown as round-headed and the first-floor window as having acquired Y-tracery and a pointed head.[12] Assuming that the window which survives today is the same as, or a replica of, this window, its height is exaggerated, as is that of the door to its right. Next to the window is a new feature, still extant, the Revd

Walker's plaque explaining the hospital's history. The doorway and blocked arch in the lean-to are as before, and the change in wall construction is also indicated, although further to the right than in the earlier engraving. It is again impossible to be sure whether the 'lean-to' was roofed. To the right of the cottage the hedge and post and rail fence are again depicted, although the perspective is odd, and a path is shown from the door nearer the north-east gable heading towards Westhampnett Road. On the left the well windlass is shown, and behind it is either a low-walled structure or a ruin.[13]

Neither illustration is necessarily very trustworthy and differences in detail mean that it is impossible for both to be accurate. By comparing both with the plan and elevation (see below) the earlier seems the more believable but the two-storey element is too short and the 'lean-to' possibly too long.

A third pictorial source is a watercolour and ink sketch (Fig 6.5) measuring *c* 230 × 140mm by G Shepheard dated 18 July 1805 and now in Chichester District Museum.[14] The view is again of the south-east façade, but this time seen from the south, from what would today be the area behind Swanfield Chapel. There are again reasons to doubt its accuracy. The plaque (which is transcribed in abbreviated form[15] in the top left corner of the painting) is as big as the adjacent window, and both are disproportionately large. All the features discernible in the earlier

Figure 6.1 (opposite, above) *Yeakell and Gardner's map 1769 (inset) and its main features superimposed on the OS 25 inch map of 1875. Survey mistakes in the earlier map become more pronounced towards its edges, where St James' lies, and there is consequently some scope for error in correlation. The only excavated feature drawn is one of the tombs, to show that its alignment is quite different from that of the other structures. Scale 1:2000*

Figure 6.2 (opposite, below) *The extra-parochial Liberty of St James in the 19th century on the OS 25 inch map of 1875 (not to original scale). The area still lies beyond Chichester's expanding suburbs*

UNIVERSITY OF WINCHESTER LIBRARY

Figure 6.5 St James' Hospital in 1805. The roofed structure, if the painting is to be believed, is the northern half of an otherwise derelict range

Figure 6.7 The Leper Cottage in 1986, during its ownership by Chichester District Council

Figure 6.6 St James' Hospital in 1825, according to Rouse

Figure 6.8 The Leper Cottage, rear elevation. The recent history of the hospital deduced from its main façade is reflected in the two major building phases prominent in its rear wall

engravings are indicated, others are made clearer and there are a few new features of note. A further blocked opening to the left of the arch in the lean-to is indicated, and this seems to be the gap blocked by timbers in 1792. The lean-to, or at least most of it, is clearly thatched, and at its south-west end is a gate. As in all previous illustrations, the cottage and its lean-to together make a longer building than the cottage is today.

A fourth source is a drawing in Rouse's *Beauty and Antiquities* (351, pl 124) published in 1825 (Fig 6.6). The view is from St James' Road (then Bottle Lane). On the left-hand side is a pillar with ashlar facings, perhaps the corner of a boundary wall, and to its right is the bridge carrying Westhampnett Road over the Lavant. The right-hand side of the picture shows the south-east wall of the hospital and its north-east gable. As usual, not all the detail is independently verifiable or believable. Both sides of the bridge, for example, have gained brick piers with pyramidal tops that are otherwise unattested. The cottage proportions are about right although the

openings look wrong. The door near the north-east gable seems to have acquired a pointed arch, and the Gothick window on the first floor and the plaque are too big. The main point of interest is that the lean-to is much truncated and of a length corresponding to the south-western part of the present cottage. In other words, it appears as if the long lean-to shown in 1804 and earlier had been shortened by 1825.

Discussion

The cottage today (Figs 6.7 and 6.8) looks quite different from its early 19th-century appearance, but as the major changes have been to the superstructure rather than to the ground-plan, they cannot be dated by reference to maps and it is not known exactly when it assumed its present form, although it was later than 1825. The major alteration has been the building up of the lean-to section to eaves level so that the cottage is two-storey throughout. This cannot, however, have been done to the whole of the lean-to unless all the illustrations before 1825 exaggerate its true length, and it must be suspected that the building as depicted up to 1805 was further truncated. The building is still thatched, with a hipped roof at the south-west end. The structural history of the cottage as deduced from illustrations of its south-east façade is reinforced by an examination of the back wall of the cottage (Fig 6.8), which is also of two phases, the earlier (Fig 6.9, phase 3), belonging with the two-storey building of 1792, incorporating architectural fragments and burnt stones and ending with brick quoins. The section corresponding to the lean-to (Fig. 6.9, phase 4) is of regularly coursed flints, and the buttresses were added when or after this had been built.

In 1983 the Leper Cottage was owned by Chichester District Council and accurate 1:50 plans and elevations were made in advance of a refurbishment scheme that included the installation of an inside toilet. These are the basis of the phase plan (Fig 6.9). The greater part of the south-east wall (ie the front elevation) is up to a metre wide, much thicker than the other walls, at both ground-floor and first-floor levels and corresponds with the two-storey part of the cottage depicted in the *Gentleman's Magazine* engravings and the 1805 watercolour. The thick wall ends to the right of the south-westerly doorway (Fig 6.9), which seems to correspond to the round-headed door of the 1792 engraving, and the only solid internal wall, which is two storeys high, lies approximately at right-angles to it. From its thickness, it may be concluded that the south-eastern wall is of an earlier constructional phase to the rest of the cottage.

The former lean-to section has walls of comparable thickness to the rest of the cottage, except for the door jambs, but its later date is apparent in the north-west wall not only from the different materials used to build it but also its width, for it is slightly narrower south-west of the only internal wall than north-east of it. The door in the front wall that had a round-headed arch in 1792 has a flatter top today and the original arch may have been lost when a second pointed arch mock-ecclesiastical window was inserted more or less above it. The door-jambs are, however, of comparable thickness to the wall ascribed to phase 1 (Fig. 6.9) and may represent a fragment of ancient masonry that has survived. The position of the blocked arch of the engravings corresponds to the privy door opening of 1983 and must be assumed also to have been lost. The whole façade is cement-rendered and colour-washed and much helpful detail may be concealed behind the plaster.

Whether the lean-to is as old as late 18th- and early 19th-century illustrations appear to indicate or if it began essentially as a folly constructed after the fire on old foundations is a matter for conjecture; the narrowness of the walls suggests the latter. The three possibilities are:

- the lean-to wall as depicted *c* 1800 is genuine, in that it represents a building of several phases that was derelict by 1769;

- the lean-to wall as depicted *c* 1800 was constructed after the fire of 1781 out of architectural fragments found elsewhere on site;
- whatever its age, the lean-to wall shown *c* 1800 was demolished, apart from the door jambs, by 1825.

The round-headed doorway, if it is not in situ, could be explained as a useful feature worth salvaging, but the blocked arch, if not in situ, would seem to have no function other than to give a spurious air of antiquity.[16] It brings to mind an instruction given earlier in the 18th century that the chapel door should be blocked up, but the building in its 1792 form does not otherwise look convincing as part of a chapel.[17] The cottage as a whole does, however, appear to be exactly on the site and of very similar dimensions to the larger of the ruins shown in 1769 and the thickness of the south-east wall appears to vindicate the Ordnance Survey's caption that it incorporates 'remains of' the hospital. The antiquity or otherwise of what was the lean-to wall could be readily established by removing the cement render that now conceals it. The best guess from present information is that phase 1 is ancient, phase 2 may be so but phases 3 and 4 are post-1781.

The lesser ruins of the 1769 map should have been detected in the course of excavation in 1993 but there was nothing surviving that might have corresponded with them. It may have been a relatively late structure as it lay above the cemetery area, and perhaps had slight foundations that gardening subsequently destroyed. A less likely explanation is that the 1769 map has been wrongly superimposed on the 1875 map and both the ruins and the Spittle House should be shunted north-eastwards. This would put the lesser ruins on the site of the present cottage.

6.3 Cemetery features other than graves

Excavations in 1986–87 and 1993 (for location, see Fig 6.1) revealed a number of features apart from individual graves. Features earlier than and irrelevant to the hospital are omitted from the discussion below but shown on Figure 6.10; the rest are briefly described and discussed. The main feature to pre-date the cemetery was a very substantial Iron Age north–south ditch that had still been partly open in the Roman period. Although parts of it appeared to be reflected in field boundaries down to modern times to the north of the site, its course seems to have had no effect on the bounds of the hospital or its cemetery and it is not further described here.

Remaining features may in theory be subdivided into those that pre-dated the cemetery, those contemporary with its period of use, and those that post-dated it. In practice, many are less easy to categorise. One of the more important pottery assemblages was recovered from the backfilled lime kiln described below; it demonstrated either that

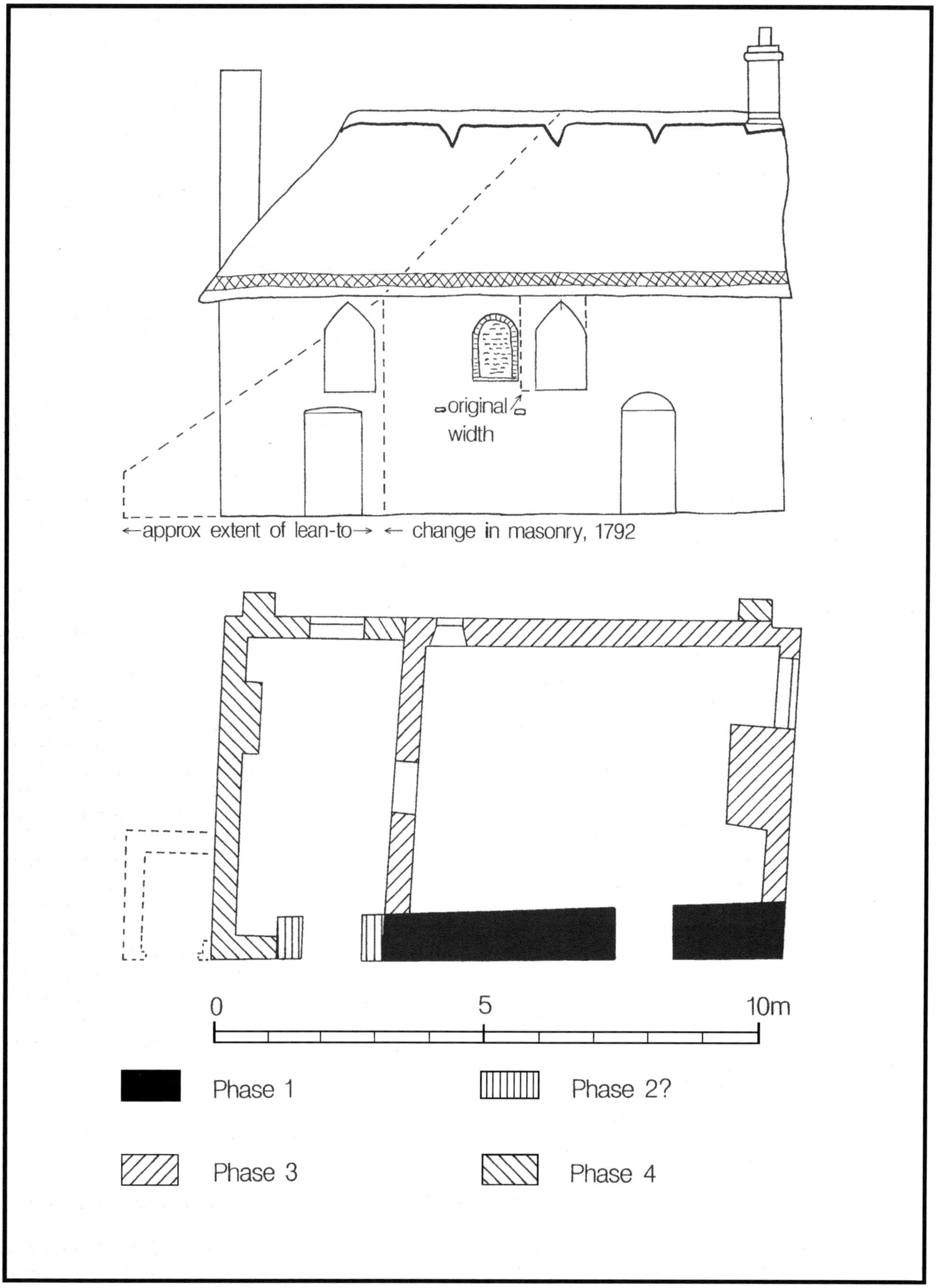

original
width

←approx extent of lean-to→ ← change in masonry, 1792

0   5   10m

Phase 1   Phase 2?

Phase 3   Phase 4

Figure 6.9   The Leper Cottage. Elevation, plan and interpretation of existing building. Scale 1:100

the whole cemetery was late medieval or, much more probably, that the excavated area was part of a late cemetery, its predecessor lying elsewhere. The Iron Age ditch excepted, this was the only significant archaeological feature to lie beneath the cemetery.

Features earlier than the cemetery

The lime kiln 827 (Figs 6.11 and 6.12)

The 1993 excavations revealed a lime kiln (827) about 20m east of the Leper Cottage beneath a number of graves (Fig 6.11). The bottom of the kiln was more or less square, about 3m across at the base, but the walls had collapsed in such a way as to suggest a roughly circular structure when it was first seen in plan. A stoke hole lay to the east. It was not initially appreciated that the kiln and stoke hole were components of the same feature and both features were half-sectioned from north to south rather than along the long axis of the kiln, which would have been preferable.

The kiln had been extensively damaged. At the base, which was more or less flat, a little over 1.5m below the modern ground surface, the small pieces of sandstone 774 lining the lower parts of the north and south sides survived generally only to a height of around 0.25m. The stoke hole 776, constructed of larger blocks of sandstone and about 0.5m wide, had fared little better. The lowest layer within the kiln consisted of charcoal, above which was a layer 777 of chalk lumps and some lime but both were restricted to the bottom 0.25m or so of the structure. Above were more or less uniform layers 775 of very gravely soil that had been tipped in from the north side (Fig 6.11, section 2). The impression was that the kiln had been thoroughly emptied following its last firing and that it had been subject to weathering, during which time the upper parts of the sides had collapsed, before deliberate backfilling had taken place.

The stoking pit 765 was about a metre wide. Its base was 2m long and, like the kiln, its walls were lined with stones. It lay at about the same depth as the kiln base and was approached by a step 0.45m deep on the north-east side. The filling was much the same as for the kiln, with a 300mm layer of mainly charcoal 767 in the base capped by chalk and lime (826) corresponding to 777 in the kiln. The upper layers 766 were again the result of deliberate backfilling. Interestingly, a triangular wedge of clay blocking the flue arch remained in situ (Fig 6.11, section 2). Although they were not seen in plan, there were stakeholes against the sides of the pit (Fig 6.11, section 3), perhaps indicating that its sides were either revetted or fenced off with, for example, hurdles as a safety precaution when it was partly infilled. This seems uncharacteristically safety-conscious for the Middle Ages, but some of the hospital inmates may have been blind. On the south side of the stoking pit, towards the top, was the lower

filling 760 for the grave of burial 349, incompletely excavated when the skeleton was lifted.

Lime is produced by strongly heating limestone or chalk to leave calcium oxide, a white powder also called quicklime. When combined with water it reacts to form calcium hydroxide, also known as slaked or hydrated lime which, when mixed with sand and water, makes mortar. It was normally made on site for building projects in the Middle Ages and the kiln was presumably constructed for a campaign of extending or rebuilding the hospital. From pottery recovered from its filling, assuming that the back-filling did not long post-date the last use of the kiln, it cannot relate to the foundation of the building in the 12th century and, as virtually nothing is known of the structures of the hospital, the kiln cannot be associated with any later ancillary buildings. The kiln points to some building activity in the 13th or 14th centuries, but the structure has yet to be found. Slaked lime can be mixed with water alone to make a whitewash, used externally on many medieval buildings as well as on inside walls. It has a disinfectant value and was perhaps used extensively at St James', although not perhaps on a scale to justify a kiln load.

Parallels for the kiln include a circular example about 3m across excavated next to Doncaster parish church and the river on the edge of the medieval town in 1978 (Buckland *et al* 1989, 205–7). A monastic example has been published from St Mary Stratford Langthorne, formerly Essex, now Greater London (Barber *et al* 2004).[18] There is no example of a lime kiln from excavations in the city of Chichester and lime burning may have been discouraged or forbidden in built-up areas of predominantly timber-framed buildings. In early 17th-century Worcester it was the responsibility of the mason in charge of a building project to supply 'lyme' (Carver 1980, 283) and this had presumably been so in the Middle Ages too, although in the post-medieval period lime was normally made in primitive kilns near the stone source. Rural kilns producing lime for agriculture were common in the 18th and early 19th centuries and were more or less permanent structures, the detailed features of which were much discussed by agricultural 'improvers' of the day, but the use of lime for neutralising acid soils was not a medieval custom.

Features contemporary with the cemetery (Figs 6.10 and 6.13)

Robber trench 770: the hospital precinct wall?

The 1993 site in the garden of the 'leper cottage' revealed a number of linear features, some of which may be interpreted as cemetery boundary ditches. They were not investigated in any detail because the excavation brief was to record and remove human remains before the sale of the plot (see Chapter 1 for background).

The southernmost linear feature lay about 7m

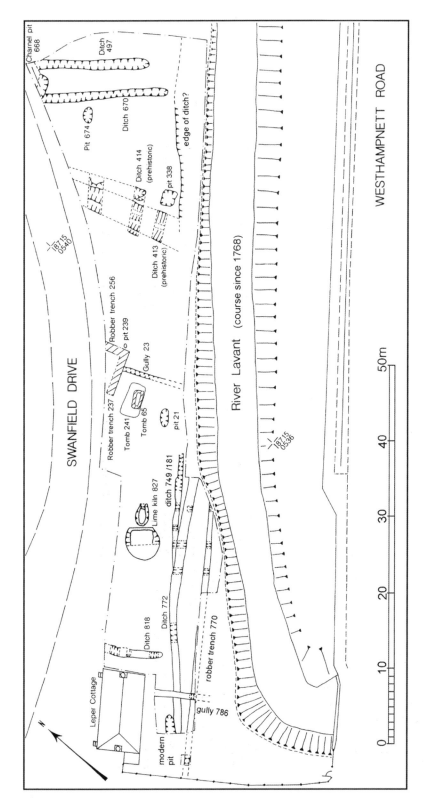

Figure 6.10 Excavations at Swanfield Drive 1986–87 and 1993, showing negative features (apart from burials) of all periods. Three trenches opened up in 1986–87 north-east of this area (for location, see Figure 1.4) contained no archaeological features. Scale 1:500

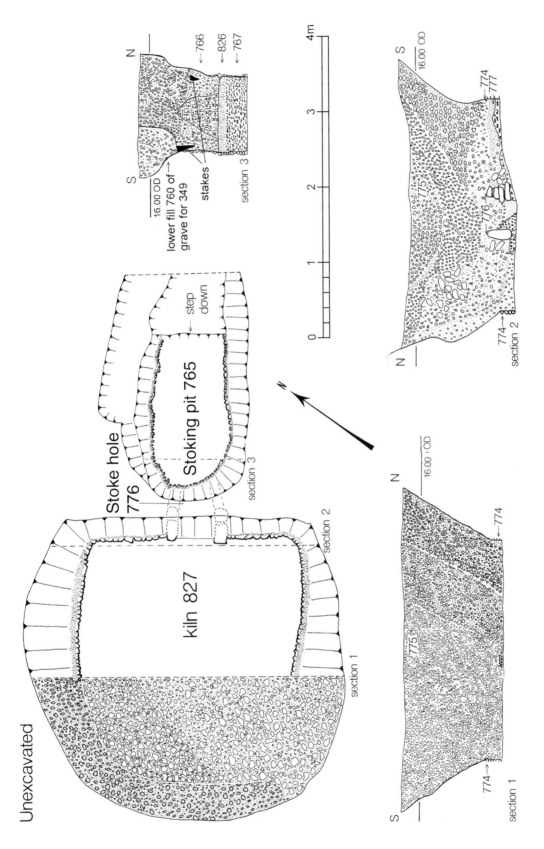

Figure 6.11 Lime kiln 827, plan and sections. Scale 1:50

Figure 6.12 Photograph of lime kiln 827. The photographic scales are in the part-excavated kiln chamber and the stoke hole is visible beyond

south of the 'leper cottage' and shared its alignment, also lying more or less parallel to the Westhampnett Road, as Stane Street is designated at this point. Feature 770 was traced from a sondage south of the west wall of the cottage to a point where it had been cut away by the culverted River Lavant, a distance of about 35m. The greater part of its line was seen in plan only but four narrow sections, three of them at its north-eastern end, were excavated to try to determine its nature and date. The drawn section (Fig 6.13) showed the feature at this point to be about 1.2m wide and 0.6m deep with a broad V-shaped profile and a rounded base. The upper filling, containing flints, was partly capped by a lens of mortar,

and at the time of excavation it was thought to be a robber trench for a wall. To the south, just within the excavated area, was the edge of a cut associated with the canalised river.

Although neither the profile nor the filling would rule out its interpretation as an infilled ditch, Feature 770 was absolutely straight for the whole of its recorded length, a characteristic rarely seen in ditches, and its interpretation as a robber trench remains the more likely. It cannot have been the boundary wall of the cemetery since the closest graves are about 6m north of it, extending no further south than the line of the south wall of the 'leper cottage', and it may have served as the south-east wall of the hospital precinct. Whether the whole precinct was so defined is open to question since, for economy, it is possible that only the side nearest the road was given this relatively prestigious treatment. Alternatively, it may have swung northwards at some point beyond the 1986–87 excavations to form the north-east wall of the enceinte. There is no hint of either wall on the 1769 Yeakell and Gardner map (Fig 6.1), which shows a field boundary on the alignment of the south wall of the cottage, and although there appears at first glance a boundary on about the right line on the 1875 1st edition 1:2500 plan (Fig 6.2), it is a little too far south.

The southern ditches 772 and 749 /181

North of the supposed wall 770 but south of all the burials were two north-east/south-west ditches. The larger and later of these, 772, was slightly curving, lying about 3m away from 770 in the middle but

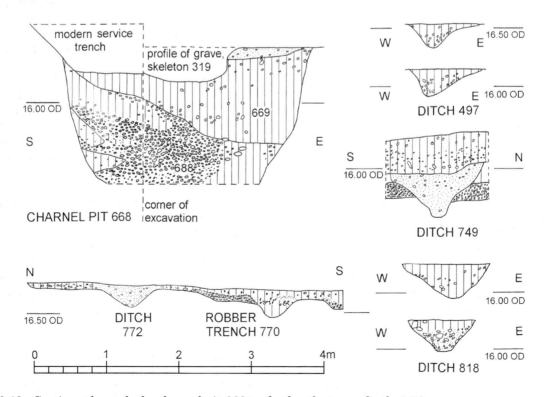

Figure 6.13 Sections through the charnel pit 668 and other features. Scale 1:50

slightly closer at both ends. It was traced for 34m across the whole of the 1993 site, where it was cut by a modern pit on the south-western edge of the excavation, but was not seen in 1986–87 as its projected line lay outside the excavated area. As with 770, the greater part of the ditch line was seen only in plan but four short sections of it were excavated in order to record the profile and in the hope of obtaining datable artefacts. The profile where recorded (Fig 6.13) was about 1.6m wide at the top and slightly irregular, and there was a single uniform filling containing few stones.

It was cut through an earlier, narrower ditch 749 to the north that was traced for 15m to the edge of the 1993 site, its terminal lying just within the 1986–87 excavations (Fig 6.10). Beyond the terminal it continued as a narrower gully 181 for about 3.5m only, the remainder of its course having been destroyed by a modern pipe trench. Ditch 749, 0.7m wide at its western end and filled with dark brown silty loam, was more or less straight and on the 'cottage alignment', being precisely parallel to the feature interpreted as a robbed wall 770 (see Fig 6.10). As the narrower gully 181 pre-dated the ditch, 749 may be regarded as a recutting of the same feature. The south-western end of 749/181 was cut away by ditch 772. At the north-eastern end of the 1986–87 site, and on the same alignment as 749/181, was the northern edge of a linear feature that effectively formed the southern limit of the cemetery. At the time of excavation it was thought to be a relatively late feature associated with the canalised course of the River Lavant, but it may well be a continuation of ditch 749/181, its north-east edge having been destroyed by canalisation.

Neither the dating nor interpretation of either ditch is certain. They do not cut through, nor are they cut by any graves, although a north–south gully possibly contemporary with gully 181 does post-date graves in its vicinity (see 'The middle ditch' below) and yielded post-medieval pottery. If 770 is correctly interpreted as a robbed medieval precinct wall, it is difficult to see why this was not taken as the cemetery limit for, even if it was not a primary feature, it must have been extant long before the latest interments took place. A possible clue is given in the drawn section (Fig 6.13) where a gravel layer containing some tile fragments is shown between the robber trench, which cuts it, and the ditch, although it was not noted in plan; it could represent a metalled track or narrow lane between the precinct wall and the cemetery boundary, but it is very difficult to imagine why such a feature would be needed. As the layer, or one very similar, also occurs just south of 770, it may be construction debris from the wall although it seems to have spread a long way from the wall line on the north-west side.

The western ditch 818

About 2m beyond the east wall of the 'leper cottage', and parallel with it, was a north–south ditch 818. Its southern terminal was about 1.5m north of the line of ditch 772, and it was traced northwards for about 7m to the edge of excavation. Its width and depth were both variable and it became shallower and narrower to the south, although at its northern end it was around 1.1m wide and 0.8m deep (Fig. 6.13), proportions similar to those of 772. A seeming spur on its eastern side, a natural feature excavated in error, has been omitted from the drawing (Fig 6.10). The nearest burials lay about 3m east of the ditch.

An association with the graveyard seems probable and this ditch, with a bank on its eastern edge, may have delineated the western limit of the cemetery. The gap between the southern terminal of ditch 818 and the northern lip of 772 may be explicable by a pre-existing bank belonging with either 772 or its predecessor, 749/181. If so, ditch 818 is at best more or less contemporary with ditch 772, with which it is broadly similar, or it post-dates 772. The existence of ditch 818 is of relevance to the plan of the medieval hospital, since its presence rules out the possibility of a structure immediately adjoining the 'leper cottage' to the east. What Yeakell and Gardner's 1769 map appears to show is a gap due east of the cottage and then the ruins of a smaller building beyond (Fig 6.1). Some part of the latter, if not all, should have been seen during the 1993 excavations but no trace was found. Very shallow foundations could have been removed by gardening.

The middle ditch 23

Running southwards from a robbed structure 237/256 in the middle of the site was ditch or gully 23 (Fig 6.10). It was similar to the narrower section of the southern ditch 181 and was of relatively recent date, cutting through a number of graves and containing pieces of slate. It was almost exactly half way between ditch 818 on the west side and the earlier of the two eastern ditches described below, 607, but not quite parallel with either. As the ditch or gully could not be traced northwards within 237/256 it is likely that the structure represented by the robbed walls was still extant when the ditch was dug. Pottery recovered from the ditch filling 24 included post-medieval sherds.

Ditch 23 is about 2m west of the proposed division between the old cemetery and the new (designated Areas A and B in Chapter 7). It may represent a boundary created at some time after the establishment of the new cemetery, perhaps when the old cemetery had been put to some other use. The 1539 rental (Appendix 6) implies that part of the cemetery had been put to commercial use and ditch 23 may reflect its changed function.

The eastern ditches 670 and 497

Two ditches, about 3m apart and parallel with each other, were located in 1987 on the eastern edge of the graveyard. There were no burials beyond the outer ditch 497 but the inner ditch 670 had been used for child burials. At the time of excavation it was thought that 670 represented an original limit to the cemetery and that 497 represented a slight extension, an interpretation that is still possible.

The inner ditch 670 was traced northwards for about 17m from its southern terminal. When defined it was only about 0.85m wide but the upper part had been almost completely obliterated by burials and no representative cross section could be obtained. It was perhaps the equivalent of 818 at the western end of the cemetery although its southern terminal is further north relative to the probable eastern end of ditch 749/181 (see Fig 6.10), perhaps because there was a gate at this point. If, as has been postulated for 818, there was a bank of upcast on the edge of ditch 670, it may in this instance have been on the eastern edge so that the column of predominantly infant and child burials lay just within consecrated ground. If it is correct to postulate an early graveyard with its eastern limit on or close to the line of ditch 23, ditch 670 cannot have been dug as a cemetery boundary unless it is contemporary with or later than the cemetery extension.

Ditch 497 was more than 15m long and about 1.2m wide with a steep slope on the west side and a gentler slope on its eastern side where the associated bank may have been. Its southern terminal was about 3m north of that of the neighbouring ditch 670. A modern pit 488 (omitted from Fig 6.10) containing a dog skeleton was the only feature cut through the ditch.

If the two ditches were successive, ditch 497 represents an excess of effort to extend the graveyard by a mere 3m, an area sufficient for only a single column of burials. One possibility is that the cemetery was left open-ended once 670 had been breached and that ditch 497 was dug to define the cemetery's eastern limit after the last interment had taken place. Another possibility is that 670 and 497 were contemporary and that their purpose was to provide the upcast material for a boundary bank between them, although the fact that one was shorter than the other rather militates against the idea. It might be argued that 770 and 749/772 represent the same phenomenon on the south side of the cemetery but this would require the robber trench 770 to be reinterpreted as a ditch (or 497 as a robber trench) to make the parallel valid.

Pit 239

Pit 239 was almost square, about a metre across, lying next to the robbed wall 256 in the middle of the site. As tree roots had damaged several nearby skeletons, it may have held a tree. On the other hand, a central cross[19] was a common feature of cemeteries and a focus for burials, and the area just east of the robbed wall 256 was undoubtedly sought after as a place of interment (see Chapter 7). Unfortunately it is impossible to decide whether the focus was the structure represented by 237/256, whatever feature the pit held, or some other attraction. The focus need not have been a feature of deep religious significance. Requests to be buried 'near the old oak tree' or whatever could have brought about similar clustering. From the distribution of burials, whatever stood in pit 239 must have been extant when the grave pits were dug.

Features later than the cemetery

These are surprisingly few, but their absence is in part explicable by the way the site was dug. In effect, the only features post-dating the cemetery that appear in the archaeological record are those deep enough to impinge on or cut through burials.

Gully 786

A narrow ditch or gully ran southwards from close to the south-east corner of the 'leper cottage' (Fig.6.10). Post-dating ditch 770 and the robber trench 772, it is likely to have been contemporary with the cottage (ie no earlier than the late 18th century). Its purpose was undetermined.[20]

Pit 21

This large pit, measuring about 3m by 1.7m, lay close to the centre of the site near its southern boundary (Fig 6.10). Its fill consisted of large amounts of tile and slate. Although it did not cut any graves, it was in a part of the graveyard where burials were sparse. The slate in its fill is also found, although in much smaller quantities, in the nearby ditch or gully 23 (see above), which does post-date a number of graves. Pit 21 seems best interpreted as a post-medieval rubbish pit dug when the part of the cemetery in which it occurs had gone out of use.

Pit 338

This pit was demonstrably modern containing, *inter alia*, a Shippam's paste pot. It is listed here only because it partly cut away two grave pits.

Pit 674

An oval pit in the eastern end of the cemetery, it post-dated the graves on stratigraphic grounds. Measuring 1.9m by 1.2m, its fill included animal bone and oyster shell and it is best interpreted as a rubbish pit.

Notes

1. A vegetable garden is specifically mentioned in a 12th-century grant to St Nicholas, York (Farrer 1914–16, **1**, 251, no. 329).
2. Water-borne traffic using the rivers was of course another potential source of alms.
3. The Peculiar and Liberty are mutually exclusive apart from a triangle of the latter which bisects the Peculiar to incorporate St James' Cross.
4. At the time of the hospital's foundation Oving parish may not have extended so far west as to embrace the town fields Portfield and Guildenfield (Munby 1984, 325). Before 1212 they too may have been in Subdeanery.
5. Confusingly, the road itself is now called St Pancras where it passes through the parish. It is, however, a small part of Stane Street, the name given to the Chichester–London Roman road. Other stretches also have local names (eg Westhampnett Road).
6. The only West Sussex manor retained by the Crown in 1086 was part of Bosham.
7. Fishbourne acquired its right to burial as late as 1442 and Rumboldswick was never granted the privilege (Peckham 1933, 67) but both are peripheral.
8. Morgan (1992, 8–9) uncharacteristically has difficulties with the derivation of the field name and derives it from Latin *porta*, 'gate', noting that it lies near a gate. It is far more likely Old English *port*, 'market', used here in the sense of 'town', the whole meaning simply 'town field'. Oxford has a 'Port Meadow' (Butler 1993, 80).
9. The term is from Spershott's Memoirs. From his entry for 13 December 1781 ('The large old Spittle House belonging to St James' Chapel burnt down') it may be inferred that the chapel and hospital were by this date separate buildings. The chapel walls were still standing 'showing the form of its windows and door &' in 1721, 'but are since demolished'. As Spershott did not die until 1789, they may have been extant when Yeakell and Gardner's map was drawn.
10. They do not quite match up and there are few features in the immediate vicinity common to both maps.
11. If the perspective is a little awry, as it is elsewhere, this ruin could be the east corner of the Spittle House with the wall lying at right-angles to the Leper Cottage and the gate blocking a continuation of the lane or track shown on the 1875 map.
12. The first-floor plan of the cottage (not shown) makes it clear that the earlier, wider window was narrowed on the left-hand side. The window shown in 1792 had its south-western edge corresponding to the line of the north-east edge of Revd Walker's plaque and was 1.2m wide at the wall face with an internal splay of 2m. The second window is fractionally wider and seems to be contemporary with its opening, which is unsplayed.
13. Again, possibly the Spittle House. See note 11.
14. Accession number 1169.
15. The complete text is as follows: THESE/ARE THE/ SACRED REMAINS OF/ ST JAMES'S HOSPITAL/ WHICH WAS FOUNDED/ IN THE REIGN/ OF HENRY THE FIRST/ FOR THE RECEPTION/ OF PERSONS AFFLICTED/ WITH THE/ LEPROSY
16. One person who may have been responsible is the Revd Walker.
17. Burials did not cluster against its walls as they undoubtedly would have done if it had been a chapel.
18. I am grateful to Barney Sloane for bringing this to my attention.
19. The only cross to survive from an English leper hospital cemetery is at St Giles', Wenlock Road, Shrewsbury. The present Victorian church contains substantial remains of a leper hospital founded *c* 1154–62 (Pevsner 1958, 262) or perhaps as early as 1136 (Prescott 1992, 153) and the churchyard cross has been re-erected in its cemetery (for an illustration, see Gilchrist and Sloane 2005, 39, fig 17). Although closely associated with Shrewsbury Abbey, the hospital escaped the Dissolution.
20. Thatched buildings do not have guttering, so the feature cannot have been a rainwater gully leading to the river.

7 The cemetery *by John Magilton*

7.1 Cemetery dating, organisation and layout

Written sources

The earliest reference to the cemetery is in the Cathedral Chartulary (Peckham 1942–43, 7) where it is recorded incidentally in a dispute between the rector of Itchenor and his parishioners that a certain Richard son of the clerk rests in the graveyard of the Hospital of St James in the suburbs of Chichester, and that his mother and her husband are also buried there. This was in the very late 12th or early in the 13th century, and it is a salutary reminder that some early female skeletons may be expected in a predominantly male graveyard. Agreeing to bury the wealthy in their cemeteries was potentially lucrative for leper hospitals but, it must be suspected, little sought after. This was certainly the case in Bristol (Price 1998, 212), where medieval wills survive in much greater numbers than at Chichester. For those who did seek this, burial amongst lepers who had suffered purgatory on earth meant, perhaps, the possibility of escaping judgement and enjoying a direct journey to heaven with the rest of the brethren.

From the general history of the hospital, the earliest cemetery occupants would be expected to be predominantly male and many of them lepers. In time, as the hospital became an almshouse, the number of leprous skeletons would be expected to decline but the skeletons would still mostly be male. Later, female burials would become perhaps equally common as the hospital began to admit women. There is no historical record of the admission of children, and the 1594 list of inmates records no one under fifteen (see Appendix 3). It cannot be assumed that there were no children at the hospital at this time, but neither can it be assumed that the children's graves that appear in the archaeological record are necessarily those of inmates. Conversely, there may have been adults, and not just the healthy brothers and sisters, resident at the hospital who were buried elsewhere.

Wills give rough dates for these hypothetical phases of burial. The hospital inmates are called 'the poor' in a will of 1366–67 and are last referred to as lepers in 1418. At least as late as 1478, when a bishop's visitation was held, the inmates were still all male, but Walter Maryng's will of 1493 speaks unequivocally of the 'poor men *and women*' of the hospital, and in 1527 John Cressweller leaves money to 'every brother *and sister*' (see Appendix 4). From a date somewhere between 1478 and 1493, then, women were first admitted and, as far as is known, were accepted for the remainder of the hospital's existence. The reason for its foundation was, however, still remembered in the 16th century and in 1535 it was called 'The hospital or House of poor lepers'.[1] The sexes were represented in more or less even numbers in 1594 and the last known inmate in *c* 1685–89, under the mastership of Peter Edge, was a woman, although she seems to have been buried in St Pancras cemetery (McCann 1987).

The only specific reference to the graveyard, in the 1539 rental (Appendix 6), is not fully understood. Jacob West (possibly the 'prior' or senior inmate) and the others were collectively paying 1s for its lease but had to repair the cemetery wall. The use to which they put the cemetery is not given. As there is no reason to suppose that the graveyard was disused by this date, it seems most likely that the older part only was involved, perhaps utilised as a garden or for grazing.[2] There is a certain logic in the order of entries in the rental, with buildings listed before land and gardens, and the entry for Jacob West *et al* occurs at the end of the lands and gardens section. The shilling income that it produced for the hospital is the sort of money that was generated by the lease of a garden in St Pancras; perhaps the able-bodied inmates were cultivating the older part of it and selling the produce for profit. It seems that some rent had been remitted on condition that the wall was repaired, and this is the only written reference to a cemetery wall.

The archaeology: tombs

Excavations in 1986–87 and 1993 (for location, Fig 1.4) revealed a number of mortuary structures apart from individual graves, some of which seem to have influenced the cemetery layout. For this reason they are described and discussed in advance of an overview of the graveyard's layout and organisation. In this report the word 'tomb', ultimately derived from a Greek word meaning 'mound over a grave', is used for any burial other than those (the vast majority) that took place in pits in the ground.

The robbed northern structure 237/256 (Figs 7.1 and 7.2)

Two robbed walls at right-angles to each other were discovered on the northern edge of the 1986–87 site. The southern wall (237) was externally 6m long and the eastern (256) at least 3.6m, extending beyond the northern limit of the excavation. Both robber trenches were vertically truncated and as shallow

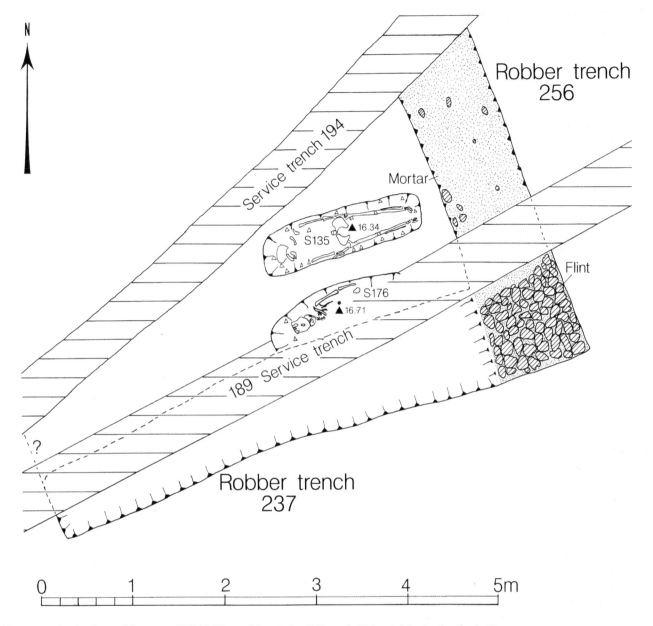

Figure 7.1 A plan of feature 237/256 and burials 135 and 176 within it. Scale 1:40

as 0.1m in places. Two modern service trenches had been dug through them, one, a pipe trench (189), mostly destroying the north edge of the southern robber trench and the other, a British Telecom trench (194), effectively delimiting the edge of the excavation.

The robbed east wall was about 1m wide and the south wall similar, as far as could be determined; it had been partially destroyed by the pipe trench 189. Where the two joined, a patch of flint nodules in lime mortar about 1m^2 survived; it was presumably the very base of the foundations. To the north, only loose mortar was found and to the west the backfill 238 was mainly gravel containing many flint nodules. That there was no hint of any associated floor is hardly surprising, given the shallowness of the trenches.

Although this part of the cemetery is almost exclusively male, the two skeletons enclosed by the walls,

135 and 176, were both of women aged 30 years or more (Fig 7.1). Nails indicated that both had been in wooden coffins. Eight small bronze pins, perhaps hairpins, were found around the skull of 176, some staining it green. This was a unique find in the cemetery, and reinforces the suggestion that this was a distinctive area for special burials. Such pins are elsewhere associated with the skeletons of nuns (see 'pins' under 'Grave Goods' below, and Chapter 8). A third grave, not shown in Fig 7.1, for skeleton 145, an adult male, partly lay across the supposed line of the west wall of the structure, apparently post-dating its robbing. There was room for a second column of burials in the structure west of 135 and 176 and, if a tomb, it may have been designed for at least four burials.

One of the greatest concentrations of burials in the cemetery lay due east of the structure. They

Figure 7.2 Feature 237/256 from the south-west. The vertical scale is in grave pit 135 and the other scale is in robber trench 237

included a few females. By contrast, to the south there was a strip up to 2m wide that was free of burials and may have been a path or processional route. The alignment of the structure may have been responsible for the orientation of burials in Area A east of the lime kiln which are closer to 'correct' than those at the western and eastern limits of the graveyard.

That the structure was in some sense 'special' seems plain since it acted as a focus for burials to the east. It could be argued that the two women within the structure were fortuitously incorporated and really pre-date it, but given the sparseness of female graves in the vicinity this would be difficult to sustain. It could equally be argued that the female burials are late and post-date the robbing of the structure. This is more supportable as a quantity of slate and decayed mortar recorded from the fill (293) of the grave for skeleton 135 could be interpreted as debris from robbing; it might, however, be construction debris. The most likely explanations seem to be either that the structure was mortuary and built specifically for the two women and perhaps others, or that it was built for some other purpose and the two females were granted the privilege of burial within.

The width of foundations would be appropriate for a substantial stone structure but their seeming shallowness, assuming the medieval and modern ground surfaces to have been similar, contradicts the idea. Perhaps some kind of mortuary house, what might today be called, inaccurately, a family vault, is to be envisaged, and the women within it were benefactresses of the hospital or otherwise

locally renowned for their piety.[3] At its simplest, it may have been no more than a walled enclosure although a wall width of around 0.6m would have been sufficient for that purpose. Alternatively, it could have been a side chapel or chantry of the hospital church, robbed in post-Dissolution days. The two pottery sherds recovered from the robber trench fill 238 were not diagnostic and could be dated no more closely than the 13th to 16th centuries. The graves within and associated with it yielded sherds of the 12th to 14th centuries and the late grave 145 overlying the supposedly robbed west wall was of 16th-century or later date. As the structure became a focus for subsequent burials it is regrettable that it cannot be dated more closely, but it is noteworthy that nearly all the burials north-east of this point could, on the basis of pottery alone, be as late as the 16th century. Some were almost certainly later.

A second mortuary structure 241 (Figs 7.3 and 7.4)

There was a second cluster of graves in the centre of the cemetery above and south of feature 241, which lay south of and on the same alignment as the structure described above. Feature 241 (Fig 7.3) was essentially a shallow rectangular pit, its base at about 16.12m OD, measuring 4.3m from east to west by 1.9m from north to south. On the north side were the remains of an insubstantial wall foundation composed mainly of flints and occasional fragments of tile and limestone that may once have enclosed the whole structure, and on the south side was a strip of gravel, perhaps the remains of its counterpart.

Central within the structure, and presumably the primary burial, was skeleton 88, a young to middle-aged adult with lepromatous leprosy. To the south was another burial, skeleton 115, a mature adult male with leprosy (Fig 7.4). The relationship between the two skeletons was undetermined and both were intact. In Figure 7.3 it has been assumed that 115 was the earlier, mainly to show full details of the supposed primary grave, but the opposite is at least as likely and it should be noted that 115 was shallower than 88. To the north was a further mature adult male, 55, whose skeleton carried no trace of the disease. The central and southern burials, as well as several others overlying the southern and eastern edges of 241, were both sealed beneath a later stone-lined tomb (65) containing skeletons 71 and 72 but the non-leprous northern burial was not, and may be intrusive.

The plot allocated for skeleton 88 is very close in internal length to the robbed northern structure 237/256 described above and reinforces the suggestion that the latter was essentially mortuary in nature. The skeleton was that of a tall man (1.8m) when compared to the site norm. No pottery was recovered from any associated contexts to help with dating the feature.

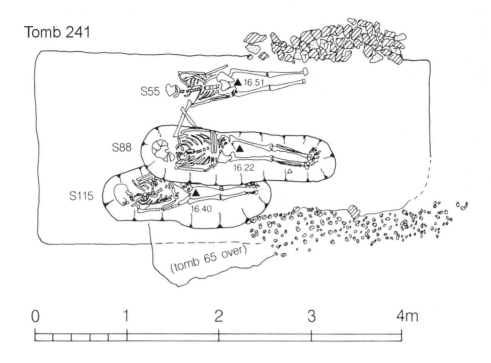

Tomb 241

0   1   2   3   4m

Figure 7.3 (above)   Tomb 241. Skeleton 115, a mature adult male, has early rhinomaxillary and other changes associated with leprosy. Skeleton 88, perhaps the earliest burial, is a young to middle-aged adult with similar changes. Skeleton 55, a mature adult male, has no trace of leprosy. Scale 1:40

Figure 7.4 (left)   Skeleton 115 in tomb 241. The burial was noteworthy for the number of pathological changes that had taken place (for an interpretation see Knüsel and Göggel 1993). Obvious in the photograph is remodelling of the distal end of the shaft of the right femur, a process that was ongoing at the time of death

The stone-lined tomb 65 (Figs 7.5 and 7.6)

On the south side of the feature described above, overlying its southern edge, was the shallow stone-lined tomb of skeleton 72, a mature adult, probably male, but with no other distinguishing characteristics. The interior of the tomb measured about 1.65 by 0.45m and the skeleton was a tight fit within it. Inexplicably, the rectangular space left for the corpse was misaligned within the tomb (Fig 7.5). The walls, mainly of mortared flints, were up to about 0.5m wide in places, their inner faces of dressed blocks of chalk and lime mortar, an unusual choice of building stone but probably dictated by the desire to give the tomb a white lining, a feature found at Bermondsey and elsewhere (Gilchrist and Sloane 2005, 135). The tomb was presumably marked above ground in some way, perhaps with a slab. No dating material was recovered. The tomb belongs to the final phase of use of this part of the cemetery, to a period when the

Tomb 65

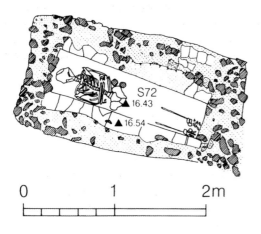

0   1   2m

Figure 7.5. Skeleton 72 in the stone-lined tomb 65. This was partly overlying tomb 241. Scale 1:40

mortuary structure 241 was still a focus for burials. Directly above this burial, and probably also deliberately interred in the tomb, was a second mature adult (71) of undetermined sex.

It has been suggested (Chapter 3) that normal practice was to dig the grave pit in the presence of the cortège. Where graves were stone-lined they had plainly to be prepared in advance of the burial party's arrival in the cemetery, and in this case the mismatch between corpse and grave pit is further confirmation that the corpse was elsewhere when the grave pit was dug. Stone-lined graves, sometimes described as 'cists', in cemeteries are apparently pre-Reformation and many seem to have been capped with slabs (Gilchrist and Sloane 2005, 134–40).

The charnel pit 668 (Figs 6.13 and 7.7)

What may for convenience be described as a charnel pit (668) was located in the north-east corner of the 1986–87 site. It was later than ditch 670 but earlier than grave 319, which had been cut through its upper

Figure 7.6 Skeleton 72 in tomb 65. The body was that of a mature male with a well-healed fracture of a rib but no other noteworthy features apart from degenerative conditions due to age

Figure 7.7 Bones within the charnel pit 668. An attempt had been made to gather up skulls and long bones but smaller bones were very much under-represented. The redeposition of the bones was apparently random with no attempt, for example, to put legs at one end and skulls at the other

filling. A modern service trench lay on the north-west side of the pit, and its closeness to the pavement and road, both still in use at the time of the excavations, meant that for safety reasons only the upper part of the pit could be investigated. The deepest level examined was about 2m below the modern ground surface. The complete plan of the pit could not be recovered as an unknown percentage of it lay beyond the excavated area, but it was around 3m across from west to east. The section illustrated (Fig 6.13) is composite, consisting of two sections at an angle to each other in the corner of the excavated area (see Fig 6.10).

The uppermost layer, cut by grave 319 but perhaps originally capping the whole pit, was of mortar with some gravel. Below it and more than 1m thick at its deepest was a layer (669) predominantly of clay with occasional flints. This too looked like deliberate infilling to level up the pit. Below it were alternating layers of gravel and loam above a layer consisting of mainly gravel and human bone at the lowest excavated level 688. The layers had plainly been tipped in from the north-western or cemetery side of the pit. The bones

represented a minimum of eight individuals. Five were adults of whom at least three were male, an adolescent, a child and a second child aged between one and three years. One of the adult males had evidence for leprosy and another individual had changes to the lower thoracic and upper lumbar vertebrae consistent with a diagnosis of tuberculosis. The bones were not laid out in any particular order (such as skulls to the west, legs to the east) and, as might have been expected, they were unrepresentative of the human skeleton, with skulls predominating.

The pit cannot be independently dated and its stratigraphic position relative to other features does not help as they are similarly undated. From the presence of children's bones it may be inferred that the burials were originally from the later cemetery which has been designated Area B (see below) as children are virtually absent from Area A. Charnel pits were often dug when a building extension resulted in the disturbance of a mass of burials, but the circumstances at Chichester must remain speculative. The depth of the pit and the depth at which burials occurred are both inexplicable. It would appear that when the pit was originally dug a very large number of bones was anticipated but in practice few were recovered. The first bones were encountered at about 1m below normal graves in the cemetery. It is just conceivable that the pit was dug for some other purpose and subsequently used as a charnel, but it seems too big for a well, for example, and it is equally difficult to imagine a use for the clay and flints that would have been excavated to make the hole. The pit may have been dug in a corner of the cemetery; this would be an obvious spot for a feature that was perhaps intended to be unobtrusive. If so, assuming the cemetery to have been rectangular, a rough guess could be made as to its total capacity, annual mortality rates and so on, assuming an average number of inmates, but this would be to pile speculation on top of speculation.

Charnel pits, a common feature of medieval cemeteries, represent a step beyond collecting up any stray bones for reinterment when a grave was next dug, but are relatively *ad hoc* when contrasted with charnel houses, ossuaries sometimes incorporating chapels that were an occasional feature of large medieval cemeteries. Charnel pits could occur both inside and outside buildings and were typically grave-shaped pits containing a miscellany of bones that had been collected and stored pending their eventual disposal. The choice of bones for retention and their disposition within the pit were occasionally bizarre. Within the church and churchyard of St Helen-on-the-Walls, York, were four charnel pits, the largest containing remains from about 70 skeletons but the most unusual was an arrangement of tibiae, femora and a humerus to form a square (Dawes and Magilton 1980, 17 and pl Vc). The Augustinian priory of St Mary, Merton (Surrey), has a careful arrangement of skulls and long bones (see Gilchrist and Sloane 2005, 195, fig 142), presumably a slightly odd act of piety rather than a joke in questionable

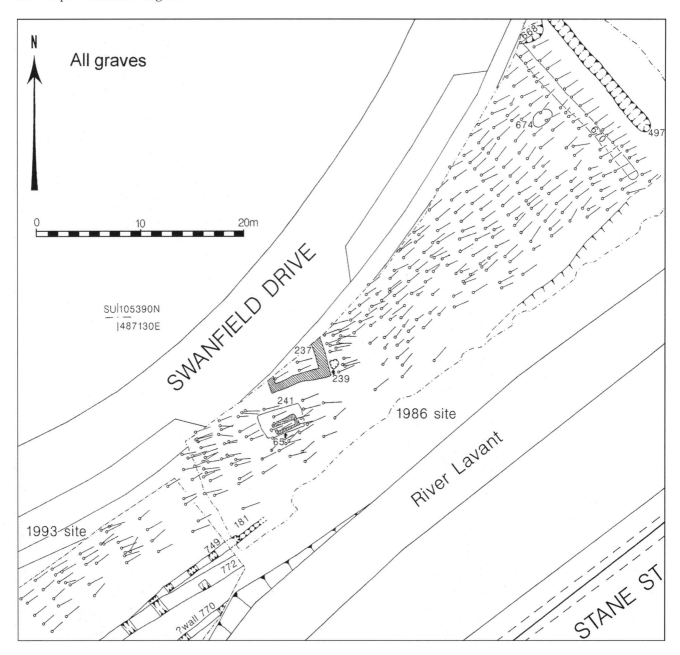

Figure 7.8 'Matchstick' plan of all graves for which an orientation could be recorded

taste by the gravedigger. The contents of charnel pits are generally skulls and long bones, the largest and most easily identifiable human bones.

If the charnel had been left open for a time, it may have had a minor role in focusing the minds of inmates on the common fate of mankind. Hermits, anchorites and other solitary religious had graves dug as part of the ceremony for their enclosure and the anchoress at St Anne's church, Lewes (E Sussex), had to kneel in an open grave to view the high altar through a squint (Godfrey 1928, 166–8).

General characteristics of the cemetery

Scrutiny of a plan showing graves of all periods (Fig 7.8) reveals a difference between the mainly

orderly layout of graves at the north-eastern end, a seemingly more chaotic area in the centre where grave intersections were common, and an area to the south-west, approximating to that of the 1993 excavation, where graves were sparser and intersections few. There is also an evident difference in the alignment of burials, with those in the north-eastern half approximating to south-west/north-east in orientation.

An interim report written after the 1986–87 excavations (Lee and Magilton 1989) postulated that the cemetery, as far as it was then known, exhibited a relatively simple sequence of development, the earlier graves being those to the south-west with a gradual expansion of the cemetery north-eastwards, although it was recognised that this hypothetical horizontal stratigraphy might not be true in

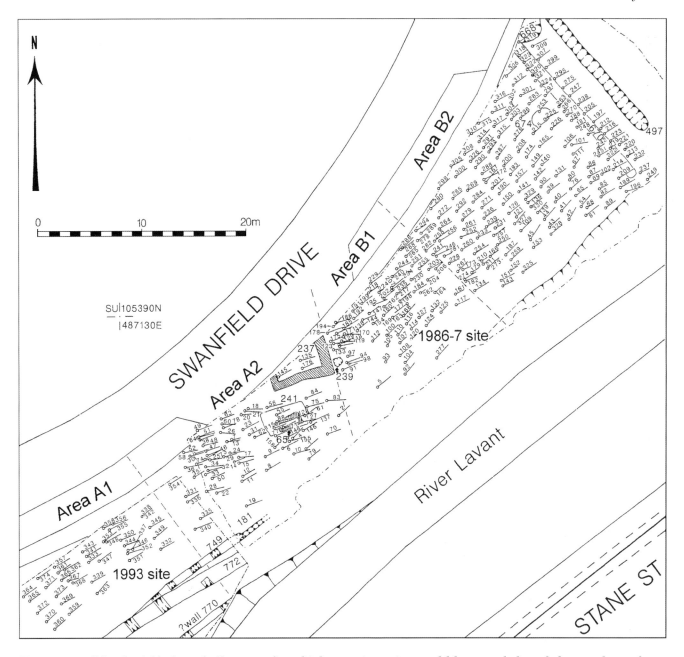

Figure 7.9 'Matchstick' plan of all graves for which an orientation could be recorded, and the numbers of each skeleton. The site is shown subdivided into Areas A and B, and each is further split into A1, A2, B1, B2

detail. The overall picture seemed to be borne out by the study of the skeletons themselves: the south-western burials were almost exclusively male and many had changes compatible with leprosy but the disease had seemingly become less prevalent by the time that female burials began to occur regularly in the central and north-eastern parts of the cemetery. There was a band of infant and child burials at the north-eastern edge of the cemetery of uncertain relative date.

This simple explanation was later criticised on the grounds that the argument was circular (Gilchrist 1992, 111–12). It was said, for example, that the predominantly male burials might be a product of a policy of segregation by sex within the cemetery at one stage in the hospital's existence and might not reflect the true population mix. Subsequent research using a variety of criteria has, however, confirmed the authors' original views to their satisfaction at least, and we still believe the general picture to be one of north-eastward expansion. We have abandoned an earlier subdivision of the site into three zones (Lee and Magilton 1989, 276, fig 3) in favour of a simpler division into Areas A and B (Fig 7.9) although each may be subdivided into two parts.[4] The mixed north-eastern half of the cemetery is thereby separated from the mostly male south-western half and, whilst a case can be made for other or extra divisions, depending on what criteria are employed, a line approximating to the one suggested has regularly reappeared when such apparently unrelated factors as the number of coffin nails in primary grave pits or the distribution of individuals under ten years old is plotted. What it means is

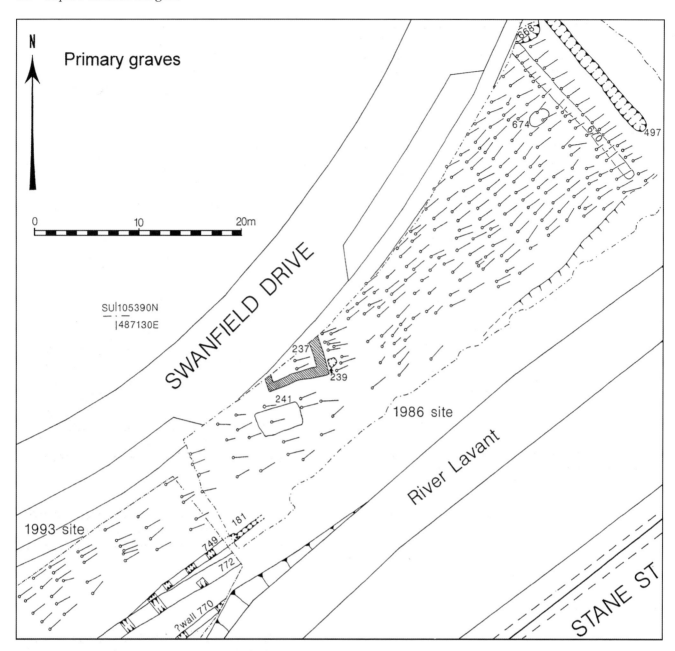

Figure 7.10 'Matchstick' plan of all primary graves for which an orientation could be recorded. The omission of secondary graves makes the organisation of the cemetery appear much clearer, particularly in the middle of the site. The burials of Area B are much more tightly packed than those of Area A. There are absences of burials that may reflect paths or processional ways across the site

open to question. No physical evidence survived for a division between 'new' and 'old' cemeteries unless gully 23 performed the function,[5] although one may have existed hereabouts, and what can be seen is most likely the product of a process rather than an event. There is not, for example, a dramatic reorganisation of the layout of the cemetery when women's and children's graves first appear, but they may be distinguished from those to the south-west by their alignments, which are closer to south-west/north-east than the liturgically correct orientation.

A potential subdivision within Area A is approximately that between the 1986–87 site and the 1993 excavation. There is a gap between a column of five graves, two of which were cut into the stoke hole of

an earlier lime kiln, and those to the north-east. The south-westernmost graves are aligned south-west/north-east but those beyond the gap are slightly closer to true west–east. The graves south-west of the line are relatively widely spaced with few intersections whilst those to the east are practically shoulder-to-shoulder. These south-westernmost burials may be termed for convenience the 'leper cottage group' and are referred to below as Area A1 and the north-eastern group as Area A2.

There is a similar although less easily defined distinction within Area B between the orderly graves in the north-eastern half (hereafter Area B2) and the seemingly chaotic graves of the south-western half (Area B1). At first glance the adjacent Areas A2 and B1 appear to have more in common with each other than the eastern and western extremes of the cemetery but, whilst the impression is sustainable when cemetery organisation is the only criterion, their composition is quite distinct.

It might be thought that enough is known about the history of the hospital in general, and of the turmoil created by the Reformation, to allow us to speak of old and new, or even Catholic and Protestant, parts of the cemetery, the disturbed burials in the centre representing that long period of uncertainty when no one could be sure that Protestant innovations would stick. Secondary graves in the 'old' cemetery could be interpreted as those of die-hard Catholics who sought a final resting place with their co-religionists, for example. Yet the archaeological evidence is less secure. No distinction can be seen between the 'Catholic' graves of the south-westernmost part of the cemetery and the 'Protestant' graves at the other end. It is very difficult to come up with absolute dates. Whilst the time span for the pottery fabrics in Area A is predominantly 12th to 14th century and that of Area B is 12th to 16th century, it does not follow that Area B is later (although other criteria indicate that it is). Nor is that other major change, the admission of women on a regular basis, necessarily a marker for the Reformation as one will, admittedly ambiguously worded, seems to note their presence by 1493 and another, not ambiguous but just possibly mistaken, puts them here in 1527 (see Appendix 4). Whilst it would be unreasonable to ignore the Reformation, it is a historical process that has no discernible impact on the cemetery archaeology.

A description of the cemetery

The general pattern

Cemetery layout, especially in the middle, at first appears chaotic although columns of graves can be made out, particularly at the extremes of the cemetery. Figure 7.10, which shows the cemetery with the secondary graves removed, immediately reveals two characteristics: first, that the primary burials in the south-western part (Area A) are less densely packed than those to the north-east, and secondly that many are slightly differently aligned. As it happens, many of the Area A burials are closer (but not very close) to true east–west as determined by the Ordnance Survey, but the governing factor is probably not a slavish adherence to the compass by gravediggers but a tendency to align graves parallel to the nearest straight line approximating to the correct orientation. It is perhaps the (unlocated) hospital chapel or the stone tombs in the vicinity that account for the alignment, just as, in Area B2 to the north-east, it is probably the line of Stane Street that dictates the alignment and, in the extreme south-west (Area A1), a precursor of the 'leper cottage'. The mean alignment of the cemetery as a whole was 240° (or south-west/

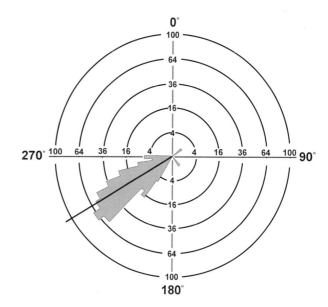

Figure 7.11 The orientation of burials. Three hundred and fifty-two skeletons were sufficiently well preserved for their orientation to be assessed. In the absence of any other influences, the mean for burials would be expected to be 270° (true west–east), but the Roman road, both directly and through structures built more or less parallel to it, has influenced orientation to the extent that the mean is south-west/north-east (Robinson 2003)

north-east; the 'correct' orientation is, of course, 270°) but more burials lay south of the mean than north of it. Figure 7.11 shows the mean alignment of graves (from Robinson 2003).[6]

Secondary burials

A secondary burial is defined as any grave that cuts or overlies an earlier grave; primary graves, in other words, are those cutting only natural earth or archaeological features pre-dating the cemetery. This is a simplistic definition since it is likely that, in a tightly packed graveyard with burials lying shoulder to shoulder in columns, there will have been accidental intersections where a new grave was dug so closely to its neighbour as to clip either the grave pit or the skeleton within. The new grave, technically secondary, will nonetheless properly belong with the primary organisation of the cemetery, as would a deliberate second burial in an earlier grave pit. Some of these suspect 'secondary' graves were identified with varying degrees of confidence during excavation and retrospectively from site records, but their identification can become subjective. A similar problem arises with burials such as 277, a young person with syphilis, in Area B (see Fig 7.17) that are geographically distant from the main concentrations. By the criterion used above, they must be considered primary but in practice, unless datable by associated

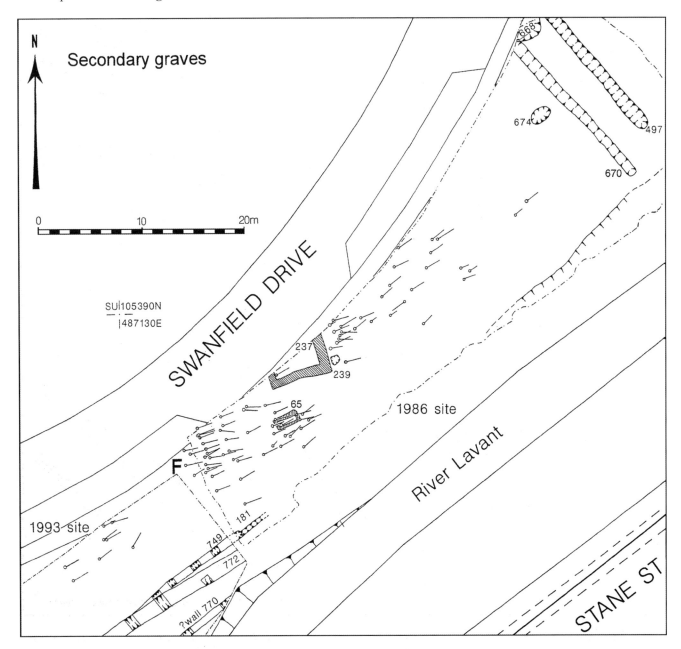

Figure 7.12 'Matchstick' plan of all secondary graves for which an orientation could be recorded. Most of the secondary burials were in the vicinity of the tombs in the middle of the site and an unknown focus ('F' on the plan) just outside the excavated area. Some of the burials, particularly those near 'F', represent a planned reuse of the cemetery, whereas others seem to occur randomly

artefacts, they could be of any phase. If they chance to line up with a column of graves considered secondary they have been assigned to that phase.

All the secondary graves for which an orientation could be recorded are shown on Figure 7.12. The extremes of the cemetery, particularly its north-east end, contain few secondary burials. Some secondary burials are misaligned when compared with primary burials and these may be late interments of a period when mounds[7] marking earlier graves had all but disappeared and the 'correct' alignment could not be discerned. Whether individuals occasionally actively sought burial in a disused part of the graveyard or were interred there because they were strangers, suicides or for some now irrecoverable reason not

welcome in the main area is unknown. They have no characteristics to suggest that they were in any way irregular burials (for example, interred by relatives at night because burial in the current part of the cemetery was likely to be refused).

Not all secondary burials were seemingly random intrusions. Those columns on the south-west side of the 1986–87 site (Area A2) represent phases of organised reuse of the cemetery by individuals wanting to be interred as closely as possible to some focus (its approximate position 'F' on Fig 7.12) just outside the excavated area. Tomb 241 and its successor tomb 65 were the foci for another group of burials, as was the east end of structure 237/256 or perhaps pit 239. Equally interesting are the

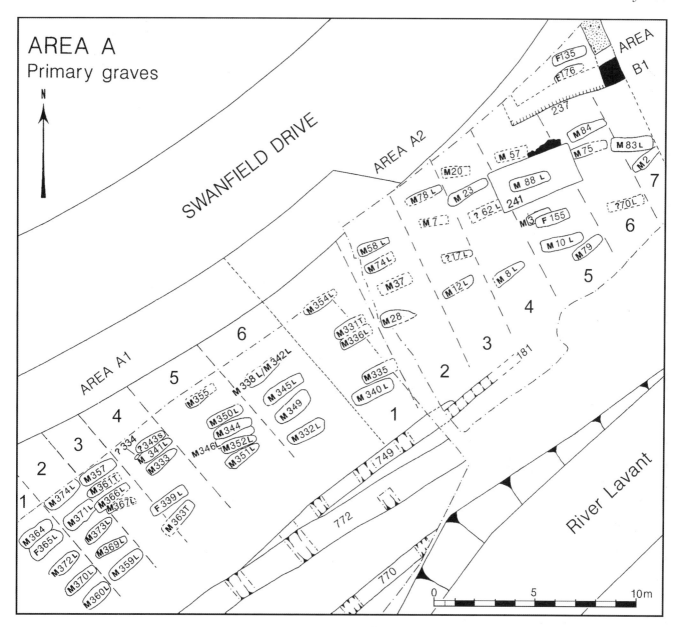

Figure 7.13 The primary graves of Area A. They have been subdivided into columns for ease of identification
Key: M = certain or probable male; F = certain or probable female; ? = undetermined sex; L = leprosy;
T = tuberculosis; S = ?syphilitic lesion

absences of graves. For example, as noted above, there is a strip clear of graves, both primary and secondary, just beyond the south wall of 237/256 where there had perhaps been a path, although it left no archaeological trace.

The relative dates of secondary graves are discussed further below (this chapter).

7.2   The dead: distribution by age, sex and disease

Area A1 (Fig 7.9)

The south-westernmost burials forming Area A1 are those of the 1993 excavations with the exceptions of skeletons 331, 335, 336, 340 and 354 on

the north-east, which are separated from the rest by a grave-free zone about 2m wide but adjoin the burials designated Area A2 (Figs 7.9 and 7.13). The burials of A1 are initially orderly and in shoulder-to-shoulder columns (see Fig 7.13 for the primary graves). The clearest column is the westernmost. Consisting of five skeletons (360, 364, 365, 370, 372), it is composed entirely of adults, at least three of whom (360, 365, 372) had skeletal changes due to leprosy by the time of death. The odd one out is 365, a young female with rhinomaxillary syndrome, since the others were certain or probable males. Although this skeleton lies closer to 364 than would be the case if spacing were exact, there is no reason to consider the female skeleton intrusive.

The second column (374, 371, 373, 369, 359) is almost equally distinct. All five were adult males,

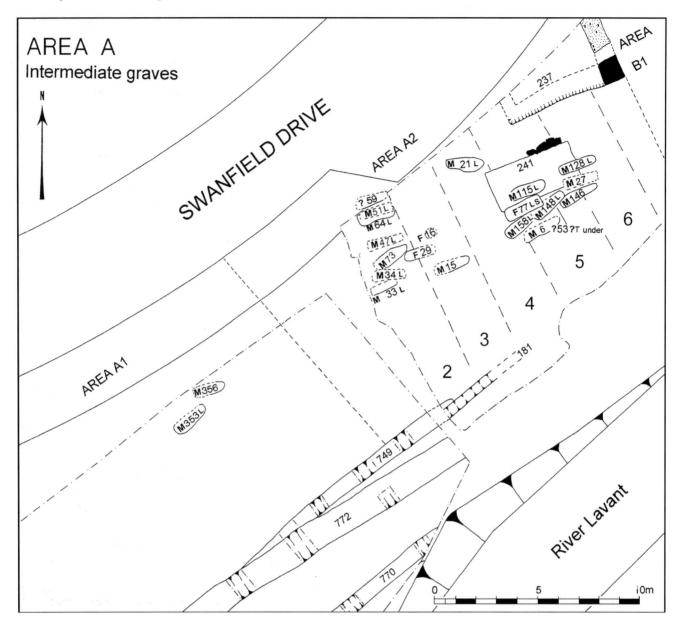

Figure 7.14   The intermediate graves of Area A, subdivided into columns for ease of identification. Nearly all lie in the vicinity of the tombs in Area A2

and all had changes consistent with a diagnosis of leprosy. The third column seems initially to have consisted of 357, 361, 366 and perhaps 367, all of them adult males. The grave pit of 367 appeared to clip that of 366 to the north but the skeleton was not disturbed. Two of the skeletons (366, 367) had leprous changes. Secondary burials (Fig 7.15), intrusive into the column and cutting away respectively the lower parts of 361 and 367, were 362 and 368, both mature adult males displaying no sign of leprosy. The fourth column is slightly less satisfactorily defined but probably comprised 343, 341, 333, 339 and 363, the skulls of which are more or less on a common line although it is not parallel to the first three columns. Two were leprous, 341, an adult, probably male, and a young female, 339. 343 was a mature adult, perhaps with a syphilitic lesion. 334, a piece of skull, may also have been primary. Skeleton

347 (Fig 7.15), an adult male with leprosy, appeared to be a secondary burial intruding into the line.

The fifth column appears quite confused. Potentially the latest burials, as no others cut them, are 358, 348, 337 and 352. This is, however an instance where a slavish adherence to stratigraphy may obscure the truth. Visual scrutiny suggests that 350, 344, 346, 352 and 351 form a column of burials. They are tightly packed with heads to a common line and most are demonstrably earlier than 337, an adult male on a different alignment. All five were adult males, four of which have certain or probable leprous changes (the exception was 344). To the north, 355, a young adult male, may also belong to this group. It was cut by 356, another adult male, and that in turn by 358, an adult, probably female. In the vicinity, and in effect between columns 4 and 5, were 353 (with leprosy) and 348 (with early rhinomaxillary

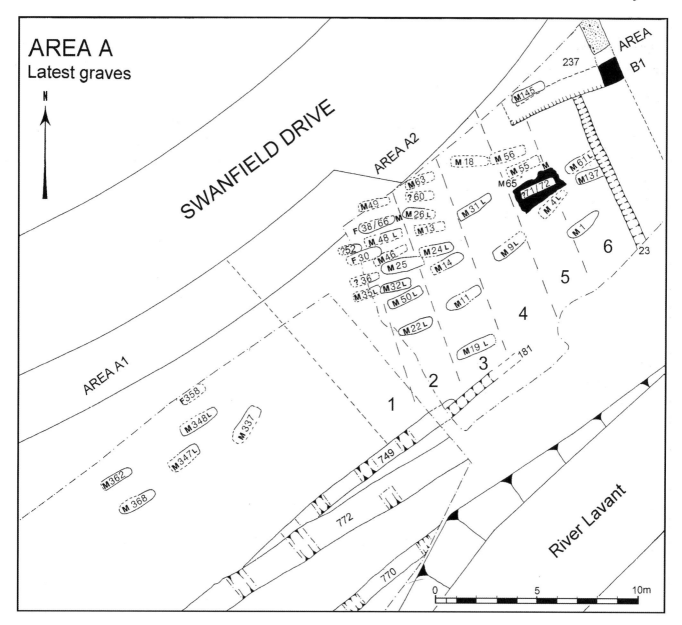

Figure 7.15 The latest graves of Area A, subdivided into columns for ease of identification. Like the intermediate burials, nearly all lie in the vicinity of the tombs in Area A2

syndrome) cut through it; both are adult males. The sixth and final column is again an orderly one, consisting of 338/342, 345, 349 and 332. The double grave consists of two males (342 and 338) both with evidence for leprosy; these are perhaps kinsmen. The other three burials were all adult males, and 345 has leprosy.

A number of features invite comment, but at this stage it will be restricted to matters of cemetery organisation. Perhaps the first necessary observation is that the cemetery is managed. There are some burials, usually demonstrably secondary, that on occasion obscure the pattern, but overall the graves consist of columns of (liturgically) west–east inhumations (in practice, south-west/north-east) with heads to a common line. The burials were all adult and nearly all male. The only certain females amongst the primary burials (339, 365) had leprous

changes. The graves become more ragged in terms of spacing and orientation from south-west to north-east, and this could represent increasing carelessness over time. It must be emphasised that the excavated graves represent the southern ends only of columns, each column with perhaps 20 or more graves in it, so the retreat from orderliness may not have been rapid.

The chronology of the primary graves (Fig 7.13) seems to be demonstrated by the incidence of leprosy. Of the fourteen skeletons in the first three columns, only three (364, 357, 361) are apparently unaffected by the disease. This represents 78.5% lepers. The seventeen skeletons in columns 4–6 have ten cases of leprosy between them (59% lepers). The north-eastern graves, columns 4–6, apparently date to a period when leprosy was fractionally less prevalent but, given the small sample size, this is no more than

Figure 7.16   Skeletons 32–36, some of the first burials to be uncovered in 1986 in Area A2. They were mostly men with leprosy. Scale divisions 0.5m

a statistical quirk. It must always be remembered that what we can distinguish between are individuals so badly afflicted with leprosy that the skeleton was affected and others who may have been disfigured by the disease but suffered no skeletal changes. In practice, all the individuals in Area A1 may have been lepers, and their contemporaries would have made no distinction between those who suffered skeletal change and those in whom the changes were more superficial. Even in legal terms, it was the degree, not the nature, of deformity that determined how individuals were to be regarded.

The eight secondary burials (Figs 7.14 and 7.15) have features in common with each other. There were only three demonstrable lepers amongst them (38%), although 'lepers' formed 68% of the primary burials.[8] The secondary burials do not respect the earlier layout of the cemetery and they may also be differently aligned, perhaps because the original layout had become obscured. Nor do they resemble a second planned graveyard superimposed on the first and they do not appear to be clustering around any particular focus. *All* the graves are secondary in the sense that this part of the site was first used for a

lime kiln and, as a group, they cannot belong to the earliest phase of the hospital.[9]

It is just conceivable that, as a group, all the burials of A1 are later than the primary burials of A2, marking a phase in the hospital where badly afflicted female lepers for whom there was no local institutional provision were first admitted. If so, it was never a particularly popular part of the cemetery when its few secondary burials are contrasted with those from Area A2.

Area A2

The north-eastern half of Area A looks at first sight impossibly jumbled (Fig 7.9) but analysis has revealed a much more orderly picture, albeit one where clustering around foci has occurred.

One focus is assumed just beyond the western corner of the 1986–87 site ('F' on Fig 7.12). A dense concentration of graves just within the excavated area, many on a different alignment to those of Area A1, was recorded (Fig 7.16). As lower legs were seen protruding from the section, this hypothetical focus, whatever its nature, must be assumed to lie at least 1m beyond the excavated area. The clustering of graves in the vicinity of tomb 241 and its successor, 65, also in Area A2, attests to another focus, and structure 237/256 on the western edge of Area B1, where the same phenomenon may be observed, is a third. Although this last structure may be a further tomb, a hospital building, particularly part of the chapel, would in all likelihood have had a similar influence.

It was here that construction work began in 1986, and the machine excavation of foundation trenches damaged many burials. However, by restoring these skeletal fragments to their approximate original size and estimating the dimensions of the grave pits which once accommodated them, and doing the same for burials truncated by later interments, a much more regular pattern of burials in columns emerges with essentially three phases of cemetery: early burials, which do not cut any others, intermediate burials, which cut or overlie early graves but are themselves cut by later ones, and late burials which cut or seal others but are not themselves cut by any graves.

The south-westernmost column of the early burials (Fig 7.13) in Area A2 consisted of, from north to south, 354, 331, 336, 335 and 340, all males and three of them (336, 340, 354) lepers. The next column east comprised 58, 74, 37 and 28, all of which were either cut or part-sealed by later graves. Three were certainly and the fourth probably male, and two (58, 74) had leprous changes. In the third column were 78, 7, 17 and 12, all adults, three male and the other undetermined, three of them (12, 17, 78) leprous. The column was about 2.5m away from the burials of column 2 and the distance between each grave was a fairly regular one of about 1.5m. Those assignable to the primary phase in column 4 were 20 (cut by 18) and 62 (cut by 31), respectively an adult male and an adult of undetermined sex, 8 and 23, both male, neither of which was cut by a later grave. Of the four skeletons, two (62, 8) had leprosy. Although the graves were a generous distance apart when measured shoulder-to-shoulder, the column is very close to column 3, and could almost be described as interlocking with it. The primary graves of column 5 were 57, 88 (the occupant of tomb 241), 3, 10 and 79, all male, two of them (10, 88) leprous. An early grave of a mature female, 155, is not technically primary as it post-dated 3 but its position is illustrated here (Fig 7.13) as the relevant figure is overcrowded. Those unaffected by leprosy were all adults. Column 6 consisted of three burials only (84, 75 and 70), two males and one (70) a leper of undetermined sex, and column 7 of two adult males (83 and 2), one of which (83) was leprous. In all, 29 burials have been ascribed to this primary phase (including the two women in tomb 237). Thirteen (45%) were certain or probable lepers, and these were mostly in the first four columns. Twenty-four (83%) were male or probably male and three were undetermined. Burials become generally less orderly from south-west to

north-east. The two women in tomb 237 are, as far as is known, primary but are obviously 'different', intruders in what was at the time virtually an all-male cemetery.

Next came an intermediate phase of graves (Fig 7.14) cut through one or more of the above but also cut by later interments. There were no intermediate burials in the first column of Area A2. Column 2 consisted of 59, 51, 64, 47, 73, 34 and 33. All were adult, the six for whom the sex could be determined were male and five (33, 34, 47, 51, 64) were certain or probable lepers. The only certain intermediate burial in column 3 was 15, a middle-aged man, and in column 4 the only intermediate grave was 21, a young man with leprosy. Column 5 comprised 115, 77, 158, 148 and 6, four of which were leprous (the exception was 6). All were male apart from 77, a female with leprosy. Column 6 contained only three burials (128, 27 and 146), two certain and one probable male, one of which (128) was leprous. Although these intermediate burials have been described for convenience as forming columns, they might better be attributed instead to two clusters, one around the putative western focus (columns 2 and 3, as well as burials 16 and 29, the latter both potentially female) and the other cluster, including burial 53, a child with TB, around tomb 241. Twenty burials have been ascribed to this intermediate phase, seventeen in columns and three outside. Only one of the skeletons in columns (77) was demonstrably female and none was a child. Eleven (55%) were certain or probable lepers.

The latest graves (Fig 7.15) in column 2 were 49, 38/66, 48, 46, 25, 32, 50 and 22. All were male or probably male apart from 38, a female, which shared a grave with 66, a mature male. Grave 32 contained two individuals, both males and one (32b) with probable leprosy. Three of the nine (22, 48, 50) were certain lepers. West and south of this column were the legs of four skeletons, the remainder of which were mostly beyond the edge of the site (column 1: 52, 30, 36 and 35), one of them (30) female and another (35) a leper. In column 3 the latest burials were 63, 60, 26, 13, 24, 14, 11 and 19. All were men apart possibly from 60 (undetermined) and three (19, 24, 26: 38%) were lepers. Compared with the early burials, they were close to each other and to their contemporaries in column 2. In column 4 the latest burials were 18, 31 and 9, all of them adult males and two of them (9, 31) lepers. Column 5 consisted of 56, 55, 71/72 in the stone-lined grave, 65, 4 and perhaps 1. All were adult and probably male apart from 71, which was unsexed. Skeleton 4 was leprous. Column 6 started with 145, an adult male overlying the supposed west wall of tomb 237/256 and therefore post-dating its demolition. Immediately south of the tomb was a burial-free strip over 1m wide, and to the south of this, forming the rest of the column, were 61 and 137, one of whom, an adult male (61), was possibly leprous. Thirty-four burials in all have been ascribed to the final phase, of which two were female and the remainder, where the sex could be determined, adult males. Twelve (35%) were lepers, compared to 55% of the intermediate burials and 45% of primary burials. The distribution of burials was inclined to be, as with the intermediate phase, around two foci but the first two columns were orderly and full and those in the vicinity of the tombs were less clustered.

The overall picture of Area A2 is that of a phase of more or less regular primary burials succeeded by an intermediate phase when tomb 241 acted as one focus and an unknown feature to the west of the site another, and a final phase when order was restored but a clustering is nevertheless observable around the foci of the intermediate phase. The graves were overwhelmingly those of adult males. There were fewest lepers amongst the latest burials but the percentage was not dramatically reduced.

Area B1 (Fig 7.9)

Area B effectively begins east of feature 237/256 and Area B1 is its south-western part. Defining the north-eastern edge of B1 is a more subjective matter for, although it may in theory be said to end where orderly burials in columns recommence, drawing such a line on a plan is somewhat arbitrary and for present purposes grid line 38E of the 1986 site grid has been used. Area B1 is generally distinguished from A2 by the presence of non-adults and women, who together make up well over half of the cemetery population in this area. The alignment of burials is another distinguishing feature, for although those backing onto tomb 237 are on what might be termed the Area A orientation, the remainder lie with their heads more to the south-west. The presence of infants and children makes it harder to appreciate cemetery organisation since they obviously occupy something smaller than an adult-sized grave pit.

Graves due east of 237 form superimposed columns similar to column 1 in Area A2. One distorting factor is a near-square pit 239 about 1m across lying next to the robbed wall 256. As suggested in Chapter 6, it perhaps held a tree that was standing before the first burials were made in the vicinity and perhaps even pre-dated structure 237/256. Tree roots had damaged several nearby skeletons. On the other hand, the pit is almost exactly central within the graveyard; a central cross was a common feature of cemeteries and a focus for burials.

The earliest burials (Fig 7.17) were, from north to south, 178, 175, 123, 133, 97, 94 and 91. All were adult males apart from 97, an infant of unknown sex, and 94 and 133, which were female; none of the skeletons was leprous. The infant burial had been made in an irregular earlier pit 227 east of pit 239 that may have been dug for gravel extraction. Also possibly of this group is burial 5, an adult male some distance to the south, and 130, a grave containing the remains of a mature adult male (130a) and a youth (130b) in his early teens.

The intermediate burials (Fig 7.18) were 194,

perhaps 185, 170 and 118. The first was a child of eight or thereabouts, the next a probable male, the third another child and the last a young man. Burials 194, 170 and 118 had their heads to a common line and resembled a planned column, whereas 185 lay to the north-east. The latest burials (Fig 7.19) were 186, 171a, 171b, 129, 124, 119, 113a, 113b, 113c and 98. The assemblage labelled 113 consisted of two adult males and parts of a child; the assemblage labelled 171 consisted of an adult female and a probable adult male. The rest were all adults, two males (98, 129), two female (119, 124) and one possibly female (186). The presence of both sexes and the range of ages would be appropriate for a family group, and it is possible that all were kin of the two women in structure 237/256.

The remainder of Area B1 was characterised by an apparent lack of organisation. Its western edge is, however, quite apparent when only the primary burials are plotted. One noteworthy aspect of B1 is the number of non-adult burials, many of which are primary (Fig 7.25). Most lie in a band towards the south-eastern end of the site but they do not form any other obvious pattern. They generally differ in orientation from the burials next to feature 237. No topographical feature is known to explain the alignment and even if it were, it would not explain why seemingly contemporary adult graves did not share it to the same degree. Whilst intersections between burials are not common, it is impossible to see any certain scheme of cemetery management beyond a usually successful attempt not to disturb neighbouring graves. One possibility is that the southernmost child burials (from 93 on the south-west to 161 and 206 on the north-east) pre-date the adult interments and belong to a period when, as in Area B2, it was customary to inter non-adults along the cemetery boundary. If this were so, some of the burials to the north may be seen as the ends of columns of graves with heads to a common line. For example, 240, 235, 217, 198 and 168 could form a slightly askew column.

Of the adult burials that were or could have been primary (Fig 7.17), twelve were certain or probable females, and there were seventeen certain or probable males, five of which had leprosy (117, 195, 199, 227, 235) and a sixth TB (104). The incidence of leprosy in adults is 20.5%, compared with 35% for the latest burials of Area A2. Subadults slightly outnumbered adults, totalling 33 burials in all.

The intermediate burials of B1 (Fig 7.18) had little in common with each other. If grave 185 is included, they comprised two probable (185, 243) and one certain (118) adult males, two adult females (138, 177), an adult of undetermined sex (234) and five children. A noteworthy grave was the one containing 177, a young adult female, who was interred with her head to the east, presumably in a coffin in which head and foot could not be distinguished.[10] There were no lepers at all in this assemblage.

The latest graves (Fig 7.19) were similar, consisting of seven women, two of them (144, 202) with

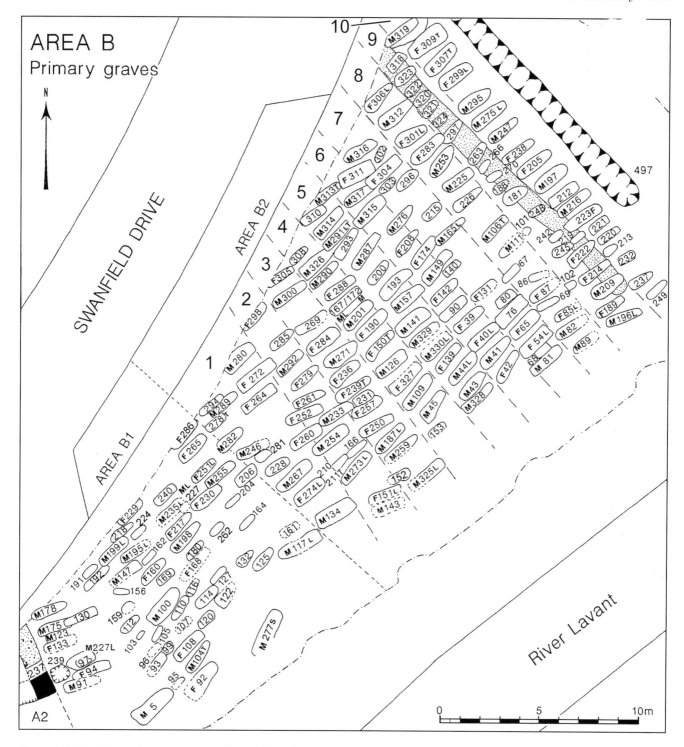

Figure 7.17 The primary graves of Area B, subdivided into columns for ease of identification. Area B2 in particular is plainly a 'managed' cemetery with regular columns of graves

leprosy, and six men (98, 113a, 113c, 171b, 244, 268). Of the two non-adults, one was a baby (183) buried alongside, perhaps with, one of the leper women. The adult of undetermined sex (203), perhaps suffering from TB, lay on the arbitrary boundary between B1 and B2.

The children of Area B1 are of all ages to adolescent but older children (6–12 years old) are under-represented. However, children and adolescents are not equally susceptible to disease throughout each

year of childhood and the absence of juveniles in the cemetery does not mean that they were not to be found in the hospital. Children in general are discussed further below.

A feature of some of the graves in B1 that becomes commoner in B2 is the presence of 'ear muffs' (see Fig 7.23). In other parts of England (see Chapter 3) they can be a feature of Anglo-Saxon graves but at St James' they occur with the later burials. Typically they consist of a flint on each side of the skull as if

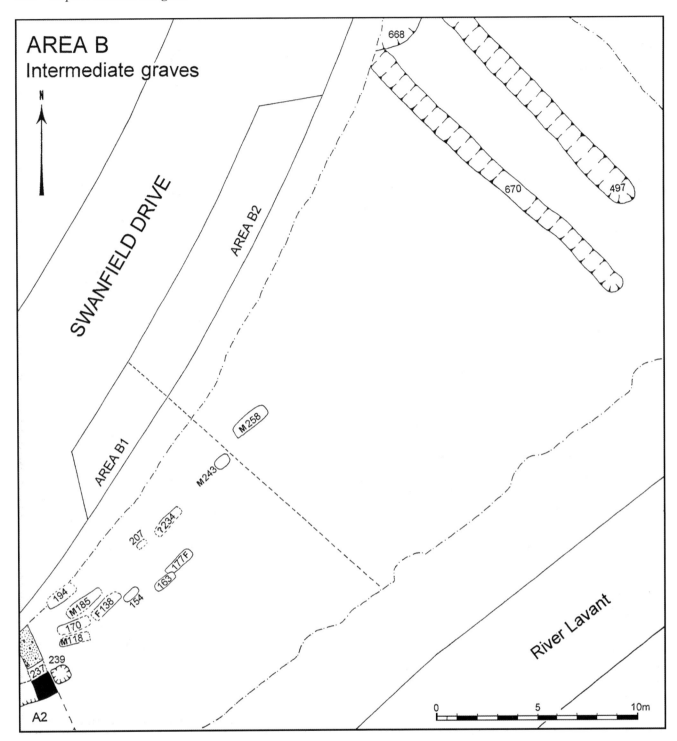

Figure 7.18 The intermediate graves of Area B. These are almost entirely found in Area B1

intended to wedge it in position. Given the flinty and gravelly nature of the subsoil through which the burials were dug, the occurrence of stones in these positions could occasionally be fortuitous although the 'ear muff' stones were generally bigger than those found naturally on the site. Examples of the practice from B1 were with 199 (adult male), 160 (adult female), 251 (probably female), 255 (adult male) and 108 (adult female), all of them potentially primary burials. There were six examples in all from Area A1, all but two from the earliest phase of graves.

Area B2

The fourth and final subdivision of the cemetery is the most obviously 'planned'. As noted, its south-western edge is somewhat arbitrary. Its north-eastern limit is the ditch 497. The burials, of men, women and children, are in columns with few intersections between graves or other noteworthy features.

Although the plan (Fig 7.17) has been subdivided into columns for convenience, it is not easy to decide where the first column of primary burials is to be

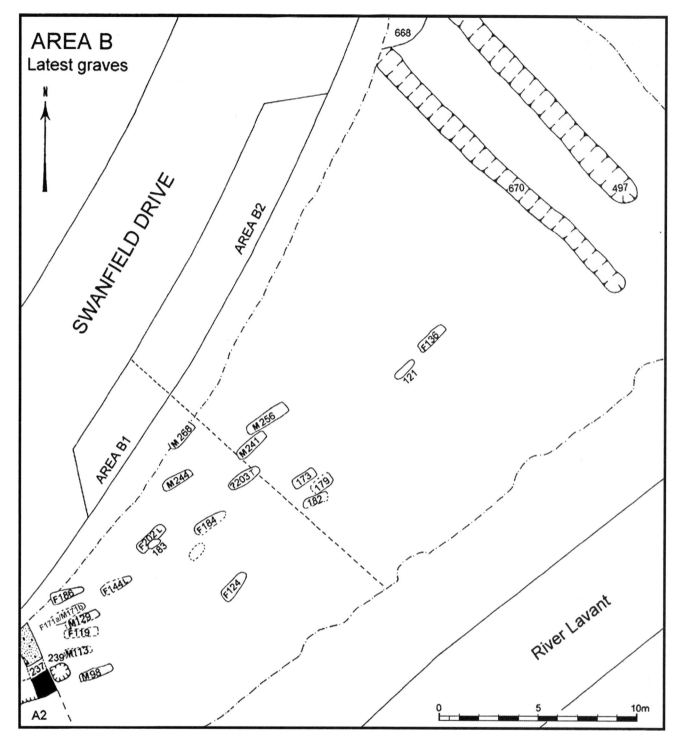

Figure 7.19   The latest graves of Area B. These, like the intermediate graves, are almost entirely found in Area B1

found. One beginning with grave 305 and ending with 325 (column 3) seems secure, and so are all those north-east of it. To the south-west is a more ragged column (column 2) extending from grave 298 to 143 but the centre is confused by burials 233, 252 and 260, which intrude into adjacent columns. They may be secondary but they do not cut or overlie any earlier graves. The westernmost column (column 1), on a different alignment to the rest, is still reasonably convincing. It begins with 294 and extends to 134. The few demonstrably secondary burials of B2

(Figs 7.18 and 7.19) are mostly above or close to this column.

The remaining columns require little comment. Column 4 contained a double burial in a single grave pit of a middle-aged to mature man (172) below a young man (167); they were perhaps kinsmen. It was otherwise an unremarkable mix of men, women and children. Most of the graves in column 5 contained men and there was one example (310) of a grave clipping the pit to the north, reinforcing the idea that the columns of graves extended from north to south.

A unique feature of Area B2 was charnel pit 668, which had been dug through the original inner ditch of the cemetery 670 but was enclosed within the outer ditch 497. It was too close to the road to be investigated thoroughly and neither its plan nor section was completely recovered (for a description, see pp.88–9). The upper fill 669, in practice a number of distinct layers, was cut by the pits for burials 309 and 319, both of them in the final column of graves.

Another noteworthy feature was a clustering of babies and young children in the inner ditch 670. It is most likely that this column of burials had been formed over a period of time, not that a single disastrous event that had wiped out a large number of children, and that many, if not most, of the burials had taken place before the column of graves to the south-west had been dug. In other words, it had long been the custom of the hospital to bury many of its infants and children on the edge of the cemetery before the graveyard went out of use. The graves themselves belonged mainly to young children including infants. There is a dearth of older children, the vast majority being no more than six and a half years old. There was only one certain intersection between these burials and those immediately to the west: the grave for skeleton 283 was later than that for 297, thus reinforcing the idea that the children were interred in the ditch before the rest of the cemetery had expanded up to the ditch edge. A similar, smaller cluster occurs outside the ditch at its south end.

The intermediate and latest burials of B2 (Figs 7.18 and 7.19) are few and apparently random in distribution. Two of the secondary burials, 121 and 136, respect the columns established for primary burials and, except in a technical sense, may well belong with the other primary burials.

The date and growth of the cemetery

There is an almost endless variety of ways in which a cemetery may be planned and infilled (for some examples, see Chapter 3, Fig 3.5). The commonest approach today would probably be to make a first interment in the north-west corner and put subsequent burials in a column until the southern boundary of the site was reached. The next burial would head the second column, and so on until the cemetery was full.

Yet, even if the general principle is burial in shoulder-to-shoulder columns, it can be carried out differently in practice. One obvious variation would be to work boustrophedon, so that when the bottom of one column was reached the first burial of the next column would be at the southern end of the site. Another way would be to start in the middle of a site and work outwards until the cemetery closed. This might well be the obvious method if the focus of a site were a churchyard cross or similar, and could result in a circular cemetery. Round cemeteries are known in the Early Christian Celtic west and this

plan of burials is attested in Ireland. Other cemeteries could well be polyfocal with, say, a chapel at one end attracting some burials and a churchyard cross in the middle attracting others, resulting in a pattern of clusters. In a culture where the orientation of burials was unimportant, these could be radial in plan.

Further variation could result from burying certain elements of the community apart from the rest. Segregation by age, sex and occupation are all possible and all attested. In the case of a hospital, a distinction might well be made between carer and inmate, the staff being buried apart from the patients. At St James' Chichester, for example, the staff may have expected and generally received burial at the Cathedral, whereas at a monastic hospital lay and religious might well have been buried on the same site but in different locations.

A generally straightforward picture may be additionally complicated by the choice exercised by individuals to do something unusual for reasons of pride or piety. In the case of a hospital, the right of burial may have been extended to the more generous benefactors and its cemetery might in theory be composed of a large majority of sick poor and a difficult to identify minority of well-to-do patrons. Alternatively, those who considered hospital burial a privilege may have foregone it for reasons of humility.

Leprosy as a chronological indicator (Fig 7.20)

As restated above, it is still contended that the earliest graves are those on the south-west of the 1986 site (Area A1) and that they grow progressively later until the most recent burials are encountered at the north-east (Area B2). However, the simple picture is confused by, for example, secondary burials and a tradition of interring children on the periphery of the cemetery. One means of checking the hypothesis is to look at the incidence of leprosy, which is universally accepted to have declined in the later Middle Ages.

There is scope for a number of complicating factors. The hospital may have favoured the admission of the sick poor rather than lepers in later medieval times, although there is no written evidence that it did, and thus lepers may be under-represented amongst the latest burials. Conversely, in the later Middle Ages and beyond, as erstwhile rivals to St James' closed down, all of Chichester's lepers may have ended up in the sole surviving hospital and their numbers may thus be inflated amongst the late burials. Nevertheless, the statistics, despite these and other caveats, seem to tell a reasonably consistent story.

Some 61.5% of the adults in Area A1 had leprosy. When Area A2 came into use, that figure falls to 43%. By the time that Area B1 was in use, the figure was 15%, staying at 15% in Area B2 (Table 7.1). The Area B figures are higher than might have been expected if, as is believed, these skeletons are amongst the latest hospital burials. These, it must

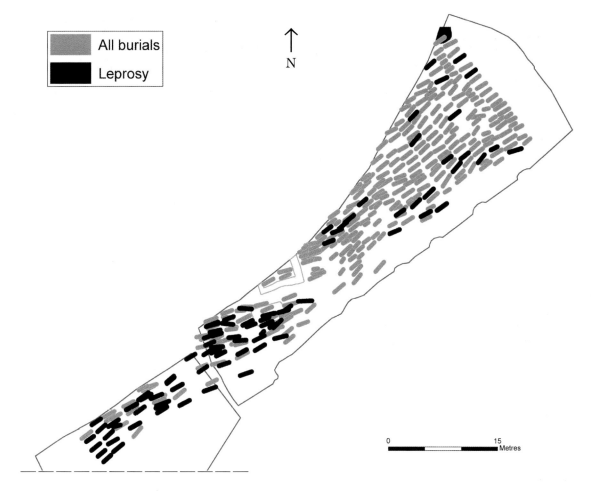

Figure 7.20   The distribution of individuals with leprosy

again be emphasised, are minimum figures as it is impossible to estimate how many had the disease but suffered no skeletal changes. Interestingly, the percentage of men and women with the disease is about the same by the time that Area B2 came into use, whereas in Area B1 leprosy had disproportionately afflicted men.

The primary burials of A1 are not particularly early and they can be reasonably well dated from pottery in the backfilled lime kiln through which some of them were dug. The whole of the excavated cemetery may be late (14th to 17th century) and an earlier cemetery with a still higher incidence of leprosy may await discovery nearby.

Pottery as a chronological indicator

On ceramic grounds the primary excavated burials of Area A1 cannot be earlier than the 14th century (pottery with skeleton 338) and this figure represents a *terminus post quem*. Most of the assemblages consisting of twelve or more sherds were from Area B and appear to represent a discrete area of domestic waste fortuitously incorporated into graves. Pottery in general is discussed in Chapter 8.

A few of the A2 graves contained pottery no earlier than the 16th century but these are all demonstra-

bly secondary and very little pottery was recovered from primary graves in A2. Area B1 is in general characterised by a pottery fabric that could be as early as the 12th century but which occurs in Area A1 only in a secondary grave and in A2 in only two or three instances. The same fabric is found, slightly less frequently, in Area B2, where one of the later graves, 54, contained pottery of 16th-century or later date. In all, the excavated cemetery seems to represent at most about 400 years of interments, the earliest excavated graves being no earlier than *c* 1300 on the basis of pottery and the latest no later than *c* 1700 on historical grounds.

The interpretation of secondary burials

Secondary burials in A1 total eight and constitute 20% of all burials. In A2, however, they are 64% of the total. In other words, when the area initially set aside for graves (Areas A1 and A2) was full, those entitled to a hospital burial much preferred interment in the north-eastern half (Area A2) of the original cemetery. As noted above, although the intermediate burials of Area A2 may be assigned to columns for convenience of description, in reality they form two clusters, one around tomb 241 and the other north-east of a focus just beyond the excavated area ('F' on Fig 7.12). For the latest burials in A2 some form of cemetery management is re-established and columns of burials are again distinguishable, albeit that those columns closest to the assumed off-site focus are the most densely packed. In Area A1 the relatively few secondary burials appear as a scatter with no particular focus and no trace of organisation.

Without secondary burials the general layout of the cemetery is much clearer and it needs to be asked when and why secondary burials, which are mostly a feature of Area A2 and Area B1, took place (Fig 7.12). In a parish graveyard it might be suspected that burial had been requested with or next to a close relative (spouse, parent or child) but this cannot have been an important factor in what was originally an all-male hospital. A wife, son or daughter may occasionally have sought burial next to a deceased inmate and paid an appropriate fine, but such instances will have been rare. Secondary graves in medieval urban cemeteries are often a consequence of overcrowding, a lack of opportunity to expand the cemetery and not infrequently contraction due to encroachment by adjacent properties. At St James', at least in theory, the whole 10-acre site could have been used for burials if needed, even if there may have been a reluctance to enlarge the area (Area A) originally set aside for burials.

One reason for the presence of secondary burials in Area A is, as discussed above, the attraction exerted by tomb 241 and its occupant and the nearby off-site focus that has been deduced. The same criterion applies in Area B1, where feature 237/256 was the focus for the earliest burials and some secondary interments. In contrast with Area A, the secondary burials of Area B (Figs 7.12, 7.18 and 7.19) have no obvious patterning and are not a consequence of replanning and reusing part of the cemetery. They are perhaps most likely a result of lax cemetery management in an era of change that saw women and children regularly admitted for the first time. There are virtually no secondary graves in B2.

Do the secondary burials of Area A represent a final use of this part of the cemetery before B1 became available for burials or are some or all of the secondary graves contemporary with the use of B1 or even later? As the two most important characteristics of B1 are the presence of women and children, the question can be rephrased to ask whether either group is disproportionately present amongst the secondary interments of Area A. Children can be ruled out immediately, but women are perhaps significant. In Area A1 there was a probable woman (358) amongst the latest burials. In Area A2 three probable women (16, 29 and 77) have been assigned to the intermediate graves. The latest graves in A2 potentially include three more women, 30, 38 and 155, although the last may be primary. A maximum of seven certain or probable women amongst the intermediate and latest burials of Area A is not at first glance impressive, but there are only two women (339 and 365), both lepers, amongst the primary burials if 155 and the two occupants of feature 237/256 are excluded. The secondary female burials included only one skeleton (77) with signs of leprosy.

Area A (in particular, Area A2) may have become available for female burials just before the cemetery was expanded into Area B1 at a time when women were still a distinct minority and children, if present, were buried elsewhere. An alternative is that certain individuals who would normally have been interred in Area B1 were allowed into Area A. If this were considered a privilege, it would more likely have been bestowed on men than women, and rarely, if ever, on children. In chronological terms, the secondary burials of Area A may be considered as intermediate in date between the primary burials of Area A and the primary burials of B1, or they may be contemporary with the burials of B1. In either case, a possible chronological sequence is A1 followed by A2 primary burials, A1 and A2 secondary, and B1 primary burials.

Finally, the secondary burials of Area B need to be considered. To some extent the pattern is a mirror image of Area A with a concentration of graves next to feature 237/256, a more general scatter over the rest of B1 and very few in B2. The simplest explanation is that the secondary burials of B1 represent individuals who would normally have been buried in B2 but who wished to be close to the focus represented by 237/256. This hypothesis seems to be supported by the relatively few (because non-privileged) subadults amongst the secondary graves. The probable overall sequence of burials is A1 primary, A2 primary, A1 and A2 secondary, B1 primary, B2 primary and B1 secondary, B2 secondary. In leper percentage terms (adult population only) this is A1 primary 68%, A2 primary 45%, A1 and A2 secondary 42%, B1 primary 21%, B2 primary and B1 secondary 15%, and B2 secondary 0%. The figures are much as might have been predicted, given the abundant historical evidence for the decline of the disease, and as the decline is less dramatic than written sources suggest, there may be distorting factors at work. It must again be emphasised that we are looking at those who died (and presumably lived) in a specific hospital and were so badly afflicted that skeletal changes had occurred. It need not reflect what was happening in society at large, although in practice it appears to do so.

Women and children as chronological indicators (Figs 7.21 and 7.22)

Another potential chronological pointer is the presence or absence of female burials, but they are

Figure 7.21 (opposite, above) The distribution of women and skeletons of undetermined sex with leprosy

Figure 7.22 (opposite, below) The distribution of men, women and children

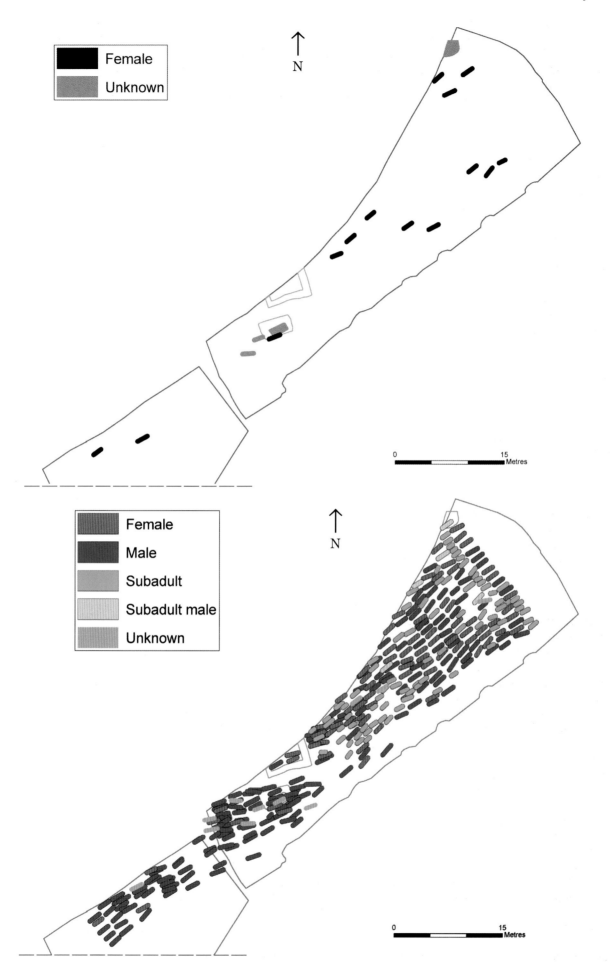

Figure 7.23   The distribution of skeletons with 'ear muffs'

so rare in Area A generally that it is impossible to say if they become increasingly frequent with time.[11] In Area B even the very earliest burials (the nine due north-east of feature 237) include two women, immediately pushing their prevalence up to 25%, and they continue to be present in significant numbers for the rest of the cemetery's period of use, apparently occurring randomly rather than being confined to a particular area.

Like women, children are virtually absent from Area A but are characteristic of Area B. In contrast with female burials, those of children appear in two specific zones as well as appearing apparently at random elsewhere. In sum, Area A is characterised by a virtual absence of women and children and Area B by the presence of both.

'Ear muffs' as a chronological indicator

Yet another indicator, alluded to above, is the presence of 'ear muffs'. They are virtually absent from Area A (Fig 7.23). Area B1 has 10 examples, and B2 36. They again seem to confirm a difference between Areas A and B as well as one, less marked, within Area B.

Coffin nails as a chronological indicator (Fig 7.24)

A final criterion to consider is the number of nails in grave fills. Since later coffins (see below) generally incorporate more nails than early ones, the intermediate and latest burials in a given area would be expected to yield more nails than primary graves. It must be remembered that many factors influence the recovery of such artefacts, including weather conditions and the experience and enthusiasm of personnel. Area A1 was dug in mid-winter, for example, but by an experienced crew and A2 mostly in late summer and autumn by a team with less experience.

In Area A2 the average numbers of nails per grave are: primary, 1.1; intermediate, 2.2; latest, 1.6, whereas the last two figures would be expected to be reversed. In contrast, the primary graves of Area A1 yielded an average of 3.2 nails per grave. It could be inferred from these statistics that the primary burials of A1 post-date the latest burials in A2, an interesting and by no means impossible idea, although unlikely on balance.

Using the greatest number of nails per grave gives the following for Area A2: primary, 10 nails; intermediate, 13 nails; latest, 19 nails. These are

Figure 7.24 The distribution of graves of all periods containing nails

in the expected order, but the figure for A1 primary graves is also 19, putting them, according to the nail criterion, contemporary with the A2 latest graves.

One final way of looking at the statistics is to ask what percentage of graves yielded nails. The figures are as follows: A1 primary, 45%; A2 primary, 38%; A2 intermediate, 31%; A2 latest, 46%. These statistics could again be taken to suggest that the primary burials of A1 post-date the latest burials in A2.

Most burials in Area B were in nailed coffins, and numerous nails secured most coffins. The division between Areas A and B seems again to be confirmed.

The distribution of men, women and children

At least 384 individuals (excluding those from the charnel pit) were excavated. The western part of the cemetery, Area A, was almost exclusively male whereas the eastern part, Area B, was characterised by the presence of infants and children, with men only slightly in excess of women. The contrast is even greater when secondary burials are removed from Area A, reducing its female population to two examples from the 'leper cottage' group, Area A1, and two from Area A2 in feature 237.

Children (Figs 7.22 and 7.25)

The pathology of children is the subject of Chapter 12. The aims here are to try to understand the distribution of children within the cemetery and to account for their presence, as they are nowhere documented as inmates. Nearly all children came from Area B and most (over 85%) were or may have been primary burials. In Area B1, infant and child burials were concentrated in the south-eastern part of the cemetery and more thinly scattered elsewhere. Child burials were fairly sparse due east of feature 237/256 but this may not be significant as there was a similar but inexplicable lacuna in the northern corner of B1.

There may be two patterns of child burial in Area B1, the earlier consisting of an infants- and children-only zone of interments along the cemetery edge extending north-eastwards from burials 93 and 96 as far as 166 in Area B2 and the later consisting of the rest of B1 where children were intermingled with men and women in what was, except next to 237/256, a seemingly fairly chaotic part of the graveyard.

In Area B2, the main concentration of child burials was at the extreme north-eastern end,

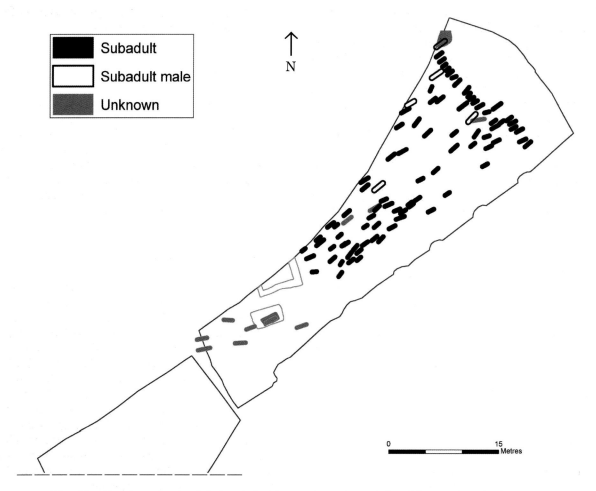

Figure 7.25 The distribution of subadult burials. Except for a few of the oldest individuals it is impossible to assess the sex of the deceased

above and beyond ditch 670. Where child graves are intermingled with those of adults in the rest of B2 they appear sparser than in Area B1 and they form elements in regular columns of burials. About half of the burials in the ditch consisted of infants under a year old, including perhaps three neonates, with the remainder aged up to about seven years. The burials in columns tended to be of older children aged twelve or even fifteen at the time of death. If a line is imagined from the south-east corner of feature 237/256 in Area B1 to the terminus of ditch 497 in Area B2 (Fig 7.17), the older children and adolescents tend to lie north of the line and infants and younger children to the south. If the age of seven is taken as a cut-off, there are three burials of children of seven or over south of this line and nearly seven times as many to the north, although there are burials of infants and younger children there too. Whether burial in ditch 670 and at the cemetery edge was sought after or avoided, it was generally the place where children up to around seven years were interred.

There is no good parallel for this burial pattern in any English graveyard excavated to date. There were certainly favoured and unfavoured spots within cemeteries of all kinds, but the closest in

concept to the segregation of children are the *cillin* of the Gaelic west, similarly reserved for (unbaptised) children. The thinking behind these is equally obscure. They may once have been regular graveyards that somehow became redundant and came to rank as burial grounds of secondary importance.[12] The presence of children in the hospital graveyard need not imply their residence at the hospital and some possibilities to explain their presence are explored below.

Foundlings

Technically suicides, the non-baptised and other theologically suspect individuals were denied burial in consecrated ground but in practice the rules were bent where possible to allow a decent burial in almost all cases, whether through compassion or a less praiseworthy desire to collect soulscot. In dire need, lay baptism could be carried out by a midwife or other individual, so non-baptised infants should have been few and, in cases of uncertainty, given benefit of the doubt. Abandoned babies were often accompanied by a quantity of salt, a substance taken to church by the christening party for the priest's use in the service, as a token that the mother wished them to be baptised (Orme 2001, 96).

Amongst the poorest, particularly single mothers, there may have grown up a custom of leaving foundlings at the hospital gate in the hope that they would reared at the institution's expense. St Leonard's, York, had an orphanage that took in foundlings and other poor children, and Lincoln too had hospital orphans as early as 1283 (Orme 2001, 88). Other institutions that took in abandoned babies were the religious houses: Abingdon Abbey took in a small destitute boy found by Queen Eleanor of Aquitaine, and in a late 12th-century romance a baby left outside a nunnery is reared by the sisters (Orme 2001, 96).

In post-Reformation England there were many fewer institutions able to look after foundlings and St James' Hospital may have taken on this new rôle reluctantly in the 16th and 17th centuries.[13] If the cemetery can be understood entirely by horizontal stratigraphy, did the hospital in its last days cater mainly for foundlings, few of whom grew to adulthood? If the easternmost burials *are* representative of the hospital's last inmates, there is no documentation to record the new admissions policy.

Orphans

Other children may have been those whose mothers had died during childbirth at the hospital, either in giving birth to them or to a younger sibling. The two London hospitals catering for pregnant women, St Bartholomew's and St Mary's without Bishopgate, both had a policy of looking after children orphaned by their mother's death in childbirth until they were seven (Orme 2001, 88). The anonymous Spitalhouse in Copland's poem of *c* 1536 (Appendix 5), possibly St Bartholomew's, admitted 'poor women in childbed' and those who sought hospital admission may have been expecting a difficult birth. Yet other children may have had no connection with the hospital until orphaned. The Reformation greatly narrowed the options for orphans as well as for foundlings. We have no direct evidence that St James' Chichester sent out its orphans as servants or apprentices at eight years old, but there is a noticeable absence amongst the deceased of older children and adolescents that may not be explicable by biological factors.

Poor families

Another possibility is that the infants and children were the progeny of poor families that had been accommodated as a unit, albeit perhaps one headed by a single parent. Their stay, however temporary in theory, may have been long enough for mortality to strike. If the head of the family were in some way crippled, his or her children may well have been housed until they were old enough to be eco-nomically useful, a date perhaps some time after the demise of the parent in question.

Hospital staff

It is possible, if very unlikely, that hospital staff could bury their infants and children up to a certain age at the institution (and thus escape paying fees in their own parish). This would not have commended itself to the priests of adjoining parishes and it must be recalled that the privilege of burial had been granted to leprosaria on the specific condition that parish priests suffered no financial loss.

Women[14] (Figs 7.21 and 7.22)

Women are predominantly a feature of Area B although a few occur outside it. There were three in Area A1 (339, 358 and 365), of which one (358) was secondary. In Area A2, outside feature 237/256, there were only six women. Skeleton 155 was the only possibly primary grave, 16, 29 and 77 were intermediate, and 30 and 38 latest. The latter may all have been attracted by whatever focus lay just beyond the excavated area. In both parts of Area A the secondary female burials may be as late as, or later than, the first women in Area B. The two females in 237/256 are plainly in some way special as either they or the structure that contained them became a focus for later burials.

Area B had 66 women's graves. In Area B1 there were 21, and their distribution was fairly even. Most were primary, but nine were known or thought to be secondary. In contrast, the more numerous female burials of Area B2 included only one in a secondary grave (136). If primary graves only are plotted, they are much denser in Area B2 than in B1. Three secondary women's graves of Area B1 (burials 186, 171a and 119), and probably a further two (138 and 144) seem to have been attracted to feature 237/256, but there were two primary female burials (94 and 133) also in its vicinity. Female graves tended to be at their least dense where children were most numerous, but this was characteristic of adult graves in general, not just women's. There is a hint from contrasting the primary burials of B1 with those of B2 that women became more numerous towards the end of the hospital's life, but they were still slightly outnumbered by adult males.

The admission of women in general may have come about through the occasional admittance of leper women in the absence of any other local institution that catered for them (Fig 7.26). The only primary female burials of Area A1 were both lepers. The female burials of A2 included only one with leprosy that had caused skeletal changes (F77). Area B1 contained one primary probably female leper (251), and one certain (144) and one probable (202) secondary female lepers; Area B2 contained eight female lepers (40, 54, 85, 151, 274, 299, 301,

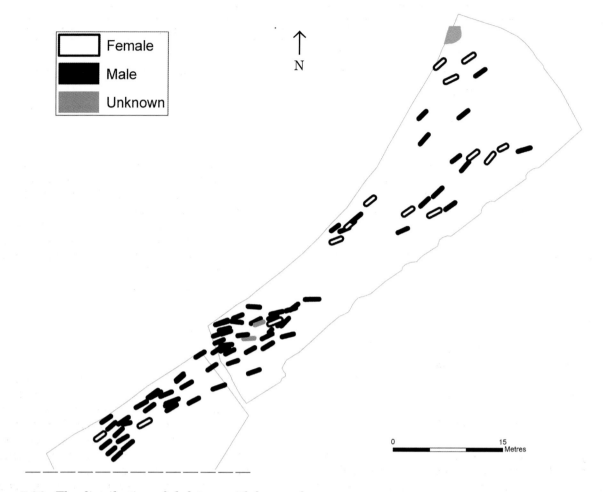

Figure 7.26 The distribution of skeletons with leprosy by sex

306), all in primary graves and spread evenly across the area.

Men

Adult males were the predominant burials in Area A, greatly outnumbering women and children combined. Even in Area B there were more men than women but child burials were here the largest category of all. Once women were admitted to the hospital, their graves were interspersed with those of the brethren with no attempt to segregate by sex and, as far as can be determined, both men and women were laid out and buried in the same manner.

The elderly

Those who lived to be elderly will have done so for a variety of reasons. For example, the better-off may have enjoyed a diet that led to more effective immune systems and greater resistance to the diseases that carried off their poorer neighbours. Conversely, a 'poor' diet by the standards of the time may have provided better nutrition than the diet enjoyed by

the wealthy. Although there was some slight difference in life expectancy between the two parts of the cemetery, there was no clustering of mature adults that could suggest an élite group other than in the tombs described above.

The distribution of the diseased (see Table 7.1)

The organisation of a cemetery could in theory be governed by the cause of death of its occupants. In a hospital graveyard, at its simplest, a distinction could have been made between inmates and staff, the two occupying discrete areas. Even in these circumstances there would have been scope for ambiguity as members of staff succumbed to infection and in practice became numbered amongst the diseased. Where were they to be buried?

Even if the custom of the house did not discriminate in death between carers and patients, there may have been some sufferers buried apart from the rest because of the nature of their affliction. Archaeologically, other than in exceptional circumstances, we can identify only diseases that caused skeletal changes and, whilst it is often possible to be reasonably sure that the symptoms evinced in the skeleton were the result of a specific infection, the

Table 7.1 Incidence of leprous skeletons amongst adult burials

	Primary %	Intermediate %	Latest %	All adults %
Area A1	**68** (21/31)	**50** (1/2)	**33** (2/6)	**61.5** (24/39)
Area A2	**45** (13/29)	**55** (11/20)	**35** (12/34)	**43** (36/83)
Area B1	**21** (6/29)	**0** (0/6)	**17** (2/12)	**15** (7/47)
Area B2	**16** (17/105)	**0** (0/6)	**0** (0/5)	**15** (17/116)

actual cause of death may have been quite different. If, for example, those who died from malaria had been interred apart from the rest, we could not at present deduce what they had in common as the condition causes no skeletal changes. The discussion below is therefore necessarily restricted to the few diseases that can be identified from skeletal remains.

Leprosy (Fig 7.20)

Lepers, certain, probable and possible examples, have been considered as potential chronological indicators and, as Table 7.1 indicates, become much less common as time progresses. Those with the disease in a sufficiently disfiguring form to produce skeletal changes by the time of admission may have been a minority and the true incidence of leprosy may have been very much higher than can be identified. On the other hand, given the medieval emphasis on disfigurement as the most important criterion for diagnosing a leper (see Chapter 2), only those with the disease in an advanced form may have sought and obtained hospital admission. The apparent absence of lepers from 'normal' cemeteries of the Middle Ages suggests that the disease could be diagnosed in its early stages when no skeletal changes had taken place; alternatively it could be argued that 'normal' cemeteries too contained lepers, but only those with early symptoms that had caused no skeletal alteration.[15] Even if current work on preserved leprosy DNA in bones could identify all those with Hansen's disease, including those whose skeletons were seemingly unaffected, it would not solve all the problems as a major area of interest is not its actual incidence but the accuracy of diagnosis and responses to it.

In considering the prevalence of the disease at St James' (discussed in more detail in Chapters 14 and 15) it is important to recall the pottery evidence for the date of the earliest excavated burials. We do not appear to have investigated the earliest part of the cemetery and may be looking at a period when the disease was already in decline. If so, the hospital's capacity may already have exceeded demand. Others with a legitimate call on Christian charity, perhaps starting with female lepers, for whom there was no local provision, and the sick poor in general, at first men only and then the community at large, may have been admitted. As already noted, the relatively high incidence (15%) of lepers in the latest

part of the cemetery may be misleading since they occur in a period when other local leprosaria were no longer operating and St James' was the only dedicated hospital available.

In terms of distribution, lepers with the disease in a form severe enough to cause skeletal changes appear to occur throughout the cemetery without any clustering although they represent an unknown percentage of actual sufferers from the disease.

Tuberculosis (Fig 7.27)

Tuberculosis (see Chapter 16), often a disease of childhood, can also affect the skeleton but does so only in about 3–5% of cases; for each victim identified by skeleton at least another twenty may be surmised. Unlike leprosy, TB can be fatal and it was probably always a much greater check on population growth than leprosy at its most widespread.

Confirmed and probable cases of TB[16] and skeletons with rib lesions[17] from Chichester numbered 30. Rib lesions may be caused by afflictions other than tuberculosis but many will have been due to TB. Based on a multiplier of 20, the disease was potentially more common than leprosy at St James'. At least one leper (291) had TB and there were seven lepers with rib lesions that may have been due to TB (8, 26, 31, 187, 325, 341, 365). In terms of distribution, TB was commonest in that part of the cemetery (Area B2) where lepers were not only fewest but also elderly, and rib lesions were also more abundant there than elsewhere. The pattern is, however, a consequence of complex social and biological factors that seem to have led to an increase in cases of TB in a period when leprosy, for similar reasons, was in decline, not a consequence of singling out TB sufferers for special treatment.

Syphilis

Although only three cases have been identified, one (no. 277 in Area B1), a young man, had been buried some distance from the rest of the graves, perhaps to express society's horror at what, when he died, was perhaps a new disease to which society responded much as it had to leprosy in earlier centuries. The latter, like syphilis, was still popularly supposed to be sexually transmitted, so some equation between the two is understandable. It is only in its advanced stages that syphilis affects the skeletal structure.

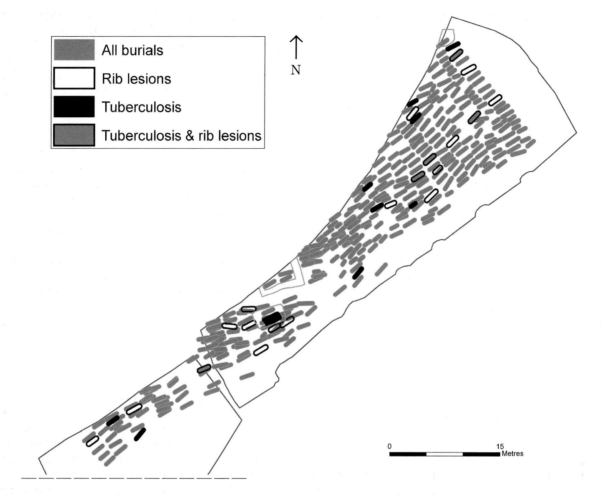

All burials
Rib lesions
Tuberculosis
Tuberculosis & rib lesions

N

0   15
Metres

Figure 7.27   The distribution of skeletons with tuberculosis and rib lesions

Degenerative disease

Although there were ample cases of degenerative disease resulting from 'wear and tear' (see Chapter 18), there was no clustering of skeletons that could be correlated with the 1594 list of inmates (Appendix 3) and, with a few notable exceptions (eg no. 115 with both leprosy and multiple fractures: Knüsel and Göggel 1993) the inmates' afflictions, as far as they were reflected in their skeletons, were not particularly horrendous in the almshouse phase. The only case of surgical intervention (an amputation, skeleton 137a, disarticulated bone from the fill of tomb 65) was from Area A2, but belonged to the latest phase, as might have been expected, and is the only indication that the hospital ever offered more than bed-rest and nursing; the surgery may, however, have been done elsewhere.

7.3   The dead: burial practice and beliefs

Grave pits

Size and shape

There is very little to be said about the size, shape or depth of most grave pits. As nothing survived to indicate the likely medieval ground surface,[18] for most graves all that can be given is a minimum depth. The variation within the cemetery, itself roughly level, between the deepest and shallowest graves was not very great and the distribution of deep and shallow graves appears to have been more or less random, although there was a tendency when graves were cut into earlier features such as the lime kiln in Area A and an Iron Age ditch in Area B for the gravedigger to go a little deeper where the digging was easy. The subsoil in general was flinty, not easy to dig and even more difficult for the archaeologist to distinguish between grave cut and fill. Grave pits, except in rare instances, could not be identified with confidence and an area around each skeleton was dug, probably over-dug, until the excavator was satisfied that the likely area of the original pit had been completely excavated. Those graves containing coffin nails indicating the outline of the coffin (see below) gave an idea of the minimum size for each grave pit. There was no evidence of a mismatch in size between grave pit and contents, as has been noted in other graveyards (see Chapter 3), but this may simply reflect our inability to identify grave pits. In a cemetery where many of the bodies were in coffins, the evidence would normally take the form of an over-large pit since coffins, unlike shrouded burials, cannot be squeezed into holes that are too small.

Alignments

The alignment of each pit was most likely dictated by that of its neighbour and the number of burials every year was undoubtedly sufficient for the alignment of previous graves to be seen even without formal markers. In general, groups of contemporary burials conform to a common alignment, but secondary burials may not. In Area A1, for example (Fig 7.15), the secondary burial 337 has a very different orientation to the rest of the burials and, even without any stratigraphic information, it would be suspected either to pre-date or post-date its neighbours. Other secondary burials here are much more closely aligned to the norm, presumably because a common linear feature influenced both them and the primary burials and all lay roughly parallel to it.

In areas such as A2, which were formally replanned and reused, the primary, intermediate and final period burials nearly all shared a common alignment, presumably because each successive phase had been laid out parallel to the same line. The odd ones out tended to be those of uncertain stratigraphic position that were some distance from their neighbours. Grave 83, for example, is an eastern outlier of Area A2 and on the appropriate alignment but its nearest neighbours to the south, 70, 2 and 79, all of them near to the graveyard's edge, are on what could be termed a B1 alignment (Fig 7.13). All that has happened is that the sexton has dug three pits parallel to the nearest straight line, in this case the edge of the graveyard, which approximated to the liturgically correct orientation.

Not all alignments can be explained. For example, grave 149 in Area B2 seems to be sited to avoid child burial 140 to the east (Fig 7.17). Both are technically primary in the sense that neither cuts the other and neither is cut by any other grave. Apart from its strange alignment, 149 forms part of a column of burials with heads to a common north–south line. Grave 140 too can be ascribed to the next, slightly more ragged, column. Yet it is difficult to understand the orientation of 149 unless it post-dates 140 and the latter was still visible, and such an explanation is contrary to our understanding that the general expansion of the cemetery was from south-west to north-east. Perhaps 140 belongs with the cluster of child burials at the eastern edge of the cemetery that had been established before the adult burials of Area B2 had expanded as far as the graveyard boundary, but it is a little apart from most of them.

Burials in coffins

From the start of the excavations nails in grave pits were diligently recorded on plan and by grid reference in the hope that the number and the nature of coffins could be ascertained, with perhaps evidence of changing coffin shapes over time. Nonetheless, as recovery will have depended on the alertness of the individual digging the grave and conditions (of light, for example) on a given day, the record cannot be wholly objective. Preservation across the site seemed to be uniform, and there is no reason to suppose that the greater numbers of nails recovered from more recent burials were due to better survival. It was appreciated that although the presence of nails, especially in quantity, might be taken as evidence for a coffin, an absence of nails could indicate no more than the use of dowels or some other means to hold the box together. Coffins of composite construction, with a dowelled box but a nailed lid, are by no means improbable and 40 such have been found in an Anglo-Saxon context at Barton-on-Humber (Taylor 2001, 176) where waterlogged conditions preserved them. Nails apart, no physical evidence for coffins survived at Chichester.

Coffin nails, their distribution and interpretation

Figure 7.24 shows all grave pits that yielded at least one nail, and those containing twenty or more nails are emphasised. Very many grave pits in Area B yielded nails but they were less common in Area A. Nearly all the graves containing twenty or more nails also occurred in Area B. If it is simplistically assumed that nails equal coffins, it could be concluded that many burials of the almshouse phase (Area B) were in coffins but only about half were in coffins in the leper hospital phase (Area A). Nails found in grave pits may, of course, have been used to attach things to coffins rather than to hold them together.

Figure 7.28 shows the picture with primary graves emphasised. It was drawn to see if excluding secondary graves from Area A, the earlier part of the cemetery, increased the ratio of apparently uncoffined to coffined burials, so confirming that burial in a coffin became more usual as time progressed. In fact, the number of burials seemingly in coffins in Area A actually increased as a ratio of the whole to the extent that they became a majority,[19] but the picture for Area B was largely unchanged. The story from this figure would seem, at first glance, to be that most primary burials from Area A were in coffins, as were nearly all from Area B.

A more detailed scrutiny, however, reveals differences. A number of Area A burials had only one or two nails in their fills and if, as is possible, some were residual objects incorporated by chance, the number of apparent coffins is reduced considerably. If graves with no more than two nails are excluded from consideration, an additional effect is to emphasise the separateness of the 'leper cottage' group (Area A1) where grave fills tend to incorporate either a number of nails or none at all. There were a few graves in Area B containing no more than two nails,

Figure 7.28 The distribution of primary graves containing nails

but omitting them from consideration makes little alteration to the overall picture. The only hypothesis that seems to emerge is that the secondary burials of Area A are likely to be of the same general period as the primary graves since, using the nail criterion, they consist of a mixture of coffined and uncoffined skeletons, whereas (the later) burials of Area B are predominantly in coffins. Either Area A received few further burials once the almshouse cemetery, Area B, had been established,[20] or if it did, they were uncharacteristically uncoffined.

A similar distribution diagram (not published), but for secondary graves only, reinforced the impression from Figure 7.28. Those secondary graves in Area A that contained nails usually had only one or two, occasionally three or four, in their fills, but those in Area B contained more numerous nails. The only two secondary graves in Area A to contain more than ten nails both lay just south of tomb 241.

The position of the body as an indicator of a coffined burial

It might be argued that hospitals, institutions with a quasi-monastic rule, would have a standard burial practice, although subject perhaps to change over

time. If it could be demonstrated that some inmates were buried in coffins, it might be assumed, in the absence of evidence to the contrary, that all were. The weakness of the argument is demonstrated by the presence of 'special' burials such as those in tombs. They are unlikely to have been the graves of ordinary inmates and are proof of some kind of social or religious stratification. Accepting that a failure to recover (coffin) nails from a grave fill for whatever reason does not conclusively indicate that the burial had no coffin, it may be asked whether there are other characteristics by which burials in coffins can be recognised.

One possibility to explore is whether the position of the body in the grave varied according to whether the burial was demonstrably in a coffin or not. In practice, although differences in leg positions occur (Fig 7.29), it is the position of the arms that varies most. The broad division is between skeletons where the arms lie beside the body (hereafter Type A) and those where the arms are laid on the body. The latter may be subdivided into three types: B, where the arms are bent as if in prayer with the hands at the throat or thereabouts; C, where the arms are folded at the waist; and D where the hands overlie the pelvis, often with the wrists crossed (Fig 7.30). There are also a few hybrid examples. Two skeletons may

Figure 7.29 Skeleton 332, an adult male. This is one of a very few burials where the legs were other than straight. The individual was a middle-aged to mature man but there is no pathological explanation for the bent legs

be classified as A/D, having one arm on the body and the other beside it, but these are presumably Type D skeletons in which an arm has been displaced. Less readily explicable are B/A skeletons (one example), B/C skeletons (2) and C/D (5).

The distribution of burials thus classified is shown in Figure 7.31. It is immediately apparent that no single practice has an exclusive distribution, with Type A burials (15%, total 31: Fig 7.32), for example, occurring across the whole site, and also that the 'arms on body' methods of laying out are collectively far commoner than Type A. There are patterns within the cemetery. Type C burials (arms folded: Fig 7.34) are the commonest (54%, total 115) and are very common in Area B2, the easternmost part of the graveyard, and Type D (hands on pelvis: Fig 7.35, 26%, total 56) are second in that area. Type B (arms bent as if in prayer: Fig 7.33) are the rarest (5%, only ten examples, excluding hybrids) but, like Type A, are found at both ends of the site.[21] Figure 7.36 demonstrates variations in arm positions.

Although nine Type A graves had no nails associated with them, others yielded up to 26 nails and unquestionably contained coffins and, of the total, there were seven graves with ten or more nails. Four of the Type B graves contained no nails, but one contained ten nails and another 30. Thirty-five of the Type C graves yielded ten or more nails, and fifteen Type D graves also had ten or more nails in their fills. All four types of laying out are therefore to be found in association with graves very likely to have contained coffins, and the position of the skeleton is thus of no assistance in determining

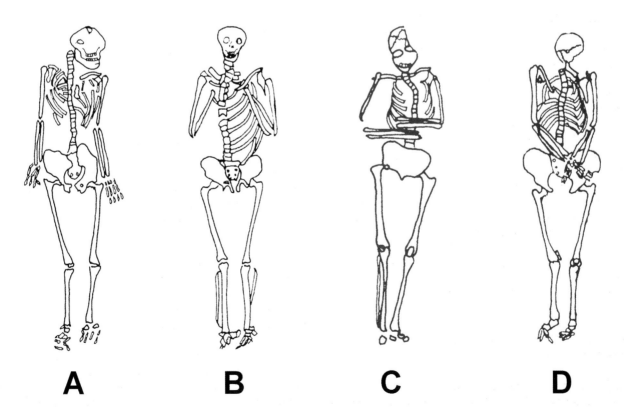

A   **B**   **C**   **D**

Figure 7.30 Arm positions of skeletons: A with arms beside body and B–D on top of body

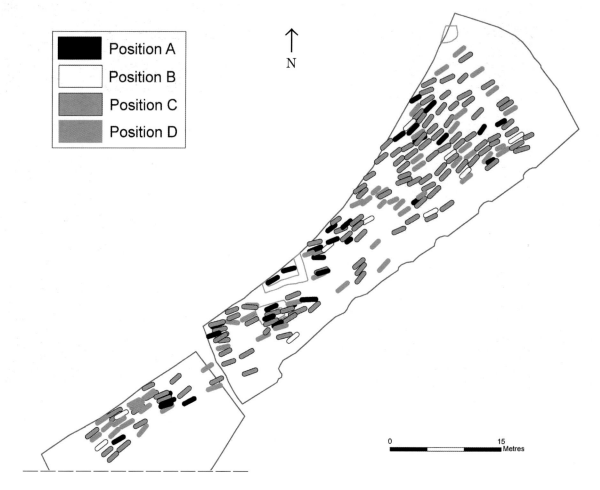

Figure 7.31 The distribution of skeletons with arm positions A–D

whether a burial with no associated nails was likely to have been in a coffin or not.

'Ear muffs' and coffins

A number of graves contained what could be described as headphones or ear muffs (see Figs 7.23, 7.37), and it is the latter term that is current in archaeological literature. Typically, the skull had a small flint on each side, as if to hold it in position, looking upwards, in a box that was wider than the skull itself. Although found throughout the cemetery, they were most common in Area B2 and scarce elsewhere. Some graves appeared to contain only one stone and, given the gravelly and stony subsoil through which the graves had been cut, it could be argued that the apparent association of stone and skull was fortuitous. Removing from the distribution map all but examples of 'ear muffs' composed of two or more stones virtually restricts the distribution to Area B, with examples again commonest in B2.

Sixty-six 'ear muffs' were identified. Excluding examples where the 'ear muff' consisted of a single stone reduces the total to 39. Of these, five 'ear muffs' came from graves which yielded no nails but the rest were mostly from graves where nails were numerous, twenty of them containing ten or more nails. An association between 'ear muffs' and coffins seems to be demonstrated. Interestingly, the more doubtful examples of single 'ear muff' stones were also disproportionately associated with coffin nails. Four were found in graves with no nails but the rest were from graves with at least one nail, eight belonging to graves where the nails reached or exceeded double figures. This association with nails in graves helps to validate these more dubious examples of 'ear muffs', perhaps indicating that a corresponding stone had been displaced or was otherwise unrecorded rather than that the surviving stone had been 'invented'.

How the stones were used is a matter for speculation. If they came from a ruin invested with an aura of sanctity, a single stone may have been as efficacious as the commoner pair. In 19th-century Ireland the custom of burying a stone from an ancient church or tombstone is said to have led to the disappearance of several early monuments at Clonmacnoise, Co. Offaly, and was also seen at Tuamgraney, Co. Clare (Westropp 2000 [1912], 78). Such an explanation could apply in Chichester, given that 'ear muffs'

Figure 7.32 Skeleton 145, a Type A burial with arms at the side. The individual was a young to middle-aged man

Figure 7.33 Skeleton 326, a Type B burial with arms as if in prayer. The individual was a middle-aged man

Figure 7.34 Skeleton 335, a Type C burial with folded arms. The individual was a mature man

Figure 7.35 Skeleton 367, a Type D burial, with hands in the pelvic region. The individual was a mature male

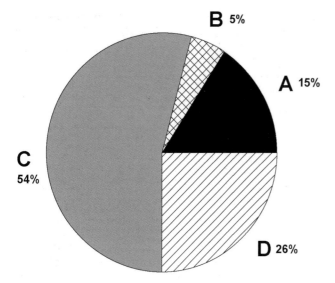

Figure 7.36 The arm position of skeletons expressed as percentages

Figure 7.37 A burial with 'ear muffs'. Skeleton 251 was a probable woman with some early rhinomaxillary changes attributable to leprosy

are a relatively late feature, found when the earliest hospital buildings may have become ruinous.

Yet, whilst it is easy to invest some religious symbolism in the stones (the Roman brick in 254 might present a challenge), their purpose was perhaps strictly practical, as wedges to hold the skull in place. As it is difficult to imagine bare stones used as wedges in the coffin, they may have been cloth-wrapped.[22] If so, other, perishable materials may have occasionally been employed for the same purpose and the single stones may have had as their counterparts some organic equivalent. Such a function is seemingly reinforced by the broad distribution of 'ear muffs' since they occur in that part of the cemetery where coffin nails were most numerous. It has been said that stone settings of one sort or another are 'symptomatic of the care given to the proper positioning of the body' (Taylor 2001, 176). If they really were merely to stop the skull lolling about in the coffin, the implication must be either that burial took place very soon after death, before the onset of *rigor mortis* or, more likely, that burial was commonly delayed until its effects had worn off.

Whilst the custom is a late arrival at St James', it is recorded in Anglo-Saxon contexts at Winchester Old Minster and elsewhere (Taylor 2001, 176). At St Andrew's Fishergate, York, the cobbles cradling one skull may be strictly functional, as the individual had been decapitated. The custom is said to be unusual after the 11th century although there are late examples at St Mary's, Stow (Lincs), and St Leonard's Hospital, Chesterfield (Derbys) (Hadley 2001, 118). Closer to Chichester, the hospital originally for leper men at Bidlington (E Sussex) contained one burial with three chalk blocks around the skull, another with a chalk 'pillow' with blocks on both sides and a third with a large flint nodule under the skull (Lewis 1964). The general date

range for the cemetery is 13th to 16th century, but the institution became an almshouse before 1366.

Coffin shapes and their distribution

In many graves there were sufficient nails to attest the presence of a coffin although its form could not be recovered. In 64 cases it seemed possible to recover the coffin outline by linking the nails to make a symmetrical or near-symmetrical pattern. However, before examining the detail, it is worth considering how nails could have been used in coffin construction.

Iron nails were handmade and perhaps relatively expensive throughout the existence of the graveyard. As they are amongst the goods imported through Dell Quay in 1661/62[23] it may be assumed that they were not made locally at that date, or at least not in any quantity. There was, as far as is known, no significant technological advance in nail manufacture from medieval times until the closure of the cemetery *c* 1700 and if nails were more commonly used as time progressed, this presumably reflects changing

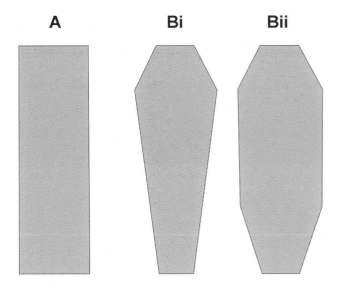

A **Bi** **Bii**

Figure 7.38 Coffin types A (rectangular) and Bi and Bii (shaped)

fashions or perhaps the use of different materials.[24] Blast furnace technology and its introduction from 1495 onwards in south-east England may have made iron cheaper, but the fact that it could now be cast was irrelevant to contemporary nail-makers, who continued to hand-forge the items.

Some of the forms that coffins could take have been mentioned in Chapter 3. All could have been constructed without nails although securing the lid, if a simple box-like coffin is envisaged, would have taken some ingenuity.[25] Where coffin nails occurred only in the upper parts of grave fills at Chichester, they may have been used exclusively to affix the lid. Relatively few[26] would have sufficed to prevent a simple broad plank or two from sliding off the top of a box. Where it seems possible to recover coffin shapes by plotting nails, these were almost always found and recorded at the level of the lowest part of the skeleton and were thus somehow used to join together the base and sides. The more effective method of manufacture would have been to nail the sides to the edge of the base of the coffin rather than the base to the lower edges of the sides, since without a generous use of nails a heavy corpse of, say, 100kg, might make an unscheduled reappearance if the coffin were to be lifted other than by its base.

Archaeologically, the nails might be expected to lie either horizontally, heads outwards, or points upwards if the less-effective method of manufacture were used. Circumstances at Chichester did not permit the graves to be excavated with the degree of meticulousness needed to determine the lie of each nail and, as in many cases it was possible to distinguish head from point (where both survived intact) only after X-raying, the effort might not have been justifiable. Two types of coffins seemed to be distinguishable.[27] Type A coffins had a simple rectangular outline whereas Type B were shaped. The latter could be further subdivided into

examples that were 'shouldered' towards the head and tapered towards the feet (ie the 'traditional' pattern), and others which were 'shouldered' at both ends (Fig 7.38).

The locations of such coffins in primary graves are given in Figure 7.39. 'Shaped' coffins (Type B) appeared to outnumber rectangular examples (by about 7:5) but neither has an exclusive distribution, their relative occurrence being more or less constant throughout the cemetery; in other words, the distribution is random (Fig 7.40).[28] Professional undertakers do not appear until the 16th century (see Chapter 3) and one unanswerable question is where the hospital acquired its coffins. A simple box should have been easily within the competence of the hospital handyman and a shaped one would have been no challenge to a general carpenter.[29] What the distribution plan may be showing is that the hospital had at least two potential sources of coffins – 'homemade' and 'professional' – and that it was a matter of chance which source was used. As the coffin lay beneath the pall from the time it was closed until the moment of interment, its workmanship may not have been considered of much importance. The relative numbers of rectangular and 'shaped' coffins rule out any suggestion of a social distinction such as 'shaped' for staff and rectangular for inmates. Where female graves occur in Area B there is no apparent correlation between sex and coffin shape,[30] nor is any particular style of coffin exclusive to non-adults.

It may reasonably be asked whether the 'shaped' coffins, Type B, really exist or whether they have been invented from incompletely excavated and recorded graves. To put it bluntly, are Type B coffins really rectangles with some corner nails missing or unrecorded? In favour of their existence, it might be pointed out that the Type Bi coffins, shouldered towards the head and tapering at the feet, are of exactly the outline that a person asked to look for shaped coffins might seek: they are 'traditional' in shape and are perhaps as close as one can get to the type of stone coffin with a head niche if a slab-sided box is the basic constructional form. The archaeologist, it might be argued, has come up with a traditional shape because that is what he expected but, to reverse the argument, the shape may have become 'traditional' because many coffins were once of that form. Type Bii coffins, on the other hand, are distinctly non-traditional in shape and are less likely on that count to be the construct of an archaeologist's mind. In reviewing the evidence, the present writer was convinced that (a) it supports the proposed distinction between rectangular and shaped coffins but (b) although the latter characteristically taper towards the feet, the evidence is not adequate to support further subdivision.[31] There seems to be a typology emerging for stone coffins (Bruce-Mitford 1976, fig 2) that may one day be applicable to their much commoner wooden counterparts.

UNIVERSITY OF WINCHESTER
LIBRARY

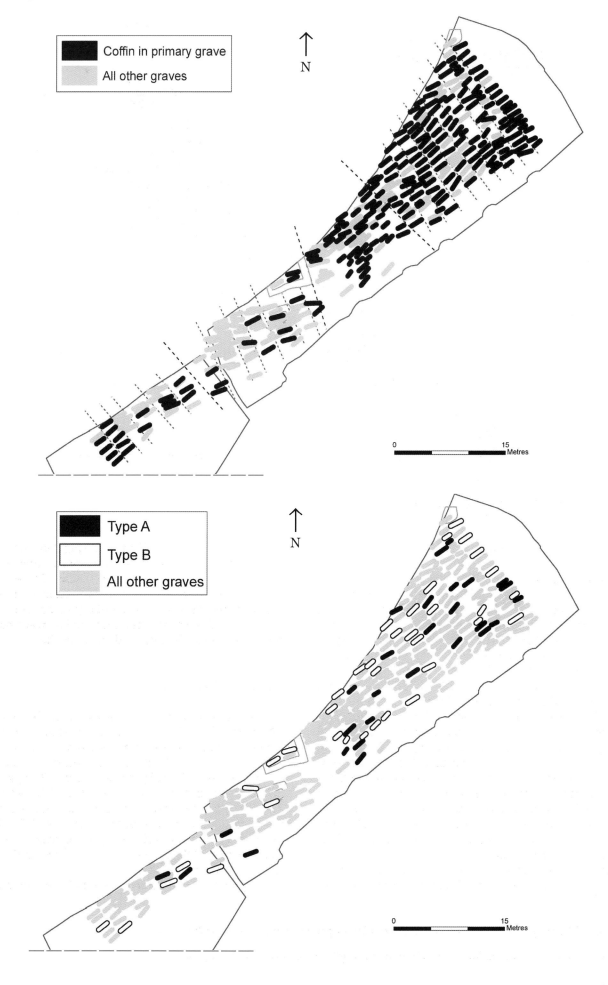

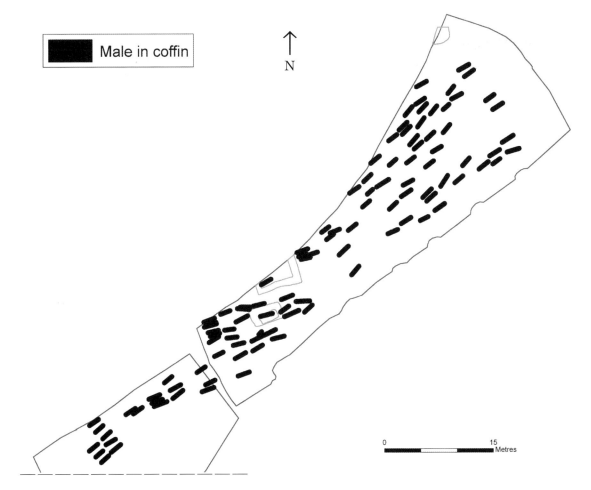

Figure 7.41 The distribution of male skeletons in coffins

Coffins and their occupants

In any hospital cemetery it is fair to assume that most graves are those of inmates and, in an era when hospitals were run on monastic lines, that all were treated equally in death. It is even possible, as suggested above (Chapter 2), that the prospect of a decent send-off was an inducement to those who might otherwise find the regular round of hospital life less than enticing. Most burials, then, should have been similar. The odd pious inmate may have sought burial in a simple shroud, and at the other extreme the heirs of a wealthy inmate may have sought to use a better than average coffin, but on the whole, uniformity is to be expected. The absence of evidence for coffins in some graves is not evidence of absence and, whilst the archaeologist may make much of the presence or otherwise of coffin nails in a grave fill, it would not have mattered a jot to the mourners or the deceased whether the coffin had been nailed or dowelled.

This section looks at correlations between burials containing nails thought to be coffin nails and other features. Much of the initial work was done after the 1993 excavations[32] using a very simple database. The questions posed were along the lines of 'Are leper burials more likely to be in coffins than non-leper burials?' and 'Are men more likely to be in coffins than women?' and assumed that burials were not in coffins unless nails indicated the opposite.

Men and coffins (Fig 7.41)

There were 190 male or probable male burials covering all periods of the excavated cemetery. Seventy-seven (40.5%) male graves, many in the south-western part of the cemetery (Area A), contained no nails. Fifty-three graves (28%) yielded between one and five nails, and 32 (16.8%) between six and ten. Nineteen graves (10%) had between eleven and twenty nails and nine graves (4.7%) had between 21 and 35 nails. No grave contained more than 35 nails. Of the graves that yielded nails, few contained more than ten.

Compared with women (see below), relatively

Figure 7.39 (opposite, above) The distribution of primary burials in coffins

Figure 7.40 (opposite, below) The distribution of Type A and Type B coffins

Female in coffin

N

0   15
Metres

Figure 7.42   The distribution of female skeletons in coffins

fewer men were buried in coffins, the figures being 80% of women and 59.5% of men, but the raw figures take no account of the fact that women were not generally admitted to the graveyard until coffined burials were usual. Looking at the north-eastern part of the cemetery only (Area B), however, reveals that the difference is real. Of all the adult graves, about 75% were in coffins, assuming that the presence of a single nail indicates a coffin. Of the 25% that were not in coffins, nearly 20% were men and only around 5% women. Put another way, 33% of male burials were uncoffined as opposed to 6.3% of female burials if the recovery of a single nail is used as the criterion.

It would be perverse to argue that males were normally interred in dowelled coffins and women in nailed ones, for example, and it seems that over a third of all men were in winding sheets alone, perhaps as a sign of humility. Male graves without nails are too numerous to be those of successive chaplains or masters, even allowing for a rapid turnover before 1244 when the first is recorded, and, if they do form a distinct group, they must represent a broader category of persons. Interestingly, around 30% of the mostly male leper graves were similarly uncoffined if an absence of nails is taken to indicate an absence of coffin (see below).

This difference between the sexes is reflected at other sites (see Gilchrist and Sloane 2005, 114, table 7). At St Mary Graces, London, for example, 33% of females, 25% of subadults and only 20% of males were apparently in coffins, and at St Mary Stratford Langthorne (formerly Essex, now Greater London) the division was even more acute, with 5.6% of males but 32% of females coffined. Perhaps understandably, the Black Death cemeteries have a high proportion of coffined burials compared with those of other periods. What is surprising is a decline in the use of coffins after *c* 1370 recorded at Hull Augustinian Friary when the Black Death was in abeyance (Gilchrist and Sloane 2005, 209). This appears to contradict the evidence from Chichester and may be indicative of regional burial traditions.

Women and coffins (Fig 7.42)

If coffins were considered prestigious and women, on the whole, were not, were their chances of burial in a coffin thereby diminished? As already noted, the opposite seems to have been the case. Sixty certain or probable female graves contained at least one nail, and 51 contained three or more nails. Females as a

Child in coffin

N

0   15
Metres

Figure 7.43   The distribution of children's skeletons in coffins

whole numbered only 75 so it might be concluded that 80% of women, according to the nail criterion, were buried in coffins. Again the figure is distorted by geography, for the first female burials mostly do not appear until burial in a (nailed) coffin in Area B was normal for all.

Children and coffins (Fig 7.43)

As with the statistics for women, those for children are distorted by the fact that they first appear in this cemetery at a time when burial in a nailed coffin had become the norm. Whereas adult-sized wooden chests apart from coffins must have been rare, child-sized boxes were perhaps available for reuse and may have served as coffins, although there is no specific evidence that they did so. If coffins were in part provided to make it easier to handle the body, they may again have been less necessary for non-adults, and if they were to some extent still prestige items, the privilege of burial in a coffin may have been extended to children less often than to adults. Given that children's coffins were smaller, they may have been held together with fewer nails and may thus be under-represented if nails are the sole criterion for coffins. All in all, one would expect,

for a variety of possible reasons, evidence of fewer children buried in coffins than adults.

If children are defined as being fifteen years old or younger, there were 94 of them. Nineteen percent came from graves that yielded no nails, a figure very close to that for women (20%) who form a con-temporary group. Of the remainder, a quarter were from graves containing 1–5 nails, very slightly more from graves containing 6–10 nails, around 14% from graves with 11–15 nails and fewer than 4% from graves containing 16 or more nails (Fig 7.43). Even if those graves yielding fewer than four nails are dis-counted, and in practice these may have been more than outweighed by graves where, for a variety of reasons, traces of nails were not recovered, the figure still exceeds 70%. Within those defined as children, there did not appear to be any distinction between the number of nails associated with the very young (ie those with ages reckoned in months) and those who could be termed subadults.

The statistics can again be paralleled elsewhere. At St Mary Graces, London, the number of subadults in coffins was fewer than that for adult females but greater than that for adult males (Sloane and Gilchrist 2005, 114). However, as the total burials number fewer than 100, the statistics may be unrepresentative.

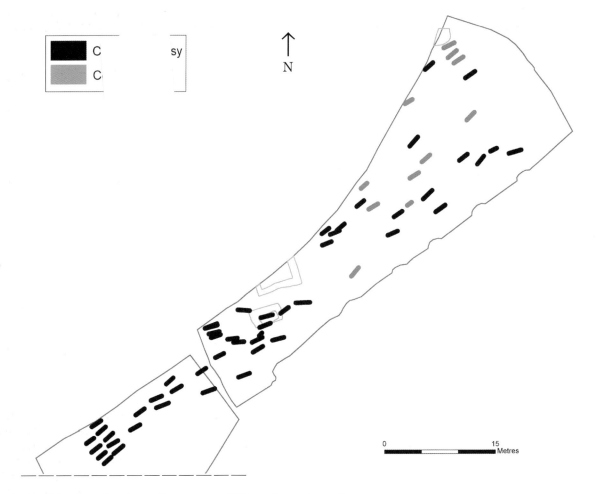

Figure 7.44   The distribution of leprosy and TB sufferers in coffins

Coffins and disease (Fig 7.44)

Not all inmates of a leper hospital will necessarily have had the disease and it is conceivable that those with leprosy at the time of death were treated differently, either on public health or religious grounds, by being buried in coffins whereas the non-leprous minority (servants, staff and any corrodians) normally had to make do with a shroud alone.[33] By the mid-14th century it was believed in some Continental European cities that diseases (specifically, the Black Death) could be spread by noxious miasmas from uncoffined corpses (see Chapter 3) and the concept could have been current both earlier and in England. There is no obvious religious imperative to bury lepers in coffins beyond the likelihood that a 'decent' burial in a coffin was one of the privileges of hospital admission. For the archaeologist, the problems are not only those of distinguishing between coffined and uncoffined burials, which have already been discussed, but also of discriminating between non-lepers and lepers who, unless they had the disease in an advanced and disfiguring form which left some skeletal trace, cannot be identified.

Thirty-seven (42%) of the known and likely leper skeletons from discrete pits (Table 7.2) were in graves which yielded no nails at all, and a further fifteen (17%) were in graves from which no more than two nails were recovered. From these figures it looks at first sight as if there is little correlation between leper skeletons and coffins, but it is partly explicable by the distribution of lepers, which are commonest in the south-western part of the cemetery, Area A, where coffin nails are least numerous. Using 'ear muff' stones as an additional indicator of coffins does surprisingly little to alter the overall picture. Certain and probable examples were found with skeletons 50 (19 nails), 299 (11 nails), 143 (5 nails), 365 (4 nails) and two others (165 and 353) where no nails were recovered. Again, the seeming lack of correlation is partly geographic in that 'ear muffs' occur mostly in Area B, the part of the cemetery where lepers are less frequent. The overall picture, taking two or more nails in a grave as the only reliable indicator of a coffin, seems to be that around half the lepers were so interred. Taking the presence of any nail as a coffin indicator pushes the figure to 58%, but in reality it seems likely that the same method of burial was used for all inmates except in rare circumstances.

Five (33%) of those known or thought to have had TB were from graves yielding no nails at all but nine (60%) were in graves that yielded three or more nails (Table 7.3). On the face of it, TB sufferers

Table 7.2 The numbers of coffin nails recovered from lepers' graves

Coffin nails	No. of leper graves	No. of non-leper graves	No. of leper graves as % of all leper graves
0	37	96	42
1	8	24	9
2	7	11	8
3	4	12	5
4	5	12	6
5	2	16	2
6	2	12	2
7	1	14	1
8	6	14	7
9	4	9	5
10	2	12	2
11	2	8	2
12	–	6	–
13	–	8	–
14	2	5	2
15	0	9	0
16	2	2	2
17	–	8	–
18	1	1	1
19	1	–	1
21	1	2	1
22	1	–	–
23	–	1	1
24	–	2	2
25	–	1	1
26	–	3	3
30	–	3	3
34	–	1	1
35	–	1	1
Totals	**88**	**293**	

Table 7.3 The numbers of coffin nails recovered from known and probable TB graves

Coffin nails	No. of TB graves	No. of TB graves as % of total
0	5	33.33
1	1	06.66
3	1	06.66
4	2	13.33
5	1	06.66
9	2	13.33
11	1	06.66
13	1	06.66
14	1	06.66
Totals	**15**	**99.95**

logical sense do not generally occur in Christian graveyards and the term is used loosely here for objects apart from coffin nails and other ferrous items recovered from or associated with burials (Fig 7.45). In some cases the association seems to be fortuitous. For example, five Roman coins were found on the site, one from the grave of skeleton 257, but the incorporation of a coin in its fill seems to have been entirely accidental.

Listed below are potential 'grave goods' from the Chichester cemetery. There are many other classes of items that occur in medieval graveyards (papal bulls, pilgrim badges) that are simply unattested at Chichester, and it must be emphasised that the typical grave, whether at Chichester or elsewhere, contains no more than a few nails. Grave goods of a perishable or fragile nature, such as wooden or wax crosses (Gilchrist and Sloane 2005, 92–3), may of course have been commoner than the archaeological record indicates.

Although the distinction is potentially important, it is usually impossible to say whether an item was placed on the body and wrapped in a shroud, placed in a coffin with a burial, or placed on top of a coffin at the time of burial.

Non-ferrous 'grave goods'

Pins

Eight pins attached to the skull of female skeleton 176 in its prestigious stone-built tomb must have supported some type of headdress. At least six copper alloy pins were found attached to the skull of a probable female from Syon Abbey (Middlesex),

were more likely to be accorded a coffined burial than lepers, but the explanation is again chronological/geographic as TB sufferers were mostly in Area B2 where coffin nails were commonest and most numerous (Fig 7.44).

Grave goods (Fig 7.45)

All excavated 'small finds' are listed and described in Chapter 8. Grave goods in the normal archaeo-

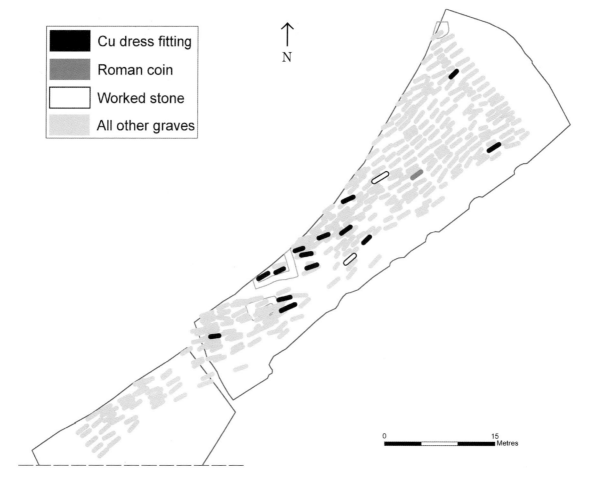

Figure 7.45 *The distribution of non-ceramic artefacts in graves*

the Bridgettine double house, but the burial was probably much later (*c* 1430–1540) than the Chichester example. Ten burials from St Clement's nunnery, York, have pins attested only by green staining (Gilchrist and Sloane 2005, 81). Nuns in general may have been buried in a particular type of headdress, but this does not mean that the Chichester skeleton was that of a woman in religious orders. The distinction between lay and religious was in any case often blurred at death; the moribund would seek and gain admission to a religious community not long before their decease, often in return for past benefactions, and a lay man or woman might thus be buried in the habit of a monk or nun.

Pins were also the commonest articles overall (ten additional examples). Their distribution was very restricted, with each occurring in the vicinity of the stone-lined tombs in the middle of the site. There were three pins with skeleton 144, a leper woman, but the others occurred singly, in male as well as female graves. Given the context, the description of these pins as shroud pins is permissible but they are unlikely to have been manufactured specifically for use in a funerary context, and alone would have been inadequate to hold together a winding sheet. Their most likely function was to tack together the winding sheet until it could be sewn up in the usual manner, and what we have recovered are a few

examples that the woman undertaking that task had omitted to retrieve. Their distribution within the cemetery may reflect nothing more than the activities of a careless individual.

Needle

An unstratified needle could have been accidentally left in a shroud after it had been sewn up, but as it had cotton thread wrapped around the shaft it is more likely to post-date the cemetery.

Lace tags

Lace tags were found in three graves and two more were found in other contexts. They could have come from ordinary items of clothing but as one was found with a man (S25), one with a woman (S94) and another with a child about eight years old (S297), a funerary rather than a fashion context seems the more probable. They may derive from the ends of cords used to tie shrouds, especially those of the 'Christmas cracker' variety (Chapter 3). Similar tags were found in quantity at the cemetery of Whithorn Priory where they were dated to *c* 1350–1450 (Nicholson and Hill 1997, 35).

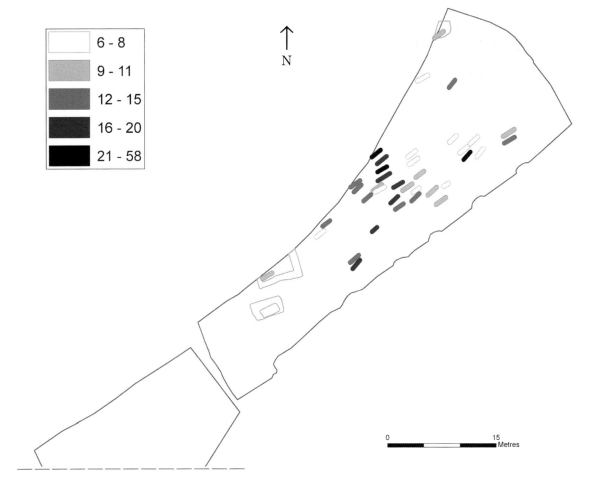

Figure 7.46   *The distribution of pottery sherds in graves*

Buckles

Six buckles were found, three of them in graves. One was a plain circular frame buckle of a type found from the late 13th century to post-medieval times that occurred with skeleton 82, an adult male. The second stratified example, with skeleton 244, another adult male, was an oval frame buckle with ornate outside edges and a plate datable to the late 12th to late 14th century, and the third, with skeleton 124, a young woman, was a subrectangular frame buckle of the late 12th to mid-15th century. All came from the centre of the cemetery but it would be unwise to make anything of the apparent distribution from so few examples. As it is generally assumed that the corpse was naked apart from a winding sheet, the reasons for the presence of the buckles are unclear.[34] It would be rash to write off all examples as intrusive.

Buttons

Two buttons were found but none in graves and the only metallic items not of bronze, a gold ring and a lead window came, were not found in graves either. The usual miscellany of unidentifiable

bronze items was also mostly from contexts other than graves.

Non-metallic finds

These may be rapidly summarised. First, there were three wood fragments, two from burials. Also from a burial was a carved chalk fragment with an incised cross, a unique find. A probable pumice stone came from one grave and a fine sandstone hone from a ditch (709) of late prehistoric origin. There were three unstratified fragments of vessel glass. A fragment of glazed peg-tile with the burial of a child about three years old may have been deliberate; it was perhaps a favourite plaything. There was no building in the vicinity.

Pottery in graves (Fig 7.46)

Broken pottery is usually a by-product of domestic sites and is a rare find in medieval cemeteries. When it does occur, the sherds tend to be small and the main diagnostic factor is consequently the fabric rather than variations in form that occur over time. As a suitable clay deposit could be, and often was, exploited for many centuries, the date of a given sherd in such-and-such a fabric may fall within a very broad chronological band such as 12th to 16th century. This is of limited help in trying to date areas within the cemetery, as has been seen above. The date of pottery is not, however, the main concern here. No complete or anywhere near complete vessels were recovered from graves, and it may be concluded with near certainty that all potsherds found their way accidentally into graves. This is discussed further in Chapter 8.

The position of the body within the grave (Figs 7.30–7.31)

The burials were supine inhumations all, apart from one, with heads to the liturgical west. Even so, there was considerable variation in how the body lay within the grave. Amongst the data examined, although the results are not reproduced here, were the positions of the skulls (leaning left, leaning right, looking straight up) and the legs.[35] Most skeletons had legs outstretched but it was concluded that variations were random and seemingly meaningless. Difficult to interpret, but possibly significant, were the positions of the arms, all of which must represent the attitude of the corpse when wrapped in its winding sheet.

Sixteen percent were Type A with the arms beside the body and the rest were variants in which the arms lay on top of the body. Least common of all were Type B (hands in prayer), which constituted only 5% of the total. Type C (arms folded) accounted for over half of all burials, and Type D (hands over pelvis) a quarter.

There are numerous theoretical possibilities to explain these differences, ranging from the customs and usages of individuals who laid out the dead to the application of differing practices to discrete sections of the graveyard population. In a few instances the nature of the disease may account for the position. A probable male hunchback from Doncaster West Street with Pott's Disease (spinal TB) was, not surprisingly, buried on his side (Buckland *et al* 1989, 134–5 and 424–7). It might be assumed, for example, that the least common method of laying out, with hands beneath the chin (Type B), was reserved for individuals who had something in common with each other (eg they were priests, priors, proctors, women religious etc) and were therefore privileged to be marked out in death by this distinctive feature. In terms of grave distribution, half the examples

(five) occur in Area B2, and only one occurs in A2, B1 and A1 containing two examples apiece. The two such (female) burials in Area B1 are both secondary, reinforcing the idea that the practice was, at least in Chichester, a late one. This hypothesis seems to be undermined by (male) burial 79 in Area A2, which in theory is primary (it cuts no earlier grave) but in practice may be quite late, lying, as it does, on the periphery of the area used for burials. In Area A1, one of the examples is again a secondary grave, but the other (372) is inescapably primary. The practice may have been confined to adults, but the total number of examples is so small that the absence of a child burial of this type is statistically insignificant. Although more men than women were buried in this manner (the numbers are 6:4), the rite seems overall to be more commonly associated with women, given the imbalance between the sexes in the cemetery. Again, the numbers are so small as to render any such conclusion at best questionable. About all that can be said for certain is that the custom was not specific to either sex nor confined to a short period. Two of the graves were demonstrably those of lepers, so it was not restricted to strangers who sought burial here, and one grave at least (136) is stratigraphically so late that it, and perhaps as many as half of all examples, are of the post-Dissolution period.

Robinson's study (2003) concluded that a correlation existed between diseased individuals and certain arm positions, Type C being most commonly used for the diseased, followed by Type D, but as these are respectively the commonest and next commonest positions, the raw figures are unsurprising. In practice, nearly every cemetery occupant is likely to have been diseased, and the only valid distinction is between those with diseases that had affected the skeleton and those that had not (because the disease was insufficiently advanced) or did not. The former include leprosy, TB and syphilis. A re-examination of the data, treating probable examples of disease as confirmed, produced the following (Table 7.4).

Studies of arm positions in other cemeteries have indicated a possible correlation between position and sex. The best evidence is at Ipswich Blackfriars, where 21 of 24 burials with arms across their chests/stomachs were male and the other three possibly female, indicating that this position may be a male phenomenon (Mays 1991). However, the closely dated cemetery (1235–80) at St Mary Spital, London, had just over half the bodies with hands in the pelvic region and none at all with their arms crossed over their chests, and no correlation could be

Table 7.4   Arm positions and skeletal evidence for disease

Position A		Position B		Position C		Position D	
disease	no disease	disease	no disease	disease	no disease	disease	no disease
7%	9%	1%	4%	17%	38%	12%	13%
13	18	2	8	32	72	23	24

found with any variable such as age, sex or location (Thomas *et al* 1997, 121).

Others have suggested that the body position changes through time. At Hereford cathedral the earlier burials are said to have arms at their side or hands in the pelvic region, but the later ones had arms either over the chest or across the stomach (Stone and Appleton-Fox 1996). In the same region, at St Oswald's Priory Gloucester, a similar pattern has been noted (Heighway and Bryant 1999, 204). Both samples are very male-biased.

Finally, a correlation between laying out and the place of burial has been proposed at St Andrew's, York (Stroud and Kemp 1993, 150), where skeletons east of the church were much more likely (76%) to have their hands on the body than those south of the church (43%). Overall, there is as yet no convincing evidence that the position of the body is governed by any such factors as sex, age or location, but when the corpus of evidence is larger, laying-out practices may be seen to have a regional and perhaps chronological component.

Notes

1. Hospitale sive Domus Pauperu' Leprosoru' Sanctoru' Jacobi et Marie Magdalene juxta Cicestria Ricardus Odeby Magister inde (*Valor Ecclesiasticus temp. Henrici VIII auctoritate regia institutus* (1810), **I**, 304).
2. By the 15th century the inhabitants of Holy Innocents leper hospital, Lincoln, habitually used their cemetery for grazing (Pugh 1981, 567).
3. Barney Sloane (pers comm) has suggested that the burial with the pins may be that of an anchoress attached to the hospital, or that both may be the graves of non-inmates who took the veil *ad succurrendum*.
4. Area A2 corresponds approximately to zone 1 in the original scheme, and Areas B1 and B2 to zones 2 and 3 respectively.
5. As it cuts a number of skeletons of the early, predominantly male, cemetery its earliest date must be the period of graveyard extension. It was quite clearly not the boundary of the early cemetery when that cemetery was in use.
6. Her text gives the mean as 230°, but her diagram contradicts this.
7. A headstone cross was found at the New Romney (Kent) leper house (Rigold 1964) but such finds are rare.
8. Probable lepers are counted as certain for these crude statistics.
9. In the absence of historical record, it could have been argued that the hospital was either late to acquire or late to exercise its right to its own cemetery, but the first burial, of Richard son of the clerk, is recorded before the end of the 12th century (Chapter 5).
10. This is unlikely to have been a deliberate act of disrespect since the reversed position became traditionally reserved for a priest to face his congregation on Judgement Day: see Chapter 3. Prone burials (not recorded at this cemetery) are more likely to represent society's disgust with the deceased.
11. The figures are as follows: A1 primary, two; A1 intermediate, none; A1 latest, one; A2 primary, two in feature 237; A2 intermediate, three; A2 latest, three, a figure of 9% of all adult burials in Area A.
12. In parts of Co. Clare these are known as strangers' graveyards. It is said that those suicidally inclined, knowing their own church would deny them burial in the parish graveyard if they killed themselves, would travel to somewhere they were unknown before doing the deed and thus hope to qualify for a Christian, if low-status, burial. They also served for the burial of shipwrecked sailors whose bodies were unclaimed by their kin.
13. The more obvious local institution to take on the role was St Mary's, in the middle of the city.
14. For the purposes of this discussion, probable women are counted as certain examples, as are probable men.
15. There was no theological bar to burying lepers in their parish cemeteries and it must have been the custom before hospitals acquired their own cemeteries.
16. Nos 53, 104, 106, 137a, 150, 203, 211, 239, 278, 291, 307, 309, 331, 361.
17. Nos 8, 18, 26, 31, 121, 142, 146, 148, 187, 197, 228, 295, 314, 325, 341, 365.
18. Although it was almost certainly higher than the garden of the 'leper cottage'. The 1986–87 site had been stripped for construction work before archaeologists were alerted to the site's potential.
19. Were the secondary burials therefore of lesser status?
20. This conclusion seems to agree with the 1539 rental (Appendix 6), which implies that a part of the cemetery, presumably no longer in use, was available for rent.
21. Amongst other things, it is interesting that the Reformation brought about neither a radical nor a gradual change in laying-out practices, presumably because there was nothing objectionable about what had been inherited from Catholic times.
22. At St John's Norwich there were hints of possible organic matter ('pillows') by skulls or feet in some burials (Elizabeth Popescu, pers comm).
23. Morgan 1992, 46.
24. For example, imported timber. Its use in such a well-wooded county as Sussex before *c* 1700 may have been limited but it must be remembered that it was the Kentish port, Deal, which supplied its generic name.
25. One way round the problem would have been to cover an open 'box' with planks immediately

before backfilling. The plank-covered burials from St Andrew Fishergate, York, referred to in Chapter 3, may indirectly attest such a practice.

26. One nail on each corner and three down each side, perhaps ten in all.

27. The initial investigation of coffin shapes was by Robbie Browse, a field officer with Southern Archaeology at the time of this work. Although the writer does not totally accept his findings, his research records have been most useful.

28. Robinson (2003) thought she could see clusters but the writer is unconvinced.

29. It may be asked where the normal medieval parishioner obtained his or her coffin. The sacristan or verger seems to have been one source of supply, although whether he himself was the manufacturer is unclear.

30. There is a slight tendency for women to be buried in Type A coffins but the numbers are so small as to be statistically questionable.

31. To confuse matters further, the writer could see examples of coffins that, to his eye, were essentially wedge-shaped with the point removed.

32. By Robbie Browse and James Kenny, both then of Southern Archaeology.

33. Alternatively, non-lepers may have been permitted to choose a shroud burial but lepers were not.

34. One possibility is that the deceased's belt was used to secure the winding sheet.

35. Robinson (2003) also looked at leg position and she too concluded that it was random.

8 The finds

8.1 Pins: a report on associated textile remains *by R C Janaway*

Finds list

Table 8.1 List of copper alloy objects with associated textile remains

Description	Small find no.	Context no.	Skeleton no.
Copper alloy pin	127	258	118
Copper alloy pin	131	287	Area of 118, 119, 123, 129, 130, 133
Copper alloy pin	147	311	144
Copper alloy pin	157	311	144
8 copper alloy hair pins	191	376	176
Copper alloy needle	155	U/S	
Copper alloy lace tag	22	54	25
Copper alloy lace tag	97	200	94

Methods

The metal alloy composition of the objects was determined by a semi-quantitative energy dispersive X-ray fluorescence analysis. The surfaces were examined under a stereo-microscope at magnifications between ×10 and ×75. Fragments of adhering organic material were detached by scalpel and forceps. These were soaked in a 10% solution of di-Na EDTA for 24 hours. The residue was then washed and mounted for light microscopy. The samples were examined using plain and polarised incident light at ×400.

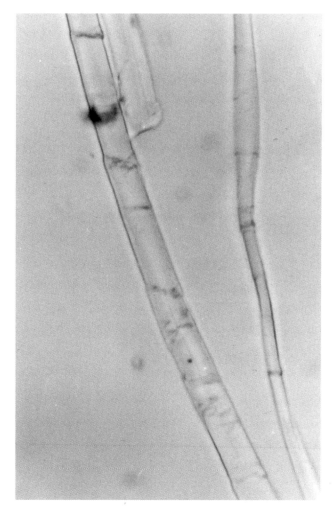

Figure 8.1 Small find 127. Mass of bast fibres after corrosion matrix removed with EDTA. Original magnification ×10. Photo: Bradford University

Figure 8.2 Small find 127. Bast fibre. Original magnification ×400. Photo: Bradford University

Table 8.2   Catalogue of metallic small finds with their associated textiles

For pin use types, see Figure 8.5

Small find number	127 (Figs 8.1–8.2)
Description	Shroud pin
Metal composition	Brass 70/30
Pin head type	Missing
Shaft complete?	No
Shaft length	17.8mm
Textile description	Textile on all surfaces of shaft for whole length. Thick wad of textile remains 2.4mm in diameter around head end of shaft. Z spun single ply. Use type C.
Fibre type	Bast
Small find number	131
Description	Shroud pin
Metal composition	Brass 80/20
Pin head type	Missing
Shaft complete?	In two fragments
Shaft length	19.9mm, 5mm
Textile description	Woven textile on all faces of shaft middle, one side of head and end of tip. Spin and weave indiscernible
Fibre type	Unidentifiable
Small find number	147
Description	Shroud pin
Metal composition	Brass 70/30
Pin head type	Missing
Shaft complete?	No
Shaft length	11.7mm
Textile description	Fibres mainly adhering to one face of shaft, but towards head some evidence of shaft having been inserted through cloth thickness. Spin and weave indiscernible. Use type A or B
Fibre type	Unidentifiable
Small find number	157
Description	Shroud pin
Metal composition	(leaded) brass
Pin head type	Missing
Shaft complete?	No
Shaft length	18.3mm
Textile description	Fibre remains on all surfaces except point. Use type C
Fibre type	Bast
Small find number	191.1
Description	Hair pin
Metal composition	(leaded) brass
Pin head type	Round
Shaft complete?	Point missing
Shaft length	28.8mm
Textile description	Organic material around shaft. Very degraded and possibly not textile

Small find number	191.2
Description	Hair pin
Metal composition	(leaded) brass
Pin head type	
Shaft complete?	Yes
Shaft length	23.1mm
Textile description	No textile remains

Small find number	191.3
Description	Hair pin
Metal composition	(leaded) brass
Pin head type	Missing
Shaft complete?	Head and point missing
Shaft length	1.7mm
Textile description	Some organics, possibly not textile, probably reed or grass

Small find number	191.4
Description	Hair pin
Metal composition	Brass 80/20
Pin head type	Round
Shaft complete?	Yes
Shaft length	21.8mm
Textile description	Very degraded organic material adhering to part of shaft. Impossible to identify
Fibre type	Unidentifiable

Small find number	191.5
Description	Hair pin
Metal composition	(leaded) brass
Pin head type	Missing
Shaft complete?	Head and point missing
Shaft length	9.8mm
Textile description	No organic material

Small find number	191.6
Description	Hair pin
Metal composition	(leaded) brass
Pin head type	Round
Shaft complete?	Point missing
Shaft length	17.9mm
Textile description	Single fibre adhering to shaft
Fibre type	Unidentifiable

Small find number	191.7
Description	Hair pin
Metal composition	(leaded) brass
Pin head type	Round
Shaft complete?	Point missing
Shaft length	9.6mm
Textile description	Organic material (not textile) adhering to shaft

Small find number	191.8
Description	Hair pin
Metal composition	Low Zn brass
Pin head type	Missing
Shaft complete?	Head missing
Shaft length	15.3mm
Textile description	Organic material (not textile) adhering to shaft

Small find number	155 (Figs 8.3–8.4)
Description	Needle
Metal composition	(leaded) brass
Textile description	Has been discarded with shaft inserted into cloth or used as a pin? There is evidence of woven fabric on one face of shaft but also spiral ridges in the corrosion that may indicate that the needle had thread inserted through eye and wrapped around the shaft.
Fibre type	Cotton

Small find number	22
Description	Lace tag
Metal composition	(leaded) brass
Description	Rolled brass sheet rolled into tube with fibrous material in centre
Textile description	Unidentifiable

Small find number	97
Description	Lace tag
Metal composition	Brass 80/20
Description	Rolled brass sheet rolled into tube with fibrous material in centre
Textile description	Unidentifiable

Figure 8.3 Small find 155. Detail showing spiral from cotton thread wrapped around shaft. Photo: Bradford University

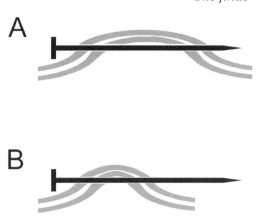

Figure 8.5. Pin use types

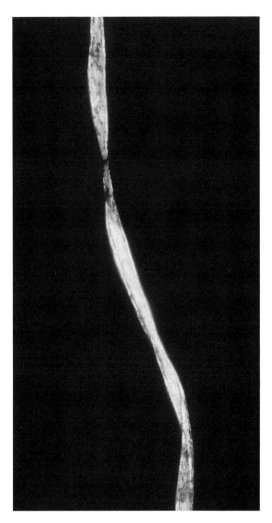

Figure 8.4 Small find 155. Cotton fibre, polarised light. Original magnification ×400. Photo: Bradford University

A note on cotton in Britain *by John Magilton*

Cotton is said to have been first imported to England for yarn in the 16th century, although there are earlier records of its use as padding. Up to *c* 1750 it was generally mixed either with linen or worsted, but from the later 18th century onwards pure cotton garments, the raw materials imported from the American colonies or West Indies, became common (Baines 1835).

8.2   Non-metallic small finds *by James Kenny*

Table 8.3   Catalogue of non-metallic small finds

Description	Small find no.	Context no.	Skeleton no.	Date
Wood fragments	56	119		
Wood fragments	62	137	72	
Carved Malmstone (Upper Greensand) object: crudely carved human lips or vulva with, on the smoothed flat base, a series of rows of drilled dots. A toilet abrader, akin to a modern pumice stone?	113	230	108	? P-med
Green-glazed peg-tile fragment	136	286	132	Med
Fragment of Roman brick, 'packing for skull'	280	538	254	R-B
Chalk block incised with crude cross. Under skull	282	542	256	Med?
Clear green glass fragment	324	U/S	–	–
Bottle glass	360	U/S	–	P-med
Whetstone, Horsham Stone	362	709		Med?
Wood fragments			281	?

8.3   Non-ferrous metallic small finds (Fig 7.45) *by James Kenny*

Table 8.4   Non-ferrous metallic small finds
In column 4 (m) = male skeleton, (f) = female skeleton, (ch) = child burial

Description	Small find no.	Context no.	Skeleton no.	Date
Copper alloy shoe buckle with cast foliate decoration on frame	4			C17
Copper alloy lace tag	22	54	25(m)	
Copper alloy D-shaped buckle loop	28	U/S		C14
Simple yellow metal wire finger ring with small bezel set with a small, round, red stone or glass fragment	35	U/S		P-med
Copper alloy double-looped asymmetrical buckle	36	U/S		P-med
Copper alloy object, too corroded to identify	40			
Copper alloy object, too corroded to identify	41			
Copper alloy button, disc-shaped with 'cone shank'	55	U/S		C18
Copper alloy dress pin	67	157	75(m)	
Copper alloy plain, circular-framed buckle	76	171	82(m)	Late C13–p-med
Copper alloy lace tag	97	200	94(f)	
Copper alloy object, too corroded to identify	106	228		
Copper alloy subrectangular frame buckle with ?zoomorphic roller	124	270	124(f)	Late C12–15
Copper alloy dress pin fragment	127	258	118(m)	
Copper alloy object, too corroded to identify	128	258	118	
Copper alloy blazer button, disc-shaped with 'alpha shank', face coated with white metal	130	U/S		C19
Copper alloy dress pin fragment	131	287		
Lead window came fragment	132	287		
Copper alloy lace tag	135	287		
Copper alloy dress pin fragment	140	297	137(?)	
Copper alloy dress pin fragment	146	311	144(f)	
Copper alloy dress pin fragment	147	311	144(f)	
Copper alloy dress pin	154	313	145(m)	
Copper alloy needle, 70mm long	155	U/S		
Copper alloy dress pin fragment	157	311	144(f)	
Copper alloy pierced circular sheet object	174	338		
Copper alloy lace tag	177	189		
Copper alloy dress pin	190	374	175(m)	
8 copper alloy hair pins	191	376	176(f)	
Copper alloy dress pin	196	378	177(f)	
Copper alloy coin, Antoninus Pius, *as*	212	U/S		*c* AD 138–61
Copper alloy coin, illegible	257	U/S		Mid-C4
Copper alloy oval frame buckle with ornate outside edges, and plate	266	518	244(m)	Late C12–late 14
Copper alloy coin, Æ3, Constantius II	274			*c* AD 337–61
Copper alloy coin, Æ3, Constantine I	284	544		*c* AD 335–37
Copper alloy twisted wire object	293	563	267	
Copper alloy lace tag	326	623	297(ch)	
Copper alloy coin, Æ3, Constantine I	345			*c* AD 307–24
Copper alloy object, too corroded to identify	366	707		

8.4 The medieval and later pottery (Fig 7.46)
by James Kenny

Given the nature of the site it is not surprising that pottery finds, as indicators of domestic activity, were virtually absent. The quantities that were recovered are so small as almost certainly to represent either a light scatter of residual refuse deposited before all or parts of the cemetery were in use or intrusive material brought in after partial or complete disuse, or both. In order to identify the secure contexts which might contain primary deposits of pottery, those producing five or fewer sherds have been disregarded as statistically insignificant: this accounts for 261 of a total of 917 sherds. For the secure contexts that produced more than five sherds, the catalogue is as follows (the complete catalogue is held in archive).

Table 8.5 Medieval and later pottery

Context	Context description	Skeleton no.	Sherd nos by fabric	Quantity	Date
24	Fill of pit 23		1F6; 3F9; 1F8E; 2F11	7	C19
85		40	7F1; 1F6	8	C13–14
86		41	40F2	40	C11–12
113	(1F2; 2F1 directly below skeleton)	54	2F2; 5F1	7	C11–14
159		76	6F1; 1F6; 1F10	8	C12–14; P-med?
191		90	5F1; 1F6	6	C13–14
220		104	13F1; 7F6	20	C13–14
230		108	10F1; 2F6; 1F4	13	C13–14
286		132	7F1; 8F2; 2F7	17	C13
313		145	5F1; 2SF1; 2F6*; 1F10	10	C18
329		153	6F1	6	C12–14
356		166	5F1; 1F6; 2F9	8	C13–14; P-med
402		189	10F1; 2F4; 1F6	13	C13–14
408		192	7F1; 1F6	8	C13–14
415	Fill of ditch 413		30F1; 1F7; 3F10	34	C12–14; P-med?
425		199	5F4; 7F1; 3F6	15	C14
445		209	10F1; 1F3	11	C12–14
502		236	7F1, one with applied thumb-impressed strapwork decoration	7	C12–C14
512		241	9F1	9	C12–14
522		246	7F1	7	C12–14
536		253	10F2/F1; 1F4 with applied thumb-impressed strapwork decoration; 1F6; 1F10	13	C11–14; P-med?
538		254	10F1, including one cooking pot rim	10	C13–14
540		255	13F1; 2F6	15	C13–14
542		256 & 258	18F1, some ?F2 including two decorated with incised wavy lines	18	C11–13?
544		257	2F2; 7F1; 1F4	10	C10–14
547		259	6F1; 2F4; 1F2	9	C11–14
549		260	20F2/F1	20	C11–13?
557		264	38F2/F1, some applied thumb-impressed strapwork decoration; 2F6; 2F10	42	C13–14
559		265	10F1; 2F6	12	C13–14

Table 8.5 (*cont.*)   Medieval and later pottery

Context	Context description	Skeleton no.	Sherd nos by fabric	Quantity	Date
563		267	18F1; 1F6	19	C13–14
565		268	12F1	12	C12–14
571		271	6F1; 1F4	7	C12–14
573		272	14F1, including range of C12–13 cooking pot rims; 1F4; 2F6	17	C13–14
575		273	13F1; 1F6; 1F9	15	C12–14; P-med?
577		274	9F1; 4F6 with overglaze white-painted decoration	13	C14–15
589		280	57F1, including range of C13–14 cooking pot rims and some applied thumb-impressed strapwork decoration; 1F6	58	C13–14
667		S319	10F1; 1F6	11	C13–14
669	Fill of charnel pit 668		31F1, including range of C10–12 and C13–14 cooking pot rims; 5F7	36	C13–14
671		316	7F1; 1F6	8	C13–14
675	Fill of pit 674		13F1, 2F6	15	C13–14
685		325	8F1; 3F6	11	C13–14
766	Fill of lime kiln 827		31 F7 (conjoining: jug)	31	C13–14

(*Three conjoining sherds from the base of tripod-based pitcher in fabric EGGSG (F7), probably a Chichester Southgate product, *c* 13th century, found in the adjacent graves of skeletons 135, 145 and 176)

Pottery fabrics

The assemblage is dominated (82% by sherd count) by flint-gritted, coarseware cooking pots that are not particularly period-specific but are probably local products. Characteristically 'Saxo-Norman' fabrics, thought to date from the 11th to 12th centuries, are represented, as are forms and decoration typical of the 12th to 13th and 13th to 14th centuries. The majority of the remainder (13%) are green-glazed locally produced jugs and pitchers that start to predominate in the later 13th and 14th centuries. The rest are either sandy medieval coarsewares (2.5%) or post-medieval (and later) terracottas, white earthenwares and stonewares (2.5%). The assemblage is notable for its poverty, the only fine wares being represented by later post-medieval and 19th-century wares that probably post-date the use of the cemetery.

The extremely limited nature of the assemblage is illustrated by the fact that 4.7% of the green-glazed jug sherds came from a single pot in a single context (a possible tuyère in the stoke hole of the lime kiln).

Table 8.6   Pottery fabrics

No.	Name	%	Description
F1	coarse medieval	74	Coarse earthenware with moderate to frequent medium to large angular flint grit, usually fired to reddish- or pinkish-buff or dark to very dark grey. Either simple, long, everted rims typical of the 12th to 13th centuries or angular, developed rims of the 13th to 14th centuries. Sometimes has applied thumb-impressed strapwork decoration on the exterior. Local.
F2	Saxo-Norman	8	As CM (F1) but with occasional small, well-rounded voids (due to the leaching out of a mineral?). Simple, long, everted rims. 11th to 12th centuries? Local.
F3	sandy coarse medieval	0.5	Coarse, sandy, flint-gritted earthenware. Angular, developed rims of the 13th to 14th centuries. Local?
F4	sandy medieval	2	Sandy medieval earthenware.
F5	very sandy medieval	0	Very sandy medieval earthenware, with very large, rounded grains of sand. Midhurst/Graffham area? 13th to 14th centuries?

Table 8.6 (*cont.*)   Pottery fabrics

No.	Name	%	Description
F6	green-glazed sandy	7	Externally (and occasionally internally) green-glazed sandy earthenware. Jugs and pitchers. 13th to 14th centuries. Chichester or Binsted kilns? Similar with overglaze white-painted decoration probably a later product of the same kilns. 14th to 15th centuries?
F7	green-glazed flinty	6	Externally green-glazed coarse, sandy, flint-gritted earthenware. Jugs and pitchers. 13th to 14th centuries. Chichester or Binsted kilns?
F8	'Tudor green'	0	Cream-coloured sandy earthenware with thick, bright apple-green glaze on exterior and interior surfaces. Late 15th to early 16th century.
F9	green-glazed terracotta	1	Externally (and occasionally internally) dull apple-green-glazed terracotta. Graffham product? 18th century?
F10	salt-glazed stoneware	0.3	Salt-glazed stoneware. 18th to 20th century.
F11	red-glazed terracotta	0	Red-glazed terracotta. Local. 18th to 20th century.
F12	terracotta	1	Unglazed terracotta, sometimes with external white-painted decoration. Local, 19th to 20th century?
F13	Tin-glazed earthenware	0.2	Tin-glazed English white earthenware. 19th to 20th century.

Discussion

The quantities of sherds in some of the graves, especially nos 41, 264 and 280, are too high to be intrusive. It is therefore likely that all the medieval pottery is residual. Figure 7.46 seems to indicate a concentration near the centre of the north-eastern half of the site, presumably the location of a group of rubbish pits or a midden-like deposit that was virtually eradicated by the cemetery and subsequent use of the site. Unfortunately the quantities of pottery are so small that complete absence may not be significant.

The pottery assemblage is very similar to the sort that might be expected to be collected from the surface of a ploughed field near to a minor, impoverished medieval settlement. Using this analogy the small quantities, poor quality and distribution might represent the deposition of domestic refuse thinly across the surface of an open area, in this case perhaps a garden. This was subsequently reused as a cemetery. It is instructive that the only contexts that might contain secure assemblages – the charnel pit 668 and the lime kiln 827 – both post-dating the late 13th century, were both subsequently overlain by graves, clear evidence for the spread of the cemetery into areas not originally used for burial.

Roman pottery

Roman pottery and tile were also recovered but are not discussed above. They contrast with the medieval material in indicating the likelihood of an occupation site nearby, reinforcing what might be inferred from the coins.

Part 3

The human skeletal remains

Foreword *by Frances Lee*

Shortly after the excavations at Chichester in 1986 the human remains were sent to Bradford University. At the time, Dr Keith Manchester had newly created the Calvin Wells Laboratory for Burial Archaeology in the Department of Archaeological Sciences. Keith, a world authority on the bone changes of leprosy, and his research assistant, Charlotte Roberts, had recently completed a SERC research project on *The Palaeopathological Evidence for Leprosy and Tuberculosis in Britain*. It was therefore decided that the best place for the burials to be studied was at Bradford under the supervision of Keith Manchester. The analysis and bone report was carried out by Frances Lee in consultation with Keith. His contribution to this volume has been fundamental, all of the authors having benefited from his expertise and enthusiasm; Keith's influence cannot be over-emphasised. Indeed it would be fair to say that most of the initial diagnoses were either made or verified by him.

The interest in this extraordinary collection has meant that soon after the publication of the interim reports (Lee and Magilton 1989; Magilton and Lee 1989) many visiting researchers and students began to work on the material. This has greatly enhanced our understanding of leprosy, in particular the collaboration of Dr Keith Manchester and Dr Johs Andersen, a clinician in Denmark, and Professor Donald Ortner of the Smithsonian Institution in Washington DC who have all have worked on refining the criteria for the diagnosis of this disease in human bone.

Charlotte Roberts, now Professor of Archaeology at Durham University, along with Zoe Chundun, curated the assemblage and made it possible for MSc students to work on the collection. Charlotte has supervised many original pieces of research on the assemblage and also carried out her own studies. In 1999 she ran an important conference at Bradford entitled *The Past and Present of Leprosy* which brought together experts from all over the world; many of the papers featured work on the Chichester collection. Dr Chris Knüsel has now taken over Charlotte's role at Bradford encouraging and offering advice to many more research students using the material. He has also made contributions to our understanding of the disease processes visible in the collection through his own research. The students' theses are listed on the CD, as are the publications that have emerged since the excavations in 1986.

Much more is still to be written on the pathology of Chichester and this volume is in no way the last word on the subject. However, it represents years of investigation by many researchers and the foresight and dedication of Dr Keith Manchester to the palaeopathology of leprosy. Finally the human bone chapters would have taken a very different form if it had not been for the vision and drive of Anthea Boylston who has patiently advised, edited and encouraged the writers of this section of the book.

Note

In Part 3 the term burial has been used to distinguish individuals, rather than skeletons, eg burial 78.

Glossary of medical terms

A

ABSCESS   A localised collection of pus.

ACUTE   Having a short and relatively severe course.

AETIOLOGY   The cause of disease.

ALVEOLUS   The sockets or hard tissue in which the teeth are set.

AMELOBLAST   A cell in the innermost layer of enamel.

ANAESTHESIA   Loss of bodily sensation especially pain.

ANAEMIA   A condition characterised by inadequate red blood cells or haemoglobin in the blood.

ANKYLOSIS   A condition in which the movement of a joint is restricted by fibrous or bony union of the bones.

ANTRUM   A natural hollow or cavity.

APOPHYSIS   A bony outgrowth that has not separated from the bone of which it forms a part, such as a process or tuberosity.

ARTHRITIS   Inflammation of the joint or joints.

ARTHROPATHY   Any form of joint disease.

ASYMPTOMATIC   Without symptoms.

ATROPHY   A wasting away.

ATTRITION   The natural process of wearing down the biting surface of the teeth by mastication.

B

BACTERIA   A large group of unicellular micro-organisms.

BENIGN   Not threatening to life or health.

BRACHIAL   Relating to the arm.

BRONCHUS   The air passages of the lungs.

BRONCHIECTASIS   A condition characterised by dilation of the bronchi. This is generally as a result of infection of the bronchial tree leading to obstruction of the bronchi.

BUCCAL   Relating to the cheek.

C

CALCULUS   A solid pathological concretion on the teeth.

CARIES   Process of gradual decay in the dental hard tissues.

CARTILAGE   A hard but pliable substance forming the joint surfaces.

CERVICAL   Relating to the neck.

CHONDRAL   Relating to cartilage.

CHRONIC   Continuing for a long time, constantly recurring.

CLOACA   An opening in the involucrum of a necrosed bone.

CONGENITAL   Conditions which are either present at birth or appear shortly after.

CORTICAL BONE   Part of the cortex or outer, more compact, bone.

CRURAL   Relating to the leg.

CYST   A hollow tumour containing fluid or soft material.

D

DEGENERATION   Breakdown of organised structure into a less organised form.

DENTINE   The hard portion of tooth surrounding the pulp and covered by the enamel.

DEVELOPMENTAL   Pertaining to the series of changes by which the embryo becomes a mature organism.

DIAPHYSIS   The shaft of a long bone.

DIPLOE   The layer of spongy bone that intervenes between the compact outer and inner tables of the skull.

DISTAL   Farthest from the centre or midline of the body.

DORSAL   Relating to the back.

E

EBURNATION   A degenerative condition in which the bone becomes hardened and polished. It is a consequence of osteoarthritis and the wearing away of the cartilage to expose the bone beneath.

ECTOCRANIAL   The outside of the skull.

EMBRYONIC   In an early stage of development, relating to the embryo.

ENDOCRINE   Relating to internal secretions.

ENDOSTEUM   The tissue lining the medullary cavity of bone.

ENTHESOPATHY   A bony outgrowth at the site of a tendon or ligament attachment on bone.

EPIPHYSIS   Secondary growth centre attached to a bone and separated by cartilage.

EROSIVE   Relating to superficial destruction and wearing away of the tissue.

G

GANGOSA   'Muffled voice' – grossly mutilating ulcerative destruction of the nose, soft and hard palates and pharynx; a late sequel of yaws, endemic syphilis or leprosy.

GASTROINTESTINAL   Relating to the stomach or intestinal tract.

GENOME   The complete gene complement of an organism.

GINGIVAL   Pertaining to gums.

GRANULOMA(TA)   A chronic inflammatory response initiated by infectious and non- infectious agents.

GUMMA(TA)   Chronic focal areas of inflammatory destruction seen in treponemal disease.

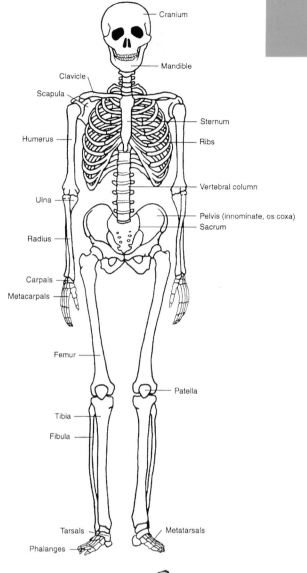

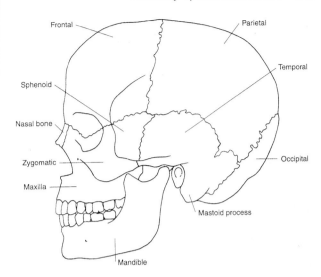

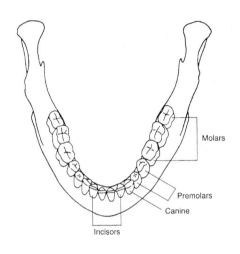

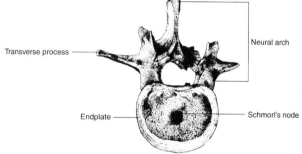

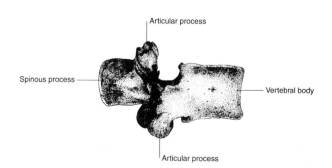

Buccal - towards cheek

Occlusal - biting surface

Mesial - towards midline

Distal - away from midline

Lingual - towards tongue

H

HAEMATOMA A localised collection of blood.

HAEMOPTYSIS Spitting up blood-stained sputum.

HAEMORRHAGE Any escape of blood from the vessels that naturally contain it.

HOMEOSTASIS The maintenance of metabolic equilibrium.

HYPEROSTOSIS An overgrowth of bone.

HYPERPLASIA An abnormal increase in the number of cells of a tissue.

HYPERTROPHY An increase in size.

I

IMMUNITY The ability of an organism to resist disease.

INCUBATION PERIOD Time between exposure to an infectious disease and the appearance of the first signs.

INFECTION The invasion of the body by a pathogenic organism and its subsequent multiplication in the body.

INFLAMMATION The reaction of tissues to injury.

INTERVERTEBRAL DISC Fibro-cartilaginous tissue between successive vertebrae.

L

LABIAL Towards the lip

LAMINA A thin plate of material.

LESION A pathological disturbance such as an injury.

LINGUAL Towards the tongue.

LYTIC Destruction of bone cells.

M

MACULES A stain spot or thickening.

MALIGNANT Cells which are uncontrollable or resistant to therapy and rapidly spreading.

MASTOIDITIS Inflammation of the mastoid antrum (part of the temporal bone) and cells.

MEMBRANE A thin pliable sheet of material.

MENINGES The membrane surrounding the brain and spinal cord.

METABOLIC The chemical processes that are essential to life.

METASTASISE Spreading of disease from one part of the body to another.

METAPHYSIS The growth zone of bone adjacent to the growth plate (epiphysis).

MORBIDITY Relating to or characterised by disease.

MORPHOGENESIS The evolution and development of form.

MORPHOLOGICAL The structure and form of the organism.

MORTALITY The number of deaths in a given period.

MUCUS The free slime which is secreted from the mucous membrane, comprised of a mixture of secretions from glands, inorganic salts, cells and leukocytes.

N

NECROSIS Death of a limited portion of tissue.

NEONATAL Newborn (0–3 months).

NEURAL Relating to the nerves.

NEUROPATHY Any disease of the nervous system.

O

OEDEMA An abnormal localised accumulation of fluid beneath the skin or in one or more cavities of the body.

OSSICLE A small bone.

OCCLUSION Contact between the upper and lower teeth during normal movement of the mandible.

OSSIFICATION The formation of bone.

OSTEOMA A tumour composed of bone tissue.

OSTEITIS Inflammation of the bone as a result of infection or injury.

OSTEOID Like bone; organic matrix of bone.

OSTEOARTHROSIS Chronic arthritis of a degenerative type, usually but not invariably associated with increasing age.

OSTEOBLAST A bone-producing cell.

OSTEOLYSIS A localised destruction of bone.

OSTEOMALACIA A condition which results in the softening of the bone.

OSTEOMYELITIS Inflammation in the marrow of the bone.

OSTEOPENIA A condition in which there is a loss of bone density.

OSTEOPOROSIS Condition in which there is a loss of bone matrix.

OSTEOPHYTE An exostosis or outgrowth of bone.

P

PAGET'S DISEASE A chronic disease of unknown cause in which the bones, particularly those of the skull, limbs and spine, gradually become thick and also soft, causing them to bend.

PALAEOPATHOLOGY The study of diseases in the past.

PATHOGEN Any disease-producing organism.

PATHOLOGY The cause of disease and its effects on the structure and function of the body tissues.

PERINATE Shortly after birth.

PERIODONTAL Relating to the tissues around the dentition.

PERIOSTEUM The membrane surrounding a bone.

PERIOSTITIS An infection of the periosteum.

PHENOTYPE The physical, biochemical and physiological make-up of an individual determined both genetically and environmentally.

PHYSIOLOGICAL Relating to the healthy functioning of organs and the changes that the whole body undergoes in the course of its activities.

PIRIFORM Pear-shaped.

PLAQUE A small abnormal patch on the tissues of the body.

PLEURA The membrane that forms a covering for the lung.

PULMONARY Affecting the lungs.
PUS A thick fluid that is found in abscesses or ulcers.
PYOGENIC Producing pus.

R
RESORPTION The loss of substance through physiological or pathological means.
RHINOMAXILLARY Relating to the nose and maxilla/upper jaw.

S
SACRALISATION Fusion of the 5th lumbar vertebra to the first segment of the sacrum.
SCLEROTIC A hardening or thickening of organisms as a result of chronic inflammation.
SCOLIOSIS A deviation from a normally vertical straight line of the spine.
SEPSIS Poisoning by the products of growth of micro-organisms.
SINUS Narrow cavities of various kinds occurring naturally or resulting from disease.
SPUTUM Saliva mixed with mucus.
SPONDYLOSIS Pathological changes to the intervertebral plate.
STRAIN To overtax a faculty of the body.
STRESS Any potential damaging strain, force or agent which stimulates a physiological defence reaction.
SUBCHONDRAL Beneath the cartilage.
SUBLUXATION An incomplete or partial dislocation.

SULCUS A linear groove, furrow or slight depression.
SYNOSTOSIS Union by bony material of adjacent bones normally separated.
SYNOVIAL A transparent lubricating fluid found in the joints.

T
THORACIC Relating to the thorax, the area between the neck and respiratory diaphragm.
TRABECULAR The sieve-like inner or supporting tissue of the bone.
TRAUMA An injury inflicted by force or some physical agent.
TUMOUR A swelling, but not as a result of inflammation.

U
ULCER A breach in the surface of the skin or membrane that does not heal quickly.

V
VASCULAR Relating to blood vessels or blood supply.
VENTRICLE The term applied to the lower two cavities of the heart and also the cavities within the brain.
VIRUS One of a group of infective agents responsible for some of the most important diseases affecting man.
VISCERAL Relating to the larger organs lying within the cavities of the chest and abdomen.

Reference

W A R Thomson, 1984 *Black's Medical Dictionary*. London: Adam & Charles Black

9 Physical anthropology
by Frances Lee and John Magilton

Introduction

In 1986 building contractors discovered burials known from a previous development in 1947 to be from the former leprosy hospital of St James and St Mary Magdalene. Subsequent investigation by Chichester District Archaeological Unit identified 330 distinct graves. In December 1993, further excavations in advance of building work yielded 44 additional graves. The assemblage is of great importance for understanding the history of leprosy in medieval and early modern times (Magilton 1986, 14). No excavations on this scale had taken place in known leper institutions since the 1950s when a study of Danish medieval cemeteries by Møller-Christensen (1953, 1961, 1978) defined new criteria for diagnosing leprosy in skeletal remains.

The aims of the study were to:

- establish the sex and age at death of each individual,
- identify the range of diseases present at the site and to consider evidence for possible treatment in the medieval period,
- establish what evidence for leprosy and other diseases at Chichester could tell us about the way these conditions have changed over time, and
- ascertain if the skeletal pathology could provide information on occupation, lifestyle, nutrition and/or diet of the community.

The following chapters include sections on various aspects of the osteology and palaeopathology contributed by scholars who have studied these features of the Chichester collection in detail. Appendix 7 (on

Figure 9.1 Post-mortem damage to the cranium of burial 78, possibly caused by beetles

CD) contains much of the raw data, including the catalogue of skeletons, so that future researchers should be able to make comparisons with other sites.

Burial was carried out in the cemetery from west to east and was a fairly continuous process. Therefore the division into phases was somewhat arbitrary. However, for demographic and palaeopathological comparisons, it was considered that a distinction could be made between those interred at the western end when the hospital functioned as a leprosarium (Area A) and those in the eastern zone when it was an almshouse (Area B) (see Chapter 7).

Results

Preservation

The burial conditions prevailing in a cemetery and the care with which the skeletons are retrieved will determine how much information can be gained from archaeological human bone. In addition, the completeness of each skeleton decides whether sex and age estimation techniques, necessary for demographic study, can be reliably undertaken and whether a picture can be obtained of the distribution of pathological lesions in a particular individual. Medieval cemeteries are notorious for the amount of intercutting between the graves but the situation at Chichester was much better than is usually the case. Retrieval of the small bones of the hands and feet is essential for consideration of pathological changes in a highly unusual assemblage such as St James' Hospital. To this end, the areas surrounding the hands and feet were sieved and the tiniest phalanx or sesamoid bone was collected.

Each inhumation was categorised by its state of preservation and degree of fragmentation, and scored accordingly. Most were in a good (41.7%) to fair (36.5%) condition (Table 9.1) with some post-mortem breakage and weathering of the cortical bone. Individual elements displayed surface erosion as a result of physical, chemical or biological processes, which had affected the bones in the burial environment (eg Fig 9.1). Those individu-

Table 9.1 Comparison of the degree of preservation of burials between Areas A and B

Area	Good	Fair	Poor	Total
Area A	62 (49.2%)	45 (35.8%)	19 (14.9%)	126
Area B	98 (38.0%)	95 (37.0%)	65 (25.0%)	258
Totals	**160 (41.7%)**	**140 (36.5%)**	**84 (21.8%)**	**384**

Table 9.2 Proportion of each burial present in the two areas

Area	0–25	%	25–50	%	50–75	%	75–100	%	Complete	%
A	15	3.91	26	6.77	12	3.13	25	6.51	48	12.50
B	25	6.51	21	5.47	44	11.46	76	19.79	92	23.96
Total	40	10.42	47	12.24	56	14.58	101	26.30	140	36.46

als buried at the western, or earlier, end of the site were better preserved than those in the later part of the cemetery, although the proportion of complete burials varied little between the two areas (Table 9.2). As might be anticipated, the better organised parts of the site, at the extreme eastern and western ends, had the greatest number of complete burials, 45% (68) and 65.9% (29) respectively. Individuals with the poorest preservation and completeness were found in the central, or transitional, parts of the site. These areas had not only a higher number of juveniles, but also considerable intercutting of graves and disturbance of the burials. Looking at the site as a whole, 62.8% (241) of burials excavated were complete or almost complete and most, 77.3% (297), had more than half the skeleton preserved. The most notable feature of this population was the excellent preservation of the hands and feet. This was extremely important for the diagnosis of leprosy to be made, since without these parts of the body being present many cases would have been missed.

Counting the dead

Three hundred and seventy-four graves were excavated, producing at least 384 individuals. Cranial and postcranial bones were counted not only to establish the minimum number of those present but also so that accurate prevalence rates for particular pathologies could be estimated. The results of these counts are shown in Appendix 7, Tables 1–4. Occasionally graves had additional remains in the cut or fill. Where possible, neighbouring skeletons were checked to see if the material came from the later burial cutting the earlier one, and in most cases these additional bones could be allocated to an existing skeleton number. Rarely do they represent a new or separate burial.

However, extra skeletons were found in several contexts. Incomplete burials 137a, 137b and 137c were contained within the fill of the masonry structure above the stone-lined tomb 65. All three were considered to be late in date as they were associated with a 17th-century sherd. A second individual, an adult male, was excavated from the fill (context 52) of grave 51, which has skeleton 24 as its primary burial. Likewise context 54 contained the fragmentary remains of a minimum of two adults. This context is the fill for grave 53 containing burial 25 which is already recorded and complete; these are therefore extra individuals. At least eight graves contained the remains of more than one individual.

These include burials 32 (a and b), 67 (a and b), 113 (a, b and c), 130 (a and b), 137 (a, b and c), 171 (a and b), 311 (a and b), 313 (a, b and c). Fragments of five individuals were excavated from context 55, a pit which cut several burials. These remains were found to be parts of skeleton 28, 32b, 37 and 73 and do not add to the total number of individuals.

The partially excavated charnel pit 668 contained a minimum of eight individuals. These included five adults, three of whom are male and two unsexed, in addition to an adolescent, a child and a young child/infant. The bone counts from the partial excavation of this pit, along with other unstratified disarticulated material, have not been included in the minimum number counts, but descriptions of the pathologies are discussed in the relevant chapters.

Age and sex

The age and sex of individuals were determined by as many criteria as possible following recommendations published in the *Journal of Human Evolution* (Workshop of European Anthropologists 1980), in conjunction with Krogman (1978) and Phenice (1969).

Sex estimation

An indication of sex was attempted for adults and late adolescents only, since the definitive traits used in sexing skeletal remains are not present until the onset of puberty. Consequently no attempt was made until the three parts of the *os coxa* had fused. The determination of sex in an adult relies on the differences in robusticity between the male and female skeleton and the adaptation of the female frame for childbearing. The skull and pelvis are therefore the most reliable indicators and accurate sex estimation relies on these two elements being well preserved. Table 9.3 shows the results for the site with five categories: male, probable male, female, probable female and unknown. When the site is considered in its entirety, 49.8% of the burials (190) were male or probably male, 20.8% (81) female or probable female, and 29.4% (113) were of undetermined sex.

The ratio of male to female burials is clearly abnormal and is in the region of 1 female: 2.3 males. There are also differences when the two major subdivisions of the site are considered (Table 9.4). The western part, Area A, has a very high proportion of males with a ratio of approximately seven males to every female (Fig 9.2), although eight adults were

Table 9.3 Demography of the entire Chichester sample

Age group	Male		Probable Male		Female		Probable Female		Unknown		Total	
	n	%	n	%	n	%	n	%	n	%	n	%
Birth–1.0									17	4.43	17	4.43
1.1–2/5									24	6.25	24	6.25
2.6–6.5									27	7.03	27	7.03
6.6–10.5									16	4.17	16	4.17
10.6–14.5			1	0.26					10	2.60	11	2.86
14.6–17.0			4	1.04					2	0.52	6	1.56
Child									4	1.04	4	1.04
Young adult	41	10.68	7	1.82	13	3.39	2	0.52	1	0.26	64	16.67
Middle adult	54	14.06	6	1.56	24	6.25	4	1.04	1	0.26	89	23.18
Mature adult	58	15.10	5	1.30	30	7.81	4	1.04	2	0.52	99	25.78
Adult	9	2.34	5	1.30	2	0.52	2	0.52	9	2.38	27	7.03
Total	**162**	**42.63**	**28**	**7.28**	**69**	**17.83**	**12**	**2.84**	**113**	**29.46**	**384**	**100**

Table 9.4 Comparison of demographic profile between Areas A and B (percentages of total sample)

Age group	Area A		Area B		Area A		Area B		Area A		Area B	
	M	%	M	%	F	%	F	%	U	%	U	%
Birth–1.0											17	4.43
1.1–2/5											24	6.25
2.6–6.5											27	7.03
6.6–10.5									1	0.26	15	3.91
10.6–14.5			1	0.26							10	2.60
14.6–17.0			4	1.04					1	0.26	1	0.26
Child									4	1.04		
Young adult	26	6.77	22	5.73	4	1.04	11	2.86	1	0.26		
Middle adult	30	7.81	30	7.81	2	0.52	26	6.77			1	0.26
Mature adult	39	10.16	24	6.25	7	1.82	27	7.03	1	0.26	1	0.26
Adult	7	1.82	7	1.82	1	0.26	3	0.78	6	1.56	3	0.78
Total	**102**	**26.56**	**88**	**22.91**	**14**	**3.64**	**67**	**17.44**	**10**	**2.60**	**103**	**26.82**

of unknown sex. In the eastern area (B), the ratio of males to females is much more representative of a normal population structure. The explanation for a predominance of males at the western end of the site has a clear historical basis; the hospital was originally founded for eight leper brethren and the sex profile reflects this. At the time it was an institution based on monastic principles. Indeed, the lepers of St James' Hospital were adjured in 1408 to rise from their beds and perform the night offices (Appendix 2).

Age estimation in adults

Assessment of age in skeletal remains depends upon the developmental phase that each person has attained. The age assigned to an individual is the biological age, not an exact chronological one, and tends to reflect the demographic pattern of the reference population from which the method is derived. Hence there are problems detecting older individuals in a skeletal assemblage because at this stage of life the only reference points are degeneration of the bones and joints together with the degree of dental attrition. The rate at which these processes affect an individual has been found to vary greatly from person to person. Many of the methods of age estimation have been devised from the study of recent populations and there are differences in lifestyle between the present time and the medieval period, which may cause inaccuracies. The role a person plays in society varies according to their time of life and therefore landmarks such as puberty, marriage,

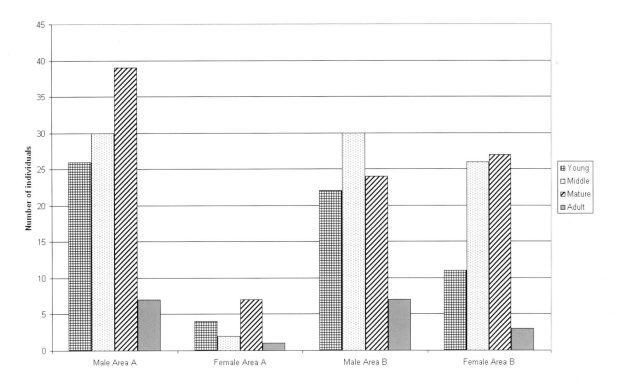

Figure 9.2   Age and sex profile of the cemetery contrasted between Areas A and B

the menopause and old age are considered more important than the exact chronological age of the individual when studying archaeological groups (Cox 2000).

Estimation of age in adults from Chichester depended upon:

- assessment of the pubic symphysis (Katz and Suchey 1986; Suchey *et al* 1988)
- changes to the sternal ends of the ribs (Iscan *et al* 1984; 1985)
- scoring of dental attrition (Brothwell 1981; Murphy 1959 adapted by Hillson 1986)
- cranial suture closure (Meindl and Lovejoy 1985).

The problems involved in age assessment of adults have been widely discussed (Molleson and Cox 1993; Brooks and Suchey 1990; Iscan and Loth 1986). Osteologists and physical anthropologists are now more acutely aware of the pitfalls in assigning a specific age for an individual. Three broad age categories were therefore employed: young = 17–29 years of age, middle = 30–45 years and mature = 46 years and over approximately. A fourth category of adult was reserved for those whose late epiphyses had fused but who could not be further classified.

The mortality curve reflects the history of the hospital; only a small number of children (2/126) were present in the western area (A) whereas 40% (103/258) of the population died before reaching adulthood in the eastern and more organised area (B) of the site. These figures are much more typical of a cross-section of the population, where one

would expect to see around 50% mortality before adulthood in the historic period (Gilchrist 2003). These figures may reflect not so much a decline in nursing standards as a difference in the conditions of those admitted since, as has been noted, leprosy in itself is not fatal whereas other conditions, tuberculosis for example, may have been.

Once more, different parts of the site present an interesting and varied picture (see Fig 7.22). In particular, the distribution of children's graves is notable, with two discrete areas where juveniles are interred. The first concentration is seemingly on the western margin of Area B, in the early part of the use of the site as an almshouse and possibly a transitional area between this and the leprous phase of the cemetery. There is a greater proportion of immature individuals in this region than anywhere else. The second area is a column of graves at the eastern edge of the site following the line of the boundary ditches. A few other immature burials are scattered throughout the eastern, more formal part of the cemetery. One possible explanation is that the western and eastern areas represent two separate, but consecutive, cemeteries. This hypothesis would require the admittance of non-adults for burial at a relatively early date in the history of the burial ground. It may be that the interments of children close to the western and southern boundaries are peripheral to the second phase of its existence.

There is only one child under 10 years of age buried in the western part of the cemetery. This probably reflects the long incubation period for leprosy, and the fact that the admissions policy did

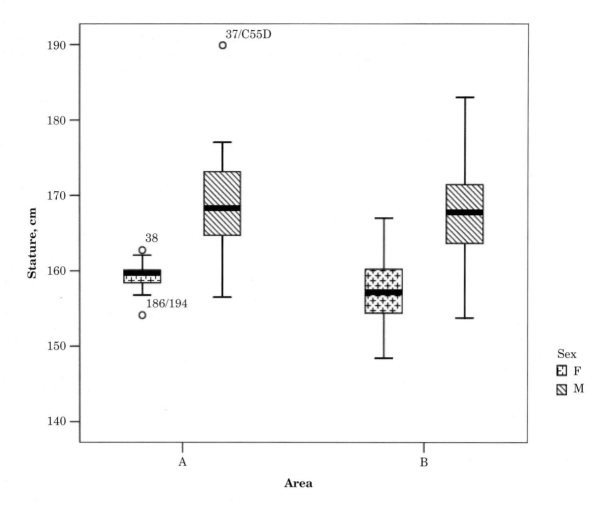

Figure 9.3 Box plot of stature variations by sex and area in the Chichester adult sample (Marianne Schweich)

not include children under a certain age. If juveniles were rarely admitted to this institution, they may nonetheless have been eligible for care in one of the other hospitals in Chichester.

The contrast between men and women in Area B is of interest, for it seems that far fewer women than men died at a young age. This is surprising as relatively greater mortality might have been suspected during a woman's child-bearing years, especially if the hospital offered assistance when difficult births were expected.[1] There are numerous possible explanations. It may be, for example, that women who died in childbirth normally sought and obtained burial in their home parish where they expected their spouses eventually to join them, thus distorting the figures. The distribution of adults appeared to be random. There was no clustering of, for example, mature adults that could suggest an élite group within the cemetery other than in the tombs described in Chapter 7. In one respect, events within the hospital cemetery ought to reflect society at large, for high mortality rates in the outside world (such as have been claimed for the 15th century: Gilchrist 2003, 400) are likely to be reflected in the frequency of burials.

Stature

An estimation of adult stature was made from long bone measurements using the regression formulae devised by Trotter (1970). Wherever possible the femur and tibia were employed, as the long bones from the lower limb give the smallest standard error. Stature was estimated for 81.5% (66/81) of the female population and 88% (167/190) of the male; subadults were excluded from the study. The overall mean statures and those for the different areas are given in Table 9.5 and Figure 9.3.

Male stature ranged from 155.2 to 190.1cm (5ft 1in to 6ft 2in) with a mean of 170.6cm (5ft 7in), whilst females ranged from 152 to 169cm (5ft to 5ft 6½in) with a mean of 160.2cm (5ft 3in). There were no significant differences in male stature between Areas A and B and the females were similar in this respect.

Although growth curves for the children buried in the Chichester cemetery and their indicators of general health suggested a considerable degree of deprivation, this was not reflected in adult stature. While it has occasionally been suggested in the literature that an inadequate diet may result in lower

Table 9.5 Stature estimation (cm)

Sex	Mean	Range	sd	Number of Individuals
Male (all)	169.7	155–190	6.3	167
Female (all)	159.4	152–169	4.2	66
Male (A)	170.6	155–190	6.2	92
Female (A)	159.2	156–162	2.4	7
Male (B)	168.7	155–186	6.3	75
Female (B)	158.6	152–169	4.3	59

final stature, this argument may be too simplistic. It is more likely that a poor diet would have simply delayed the age at which an adolescent ceased to grow (Mays 1998). As recently as the Second World War, long bone growth was continuing well past the age of 20 years (McKern 1970); nowadays most boys have stopped growing by eighteen and girls even earlier. When the results of stature estimation for St James' Hospital, Chichester, are compared with other sites dating to the late medieval period and earlier, they are found to be very similar. It was not until the middle years of the last century that any appreciable increase in average stature was noticed in Britain (Table 9.6).

Metric and non-metric data

Metrics

A series of anthropological measurements was taken from all adult skulls and postcranial bones where complete. Cranial and infracranial indices were calculated according to Bass (1981) and Brothwell (1981). The results of these measurements are recorded in Appendix 7 (Tables 5–7) but discussion has been kept to a minimum in this volume, which is primarily concerned with palaeopathology.

Measurements of the cranium are normally used to study variability in cranial shape within the population and for interpopulation comparisons. In the past, cranial measurements were used to show how the cranium has evolved through time and to compare groups which are separated geographically. However, more recently it has been shown that cranial shape is not only determined by genetic factors but can vary as a result of disease, deformation, diet and climate (Mays 1998). Indeed, such applications for craniometrics are considered in Chapter 11.

Individual cranial measurements are listed in Appendix 7, Table 5. Indices, which give further information on cranial shape, are shown in Appendix 7, Table 6. Males and females were recorded separately, as were the two areas of the cemetery. Three of the facial measurements should be treated with caution. These are the upper facial height, nasal breadth and nasal height, all of which may be altered by leprosy.

The results of the postcranial measurements, which include the means and ranges for the long bones, are given in Appendix 7, Table 7.

Non-metric variation

These traits are not pathological but anatomical anomalies and result from normal but varied developmental processes. They are scored on a present or absent basis and not on a continuous scale, unlike metrical analysis. As yet their exact relevance is not fully understood. The results are recorded in Appendix 7 (Tables 8–11) for use as comparative data; however, their discussion is limited

Table 9.6 Intersite stature comparison

Site	Males		Females		Reference
	Stature (m)	n	Stature (m)	n	
Trentholme Drive, York (Roman)	1.70	>100	1.56	30	Warwick 1968
Raunds Furnells, Northamptonshire (Anglo-Saxon)	1.67	50	1.62	33	Powell, in Boddington 1996
Worthy Park, Kingsworthy, Hants (5th–8th century)	1.74	23	1.61	27	Hawkes and Wells, 1983
Hull Magistrates' Court (14th–16th century)	1.69	79	1.59	27	Holst *et al* 2001
Fishergate, York (Period 6, 12th–16th century)	1.71	205	1.59	73	Stroud and Kemp 1993
Jewbury, York (12th–13th century)	1.67	135	1.56	116	Lilley *et al* 1994
St Nicholas Shambles, London (11th–12th century)	1.73	*c* 50	1.58	*c* 40	White 1988
St James' Hospital, Chichester	1.70	167	1.56	66	This study
Christ Church, Spitalfields	1.69	182	1.58	180	Molleson and Cox 1993
Modern – Britain	1.77		1.63		

to where they are considered to relate to pathology (see Chapter 10).

Non-metric traits were recorded for the present study using the descriptions set out in Berry and Berry (1967) and in the postcranial skeleton as described by Finnegan (1973). Twenty-six cranial and 28 postcranial traits were routinely recorded and a few extra anomalies were also noted as occasional observations. The results are broken down for each area with males and females recorded separately as some lesions are known to be more common in one sex or the other (Corruccini 1974), while others are considered to be side-related.

Notes

1. At St Helen-on-the-Walls, York, female mortality peaked in the 25–35 age range, as might have been expected, but male deaths peaked in the 35–45 years bracket (Dawes and Magilton 1980; Grauer 1991).

10 Congenital and developmental conditions
by Judi Sture

Introduction

The World Health Organisation (WHO 1997, 53) has defined a birth defect as 'any structural, functional or biochemical abnormality present at birth, whether detected at that time or not. This includes the overlapping categories of genetic disorders and birth abnormalities'. The situation is somewhat confused by the continuum-like nature of birth defects. When is a condition a defect, and when is it an extreme of normal development? Brothwell and Powers referred to a 'no man's land' from so-called normal variation through minor to major abnormality (Brothwell and Powers 1968, 173). For the purposes of this chapter, defects are defined as malformations of bone that may be diagnosed using clinical criteria (Barnes 1994; Cailliet 1995; Resnick and Niwayama 1988).

The majority of developmental defects originate during the early stages of embryonic development, and may occur in both the skeleton and the soft tissues. They may range from the most minor anomalies, which are asymptomatic, to the very severe, which are incompatible with life (Levene and Tudehope 1993).

Causes of developmental defects

It is estimated that about 2% of babies today present with a major birth defect but when minor defects are added, the figure rises to 7% (Carter 1971; Levene and Tudehope 1993). The incidence is highest in preterm babies (born before 37 weeks gestation), and in babies that are 'small for gestational age' (SGA), including low birth weight (LBW), which is linked to maternal health and nutrition (Levene and Tudehope 1993). Genetically mediated defects may be passed on to the foetus due to the parents' chromosomal make up. Alternatively, they may be induced as a result of some environmental factor acting on the constitution of genes or chromosomes in the foetus, leading to mutations in the affected or subsequent generations (Moore 1978, 63). Environmental causes include any agent that acts on the foetus while it is *in utero*, leading to a departure from normal development and growth. However, most authorities are agreed that the majority of birth defects are most likely the result of a combination of genetic and environmental factors, interacting in some complex manner which is yet to be identified. Levene and Tudehope (1993, 194) estimated that 20% of defects were of genetic origin alone, with environmental causes, including maternal infection, responsible for 2–3%, drugs and chemicals 2–3%, and maternal metabolic disease responsible for 1–2% of defects. The remainder of defects are assumed to be multifactorial, that is, due to a combination of both genetic and environmental causes.

Frequency of developmental defects

The clinical literature reveals variations in frequency, usually given as the incidence, of many defects depending on the sex of the individual (*not* the gender), geographical location, time of year at birth, age of the mother, and many other variables. Most of these cannot be identified in archaeological contexts. However, it is possible to identify certain patterns of defect frequency among archaeologically derived human remains (eg Sture 2001).

The medical literature shows that males appear to be more frequently affected with defects than females, although this varies depending on the type of defect. For example, cleft palate is reported to affect twice as many males as females (Levene and Tudehope 1993); but Jorde *et al* (1987) found that more females than males are affected with neural tube defects. The Chichester cemetery population followed the higher male defect rate trend overall, with 61% of males and 45% of females having one defect or more. There are often disagreements on sex-based frequencies in the literature depending on the area and scope of the relevant studies. There are also recognised geographical variations in the frequency of many defects (for example, neural tube defects and facial cleft defects), as well as variations along ethnic lines (Laurence 1966; Laurence *et al* 1968; Laurence and Tew 1971; De Beer Kaufman 1977; Levene and Tudehope 1993; Murray *et al* 1997).

Sources of data

Much of the work described in this chapter was undertaken as part of a wider study focusing on patterns of developmental defects between rural and urban communities in medieval England (Sture 2001). The other samples investigated in the study were derived from excavated early to late medieval cemeteries at Rounds Furnells, Northamptonshire (Boddington 1996); Wharram Percy, East Yorkshire (Hurst *et al* 1979); St Helen-on-the-Walls, York (Dawes and Magilton 1980); and the Augustinian Friary, Hull (Holst *et al* 2001). The work focused on a range of anomalies of the axial skeleton, most of which are found in the vertebral column. While

Figure 10.1   Occipitalisation of the atlas vertebra in burial 369, a young adult

some of the anomalies examined are not necessarily symptomatic, they were taken as variables that are subject to environmental variation, and as such may be seen as indicators of the environmental susceptibility of the foetus and its parents. In addition, as these defects are occult, they are less susceptible to cultural influence in social and burial practices (Post 1966).

Defects of the axial skeleton at Chichester

Craniocaudal border shifts

This phenomenon is most commonly found at the lumbosacral border, although it does occur at higher borders. It is often considered that transitional vertebrae are clinically insignificant, but the medical literature shows that this is not the case (Cailliet 1995; Castellvi *et al* 1984). Sacralisation is particularly related to back pain and nerve impairment, especially if it is unilateral. Lumbarisation, on the other hand, offers greater flexibility at the lumbosacral junction, and may be beneficial in childbirth and certain occupational activities involving lifting and bending.

Transitional vertebrae

Transitional vertebrae represent a segmental anomaly which is due to a delay in the formation of the embryonic vertebrae at the segmental borders. They are often found in association with a supernumerary vertebra either at the same junction, or in another segment of the vertebral column. Barnes (1994, 79–80) believes that mild to severe anomalies equate to the 'strength' of the factor that acted on the embryo to cause the anomaly. Burial 369 at Chichester displays transitional vertebrae at three segmental borders: there is occipitalisation of C1

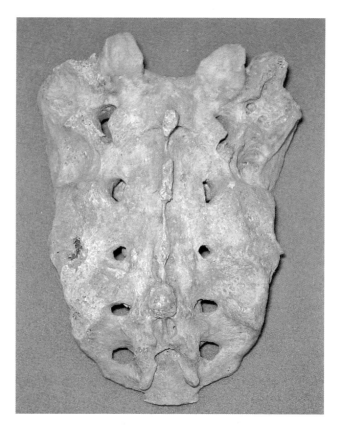

Figure 10.2   Complete sacralisation in burial 350

(Fig 10.1) in addition to transitional vertebrae at the thoracolumbar and lumbosacral junctions.

At the lower end of the vertebral column transitional vertebrae or border shifting exhibit as either sacralisation, a partial or complete (Fig 10.2) attachment of the lowest lumbar vertebra to S1, or lumbarisation, a partial or complete separation of S1 from S2, as the upper sacral element undergoes an inappropriate segmentation (Barnes 1994). The transverse process(es) of L5 may be abnormally defined, taking on the appearance of the S1 ala, being occasionally fused to the upper surface of the first sacral element, indicating an incipient sacralisation; alternatively, there may be some more or less distinct posterior arch development on the posterior face of the sacrum at S1.

The high sacralisation rate seen in Chichester males (29%) may be related to admission to the Chichester hospital/almshouse, particularly for the four individuals affected with a unilateral lumbosacral malformation (Jonsson *et al* 1989; Cailliet 1995). Transitional defects are closely associated with low back pain syndrome today and with a generalised reduction in mobility at the lumbosacral junction, either due to the fusion of the elements involved, or to pain inhibiting movement. These effects can have an impact on higher or lower levels of the vertebral column in the form of secondary changes. Transitional vertebrae may also be related to the appearance of Schmorl's nodes in archaeologically derived materials. The four individuals affected by unilateral sacralisation were 81, 335, 346 and 371 (Fig 10.3).

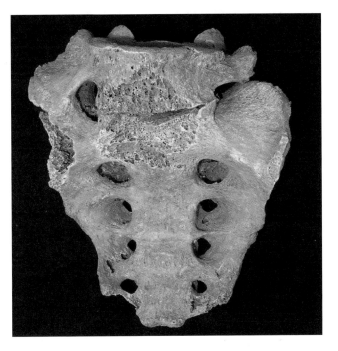

Figure 10.3   Partial sacralisation in burial 335

Figure 10.4   Compression fracture of L5 which is fused to a sacralised L6 in burial 190

In addition, 77% of those with sacralisation at Chichester also had other spinal anomalies. As co-occurrence of soft-tissue anomalies is associated with skeletal defects (Warkany 1971), such a co-occurrence frequency may equate well with a hospital/almshouse population. This suggests that a proportion of those affected with lumbosacral border shifting at Chichester may also have had soft tissue anomalies that rendered them less than healthy, and possibly unable to support themselves.

There were 64 cases of border shifting at the lumbosacral border at Chichester, affecting both males and females. This covers sacralisation (n = 47) and lumbarisation (n = 17). Nine individuals had signs of more than one vertebra being sacralised (Fig 10.4). As has been noted at other sites, border shifting was frequently associated with a supernumerary vertebra (n = 22, 4% of overall attributable border shifts), most commonly involving a sixth lumbar vertebra. Only six cases of sacralisation involved a simple fusion, partial or complete, of L5 (10%); the remainder were associated with an absent lumbar vertebra (sacralisation of L4, n = 1); sacralisation of the first or more coccygeal elements (n = 16, 27% of attributable border shifts), and with vertebral arch non-fusion being the most commonly associated defect (n = 21, 36% of total border shifts).

Numerical variation of vertebrae

The normal number of vertebrae in the pre-sacral vertebral column is 24. However, not all individuals have a full complement of vertebrae. Any segment of the column may exhibit fewer than the usual number of vertebrae, although this can only be diagnosed when the whole segment, and preferably the entire

column, is present. An absent element in one segment is often balanced by an 'extra' element in another, resulting in the usual number of vertebrae (for example, burial 217 with six lumbar and four sacral elements or C2). A few cases of numerical variation were noted overall, some with segmental variations making up the usual 24 pre-sacral number, others resulting in extra elements. The most common additional vertebra observed was a sixth lumbar element, which in 12/19 cases were partially or completely sacralised. Vertebral arch non-fusion was also present in the extra element in 6/19 cases.

Vertebral arch non-fusion (VAN)

This condition is variously described in the literature as 'cleft neural arch' or, more frequently, *spina bifida occulta*. The defect consists of a failure to unite of the two halves of the neural arch. There may be a complete absence of one or both arch halves, hypoplastic (shortened) arch halves, or a non-fusion in which one half crosses the midline to attempt a union with the opposite side. A bifid spinous process represents a minor developmental delay. VAN commonly occurs at segmental borders and in supernumerary vertebrae, which was the case at Chichester. It is particularly common at the lumbosacral junction, but also occurs elsewhere (Fig 10.5).

A vertebral arch non-fusion is a distinct entity from *spina bifida occulta*. It originates from a formation delay of the vertebral arch and has no relationship at all with the neural tube developmental field which

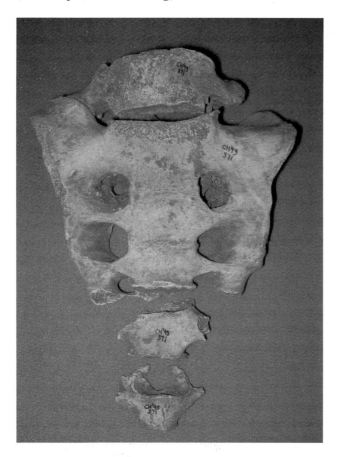

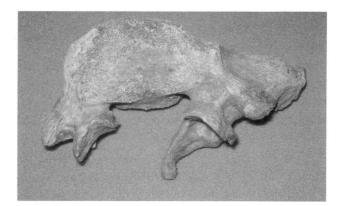

Figure 10.5 (a) Unfused and lumbarised first sacral vertebra (left), and (b) detail of neural arch deficit in S1 (above) in burial 371

produces *spina bifida occulta* (Barnes 1994; Sture 2004). A cleft sacrum, in which there is no formation of the arches at all, is an example of a VAN originating in the paraxial mesoderm field (Barnes 1994; Sture 2004). At Chichester there was a high rate of VAN, with 34% of individuals affected.

Defects of the neural tube developmental field (NTD)

Spina bifida occulta

A case of *spina bifida occulta* may be diagnosed by the outwardly (dorsally) flared nature of the resulting arch halves. This flaring formation results from the bone forming over the extruded tissues, which comprise the actual NTD, even if it is asymptomatic. Using this diagnostic criterion, six cases of *spina bifida occulta* were diagnosed at Chichester, comprising four males and two females. In only one case (a female) was the defect associated with another developmental anomaly, a partial lumbarisation of S1, which was itself the site of the SBO (Fig 10.5). None of the affected individuals was aged above 44 years.

A 'monstrous child' with apparent *spina bifida cystica* and showing the spinal cord and meninges extruding through the skin, appears on a notice dating to AD 1568 (Fig 10.6). The child is described as having 'a lump of flesh' in the centre of his back which looked like a rose, in addition to deformities of the lower limbs. He only lived for 24 hours. This strongly worded document provides evidence of how such congenital defects were feared at the time.

Miscellaneous vertebral defects

Burial 166, a child aged 8–9 years, has a notochord regression failure defect (sagittal cleft centrum) to the superior aspect of the seventh thoracic vertebral body with a cleft running towards the centre of the vertebral body. This represents an incipient butterfly vertebra. This condition has been associated clinically with gastrointestinal and central nervous system defects, as well as other vertebral defects (Barnes 1994). This child also has a developmental anomaly of the second and third cervical vertebrae in which the right side of the neural arch is rudimentary and retarded in development (see Fig 12.11). Four individuals have vestigial transverse processes on a single vertebra (337, 354, 360, 371). All of these cases are found in Area A.

Miscellaneous vertebral anomalies

Burial 21, a male aged 17–25, has a very narrow neural canal in the lumbar segment.
Burial 350, an adult male, has an absence of the left facet to the transverse process of the tenth thoracic vertebra.
Burial 368, an adult male, has a vestigial apophyseal joint to the twelfth thoracic and first lumbar vertebrae.

Accessory ribs

Thirteen individuals had evidence of extra ribs associated with either the seventh cervical or the first lumbar vertebrae. The exact position cannot always be identified, but in some instances facets to the vertebrae indicate their location. Cervical ribs were present in eight individuals (55, 91, 146, 209, 222,

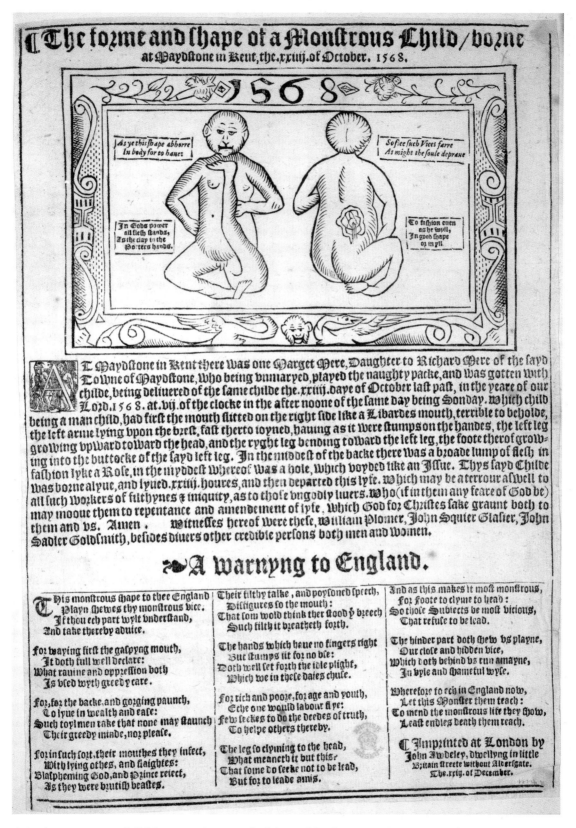

Figure 10.6   A monstrous child born with spina bifida at Maidstone in Kent on 24 October 1568

275, 349, 350), with five having bilateral lesions. Six individuals have lumbar ribs (23, 26, 27, 175, 263, 354), of which four are bilateral. Cervical ribs are a congenital over-development of the costal process of the seventh cervical vertebra. These may be asymptomatic, but can cause neurological or vascular (circulatory) disturbances in the upper limb. They may be the cause of local damage to the subclavian artery, and pressure against the rib can cause damage to the nerves supplying the arm (Adams 1981, 167). Rudimentary ribs in the lumbar region are probably of little or no importance. Krogman

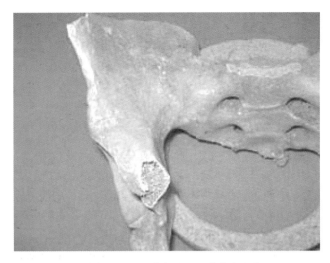

Figure 10.7 Congenital fusion of the right sacroiliac joint in burial 250

(1978, 220) notes that the incidence of cervical ribs from 559 individuals studied was 1.1%, with a rate of 8.8% in lumbar ribs.

Vestigial ribs

Incompletely formed vestigial ribs were noted in two individuals in the far west of Area A. They both have rudimentary 12th ribs (346, 353).

Pelvic anomaly

Congenital ankylosis of the right sacroiliac joint was seen in a middle-aged female from Area B (Fig 10.7). The bone in this area is extremely smooth and there is no evidence that there ever was a joint at this site.

Discussion

There was no significant difference statistically between the overall frequency of defects between Area A and Area B. However, there were significant differences between the two areas in terms of the frequency of sacralisation and supernumerary vertebrae (Table 10.1). There was also a significant difference in the frequency of females with defects between the two areas. This does seem to indicate a change in the health of female residents, possibly as a result of alterations in admission criteria. It could be that the majority of females buried in Area A were benefactors or relatives of the wardens, and the female burials from the eastern end (Area B) mainly residents of the almshouse. In terms of absolute figures, the females from Area B had a much higher burden of defects than those in Area A (which contained fourteen females, of whom three had defects; the

Table 10.1 Chi-square results for significant differences in prevalence between Areas A and B. Defects not mentioned here were all below 95% C.I.

Variable	Sex	Chi-sq value	p =
Overall defect prevalence	F	6.39	0.01
Paraxial mesoderm defect prevalence	F	4.87	0.05
Sacralisation	M and F	3.86	0.05
Supernumerary vertebra(e)	M and F	8.11	0.005

almshouse contained 66 females, of whom 28 had defects).

The pattern of higher male frequency of defects was mirrored across all of the other sites studied by the author (Sture 2001) except for Wharram Percy, where a higher proportion of females was affected. It could be that males are less buffered against environmental insults than are females when *in utero* (Saunders and Hoppa 1993).

Comparison with other sites

When compared with the four other sites studied by Sture (2001), the cemetery population at Chichester had the highest rate of developmental defects, among both adults and juveniles (Fig 10.8). Moreover, paraxial mesoderm defects (involving craniocaudal border shifting) were the most commonly observed anomalies and the most susceptible to environmental variation (Table 10.1).

A total of 52% of adults in the cemetery had one or more developmental defects, compared with 30–40% at the other sites. This high frequency of defects was not unexpected in a hospital/almshouse population, which was the focus of the sick and poor of the area. It should be remembered, however, that not all burials in the cemetery were those of the sick or poor – benefactors and the various wardens and their families are also likely to be present, although unidentified. Fig 10.9 and Tables 10.2 and 10.3 show the frequencies observed at Chichester.

Associated general health issues

Stress indicators

Females with defects at Chichester were more likely to exhibit stress indicators than females without defects, although this is not statistically significant. Stress indicators noted included *cribra orbitalia*, enamel hypoplasia and tibial periostitis. This finding was also noted at the other sites investigated by the author, including stress amongst males, which was recorded at Wharram Percy, Hull and York. This association with generalised stress

Table 10.2 Frequencies of defects affecting the vertebral column

Defect	Male	Female	Juven	Unsexed adult	Total	Prevalence %
Sacralisation	38/93	7/55	1/26	1/3	47/177	27
Lumbarisation	11/109	7/46	0/23	1/4	17/182	9
Other border shifts	4/142	2/67	1/30	1/4	8/243	3
Spina bifida occulta	4/133	2/61	0/29	0/5	6/228	3
VAN	39/108	15/56	5/28	2/3	61/195	31
Supernumerary vertebrae	18/128	4/66	1/31	0/5	23/230	10
Total	**114**	**37**	**8**	**5**	**162**	**–**

Table 10.3 Percentage frequencies of defects affecting the vertebral column

Defect	Male	Female	Juvenile	Unsexed adult
Sacralisation	41	13	4	33
Lumbarisation	10	15	0	25
Other border shifts	3	3	3	25
Spina bifida occulta	3	3	0	0
VAN	36	27	18	66
Supernumerary vertebrae	14	6	3	0

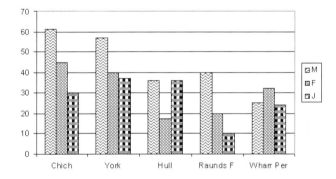

Figure 10.8 Percentage of individuals having one or more defects among five cemetery populations

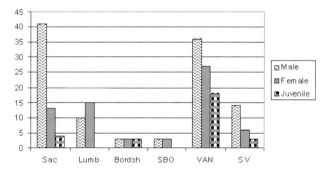

Figure 10.9 Percentage of defects of the axial skeleton observed at Chichester, showing affected percentage of observable population

suggests that the presence of defects is associated with other health-inhibiting factors, perhaps some soft-tissue or metabolic anomalies invisible to the anthropologist, or an overall increase in susceptibility to disease.

Summary

The high defect frequency of the Chichester population could reflect the fact that it derives from a leprosy hospital and almshouse. Most of the conditions and trends noted here are also found elsewhere, but it is argued that there is a greater concentration of developmental defects at St James' Hospital. As all the vertebral defects are invisible in life, and therefore free from cultural bias in terms

Key:
Sac = sacralisation
Lumb = lumbarisation
Bordsh = border shifting above lumbosacral level or unascribed lumbosacral shifts
SBO = spina bifida occulta (with neural involvement, ie neural tube field)
VAN = vertebral arch non-fusion (paraxial mesoderm field)
SV = supernumerary vertebrae

of discrimination in any way regarding burial, it is suggested that some or all of these defects may be accompanied by the presence of other, soft tissue anomalies. This is the subject of further research by the author. Individual case studies are described in detail in Appendix 8 (on CD).

11   Cranial asymmetry and developmental abnormalities *by Rebecca A Storm*

Introduction

Asymmetries and developmental abnormalities in the cranium can provide insight into the health of a past population. The cranium is a delicate and malleable structure and any insult during development can modify its shape and size (Herring 1994). In almost all bilateral structures, like the human body, the normal process of development is that each side of the structure should be a mirror of the other, thus creating perfect symmetry. During growth, in the need to retain symmetry all organisms have a self-correcting process, or developmental homeostasis. Any breakdown in this communication or deviations away from the intended symmetrical phenotype is considered to be a developmental instability (Van Valen 1962; Larsen 1997a; Møller and Swaddle 1998; Nijhout and Davidowitz 2003). These disruptions in stability are caused by mutations within the genome, biomechanical adaptations, and variations in the environment of the developing structure (Palmer 1994; Fields *et al* 1995; McManus 1982; Møller and Swaddle 1998).

One of the best measures of developmental instability is through the analysis of fluctuating asymmetries (FA). These are small variations in the two sides of bilateral structures that occur when an individual's homeostasis has been disrupted (Van Valen 1962). These variations are random, as they can occur on either side of the body, and are usually small differences, amounting to less that 1% of the measurable trait (Van Valen 1962; Møller and Pomiankowski 1993; Palmer and Strobeck 1997). Those individuals with higher fluctuating asymmetry frequencies will have had a higher level of disruption during their development. Many studies have established a direct negative relationship between asymmetry and health, fitness and sexual selection (Swaddle *et al* 1994). Further, it has been noted that those individuals with congenital abnormalities will tend to have a higher level of asymmetry (Cohen 1986; Livshits and Kobyliansky 1991; Møller and Swaddle 1998).

Although the human cranium has been widely studied by anthropologists, only now is its true complexity becoming better understood. Most crania have at least some degree of asymmetry, usually favouring the right side, due to the asymmetrical growth of the brain; but this normally differs only by a millimetre or less (Woo 1931; Hershkovitz *et al* 1997). Abnormal cranial asymmetry can have many causes – both congenital and developmental – including craniosynostosis, positional deformity, cleft lip/palate, torticollis or paralysis; or it may be a response to postcranial asymmetries. Further,

asymmetries often derive from longstanding pathological conditions. Many of these asymmetries can be so greatly deforming that they contribute to negative social stigma and can lead to the individual becoming an outcast from society. Previous osteological studies have identified some of these conditions in the crania of the population of St James' Hospital. These include a study conducted by Ward (1996) on mental retardation and more recently Leighton's (2005) research on diagnosing congenital conditions by a study of cranial size and shape.

Not only is there the physical osseous evidence from the hospital of St James and St Mary Magdalene, discussed below, there is also historical documentation of congenital conditions of both patients at this institution and of individuals from the wider Chichester area. This provides an indication of the negative reaction of the people of the time to such afflicted individuals. Although used as a leprosarium throughout most of its history, with the decline of leprosy during the late medieval period this hospital, like other similar institutions, became a home for people with a variety of afflictions, including those who suffered congenital conditions, of which some were deemed to be mentally disabled (Foucault 1965; Bishop 1970; Rubin 1987; Mora 1992). It is known that the function of the leprosarium and the almshouse was not only to provide care for the aged and infirm, but also to separate individuals who were seen as unacceptable members of society from the rest of the community (Rubin 1987). After the decline of leprosy in the 15th century, those with mental disabilities became the new ostracised class to be housed in such hospitals (Foucault 1965). As Mora (1992, 42) relates, 'rather than a sign of stigma, the mentally ill were seen as a living witness of the frailty of the lowest level of mankind'. There is documentary evidence that three individuals with mental deficiency were patients at St James' Hospital. In 1594 a list of inmates included 'John Pellard a diseased idiot, 30' and 'Elizabeth Vody an idiot, 17' (see Appendix 3 on CD). Records also indicate that the last admission in 1685–89 was that of a 'miserable idiot' (Turner 1861). Although the presence of abnormal cranial asymmetries does not necessarily indicate that an individual is mentally deficient, abnormally extreme asymmetry values may serve as evidence, as a large number of the congenital conditions associated with mental deficiencies have also been found to be also associated with abnormal asymmetries (Renier *et al* 1982; Malina and Buschang 1984; Jones 1997; Sun and Persing 1999). This being the case, it is possible that the three named 'idiots' comprise one of the asymmetric outliers described below.

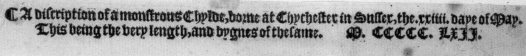

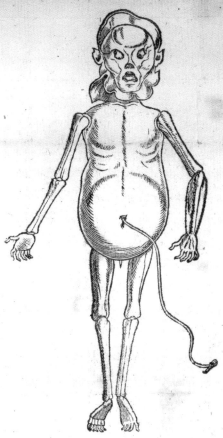

Figure 11.1 Warnings of a monstrous child born in Chichester 1562 (Anon 1562)

Further documentary evidence of medieval perceptions of these individuals includes two notices about monstrous children issued at Chichester, both of which mention and depict cranial abnormalities. The first is a document from 1562, pictured in Figure 11.1, that warns of a 'monstrous chylde' born in Chichester to a father named as 'Vyncent, a boucher' (Ihon 1562). This warning depicts a child whose misshapen frontal and parietals has the appearance of craniosynostosis, similar to individuals found at the hospital. The second, entitled *The Doome Warning all men to the judgement*, describes a child born in Chichester in 1580 as possessing

> *little shape of body, trussed together, the head verye great, bigger than the body, the body in compasse 9 inches, the arme an inche long, and two inches about the face, of indifferet favour, on the cheeke and chin the likenesse of a blacke beard, the legs wanted thighs, the toes crooked* (Batman 1581).

Although these two monstrous children's abnormalities were not compatible with life, there is a high probability that there were others born with congenital conditions associated with cranial asymmetries who did survive and who were housed at St James' Hospital.

Cranial asymmetry in Chichester

One hundred and ninety-four crania were examined for cranial asymmetry in the Chichester population, through 22 standard measurements taken on both the right and left sides (Table 11.1). Measurement error was assessed by repeating each measurement, on ten separate occasions, on both left and right sides of ten individuals. Technical error of measurements was then figured using the formula: $TEM = \sqrt{\Sigma(d^2)/2n}$, where d is the difference between repeated measurements and n is the number of replicated measurements (Dahlberg 1940; Knapp 1992). All measurements were found to have insignificant levels of error (p<0.01) (Table 11.2). FA was ascertained using a basic asymmetry formula of R-L, where R is the right side and L the left side of the measured trait; and by using the formula $|R-L| / (R+L/2) *100$, which calculates a percentage of asymmetry within a measured trait and thus compensates for the size of that trait (Palmer 1994; Palmer and Strobeck 2003). An asymmetry index for multiple traits for each individual was then calculated: $\Sigma|\ln(R_j/L_j)|/T$, where R_j and L_j are the measurements of the right and left side of each trait and T is the total number of traits (Palmer and Strobeck 2003). The results are reported to the 0.001 as FA scores represent a percentile of the asymmetry to the trait's size. After this, the results were subjected to the Grubb's test statistic (T_G) for population outliers for each measurement using the formula $T_G=(X_i-\mu)/SD$, where X_i is the observed value of the potential outlier,

Table 11.1 Measured bilateral traits

Measurement
Orbital breadth, ectoconchion (ec) to dacryon (d)
Orbital height, bisection of orbital breadth
Nasion (n) to orbitale (or)
Frontomalare temporale (fmt) to nasion (n)
Frontomalare temporale (fmt) to nasospinale (ns)
Cheek height, least superior and inferior height of the zygomatic
Mastoid length, mastoidale (ms) to porion (po)
Mastoid breadth, porion (po) to the posterior extent of the mastoid
Mastoid height, mastoidale (ms) to the floor of the digastric groove
Mastoidale (ms) to asterion (ast)
Maximum length of the digastric groove
Maximum length of the occipital condyle
Ectomolare (ecm) to the internaxillary suture
Opisthion (o) to porion (po)
Basion (ba) to porion (po)
Frontomalare temporale (fmt) to bregma (b)
Bregma (b) to porion (po)
Bregma (b) to zygoorbitale (zo)
Nasion (n) to mastoidale (ms)
Bregma (b) to asterion (ast)
Lambda (l) to frontomalare temporale (fmt)
Lambda (l) to asterion (ast)

μ is the population mean, and SD is the standard deviation (Palmer and Strobeck 2003). These scores were then assessed by a Levene's test for heterogeneity of variance.

With a mean value for multiple trait indices of 4%, fluctuating asymmetry in the Chichester population is above the expected value of <1% for the measured traits (Van Valen 1962; Møller and Pomiankowski 1993; Palmer and Strobeck 1997), indicating this population has very high levels of developmental instability (Tables 11.2–11.3). Differences between the sexes indicate that males from this site have a slightly higher FA at 4.1%, with females at 3.5%. Children at this site were found to have higher FA than adults, with those in late childhood showing the highest levels at 4.6%. In a comparison of cranial fluctuating asymmetry with six further populations (Table 11.4), individuals from Chichester were found to have the second highest FA (Fig 11.2). The only site with higher asymmetry values was found to be St Peter's Church, Wolverhampton, a Victorian group, which is known to have been under high levels of stress and of poor economic status (Storm forthcoming). The Chichester population was found to differ significantly from St Helen-on-the-Walls, Fishergate and York Minster populations; but it

**Table 11.2   Descriptive statistics of asymmetry scores
for each measurement, indicating the population norm**

Measurement	Intra-observer Error*			N	R-L		|R-L| / (R+L/2)	
	TEM	SD	P		Mean	SD	Mean	SD
Orbital breadth (ec-d)	0.3	3.0	0.01	41	0.3	0.8	0.015	0.014
Orbital height	0.2	2.8	0.006	41	0.2	0.7	0.017	0.014
n-or	0.3	2.5	0.01	40	0.2	0.7	0.011	0.007
fmt-n	0.3	2.6	0.01	119	0.3	1.1	0.013	0.015
fmt-ns	0.2	3.8	0.003	47	0.2	1.2	0.012	0.012
Cheek height	0.3	2.7	0.008	123	0.0	0.8	0.028	0.024
Mastoid length	0.3	3.3	0.007	123	0.5	1.6	0.038	0.038
Mastoid breadth	0.3	3.7	0.007	143	0.2	1.4	0.04	0.041
Mastoid height	0.3	2.7	0.01	120	-0.2	1.9	0.148	0.141
ms-ast	0.2	4.5	0.002	126	0.3	1.9	0.034	0.022
Digastric groove length	0.4	3.5	0.01	131	-0.8	2.8	0.091	0.093
Occipital condyle length	0.2	2.3	0.006	82	0.3	1.6	0.048	0.046
ccm-intermaxillary suture	0.3	2.4	0.01	90	0.1	1.2	0.028	0.028
o-po	0.3	3.8	0.008	49	0.0	2.0	0.019	0.020
ba-po	0.3	3.5	0.007	48	-0.4	1.8	0.023	0.020
fmt-b	0.3	5.3	0.003	96	0.2	1.9	0.009	0.014
b-po	0.4	5.1	0.005	52	0.9	2.1	0.013	0.012
b-zo	0.4	5.1	0.005	34	0.7	1.3	0.007	0.009
n-ms	0.3	5.5	0.004	42	0.3	2.3	0.012	0.015
b-ast	0.3	5.6	0.003	84	0.7	2.2	0.012	0.012
l-fmt	0.4	6.7	0.003	75	0.4	1.9	0.008	0.009
l-ast	0.3	4.7	0.002	86	0.5	2.1	0.017	0.017
Mean trait index				194	–	–	0.04	0.032

*TEM=Method error statistic $\sqrt{\sum (d^2)/2n}$, SD=the population's standard deviation of the measurement, p=TEM^2/SD^2

**Table 11.3   Fluctuating asymmetry values in Chichester, which are above normal
expected value of <1% (Van Valen 1962; Møller and Pomiankowski 1993; Palmer and Strobeck 1997)**

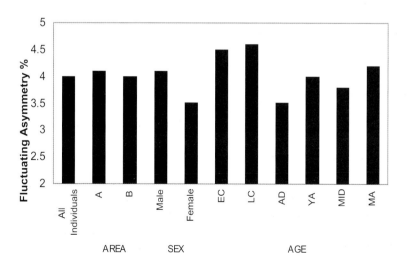

Area: A, Leprosarium phase of the site; B, Almshouse phase of the site
Age: EC, early childhood (2–6 years); LC, late childhood (7–12 years); AD, adolescence (13–17 years); YA, young adult (18–25 years);
MID, middle adult (26–45 years); MA, mature adult (46+ years)

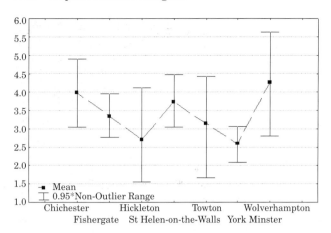

Figure 11.2 Chichester's mean fluctuating asymmetry score compared with six other archaeological sites in England

more closely related to highly stressed groups of medieval soldiers and Victorian populations.

Furthermore, the Grubb's statistic for outliers indicated that the Chichester population had a high number of significant outliers, that is, those with asymmetry measurements well above the mean and standard deviation for the population (Storm 2006a, 2006b). There are 42 crania from Chichester with individual measurements that fall outside the normal FA values for the populations. On close examination, these individuals were found to have had suffered from certain forms of congenital or developmental abnormalities. This could be evidence that this institution was used either to care for, or for the segregation of, those afflicted with phenotypically expressed and/or disabling congenital conditions (Storm 2006a). As a definite diagnosis of specific congenital syndromes from the skeletal remains is not possible in the majority of cases, only symptoms are recorded here and some tentative inferences drawn from them. There are three main expressions of developmental abnormality in those individuals exhibiting extreme asymmetry in the Chichester population discussed below. These are torticollis, craniosynostosis, and other sutural and shape abnormalities.

did not differ from the highly stressed populations of Wolverhampton, Hickleton, and Towton groups (Table 11.5). This indicates that Chichester was affected by higher levels of developmental instability than other contemporary populations, but was

Table 11.4 Comparative populations

Skeletal Population	N	Mean Asymmetry*	Period	Notes
Gilbertine Priory of St Andrew Fishergate, York	181	3.3%	Medieval	Lay population, priors, and influential families (Stroud and Kemp 1993)
St Wilfrid's Church, Hickleton	16	2.7%	Medieval to Victorian	Rectors or parsons of the church and influential families, most dating to the Victorian period (Sydes 1984; Dabell 1999)
St Helen-on-the-Walls, York	128	3.7%	Medieval	Poor lay population (Dawes and Magilton 1980)
Wars of the Roses battle site, Towton	24	3.3%	Medieval	Soldiers and conscripts (Fiorato et al 2000)
St Peter's Church, Wolverhampton	49	4.3%	Victorian	Poor industrial population (Neilson and Coates 2002)
York Minster, York	123	2.6%	Late Anglo-Saxon to late medieval	Clergy and prestigious families (Phillips and Heywood 1995)

* $\sum |\ln(R_j/L_j)|/T$

Table 11.5 Intersite comparisons

Chichester VS	N	Levene F(1,df)*	df	p value
Fishergate	181	7.75298	371	0.005637**
Hickleton	16	3.05338	206	0.082060
St Helen-on-the-Walls	128	4.45266	318	0.035628**
Wolverhampton	49	0.06884	239	0.407525
York Minster	123	26.98107	313	0.000000**
Towton	24	0.07199	214	0.788715

* Comparisons of mean trait scores $\sum |\ln(R_j/L_j)|/T$
** P<0.05

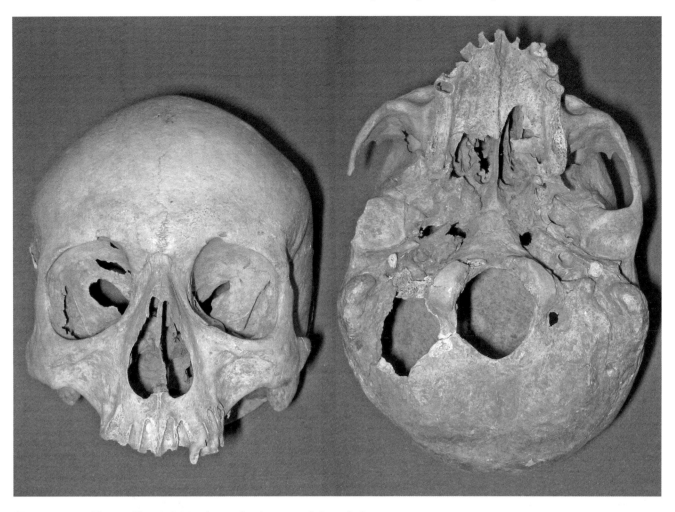

Figure 11.3   View of burial 32a from the front and from below

Torticollis

Torticollis is the abnormal lateral positioning of the neck with a degree of head rotation and tilt. This condition is usually indicative of an underlying congenital, developmental or pathological disorder, or it could be a response to a traumatic injury. It can have either a muscular or non-muscular involvement (Skinner *et al* 1989; Karmel-Ross 1997; Freed and Coulter-O'Berry 2004). Even today, with advances in our medical knowledge and better childbirth practices, as many as 18% of all children are born with a form of torticollis. Of these, muscular torticollis is considered to be the third most common congenital abnormality of the musculoskeletal system, with a prevalence of about 1 in 300 live births (Karmel-Ross 1997; Cheng *et al* 2000; Freed and Coulter-O'Berry 2004). Skeletal evidence of torticollis includes flattening of the frontal and occipital bones, torsion of the sagittal axis, facial asymmetry, dropped orbit, one enlarged and one atrophied mastoid process, recessed malar, posteriorly placed ipsilateral ear, bulging of the occipital on the affected side, cervical scoliosis, degenerative changes in the cervical vertebrae, mandibular asymmetry, changes to the clavicle and postcranial asymmetry (Skinner

et al 1989; Douglas 1991; Storm and Knüsel 2005; Knüsel 2002; Yu *et al* 2004).

The Chichester population has a relatively high prevalence of torticollis: 23 of 100 observable individuals have a degree of abnormal torsion of the cranium. The extent to which it is expressed is variable, but many of these peoples would have had a noticeable head tilt and rotation in life. These include burials 2, 5, 12, 25, 32a, 42, 43, 61, 74, 109, 117, 142, 71, 267, 272, 274, 295, 327, 346, 348, 349, 354 and 362. All of these individuals have at least four or more of the asymmetries and shape changes that are typical of torticollis. Of special note is burial 32a, which is a possible case of acquired muscular torticollis (Storm and Knüsel 2005) (Fig 11.3 and Appendix 9 on CD).

Craniosynostosis

Cranial asymmetry can be the result of compensational changes due to craniosynostosis, the premature closure of the cranial sutures. Today, craniosynostosis affects an average of three in 10,000 births worldwide (WHO 2002; Mossey and Castilla 2003). This condition occurs during the

Table 11.6
Terminology associated with cranial shape

Terminology	Skull Shape
Plagiocephaly	Obliquely and laterally deformed
Scaphocephaly	Narrow and elongated
Trigonocephaly	Triangular
Brachycephaly	Short in respect to breadth

cranium's growth period, which begins during early foetal development and continues until the age of seven when the brain has reached 90% of its adult size. When a suture is prematurely closed, the cranium will still continue to grow normally as the brain expands, forcing some areas to compensate for the disruption and thus deforming the overall shape (Cohen 1986; Kabbani and Raghuveer 2004). Tables 11.6–11.7 summarise the normal closure times of each suture and the distinct shape created by premature closure. The exact aetiology of premature suture closure is hard to determine, but can be separated into primary and secondary synostosis. Primary craniosynostosis can either have an isolated cause, like birth trauma, or can be related to a congenital syndrome, for example, Apert and Crouzon syndromes. Secondary craniosynostosis can be caused by thalassaemia, metabolic conditions (such as rickets and hyperparathyroidism), bone dysplasias or foetal insults (Aviv *et al* 2002; Kabbani and Raghuveer 2004).

Table 11.7 **Estimated ages when sutures begin to close and cranial shapes associated with early closure**
(Aviv *et al* 2002; Kokich 1986; Jimenez *et al* 1994)

Suture	Age closure begins	Skull shape associated with early closure
Metopic	9 months–2 years	Trigonocephaly
Coronal	24	Unilateral: Plagiocephaly Bilateral: Brachycephaly
Sagittal	22	Scaphocephaly
Lambdoid	26	Unilateral: Plagiocephaly Bilateral: Brachycephaly
Squamosal	35–39	Plagiocephaly
Occipitomastoid	26–30	Plagiocephaly

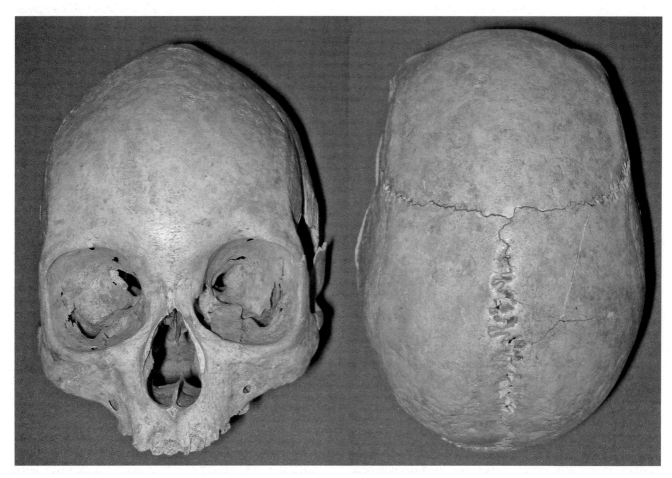

Figure 11.4 View of burial 38 from the front and from the side (scaphocephaly)

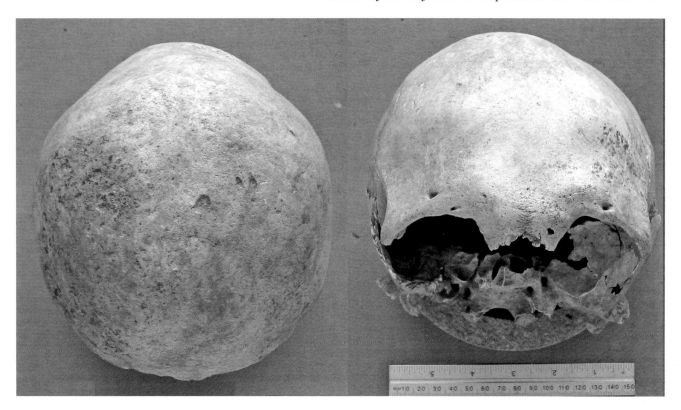

Figure 11.5   View of burial 74 from the front and from behind (plagiocephaly)

The effect of early closure of a suture on cranial shape is variable. In many cases these individuals would have a recognisable deformity; others would have been completely unaware of any abnormality. Today, craniosynostosis is usually corrected with surgical intervention, as it has been found to affect a child's psychological health and has an adverse isolating social stigma (Sun and Persing 1999), but this was not possible in the past. Furthermore, it has been found that with around 50% of premature closure of one or more sutures, there is increased pressure placed on the developing brain and this can result in deficiencies in a child's mental and cognitive abilities (Renier *et al* 1982; Sun and Persing 1999). This being the case, it is possible that one or more of the three named 'idiots' from the hospital of St James and St Mary Magdalene, mentioned in the introduction, could have been one of the individuals found to have premature craniosynostosis. No matter what their intelligence, those individuals with noticeable premature suture closure may have suffered social ostracism. This becomes clear with the negative documentary evidence of the monstrous child from Chichester, Figure 11.1, which appears to depict an individual who suffered from plagiocephaly, as can be seen in the cranial bossing on the right side of the head and an odd curvature on the left.

Of the 108 crania complete enough for examination of premature suture closer, there are eight individuals with clear cases of craniosynostosis within the Chichester population. This provides a very high prevalence of 7% of the observable population. Of these, at least four individuals (burials 38, 74, 109 and 374) are of special note as they would have had noticeable deformity, which may have affected their social interactions. A further six may have suffered early suture closure and asymmetries but were discounted in this assessment due to their age. Those individuals in Chichester with clear evidence of craniosynostosis include burials 38 (Fig 11.4), 74 (Fig 11.5), 109, 142, 327, 340, 370 and 374 (see Appendix 9 on CD).

Other sutural abnormalities

Other sutural anomalies found within the Chichester population that are associated with extreme asymmetry values include accessory wormian bones, metopism and positional head deformity. Wormian bones are extra osseous islands located within the sutures. These bony islands can be caused either by genetic predisposition or by excess stress placed on the cranium during growth and have been found to co-occur with cranial asymmetry, metopism, metabolic conditions and congenital malformations (Hess 1946; Bennett 1965). Furthermore, a study conducted by O'Loughlin (2004) found increased frequency of wormian bones in crania affected by deformation. Similarly, although usually considered a non-metric trait, metopism has been associated with congenital abnormalities, cranial asymmetry and

UNIVERSITY OF WINCHESTER
LIBRARY

Figure 11.6 View of burial 225 from behind, with seventeen wormian bones along the lambdoid suture

increased frontal curvature (Woo 1931; Torgersen 1951). Metopism is the persistence of the metopic suture, which normally closes by the second year of childhood, into adulthood. There are five individuals with extreme asymmetry values from Chichester that have abnormally large or numerous wormian bones in their sutures: burials 12, 134, 225 (Fig 11.6), 349, 351; and there are five individuals with metopism: burials 32, 43, 142, 295, 344. There is one additional individual whose asymmetry abnormalities are of special note, burial 267 (Fig 11.7). The asymmetries present (see Appendix 9), along with an unusual surface contour, flattening of the parietals posteriorly, evidence of healed cranial lesions, and plagiocephaly, could be indicative of positional head deformity with associated torticollis as a result of prolonged periods of lying down.

Summary

The high fluctuating asymmetry levels within the Chichester group indicate that these individuals were under greater developmental stress than is normal for medieval and more recent populations. As a result, they may have been more likely to suffer from poor health and diseases, such as leprosy. Many of those with asymmetry values for the cranium that fall outside the population norm have evidence of con-

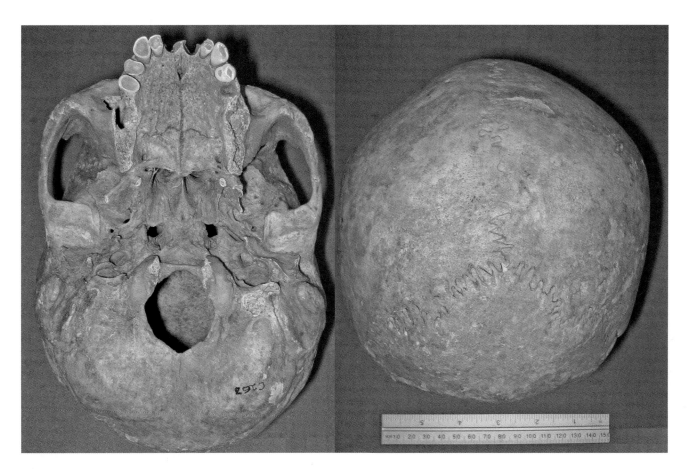

Figure 11.7 Views of burial 267 from behind and below with positional head deformity

genital or other developmental abnormalities, such as torticollis, craniosynostosis, metopism, wormian bones or positional head deformity. In many cases, these deformities can be indications of an underlying disease that required institutional care or, like leprosy, these conditions were so deforming that they would likely have affected the person's interaction with society. This may be the reason for their burial in the hospital cemetery of St James and St Mary Magdalene.

12 The children *by Mary Lewis*

Introduction

The Chichester sample comprised 104 children (27.0% of the total sample). A further two children were recorded from context 366, the plague pit, and the disarticulated material (381). The presence of children in the leprosarium and almshouse, their age at death, growth and the nature of the pathologies they exhibit are discussed in this chapter.

Age at death

The children were assigned an age at death based on the development of their deciduous and permanent dentition (Moorrees *et al* 1963a, 1963b; Smith 1991). Where no teeth were present, diaphyseal lengths and skeletal maturation were used to assign an age (Scheuer and Black 2000). Age estimates for the perinates were derived from the British standards for diaphyseal lengths (Scheuer and Black 2000). The skeletons were divided into seven age categories: perinate (under 38 weeks gestation), birth to 1.0 year (or infant), 1.1–2.5 years, 2.6–6.5 years, 6.6–10.5 years, 10.6–14.5 years and 14.6–17.0 years. In the last age category, individuals were estimated to be older than 17.0 years when the root of the third molar was complete (R_c = 17.5) but the apex remained open (Moorrees *et al* 1963b). By using broad age categories it was hoped to reduce the errors introduced by inter- and intra-population variability. Nevertheless, differences in maturation and dental development between the sexes may have resulted in some older males being included, and some younger females being excluded from the child sample. In four cases, poor preservation meant that only a suggestion of whether the child was 'younger'

or 'older' (ie over 10 years) could be given. Table 12.1 summarises the age profile of the children within specific age categories.

The majority of the children at Chichester are aged between 1.1 and 6.5 years. This is not an uncommon pattern in many later medieval cemeteries that often show a rise in number of children between 1 and 9 years of age (Lewis 2007). Only seventeen of the non-adults fell into the infant age category (16.2%) suggesting an under-representation of this group. In addition, if we accept that between 30 and 70% of individuals in the past died before the age of 15 years (Weiss 1973), then overall, children are under-represented in the Chichester sample (27%). This is not unexpected considering the function of St James and St Mary Magdalene as a leprosarium and almshouse, where people were selected to enter the institution and hence the cemetery, rather than reflecting the demography of a lay community.

The leprosy sample

Only two children (2%) came from the earlier part of the cemetery (Area A) used by the leprosarium (burials 53 and 334). Both were over 7 years of age when they died (Table 12.2). This is low when compared to the 73 children excavated from St George's leprosy cemetery at Naestved, Denmark (Bennike *et al* 2005), but again the majority of these children (66%) were over 7 years. The presence of these children in the leprosarium has raised questions as to whether or not they were recognised by the community as suffering from the disease.

Documentary evidence for admissions to Chichester is not available, but records do exist from similar institutions in Scandinavia. Richards (1977,

Table 12.1 Number and percentage of children in each age category

Age category (years)	Number	% total children
Perinate	3	2.9
Birth–1.0	14	13.5
1.1–2.5	24	23.1
2.6–6.5	26	25
6.6–10.5	16	15.4
10.6–14.5	11	10.6
14.6–17.0	6	5.8
? Child	4	3.8
Total	**104**	

Table 12.2 Numbers of children in each area of the cemetery compared with the children from Naestved

Age category (years)	Area A	Area B	Naestved
Perinate	0	3	–
Birth–1.0	0	14	–
1.1–2.5	0	24	(0–2.5) 14
2.6–6.5	0	26	11
6.6–10.5	1	15	17
10.6–14.5	0	11	11
14.6–17.0	1	5	20
? Child	0	4	–
Total	**2**	**102**	

Figure 12.1   Baldwin (later Baldwin IV, King of Jerusalem) wears a dark robe and fights with another boy (left). He shows his injured arm to William of Tyre who discovers he has leprosy (right)

69) cites an entry from Denmark where 'even two small leper children reported to a meeting of the parish...in 1658...were admitted to the hospital'. In 17th-century Finland, records from the leprosarium in Sjählö indicate that twelve children with signs of the disease were living there (Fagerlund 1886). It is clear that children were also admitted to leprosaria with their sick parents to prevent them from becoming orphaned and destitute. For instance, a young woman from Sweden entered the hospital with her parents as a child and, although she never developed the disease, remained there for sixteen years (Richards 1977, 60).

Children in the medieval period were considered particularly vulnerable to leprosy, both morally and physically, and this is indicated by edicts dating from the 15th century, which state that people with leprosy were not to touch children, not even their own (Mercier 1915). Documentary evidence of leprosy in children also exists in illustrations such as that of Baldwin IV, King of Jerusalem (Fig 12.1), who was discovered to have leprosy as a boy when another child pinched him and he felt no pain.

Clinical studies have shown that of all the children born into lepromatous families, 25–50% develop clinical signs of the disease before the age of 5 years (Melsom *et al* 1982). In many cases, lesions heal spontaneously but may recur when the child is older

(Lara and Nolesco 1956). Young children with the disease commonly develop single lesions with some loss of pigmentation, or 'macules', and active bacilli are rarely found in the nasal region. By the age of 13 years, nasal lesions become more apparent and infiltrations, loss of feeling in the limbs, and nodules are common symptoms (Noussitou et al 1978). Archaeological evidence for leprosy in children is limited (Lewis 2002a). At Naestved, 27% (n = 16) of the 60 children who could be fully examined had evidence for lepromatous leprosy before the age of 17 years (Bennike et al 2005). Three were young children with rhinomaxillary syndrome and dental stigmata (leprogenic odontodysplasia), aged 8–10 years (Lewis 2002a). At the medieval cemetery of St John's Timberhill in Norwich, Anderson (1996) reported 36 individuals with leprosy and lesions diagnostic of the disease were found in eleven children (aged 12–20 years).

None of the children in the early Chichester group had definitive skeletal evidence for leprosy, but may have been displaying soft tissue manifestations that prompted their admission to the leprosarium. Interestingly, one of the children from this group, buried in area A2 (burial 53), was a 7- to 8-year-old child with suspected tuberculosis of the elbow joint (see below). This child was buried with a cluster of other interments around tomb 241. In addition to the swelling and inflammation of the elbow, infection of the right leg indicated by new subperiosteal bone on the right femur may have been interpreted as leprosy by the community. The child would certainly have been visibly ill. However, there is some debate about the date of this burial (see Chapter 7). An older adolescent (burial 334), also from Area A, had new bone formation on the external cranium that may indicate an active scalp infection at the time of death. The skeleton is too poorly preserved to assess for signs of leprosy.

Growth

Growth is a highly regulated process controlled by the endocrine system. It begins rapidly at birth and gradually slows and stabilises at around 3 years of age. At puberty there is another episode of growth acceleration which, after a period of peak velocity, slows until the epiphyseal ends of the long bones fuse and growth ceases (Karlberg 1998). The final growth outcome of an individual is the result of a complex interaction between genetic and environmental factors. The physical growth and development of children is a sensitive indicator of the quality of the social, economic and political environment in which they live. For this reason child growth standards are regularly used as measures of the general health status of the overall community, where poor growth is taken as an indicator of unfavourable conditions (Johnston and Zimmer 1989).

Mean diaphyseal lengths were plotted against dental age estimates to produce skeletal growth profiles. All of the samples used in this part of the analysis were aged using the same method (Moorees et al 1963a; 1963b). The lower limbs are considered to be the most sensitive to environmental stress as the femur and tibia are some of the fastest growing bones of the body (Eveleth and Tanner 1990). Therefore, femoral diaphyseal length measurements were chosen to assess growth, as they also provided the largest data set in the sample (n = 36). The growth profiles were then compared with two contemporaneous later medieval samples, Wharram Percy and St Helen-on-the-Walls in York. As children buried in lay cemeteries, it might be expected that they would suffer less from chronic diseases than those from the almshouse interred at Chichester. Figure 12.2 shows that the children from Chichester fell below the other children in their age group for diaphyseal length after the age of 5 years. In fact, the four children with the smallest femoral lengths for age all had pathological lesions, indicating that they were chronically ill at the time of their death (166, 200, 215 and 232). Mean femoral diaphyseal lengths for each age group were then compared with the only available growth data for the Danish Naestved children, who may be considered to have been suffering from similar poor health (Fig 12.3). Genetic difference in growth may exist between these two groups; however, again the Chichester children are short in comparison and lagged behind in their growth, after an initial advantage in the 0–2.5-year age category.

Child health

There are many pathological conditions commonly recorded on the adult skeleton that can be identified on non-adult remains. However, not all childhood diseases will become chronic and be evident in the skeletal record. Preservation, rapid growth and the nature of paediatric bone can both aid and limit the diagnosis of diseases in child skeletons. With these caveats in mind, the general health of the children was assessed by recording the prevalence of *cribra orbitalia*, dental enamel hypoplasia, endocranial lesions and non-specific infections (ie periostitis). The rates of these conditions were compared with similar sites where appropriate. Evidence for specific diseases such as tuberculosis and rickets in the adults is given in subsequent sections.

In children, we have the advantage of examining *cribra orbitalia* in small age groups, at the time that the lesions develop, during childhood. Indicative of a systemic condition, perhaps iron deficiency anaemia, the prevalence of healed and active lesions is commonly recorded. At Chichester, 56% (n = 35) of the 62 children examined for *cribra orbitalia* had the condition. Active (sharp-edged) and healed (remodelled) lesions occurred equally throughout the age groups. This is different from the usual pattern where healed lesions are more common in the older age groups, and may reflect the nature

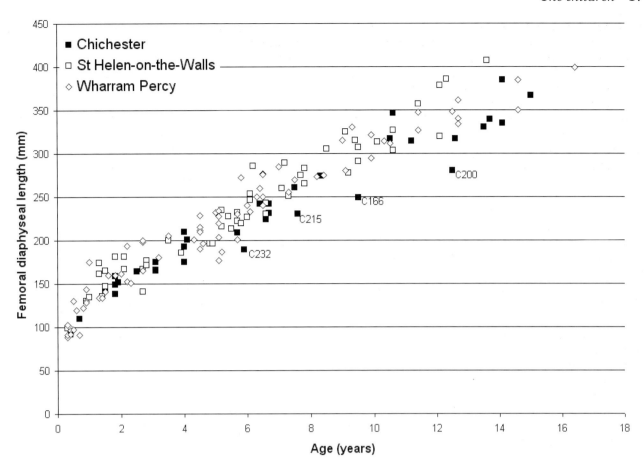

Figure 12.2   Growth profile of the Chichester children (individuals plotted) compared with other later medieval samples

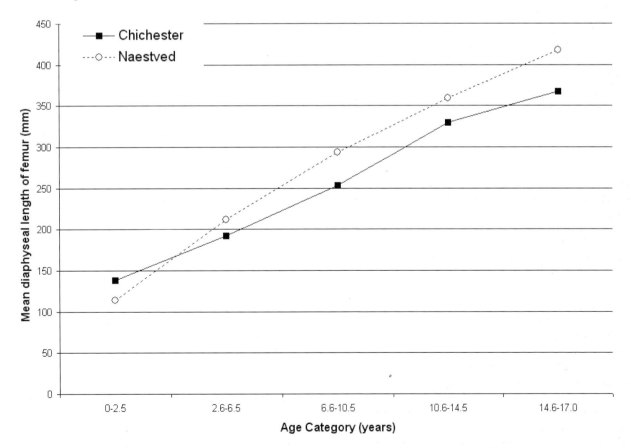

Figure 12.3   Comparison of growth profiles of the Chichester and the Danish Naestved children

Table 12.3   Percentage prevalence of pathological lesions at Chichester compared with other later medieval sites

Site	Enamel hypoplasia		Cribra orbitalia		Endocranial lesions		New bone formation		TB cases
	na/nb	%	na/nb	%	na/nb	%	na/nb	%	number
Chichester	(18/57)	32	(35/62)	56	(9/91)	10	(8/99)	8	7
Naestved	(23/55)	42	(36/60)	60	(11/64)	17	(14/39)	35	–
Jewbury	–	–	(38/93)	41	–	8	(14/85)	16	2
Fishergate	–	–	(32/50)	64	–	–	(5/50)	10	3
St Helen's	(31/95)	33	(49/87)	56	(11/92)	12	(21/104)	20	2
Wharram Percy	(36/120)	30	(112/200)	56	(33/217)	15	(21/166)	13	1

na = number of individuals affected; nb = number of individuals observed

of the institution that took children with ongoing illnesses, who probably had active anaemia. Dental diseases are discussed in full elsewhere but, of the 57 children with anterior teeth, 32% (18) had dental enamel hypoplasia. This prevalence is similar to that at Wharram Percy and St Helen-on-the-Walls (Table 12.3) (Lewis 2002b), unlike Naestved, where the prevalence of enamel hypoplasia was 42% (Bennike *et al* 2005).

Non-specific infections

New bone formation (periostitis)

The diagnosis of periostitis in non-adult skeletal remains is problematic. In the long bones, appositional (normal) growth involves the deposition of immature disorganised bone on the cortical surface. This new bone is macroscopically identical to the fibre bone deposited during an infection or after trauma. In the few archaeological studies that have identified non-adult periostitis, it is characterised as a unilateral, isolated patch of bone raised above the original cortex. Eight children in the sample (8%) have evidence of periostitis, although this is probably an underestimate due to poor preservation of some remains. Compared with the rates in other later medieval cemeteries this is low (Table 12.3), and this may be because, at Chichester, new bone that could be assigned to a specific condition (eg scurvy) was not included in this category.

Burial 258, a 14-year-old, has active new bone formation on fragments of the tibia and fibula, indicative of trauma or infection to the lower leg. This is also evident on another 14-year-old, burial 293, with new bone on the right tibia; this child also has *osteochondritis dissecans* of the left distal tibial epiphysis. Burial 159, a child estimated to be 1.5 years old, has active new bone formation along the midshaft of the left tibia, and plaque-like new bone and vascular endocranial lesions on the parietals and occipital. Burial 320, around 3 years of age, had bilateral woven (active) bone on the medial aspects of both tibiae, and along the *linea aspera* and lateral aspects of both femora. The location of the new bone

on one side of the tibia may suggest growth, but the new bone deposits are thicker than would normally be expected. There was a similar problem with the diagnosis of burial 322. This newborn infant has woven bone formation covering all the surviving bones that seems more profuse than is usual for a child of this age, and may relate to an infection that killed it. However, it may also be a snapshot of rapid growth in the child before its death. Even in an acutely sick child, we would expect growth to slow before death and therefore, if this new bone formation is part of the normal growth process, death was probably accidental.

Three children exhibited more unusual distributions of new bone formation that may be linked to specific conditions. Burial 334 is aged around 17 years and exhibits widespread periostitis on the parietals and occipital bones that may indicate trauma or a scalp infection. This individual comes from the early part of the cemetery (Area A) and there is possible evidence for a blade injury on a fragment of frontal bone. Burial 232, a 6-year-old from Area B, has new bone formation on the nasal aspect of the maxilla near the opening of the maxillary sinus, but the infection has not extended into the sinus. This is probably evidence for an active nasal infection (rhinitis). The most unusual case of new bone formation is in burial 181, a 6-year-old child, who has a profuse layer of active new bone formation on the internal and external aspects of the mandible body, on the right posterior aspect, below the first premolar. The infection lies below the attachment of the oral mucous membrane, so it is unlikely to have spread from a dental or mouth infection. The cause of the new bone may be trauma to the jaw, or may be suggestive of a more serious condition such as cancer (Fig 12.4).

Endocranial lesions

Reactive new bone on the internal surface of the skull in children is becoming more widely recognised as an important factor in assessing health in the past. These lesions vary in their appearance from layers of new bone to vascular-type lesions or

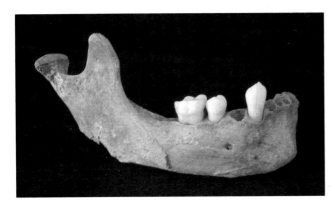

Figure 12.4 *New bone formation on the mandibular body of burial 181*

Figure 12.5 *Probable mastoiditis in burial 68, evident as a smooth-walled lytic lesion on the left temporal bone*

'hair-on-end' extensions of the diploe. Various aetiologies have been suggested for these lesions in the literature, including chronic meningitis, trauma, anaemia, neoplasia, scurvy, rickets, venous drainage disorders and tuberculosis (Lewis 2004). All may cause inflammation and/or haemorrhage of the meningeal vessels (Schultz 2001).

Nine children (10%) of the 91 with skulls exhibit vascular or hair-on-end lesions on the internal aspects of their skulls (burials 80, 105, 122, 159, 200, 207, 215, 231, 249). In several cases, these lesions are associated with more extensive changes to the rest of the skull and are discussed below. More unusually, burial 200, a 12-year-old, has arachnoid granulations on the frontal bone. These are too extensive for a normal child of this age. The child also has active *cribra orbitalia* and severe pitted enamel hypoplasia on the molars that mimic the mulberry molars seen in congenital syphilis.

Mastoiditis

Today, nearly 80% of all children experience some form of middle ear infection (*otitis media*) between the ages of 3 months and 6 years, making it one of the most common childhood conditions in the modern world (Harley *et al* 1997). Recurrent infections result in tinnitus, hearing loss and, in severe cases, meningitis. Untreated, the disease frequently settles following perforation of the eardrum and a discharge of pus from the abscess beneath. Interior drainage of the infection leads to fatal meningitis. Otherwise, the infection tracks externally into the air cells of the mastoid process behind the ear, resulting in mastoiditis (Roberts and Manchester 2005). Despite mastoiditis being reported in 20% of children in the pre-antibiotic era (Kiple 2003), archaeological evidence for ear infections is usually confined to adult skeletal remains. However, one possible case of mastoiditis was identified in a child under six months old at Chichester. Burial 68 displays a lytic, smooth-walled lesion on the left mastoid process directly behind the auditory meatus, with possible inflammation of the greater wing of

the sphenoid (Fig 12.5). The presence of a draining sinus, with sclerotic healed margins, suggests that the condition was resolved at the time of the child's death.

Otosclerosis

This is a condition which may affect the ears of older children and cause one of the ossicles which conduct the sound in the inner ear to change from hard, mineralised bone to woven bone. If the condition is bilateral it may cause deafness. The stapes, or stirrup, fuses to the oval window and is visible with an endoscope (Dalby *et al* 1993). Two children were affected by otosclerosis at St James' Hospital. Burial 192 is a child aged 6.6–10.5 years and 302 is *c* 2 years old. They are thus considerably younger than expected for children suffering from this condition today.

Metabolic disease

Rickets

Rickets usually results from a deficiency in vitamin D which is produced by the body, primarily through exposure to sunlight, and foodstuffs such as fish oil and egg yolks. Vitamin D is essential for the normal turnover of bone during bone growth and maturation, and bone remodelling (Pitt 1988). Rickets is most common in children after six months, when fetal stores of vitamin D begin to deplete and the mother and child need to ensure exposure to sunlight to make up for any dietary deficiency (Foote and Marriott 2003). However, premature, twinned and low birth weight babies are susceptible to rickets earlier in life as they have smaller fetal stores and have rapid 'catch-up' growth after birth (Bishop and Fewtrell 2003).

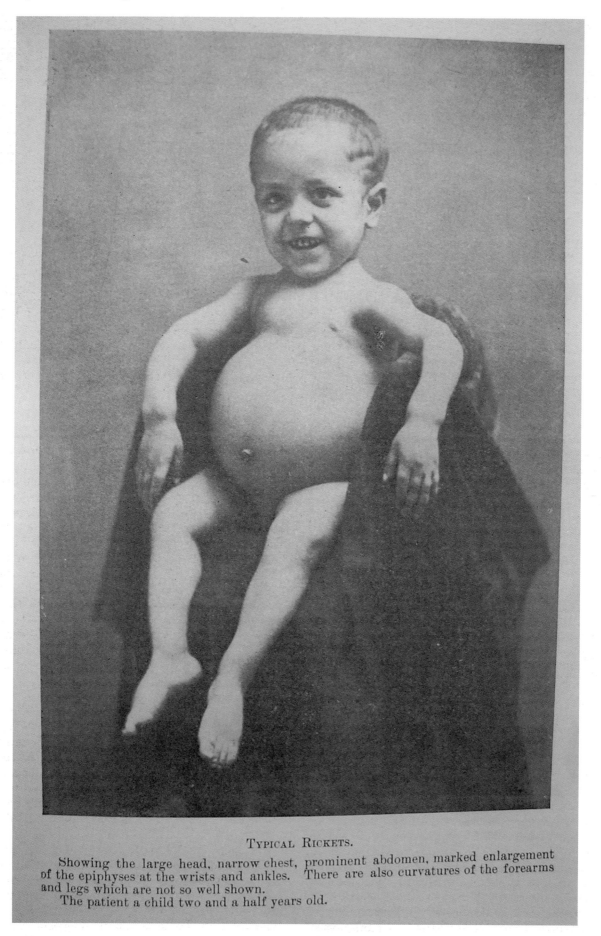

TYPICAL RICKETS.

Showing the large head, narrow chest, prominent abdomen, marked enlargement of the epiphyses at the wrists and ankles. There are also curvatures of the forearms and legs which are not so well shown.
The patient a child two and a half years old.

Figure 12.6 Child with rickets demonstrating the classic features of this condition which include swelling of the wrists and bowing of the lower limb bones (from Holt 1906, 259)

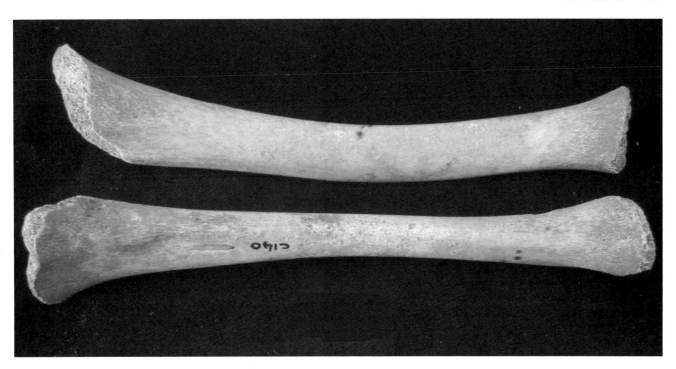

Figure 12.7   Abnormal bowing of the tibiae indicative of healed rickets in burial 140. Note exaggerated angle at the distal ends of the bones

Figure 12.8   Porotic hyperostosis, probably indicative of rickets, on the ectocranial surface of burial 218

The skeletal manifestation of rickets is related to the general nutrition of the child, the age at which the condition occurs, rate of growth, and mobility. Uncalcified osteoid laid down on the growth plate and during the remodelling process causes the bones to 'soften' and they become susceptible to bowing deformities. The wrist is usually the first area where changes to the growth plate are noticed (Fig 12.6). The metaphyseal ends become widened and concave as a result of weight-bearing (trumpeting), the cortical bone is thinned and the metaphyses develop frayed edges, resembling 'bristles of a brush' (Caffey 1978). Macroscopically, the characteristic

smooth epiphyseal surface of the metaphysis is lost. Children who maintain good muscle tone and remain mobile during the course of their disease have been shown to develop more severe bowing, cupping and flaring deformities than those with poor muscle tone who remain stationary (Stuart-Macadam 1988). In the infant, bowing of the arms, where the humeral head is bent medially and inferiorly, suggests the child may have been crawling at the time of onset (Pettifor 2003). An abnormal anterior-lateral concavity of the femoral shaft, a bowed tibia, and anterior-posterior flattening of the fibula may indicate that the child had begun to walk (Stuart-Macadam 1988). Hence, examination of bowing deformities can aid in assessing an age of onset for the condition.

At least three children display evidence of vitamin D deficiency. Burial 140 (aged 4 years) has abnormal bowing of the tibiae but an intact metaphyseal surface, suggesting this disease had occurred after the child had begun to walk, but had resolved by the time it died (Fig 12.7). Two infants (under 1 year), burials 266 and 270, exhibit cupping and widening of the epiphyseal ends of the long bones, cranial bossing and thickening of the ilia associated with active rickets. A further two individuals, 218 and 224 aged 7 and 1.5 years respectively, display new bone formation on the external surface of the skull, similar to porotic hyperostosis that may indicate a build up of unmineralised bone in rickets (Fig 12.8). The age at which this condition appears and heals in the child sample suggests that they suffered from the condition after six months of age, when fetal stores have been depleted, and suggests that mother and child were not getting access to sunlight. It does not follow that the children were all undernourished, as the bowing of the limbs of the older children suggests that they were mobile, and were then able to play out of doors, resulting in the condition being resolved as little as a year later.

Scurvy and anaemia

Scurvy results from a dietary deficiency of ascorbic acid, or vitamin C, present in wide variety of fruits and green vegetables. The disease is clinically recognisable when the vitamin has been deficient for 4–10 months, or in children, once birth stores have been depleted (Ortner 2003). Hence, scurvy is most common between 6 months and 2 years of age. But, as with rickets, premature, low birth weight babies and twins are susceptible.

The skeletal changes are most marked in the areas of rapid growth and result from two separate processes: (1) new bone formation as the result of haemorrhage caused by the vitamin deficiency and, (2) the traumatic effects on the weakened scurvy bone. Scurvy has not been recorded commonly in the palaeopathological literature although adult scurvy has been described throughout history occurring particularly in sailors who were at sea for long periods without fresh fruit or vegetables. Recent research into lesions on the skulls of children with known scurvy has improved our diagnostic criteria to include new bone formation and pitting on the orbital roof, maxilla and the greater wing of the sphenoid, due to haemorrhaging (Ortner *et al* 1999). Ossifying haematomas, or 'Parrot's swellings', may form on the parietals, occipital, and in some cases, the frontal bones and mimic porotic hyperostosis (Ortner *et al* 2001; Melikian and Waldron 2003). Some endocranial lesions may also be the result of slow haemorrhage into the dura as a result of scurvy (Lewis 2004).

Parrot's swellings may be evident in burial 207, a young child with new bone bossing on the parietals, in addition to a thin layer of woven bone internally. Another possible case of infantile scurvy was recorded in an 18-month-old child from the western end of Area B. Vertically arranged trabecular and subperiosteal new bone formation was recorded on the roof of the orbit of burial 105 giving a hair-on-end appearance (Fig 12.9). These lesions are also accompanied by hair-on-end lesions on the endocranial surface. However, some form of severe anaemia accompanying the condition cannot be ruled out. There are also unusual lesions in both orbits of burial 154, a child aged over 1 year. Porous lesions extend from the roof of the orbit, where *cribra orbitalia* is commonly located, to the orbital floor.

One of the most dramatic cases of pathology in the non-adult sample was in burial 215, a child aged 8–9 years old. The child shares similar lesions to

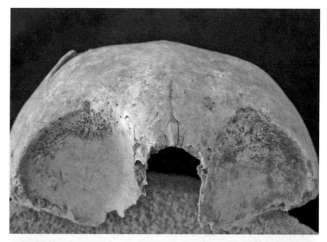

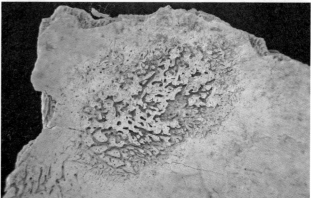

Figure 12.9   Hair-on-end endocranial lesions (a) (above) and new bone formation on the orbits of burial 105 (b) (below), indicative of scurvy and / or anaemia

those displayed in burials 105 and 154, but these are far more extensive. In this case some form of systemic bone marrow condition is suspected, but the aetiology is unknown. There is hair-on-end expansion of the diplöe on the roofs of the left and right orbits, with similar lesions on the endocranial aspect of the frontal, left and right parietal bones and occipital. There is some evidence for remodelling of the lesions and the remaining parts of the inner table (Fig 12.10). In addition, there is woven new bone formation limited to the parietal suture line. Pitting is evident on the zygomatic (cheek) bones and on the maxilla, and the developing canines have enamel hypoplasia. The condition certainly appears metabolic and may be the result of severe anaemia, with scurvy suggested by the pitting on the facial bones.

Congenital defects

A full discussion of congenital conditions in the sample is presented in Chapter 10. However, there were several cases of congenital defects in the non-adult sample. Burial 90, aged around 15 years, has ossification defects on the left and right

Figure 12.10a Endocranial (internal) view of the occipital bone of burial 215. Note hair-on-end-expansion of the inner diploe and rounded margins of the lesion suggesting healing

Figure 12.10b Endocranial (internal) view of the frontal bone of burial 215. Note hair-on-end-expansion of the inner diploe and rounded margins of the lesion suggesting healing. There is post-mortem damage to the central aspect of the lesion

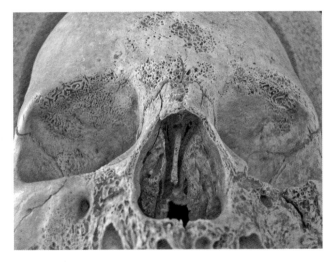

Figure 12.10c Orbital lesions on burial 215. The extensive and thickened nature of the cribra orbitalia *suggests that before remodelling, the orbits displayed hair-on-end lesions corresponding to Type 5 on Stuart-Macadam's (1991) scheme*

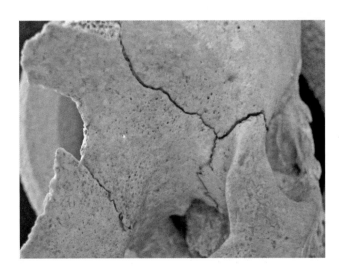

Figure 12.10d Abnormal pitting on the temporal and zygomatic bones of burial 215

proximal epiphyses of the first metatarsal and the first proximal phalanx, mimicking *osteochondritis dissecans*. The left femur is also 7cm shorter than the right, which may have resulted in a limp, but this shortening is not evident on the tibia and fibula, and soft tissue may have compensated for this difference.

Burial 166, an 8–9-year-old child, has a series of lesions on its spine. There is a cortical defect on the left superior facet of the axis that does not correspond to the atlas facet. The left posterior arch also appears thinner (hypoplastic) in comparison with the right side, resulting in deviation of the spinous process. Further down the spine, at T7, there is a deep linear depression on the left aspect

of the superior body which also appears to be compressed, suggesting trauma. This is likely to be the result of a problem during the early development of the vertebrae (notochord regression failure), with incomplete development of a 'butterfly' vertebra (Fig 12.11). Also affecting the spine, burial 297 has an unfused spinous process of L5. This lesion would probably have been asymptomatic, but may have been accompanied by soft tissue defects that may account for the early death of this child, also around 8 years. Finally burial 319, an adolescent, exhibits what appears to be a developing case of spondylolysis at L5. Deep grooves lie in the area where the neural arch usually becomes detached from the rest of the vertebral body in this condition (Fig 12.12).

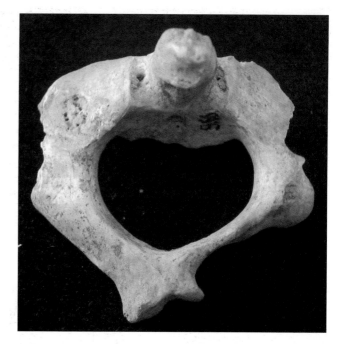

Figure 12.11   Congenital defects in (a) (left) the axis and (b) (right) the 7th thoracic vertebra of burial 166

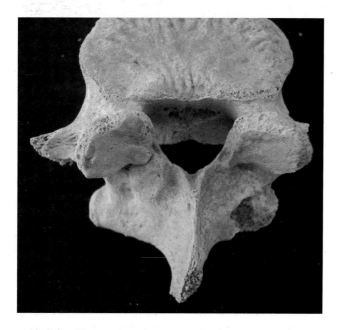

Figure 12.12   Possible developing spondylolysis in 5th lumbar vertebra of burial 319

Such a lesion may add weight to the theory that this 'fracture' is the result of a congenital weakness (Ortner 2003, 148).

Tuberculosis

Tuberculosis usually has its onset in childhood and the identification of tuberculosis in non-adult remains is significant. Infected children represent the pool from which a large proportion of infected adults will arise and, because children are usually infected by adults, child cases indicate an ongoing transmission of TB within a community. Children are more likely to develop TB after exposure than adults, and modern estimates put the likelihood of infection after exposure at 5–10% for adults, 15% for adolescents, 24% for 1–5 year olds and as high as 43% for infants (Walls and Shingadia 2004). In the past it was children who were most susceptible to the gastrointestinal form of the disease (Griffith 1919). Gastrointestinal tuberculosis is usually fatal in the first two or three years of life, and results from the ingestion of the human or bovine strain of the bacillus. The bovine form of TB is usually transmitted through infected meat or milk, but may also have spread via the respiratory tract to people in close contact with their livestock. One of the major causes of gastrointestinal TB in the past was the use of cows' milk for infant feeding (Atkins 1992).

There are seven cases in the non-adult sample where tuberculosis is suspected (c 6.6%). The children are mostly aged between 6 and 12 years of age, with one child exhibiting changes at 4 years. Two skeletons (228 and 121) have active new bone formation on the visceral surface of the ribs, indicative of a respiratory infection, which is most likely tuberculosis (Santos and Roberts 2006). Burial 121, aged around 4 years, has the most severe changes with scalloped lytic lesions to three right and one left rib (Fig 12.13). In addition, the child has active new bone formation on the external aspect of the left maxilla above the first and second deciduous molars.

Pulmonary tuberculosis is also suspected in burial 278, a 12–15-year-old with destructive infective lesions to consecutive lower thoracic vertebrae. Bone formation is limited and a draining sinus (cloaca) indicates the presence of an abscess. The major area of destruction is to the posterior aspect, resulting in

Figure 12.13   Burial 121 with scalloped lesions on the visceral surface of the ribs, probably indicative of pulmonary tuberculosis

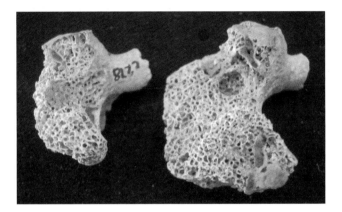

Figure 12.14   Pott's disease in burial 278, indicative of pulmonary tuberculosis

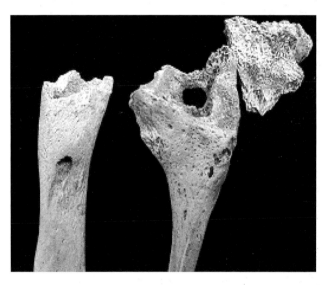

Figure 12.15   Extensive destructive changes to the right elbow of burial 53, indicative of tuberculosis in the joint

the infection extending into the neural canal. These lesions would probably have resulted in collapse of the vertebral column and a kyphosis, the hunched back appearance characteristic of a Pott's spine (Fig 12.14). Burial 313a, an adolescent aged 11–12 years, exhibits a lytic lesion at the junction between the right ilium and ischium. This is associated with reactive bone to the ischial aspect. The unusual location of this lesion probably indicates abscess formation in gastrointestinal TB, or may be the result of an extension of infection from a pulmonary site (ie psoas abscess). However, the ribs and spine are unaffected.

The spread of *Mycobacterium tuberculosis* in the bloodstream can lead to abscess formation in the joints. In children, the rapid growth of their bones means they are particularly susceptible to joint lesions, which are generally unilateral and characterised by minimal new bone formation. Burial 53, a child 7–8 years old, exhibits extensive destruction and abscess formation in the right humerus and ulna, leading to total destruction of the joint surface (Fig 12.15). There is also active new bone formation on the right femur, but there are no rib or vertebral lesions to suggest pulmonary tuberculosis.

Burial 211 is an intriguing case of possible tuber-culosis or mycotic (fungal) infection (also see Ortner 2003, 256–8). This 12–13-year-old has evidence for limited, but active, new bone formation on the anterior aspect of all the lumbar vertebrae and the sacrum, with patches of woven bone on the right spinous processes of L2, 3 and 5 (Fig 12.16). A shallow groove, possibly representing a draining sinus, is evident on the right wing of the sacrum. Involvement of the lower vertebrae and sacrum argues towards gastrointestinal TB. Ortner (2003, 257) warns that new bone formation to the posterior aspects of the spine is rare in TB and that a mycotic infection should be considered as a differential diagnosis. Mycotic infections tend to occur in immu-nologically compromised people, and are acquired by inhaling spores that grow freely in nature (Harrison *et al* 1962, 1051). Burial 211 also has evidence of infection in the nasal area, with the left maxillary sinus and left aspect of the nasal surface exhibiting new bone formation indicative of inflammation. If it is a mycotic infection, this may be where its spores

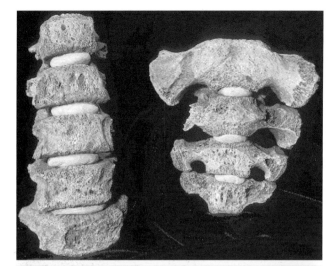

Figure 12.16 New bone formation and destruction on the lumbar vertebrae and sacrum of an adolescent (burial 211), probably indicative of gastrointestinal tuberculosis

undermined by a draining sinus caused by TB (Fig 12.17).

Discussion and conclusions

Of the 105 child skeletons in this sample, 26 (24.8%) show some evidence for chronic disease at the time of their death. For individual lesions, the prevalence rates in comparison to other medieval sites are given in Table 12.3. The prevalence of enamel hypoplasia and *cribra orbitalia* is comparable to other sites, but figures for new bone formation are more problematic, as at Chichester new bone formation that could be attributed to a specific condition (ie rickets, scurvy or tuberculosis) was not included.

Congenital conditions would have probably been accompanied by more life-threatening soft tissue defects, and the severe cases of 'anaemia' in at least two individuals would suggest that these children were clearly ill when they entered the almshouse. Of the infectious diseases, the most prominent in the sample was not leprosy, as might be expected, but its cousin tuberculosis. The slowly debilitating nature of leprosy probably means that,

were inhaled. However, mycotic infections are usually reported in North American samples, and as there is already evidence for tuberculosis at this site, it is generally accepted that this child exhibits a more unusual form of TB.

A similar spread of lesions is also apparent in burial 106, an adolescent aged around 17 years of age. L4 and 5 exhibit lytic lesions on the vertebral surface and Schmorl's nodes, with compression to the left aspect of the body of L5. The first sacral vertebra shows a similar lytic lesion on the posterior aspect of the body. The compression of L5 suggests acute trauma and the unilateral fusion of the right tibial epiphysis may also indicate that this adolescent experienced a traumatic incident. However, the lytic appearance of the body and a smooth channel on the left aspect of the body could signal secondary trauma after the spine had been

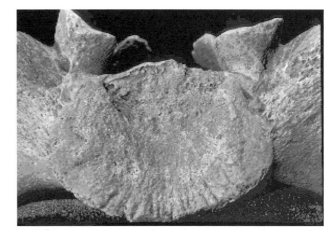

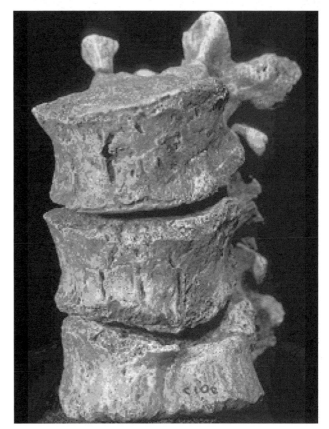

Figure 12.17 Trauma and/or infection on the lumbar vertebra and first sacral vertebra of a 17-year-old adolescent (burial 106)

even if the children had the skin lesions of leprosy, skeletal lesions did not have time to develop before they died, making this condition invisible to the palaeopathologist. In contrast, the number of cases of both pulmonary and gastrointestinal TB in the children at Chichester is higher than has been reported elsewhere. More generally, the children are considered to be particularly disadvantaged through their growth profiles, which show them to be shorter than other later medieval children from lay cemeteries and the leprosy sample from Naestved in Denmark.

13 Dental health and disease *by Alan Ogden and Frances Lee*

Introduction

The majority of the data were prepared and analysed some twenty years ago, and so what follows is a report of the main findings, with some interpretation to bring it into line with more modern thinking. Inevitably there have been huge improvements in our understanding of caries, periodontal disease and enamel hypoplasia over this time, but publication of these carefully recorded data is important, especially as there has been inevitable deterioration of the skeletal material. The dental findings are very similar to those from other contemporary sites in England. However, the many cases of rhinomaxillary remodelling give this collection a unique importance. It is hoped that this report will be of use as a foundation for future researchers wishing to use new techniques to re-examine the Chichester material.

Teeth present

Table 13.1 summarises the number of individuals with dentitions from the site. Some 304 individuals (79.2%) out of a total of 384 had at least part of the dentition present. Figure 13.1 reports the fate of the permanent teeth (4417 in all), showing a breakdown of the teeth present, lost ante-mortem, post-mortem and unerupted. Sixty-six percent of the adults with teeth were male (171) while only 28.6% (74) were female. Forty-five subadults had 527 deciduous teeth present.

Ante-mortem tooth loss

This had occurred in 186 individuals (Table 13.2; Fig 13.1), representing 71.3% of permanent dentitions with a loss of 1231 teeth. Women were slightly more susceptible with 78.4% (58) of them having one or more teeth lost compared to 71% (122) for the adult male population. However the males have rather more teeth lost per individual than the females. The maxillary first and second molars were the most commonly absent teeth. In modern dentitions, ante-mortem tooth loss before middle age almost invariably results from dental caries. This is not necessarily so in medieval dentitions where a combination of severe attrition, caries and periodontal disease may all be responsible. There is possibly an association between tooth loss and apical abscesses at Chichester, but this is difficult to illustrate as the infected tooth may have been lost and the associated socket and lesion totally remodelled well before death.

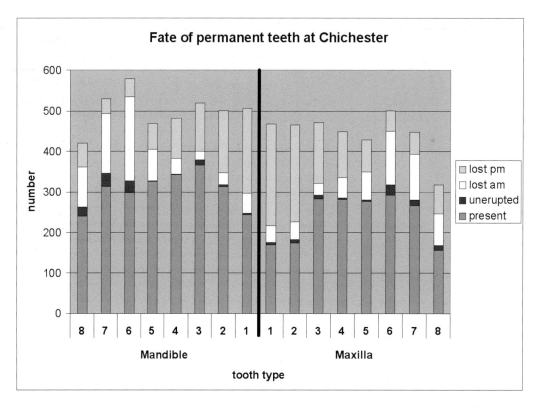

Figure 13.1 Chart showing the fate of the adult teeth in the individuals from Chichester

188

Post-mortem tooth loss

About 30% of all teeth had been lost post-mortem, with substantially more lost from the maxilla than the mandible. This is because the bone of the maxilla is so much thinner and more fragile than that of the mandible. By its very thickness and density the mandible tends to survive and retain the teeth *in situ* long after the maxilla has fragmented and released its teeth into the interstices of the soil. The most commonly lost teeth from both jaws were the incisors, which have a single straight and tapered root that is easily dislodged (Fig 13.1).

Dental pathology

Tables 13.3 and 13.4 record the occurrence of a range of dental pathologies found at Chichester, in relationship to the age and sex of the individual. The severely abrasive nature of diets up to and including the 17th century meant that dentitions rarely remained intact beyond the age of 40 to 45 years, after which age the teeth were exfoliated. Wear, and not caries and periodontal disease, was the principal destructive agent of dentitions in this country prior to the 17th century (Kerr 1998). Figure 13.2 is an example of how several pathologies sometimes occurred in a single dentition.

Table 13.1   Permanent dentition

Sex	No. of dentitions
Male adults	171
Female adults	74
Adult, sex unknown	14
Subadults	45
Total	**304**

Calculus

In life a bacterial carpet (plaque) is constantly colonising the tooth surfaces. Calculus is the hard deposit that forms on teeth through the calcification of undisturbed areas of this plaque. Almost ubiquitous in archaeological material, its presence in quantity is frequently taken as an indicator of poor oral hygiene (Fig 13.3). The teeth of 191 individuals show some evidence of the presence of calculus. Whether this brittle and porous material survives to be recorded depends, however, on taphonomic processes, excavation and cleaning techniques, and curation care (Ten Cate 1989; Lieverse 1999). In some cases large deposits may be due to pathological conditions, preventing oral hygiene, or to dietary factors.

The pH or acidity of the mouth depends upon the amount and type of carbohydrate in the diet. Plaque grows faster on the surfaces of the teeth when

Table 13.2   Ante-mortem tooth loss

Adults – Sex	Mandibles								Maxillae							
	8	7	6	5	4	3	2	1	1	2	3	4	5	6	7	8
Male and ?male	73	97	128	54	27	17	23	36	32	31	19	38	43	88	74	55
Female and ?female	23	44	69	18	8	5	6	13	8	10	8	11	22	38	35	20
Unknown sex	4	6	9	4	4	0	0	0	2	3	2	2	4	7	4	3
Total	**100**	**147**	**206**	**80**	**39**	**22**	**29**	**49**	**42**	**44**	**29**	**51**	**69**	**133**	**113**	**78**

Table 13.3   Distribution of dental pathologies by age

	Calculus	Periodontal disease	Caries	Granuloma/ Abscess	Enamel hypoplasia
Infant	0	0	0	0	1
Child	0	0	17	4	17
Adolescent	5	1	5	6	13
15–18yrs	2	0	2	8	4
Young adult	47	35	45	27	50
Middle adult	76	59	73	52	72
Mature adult	52	61	61	64	50
Adult age unknown	9	3	8	4	4
Total	**191**	**159**	**211**	**165**	**243**

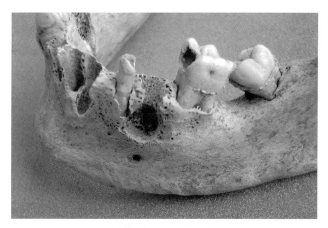

Figure 13.2 Young male 344 displays several pathologies. The lower left first molar contains a large mesial carious cavity. The porous bone and the smooth hollow related to the missing root of the lower left second premolar show this tooth to have been dead and infected, with an apical granuloma, probably because of distal caries. The left third molar has tipped forward after loss of the second molar in this individual's early twenties. This individual was very prone to caries with gross lesions in nine teeth, and an oro-antral fistula on an upper molar. The narrow rim of supra-gingival calculus, marking the level of the gingival crevice around both molars, was a common finding in this population

Figure 13.4 Mature male 368 showed an extremely unusual pattern of calculus formation, with nodular clumps of calculus. This plaque was never moulded by the tissues of the cheek and it is certain that this individual was either suffering from paralysis of the facial muscles or had lost his cheek altogether, which can occur in the severe rhinomaxillary syndrome of leprosy

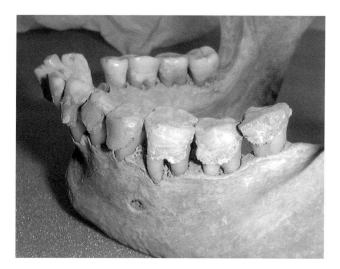

Figure 13.3 Severe calculus in mature male 315. The surface of the plaque has been moulded by the lips and cheeks before it calcified and hardened. The calculus on the occlusal surface of the left third molar shows clearly that this tooth was functionless and had no contact with an opposing molar

sucrose is added to the diet than when other sugars, such as fructose or glucose, are added. Large quantities of sugars depress the pH levels close to the teeth, decalcifying the enamel and leading to caries, but paradoxically give an adverse environment for the calcification of thick, mature and highly complex bacterial plaque and the formation of calculus. Dental caries and large quantities of dental calculus tend to be mutually exclusive (MacPhee and Cowley 1975).

An explanation for the greater quantity of calculus in some individuals might be a combination of inmates being fed a soft pulpy diet and poor oral hygiene due to leprous involvement of the mouth. The most interesting case is that of burial 368, a mature male who had nodular calculus on his lower right molars (Fig 13.4). This appearance is unique in the literature and suggests that he had probably lost his cheek, for there is no sign of the plaque which formed the calculus having been moulded by soft tissues. Lingually the calculus was smooth and rounded by movement of his tongue.

Woodward (1995) looked to see if it was possible to discern either dietary and/or bacterial differences between the calculus in leprous and non-leprous individuals, using scanning electron microscopy, but results apparently showed no significant difference.

Table 13.4 Distribution of dental pathologies in adults by sex

	Calculus	Periodontal disease	Caries	Granuloma/ abscess	Enamel hypoplasia
Male and ?male	124	109	123	97	120
Female and ?female	54	46	54	45	53
Sex uncertain	6	3	9	5	35

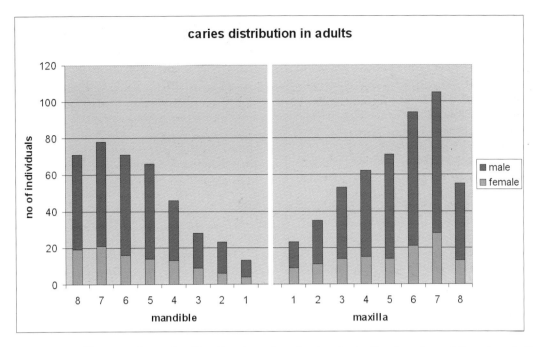

Figure 13.5   *Chart to show the distribution of caries in the teeth of male and female adults*

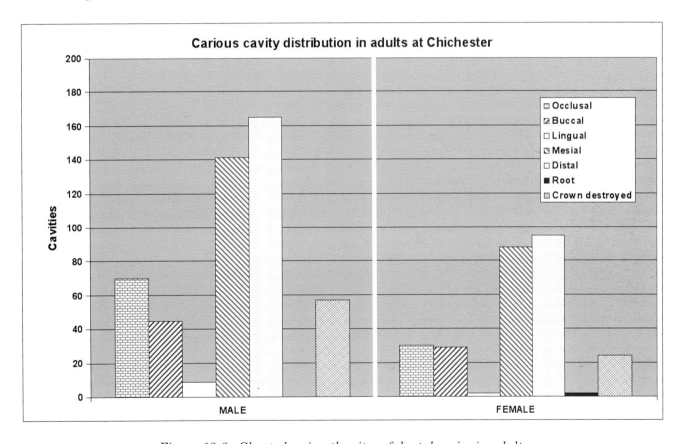

Figure 13.6   *Chart showing the sites of dental caries in adults*

Caries

Dental caries is the progressive decay of the dental hard tissues exposed to the mouth. It is one of the commonest of all pathologies and is also a major route by which bacteria can invade the living tissues, producing infection and inflammation of the dental pulp, the periapical tissues and the jaw bone itself. Hydroxyapatite, the form of calcium phosphate that composes the mineral in enamel, dentine and cement, dissolves when the overlying plaque produces a drop in the local pH to between 4 and 5.5 (Hillson 2005). In archaeological populations caries occur in three main areas: between the crowns of adjacent teeth; in later life, around the neck of the tooth especially after recession of the alveolar margin; and in wear facets in exposed dentine (Hillson 2005, 293).

The caries was not recorded in the detail now required (Hillson 2001), but it is still possible to build up a picture of the pattern of caries distribution in this group. Seventy-two percent (186) of all adults with dentitions had one or more carious lesions affecting 15.8% (67) of teeth. Although the number of adult males and females suffering from caries was similar (72–73% of the sample), 21.0% of all female teeth had a carious lesion compared to only 12.8% of male teeth. The number of individuals with caries and the teeth most commonly involved can be seen in Table 13.3 and Figure 13.5. The molars, particularly the first and second, were the most commonly affected teeth, followed by premolars. This pattern is almost universal for caries, due mainly to the complex morphology of the molars and premolars where the teeth do not fit snugly against each other and the crowns contain hollows and fissures where food and bacterial plaque can accumulate. Many of the teeth lost antemortem may have been shed as a result of caries.

Figure 13.6 records the location of carious lesions on the permanent dentition. The majority of cavities, 64% (503), occurred at the interproximal margin where the crown meets the tooth immediately adjacent to it. Lesions at the cemento-enamel junction are associated with age for as the alveolar bone recedes, the exposed root dentine creates a site for caries. In the mature individual, with the abrasive foodstuff of the Middle Ages, attrition will almost certainly have removed the occlusal pits and fissures favoured by caries in the young, but large areas of wear-exposed dentine provide new opportunities for occlusal caries to develop (Hillson 2005, 293). Twenty-four subadults had carious lesions affecting 37 deciduous teeth, predominately their second molars.

Periodontal disease and alveolar recession

Recession and loss of contour of the alveolus and inflammation, visible as pitting and lipping of the alveolar margin (Fig 13.7), are the main features of periodontal disease. This results in the loosening and eventual loss of the teeth (Costa 1982; Clarke *et al* 1986; Kerr and Ringrose 1998; Kerr 1998). It is a common condition and affects most individuals over the age of 35 years (Hillson 2005, 306).

Prior to the 17th century in Britain, few individuals retained their dentitions intact much into the fifth decade (Kerr and Ringrose 1998). As caries prevalence was low, the reason for this early disintegration of the dentition has been invariably attributed to periodontal disease with the observed root exposure in skulls being interpreted as inflammatory alveolar bone loss. It has only been in the past decade or so that it has been appreciated that, in dentitions with severe occlusal attrition, compensatory coronal movement of the teeth occurs, and that this further eruption of the teeth is bodily movement of a basically healthy periodontium

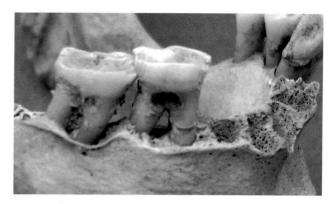

Figure 13.7 Gross periodontal disease showing loss of contour of the alveolus, with horizontal bone loss leading to a flattened plateau with slightly rolled margins. Burial 348, a mature male, also has severe wear and a large buccal cervical carious cavity in the lower right first molar

and socket through the alveolus. It is not possible, therefore, where there is also severe attrition, to assess simply from estimates of the amount of root exposure in skeletal material, whether this loss of attachment has been because of compensatory tooth eruption, or because of alveolar bone loss, or a combination of both (Newman 1999). Fortunately in this study periodontal disease was diagnosed by destruction, porosity and irregularity of the alveolar margin, rather than simple root exposure.

At Chichester 159 individuals were affected by some periodontal disease, representing just over half the dentitions (Table 13.3).

Rhinomaxillary change in leprosy

The Chichester collection enables the examination of many cases of this distinctive condition (Manchester and Roberts 1989; Lewis *et al* 1995). Seventy-two of the 374 individuals have some form of change to the facial region (Fig 13.8). In the maxilla of these cases, where root exposure by the alveolus was >2mm, the alveolar margin was often a thin knife-edge in type, with no sign of bony proliferation, nor of the porosity and ragged edge that would be expected at the margins in advanced periodontal disease (Lukacs 1989). This smooth atrophy occurs both at the alveolar margins and at the margins of the pyramidal aperture of the nose. The commonest appearance is one of atrophy, with the bulk of the cancellous bone disappearing, with a smooth, relatively non-porous cortex surrounding the resorbing core. The predominant process appears to be atrophic, the bone mass decreasing, but with the surface layer of compact bone remodelled, and little porosity. This is suggestive of a reduced blood supply, with fewer vessels perforating the bony cortex.

The leprosy bacillus is known to favour situations appreciably cooler than 37°C and a similar pathogenesis to that proposed for concentric diaphyseal

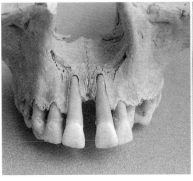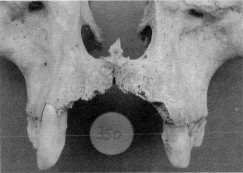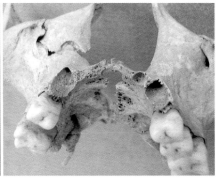

Figure 13.8 Three young males from Chichester with facies leprosa, *burials 347, 350 and 360, show the progression of this condition, with first loss of the teeth and nasal spine, then loss of the anterior alveolus and finally the loss of alveolus and palate. More severe cases than this could not be clearly identified as only the upper cheek teeth in remnants of maxilla would be left*

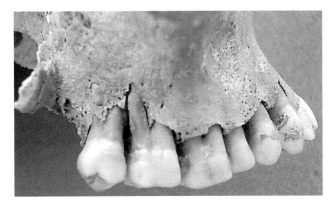

Figure 13.9 Many individuals with rhinomaxillary syndrome also showed a similar pattern of alveolar atrophy around the posterior teeth (young male 347)

remodelling of the phalanges and metatarsals may apply (Andersen *et al* 1992; Scheepers *et al* 1993; Scheepers 1998), that is, damage to the autonomic fibres travelling with the nerve and artery supplying the region. Smith (1999) therefore suggested that as the anterior premaxilla is relatively cool, it may be of critical importance for the lodgement and multiplication of this bacterium, as it is in other body sites (Rendall *et al* 1976; Rees and McDougall 1976; McDougall and Salter 1977; Scheepers 1998). Smith and Manchester considered that infection and resultant fibrosis of the nasopalatine nerve would lead to increased sclerosis, similar to that seen in concentrically remodelled phalanges/metatarsals, by producing autonomic neurovascular dysfunction, leading to atrophy of the labial alveolus and the characteristic loosening and loss of upper anterior teeth. This was not supported by Smith's (1999) study, but she felt that was probably because of the relatively small population available.

There may be some connection too with the almost total absence of periosteal reaction and callus formation in pathological fractures, which is characteristic of leprosy (Aufderheide and Rodríguez-Martín 1998, 150). The development and

repair of microcracks due to function are now seen as an intrinsic part of bone remodelling (Vashishth *et al* 2000). It appears then that, in leprosy, the normal simultaneous repair processes seen in periodontal disease are overridden by the presence of *M. leprae* in quantity, and the inflammatory processes and autonomic dysfunction that go with it.

Resorptive and inflammatory lesions are going on simultaneously, but in different locations, with resorption of the labial and buccal alveolar plates being strongly associated with inflammation and porosity of the palate. Møller-Christensen (1974) considered the changes in the maxillary alveolar bone and anterior nasal spine to be part of the same process causing atrophy to the phalanges of the fingers and toes, and therefore associated with neuropathy. However, tests on the nasal mucous membrane apparently show no loss of sensation.

Rhinomaxillary remodelling cases identified in the Chichester material by Smith (1999) were examined by Ogden (2001). The surprising lack of porosity on the labial and buccal aspects of the alveolar bone, despite the intense resorption, was one of the first features noticed. It is interesting to note that Smith and Manchester's microscopic examination revealed porosity levels of the anterior premaxilla to be significantly lower in their leprous sample than those found in the control sample (p < 0.05) (Smith 1999).

Many similarities to the processes occurring anteriorly were also apparent posteriorly, with bone loss around the most posterior molars, and gross recession around apparently healthy teeth (Fig 13.9). Haas *et al* 2000 have shown that *M. leprae* DNA is retrievable from the nasal cavity in 1000-year-old archaeological specimens and so it does seem possible that such a massive infection may have more widespread effects on the maxilla than has been realised.

Smith (1999) believed that the dramatic atrophy of the premaxilla region seen in the rhinomaxillary syndrome is not due to arterial wall inflammation (Møller-Christensen 1978) but, more likely, to destruction of the autonomic function of the nasopalatine nerve, which descends the incisive canal. Smith claimed that although the premaxilla develops separately to the maxilla, it takes no role in the formation of the *anterior* walls of the incisor sockets. She felt it was of great significance that the terminal branches of the nasopalatine nerve innervate the anterior nasal spine which also becomes resorbed in leprosy.

However the premaxilla is innervated not only by the nasopalatine nerve, but also by the anterior superior alveolar branch of the infra-orbital nerve, stemming from the maxillary nerve. The anterior fibres cross the midline. The maxillary nerve is a sensory branch of the trigeminal nerve (C5) which is known to be affected in leprosy (Jopling and McDougall 1988) and is intimately related to the maxillary artery and its branches, using the same channels and foramina, and an infection of one is likely to have effects on the other. Ogden (2001) suggested that the alveolar atrophy is widespread throughout the area supplied by the maxillary nerve and artery, and greatest at the extreme ends of their distribution, that is, in the incisal and third molar regions. The resorbing alveolus shadows the course of the main maxillary vessels. As the smaller side-branches close so the bone retreats to remain a survivable distance from its blood supply.

Ogden (2001) also noted that the first and most dramatic appearance of resorption in the anterior region may also be simply a function of the extreme thinness of the normal labial plate in this region. The high incidence (67%) of rhinomaxillary syndrome found by Smith (1999) in young males in the 1987 Chichester material may also be because their bone was thinner, and less stable and consolidated than that of more mature individuals.

Leprogenic odontodysplasia

This deformity of the permanent dentition was first described by Danielsen (1970). An early invasion of leprobacilli whilst the crown is still forming results in defects in ameloblasts and subsequent hypoplasias. If the dentition is invaded after the crowns have formed (around five years of age) the roots become concentrically constricted. No clear evidence of this condition was seen at Chichester.

Granulomata and abscesses

The dental pulp in a mature tooth has virtually no ability to repair itself when damaged, whether by trauma, caries or exposure to the oral environment. The dental pulp undergoes autolysis, which will be aseptic if bacteria or fungi cannot gain access. This is enough to trigger development of a granuloma, a mass of fibroblasts, capillaries and polymorphs, as pulpal breakdown products leak from the root apex. This usually spherical mass of soft tissue creates and maintains a void in the bone (Fig 13.10). If there is an apical bony cavity the dental pulp, or, at the very least, the pulp in that root, must have been dead even if there is no obvious sign of trauma or disease.

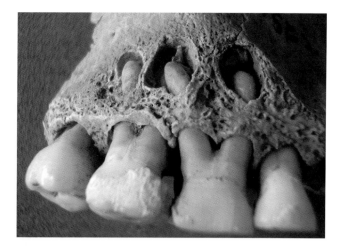

Figure 13.10 Middle adult female 250 had large voids around the apices of the upper first and second molars. These will have been filled with granulomas, following death of the dental pulps due to gross interproximal caries

The clump of granulation tissue can become cystic, undergoing slow enlargement, when the interior becomes necrotic and osmotic pressure leads to fluid build up in the interior. A symptomless non-vital pulp is likely eventually to become infected by blood-borne organisms, which find such necrotic material a haven from the body's defence mechanisms. In the absence of a smooth-walled sinus tracking out through the cortical bone, which indicates the presence of a chronic abscess, all that can be proved for sure by the presence of an apical void is that the tooth was non-vital (Dias and Tayles 1997). Whether or not it was causing pain at the time of death is impossible to determine. However, the presence of a remodelled buccal or lingual sinus, lined with a layer of cortical bone, is evidence that, at some time, there was an abscess, painful at first, which has since drained and become chronic and painless.

Just under half the dentitions at Chichester had evidence of at least one dental granuloma. Eighteen subadults had 74 in the deciduous dentition. Some 147 adults (97 males, 45 females and 5 unknown) had a total of 387 granulomata in the permanent dentition. The most noticeable feature is that the maxillary teeth are almost twice as often involved as the mandibular, but this is partly because they are more easily exposed to observation behind the thin maxillary cortical plate. However, radiographs would probably reveal many undetected lesions in the mandibles. The maxillary first molar is much the most common tooth to be affected, followed by the first mandibular molar and the maxillary first premolar. As with all the other plaque-related dental pathologies, there is a direct correlation with the length of time the teeth have been exposed to the oral environment. The first molars erupt at least six years earlier into the mouth than the other molars. The age of the adult is also a significant factor: 44% of the dentitions with granulomata occurred in the mature age group and 80% in the middle and mature age ranges.

Abscesses are localised areas of infection resulting in the build up of pus with the formation of an osteolytic (bone-destroying) lesion. They may be secondary to pulp death from dental caries or exposure of the pulp cavity as a result of trauma or extreme attrition. If wear is very rapid the pulp may not be able to deposit secondary dentine fast enough to retreat out of harm's way. In advanced cases the build up of pus bursts through the bone and drains into the soft tissues forming a sinus or 'gum-boil' which usually fails to heal completely and becomes chronic. Oro-antral fistulas produced by abscesses creating a channel from the upper teeth into the maxillary antrum were seen in burials 41, 344 and 348. This will have enabled the passage of fluid from the mouth into the nose and *vice versa,* and will have established a maxillary sinusitis detectable on the floor of the sinus.

Enamel hypoplasia

This is a defect that occurs during the enamel-forming processes of the teeth and is caused by a cessation or decline in enamel formation and mineralisation. Enamel hypoplasia may be due to a variety of causes including nutritional deprivation, sometimes secondary to parasitic infection, and systemic disease. Defects are visible macroscopically as lines or pits on the surface of the teeth, and are considered an indicator of stress during early life. Bouts of malnutrition, disease and fever are known to depress the activity of the enamel-forming ameloblasts and result in the formation of thin and poorly calcified matrix, with the formation of pits or grooves of defective enamel (Goodman and Rose 1990; Skinner and Goodman 1992; Hillson and Bond 1997; Hillson 2005). Once formed, the enamel gets no further chance to develop, as the 'active front' of ameloblast matrix formation has moved on towards the cervical margin. Since enamel, unlike bone, is not remodelled during life, each person's enamel is a record of the first seven or eight years of their life when the enamel of their tooth crowns was formed.

However enamel hypoplasia in an individual is often underestimated for the following reasons:

(1) The high level of tooth wear in archaeological populations has often removed evidence of hypoplasia from the first-formed regions of each tooth (the cusp tips) in those individuals who die in adult life. This certainly applies to the Chichester material.
(2) Overlapping of poorly formed enamel by later-formed sleeves of enamel means that lesions may not be visible on the surface (Hillson and Bond 1997). These can only be revealed by destructive sectioning of the teeth.

In this study hypoplasia was simply assessed as being present or absent. Two hundred and eight individuals (80.3% of the dentate population) had some observable enamel hypoplasia in the

Figure 13.11   Seven-year-old individual 122 had a fully formed mesiodens palatal to the permanent upper central incisors

permanent dentition, but little was severe. As would be expected, the most commonly affected teeth were the canines as their crowns are forming for longer than any other tooth (Goodman and Rose 1990) and are therefore at greatest risk of having their growth interrupted by bouts of ill health.

Developmental anomalies

Hypodontia

In many cases there may be a failure of one or more teeth to develop (hypodontia). The most common is the absence of the third molar. In humans the absence of the third molar may be as high as 20% of the sample and there is some indication that this may be directly related to the tooth size and contain an inherited element. Other teeth frequently missing are the second premolars or maxillary second incisor (Lavelle and Moore 1973).

At Chichester, 63 individuals had absence of one or more third molars: 70 mandibular and 53 maxillary. Two individuals (burials 33 and 77) had abnormally small left maxillary third molars. Five individuals had congenital absence of teeth in other positions. Burial 253 had the right mandibular central incisor absent, while 311 had the left and right lateral mandibular incisors missing and 326 the left second mandibular premolar. In the maxilla the left and right lateral incisors are absent in burial 243 and the second premolars in 211, with the left deciduous second molar being retained in this position.

Supernumerary teeth

These are much rarer than teeth that have failed to develop (Lavelle and Moore 1973). Additional teeth were recorded in two individuals: burial 122, a 7-year-

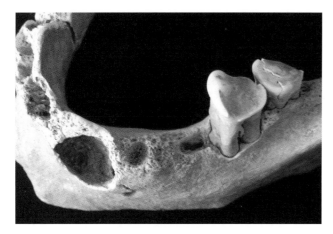

Figure 13.12   In burial 300, a mature male, there is a large smooth-walled lesion measuring 16 × 25mm and 10mm deep in the left anterior region of the mandible. This is probably a cyst that has developed from a granuloma on the apex of the left canine

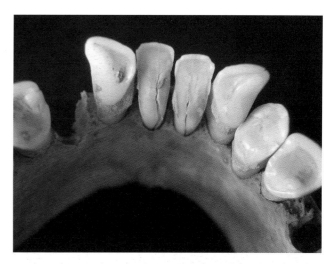

Figure 13.13   In burial 40, a mature female, the anterior mandibular teeth were heavily worn lingually, showing the presence of a reverse overjet, combined with a complete overbite, suggesting a small maxilla

old, has a supernumerary tooth (mesiodens) erupting posterior to the central incisors (Fig 13.11); burial 346, a young adult male, has an additional central mandibular incisor which is so well aligned in the arch that it could easily be missed by the observer.

Cysts

Cysts were present in two individuals (burials 123 and 300). These are fluid-filled cavities lined by epithelium and are the commonest cause of painless swellings of the jaw (Cawson 1968, 236). In burial 123, a mature male, there is a smooth cyst-like cavity to the left maxilla in the region of the second premolar. There is no evidence for infection. In burial 300, a mature male, there is a large smooth-walled lesion in the left anterior region of the mandible (Fig 13.12).

Impaction

Impaction of teeth occurred in four individuals (burials 100, 124, 253, 287). The mandibular third molars and upper canines are the teeth most often misplaced; they rarely cause symptoms if they fail to erupt, but partial eruption often leads to infection and pain (Cawson 1968, 151). Two lower third molars were horizontally impacted. In burial 287 a left maxillary canine had developed horizontally in the palate and failed to erupt.

Rotation

Rotation of teeth may be the result of overcrowding, particularly in the incisor region or where

movement has resulted from loss of a neighbouring tooth. Paradoxically it can also occur due to natural spacing when the teeth are not forced to line up in the normal catenary arch. Rotation was noted in a minimum of five individuals: to the right mandibular canine in burial 356, to the mandibular second premolars in 293 and to the left first and second maxillary premolars in 328; the right lateral incisor in 272 and right maxillary third molar in 178 were also affected.

Malocclusion

Unusual wear to the maxillary incisors in burial 272 indicates a protrusion of the mandible or prognathism. Associated with this is rotation and overcrowding of the right maxillary anterior teeth. In burial 40, a mature female, the anterior mandibular teeth were heavily worn lingually, indicating a small maxillary arch meeting this normal-sized mandibular arch (Fig 13.13).

Overcrowding

Overcrowding of one or more teeth was not uncommon but was particularly marked in four individuals: to the anterior mandibular teeth in three (burials 2, 92 and 122) and the maxillary anterior teeth in burial 272.

Miscellaneous

Individual 198, an adult male, has a much larger maxillary central incisor on the left than on the right (Fig 13.14). Burial 240, a child aged 11–12 years, has

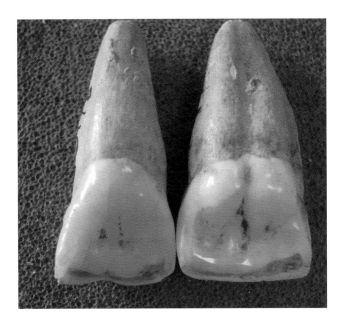

Figure 13.14 Burial 198, an adult male, has a large left maxillary central incisor. This has the appearance of two fused teeth, producing a wide crown, with a groove to the posterior aspect of the root. The normal-sized right central incisor is included for comparison

both maxillary canines erupting palatally. An 11- to 12-year-old (burial 313a) has had the position of the right mandibular second premolar affected by a large apical abscess at the root of the deciduous molar. This has forced the developing premolar to erupt buccally. Young adult male 338 has upper canines with very large cingulae and relatively short roots, resembling premolars. Young adult male 346 has three-rooted upper first premolars as well as an additional lower central incisor. Burial 370, a young adult, probably male, may have had a developmental midline cleft of the posterior two-thirds of the hard palate.

Conclusions

The skeletal material from Chichester, carefully excavated and well preserved, forms a valuable resource for the study of the dental and oral health of the chronic sick in medieval society. In particular the many skulls showing rhinomaxillary remodelling will be invaluable for years to come as new techniques develop for the investigation of leprosy.

14 Skeletal manifestations of leprosy
by Donald J Ortner

Introduction

Evidence of skeletal disease in human archaeological burials provides important data on human health in past human populations. Admittedly the evidence does not lend itself to easy interpretation but with the dramatic increase, both in the quality and quantity, of research on human skeletal palaeopathology in the past twenty years we are in a much better position to identify the diagnostic options for archaeological burials with skeletal disorders. We are also more aware of the pitfalls in interpreting evidence of disease and better able to understand the significance of disease when we encounter it in these burials.

Leprosy is one of the infectious diseases that can affect the human skeleton. It is caused by *Mycobacterium leprae*, a bacterial species closely related to the pathogen that causes tuberculosis. Of the people who are exposed to the pathogen most never have any evidence of disease. Spouses living with infected patients only acquire disease in between 5 and 6% of cases. Similarly about 8% of children living with one or more parents who have leprosy will develop this disease (Binford and Meyers 1976). Those that do exhibit morbidity will range from very mild symptoms (tuberculoid leprosy) to individuals with severe disfigurement of the face, deformity with disability of hands and feet, secondary infections and blindness (lepromatous leprosy). This broad range in the variable expression of disease is not caused by differences in the organism but depends entirely on the immune response of the patient (Jopling 1971).

What is known about the history and archaeology of the medieval hospital of St James and St Mary Magdalene in Chichester is presented in other chapters and will not be reviewed here except to note that the early use of the hospital was for patients with leprosy. As the prevalence of leprosy declined in the latter part of the medieval period, the prevalence of patients with other disorders increased. Nevertheless, given the history of the hospital, one expects that the predominant disease represented in the burials is leprosy but other skeletal disorders have been identified. These other diseases are presented in other chapters and highlight the fact that over the long use of the hospital the occupants were not limited to patients with leprosy. Nevertheless the substantial number of burials for which a diagnosis of leprosy is at least plausible provides a remarkable view of the range of skeletal manifestations associated with the severe end of the spectrum of morbidity in this disease. It is the primary purpose of this chapter to review the range of skeletal abnormalities with the expectation that this information will both increase our knowledge of the bone lesions associated with leprosy and also aid in the diagnosis of leprosy in other palaeopathological cases where leprosy is a diagnostic option.

Much of what we know about the skeletal evidence of leprosy in archaeological burials was first observed by the late Prof Vilhelm Møller-Christensen, a Danish physician who based his research on burials excavated from cemeteries associated with Danish medieval hospitals for patients with leprosy. He was the first to describe the abnormalities apparent in the bones of the face and particularly those affecting the nose and anterior alveolar bone (Møller-Christensen 1953; 1974). He used the Latin term *facies leprosa* to describe the destructive remodelling that occurs in the face of patients with leprosy. He described the rounded and typically enlarged margins of the piriform aperture, the destruction of the anterior nasal spine and the resorption of the maxillary alveolar process associated with the premaxilla. He also identified the effect leprosy can have on the development of tooth roots in young children. In this abnormality, which Møller-Christensen called *leprogenic odontodysplasia*, the tooth roots, particularly those of the maxillary central incisors, fail to develop fully and are easily lost particularly if the anterior maxillary alveolar bone undergoes destructive remodelling as the result of a focus of chronic infection of the rhinomaxillary tissues.

Additional research on the skeletal palaeopathology of leprosy was conducted by Johs Andersen, a Danish surgeon who had studied with Møller-Christensen. Andersen spent much of his life in Ethiopia treating patients with leprosy. In collaboration with Keith Manchester, an English physician, they published several papers on various manifestations of skeletal leprosy that combined Andersen's experience both as a surgeon caring for patients with leprosy and extensive knowledge of Danish medieval cases of skeletal leprosy as well as Manchester's research on skeletal manifestations of leprosy in medieval English skeletal samples (Andersen 1969; Andersen and Manchester 1987; 1988; 1992; Andersen et al 1992; Andersen et al 1994).

In 1988, at the invitation of Keith Manchester, I began an analysis of the medieval Chichester skeletal sample as a visiting professor at the University of Bradford where this skeletal sample is curated. Until that time my exposure to archaeological evidence of skeletal leprosy was a brief encounter in 1985 with some of the burials from the Danish leprosy hospitals through the courtesy of Prof Vilhelm Møller-Christensen. At that time, no evidence of leprosy had been reported in preColumbian Native American burials that had been a focus of much of my research. Very recent, and thus far unpublished, research on Native American burials from the Kodiak Island, Alaska, USA, provide possible evidence for the presence of leprosy in a single skull (Wilczak and Ortner 2006). The burial (NMNH 366639) is the skull with lower jaw, right scapula and both clavicles of an adult female. It was excavated in the early part of the 20th century with field methods that raise questions about the archaeological context. However, the field notes and catalogue information state that the burial was from the pre-Koniag period which, if correct, would be well before Columbus and the introduction of leprosy into the New World by African slaves. During my tenure at the University of Bradford, I was interested in all skeletal evidence of disease but the opportunity to work with Manchester, as well as the very high prevalence of leprosy in the Chichester skeletal sample, provided a remarkable prospect of obtaining a much better understanding of the range of skeletal manifestations in archaeological burials of people with leprosy.

What emerged from this experience was a better knowledge of the effect of leprosy on the human skeleton in different stages of the disease. Of particular importance were the manifestations of early stage skeletal involvement in some of the lesions encountered in this remarkable archaeological skeletal sample (Ortner and Connell 1996; Ortner 2003). The primary objective of this chapter is to summarise the effect of leprosy on the human skeleton as revealed by the burials excavated from the medieval cemetery of the Hospital of St James and St Mary Magdalene in Chichester. To some extent this will duplicate the research and publication of others but it will add further observations and depth to our knowledge as well as provide the reader with diagnostic information useful in identifying leprosy in human skeletons from other archaeological sites.

A brief word is necessary about the descriptive terminology used in this chapter. Evidence of both abnormal bone formation and abnormal bone destruction can occur in the skeletons of people who had leprosy. Several terms have been applied to these skeletal abnormalities in other publications. Ideally terminology about skeletal abnormalities should be descriptive without implying a diagnosis unless there is relative certainty about the cause. Also, the terminology should address all the variation in anatomical abnormality that the observer encounters.

I am not completely satisfied with the terminology regarding skeletal leprosy generally found in the medical and bioanthropological literature. For this reason I use terms that, in my judgement at least, accurately describe the abnormality encountered. In some cases I have included, in parentheses, the terms used by others for the same abnormality. Only two basic skeletal abnormalities occur in burials of individuals that had leprosy; these are abnormal bone formation and abnormal bone destruction. I refer to abnormal bone formation as reactive bone

formation. The bone formed may be rapidly formed woven bone or more slowly formed compact bone. Woven bone indicates active pathology at the time of death since this type of bone begins to be remodelled into compact bone within a few weeks of formation. Woven bone is poorly organised and very porous. As woven bone is remodelled into compact bone the evidence of its rapid development, including some porosity, is often retained. Abnormal compact bone formation can also occur and may be porous if there is vascular stimulation caused by disease. One manifestation of reactive bone formation is known as porotic hyperostosis which has been linked to anaemia but also occurs in other pathological processes. It is a common bone abnormality in relatively chronic, inflammatory and vascular disorders.

Abnormal bone destruction of compact bone may be expressed as pitting in which fine defects in the cortical surface do not penetrate the entire thickness of the cortex. Another manifestation that may resemble pitting is porosity in which the compact bone is completely penetrated by holes. This type of bone destruction is usually associated with increased vascularity in response to an inflammatory stimulus at the site of the porosity or another pathological stimulus such as trauma or chronic bleeding at the site. Both porosity and pitting occur in some of the Chichester cases of leprosy. However, the major destructive feature is a very gradual enlargement of the nasal aperture and the gradual loss of bone in the diaphyses of the hands and feet. I prefer the term destructive remodelling for this process since it clearly describes what happened but is more inclusive than some of the other terms used in the literature.

The Chichester skeletal sample

Of the at least 384 medieval burials recovered from the Chichester site, a firm estimate of the number of cases of leprosy cannot be made. This reflects the fact that there is a range of skeletal involvement that at one end of the scale contains easily diagnosed cases that have multifocal skeletal abnormalities with a pattern of bone involvement typical of leprosy. At the other end of the diagnostic spectrum there are cases with a type and distribution of lesions that cannot be distinguished among the several infectious and other diseases that affect the skeleton. We do have clear evidence that other skeletal disorders including tuberculosis and carcinoma were present in the sample so caution is needed in assigning a specific diagnosis when the evidence is ambiguous.

It is also important to recognise that the Chichester sample does not reflect the population of medieval England as a whole. There are few subadult skeletons and female burials are also under-represented in the western half of the cemetery. The limited subadult skeletons reflect the fact that leprosy is very slow to develop, typically with incubation periods measured in years (Jopling 1971, 1), although documentary records suggest that juveniles may not have been admitted to the hospital. The diagnostic features necessary for a diagnosis of leprosy are much less likely to occur during childhood.

A substantial number of the skeletons that show evidence of skeletal disease can be attributed to leprosy and the likely minimum number of cases of leprosy in the sample is about 75 burials. This is a substantial subsample and provides considerable insight regarding skeletal abnormalities that occur in leprosy in stages of development from early involvement of the skeleton to late stage severe involvement. It is important to emphasise that leprosy is a chronic disease with long-term survival of individuals with the disease. This means that several of the occupants of the leper hospital could have been there for many years and most of the cases with skeletal involvement will represent late-stage manifestations of lepromatous leprosy. However, there are a few cases suggestive of early stages that provide the basis for further research on this phase in the development of skeletal leprosy. These patients probably died from disorders other than leprosy.

What is clear from my research on the Chichester sample is that criteria for a specific diagnosis of leprosy are likely to vary among observers. For example, reactive periostitis, a bone-forming abnormality caused by infectious pathogens, of the distal tibia and fibula is a common feature in skeletal abnormalities caused by leprosy. When this is associated with abnormalities occurring in the rhinomaxillary region as well as the bones of the hands and feet a diagnosis of leprosy is virtually certain. However, abnormal bone-forming lesions of the lower leg can be caused by other infectious disorders and by non-infectious abnormalities. When bone-forming abnormalities occur on the distal tibia and fibula but are the only abnormality, a diagnosis of leprosy may be plausible in some cases but not others and there is likely to be disagreement between observers.

Skeletal abnormalities associated with leprosy

The major sites for skeletal involvement in leprosy include the bones of the face, hands, the lower legs and feet. I will review the skeletal abnormalities associated with each of these anatomical sites. In living patients the initial disorder associated with leprosy is a skin rash. This abnormality is also present in several other skin diseases such as psoriasis. However, skin rash was probably the basis of the initial diagnosis of leprosy in medieval Europe (Richards 1977). The misdiagnosis of leprosy in some cases is probably the basis of reports of some patients who recovered from the disease. The potential of misdiagnosis based on a skin rash must have been a troublesome possibility. Given the fact that leprosy is not easily transmitted between people, the social reaction to leprosy in most human societies seems severe particularly in the context of other diseases that can affect the skeleton, such as tuberculosis, which are more contagious and cause more serious morbidity and mortality.

Typically a diagnosis of leprosy led to banishment from society often with a funeral ceremony to mark the patient's loss of all rights (Richards 1977). In medieval society, options for people with leprosy were very limited and many were condemned to life as a beggar. The more fortunate might find a home in one of the hospitals scattered throughout the British Isles. Undoubtedly in many cases the abnormalities did not progress to more severe manifestations and this at least partially explains the presence of many skeletons in the Chichester sample that have no evidence of significant skeletal disease. Other factors, however, including the decline in the prevalence of leprosy in the latter stages of the medieval period, with the resulting inclusion of patients with other diseases that may not have affected the skeleton, need to be considered in interpreting the evidence for leprosy.

Abnormalities of the face

Møller-Christensen (1953; 1961; 1978) described very well the basic abnormalities that can occur in the facial area of skeletons of individuals who had leprosy. He noted that porous lesions were found in the orbital roof of some skulls which also had other skeletal evidence of leprosy. He called this condition *usura orbitae* but this lesion is better known as *cribra orbitalia*. He hypothesised that the condition might be secondary to an enlarged lacrimal gland (Møller-Christensen 1953, 128), presumably caused by chronic infection of the eye. In the scientific literature on palaeopathology lesions of the orbital roof have been associated with other disorders including anaemia and scurvy (eg Stuart-Macadam 1987a, 1987b; Ortner *et al* 1999; Ortner *et al* 2001). Møller-Christensen's link between this condition and leprosy highlights the importance of infection in producing these lesions. In patients with leprosy they are in all likelihood caused by chronic infection of the eye which is a well-known complication of chronic lepromatous leprosy (Jopling 1971, 26). It seems likely that other chronic infectious conditions of the eye such as trachoma will result in similar lesions. *Cribra orbitalia* also occurs in the Chichester leprosy cases (Fig 14.1) although it is not common and, when present, is a relatively mild expression.

Perhaps the most noticeable abnormality of the face is the destructive remodelling associated with the piriform aperture. Typical abnormality involves an enlargement of the aperture linked to a rounding of its normally sharp margins (Fig 14.2). The anterior nasal spine participates in this destructive process and is often completely eliminated. Andersen and Manchester (1992) have provided a review of both the pathogenesis and the anatomical abnormalities that occur in the facial area of patients with

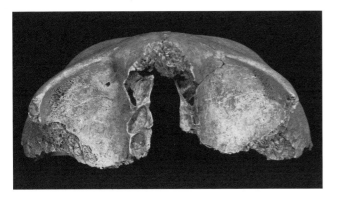

*Figure 14.1 Porosity of the orbital roof (*cribra orbitalia*) probably associated with chronic infection. Chichester burial 64, an adult male about 20 years of age*

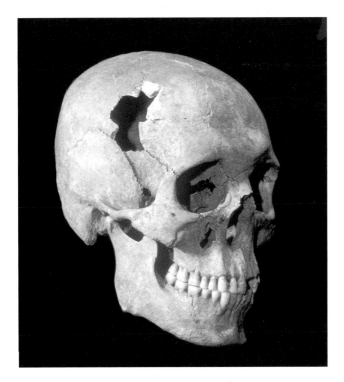

Figure 14.2 Destructive remodelling of the nasal aperture with rounding of the piriform aperture margin and loss of the anterior nasal spine. Chichester burial 48 is a mature adult male

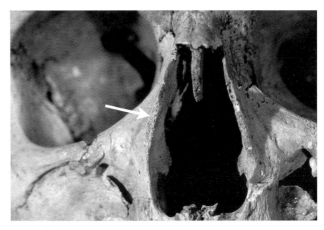

Figure 14.3 (a) (above) Probable early stage of destructive remodelling of the nasal aperture. Note the flattening of the aperture edge and the porous surface of the edge particularly apparent on the right margin (arrow). (b) (below) Interior right wall of the nasal passage. Note the porosity and pitting of the cortical surface indicative of inflammation and osteoclastic activity. Chichester burial 354, an adult male about 27 years of age

leprosy. Møller-Christensen (1961, 13) thought the destruction of the nasal spine was pathognomonic for leprosy. Unfortunately this is not the case; the nasal spine as well as the margins of the piriform aperture may undergo destructive remodelling in tuberculosis, treponematosis, leishmaniasis, cancer and probably other conditions as well. However, in combination with other abnormalities of the face, it is an important diagnostic feature in skeletal leprosy.

In most cases of destructive remodelling around the piriform aperture, the margins are smooth compact bone indicating a very chronic stage of lepromatous leprosy. An important question is, what is the appearance of this destructive remodelling process in the early stage of nasal involvement? Two cases (burials 187 and 354) of what is probably early stage destructive remodelling occur in the Chichester sample. A brief report on one of these cases has been published (Ortner and Connell 1996).

In both cases the margins of the piriform aperture are still relatively intact and the anterior nasal spine is present in burial 354 (in burial 187 the spine is missing post-mortem), supporting the hypothesis that nasal involvement is in the early stage of skeletal leprosy. What seems to be the earlier manifestation of piriform aperture destructive remodelling occurs in burial 354. The individual represented by these bones was a male about 27 years of age at the time of death. Abnormalities of the bone forming the margin of the aperture include porosity of the maxillary bone at the aperture margin (Fig 14.3a) as well as pitting and porosity of the inner surface of the nasal passage (Fig 14.3b).

Burial 187 was a male about 18 years of age at the time of death. The external maxillary bones of the

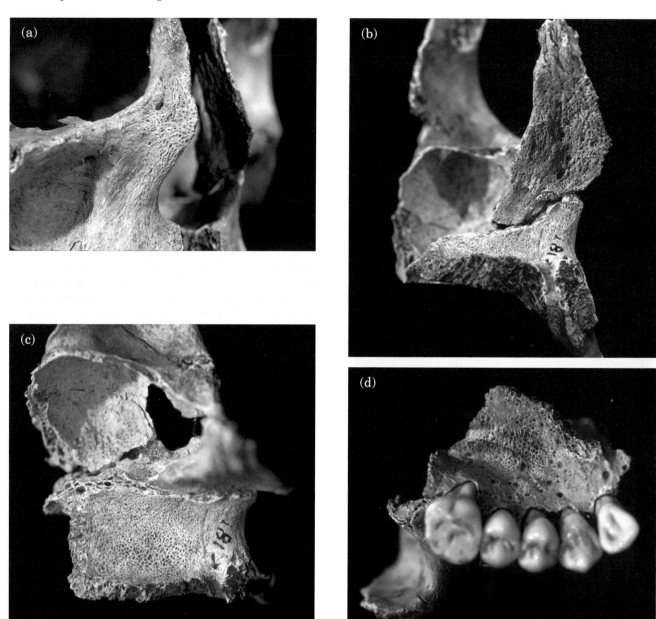

Figure 14.4 (a) External surface of the maxillary bone adjacent to the piriform aperture. Pitting predominates the destructive remodelling but some abnormal porosity is also present. (b) Interior surface of the nasal passage showing abnormal porosity of virtually the entire surface. (c) Abnormal porosity of the left nasal floor. (d) Abnormal porosity of the left hard palate. Chichester burial 187, a young adult male about 18 years of age

aperture margin are abnormally porotic, indicating a vascular response to an infectious stimulus. But the much more prevalent feature is a series of depressions in the cortical surface indicative of osteoclastic activity (Fig 14.4a). Both these abnormal manifestations are bilateral and symmetrical. The maxillary bone lining the nasal passage is highly porous (Fig 14.4b), as is the nasal floor (Fig 14.4c) and the hard palate (Fig 14.4d). The skeletal evidence supports the observation that nasal infection by *M. leprae* was in the early stages of development and very active at the time of death.

The anterior alveolar process also undergoes destructive remodelling in some cases (Fig 14.5). This remodelling occurs in association with remodelling of the piriform aperture. The recession of alveolar bone affects the area associated with the premaxilla and, thus, the support for the upper incisors is compromised and these teeth may be lost ante-mortem because of this destructive remodelling. The most prevalent manifestation of nasal involvement in leprosy is an enlargement of the piriform aperture. However, in some cases the destructive remodelling phase is followed by limited bone formation that can result in abnormal narrowing of the aperture (Fig 14.6).

If the onset of leprosy occurs during dental development, growth of the tooth roots may be impaired

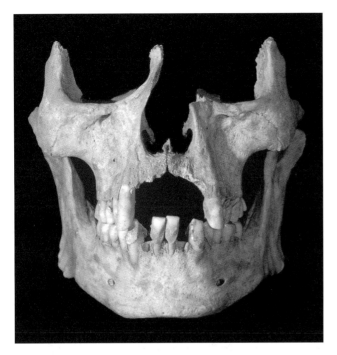

Figure 14.5 Destructive remodelling of the anterior maxillary alveolar process. Note that little remodelling is apparent in the margins of the piriform aperture and the remaining cortical bone of the anterior alveolar process is abnormally porous. Chichester burial 350, an adult male about 26 years of age

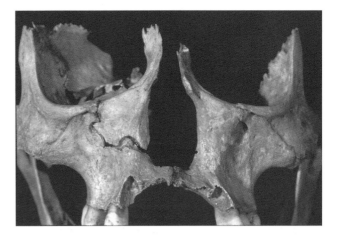

Figure 14.6 An unusual manifestation of remodelling at the margins of the piriform aperture. Destructive remodelling has removed the original margins but reactive bone formation has partially filled in the aperture, greatly narrowing the nasal passage. Note also the severe destructive remodelling of the anterior maxillary alveolar process. Chichester burial 360, a young adult, probably male

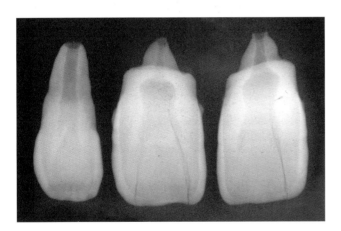

Figure 14.7 Failure of dental root development (leprogenic odontodysplasia) in a child with leprosy. Naestved, Denmark medieval cemetery case 1, child 9 years of age

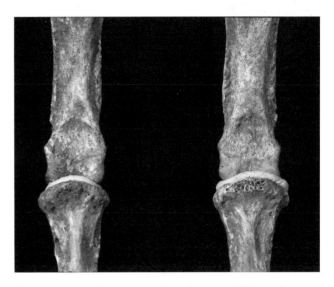

Figure 14.8 Pressure-induced remodelling of the volar metaphysis of the phalanges in the left and right proximal third interphalangeal joint secondary to severe flexion contractures. Note the reactive porosity apparent in the proximal joint margins of the distal phalanges. Chichester burial 44, an adult male about 40 years of age

resulting in what Møller-Christensen (1978, 123) called *dens leprosus* or *leprogenic odontodysplasia* (Fig 14.7). I have not seen evidence of this abnormality in the Chichester sample.

Abnormalities of the hands

There are both similarities and differences in the skeletal abnormalities that occur in the hands

and feet. The pathogenesis for diaphyseal destructive remodelling (concentric atrophy) occurs in both extremities but is more pronounced in the metatarsals and phalanges of the feet. Nevertheless abnormal remodelling of the metacarpals and phalanges of the hand can be severe. The neuromuscular degeneration associated with lepromatous leprosy can cause severe flexion contractures of the phalanges of the hand (Andersen and Manchester

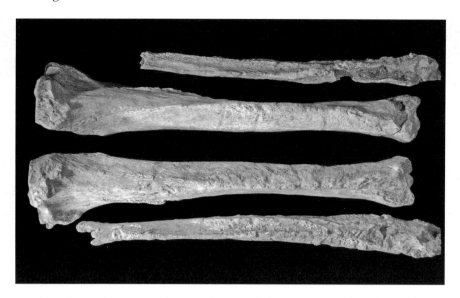

Figure 14.9   Secondary periostitis of the tibiae and fibulae secondary to infection of the feet following injury introducing infectious pathogens. Chichester burial 48, a mature adult male

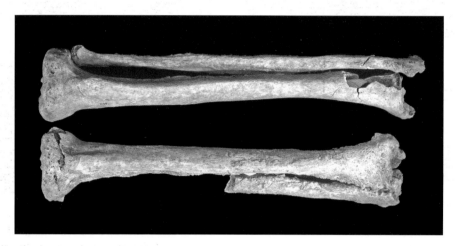

Figure 14.10   Septic arthritis of the right ankle with secondary periostitis affecting the distal tibia and fibula. Infection has resulted in destruction of the joint with fusion of the talus remnant to the tibia and fusion of the distal tibia and fibula. Chichester burial 35, an adult male

1987). This results in a pressure erosion of the volar metaphysis of the proximal component of the joint (Fig 14.8).

Abnormalities of the lower legs

A very common abnormality in leprosy burials that occurs in the lower legs is a reactive periostitis (Fig 14.9). The most likely cause is a neurovascular response to chronic secondary infection of the foot (Andersen *et al* 1994). Pathogenic bacteria invade through damaged skin and create a chronic infection as the impaired immune response associated with leprosy may be inadequate to eliminate the pathogens. Andersen *et al* (1994) emphasise that these lesions of the tibia and fibula could be a result of either direct infection spreading from a focus in the foot or toxins secondary to the infec-

tious focus spreading well beyond the infectious focus and stimulating a generalised inflammatory response in the tibia and fibula. The important anatomical feature, relative to other infectious diseases that produce reactive periostitis of the lower leg, is that in leprosy the lesions are located primarily on the distal end of the bones reflecting the pathogenic stimulus in the foot. However, these lesions may extend a considerable distance proximally and the observer needs to pay particular attention to the area of the bone where the most severe manifestations occur. If the major focus of the reactive bone is in the mid-shaft or proximal end of the bone, diagnostic options other than leprosy are more likely. Commonly these lesions are composed of woven bone indicating that the disorder was active at the time of death. Since these lesions may be caused by bacterial pathogens with a potential for serious morbidity

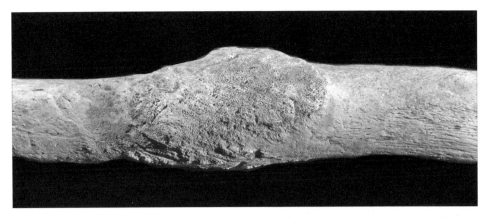

Figure 14.11   Localised periostitis associated with a skin ulcer. Note the extensive porosity of the lesion and the very distinct margin between the site of the ulcer and the adjacent normal bone. Chichester burial 4, an adult male of unknown age

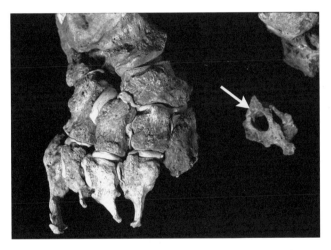

Figure 14.12   Concentric destructive remodelling of the metatarsals of the feet. The phalanges were destroyed ante-mortem. Note the tarsal fragment (arrow) with a large cloaca resulting from a focus of osteomyelitis. Chichester burial 62, an adult of unknown sex or age

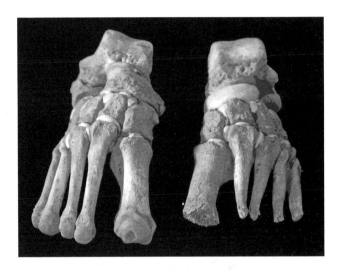

Figure 14.13   Unilateral blade-like destructive remodelling of the metatarsals of the left foot. There is a small destructive focus in the subchondral bone of the right first metatarsal. Chichester burial 21, an adult male about 25 years of age

that is greater than *M. leprae*, they may have given rise to a septicaemia which would be a probable cause of death.

Secondary infection of the feet may result in septic arthritis with severe joint destruction and fusion, as seen in the bones of the right ankle of burial 35, an adult male (Fig 14.10). Another secondary infection that may be associated with neurological degeneration and the diminished vascular function linked with leprosy is chronic ulcer. An example of this is seen in burial 4 which is the skeleton of an adult male of unknown specific age. A common site is the lower leg and particularly the tibia. The unique features of the bony response to an overlying ulcer include an area of reactive bone formation that typically has a well-defined border with the adjacent normal bone (Fig 14.11). The surface of the bone lesion is very porous which is indicative of the pathology being active at the time of death.

Abnormalities of the feet

There are two major abnormalities of the foot directly associated with neurovascular disorders linked with leprosy. The first of these is destructive remodelling (concentric and blade-like) of the metatarsals and phalanges. The second is degeneration of one or both arches of the foot, with collapse of the foot and reactive remodelling of the tarsal bones (Andersen and Manchester 1988).

Destructive remodelling of the metatarsals and phalanges tends to be concentric (Fig 14.12) and most severe in the distal ends and diaphyses of the metatarsals and phalanges. However, the remodelling may result in a blade-like abnormality of one or more metatarsal bones (Fig 14.13). Severity varies from a barely distinguishable abnormal reduction of diaphyseal diameters to cases where the phalanges may be entirely missing and the metatarsal bones greatly reduced in size with

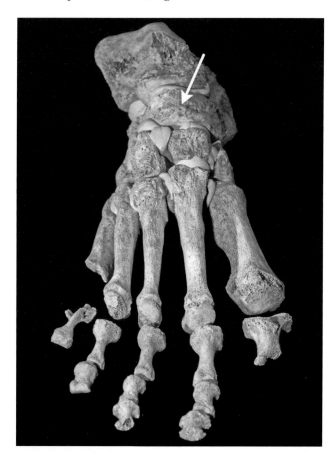

Figure 14.14 A dorsal exostosis (arrow) on the superior surface of the right navicular. Chichester burial 88, an adult male about 35 years of age

Table 14.1
Skeletal lesions and locations for leprosy

Lesions of the skull
  Skull vault usually not involved
  Orbital lesions – porosity and porous reactive bone formation on the orbital roof
  Nasal lesions
    Destructive remodelling of the nasal aperture
    Destruction of the anterior nasal spine
    Abnormal porosity of the nasal floor
  Maxilla
    Abnormal porosity of the alveolar process
    Destructive remodelling of the anterior alveolar process
  Palate
    Abnormal porosity
    Lytic defects
Abnormalities of the teeth
  Odontodysplasia – failure of root development in children with leprosy
Bones of the hands
  Destructive remodelling (concentric atrophy) of the metacarpals and phalanges
  Flexion contractures resulting in volar grooving
Bones of the lower leg
  Periostitis caused by secondary infection of the feet
Bones of the feet
  Destructive remodelling (concentric atrophy) of the metatarsals and phalanges
    Concentric remodelling
    Blade-like remodelling
  Dorsal exostoses of the tarsal bones, particularly the navicular
  Secondary infection following trauma

only a small remnant of the proximal metaphysis remaining.

The general loss of muscle control associated with nerve destruction in leprosy results in a loss of ligament function in the sole of the foot. This affects the transverse and plantar ligaments but the effect is more apparent in bone components associated with the plantar ligament. The result is a breakdown in the normal arch configuration of the foot. Bone changes associated with this abnormality have been described by Andersen and Manchester (1988) and consist of abnormal bars of bone on the superior surface of the navicular bone (Fig 14.14).

Discussion and conclusions

The ability to diagnose leprosy in archaeological human skeletal remains ranges from problematic to highly likely. Andersen *et al* (1994) distinguish between bone lesions that are a direct response to *M. leprae* and those that arise as secondary infections from exposure to pathogens through skin ulcers. These secondary infections are similar to other infectious diseases that can affect the skeleton and differentiation of leprosy from other disorders without additional evidence elsewhere in the skeleton may not be possible. The range in certainty

regarding a diagnosis of leprosy in archaeological remains is the result of great variability in the effect of leprosy on the human skeleton associated with variation in the immune response, age of onset and other factors such as adequacy of the patient's diet. The probability of a correct diagnosis of leprosy in a given archaeological burial greatly increases as the number of skeletal abnormalities associated with this disease increases, because the overall pattern of skeletal lesions in multifocal leprosy is relatively distinctive. The importance of carefully evaluating both the type and distribution of these abnormalities in the skeleton cannot be overemphasised. A summary of the skeletal manifestations of leprosy is provided in Table 14.1.

My experience with the leprosy cases from the Chichester sample very clearly indicates that the feet were more often and more severely affected by leprosy than the hands. Part of this difference is probably due to the secondary infections that are more common in the feet than the hands. It is also possible that vascular insufficiency is likely to be more of a problem in the former than the latter.

It is important to emphasise the association of *cribra orbitalia* and leprosy. The well-established complication of chronic eye infection associated with leprosy results in blindness but will also stimulate hypervascularity that will affect the bones of the orbit resulting in increased porosity and possibly porous reactive bone formation. The probable link between leprosy and *cribra orbitalia* raises an important caution about the specificity of this abnormality which has often been linked to anaemia and used as an index of anaemia. Lacking evidence of marrow hyperplasia such a conclusion is unwarranted and should be abandoned in research conducted on palaeopathology. There are several diagnostic options for *cribra orbitalia* including infection, scurvy and anaemia if there is evidence of marrow hyperplasia in other parts of the skull and/or skeleton.

Andersen *et al* (1994) discuss the differences in the skeletal manifestations of tuberculoid as opposed to lepromatous leprosy. These authors emphasise that tuberculoid and lepromatous leprosy represent a continuum in the immune response of the patient and skeletal manifestations will vary between absent in some cases of tuberculoid to extensive skeletal involvement at the other end of the spectrum. They state that rhinomaxillary destructive remodelling is only seen in lepromatous leprosy and is diagnostic for this disorder. In lepromatous leprosy, skeletal lesions are bilateral and often symmetrical. We have seen some evidence in the cases presented above that have unilateral involvement or severe involvement of the foot but no rhinomaxillary involvement. These manifestations reflect a more effective immune response relative to those that occur in severe lepromatous leprosy.

The role of the immune response in determining the severity of leprosy raises interesting options for evaluating genetic differences between populations, for example, the Danish medieval expressions of skeletal leprosy relative to skeletal manifestations found in the Chichester sample. Some population-based differences in the immune response and the prevalence of tuberculoid versus lepromatous skeletal manifestations would provide at least a small window on genetic differences between populations in the immune response to leprosy.

15 Leprosy: a review of the evidence in the Chichester sample *by Frances Lee and Keith Manchester*

As a refuge for the despised the leper house was ubiquitous in medieval Europe (Dols 1983).

Few diseases have engendered such widespread fear or are as mutilating as leprosy, a chronic infectious disease caused by *Mycobacterium leprae (M. leprae)*. The bacteria primarily affect the peripheral nervous system and secondarily the skin and other tissues, causing pigmentation change. In lepromatous leprosy nodules develop which contain the bacilli. Infection of the peripheral nerves near the skin surface results in paralysis and anaesthesia of supplied muscles and skin.

Transmission

The mode of transmission is not fully understood, but the commonest source is from nasal secretions, through sputum and respiration. It is therefore a disease that is transmitted through close contact, and the risk is greatly increased where living conditions are poor and overcrowding common. Whatever the route of entry, only a proportion of the affected population develop clinical manifestations of leprosy; the majority develop a sub-clinical infection without symptoms or physical signs of the disease (Jopling and McDougall 1988). Some transmission may take place through the skin in the form of ulcerated lesions, as well as from bacillus-laden nodules, but these would have to enter the healthy individual through cuts and abrasions and would not be likely to account for many cases. Biting insects may have contributed to the transference of the condition from leprous to healthy individuals (Jopling and McDougall 1988). Jopling (1984) also suggests that infection may occur via the gastrointestinal tract, with flies conveying the bacteria to food. The rate of spread within the population is therefore proportional to susceptibility and the opportunity for contact.

Overcrowding, especially at night, is ideal for the spread of infection either through droplet infection or via the skin, and under-nourishment reduces cell-mediated immunity (Jopling and McDougall 1988, 3). The incidence of leprosy today is highest among family contacts, but transmission is not determined by intimate contact nor exposure to highly infectious cases alone (Parry 1984). Once infection has occurred, the progress of the illness is dependent upon the immune status, or resistance, of the infected individual. The incubation period is shorter than previously believed,

with between two and four years before the symptoms become manifest, but periods as short as three months have been observed (Bryceson and Pfaltzgraff 1973). There is now some evidence to suggest that placental transmission may be possible, if rare (Brubaker *et al* 1985). Children are particularly susceptible, with 60% developing the disease as young children or young adults (Jopling and McDougall 1988), most probably due to the opportunity for exposure rather than to a lack of resistance. No age group is exempt from leprosy.

The wide variety of lesions in leprosy and the way in which the disease develops is never random but is directly dependent upon the immune status of the individual. Therefore, through careful study of the leprous skeletons at Chichester, it may prove possible to make some inference about the form of the disease and its impact on the community, particularly with regard to the transmission of the disease. Resistance is highest in tuberculoid leprosy (TL) diminishing through borderline (BT-BL) to the lowest-resistance form, lepromatous leprosy (LL). The individual may not remain stable within the system of gradation; poor nutrition, ill health or pregnancy may have a worsening effect due to the depression of cell-mediated immunity. Untreated tuberculoid leprosy (TL) tends to heal spontaneously but with severe nerve damage (Parry 1984, 208). At the other end of the spectrum, the individual may pass from borderline to lepromatous leprosy.

Tuberculoid leprosy (TL)

Tuberculoid leprosy results in anaesthesia and muscle weakness. The loss of sensation leads to repeated injury to the hands and feet and ulceration may occur eventually on the pressure points of the foot. Damage to the motor nerves causes progressive paralysis of muscle groups supplied by those nerves. Early diagnoses in TL are the result of neural and dermal changes, anaesthesia, muscle weakness and paralysis.

In TL few nerves in the limbs become damaged and these are confined to a single nerve trunk or possibly two, occurring early on in the disease. The changes are either unilateral or, if bilateral, asymmetrical (Jopling, pers comm). Skeletal lesions would have been minimal or non-existent and it is therefore difficult to give a firm diagnosis of tuberculoid leprosy in the archaeological record.

Borderline leprosy (BT-BL)

In borderline leprosy the nerves are attacked but there is a higher concentration of bacilli. The nerve damage will antedate the skin lesions by months or even years (Jopling and McDougall 1988). This type of leprosy is immunologically unstable and the individual may downgrade to lepromatous leprosy if his health becomes compromised.

Lepromatous leprosy (LL)

Clinically, the hallmark of lepromatous leprosy is the presence of multiple changes in the skin, nerves and bones (if involved), with a bilateral and symmetrical distribution (Jopling, pers comm). Early on in LL, the nerves are not involved and the skin lesions are unlikely to be noticed. This is important in understanding the spread of the disease as it is at this stage that the individual is at his most infectious, with bacilli being shed in enormous numbers from the nasal mucosa. Paradoxically, the person would have felt perfectly fit.

Early symptoms include nasal congestion, and oedema or swelling of the legs. As the disease progresses the skin thickens, bacillus-filled nodules develop (Fig 15.1a), the nose may collapse and the voice become hoarse. Eventually the classic glove and stocking insensitivity indicative of sensory nerve damage in the upper and lower limbs occurs. The nerve damage is always bilateral and symmetrical although one side may become involved earlier than the other; eventually all four limbs are affected. Nerve thickening increases with time; the loss of warning sensation results in repeated injury to the hands and feet and chronic plantar ulceration is common (Fig 15.1b). Damage to the motor nerves is shown by muscle weakness, with muscles becoming wasted and paralysed. Other tissues involved in the infection include lymph nodes, eyes, liver, spleen, pharynx, larynx and trachea, and testes. Lepromatous leprosy was probably the commonest form of the disease in the past.

The nature of osteoarchaeological changes

The skeletal changes result from both the specific *M. leprae* infection and non-specific infection by

secondary pyogenic bacteria. Sensory nerve damage facilitates insensitive soft tissue injury both to the skin surface and to deep tissues. These injuries, combined with impaired arterial circulatory supply to the tissues because of autonomic nerve damage, permit the invasion of superficial and deeper tissues of the hands and feet by pyogenic bacteria. Subsequent bone and joint involvement in the process results in osteomyelitis and septic arthritis. For details of pathogenesis and palaeopathology see Appendix 10 (on CD). Seventy-five individuals excavated from the site have definite bone changes of leprosy (see Fig 7.20), another fourteen have some lesions which suggest that they probably had the disease and yet another 37 have non-specific infections which might have developed into obvious leprous change had the individual survived. This represents almost one-third of the burial population. The age and sex distribution of those with definite leprous changes in the two parts of the site is shown in Table 15.1.

Rhinomaxillary syndrome

The specific changes are to the facial region and are known as rhinomaxillary syndrome; they are secondary to oronasal infection by *M. leprae*. This type of change is only present in the low-resistant or lepromatous and near lepromatous leprosy. Clinically, the person suffers from nasal stuffiness, a bloodstained discharge and, later, destruction of the nasal cartilage and associated nasal collapse. Damage to the trigeminal nerve results in anaesthesia of the face, tongue and eyes. Damage to the facial nerve results in facial paralysis, including paralysis of the lower eyelids. The resultant lagophthalmos facilitates invasion of the orbit by pyogenic bacteria, leading to corneal damage, scarring and blindness. Seventy-two skeletons from Chichester had some form of change to the facial region, 37 with definite rhinomaxillary syndrome, six with probable and fourteen with changes consistent with an early diagnosis. A further fifteen have some features but insufficient for a firm diagnosis. Table 15.2 records the types of change to the facial region and the number of individuals affected.

Osteoarchaeologically, the changes to the face include absorption and eventual loss of the anterior nasal spine, associated with progressive smooth recession of the normally sharp margins of the

Table 15.1   The distribution of individuals with leprous change between the two areas in the cemetery

	Area A			Area B		Charnel pit
	Male	**Female**	**Unknown**	**Male**	**Female**	**Male**
Young	21	2	0	3	0	
Middle	18	0	0	2	4	
Mature	10	1	0	4	3	
Adult	1	0	3	2	0	
Total	**50**	**3**	**3**	**11**	**7**	**1**

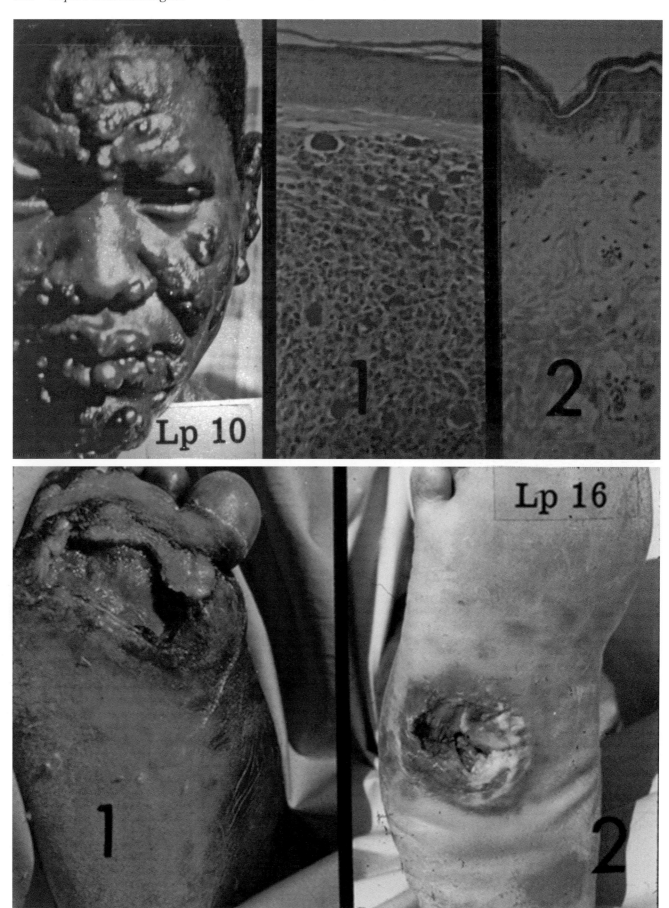

Figure 15.1   (a) (above) Skin lesions in lepromatous leprosy. Also included is histology of normal skin (1) and skin (epidermis and dermis) infected by the leprosy bacillus (2). (b) (below) Ulceration of the foot as a result of nerve damage in leprosy. Photographs: Dr Colin McDougall

Table 15.2 Number of individuals affected by the different features of rhinomaxillary change

Features of rhinomaxillary change	No. of individuals affected
Resorption of anterior nasal spine	42
Resorption of alveolar process	38
Inflammaton of oral aspect of palate	52
Inflammation of nasal aspect	58
Inflammation of oral and nasal surface	38
Inflammation of turbinates	32
Resorption of nasal septum	18
Remodelling of nasal aperture	37
Total nos with rhinomaxillary change	**72**

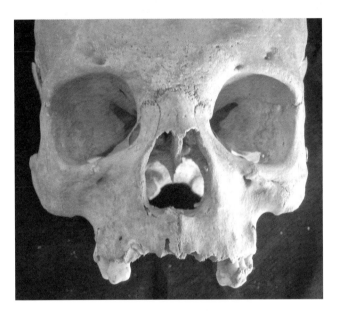

Figure 15.2 Rounding of the nasal aperture due to slow remodelling in burial 19

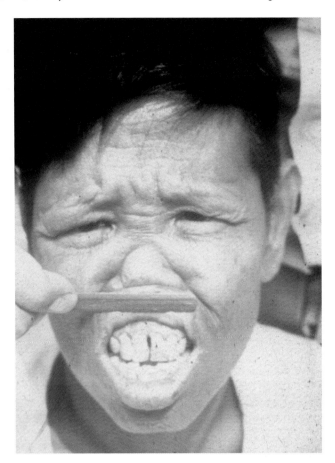

Figure 15.3 Rhinomaxillary syndrome in a patient from Ethiopia. Photograph Dr Keith Manchester

nasal aperture (Fig 15.2). Clinically this is visible as collapse of the nose. Forty-two individuals, 58% of those with rhinomaxillary change, have evidence of resorption of the anterior nasal spine, although in two this is only visible as pitting or early remodelling (151, 211). Remodelling and rounding of the margins of the nasal aperture occurred in 51% of individuals (37) with changes to the facial region.

Recession of the alveolar process of the maxilla commences at the prosthion (centre or midline) and extends to the alveolar bone of the central and lateral incisors. The resorption is progressive until the roots of the teeth are exposed, resulting in the teeth either being lost or simply retained, but loose in the soft tissue (Fig 15.3). Thirty-eight individuals had some degree of resorption; of these, twelve have slight change, leaving 26 of those with rhinomaxillary syndrome with significant alveolar resorption.

Inflammatory changes occur to the palatine process of the maxilla on both the oral and nasal surfaces. These range from slight inflammatory pitting, to ultimately ulceration and perforation of the palate (Fig 15.4). The changes occur predominantly in the median or perimedian position. The palatal aspect is affected in 52 individuals and the nasal aspect in 58, with 38 having both surfaces involved.

Inflammatory change occurs also to the turbinates and nasal septum, visible as inflammatory pitting and resulting in their ultimate loss due to a combination of infection and absorption. These are associated with a foul-smelling purulent discharge. At Chichester, 32 skeletons had evidence of changes or loss of the turbinates, while the nasal septum was affected in eighteen individuals. It must be noted that this is the minimum number of individuals affected, as these bones are particularly fragile and subject to post-mortem damage. The prevalence would certainly have been higher.

Non-specific leprous change

The indirect effects of *M. leprae* infection are the result of three main processes: acroosteolysis (the loss of peripheral bone substance through diffuse absorption, and concentric diaphyseal remodelling of the

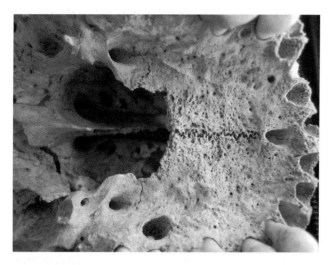

Figure 15.4 Porosity and perforation of the palate in burial 19

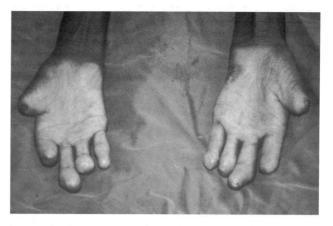

Figure 15.5 Shortened fingers in a patient with leprosy. Photograph: Dr Keith Manchester

shafts of the metatarsals, metacarpals and terminal bone absorption), sepsis (or secondary pyogenic infection) and modification of the architecture of the bones through mechanical adaptation. In this study, the osteoarchaeological evidence is viewed and described according to the area of the body affected.

Leprous changes to the arms and hands

A total of fifteen adults have periostitis of the forearm. The majority occur in the leprous area, with nine of them having a firm diagnosis of leprosy

and one of treponematosis (277). In the leprous individuals, these changes may result from infection spreading from soft tissue trauma to the anaesthetised hand. Five of these individuals have leprous infection of the hand in conjunction with periostitis of the forearm. By contrast, Jopling (1984) considered periostitis to be rare in the bones of the lower arm in leprosy. Non-specific infection of the metacarpals and phalanges of the hands occurs in 25 individuals, 76% (19) of whom are known to be leprous. The right hand was found to be marginally more often involved, which is to be expected.

Trauma and ulceration of the skin of the hands were not common. Ten individuals had definite changes resulting from a secondary leprous response.

Table 15.3   Number of individuals affected by leprous changes to their hands

Changes to the hands	Number of individuals affected
Definite leprous changes to the hands	10
Inflammatory and infective change	18
Septic changes:	
Secondary septic arthritis of joints	8
Secondary septic arthritis of interphalangeal joints	7
Metacarpophalangeal joints	3
Carpometacarpal joints	1
Wrist	1
Subperiosteal change:	20
Subperiosteal change associated with leprous change	17
Metacarpals	16
Phalanges (including 2 with osteitis)	8
Volar grooves:	51
Volar grooves associated with leprosy	43
Volar grooves with no other leprous change	9
Volar grooves are the only leprous change to hand	8
Volar gooves with other leprous changes to hand	10
Acroosteolysis and resorption	3

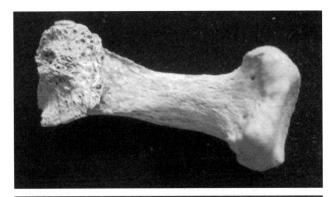

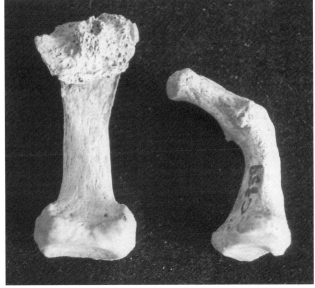

Figure 15.6   Ankylosed hand phalanges of burial 339, indicative of claw hand deformity

Table 15.3 records the types of changes that can be seen. Shortened fingers are a characteristic feature of lepromatous individuals (Fig 15.5) because the hands are insensitive and, used daily, are susceptible to trauma (Jopling and McDougall 1988). Trauma to the fingers occurs first at their tips, producing nicking of the terminal phalanges. This is the result of bone absorption leading to 'collar stud deformities'. This is a progressive feature and later extends to the middle and proximal phalanges. The proximal ends of the phalanges may eventually become cupped with circumferential osteophyte formation in the joint tissues. This is associated with subluxation of the joint resulting from muscle paralysis due to motor nerve damage. Coincidental with this, acroosteolysis may produce a peg deformity of the proximal bone in the affected joint. Concentric remodelling, the result of acroosteolysis, rarely appears to have occurred in the metacarpals and phalanges, although some bone absence could be the result of acroosteolysis.

At least three individuals had some change: in burial 58 the first proximal phalanx had been totally resorbed leaving a spike as the remains of the proximal end of the bone. In burial 148 only the proximal ends remain of two distal phalanges which are ankylosed to the middle phalanges, the tufts and distal ends

having been totally resorbed. In burial 339 the second digit of the right hand shows complete resorption of the distal phalanx and only three-quarters of the middle phalanx remains, ankylosed at a 90° angle to the proximal phalanx (Fig 15.6). Motor nerve damage results in claw hand deformity because of unopposed spasticity of the flexor muscles. The clawing of the fingers prevents damage to the palm leaving the prominent parts, in particular the joints, vulnerable to pyogenic sepsis and dorsal ulceration as the individual attempts to use the insensitive hand (Andersen and Manchester 1987). In the anaesthetised hands the individual cannot assess the friction force needed to hold objects and therefore uses the maximum force all the time, with turning, shearing and striking forces no longer regulated by warning pain (Parry 1984). Secondary bacterial infection may give rise to subperiosteal change, osteomyelitis and eventual septic arthritis. Whilst carpal disintegration does occur in leprosy, with ulceration leading to lesions in the palms and wrists if neglected, it is not common and would have been noticed by the individual and protected from further damage.

Eight individuals have changes that can be directly attributed to secondary septic arthritis of the joints. The interphalangeal joints were affected in seven of them; ankylosis was invariably the outcome and the angle of fixation suggests clawing of the finger. Burial 216 is included, although the curvature of the finger in this instance may not be as a result of leprosy. Septic change destroyed the metacarpophalangeal joint in three individuals, and in 235 the carpometacarpal joints of the second and fourth metacarpals were involved. In burial 366 the right wrist and hand, including the right distal radius, scaphoid and trapezium, second and fourth carpometacarpal joints were involved. Subperiosteal reactive bone, the result of inflammation in the soft tissues, occurred in twenty individuals, of whom seventeen had some other form of leprous change. The metacarpals were most commonly affected with sixteen individuals exhibiting lesions, the second and third metacarpal in particular. In six cases the phalanges showed some reaction, with osteitis occurring in a further two phalanges (273 and 356). The bones of the forearm were rarely involved. Burial 88 has periosteal reaction on the radius and ulna perhaps suggestive of infective spread from ulceration in the palms of the hand. Burial 50 has osteomyelitis in the right third metacarpal.

Disuse osteoporosis may affect the hands due to paralysis and/or contractures causing reduced osteoblastic, bone-forming, activity (Jopling and McDougall 1988, 34), and while widespread osteoporosis was thought to be present in many leprous individuals, localised osteoporosis of the hands alone was not noted.

Volar grooves

The claw hand deformity may result in pressure atrophy of the volar aspect of the phalanges, the so-called volar grooves (see Fig 14.8). These are visible as shallow depressions to the volar surface of the distal end of the proximal phalanges, close to the distal articular surface. They are the consequence of sustained hyperextension at the metacarpophalangeal joint and hyperflexion, or even subluxation, at the interphalangeal joint. They are a sequel to ulnar nerve paralysis resulting in the claw hand deformity, even occurring in individuals with no other leprous change to the hand (Andersen and Manchester 1987).

Fifty-one individuals have volar grooves (Table 15.3). Forty-three of these have one or more features compatible with a diagnosis of leprosy (31 are leprous or probably leprous, while a further twelve have one or more features which could indicate leprosy). Ten individuals have other leprous changes to the hand, while the remaining nine show no other indication of leprosy. This suggests that other conditions may result in volar grooves, for example Dupuytren's contracture. An alternative explanation, but hypothetical, is that these individuals are representative of the early stages of tuberculoid leprosy, since ulnar nerve paralysis occurs early on in tuberculoid leprosy. Remodelling of the metacarpophalangeal and interphalangeal joints, possibly resulting from changes in musculature as a result of claw hand deformity, may also occur. This may account for the absence or masking of volar grooves in four of the more seriously affected hands (58, 235, 115 and 77).

Of the 31 leprous individuals, seventeen have volar grooves only, suggesting that the changes had resulted in clawing of the fingers but little other damage. A possible explanation is that the individual was aware of the danger to his or her hand and so avoided injury. The feet, in contrast, were much more susceptible to accidental damage.

Leprous changes to the lower limbs

Changes to the lower leg are seen clinically as swelling of the limb and thickening of the skin. Osteoarchaeologically, they manifest as gross inflammatory changes to the tibia and fibula. Subperiosteal reactive bone occurs on the surface of the bone and involves the membrane (periosteum) surrounding the bone. The membrane becomes inflamed with the development of an associated subperiosteal oedema, new bone is then deposited on the outer surface of the original bone cortex through subperiosteal ossification. In total, 128 individuals (46% of the adult population) exhibited subperiosteal bone reaction to the surface of the tibia and fibula. Of these, two have associated osteitis or inflammation of the bone itself (151 and 251), while three (92, 108 and 290) have osteitis only in a single tibia.

Three distinct types of subperiosteal bone reaction were noted. The most significant changes, in this discussion, are typical of those seen in the lepromatous leper. The changes appear as a smooth, profuse, undulating layer of new bone applied to the

Table 15.4   Number of individuals affected by periostitis of the lower leg

Lower Leg	No. of individuals affected
Bilateral change	92
Bilateral molten lead change	31
Molten lead associated with leprosy	22
Molten lead with no other leprous change	9
Other bilateral change	61
Other bilateral change associated with leprosy	29
Bilateral change with no evidence for leprosy	32
Molten lead change and *facies leprosa*	12
Molten lead with no skull present	9
Molten lead associated with changes in foot	19

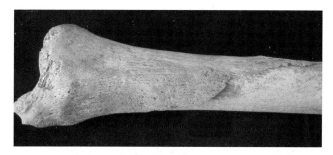

Figure 15.7   Periosteal reaction consisting of woven bone in burial 88

cortical surface of the bone (see Fig 16.12) and the deposits have an indolent appearance resembling molten lead (Table 15.4). They are bilateral and are most marked on adjacent surfaces of the tibiae and fibulae along the attachment of the interosseous membrane. Thirty-one individuals exhibit this type of change, almost all at the western end of the site (Area A). There is a close association with leprosy, with 22 of them having other leprous features, eleven associated with rhinomaxillary change. Nine had no skull available for examination; four of these burials were so incomplete that they may well have had other leprous features. The less-severe forms of subperiosteal reaction, where bilateral, may represent an earlier stage in the leprous process (Fig 15.7). Ninety-two individuals had some form of bilateral subperiosteal reaction to the lower leg, and of these 65% (60/92) had some associated leprous involvement. There is therefore an extremely strong probability that some of these bilateral changes represent an early stage in the leprous process.

The sequence of events that leads to the deposition of subperiosteal bone on the lower leg bones is not entirely clear. Andersen (pers comm) suggests that the inflammatory response may be the result of an ascending toxic 'abacterial' process from soft tissue ulceration and infection of the plantar surface of the feet. In clinical studies, tibiofibular change is only associated with infection to the foot. Moreover, the change seems to be more common in the presence of longitudinal arch collapse and midfoot plantar ulceration (Manchester 2002). A quite different scenario is suggested by Jopling (1984), who considers oedema or swelling of the lower legs along with the nasal symptoms to occur early on in lepromatous or low-resistant leprosy. This is thought to be a combination of gravity and increased permeability, probably the result of lepromatous involvement of the capillary endothelium and autonomic nerve damage resulting in arterial insufficiency (Jopling and McDougall 1988).

Osteoarchaeologically, it is difficult to add to these arguments. In archaeological populations the disease process is fixed at the time of death, with no means of telling whether the foot or facial changes occurred first, or whether tuberculoid leprosy downgraded to lepromatous.

Changes to the feet in leprosy

Changes to the feet in leprosy are secondary and result from the loss of sensation in the foot leading to painless superficial trauma, ulceration and secondary bacterial invasion, pyogenic osteomyelitis and septic arthritis. Loss of proprioception, or the dissociation of joint sensation, leads to joint subluxation, dislocation and disintegration of the architecture of the foot. Moreover, it would make trauma or accidental injury as the result of a fall more likely. Motor neuropathy also occurs, leading to paralysis of certain muscle groups, and may result in drop foot, longitudinal and transverse arch collapse and the claw toe deformity. The indirect effects of *M. Leprae* infection, probably due to metabolic and immunoreactive components, result in acroosteolysis or the loss of peripheral bone substance, concentric diaphyseal remodelling and osteoporosis (Manchester 2002).

Hyperkeratosis, or thickening of the skin of the feet, is a common feature. The skin ultimately cracks allowing pyogenic bacteria to enter; the result is ulceration with infection spreading to the bone. The absence of pain allows the individual to continue to use the foot and the infection and damage becomes worse, resulting in the eventual loss or resorption of the digits and destruction of the foot by infection and an inadequate blood supply. Thirty-five skeletons had some form of change to the feet resulting from secondary infection (Table 15.5). The position and site of the joint sepsis and bony destruction may provide an insight into the progress of the disease and its effects on the individual.

Where the mechanical integrity of the foot is maintained, pyogenic septic changes will occur to the main pressure points of the feet. These include the heel (calcaneum) and the first and fifth metatarsophalangeal joints. Twelve individuals had the integrity of at least one of the feet intact, pyogenic

Table 15.5   Number of individuals with leprous changes to their feet. The numbers in brackets represent the number of incidences

Changes to Foot	Total
Individuals with feet affected by leprous infection	35
Collapse of transverse arch	13
Change to the midfoot	9
Tarsal disintegration	15
Compression fracture	7
Changes to medial pillar	10
Changes to lateral pillar	8
Alterations to posterior pillar	5
Tarsal bars associated with leprosy	43
Tarsal bars probably not associated with leprosy	9
Ankylosis and septic arthritis	6

septic changes having occurred to the heel in two, with osteitis in the heel of a third individual (291), in the first metatarsophalangeal joint of seven individuals and in the fifth metatarsophalangeal joint in five.

The collapse of the transverse arch of the foot, visible in the destruction to the mid-metatarsophalangeal joints, in particular to the joints of the second, third and fourth digits, was present in at least one foot in thirteen individuals. Eight of these were associated with molten lead changes to the tibia and fibula and ten have some other form of change associated with leprosy. Destruction of the second and third metatarsophalangeal joints was the most common.

Nine individuals exhibited infective changes to the midfoot, closely associated with tarsal disintegration. Mid-tarsal infective change may occur without change in the forefoot associated with longitudinal arch collapse, plantar ulceration and deep spreading sepsis, as in six of the above (8, 41, 62, 115, 291 and 316), while the remaining three (227, 235 and 339) had changes to the tarsals as well as the forefeet.

Tarsal disintegration

Tarsal disintegration is a phenomenon which occurs in neuropathic or insensitive feet, where the tarsals may be so changed that the total architecture of the foot is altered, resulting in a shift in the distribution of body weight, making various parts of the foot susceptible to infection and ulceration. The causes are many and include muscle paralysis, muscle strain, bony destruction and plantar ulceration associated with secondary pyogenic infection. In all types of leprosy, involvement and loss of function of the posterior tibial nerve is common. This nerve

Figure 15.8   Navicular squeezing in burial 273

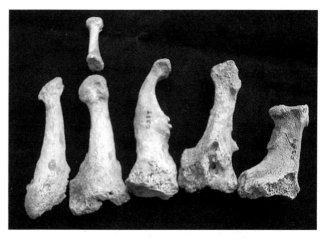

Figure 15.9   Destruction of the metatarsals and concentric diaphyseal remodelling of a phalanx in burial 339

supplies the muscles responsible for maintenance of the longitudinal arch (Johnston and Whillis 1954) and the development of a flattened or boat-shaped foot results. Primary disintegration involves the three pillars of the foot. The posterior pillar includes the body of the talus, the posterior talocalcaneal joint and the calcaneum. The medial pillar includes the neck and head of the talus, the talonavicular joint, the navicular and naviculocuneiform joint. The lateral pillar involves the anterior calcaneus, the calcaneocuboid joint, the cuboid and cubometatarsal joints (Kulkarniu and Mehta 1983).

Fifteen individuals exhibit evidence for tarsal disintegration with compression fractures in a possible seven of these. Three show alteration in the shape of the navicular, where the tarsals have been progressively dislocated and squeezed (Fig 15.8) by an antero-posterior fracture or pressure-induced remodelling (22, 273, 316), one to the first cuneiform (8), one to the head of the talus (345), one to the left cuboid (333) and another to the anterior calcaneum (356). Burial 108 is not included in these figures but was recorded as having a compression fracture of the right navicular but no evidence for leprosy. The medial and lateral pillars are the most commonly affected. Ten have changes to the medial pillar of the foot. In burial 8 there is compression and ankylosis of the first tarsometatarsal joint. The head of the talus is affected in four cases (burials 17, 22, 62, 345), ranging from early flattening of the head in burial 22 to total destruction of the head of the talus in burial 62. In three cases (35, 227 and 235), the talonavicular joint was destroyed by a septic process, and in two (58 and 316) there were changes to the navicular, although in burial 58 this maybe due to a developmental anomaly rather than associated leprous change. The lateral pillar is affected in eight individuals. One has a compression fracture of the anterior calcaneal facet (356) but little conclusive evidence for leprosy. Four have involvement of the calcanea and cuboids, two the cuboid/metatarsals (58, 227), two to the anterior calcaneum and/or cuboid (35, 62). Only five had change to the posterior pillar visible in the destruction of the calcaneum: eg burial 158 with ankylosis or a talocalcaneal bridge in burial 235, which may or may not be a result of secondary leprous infection. Tarsal disintegration may also be a secondary feature leading to generalised arthropathy of the tarsus.

Tarsal bars have been identified as an early

indication of abnormal mechanical stress on the intertarsal joints (Andersen and Manchester 1988). These are hypertrophic (bone-producing) lesions on the dorsal surface of the tarsal bones (see Fig 14.14). They are caused by chronic ligamentous strain, which results in the development of exostoses or flanges of bone at the sites of ligamentous attachment. These exostoses may develop in the absence of tarsal disintegration (Kulkarniu and Mehta 1983) and it is possible that these lesions are an early stage of tarsal disintegration (Andersen and Manchester 1988). Fifty-two individuals from Chichester had tarsal bars on one or more of the tarsal bones; nine of these had no other leprous feature. Many others had only incipient changes; for example, burials 30 and 72 had tarsal bars and volar grooves but little other change associated with leprosy. It could be argued that these minimal changes, where unilateral, indicate a possible case of tuberculoid leprosy.

Ankylosis of the interphalangeal joints may occur due to septic arthritis. Six individuals were affected, with clawing or hammer toe deformity being the main manifestations of the condition. The changes were bilateral apart from in burials 273 and 369, where the right feet were normal. Inflammatory pitting and subperiosteal reaction are not commonly seen in the foot in archaeological material, and may well represent an early stage in deep tissue spread of pyogenic infection, occurring on both the dorsal and plantar aspects of the foot. At Chichester, subperiosteal reactive bone was visible in 52 individuals (but they may not all have had leprosy). Thirty-two percent (18) of these were associated with other septic changes such as ulceration and pyogenic infection of the feet and 75% (42) were associated with bilateral changes of the tibia and fibula. Lechat (1961) claimed that periostitis is observed in lepromatous leprosy even in the absence of ulceration of the feet, in addition to where plantar ulceration had occurred (8, 17, 21, 25, 41, 58, 88, 115, 128, 148, 158, 167, 273, 316, 339, 342, 351 and 366).

Changes to the metatarsal shafts (Fig 15.9)

occurred in 49 individuals (45 associated with other probable leprous features). Whilst 29 (25 associated with leprosy) had similar inflammatory changes to the surface of the tarsals, only ten had any changes to the foot phalanges (six associated with leprosy).

The indirect effects of *M. Leprae* infection, probably due to the immunoreactive components, are absorptive bone change with gradual bone loss or resorption of the digits, that is, acroosteolysis. This progresses proximally and may lead to resorption in the absence of concentric remodelling. The process can be slow or very rapid and can occur in as little as six weeks. Forty-four individuals were affected (three with no other evidence for leprosy). Of these, most occurred at the leprosarium end of the cemetery. In the foot phalanges concentric diaphyseal remodelling, where the outer cortical bone is absorbed in the midshaft region, results in loss of the medullary cavity with eventual fracture and resorption of the element (Fig 15.9). This was noted in 34 individuals, mostly in its early stages. The metatarsals undergo a similar process with 31 individuals affected; mediolateral remodelling produces a knife-shaped appearance of the bone. Although the glove and stocking insensitivity which occurs in leprosy is bilateral, and therefore both feet are susceptible to secondary infection through trauma, one side is generally more seriously affected than the other and this was borne out in the skeletons from Chichester.

The feet exhibited some form of infection in 69 individuals. These include joint sepsis and bony destruction as well as periostitis. There is clearly a high correlation between infection in the foot and leprosy, with 56.5% (39/69) also having a firm diagnosis of leprosy. This is most clearly seen when comparing the two areas, with 68.9% (31/45) involvement in the leprous phase compared to 33.3% (8/24) in the almshouse. The less severe form of infection, periostitis, occurred in 45 individuals but even this has a significant association with leprosy (22/45). In burial 35, a male with leprosy, the right calcaneum has an osteomyelitic infection; osteitis was also present in both calcanea of 291, another male with leprosy. Two individuals (48 and 214) had osteomyelitis of the metatarsals.

In summary, there is a wide variation in the extent that the foot is affected. In early tarsal disintegration little change was noted (8, 17, 22), while widespread infection occurs in others (eg 58, 62, 148, 227 and 235) destroying the tarsals and changing the whole architecture of the foot to such an extent that some of the bones are unidentifiable.

Other skeletal changes associated with leprosy

Luongo (1997) carried out a radiological study of the right femora and right second metacarpal from leprous and non-leprous males. The results showed, in the metacarpal, a strong indication that male lepers tended to form less bone and lose it at a faster rate than their non-leprous counterparts. The femoral cortex was not so clear cut. Fracture rates support the idea that testicular atrophy is more common in the leprous individuals with a significant rise in fractures in the leprous sample presumably because of lighter, more friable bones.

Nerve thickening

Nerve thickening occurs in the cooler areas of the body. Many of these are palpable and visible as shallow grooves for the supraclavicular nerve as it crosses the clavicles and in the frontotemporal region of the skull, following the course of the supraorbital nerve. Frontal and temporal grooves were noted in many of the burials from Chichester. Goode (1993) carried out a study to consider whether the frontal grooves in this assemblage resulted from nerve thickening as a result of leprosy, and whether they were age and sex specific. Her results showed that frontal grooves were not significantly connected with leprosy. She also tested for a relationship between grooves and *cribra orbitalia*. The chi square test produced a negative correlation: in other words, where *cribra orbitalia* is present the individual is less likely to suffer from leprosy. This is in direct contrast to Jopling and McDougall's findings in modern leprosaria where they suggest that mild anaemia and raised erythrocyte sedimentation are classic features of lepromatous leprosy (1988, 21). Goode's interpretation of her findings are that iron deficiency anaemia may have been a positive response to a high pathogen load in the environment, reflecting those who had successfully fought the leprous infection or perhaps contracted the less contagious form of tuberculoid leprosy.

16   Infection: tuberculosis and other infectious diseases *by Frances Lee and Anthea Boylston*

Tuberculosis (TB)

Tuberculosis, like leprosy, is a chronic infectious disease. It has had a long history but, according to the Bills of Mortality, there was a rising incidence in the later Middle Ages that only began to fall once public health measures were introduced at the end of the 19th century. It was not until the development of effective antibiotic therapy in the 1950s that the disease really came under control. More recently, antibiotic-resistant strains of the bacterium and the advent of AIDS have caused a worldwide increase in disease frequency. Probably two strains of the bacillus were the principal infecting agents of mankind in antiquity, the human form (*Mycobacterium tuberculosis*) and the bovine form of the disease (*Mycobacterium bovis*). Bovine tuberculosis is dependent upon a close co-existence between man and cattle, with the infection spreading to humans through infected milk and meat. Traditionally children consume a large amount of milk and it is because of this that bovine tuberculosis is found more commonly in children. The digestive tract is often involved and there may be secondary changes in the skeleton. Symptoms of gastrointestinal TB include weight loss, fatigue and sweats. Specific gastrointestinal symptoms, such as bloody diarrhoea or anorexia and vomiting, are determined by the precise site of infective lesions within the intestinal tract.

M. tuberculosis, on the other hand, causes pulmonary disease spread from man to man by droplet infection, in other words it is transmitted through coughing, sneezing and spitting. As a consequence it is a population-density dependent disease thriving in close communities, with a notable increase with urbanisation. The classic symptoms of pulmonary TB include weight loss, fatigue, night sweats, cough, breathlessness and haemoptysis (spitting up blood).

Like many chronic diseases, TB mainly affects the soft tissues of the body but may also involve the skeleton so it is difficult to be accurate about its prevalence in an archaeological sample. Considerable numbers of people may have had the disease without demonstrating any skeletal lesions. Davidson and Horowitz (1970) consider that only 1% of patients with TB develop skeletal lesions, while Resnick (1995) reports it to be in the region of 3–5%. Studies at Spitalfields showed that only two individuals in a thousand had any skeletal evidence for the disease, despite TB being the most common infectious disease during the post-medieval period (Cox 1996, 78). Twenty per cent of all deaths in 18th-century London resulted from consumption,

although some of this may have been pulmonary disease misdiagnosed as TB at the time (Chundun 1991, 63). Using these figures, it is possible that individuals suffering from tuberculosis were more numerous at Chichester than those with leprosy.

The bone changes resulting from infection by the tubercle bacillus are principally destructive. Bone formative changes in the process are minimal, although they do occur, for example in Pott's disease of the spine as a biological response to mechanical instability. The bone lesions caused by tuberculous infection arise initially in the medullary cavity because of the blood-borne spread of the bacilli from the primary site of infection in the body. Involvement of cortical bone is a sequel to the changes in the medulla. There is no difference in the pathological osseous lesions caused by *M. bovis* or *M. tuberculosis*. The strain of TB in question may be inferred from their site on the skeleton. For example, it may be anticipated that the ribs adjacent to the pleural membranes would be more commonly involved in pulmonary infection by *M. tuberculosis,* and the pelvis in the bovine form where the intestinal tract was primarily infected.

In the past, TB was known by many different names. The incidence in historic records of scrofula, consumption, phthisis and white plague all suggest that TB was widespread. Diagnosis was probably reasonably accurate, although most physicians saw the disease process as stemming from many different causes. Scrofula was a common disorder in the Middle Ages. It was in reality a form of TB involving the lymph glands in the neck. The cure was said to be the touch of the king and payment in the form of a gold coin was also given to the sufferer. The disease became known as 'the King's Evil' (Fig 16.1). In Elizabeth I's reign so many coins were given out that the Royal Mint was obliged to find ways of making the coin smaller. The 'touch' was encouraged by physicians of the day who believed in its curative properties. The lesions in scrofula were very visible but in time resolved and appeared to heal, confirming to many that the touch of the king had powerful healing powers. The practice continued up until the reign of Queen Anne.

Consumption, which today we regard as pulmonary tuberculosis, probably hid a host of other chronic respiratory conditions such as bronchiectasis, pneumonia, and perhaps even some occupational conditions such as 'farmer's lung'. Undoubtedly pulmonary tuberculosis was common; indeed the London Bills of Mortality suggest that by the end of the 18th century, consumption was responsible for almost a quarter of the deaths (Roberts and Cox 2003). Treatments were many and varied: those of a

Figure 16.1   King Charles II laying his hands on a person with scrofula, the common name for tuberculosis of the lymph nodes in the neck

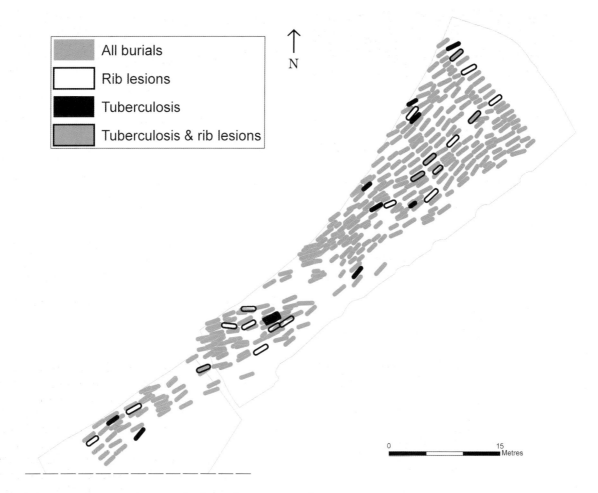

Figure 16.2 Distribution of cases of tuberculosis across the cemetery

dietary nature often involved consuming meat and a variety of milk-based drinks, which were probably often infected with the bacillus. Many medicines were based on herbal remedies, including lungwort and poppy. Another common treatment was desiccated wolf's lung and horse saliva (Roberts and Buikstra 2003).

Fifteen adults from Chichester had changes compatible with a diagnosis of tuberculosis. Furthermore,

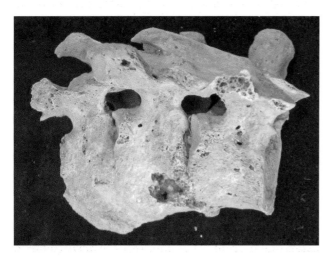

Figure 16.3 Pott's spine in burial 137a

fourteen had changes to the ribs indicative of an inflammatory process in the lungs that was probably tuberculous in origin. Figure 16.2 shows the distribution of individuals with tuberculous infection across the site. The spine is the most commonly affected part of the skeleton. This is because the vertebrae have a very good arterial blood supply in which the bacilli thrive (Roberts and Buikstra 2003). Studies have suggested that the vertebrae are involved in 25–50% of individuals with skeletal involvement (Resnick 1995), with the lower thoracic and upper lumbar most commonly affected (Roberts and Manchester 2005). Abscess formation occurs in the vertebral body, which later collapses anteriorly, giving the typical hunchback appearance of Pott's disease (Fig 16.3).

There are three parts of the vertebrae where the infection may develop (Roberts and Buikstra 2003, 94). It is thought that the disease first affects the anterior aspect of the body (Resnick 1995). This is probably because the bacteria enter the vertebral body via the intercostal arteries penetrating the anterior-longitudinal ligament (Doub and Badgeley 1932). Two spinal columns had anterior lesions which result from tuberculous infection. These are burials 137a and 309; the latter had subperiosteal reactive bone to the anterior aspect of L2 to L5.

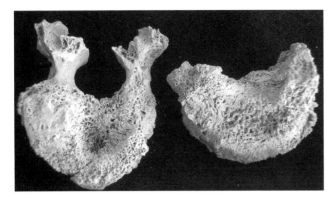

Figure 16.4 Destructive lesions of the tenth to twelfth thoracic vertebrae in burial 307

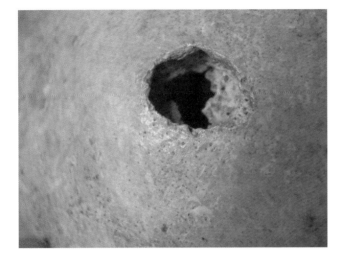

Figure 16.6 Tuberculous lesion of the cranium in burial 307

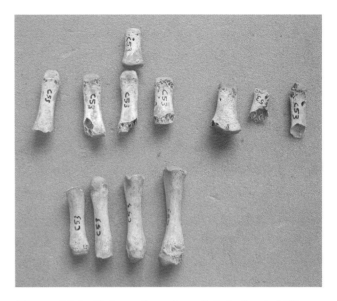

Figure 16.5 Tuberculous dactylitis in burial 53, a child aged 7–8 years

Paradiscal tuberculous lesions result in the disc space becoming narrowed with resulting damage to adjacent vertebrae. This type of lesion was present in burial 104, with destruction of the superior body of L5 and evidence for remodelling of the trabecular bone. A cloaca, or sinus, is visible draining from the right lateral aspect of the body. The adjacent L4 is also involved. Burial 291, a young adult male, also has a paradiscal infective lesion of the twelfth thoracic vertebral body.

Infection can occur in the centre of the vertebral body. The bacteria enter through the posterior vertebral artery via the spinal foramen (Roberts and Buikstra 2003). The infection is likely to spread to neighbouring vertebrae, some of which will eventually collapse forming the typical Pott's spine. Burial 307 has destructive infective lesions in the tenth to twelfth thoracic which were associated with pus formation (Fig 16.4). The infection in T11 is central, tracking posteriorly via a sinus into the spinal canal. Death was probably as a result of meningeal infection. Associated with the spinal involvement are lesions in the skull and ribs. Another individual, burial 106, has a chronic infection of T10 which has destroyed the centre of the vertebral body with

infection spreading to the disc, while the eleventh thoracic vertebra has a sinus draining anteriorly.

Occasionally the posterior part of the vertebral body is affected through involvement of the posterior longitudinal ligament. Abscess formation in this area may cause spinal cord compression and some loss of movement in the lower limbs (Roberts and Buikstra 2003). Two individuals were found to have these types of lesions. Burial 203, a middle-aged adult, has destruction of the central portion of an upper lumbar vertebra draining into the spinal canal, which, with all probability, resulted in death from tuberculous meningitis. Burial 278, an adolescent, also had involvement of the posterior part of the vertebrae.

Roberts and Buikstra (2003) hypothesise that if an individual had Pott's disease of the spine then it is possible for the heads of the ribs attached to the affected vertebrae to become involved, with evidence for new bone formation or destruction. This process can be seen in burial 331, a male with chronic infection to the left side of T2 extending into the vertebral facet and associated destructive lesions of the heads of the left and right second ribs. Tuberculosis is a possible diagnosis, although involvement of the second thoracic is unusual.

The final lesion in the spine is to burial 239, an adult female, who has evidence for subperiosteal reactive bone to the lateral aspect of second and fifth to seventh thoracic vertebrae. This was also associated with new bone on the visceral aspect of the ribs suggesting a respiratory infection, probably TB. Interestingly there is a strange lesion on the right femur at the position of the lesser trochanter, giving the impression of a large sulcus. This may result from a psoas abscess. Alternatively soft tissue trauma, such as a muscle tear, or even a bursa extending in front of the *quadratus femoris* could be responsible. Burial 150, a mature adult female, has

Table 16.1 Distribution of cases of tuberculosis throughout the cemetery

Area	No. of cases
A1	1
A2	3
B1	1
B2	10
Total	**15**

evidence for septic arthritis of the right hip. Associated with this is widespread active new bone on the external surface of the iliac bone and destruction of the ischial tuberosity, with compact sclerotic bone formation and reactive new bone on the pleural aspect of the ribs.

Bone destruction may also occur in the long bones affecting the metaphyses and epiphyses, the weight-bearing joints being particularly vulnerable to infection. A dramatic example can be seen in burial 53, although in this case it is to an arm. The child's left elbow joint has been destroyed by a very severe infective process (see Chapter 12). The bones, from the hand of the same individual, exhibit features of tuberculous dactylitis, a condition found in children and rare after the first decade. The proximal phalanges are very osteopenic and almost have the appearance of eggshell, the bone trabeculae have been all but absorbed and the shafts of the bones have a swollen or puffed up appearance (Fig 16.5). Tuberculous dactylitis may occur in 0.6–6.0% of cases of juvenile tuberculosis (Hardy and Hartmann 1947).

Destructive lesions in the cranium were recorded in two individuals, 307 and 363. The skull is involved in 0.1% of patients with tuberculosis (Ganguli 1963), with the bacilli reaching the skull through haematogenous (blood-borne) spread (Aufderheide and Rodríguez-Martín 1998). A mature female (307) has an osteolytic lesion with stellate new bone radiating from the lesion on the endocranial aspect of the right parietal bone (Fig 16.6). Associated with this lesion are destructive infective lesions in the vertebrae and ribs. Burial 363, a mature male, has a large osteolytic lesion to the endocranial aspect of the parietal bones along the sagittal suture. The lesion is smooth-walled and there is no sign of any associated subperiosteal reaction, but tuberculosis remains a possibility.

Rib lesions

Nineteen adults have subperiosteal reactive new bone formation on the visceral (internal) surface of the ribs. These are thought to result from chronic respiratory infections, the most common being pleurisy, pneumonia, bronchiectasis and TB. Kelley and Micozzi (1984) note that pneumonia alone rarely elicits a periostitic response in the ribs. Even though medical literature on tuberculosis reports low involvement rates for ribs, it is still considered to be the most common inflammatory condition observed in the thoracic cage (Tatelman and Drouillard 1953). Interestingly, Cox (1996) did not record any lesions on the visceral surface of the ribs at Spitalfields, despite pulmonary tuberculosis being one of the commonest forms of death in the 19th century, leading her to question whether these changes do indeed reflect pulmonary TB. The non-specific inflammatory changes on the visceral surface of ribs probably result from pleural involvement in pulmonary TB and in other non-specific pulmonary infections also. The visceral pleural inflammation may then, particularly in TB, progress to the production of pus within the pleural cavity (empyema) and associated inflammation of the parietal pleura. It is this inflammation of the pleura, in juxtaposition to the visceral surface of the ribs, which stimulates the inflammatory lesions on the ribs. Around 5% of all skeletal change involves the ribs (Davidson and Horowitz 1970).

At Chichester, six of the individuals with rib lesions also had other changes suggestive of tuberculous infection: three with spinal changes (106, 239, 331), two with extra-spinal joint change (53, 150) and one with a destructive lesion to the cranium (307). Subperiosteal reactive bone to the visceral aspect of the ribs in burial 18 is thought more likely to be the result of trauma to the rib cage. One adult had rib lesions of particular interest. Burial 31, a male aged 18–21 years, has a minimum of ten left ribs and nine right ribs affected by multiple depressions to the visceral surface; they are more marked at the posterior angle, predominantly along the costal groove. It is thought that these scallops or depressions may represent pressure atrophy with new bone surrounding the soft tissue lesion, the cause most probably being TB.

Kelley and Micozzi (1984) studied 445 skeletons from people who had died of TB in the first half of the 20th century. They found that only 16% exhibited skeletal lesions and 56% of these were restricted to the internal aspects of the ribs. The detection of rib lesions in cases of chronic pulmonary disease increases the absolute sample size of individuals showing osseous changes of TB by a factor of two. At Chichester, combining the figures for rib changes with those for other sites of tuberculous involvement of the skeleton, produces a figure of 30 individuals who would appear to have been infected with the disease.

Chundun (1991) carried out a detailed study of the ribs from the 1986 excavations. Her results showed that adults in the young to middle age range were most frequently affected, along with the juveniles. Tuberculosis is generally seen as a disease of young adults, which in the past would have had a tremendous impact both socially and economically. It must be remembered that individuals we consider today as 'children' would have been an important part of

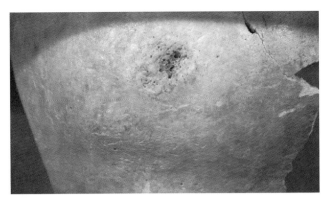

Figure 16.7 Caries sicca lesion on the right frontal bone of burial 77

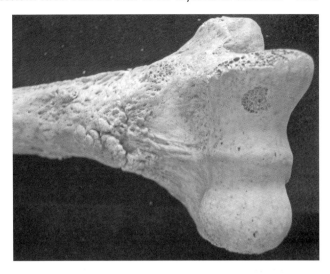

Figure 16.8 Severe periosteal reaction of the humerus in burial 277 probably representing treponemal disease

the workforce in the medieval period. At St James' Hospital almost twice as many males as females were affected, although this may be due to the preferential admission of males.

The distribution of individuals with confirmed or probable TB, although present in all areas of the cemetery, appears to show an increase in prevalence in the latest Area, B2 (Table 16.1). TB can be fatal and it was probably always a much greater check on population growth than leprosy even when the latter was at its most widespread.

Treponemal infection

A disease which might have been expect to be well represented in a site of this period is syphilis, which by Elizabethan times had seemingly become as much of a social problem as leprosy had been earlier. Syphilis is one of the treponemal diseases which consist of four syndromes. The others are yaws, bejel and pinta. Only the first three affect bone. They are caused by a spirochete of the genus *Treponema pallidum*. In 1984, the four syndromes were reclassified as *T. pallidum pallidum* (venereal syphilis), *T. pallidum pertenue*, *T. pallidum endemicum* and *T. pallidum carateum* (Norris *et al* 1993). The complete genome of the first of these was finally unravelled in 1998 (Fraser *et al* 1998). In the same year, the genetic differences between the organisms causing the four syndromes began to be clarified (Centurion-Lara *et al* 1998).

There are four hypotheses about the Old versus New World origins of venereal syphilis. All but the last depend upon whether or not Columbus and his crew transported the disease to Europe on their return from the New World in AD 1492. Certainly an epidemic of a disease fitting the description of syphilis occurred in mainland Europe at about this time. However, the Alternative Hypothesis (Livingstone 1991) postulates that treponemal disease spread from Africa, where it originated in the chimpanzee population, with the increase in trade that occurred in the late medieval period. This is an attractive theory since the cases of treponemal disease

which are being found with increasing frequency in late medieval and monastic cemeteries (eg Stirland 1994; Roberts 1994; Holst *et al* 2001) have more in common with cases of yaws described by Hackett (1951) than with syphilis. The bone changes are distinctive in yaws since many bones are involved, including those of the hands and feet (Rothschild *et al* 2000). Bejel and yaws are contracted through close contact between children and by drinking from dirty cups, unlike acquired syphilis which is transmitted by sexual contact and can be transferred from a mother to her child. In all the syndromes, the secondary infection involves the skin and bacteria are later transported to the site of tertiary infection in bone via the bloodstream, although it has been found that bone changes can also occur in secondary syphilis (Ehrlich and Kricun 1976). Periostitis was already known to be a feature in the secondary phase of yaws (Tesorieri 2006). Venereal syphilis also affects the circulatory and nervous system and in the most advanced stage of the disease the individual is given to bouts of irrational madness.

The lesions visible on the bone in both yaws and syphilis are the result of two opposing processes: a destructive phase produces erosive lesions then a regenerative one causes new bone to be laid down which becomes sclerotic. The long bones display proliferative periosteal new bone studded with focal erosive lesions due to gummatous change which are clearly seen on X-ray. The presence of a cranial vault is important for the diagnosis of treponemal disease, since stellate scars termed *caries sicca* are considered to be pathognomonic of acquired venereal syphilis. However, such changes can also be seen in yaws (Hackett 1951) and the facial features of 'gangosa' are similar, or even more severe, than the nasal destruction in syphilis.

Three individuals have probable treponemal infections. Skeleton 77, a mature female, has a cranial lesion to the right side of the frontal bone with a partly erosive and partly healed appearance. It has the features of a *caries sicca* lesion (Fig 16.7) although occasionally TB can cause the same kind of change in the cranial bones. This individual also has leprosy, with rhinomaxillary syndrome and a molten lead appearance of the lower leg associated with destructive changes of the feet, which may suggest that TB is a more likely diagnosis for this individual than treponemal disease. Burial 343, a mature adult, has a well-healed sclerotic lesion on the frontal bone and a second depression in the right parietal bone. These may prove to be early treponemal lesions or alternatively the result of healed trauma. There is associated osteitis and periostitis affecting the left lower leg.

Most convincingly, burial 277 has evidence for treponematosis with widespread inflammatory change to the skeleton, including reactive bone on the mandible, zygomatics, sphenoid and occipital bones (Lewis *et al* 1995). There are also changes to the clavicles, scapulae, swelling of the humeri (Fig 16.8), radii and ulnae, and subperiosteal bone deposition on the femora, tibiae and fibulae. The oronasal area also has destructive changes which occur in both treponemal disease and leprosy.

On chronological grounds one would assume that there would be a concentration in Area B, or more specifically Area B2. In fact there were two individuals in Area A (A1 and A2) and the other is in Area B1. This burial (277) was at some distance from its neighbour and its segregation may have been significant. Unfortunately, it is difficult to ascertain when this individual was buried in the cemetery. The grave is situated on its own, to the south of Area B and it is therefore likely that the individual was buried towards the end of the life of the hospital.

Scalp infection

Three individuals have widespread pitting of the parietal and occipital bones, with little or no evidence for expansion of the diploic space but some evidence for remodelling. Two of these are young adult males (167 and 351) while the third is a child aged around 7 years. The most plausible explanation for these lesions is a scalp infection.

Ear infection

The effect of leprosy on the middle ear is as yet largely unknown. One would expect an increase in *otitis media* in lepromatous leprosy because of the thickening of the nasal mucosa, which will eventually obstruct the pharangeal opening to the Eustachian tube. Involvement of the ear is not, however, a recognised symptom of leprosy (Jopling and McDougall 1988). Bruintjes notes that, despite a small sample, the results tentatively point towards a more than average middle ear involvement in individuals

with osseous rhinomaxillary changes due to leprosy (1990, 632).

Dalby (1993) studied the ear ossicles and temporal bones of 270 individuals from St James' Hospital. She found that 25% of the incus ossicles showed evidence of erosion. This prevalence was second only to the burials from the medieval hospital of St Giles at Brough and signs of infection were considerably more common for these two sites than at the other sites examined. Of eighteen ossicles from leprosy sufferers, the one stapes and nine mallei were normal; however of the eight incus, three showed evidence of erosion. Despite the small numbers, this represented 37.5% of ossicles which greatly exceeded the rate for the rest of the population. However, the mean size of the mastoid air cells was no different in the leprosy sufferers from the rest of the group. The development of these cells would, in any case, have been complete in childhood before they contracted leprosy. One individual suffered from otosclerosis, where the stapedial footplate fuses to the oval window of the inner ear. This condition is normally bilateral and could have caused deafness.

Mastoiditis

In modern medical practice middle ear infection, especially in childhood, is a frequent occurrence. Untreated, the disease frequently settles down following perforation of the eardrum and a discharge of pus from the abscess beneath. This must have been a common event in the past (Roberts and Manchester 2005). Infrequently, the abscess bursts through into the surrounding bone or produces mastoiditis, the long-term consequence of which is deafness. Mastoiditis is an infection of the mastoid bone, which is situated behind the ear. The pus eventually bursts through the external or internal surface of the bone. If this discharge is to the interior of the skull, death may ensue due to intracranial abscess. Burial 25, a mature male, shows destruction of the right temporal bone. There is post-mortem damage to the mastoid, though the cavity exhibits new bone deposition on the borders of the mastoid air cells.

Maxillary sinusitis

Maxillary sinusitis, in its acute form, is usually a sequel to inflammation of the nasal mucosa. This is most commonly caused by the common cold or a viral infection, which results in swelling of the nasal mucosa. If drainage of fluid from the sinuses is impaired for any reason, such as incomplete resolution of the infection, it may become chronic (Rubin and Farber 1990). In dry bone, maxillary sinusitis is visible as porosity or small irregular patches of new bone in the chamber (Lewis *et al* 1995). Two hundred and sixteen adults were studied for the presence of sinusitis. A number of sinuses were not visible as the cranium was intact and the interior could not be

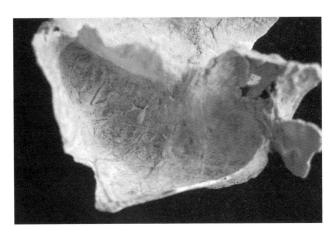

Figure 16.9   Maxillary sinusitis in burial 274

examined without the use of an endoscope. Another group proved too fragmentary to score. A total of 126 individuals had evidence for maxillary sinusitis, representing 58% of those with sinuses present. The right side is more frequently affected and in just over 50% the involvement was bilateral (Fig 16.9).

Inflammation of the nasal mucosa is a feature of lepromatous leprosy. This may spread to the mucosa of the paranasal sinuses, resulting in ulceration that in turn predisposes the sinus to secondary pyogenic bacterial attack and sinusitis. Barton (1979) drew attention to the close association between lepromatous leprosy and maxillary sinusitis. In the Chichester sample, 43 crania had evidence for rhinomaxillary change and maxillary sinusitis (63% of those with nasal antra present and *facies leprosa*). This is below the level anticipated by Barton but much higher than that seen in most archaeological assemblages (Roberts and Cox 2003). Boocock *et al* (1995a; 1995b) also studied maxillary sinusitis at Chichester and found that 54.9% of the adults had evidence for the condition and that there was no significant difference in prevalence rates between those with leprosy and those with no skeletal evidence for the disease.

Of the 21 individuals with rib lesions, representing chronic chest infections, fifteen had nasal antra present with ten of these having bilateral maxillary sinusitis (66.7%). Poor dental health, with infection draining from apical abscesses, occurred in at least four cases. Hickish (1985) suggests that dental infection is responsible for about 10% of maxillary sinusitis due to the close anatomical relationship between the floor of the sinuses and roots of the teeth.

Other causative factors include environmental conditions: a smoky atmosphere will cause ciliary paralysis that in turn will affect the drainage mechanism and predispose the individual to sinusitis. Bronchiolitis, asthma, poor health, insanitary living conditions and pollution may all have played their part (Lewis *et al* 1995). Roberts and Cox (2003, 233) record an average 13.3% involvement rates for the ten sites from the late medieval period, the highest

being found at St Helen-on-the-Walls in York, an impoverished part of the city with a great deal of industrial pollution. Boocock *et al* (1995a) suggest that Chichester's higher than average prevalence is to be expected, firstly because the community represented the unhealthy members of society and secondly because it was an essentially urban site where there would have been an increased risk of infections of all types, including leprosy.

Non-specific infections

Subperiosteal reactive new bone or periostitis is frequently seen in the archaeological record. It represents a non-specific reaction to inflammation or infection, which can be seen as a deposit of new bone on the surface of the skeletal element. Initially this is woven bone but, if the infection is of long duration, it will remodel and will have a less active and more indolent appearance. Where the compact or lamellar bone is involved, visible as thickening of the bone, the term osteitis is often employed. Osteomyelitis is a chronic infection of the entire bone, including the medullary cavity. Manchester and Roberts (2005) consider that the subdivision of non-specific infection into these categories is misleading, since they probably result from the same infective process. However, Brickley *et al* (2006) suggest that this terminology is useful as a way of describing the severity of the infection. Individual bones affected by non-specific infection at St James' Hospital are listed in Table 16.2.

Osteomyelitis

Staphylococci are responsible for most cases of osteomyelitis, which is often caused by blood-borne spread from a distant infection of the tonsil or inner ear, particularly in children. Certain conditions predispose individuals to staphylococcal infections; these include severe debilitation or malnutrition. Osteomyelitis may also be caused by a fracture or weapon injury, which causes bacteria to enter the bone by direct spread if the skin is pierced. Even with antibiotic therapy, such infections can be very resistant and may recur; in the past they would have been life-threatening. The person would have been unwell with fever, pain and immobility of the affected area (Roberts and Manchester 2005).

At Chichester, three individuals had open fractures (115, 193, 343) with secondary infection and three (71, 83, 214) had osteomyelitis of unknown origin. Roberts and Cox (2003) specify a rate of osteomyelitis in the post-medieval period of less than 1%. This was a great deal higher at Chichester, occurring in over 5% of adults. The lower leg was most commonly affected, involving four tibiae and two fibulae in five individuals. An adult male with leprosy (83) had chronic osteomyelitis of the right tibia. The shaft was swollen by widespread perio-

UNIVERSITY OF WINCHESTER
LIBRARY

Table 16.2 Prevalence of infective changes and subperiosteal reactive change to specific bones

Bone	Infective and inflammatory change	Subperiosteal reaction only	For discussion see Chapter
Mandible	3	3	13
Vertebrae	15	?	16- TB
Ribs	21	21	16- TB
Clavicle	4	4	
Manubrium and sternum	3	3	
Scapula	4	2	
Humerus	9	8	
Ulna	15	14	15
Radius	13	12	15
Metacarpals	17	17	15
Phalanges (hand)	7	7	15
Innominate	6	5	
Sacrum		4	
Femur	27	25	
Patella	1		
Tibia	128	122	
Fibula	91	91	
Tarsals	37	26	15
Metatarsals	56	48	15
Phalanges (foot)	22	9	15

steal new bone and there was evidence for abscess formation in the medullary cavity. A cloaca, or sinus, had penetrated the compact bone of the anterior tibia, forming a passage for the drainage of pus (Fig 16.10). The femur was affected by osteomyelitis in three cases (51, 115, 343), two of whom had compound fractures. In 115, a male with leprosy, an oblique fracture was evident. The shaft was swollen and there were cloacae on its anterior aspect (see Fig 17.8). In burial 343, osteomyelitis was associated with a fracture in the mid-shaft region, with sinuses draining posteriorly and medially, and new bone forming an involucrum (Fig 16.11).

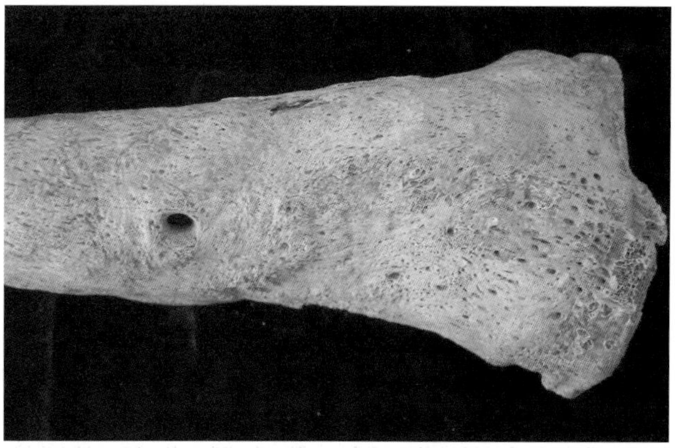

Periostitis

Roberts and Cox (2003), in their study of later medieval sites, calculated an average crude preva-

Figure 16.10 Osteomyelitis of the tibia in burial 83 with a severe periosteal reaction surrounding a cloaca

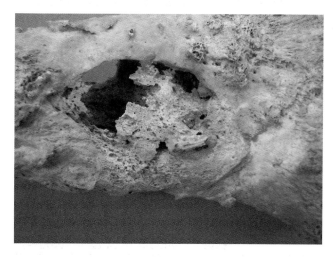

Figure 16.11 Osteomyelitis in the right femur of burial 343 with the 'classic' appearance of a cloaca, a sequestrum of dead bone and surrounding involucrum

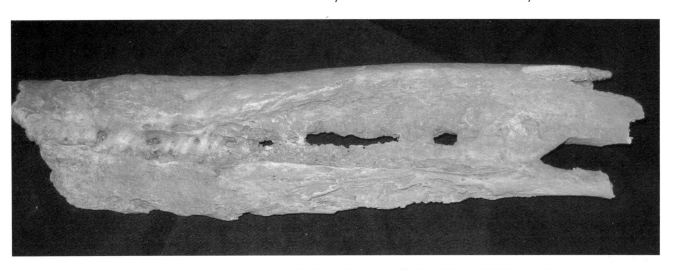

Figure 16.12   Very severe periosteal reaction of the left tibia and fibula of burial 325 with the appearance of molten lead

lence rate (CPR) for periostitis of 14%, rising to 26% in the post-medieval period. The rate for the Chichester adults was found to be considerably higher, in the region of 43% (165/384 individuals). This is similar to the figure of 44% calculated for another hospital site, St Mary's Spital in London (Conheeney 1992, cited in Roberts and Cox 2003). The prevalence for Chichester rises to 52% when adults only are considered (144/276). These figures are not altogether surprising given the nature of the site where, by definition, some individuals would have been unwell and others from the more deprived groups of society. The reason for such high rates becomes even clearer when Areas A and B are compared. Unsurprisingly, there was a higher prevalence in the earlier period when leprosy was much more frequent at around 64% of adults (79/124) compared to Area B where the rate was around 43% (65/152; p=0.0734).

Involvement of the lower limb was particularly common. In the femur, 25 adults were affected by non-specific inflammatory change. As many as a third of these also had some form of leprous involvement of the lower leg and 80% of them were males. One hundred and sixteen adults, 41% of the adult population, exhibited subperiosteal bone reaction on the surface of the tibia and fibula. The tibiae were affected in 111 adults and the fibulae in 88. The causes of this inflammation are multifactorial: the shin bone lies close to the surface and as a consequence is subject to recurrent injury. In some cases, venous stasis may cause ulceration of the lower leg,

leading to chronic low-grade inflammation. This is visible in an adult male with leprosy (burial 4). Here a large plaque-like deposit of new bone has formed on the distal end of the right tibia, the result of a large chronic leg ulcer. In burial 325, an adult male, there was also profuse subperiosteal reactive bone on the left tibia and fibula from a chronic longstanding infection (Fig 16.12). A different infective process was present on the distal end of the shaft, possibly the result of a skin lesion such as an ulcer.

The changes to the lower leg fall into distinct types. The first has the appearance of molten lead and is often associated with leprosy. The second type of subperiosteal reaction is woven or fibre bone on the cortical surface. This represents an active inflammatory process. Twenty-nine individuals exhibited this change; in eighteen it was bilateral. Four individuals had a combination of both remodelled and active new bone. The third type of change was the most common and represented well-healed new bone formation. It varied from a distinct deposit to a striated one, which merged with the cortex. Sixty-one individuals had this type of reaction, with 49% (30/61) having other leprous changes on the skeleton. The difference in prevalence of tibial periostitis between Areas A and B is well illustrated by Table 16.3. As anticipated, the condition is almost twice as common in the earlier than it is in the later period. In the tarsals of the feet, the bone most frequently affected by periostitis is the calcaneum. This is because it is one of the main pressure points of the foot and therefore more susceptible to injury.

Frequencies of non-specific infection were compared between the sexes for Area B. Here males and females were similar in number and the prevalence of leprosy was lower. There was markedly less involvement of the upper limb in this area, and it appeared to be exclusive to the males. Secondly, periostitis of the tibia and fibula was, not unexpectedly, far less common in Area B than Area A (Tables 16.4–16.5). There was a significant difference in prevalence between the Area A and Area B males

Table 16.3   Comparison of prevalence rates for tibial periostitis between Areas A and B (%)

| | Area A | | Area B | |
	Male	Female	Male	Female
Young	61.5	50	36.4	18.2
Middle	58.1	0	19.4	27.0
Mature	35.9	14.3	28.0	38.5

Table 16.4 Periostitis in the Chichester sample (%)

	Femur		Tibia		Fibula	
	Right	**Left**	**Right**	**Left**	**Right**	**Left**
Area A males	5.6	7.6	51.4	54.0	44.3	48.8
Area A females	0	18.2	25.0	45.5	20.0	50.0
Area B males	8.7	5.6	30.4	30	16.7	21.5
Area B females	3.3	3.3	22.4	28.1	13.5	16.4

Table 16.5 Periostitis and osteitis in the Chichester sample (%)

	Femur		Tibia		Fibula	
	Right	**Left**	**Right**	**Left**	**Right**	**Left**
Area A males	6.7	10.5	55.1	60.0	49.5	56.4
Area A females	0	18.2	25.0	54.6	20.0	60.0
Area B males	10.2	5.6	36.3	35.7	18.2	27.7
Area B females	3.3	3.3	31.0	35.6	13.5	18.2

in both tibial and fibular periostitis (χ^2 = 0.0025 and 0.0003 respectively). It was not possible to compare the females between the two areas since there were so few of them in Area A. Area B frequencies of periosteal reactions of all types affecting the bones of the lower limb were approximately average for medieval populations (see Roberts and Cox 2003), whereas those in Area A were considerably higher. Infections of all kinds, both specific and non-specific, were extremely common at Chichester.

17 Trauma *by Margaret Judd*

Introduction

Trauma observed among archaeological samples represents the accumulation of a lifetime of accidents, clumsiness, interpersonal conflicts and effects of ill health. The discussion presented here focuses on lesions associated with fracture, but also reports dislocation and soft tissue trauma.

Adult fractures

There are many classification schemes for fractures (Lovell 1997), but the system used here is that of Roberts and Manchester (2005). In total 97 adults from Areas A and B suffered from fractures and dislocations, with the people from Area B exhibiting the majority of trauma when the sexes were compared (Table 17.1). Area B males bore more injuries than their counterparts in Area A (χ^2 = 3.49, P = 0.060), but the difference in injury frequency only approached significance and was not significant among females (χ^2 = 0.017, P = 0.896). Males displayed the highest number of injuries in both areas, a phenomenon also observed clinically (Dimich-Ward *et al* 2004; Jones 1990; Judd 2004). There was a significant difference between the sexes in Area B (χ^2 = 5.671, P = 0.017), but not among Area A individuals (χ^2 = 0.081, P = 0.776). A total of 173 injuries were observed on the individual bones (Table 17.2). Sharp force injury was observed on two additional Area B males and the only evidence for surgical intervention or arti-ficially induced modifications is the amputation of a lower leg discussed in Chapter 19. When the age-at-death was considered the frequency of injured individuals dipped considerably among middle-aged males and females then increased dramatically among the mature adults (Fig 17.1). The higher frequency among mature adults is to be expected as older adults are more susceptible to injury with advancing age due to decreased bone mass, deteriorating senses and reflexes, and declining health (Judd and Roberts 1998).

Skull

Skull injuries are most frequently associated with violence, particularly when sharp or projectile objects, such as knife, axe or arrow are used to inflict the wounds, although accidents due to an individual's own carelessness can happen. Nine injuries were associated with the skull and of the people involved only three males were interred in Area A. The increase in skull trauma in Area B (4.3% from 2.1% in Area A) may be a reflection of the changing institutional function that admitted travellers seeking medical attention; alternatively life for individuals from Area B may have been less hospitable.

Nasal fractures are most typically associated with interpersonal violence, but may also be acquired during participation in contact sports, such as boxing (Hershkovitz *et al* 1996; Wakely 1996; Walker 1997). Nasal injuries are difficult to identify due to their

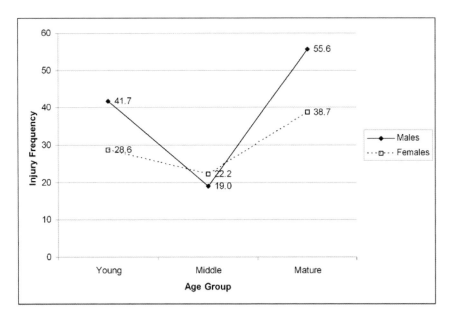

Figure 17.1 Distribution of total adult fracture frequency by age group

Table 17.1 Prevalence and percentage of individuals with injuries each cemetery area

	Males	%	Females	%	Adult	%	Children	%	Combined	%
Area A	33/102	32.35	4/14	28.57	2/8	25.0	1/2	50.0	40/126	31.75
Area B	38/83	45.78	18/67	26.87	2/5	40.0	2/103	1.94	60/258	23.26
Total	**71/185**	**38.38**	**22/81**	**27.72**	**4/13**	**32.5**	**3/105**	**2.9**	**100/384**	**26.4**

Table 17.2 Adult fractures and dislocations by bone affected

	Area A			Area B			
	Males	**Females**	**Unknown**	**Males**	**Females**	**Unknown**	**Total**
Skull	3	0	0	2	3	0	8
Mandible	0	0	0	1	0	0	1
Clavicle	9	0	0	4	0	0	13
Humerus	1	0	0	1	1	0	3
Radius	3	1	1	2	1	1	9
Ulna	2	2	1	0	2	1	8
Femur	1	0	1	0	1	0	3
Tibia	6	0	0	6	3	1	16
Fibula	3	0	1	5	0	0	9
Scapula	1	0	0	3	1	0	5
Vertebrae	12	1	0	5	4	1	23
Ribs	12	0	0	15	8	0	35
Hand bones	5	0	0	6	1	0	12
Foot Bones	3	0	0	16	1	6	26
Patella	1	0	0	1	0	0	2
Total	**62**	**4**	**3**	**68**	**26**	**10**	**173**

quick healing and the general anomalous shape of some nasal bones. One healed nasal injury was confirmed on male 57 from Area A.

Depressed skull injuries due to blunt force trauma are common archaeologically (and clinically) and may be the result of a hand-wielded implement, although fists can produce enough force to create

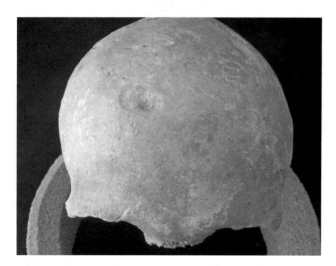

Figure 17.2 Blunt force depression fracture on left frontal of burial 205

these injuries and cause death (Fenton *et al* 2003; Shepherd *et al* 1990). Depression injuries are identified by a concave disruption on the skull surface and were observed among six individuals. This type of injury was especially distinct on the skull of a female (205) and measured 17mm in diameter (Fig 17.2). A slightly larger injury (29mm diameter) occurred on the right parietal of a female (151) who suffered from leprosy and was actively healing at the time of her death; a 5mm diameter injury was noted on a third female (307).

Three males experienced blunt force trauma. Burials 58 and 354, both from Area A, bore a 13 × 4mm and 7mm diameter lesion respectively. Another male from Area A, burial 352, eventually succumbed to a blunt force injury that produced three radiating linear fractures measuring 42mm (anterior frontal), 34mm (posterior frontal) and 51mm (parietal) (Fig 17.3). The anterior frontal fracture line was unhealed on the endocranial surface of the skull.

Sharp force trauma was identified on two young males. Individual 81 suffered from a blow to the right medial supraorbital ridge that produced a rather wide V-shaped cleft in the bone indicating that the weapon was quite heavy with a long, sharp edge (Fig 17.4). The lateral aspect of the injury was

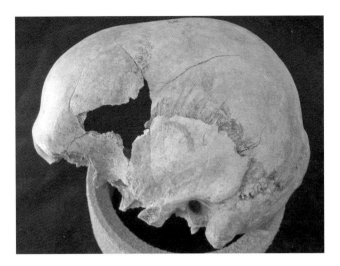

Figure 17.3 Perimortem blunt force skull injury to the left anterior skull of burial 352

healed, while the medial aspect showed an exostosis where the blade was arrested by the bone to produce crushing. A thin-bladed weapon was used to slice into the mandible superior to the gonial angle and produced a narrow cleft just prior to the death of burial 233.

Long bones

Sixty-one long bones were fractured among the 97 injured adults and overall more injuries were experienced by individuals in Area B (Table 17.3). Many of the long bone injuries among the Chichester residents were consistent with those received from falls on an outstretched hand as observed in an earlier analysis (Judd and Roberts 1998), but whether the fall was due to an accident or an intentional shove remains unresolved. Long bone injuries caused by accident typically result in a visible fracture line that produces an angle greater than 45° in relation to the longitudinal axis. This reflects the distribution of combined compression, shearing and rotational forces, such as the stress generated

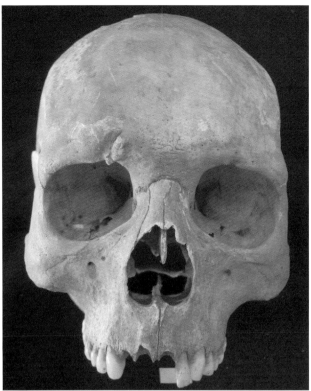

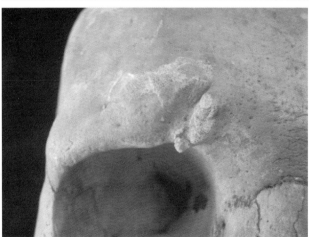

Figure 17.4 Sharp force trauma to the right supraorbital ridge (burial 81)

Table 17.3 Fractures and dislocations among adults with and without (W/O) leprosy in each cemetery area

| | Area A | | | | | Area B | | | | | |
| | Males | | Females | | Adult | Males | | Females | | Adult | |
	Leprosy	W/O	Leprosy	W/O	W/O	Leprosy	W/O	Leprosy	W/O	W/O	Total
Long Bones	10	14	1	2	3	5	16	1	5	4	61
Skull	2	1	0	0	0	0	3	1	2	0	9
Thorax	7	18	0	2	0	4	19	2	9	2	63
Hands	2	3	0	0	0	1	5	0	1	0	12
Feet	3	0	0	0	0	4	12	0	1	6	26
Patella	0	1	0	0	0	1	0	0	0	0	2
Total Injuries	**24**	**37**	**1**	**4**	**3**	**15**	**55**	**4**	**18**	**12**	**173**
Injured Individuals	**15**	**18**	**1**	**3**	**2**	**12**	**26**	**4**	**14**	**2**	**97**

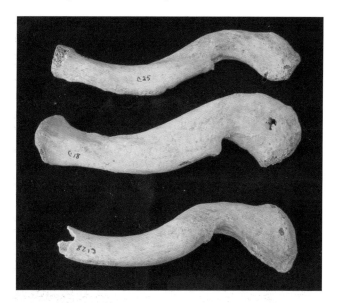

Figure 17.5   Clavicular fractures illustrate unaligned healing for burials 18, 25 and 128

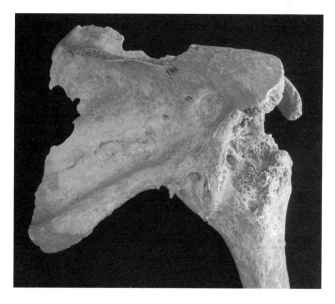

Figure 17.6   Fracture, dislocation and fusion of shoulder joint (burial 117)

on the clavicle when falling on an outstretched hand. The ends of these injured bones are displaced so that an overlap and/or rotational deformation of the bone shaft results if the bone is not properly set. Injuries caused by direct force trauma, for example, a blow with a heavy stick, are identified by horizontal bending and shearing forces that produce a fracture line less than 45° and minimal displacement (Richards and Corley 1996; Rogers 1992).

Upper body

The traumatised clavicles exhibited injuries typical of indirect force. While trauma to the forearm may also result, a sideways stress placed on the stronger clavicular ligaments during this type of event may cause the clavicular shaft to snap (Loder and Mayhew 1988). Thirteen clavicle injuries occurred among twelve males in both cemetery areas and affected the midshaft (18, 58, 98 left and right, 197, 333, 357) and lateral (9, 25, 128, 129, 145, 167) segments of the bone (Fig 17.5).

Two of the three humeral injuries observed occurred to two older males and were typical of injuries received from falling on one's shoulder so that the humeral head is crushed by the impaction. Movement within the shoulder capsule deteriorated as a result for individual 46, but remained possible as indicated by the roughened joint surface of the glenoid cavity. A similar aetiology probably caused the injury observed on burial 117 who suffered from leprosy. In this case the impact between the humeral head and glenoid cavity was so severe that the humeral head became dislocated anteriorly and eventually fused to the scapula (Fig 17.6). A less serious injury was borne by burial 136 whose medial humeral condyle may have been avulsed prior to fusion during adolescence.

Forearm

Forearm injuries, notably those of the ulna, are the most controversial among archaeological samples as their presence is used to indicate interpersonal violence (Judd 2004; Smith 1996; Webb 1995). Clinical findings show that ulna fractures that affect the distal half of the bone and are minimally displaced are most often due to fending off a blow to the head (DuToit and Gräbe 1979). These injuries, traditionally referred to as 'parry' or 'nightstick' fractures, adhere to the direct force criteria described above. In addition, the radius is rarely involved because the arm is pronated when raised to protect the skull and in so doing, it also protects the radius. The energy required to break both the ulna and radius would be exceptional, but in either case the injury configuration is that of a direct force injury. Among the Chichester group only one injury to an Area B female (76) could be attributed to a classic parry injury and it was her only injury. Oblique injuries indicative of indirect trauma sustained from the sudden transmission of excessive weight to the ulna while pronated over the radius were found among two males (57, 129), neither of whom exhibited signs of leprosy and both bore other injuries. A more severe form of this injury involved both bones of the forearm of a female (94). When these two bones are placed in anatomical position and pronated, the gross rotation indicating the position of the arm during the fracture event can be easily seen (Fig 17.7).

A combined right forearm and left radial injury was borne by an older adult of unknown sex (71) from Area A. Both radial injuries were Colles' fractures, which are usually acquired during the forward bracing of a fall. These lesions are identified by their transverse fracture line located less than 38mm from the radiocarpal joint (Connelly 1981; Rogers 1992). The distal

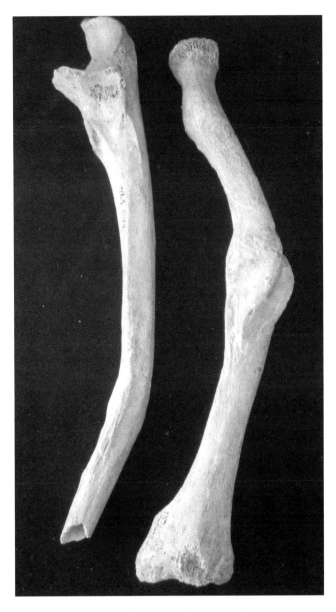

Figure 17.7   Paired forearm fracture showing gross rotational deformity (burial 94)

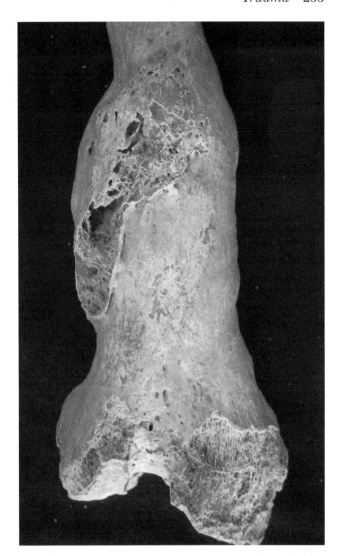

Figure 17.8   Anterior view of oblique distal femoral fracture of burial 115 that shows poor healing and osteomyelitis

segment becomes dorsally impacted when it is forced posteriorly so that the healed bone takes on a 'dinner fork' deformity. The styloid process of the right ulna was simultaneously avulsed during this event and was not recovered during excavation. Isolated Colles' fractures were observed on an individual of unknown sex (223) and a young female who suffered from leprosy (339) among others. Compaction injuries to the radial distal articular surfaces, also common outcomes of bracing a fall, were noted among four males (56, 146, 287, 292). A mature male (115) experienced a healed transverse fracture on the left radius and an oblique distal fracture on the right radius.

Femur

Femur fractures are particularly nasty as excessive force is required to break this robust bone and a similarly strong force is required to keep the bone in traction so that it may align properly during the healing process. Successful healing does not often take place in societies without access to modern medical treatment and osteomyelitis and/or gross malalignment may result.

Two Area A adults, one male with leprosy (115) and one of indeterminate sex (343), sustained open femoral injuries that resulted in considerable shortening, angulation and active osteomyelitis at the time of death. Burial 115 exhibited an oblique fracture on his right distal femur that produced a huge fluffy callus that partially mineralised at the time of death (Fig 17.8). Both individuals present other injuries and those of burial 115 are described in detail elsewhere (Knüsel and Göggel 1993). The injury constellations, though different, are consistent with similar patterns observed among traditional agricultural societies and include those received from catching a leg in an open-spoked wheel, falling from an animal, cart or height, or being mauled by a farm animal (Boyle *et al* 1997; Busch *et al* 1986;

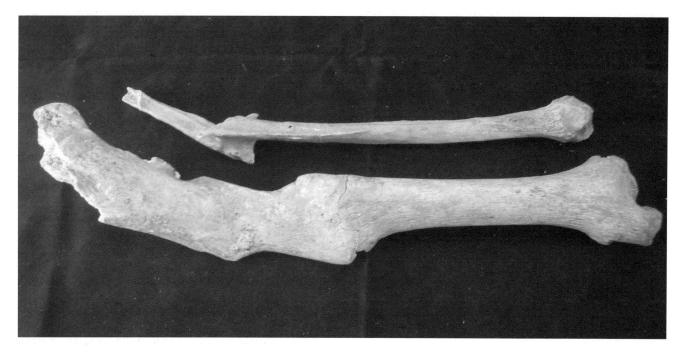

Figure 17.9   The fractures to the left tibia and fibula of burial 193 occurred simultaneously

Casey *et al* 1997; Criddle 2001; Jones 1990; Norwood *et al* 2000).

Lower leg

Lower leg injuries are commonly obtained from going over on one's ankle especially on uneven surfaces and during inclement weather, but they can also be the result of direct force trauma or accidents similar to those that affect the femur (Agarwal 1980; David and Freedman 1990; Ralis 1986). The fibula functions as little more than part of a vice to contain the ankle and, therefore, the fracture of the fibular shaft has little effect on the individual's ability to function as the weight of the body is borne on the tibial plateau. The slender form of the fibula renders it susceptible to breakage from direct or indirect forces. Eight males from both cemetery areas and one individual experienced nine isolated fibular distal or midshaft fractures, but none succumbed to fracture complications. Of the sixteen tibial injuries, the majority were minor articular surface impactions. The tibial shaft injuries of three males (55, 157 and 193) resulted in a period of incapacitation that probably made any weight-bearing activity painful. The oblique midshaft fracture of burial 55 displayed a fluffy area of undefined cortical bone when radiographed, although smooth lamellar bone was remodelling around the injury site at the time of death. The distal segment overlapped 33mm and was angled 20°, indicating unsuccessful healing according to criteria published by Grauer and Roberts (1996).

Burial 157 was one of two Area B individuals that had associated fibula and tibia injuries.

The tibia injury was unhealed at the time of death, overlapped by 27mm and angled 10° anteriorly. The medial malleolus of the articulating fibula was crushed. The tibia of burial 193 bore a double fracture that occurred simultaneously with the adjacent fibula injury during an event that mangled the bones (Fig 17.9). The tibial fractures occurred on the upper half of the bone and resulted in a doubling of the bone width at the fracture sites so that the middle connecting segment overlapped with the proximal and distal segments. A large bony spur resulted from the more distal injury that was connected to the fibula at the site of bone overlap. The distal fibula segment produced an anteroposterior angle of 20°. A cloaca, bone puffiness and periostitis indicated that osteomyelitis was present at the time of death.

Short and miscellaneous bones

Scapula

Scapula injuries are rare archaeologically and the presence of a crushed scapular body is perceived as an indicator of an injury obtained during a confrontation, or an event that mimics interpersonal violence, such as a sports injury (Wakely 1996; Wyrsch *et al* 1995; Zazryn *et al* 2003). Scapulas were fractured on five individuals. Two males (225, 333) suffered from crushed scapular bodies that may have been associated with their rib and long bone injuries (Fig 17.10). An unusually angled glenoid cavity and scapula neck with evidence of bone remodelling suggests that the scapular neck had been fractured quite some time before the death of female 137a.

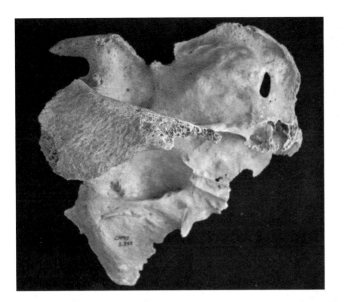

Figure 17.10 Left posterior scapula of burial 333 showing the shattered and healed body fracture. Photo courtesy of D Ortner

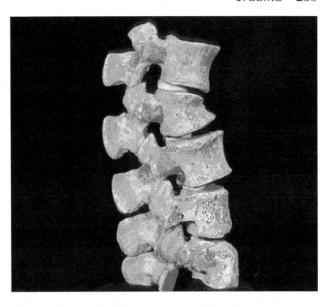

Figure 17.11 Left lateral view of lumbar vertebrae of burial 369 showing collapse due to fracture of the second lumbar element. Photo courtesy of D Ortner

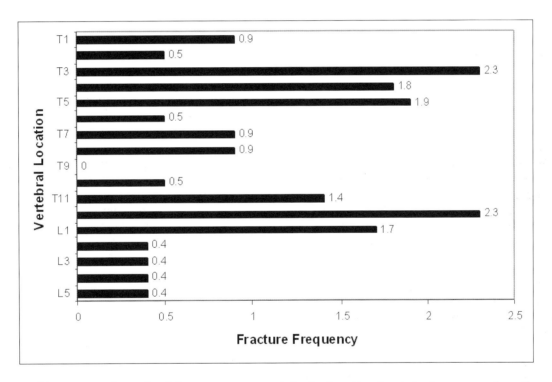

Figure 17.12 Frequency of vertebral fracture among adults by location (no injuries occurred on the cervical vertebrae)

Vertebral column

Vertebral fractures affected 23 individuals (one of unknown sex) and involved 38 vertebrae, which included 30 thoracic and eight lumbar injuries. Twenty-six of these lesions were due to vertebral collapse (Fig 17.11) and twelve involved hairline fractures that produced slight wedging of the vertebral body. Figure 17.12 illustrates that the peak fracture incidence occurs at T3–5 and T11–L1, which are located along the gravity line. The lower

vertebral injuries are consistent with those obtained following a jump or fall from a height where the individual lands on his or her feet (Richter *et al* 1996). Females suffered from more vertebral injuries with 25% (1 out of 4) from Area A affected and 19% (4 out of 21) from Area B affected. Only one female (30) was afflicted with widespread osteoporosis which predisposed her to compression injuries of thoracic vertebrae 3, 5–8 and 11–12.

The Area A males bore more vertebral injuries (11%, 12 out of 114) than their Area B counterparts (7%, 5/74), although this difference was not significant ($\chi^2 = 0.77$, $P = 0.37$). It is notable that twelve individuals (54.5%) who sustained vertebral injuries also suffered from Schmorl's nodes, which are typically associated with heavy activity and disc rupture; seven of these men were from Area A. Life in the leprosarium may not have been an easy one for its residents who may have been required to assist in daily chores involving the maintenance of the institution and the sustenance of its residents.

Spondylolysis (not included in fracture inventory)

Disruptions of the vertebral neural arch may be unilateral or bilateral and there is controversy over whether these anomalies are due to congenital weakness or habitual activity-related trauma. Among the Chichester sample, all age groups were at risk with seventeen males (8, 20, 56, 65, 84, 137b, 158, 175, 178, 197, 271, 287, 314, 319, 328, 354 and 371) and one female (238) bearing this lesion; eight of the males were from Area A. Ten of the lesions were bilateral; the fifth lumbar was most commonly affected (eight individuals). Two people had unilateral lesions of the third thoracic and first sacral vertebrae. Unilateral spondylolysis was also seen in 137b (5th lumbar), 371 (1st sacral) and 158 where an acute traumatic event had caused the left side of the neural arch of L5 to become detached.

Spondylolysis occurs with a frequency of 5–6% in many populations, but has reached endemic proportions among the Inuit (54%) and athletes (Fibiger and Knüsel 2005; Merbs 2002). A recent analysis of the Chichester vertebrae revealed that the prevalence of this anomaly at Chichester was 10% among adults, which is higher than many other British populations, but does not reach the frequency of groups associated with excessive physical exertion (Fibiger and Knüsel 2005).

Ribcage

The most frequently fractured bone in this collection was the rib. Like other injuries, rib fractures are multifactorial in aetiology and although they may be due to interpersonal violence, particularly abuse (Walker *et al* 1997; Wladis *et al* 1999), accidental falls, prolonged coughing, birth or underlying pathology, for example, osteomalacia, may also be agents (Brickley *et al* 2005; De Maeseneer *et al* 2000; Sinha *et al* 1999).

Thirty-five individuals have fractures involving 84 ribs and of these individuals 77% (27) were males. In most cases rib fractures were isolated, even when many ribs were injured. For example, one male (361) and one female with leprosy (144) experienced extensive rib trauma with seven and eight rib injuries respectively. Neither bore other long bone or skull injuries, which are to be expected from excessive interpersonal violence or a fall from

a high place. Seven males from Area A sustained other injuries in addition to rib trauma, which were typical of those obtained from falls, for example, oblique clavicular or fibular fractures. Among the Area B males, ten out of thirteen males with rib injuries had other traumatic lesions.

Hands

Fourteen wrist and hand fractures were observed among twelve individuals; with the exception of burial 358, all were male. Two carpal bones among 308 (0.6%) exhibited signs of trauma and both were associated with impacted radial articular surfaces. A hairline fracture traversed the right scaphoid of burial 287 and is a common outcome from a fall on an outstretched hand (Loder and Mayhew 1988). The left lunate of burial 115 was crushed and this along with other leprous changes to the hand probably made the manipulation of the hand difficult (Knüsel and Göggel 1993). Five out of 432 (1.2%) metacarpals were fractured and of these three were hairline injuries. The right first metacarpal of burial 3 was dislocated. Two proximal, three middle and one distal phalangeal fracture occurred among five individuals and 212 (2.8%) phalanges.

Feet

Twenty-six foot injuries were observed among fifteen individuals, fourteen of whom were male. The tarsals accounted for thirteen of the foot injuries, which is uncommon in clinical practice where the phalanges are most often injured. This phenomenon is probably attributable to the anaesthetised foot in leprosy. Four individuals bore macroscopic lesions of leprosy and a variety of foot injuries such as a midshaft right fourth metatarsal injury (burial 8) and a compressed left and right navicular (burial 373). Compressed tali and naviculars were observed among individuals whose skeleton gave no indication of leprosy, although they may have suffered from tuberculoid leprosy. The spectrum of tarsal injuries included compression fractures of six naviculars, two first cuneiforms, two calcanei and three tali. Five metatarsals out of 409 (1.2%) were traumatised in addition to six proximal phalanges and two distal phalanges recorded among 180 (4.4%) phalanges. Many of these injuries were hairline fractures.

Patella

The right patella of two males (burials 199, 348) displayed hairline fractures to the articular surface. The patella is particularly vulnerable to injury resulting from a fall, but neither individual suffered from other fall-related injuries. The anterior surfaces do not show evidence of injury so it is more likely that the hairline fractures resulted from continued stress on the posterior surface, perhaps due to kneeling.

Dislocations

Dislocations are difficult to identify in archaeological remains and are usually confirmed by the presence of a new joint surface or joint fusion. The shoulder is the most commonly dislocated joint due to the unlimited movement of the humeral head along the glenoid cavity. The head is most often displaced when the arm is abducted and extended in any direction from the body. The impact of this action results in the displacement of the humeral head and stretching or tearing of the joint capsule. If not properly reduced, a new joint surface may be created from the friction of the two articular surfaces against each other or in more severe cases the joint capsule may ossify to immobilise the humeral head in a bony shroud. Like other traumatic lesions, this injury is not limited to an individual's clumsiness, but may also occur during competitive sports, for example, boxing, or during an epileptic fit (Miles 2000; Wyrsch *et al* 1995).

Two mature males (117 and 123), one of whom exhibited DISH lesions and the other ankylosing spondylitis, bore dislocated shoulders. In each case the right shoulder was affected and the injury was quite old. The humeral head of burial 123 formed a new joint along the anterior border of the glenoid cavity and continued to be mobile as indicated by an extensive area of eburnation. The dislocation in burial 117 was described above.

Soft tissue trauma

Acute trauma may affect soft tissue as well as bone, resulting in an irregular ossified mass of bone at the site of avulsion of the muscle or tendon from the bone (Aufderheide and Rodríguez-Martín 1998). Fifty-one individuals, 39 males, ten females and two individuals of unknown sex, displayed some form of soft tissue trauma and in many cases this was associated with fractures, many of which were briefly described above.

The shoulder area of five individuals exhibited rotator cuff injuries due to the extreme mobility of the joint. Other upper body fracture-related soft tissue trauma affected muscle insertions of the clavicle (145), humerus (46, 123), ulna (57), both ulnae (115 and 330) and radius (76); the distal humerus (76 and 142) and hands (79 and 83) sustained soft tissue trauma in two isolated events. Three individuals, all males (43, 15 and 46), suffered soft tissue trauma to the innominate. The right *rectus femoris* insertion of 46 added to the extensive soft tissue trauma suffered by this individual.

The leg is most often affected by soft tissue trauma and the people of Chichester were no exception. Nine males and two females bore a diverse range of

femoral ossified tissue including the gluteal attachments (82, 145, 246, 306, 227), iliofemoral ligament (46), *vastus intermedius* (61), *gastrocnemius* (76), *psoas major* (227), *quadratus femoris* (145) and abductor (129). Tibial soft tissue trauma was even more prominent and affected fifteen males and one female. Lesions affected the distal interosseous attachment of thirteen individuals and the collateral ligaments of burials 83 and 134. Thirteen individuals had injured fibulae, which were associated with tibial soft tissue trauma or fracture in many cases. The tali of burials 46 and 79 also produced soft tissue trauma. Ossified haematomas occurred on the femoral shaft of two males (20 and 355) and tibial shafts of three males (15, 36, 255).

Children's trauma

Children's bones are particularly resilient and heal quickly so that lesions may not be visible in the archaeological record unless the injury occurred very close to the time of death. Among the 106 children observed, including one from the 'charnel pit', only three displayed some form of trauma. From Area A, one adolescent (334) experienced a 22mm incision near the coronal suture of the frontal bone. Two children from Area B had questionable traumatic lesions. Individual 140 was a young child who showed regions of periosteal bone growth on the mandibular rami. A hairline fracture occurred on the left lingual aspect of the ramus that may be due to an underlying pathology of rickets rather than blunt force trauma. Finally, the fibula of an older child (319) presented a healed distal fracture.

Discussion

St James and St Mary Magdalene was originally founded as an institution to house males suffering from leprosy and, as the individual would not recover from the disease nor be reintroduced to society, it is assumed that these individuals died and were buried there. Leprosy is a chronic infectious disease that permits the afflicted individuals to live a long life, in contrast to acute infectious diseases such as plague and smallpox, and therefore people with leprosy are exposed to a lifetime of daily trauma risk. The aetiology of injuries due to fracture is most diagnostic among the long bones. When compared to other contemporary urban British sites, the Chichester Area A and Area B groups experienced the highest frequency of long bone fractures among both groups together and when examined individually (Tables 17.4 and 17.5).

Almost all injuries sustained by the individuals from St James' Hospital were attributed to accident, most likely due to trips or falls where one extends the hand to brace oneself (Kemmlert and Lundholm 2001; Loder and Mayhew 1988). Injuries to the hands and feet were uncommon, which, at least

Table 17.4   Frequency of long bone fractures among British populations

Site	Fractures	Bones	%	Reference
Chichester Area A	31	1436	2.2	This study
Chichester Area B	30	1695	1.8	This study
Jewbury, York	8	2839	0.3	Brothwell and Browne 1994
St Helen-on-the-Walls, York	41	4938	0.8	Grauer and Roberts 1996
St Andrew, Fishergate, York	26	3235	0.8	Stroud and Kemp 1993
Whithorn, Scotland	27	9563	0.3	Cardy 1997

Table 17.5   Frequency of long bone fractures by element among British populations

Site	Humerus	Radius	Ulna	Femur	Tibia	Fibula
Chichester Area A	0.5	2.6	2.5	0.5	2.8	2.0
Chichester Area B	0.8	1.6	1.3	0.8	4.0	2.2
Chichester (Judd and Roberts 1998)	0.8	3.2	2.8	0.4	2.3	7.2
Jewbury (Brothwell and Browne 1994)	0.0	0.5	0.0	0.8	0.2	0.2
St Helen-on-the-Walls (Grauer and Roberts 1996)	0.8	1.3	1.5	0.1	0.7	0.8
St Andrew, Fishergate (Stroud and Kemp 1993)	0.4	0.8	0.8	0.2	0.5	1.7
Whithorn, Scotland (Cardy 1997)	0.0	0.5	0.1	0.2	0.4	0.8

among individuals suffering from chronic leprosy, may have been due to cumbersome coverings worn over the extremities to protect them and also to hide them from public view. Cumbersome foot wrappings and visual obstruction from overhanging tissue masses, ulceration or blindness may also have predisposed chronic leprosy sufferers to trips and falls while standing or walking (Daniel *et al* 2002; Judd and Roberts 1998).

It is unlikely that interpersonal violence would have permeated the hospital and almshouse, which were under the strict control of the church and benefactors. However, some altercations probably occurred due to the intimate communal nature of the living conditions. Even though six skull injuries and one parry fracture were observed, their frequency was negligible – interpersonal violence was the exception rather than the norm.

18   Joint disease *by Anthea Boylston and Frances Lee*

Introduction

The range of joint diseases from which a person can suffer is so wide that even clinicians with a patient in front of them, a set of X-rays and all the blood tests available may have difficulty arriving at a diagnosis (Rogers *et al* 1987). Joint diseases may be hypertrophic, that is, accompanied by production of large amounts of new bone, or erosive (Rogers 2000). Sometimes they may be a combination of the two. By far the most common conditions in the first category are those familiarly known as the degenerative joint diseases, including osteoarthritis. However, in the setting of a medieval leprosarium, other conditions such as septic arthritis are likely to be much more prevalent than in the normal population.

Degenerative joint disease (DJD)

For the first 30 years of life the bones and joints are growing and developing. Once growth is complete, a process of gradual degeneration begins. However, the rate at which this will occur varies greatly between individuals. For example, degenerative joint disease, indicated by marginal lipping, may commence in the spine as early as the third decade of life, particularly in the lower thoracic and lumbar regions where stress is greatest (Stewart 1979). Other joints in the body tend to develop sharp margins with advancing age and there is gradual formation of a bony exostosis along the attachment of the joint capsule.

There are three types of joint and their anatomy dictates the way in which they deteriorate with advancing age. Osteoarthritis affects the synovial articulations, which include not only the major joints between the long bones but also small ones in the hands and feet and the facet joints between the vertebral bodies of the spine. It was diagnosed following the criteria set out by Rogers and Waldron (1995).

Where changes to the joints are less severe, for example, indicated by slight degrees of osteophytic lipping or porosity, degenerative joint disease is the preferred term. This is important since only some individuals are more susceptible to osteoarthritis than others, whereas almost everyone eventually manifests age-related changes to the joints. This term is also used to refer to marginal lipping and disc degeneration in the spine.

Osteoarthritis

Osteoarthritis (OA) is an active metabolic abnormality of articular cartilage resulting in patchy destruction and calcification (Huskisson *et al* 1979). Its effects on the tissues lead to abnormalities of bone, tendons, ligaments and in fact all the structures surrounding the joint. After the age of 55, the incidence of OA and degenerative joint disease of the spine and other joints in the population increase exponentially (Cotran *et al* 1994) and by 65 years 80–90% of people are affected in one or more joints. From the mid-50s onwards the incidence among women rises dramatically and it seems that the menopause makes a woman more susceptible to developing OA. It may affect just a few joints or become generalised, the latter state being more common in those with a genetic predisposition to the condition.

OA may occur as a primary or secondary phenomenon. In the first situation the cause is unknown; in the second, trauma or a congenital or developmental defect may have disrupted the joint surface. In some individuals, practising various sports can lead to the development of OA in later life; the shoulders and elbows of baseball players and the knees of basketball players are some examples in point (King *et al* 1969). Secondly, there is known to be an increased local prevalence in certain occupations where a single joint is exposed to unusual stress (Dick 1972, 2; Hadler 1977). However, evidence for a direct link between OA and activity is contradictory. Early onset secondary arthritis only occurs in about 5% of cases of the disease. However, an injury to a joint in youth may lead to osteoarthritis 20 or 30 years after the event occurred. Some joints are more susceptible to age-related change and others to functional stress (Jurmain 1976; 1999).

The main effect of OA on the individual is pain, loss of function of the joint and stiffness. The pain of osteoarthritis is intermittent and mainly related to the biomechanical stress of joint activity. Thus in weight-bearing joints such as the hip and knee it is brought on by standing and walking. The loss or reduction of function is due not only to pain but in later stages to joint deformity.

Osteoarthritis of the appendicular skeleton

The synovial joints were commonly affected by degenerative change and osteoarthritis at Chichester (Tables 18.1 and 18.2). A total of 80 individuals suffered from OA of one or more of the joints in their appendicular skeleton. This represents 29% of the adult population. There was no significant difference in prevalence of osteoarthritis for any of the major joints between males and females (Table 18.1).

The acromioclavicular joint is not very stable and subject to constant shearing stresses (DePalma 1983,

Table 18.1 Comparison of prevalence rates for osteoarthritis of the appendicular skeleton between males and females

	Male			Female			Chi squared
	o	*n*	%	*o*	*n*	%	*p values*
Sternoclavicular							
R	3	145	2	3	58	5.2	0.2382
L	4	142	2.8	0	58	0	
Acromioclavicular							
R	26	129	20.2	9	46	19.6	0.9316
L	23	126	18.3	5	45	11.1	
Shoulder							
R	4	147	2.7	1	59	1.7	0.6653
L	1	156	0.6	2	58	3.4	
Elbow							
R	9	155	5.8	1	58	1.7	0.2099
L	5	154	3.2	1	56	1.8	
Wrist							
R	8	137	5.8	2	53	3.8	0.5674
L	12	136	8.8	1	54	1.9	
Hand							
R	12	145	8.3	7	54	13	0.3173
L	7	139	5	4	57	7	
Hip							
R	8	150	5.3	4	67	6	0.8496
L	15	162	9.3	4	68	5.9	
Knee							
R	3	159	1.9	2	62	3.2	0.5476
L	3	159	1.9	2	66	3	
Tarsals							
R	5	148	3.4	1	64	1.6	0.4642
L	7	151	4.6	1	65	1.5	
Foot (metatarsals and phalanges)							
R	7	128	5.5	1	54	1.9	0.2769
L	5	126	4	0	59	0	

239). Moreover, it may show signs of deterioration as early as 35 years of age in modern populations. It is also the joint most often affected by DJD at Chichester. Thirty-three per cent of acromioclavicular joints in the mature males demonstrated DJD as opposed to 26% of female ones. The changes were more likely to be bilateral in the males than the females.

Changes to the sternal end of the clavicle are rare at the present time, although this joint may be involved in rheumatoid, tuberculous and pyogenic arthritis (Adams 1981). At St James' Hospital, 4–6% of all clavicles (18) were affected but only 2% to any significant degree, and these in the mature age group. The majority of involvement was slight and asymmetrical.

True osteoarthritis of the shoulder is rare, which may be explained by freedom from pressure stresses since it is not a weight-bearing joint (Adams 1981). The glenohumeral joint is most likely to become arthritic in the wake of a traumatic event such as a fracture of the anatomical neck or dislocation. This need not be a complete dislocation since an element of subluxation of the joint can lead to the humeral head impinging on the acromion process of the scapula (DePalma 1983). However, a much more common phenomenon is an injury or tear in the rotator cuff which surrounds the humeral head (Fig 18.1). This may lead to bone spur formation, porosity and, in serious cases, eburnation (Ogata and Uhthoff 1990).

Table 18.2 Comparison of age-related prevalence rates for osteoarthritis of the appendicular skeleton between the sexes

	Male			Female		
	Young	*Middle*	*Mature*	*Young*	*Middle*	*Mature*
Sternoclavicular						
R		1/45	2/51		1/18	2/21
L			4/48			
Acromioclavicular						
R		7/39	19/48		4/15	5/17
L		5/42	17/42		1/14	4/18
Shoulder						
R			4/51		1/20	
L			1/52			2/22
Elbow						
R		1/53	8/51		1/19	
L		1/49	4/51			1/22
Wrist						
R			8/43		2/14	
L	1/43		10/44		1/14	
Hand						
R	1/43	7/48	4/50	1/12	3/16	3/25
L		2/47	4/43		1/19	3/22
Sacro-iliac						
R	1/49		2/44	1/17	1/20	4/25
L		2/51	2/44	1/18		3/26
Hip						
R		2/54	5/49		2/19	2/27
L	1/50	2/53	11/50			4/28
Knee						
R		1/48	2/48		1/20	1/25
L		1/52	1/49		1/19	1/27
Tarsals						
R	1/48		4/47			1/25
L	4/47	1/48	2/50	1/16		
Foot (metatarsals and phalanges)						
R	1/39		6/45		1/17	
L	2/41	1/32	2/44			

At Chichester, 7–8% of all shoulder joints showed evidence of degenerative change, but only 2–4% were severely affected. Just over half of these were bilateral, most simply involving minimal changes such as osteophytic lipping to the margins of the joint capsule. Eight individuals had osteoarthritis which, in burials 117 and 123, was secondary to dislocation (see Fig 17.6). In the females, the left shoulder joint was involved to some degree in 12% (7/58) of cases, almost twice as often as the right side. Prevalence rates for joint disease of the shoulder in archaeo-

logical populations are often difficult to compare, particularly when the three joints are combined into one. Rogers (2000, 167) lists figures from medieval sites varying from 0.9 to 33.5%.

The elbow is often the most asymmetrical joint in the body as far as severity of osteoarthritis is concerned and the one most likely to be subjected to functional stresses (Bridges 1991; Jurmain 1976). In total, 35 individuals were affected by degenerative change (8–10% of all adult elbows) but only 6% by osteoarthritis. Two-thirds of elbow OA

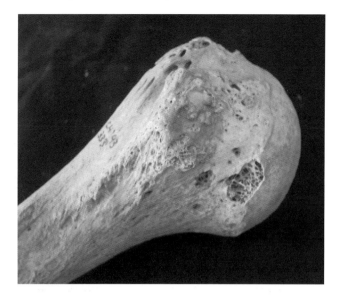

Figure 18.1 Enthesopathy of the rotator cuff (subscapularis insertion) on the right humeral head of burial 333

was bilateral, with the two sides equally affected. However, overall the right side was almost twice as likely to display advanced OA which was much more common in males than in females (5.8% of male as opposed to 1.7% of female right elbows). Two of the mature males (burials 2 and 18) from Area A were supreme examples of this asymmetry, with very severe hypertrophic OA of the elbows, particularly on the right (Fig 18.2). Clearly, the quasi-monastic nature of the institution did not prevent the inhab-

itants being involved in tasks which stressed their elbow joints. Monastic gardens had to be tilled and seasonal tasks performed in order to grow the medicinal herbs which were the main sources of treatment in the Middle Ages.

Seven per cent of male wrists were osteoarthritic as opposed to only three per cent of female ones. In most the condition was unilateral. DJD of the wrist often occurs secondary to trauma, particularly a fracture of the radius or ulna which has not been satisfactorily reduced (Fig 18.3). This is certainly the case when there is a spiral or Colles' fracture of the radius (see Chapter 17). The result is an increasing stiffness and pain in the wrist that becomes worse the more the joint is used (Adams 1981).

Nineteen individuals had OA of their right hands, which was almost twice as frequent as disease in the left hand in both sexes. The first and third metacarpals were most commonly affected as well as the interphalangeal joints. Up to a third of changes were associated with one or more leprous features in the skeleton, and some cases may be the result of motor neuron changes and a lack of feeling in the hands.

Osteoarthritis of the hip joint is common both now and in antiquity. It can be either primary, with no obvious underlying cause, or secondary to a condition such as Perthes' disease or slipped femoral epiphysis (Ortner 2003). The hip was most commonly affected by DJD at Chichester after the acromioclavicular joint, the condition occurring in 73 individuals. Twenty-four per cent of all left hips were involved, of which 8% fulfilled the criteria for OA. A third of the cases were bilateral, although in

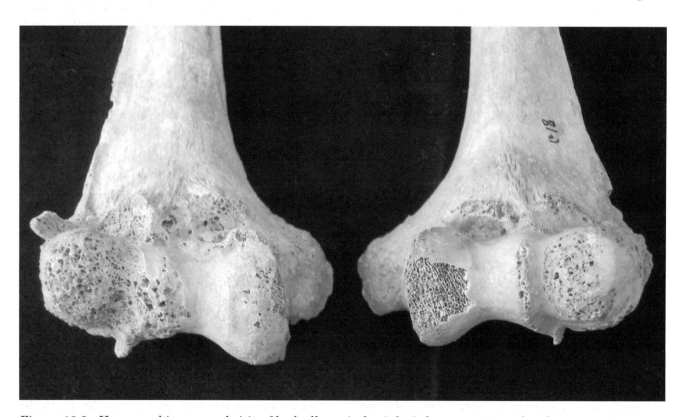

Figure 18.2 Hypertrophic osteoarthritis of both elbows in burial 18 due to activity related stress on the joint

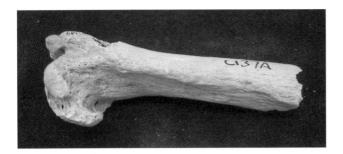

Figure 18.3 Osteoarthritis of the right distal ulna secondary to fracture in burial 137a

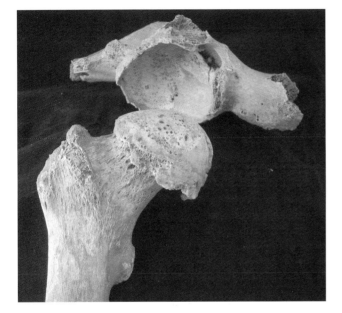

Figure 18.4 Osteoarthritis of the right hip in burial 333 demonstrating osteophytosis at the margin of the femoral head together with porosity and eburnation (polishing) on its articular surface

Figure 18.5 Secondary osteoarthritis as a result of osteomyelitis in the knee of an adult male (burial 83)

those with OA this rose to two-thirds, with considerable asymmetry in the degree of involvement.

The male left hip was by far the most commonly affected joint, with over 9% displaying OA (Fig 18.4), as opposed to 6% of female left hips. All but three of these males fell into the 46+ category. The most dramatic example is burial 13, a mature male with only the lower trunk and limbs present. The left and right hip joints have been totally destroyed by secondary OA (see Part 4) with exuberant new bone growth at the margins of the capsule, completely altering the contour of the femoral heads. Both sides of the joints display widespread eburnation and there is little or no movement in either hip, with the angle of the upper leg suggesting the individual was in a permanent sitting position (see Fig 19.7). This is hypertrophic OA, which was quite common in the past and suggests that the individual was a 'bone former' (Rogers *et al* 1997).

A serious injury to the right femur in burial 115, an elderly male with leprosy, was directly responsible for the joint disease in his right knee, which has become severely deformed owing to the abnormal loading placed upon it (see Fig 17.8). Similarly, the right knee of burial 83 demonstrates the changes of OA (Fig 18.5) owing to a severe infection of the entire bone. Osteomyelitis in this tibia is demonstrated by a cloaca surrounded by diffuse periosteal reaction (see Fig 16.10). Otherwise most of the lesions to the knee were slight with small amounts of osteophytic lipping on the femoral condyles and margins of the patellae in 21 individuals. These are a normal feature of the ageing skeleton. Between two and three percent of adult knees were affected by OA. The more severe changes were present in the mature age group. OA of the knee is very much a feature of modern lifestyles, with obesity a major predisposing factor (Leach *et al* 1973).

The ankle joint is not normally susceptible to OA unless it is severely injured. At St James' Hospital, many of the destructive changes in the tarsals were the result of septic arthritis secondary to leprosy. Some 7.3% of adults (sixteen) with feet present had joint disease of the tarsal bones; approximately half of these were osteoarthritic, most with unilateral lesions. The talus is the most frequently involved tarsal bone followed by the lateral cuneiform. There is no visible difference between the left and right sides. Males were more likely to be affected, with 6% of all male feet having DJD of the tarsals compared with 1–2% of female ones. Burial 333 had OA of the talocalcaneal joint in his left foot secondary to trauma.

Fourteen adults have OA of the head of the first metatarsal (7.5%), as a result of pressure transmission. Both left and right sides are equally involved and males are more frequently affected, with up to 15% of mature individuals having some form of DJD in the first metatarsal. In one case OA was secondary to an erosive lesion that may be consistent with a diagnosis of gout (burial 25). Other metatarsals were less frequently involved, with osteoarthritis in the phalanges of four individuals. In total, 9.3% of the adult population had changes in the foot, whereas 14.3% had alterations to the foot and ankle joints, males being more frequently and severely affected. In burial 341 a pseudarthrosis was in the process of forming between the left distal tibia and fibula.

Degenerative joint disease of the temporomandibular joint was present in 15% of adults (35). Sixty-three percent of the lesions were slight, represented by porosity of the joint with lipping of the condyles. The left joint is marginally more often affected than the right. In modern clinical practice most OA of the temporomandibular joint occurs in women, with a preponderance of 4:1. This is not the case here, with 16% of men affected compared with 11% of women.

Eight individuals have generalised osteoarthritis of multiple joints. These are mainly elderly males (2, 18, 57, 82, 115, 333), all but one from Area A. Two elderly females from Area B also had generalised OA affecting many of their joints.

Osteoarthritis may be caused by a normal force acting on an abnormal joint or vice versa; hence the high fracture prevalence at Chichester has markedly increased the number of arthritic joints in the population. Nerve damage in those with leprosy also led to loss of pain sensation so that individuals would overload their joints without realising that they were doing so. This would also have led to joint incongruity, particularly in the hands and feet. Not unexpectedly, therefore, 29% of adults with postcranial osteoarthritis represents a higher prevalence than any of the sites mentioned for the late medieval period in Roberts and Cox (2003, 282). It also exceeds the figures of 23% calculated for the post-medieval parish churchyard at St Martin's in Birmingham (Brickley et al 2006) and 11% for those interred in the crypt of Christ Church, Spitalfields, during the 18th and 19th centuries (Waldron 1993).

The acromioclavicular joint, wrist, hand and the hip were the joints which showed the highest prevalence of osteoarthritis at Chichester. The comparable figure for hip osteoarthritis in the large lay cathedral burial ground at Hereford (Boylston in prep) is 5% which is similar to figures of 5.7% calculated for a number of sites dating to the medieval period by Rogers (2000). The rate for the Chichester males is 7.4% which is not significantly different from the prevalence found at Hereford Cathedral (p=0.1232).

Spinal osteoarthritis

The synovial joints in the spinal column are the apophyseal, costotransverse and costovertebral articulations. Fifty-five per cent of all adult spines have some degree of degenerative change to the apophyseal joints. This rises sharply with age and in severity with 26% of individuals under 30 having varying degrees of change rising to 77.2% in the mature age range, with a corresponding increase in the number of joints affected and the severity of

Table 18.3 Comparison of degenerative joint disease (including osteoarthritis) of the apophyseal joints between individuals of the same sex in Area A and Area B

	Area A male	Area B male	Area A female	Area B female
C1	2.5	5.6		8.9
2	28	15.4		23.9
3	30.9	22.2	7.7	25.6
4	26.3	16	15.4	23.3
5	21.2	13.2	7.7	20.9
6	10.2	26.5	8.3	10.9
7	17.8	15.7	0	18.6
T1	21.5	10.3	8.3	20.8
2	11.8	10.5	0	18.4
3	22	15.3	8.3	22.9
4	30.1	27.1	9.1	27.5
5	34.8	29.3	9.1	35.4
6	28.6	14.8	10	22.9
7	16.5	9.4	9.1	4.3
8	14.1	14.5	9.1	5.9
9	16	16.4	0	8.2
10	20.7	14.5	0	8.3
11	12.8	9.5	0	18
12	13.8	7.8	0	6
L1	14.7	6.1	10	14.8
2	8.6	7.5	0	7.3
3	11.2	8.5	0	7.1
4	15.2	8.7	9.1	8.9
5	20.2	10.4	18.2	7

the lesions. The condition is most prevalent in males from Area A and females from Area B (Table 18.3 and Appendix 11, Tables 1–3 on CD). The upper cervical and upper thoracic regions are more frequently and severely affected in men, whilst the upper to middle thoracic is most common in women with the exception of the 4th thoracic (Fig 18.6). The pattern of OA in the apophyseal joints does not correspond with disc degeneration and vertebral osteophytosis. The causation of these two conditions is clearly quite different. Osteoarthritis of the cervical spine was seen in burial 123 who was also suffering from ankylosing spondylitis (Fig 18.7).

The costovertebral and costotransverse joints link the ribs with the vertebrae. Forty-two per cent of individuals had some change to one or other of these joints (Appendix 11, Tables 4–5). This was most noticeable on the articular surface for the first rib and on the lower ribs, particularly the eleventh and twelfth. This may be due to greater movement and increased stress that is placed on the floating ribs.

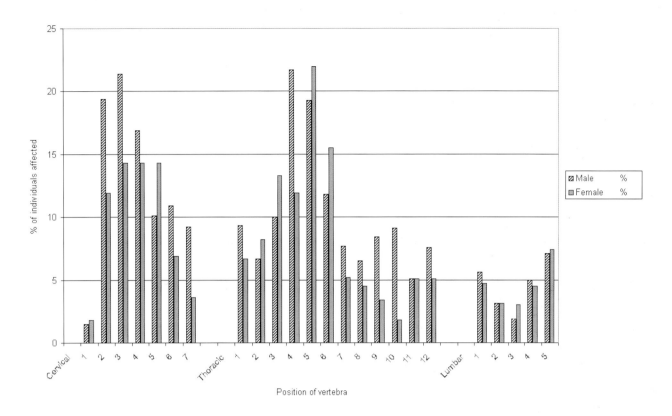

Figure 18.6   Comparison of osteoarthritis of the vertebral facet joints between males and females

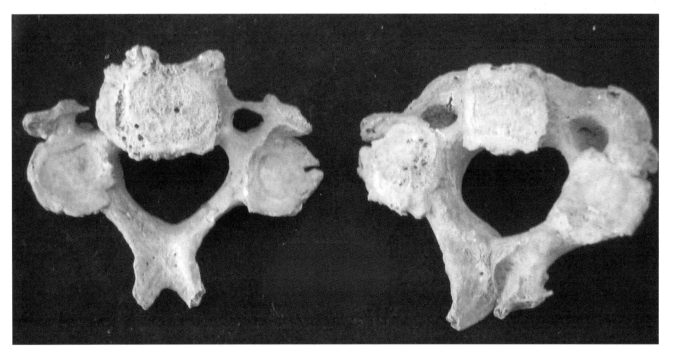

Figure 18.7   Spondylosis of the cervical vertebrae with polishing of the facet joints and osteophytosis of the vertebral bodies in burial 123

The distribution is similar for males and females, and like other DJD there was a noticeable increase in severity and prevalence with age.

The pattern for DJD on the facets of the transverse processes was quite different from the costoverte-bral facets. The eighth and ninth thoracic vertebrae were commonly affected with 22% (57) of all adults having some degenerative change to their transverse facets. More women than men were involved (27% (20) of females compared to 21% (37) of males).

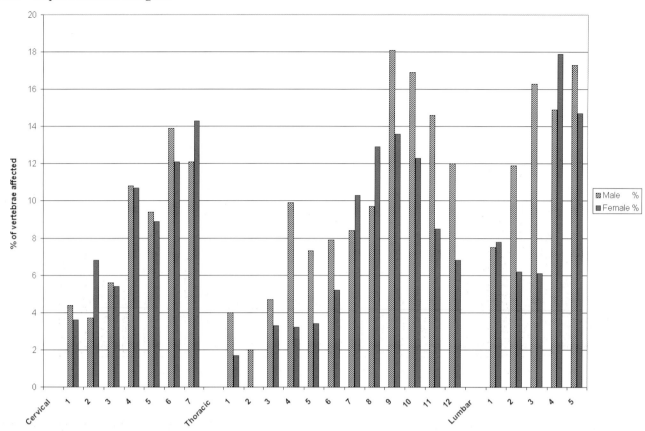

Figure 18.8   Percentage of male and female vertebrae affected by vertebral osteophytosis (moderate to severe)

There is the expected increase in prevalence and severity with age.

When the ribs themselves were considered, degenerative change was noted to the articular facets, with 36% of all adults having some alteration and 6% demonstrating osteoarthritis on one or more rib tubercles. Bilateral change occurs in approximately half of these, with a slightly greater prevalence in women.

Spinal degenerative disease

Vertebral osteophytosis (spondylosis deformans)

Vertebral osteophytes are exostoses of bone projecting from the margins of the vertebral bodies. They vary in severity from small projections to complete bony ankylosis or fusion of adjacent vertebral bodies. They are the direct result of degenerative change in the intervertebral disc. Fifty-seven per cent (102) of all adult spines recorded had some degree of osteophytosis. Figure 18.8 shows the percentage of vertebrae affected by osteophytosis, their extent, area and location within the spine. The lower thoracic and lumbar vertebrae are particularly involved, corresponding with the maximum curvature of the spine where there is increased stress on the vertebrae. A second peak occurs to the lower cervical region; these latter changes occur predominately in the older age group and are almost always associated with intervertebral osteochondrosis or disc degeneration. This is a common pattern found in most archaeological samples, though very different from that reported by Waldron (1991) for the post-medieval site of Christ Church, Spitalfields, where the cervical peak was entirely absent.

Osteophytosis is clearly age-related (Table 18.4

Table 18.4   **Comparison of males and females with vertebral osteophytosis between Area A and Area B**

| | Area A | | | | | | Area B | | | | | |
| | *Males* | | | *Females* | | | *Males* | | | *Females* | | |
	n	*o*	*%*	*n*	*o*	*%*	*n*	*o*	*%*	*n*	*o*	*%*
Young	5	28	17.9	1	4	25.0	8	20	40.0	3	8	37.5
Middle	20	33	60.6	1	2	50.0	19	30	63.3	16	25	64.0
Mature	31	43	72.1	2	7	28.6	16	20	80.0	20	24	83.3

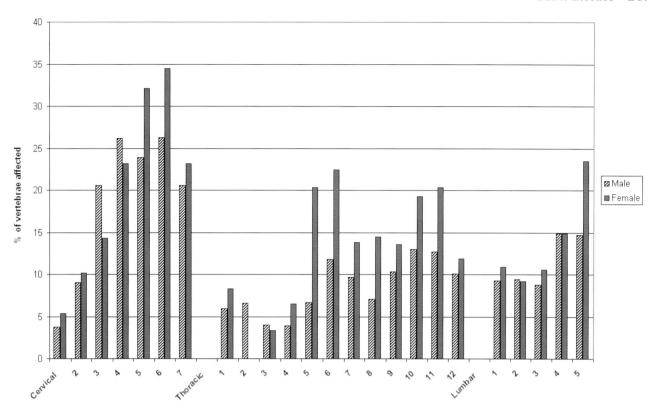

Figure 18.9 Percentage of male and female vertebrae affected by intervertebral osteochondrosis (degeneration of the intervertebral disc)

and Appendix 11, Tables 6–8); only 22.7% of young adults were affected and the lesions were minimal, rising to over 83% in the mature females from Area B and 80% in the Area B mature males, with a corresponding increase in the size of the osteophytes and number of vertebrae affected. Osteophytosis appears to be more widespread and severe in the male spine, although broadly similar percentages of males and females were affected to some extent.

Intervertebral *osteochondrosis*

This condition is closely associated with vertebral osteophytosis and results from pathological changes to the intervertebral disc, which are normally age-related. These lesions ranged from slight pitting or perforations of the vertebral body to complete destruction of the endplate with perforations and

cyst formation. Figure 18.9 shows the location of vertebrae affected by intervertebral osteochondrosis in the Chichester group and the percentage of vertebral bodies affected. The condition occurred predominantly in the middle to lower cervical vertebrae, elements of the spinal column that would have been subjected to mechanical stress because of the mobility of the neck region. Changes were also noted in the middle and lower thoracic and lower lumbar area. However, these were less frequent than in the cervicals. In contrast to vertebral osteophytosis, females were more likely to be affected by intervertebral osteochondrosis than males. Fifty percent (122) of all adults with vertebrae had one or more vertebrae affected, with an increase in numbers of vertebrae involved and increasing severity with age (Table 18.5 and Appendix 11, Tables 9–10). Fewer young adults had any involvement, rising to 75% in the mature females.

Table 18.5 Comparison of individuals affected by intervertebral osteochondrosis of the vertebral bodies between Area A and Area B

| | Area A | | | | | | Area B | | | | | |
| | Males | | | Females | | | Males | | | Females | | |
	n	*o*	*%*	*n*	*o*	*%*	*n*	*o*	*%*	*n*	*o*	*%*
Young	6	28	21.4	2	4	50.0	5	20	25.0	4	8	50.0
Middle	14	33	42.4	0	2	0.0	12	30	40.0	15	25	60.0
Mature	29	43	67.4	3	7	42.9	14	20	70.0	18	24	75.0

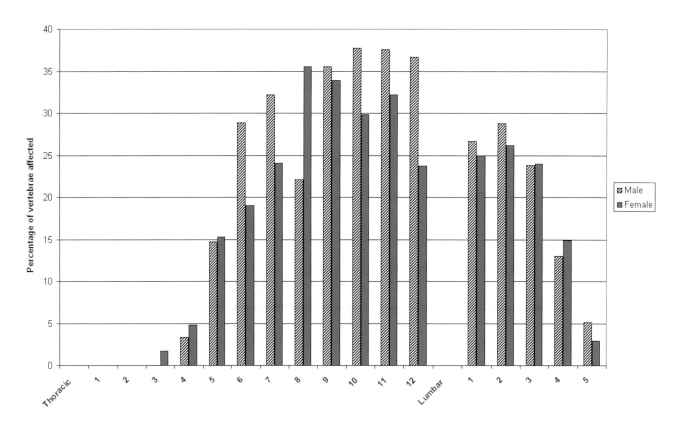

Figure 18.10   Comparison of the prevalence of Schmorl's nodes between males and females

Schmorl's nodes

These are visible as pits or depressions on the surface of the vertebral bodies. They first arise during adolescence and young adulthood and result from the protrusion of the disc into the adjacent body. Their frequency has been used to illustrate the degree to which manual labour was carried out in the past, based upon the suggestion by Schmorl and Junghanns (1971) that they are closely associated with strenuous activity. Sixty-three percent of adult spines were affected to some degree. Figure 18.10 shows the location of these lesions, with the middle to lower thoracic and lumbar vertebrae particularly affected. This is an area, predominantly the 8th–10th thoracic, where increased stress is placed on the intervertebral disc. Sixty-six percent of males had Schmorl's nodes in one or more vertebrae compared with 59% of females. Unlike the degenerative conditions, Schmorl's nodes do not increase in frequency with age; in fact in some cases the prevalence decreases (Table 18.6 and Appendix 11, Tables 11–13). The explanation for this is that they often arise during adolescence whilst the intervertebral disc is still gelatinous and some lesions will remodel in later life. These nodes occur with great frequency in the young adults of both sexes from the Area B phase, suggesting that these individuals were involved in strenuous labour from a young age.

In the medieval period it was customary for boys, in particular, to be apprenticed to craftsmen from fourteen years of age onwards (Orme 2001). However, they might be spared if they had already been occupied in agricultural work for their families since they were twelve years old. Boys might also be engaged as pages in large households when they

Table 18.6   Comparison of the prevalence of individuals with Schmorl's nodes between Area A and Area B

| | Area A | | | | | | Area B | | | | | |
| | Males | | | Females | | | Males | | | Females | | |
	n	*o*	%	*n*	*o*	%	*n*	*o*	%	*n*	*o*	%
Young	19	27	70.3	2	4	50.0	19	21á	90.4	9	9	100.0
Middle	21	32	65.6	0	2	0.0	17	31	54.8	10	25	40.0
Mature	22	41	53.6	2	7	28.6	16	22	72.7	17	24	70.8

Figure 18.11 A monk surreptitiously drinking wine (French, late 13th century, Sloane 2435). Published by permission of The British Library

could be employed in all kinds of activities which involved lifting and carrying heavy loads.

Diffuse idiopathic skeletal hyperostosis (DISH)

DISH is characterised by bony proliferation due to ossification of ligaments on the anterior aspect of the vertebral bodies, leading to eventual ankylosis.

There is also extra bone produced at the sites of tendon and ligament attachment in both spinal and extraspinal locations. This condition is rarely found in individuals below 50 years of age and these are predominantly male – in the region of 70% (Resnick and Niwayama 1988). The incidence of DISH is greatly underestimated by clinicians since the main symptoms are loss of mobility in the spine and stiffness, which can easily be confused with the normal problems of advancing age. The facet joints remain unaffected and spinal rigidity is never complete (Forestier and Lagier 1971). The cause of DISH is unknown, but impaired glucose tolerance, late onset diabetes and obesity would appear to contribute to its development. The prevalence of DISH in elderly diabetics was 21% as opposed to 4% in non-diabetics in one series (Resnick and Niwayama 1983).

DISH is only identified conclusively on the skeleton when four or more consecutive vertebrae are fused (Rogers and Waldron 1995) and this was the case in three individuals, two from Area A and one from Area B (18, 315, 357). However, a further eight had bony proliferation on the spine and other changes which appear to represent early DISH (57, 73, 82, 117, 149, 201, 348, 361). These include hypertrophic new bone on the right side of the vertebral body with a candlewax appearance, associated with enthesopathies at the insertions of tendons and ligaments on the postcranial skeleton and ossification of costal cartilages. Another male (75) was also a bone-producing individual, of mature age, with large osteophytes on the right side of his vertebral bodies but insufficient to place him in the early DISH category. It is becoming apparent from palaeopathological studies that some people have a tendency to produce extra bone, both in the form of marginal lipping on their joints and bony protuberances at the insertions of tendons and ligaments (Rogers el al 1997).

All the individuals with DISH or early DISH at Chichester were male and in the mature age range. There does not appear to be any obvious patterning with regard to their location in the cemetery. The majority of vertebrae affected are the middle to lower thoracic.

The highest number of individuals affected by DISH in the medieval period are those interred in monastic churches (Rogers and Waldron 2001). Roberts and Cox (2003) also found significant differences in the prevalence of DISH between monastic and non-monastic cemeteries. However, it is often difficult to distinguish the burials of members of the monastic order from wealthy members of the laity who have paid to be buried in such institutions rather than in the parish churchyard (Mays 2006). In the medieval period, DISH also appears to be associated with high social status in countries such as Lithuania (Jankauskas 2003). Although St James' Hospital was a quasi-monastic institution many of the inhabitants, particularly in the leprosarium, were brothers leading a relatively sheltered life. Their diet clearly did not consist of the frugal fare generally prescribed for those who have foresworn worldly comforts (Fig 18.11).

Seronegative spondyloarthropathy

The seronegative spondyloarthropathies (SNS) are a group of diseases characterised by erosive joint disease, ossification at sites of tendon, ligament

Figure 18.12 Ankylosing spondylitis, with fusion of almost the entire spine in burial 123, an elderly male

and joint capsule insertion, and a tendency to spine and sacroiliac fusion (Rothschild and Woods 1991). Although multiple genes probably increase susceptibility to these diseases, HLA-B27 is their major genetic determinant. There are now twelve known HLA-B27 subtypes. Serological tests show no evidence of circulating rheumatoid factor. Included in the SNS are ankylosing spondylitis, psoriatic arthritis, the arthritis that sometimes follows inflammatory bowel disease, Reiter's disease or reactive arthropathy and undifferentiated spondyloarthropathy.

Ankylosing spondylitis

This is a chronic inflammatory condition which affects young males in the prime of life almost exclusively. It is characterised by smooth fusion of the sacroiliac joints and spinal column, beginning at the base of the spine. The fused spine may lead to a marked kyphosis of the thoracic spine and a straightening of the normal lumbar lordosis (Böni and Kaganas 1952). Often there is also marked osteoporosis of the vertebral bodies. The small synovial joints articulating the spine and ribs also fuse and the curvature in the upper part of the spine increases until the individual can no longer look straight ahead. Meanwhile the vertebrae become osteoporotic and very brittle. The disease is very painful and at the present time is controlled with anti-inflammatory medication.

In the past, cases of DISH were often mistaken for ankylosing spondylitis so it is notable that there are two definitive cases of AS in the cemetery of St James' Hospital, both located in Area A. Burial 123 is an elderly male with ankylosis of the sixth and seventh cervical as well as the second thoracic to second lumbar vertebrae inclusive (Fig 18.12). There is ossification of ligaments throughout the spine and fusion of the left sacroiliac joint (the right ilium and lower lumbar vertebrae are missing). In the case of burial 12, most of the spine is also missing but the cervical spine is ankylosed from the fifth to seventh cervical vertebrae with the smooth fusion that is so characteristic of the disease. This individual was also an elderly male with osteoarthritis of his upper cervical vertebrae.

Undifferentiated spondyloarthropathy

There was one other convincing case of spondyloarthropathy in Chichester and that was burial 144, an elderly female with smooth fusion of four mid-thoracic vertebrae by smooth syndesmophytes. Another possible case was burial 362, an old male with fusion of one rib to the adjacent transverse process and erosions of some cervical vertebrae. It can be difficult to differentiate between the different conditions that cause erosive/proliferative changes in the spine when only the skeleton is available for study. Both psoriatic and reactive arthritis can cause this type of change.

Gout

This is the most common erosive arthropathy in men aged over 40 years, with a prevalence of about 7% in males over 65 at the present time. It has a long history, first having been described in the 5th century BC by Hippocrates. Gout involves an inflammatory response to the deposition of monosodium urate crystals in the joint leading to an acute arthritis which, if untreated, becomes chronic. It may take up to twelve years for the bony lesions to appear. Normally only one articulation is involved and this is often the first metatarsophalangeal joint. Some people who contract gout are genetically predisposed to having high levels of uric acid circulating in the bloodstream. However, the condition is also associated with obesity, excessive alcohol intake and a high-protein diet.

Three males were affected by gout at Chichester. The first was burial 25, a mature adult from Area A demonstrating erosion and destruction of the left first metatarsophalangeal joint with the classic 'punched-out' appearance that is characteristic of the disease. The second was 128, a middle-aged adult with erosive lesions of both articular surfaces of the first left metatarsophalangeal joint (Fig 18.13). The third, 273, a mature male from Area B, was also suffering from leprosy and metastatic cancer and also had bilateral lesions in the same joint.

Septic arthritis

Infection in the joints can arise either from organisms circulating in the bloodstream or as a result of

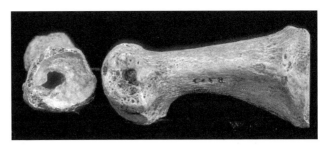

Figure 18.13 Erosive arthropathy of the left first metatarso-phalangeal joint of burial 128 probably due to gout. Photo courtesy of D Ortner

bacteria gaining direct access to the joint following injury. Normal joints in people who are healthy are seldom affected. However, if a joint is penetrated by a foreign body such as a nail or a thorn, infection can result. The latter route is common in leprous individuals who injure their extremities without realising it. Twenty-six individuals suffered from septic arthritis in multiple joints of one or both feet and nine from septic arthritis of one or both hands. Such joint infections can lead to secondary osteoarthritis.

Conclusions

Prevalence rates for osteoarthritis were calculated by Waldron (1995) for a group of over 2,500 pre-medieval, medieval and post-medieval skeletons from different sites in England. Osteoarthritis of the hip shows a decrease through time whereas joint disease of the hand rises concomitantly. The pattern of osteoarthritis in general seen at Chichester is similar to that found in the medieval cemeteries, although secondary OA is more common. This may well be explained by the fact that medieval hospitals not only housed those with leprosy but also the aged and infirm who are more likely to injure themselves. There are also changes secondary to leprosy and this infection explains the high prevalence of joint disease in the hands and feet. Other joint diseases such as ankylosing spondylitis, DISH, seronegative spondyloarthropathy and gout were also found in the burials from the cemetery. They suggest a high degree of discomfort, unalleviated by steroids and modern treatment, even if the sufferers were unlikely to die from the condition.

19 Other pathological conditions *by Frances Lee and Anthea Boylston*

Neoplasia

This category of disease includes tumours and tumour-like cysts, including the cancers, which result from the uncontrolled proliferation of cells. They may be benign or malignant. Tumours in the latter category grow faster and may spread to other tissues of the body, whereas those in the former are slower-growing, well-demarcated and localised to a small area (Roberts and Cox 2003). Physical, chemical and viral agents are all suspected of being carcinogenic (cancer forming). Today, malignant neoplasms in England and Wales account for a quarter of overall mortality, with 15% of sufferers dying before the age of 50 (Horsey 1996). Malignant neoplastic conditions are relatively uncommon in the medieval period and earlier, but are beginning to be found with increasing frequency in post-medieval cemeteries (Ogden *et al* 2005; Brickley *et al* 1999, Brickley *et al* 2006, Arabaolaza *et al* 2006).

Many forms of malignancy are age-related, with most occurring in the elderly. In the medieval period mean age at death was considerably lower than today with fewer people surviving to old age. Furthermore, in the past, the individual with a malignancy would be unlikely to survive sufficiently long for lesions to metastasise, or spread, to bone. Another reason that malignancy is not seen in archaeological samples is that, without routinely X-raying every bone, some lesions will be overlooked. Rothschild and Rothschild (1995) suggest that the pelvic bones and femora, at a minimum, should be X-rayed for a more accurate indication of metastatic disease. One final suggestion is that malignant neoplastic disease may be a relatively recent phenomenon, with certain types proving to be environmentally dependent,

Figure 19.1 (above) Large ivory osteoma on the endocranial surface of the frontal bone of burial 304

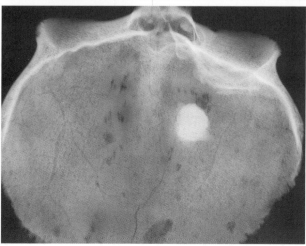

Figure 19.2 (left) X-ray of the ivory osteoma illustrated in Figure 19.1 showing the dense compact bone of which it is composed

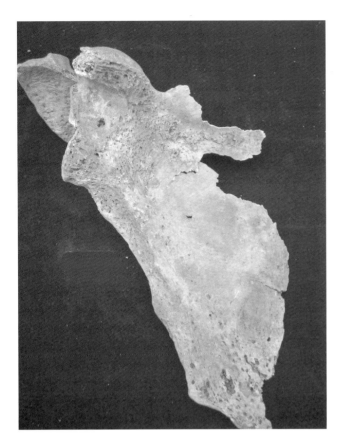

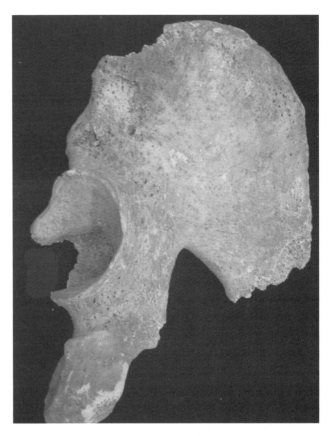

Figure 19.3 A mixture of osteoblastic and osteolytic lesions on the scapula of burial 273, an elderly male. These are indicative of metastatic cancer

Figure 19.4 A mixture of osteoblastic and osteolytic lesions on the pelvic bone of burial 273 showing the widespread nature of the disease

for example, lung cancer and its association with smoking and air pollution. This hypothesis would certainly fit with the appearance of more cases of neoplastic disease in the Victorian period when urbanisation and industrial pollution adversely affected many people's lives.

In total, 28 individuals from Chichester had neoplastic lesions of some description. The most common of these is a button or ivory osteoma. Eighteen individuals from Chichester had one or more osteomas on the cranial vault. These are small, circular projections of bone on the external surface of the cranium. They are benign bone-forming tumours occurring in bones formed by intramembraneous ossification (Steinbock 1976, 327). The frontal and parietal bones are equally affected, with the occipital bone less often. The majority (fourteen) occur in males (only three females and one unsexed individual). Most (twelve) are in the mature adult category with only three in the young or middle adult group. This is consistent with modern clinical studies, which show these tumours are more common in men than women and occur most often in the 4th to 5th decade (Aufderheide and Rodríguez-Martín 1998, 375). Burial 304, a mature female, has a very large ivory osteoma on the endocranial aspect of the left frontal bone measuring 16 × 15mm and 10mm in height (Fig 19.1). An X-ray of the lesion illustrates the density

of the cortical bone in this area compared with the surrounding osseous tissue (Fig 19.2).

Five individuals had postcranial osteomas, involving the humerus, metacarpals, femur and ribs. Burial 2, a mature male, had a small osteoma on the distal end of the shaft of the left humerus, occurring on the posterior lateral aspect. Burial 54 had a benign growth to the right third metacarpal on the lateral aspect. Burial 282 had a swelling to the lateral aspect of the left femoral midshaft. Burial 335, a mature male, had expansion to the distal third of the shaft of the right fourth metacarpal. Burial 357, another mature male, had an exostosis or irregular nodule of new bone on the superior aspect of the shaft of a single left rib.

The most dramatic example of malignant neoplastic disease is burial 273, a mature male, who had two unrelated diseases visible on the skeleton. The pathological lesions to the lower legs and feet are suggestive of leprosy. In addition, there are multiple small lytic foci (bone-destructive) and osteoblastic lesions (bone-producing) distributed widely throughout the skeleton indicating an aggressive neoplastic process (Figs 19.3 and 19.4). Precise diagnosis is rarely possible, but a strong diagnostic option is primary carcinoma of the bronchus with skeletal metastases (Ortner *et al* 1991, 97). An alternative site for the primary is carcinoma of the prostate. Many cancers do not metastasise to bone, but prostatic carcinoma is one of the exceptions and should also be considered as a possibility. It produces both osteoblastic and osteolytic lesions similar to those seen mainly on the cranium, scapulae, ribs and pelvis of burial 273.

Other forms of neoplastic lesion (cancers) are rare in the archaeological record. Burial 108, a mature female, has an osteolytic or bone-destructive lesion to the superior border of the ramus between the coronoid process and the condyle. This has a punched-out appearance with no evidence for any reparative process.

Metabolic diseases

These are the diseases of deficiency and excess of essential vitamins or minerals which produce a reaction in the skeleton, visible as a reduction in bone mass or an increase in bone density.

Rickets

Rickets is a systemic disease of early childhood caused by an inadequate intake of vitamin D. In severe and protracted or recurring cases of rickets characteristic deformities develop. In the adult skeleton, change may have been totally remodelled or simply be visible as bowing and twisting to the long bones. After healing, these bending deformities remain for the rest of the individual's life, while minor bowing can become insignificant. Burial 55, a mature male, has marked anterior bending of the proximal ends of the femora, associated with a marked curvature in the midshaft region of both tibiae, which could be the result of healed rickets. Another adult male (117) has platybasia or a flattening of the base of the skull which may also result from rickets. The weight of the head may cause bone surrounding the foramen magnum of the softened skull base to be altered in shape.

Hyperostosis frontalis interna

Endosteal thickening of the frontal bone, often nodular in appearance, was observed in nine skeletons. This best fits the description of hyperostosis frontalis interna, a relatively common finding in the ageing female skeleton. The alteration is considered to be the result of changes in the pituitary hormone after menopause, with as many as 40% of post-menopausal women affected (Resnick and Niwayama 1988). Of the nine individuals displaying these lesions (54, 77, 184, 223, 230, 260, 264, 284, 288) only seven could be reliably sexed and these were all female. Seven were in the mature age range while burials 184 and 230 were young/middle-aged. The only severe case of hyperostosis frontalis interna was burial 54, an elderly female. Henschen (1949, 85) estimates that the incidence of HFI is in

the region of 100 females to every male, which does not rule out its occurrence in males. As expected, given the profile of the population the majority of HFI lesions were to be found in Area B.

Osteoporosis and osteopenia

Osteoporosis is a condition in which there is imbalance in the processes of bone formation and resorption. The bone matrix is not qualitatively different from normal, it is just reduced in quantity with thinning of the cortical bone and the trabeculae of the spongy bone. Osteoporosis is extremely common, affecting over eight million people in the USA at the present time. Eighty percent of sufferers are women and, of these, the vast majority are elderly. Peak bone mass is attained in both males and females at around the age of 30 years and after that age there is a slow decline, with the loss of around 0.4% of bone mass each year. This is a normal process which accelerates in women, with a much steeper decline after the menopause of about 3% per year. The chief hazards of suffering from osteoporosis are fractures. The most painful of these occur in the spine with microfractures of the trabeculae in the vertebral bodies and subsequent collapse. Other bones which are commonly susceptible to osteoporotic fractures are the forearm bones which often sustain a Colles' fracture of the radius and also the femur, where the femoral neck is a frequent site of trauma at the present time.

Osteoporosis is extremely difficult to identify confidently without measurements of bone mineral content such as dual energy X-ray absorptiometry (DEXA) and/or optical densitometry (Brickley 2000), which was outside the remit of this study. An attempt was made to quantify bone loss by weighing the sacra but unfortunately these were often incomplete or damaged. In addition, 30–50% of bone mineral has to be lost before osteoporosis can be diagnosed on X-ray. As a consequence it was decided to employ the term osteopenia, which implies loss of bone density. Roberts and Cox (2003, 284) suggest that the term osteoporosis should only be used where extreme osteopenia is present and where bone loss is so severe that the individual has experienced an associated fracture.

Sixty-five individuals were recorded as osteoporotic or osteopenic (Table 19.1). Sometimes the bone loss is generalised and involves most of the skeleton, as is the case with senile osteoporosis. Fifty-nine percent (20/34) of all mature women at Chichester were noted to have widespread bone loss, compared with 27% (17/63) of mature males. Clearly, osteopenia is associated with increasing age. Eleven of these older females might also be considered to be osteoporotic. Here the quality of the bone had become so poor that the individual had sustained fractures and microfractures to the vertebrae (30, 108, 160, 223, 137a) and/or Colles' fractures to the lower end of the radius (30, 71, 76, 94, 100, 108, 171

Table 19.1   Number of individuals with osteoporosis or osteopenia by sex and age*

	Juvenile	Young adult	Middle adult	Mature adult	Adult
Male		7 (5)	5 (2)	17 (5)	
Female		3	7 (1)	20 (6)	
Unknown	2	0	1 (1)	2	1
Total	2	10	13	39	1

*Figures in brackets indicate individuals with leprosy or possible leprosy

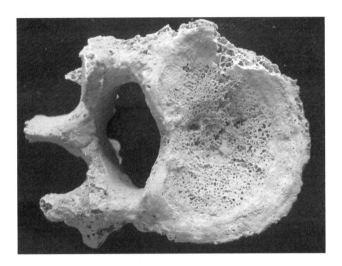

Figure 19.5   Collapsed lumbar vertebra in burial 30, an elderly female with osteoporosis

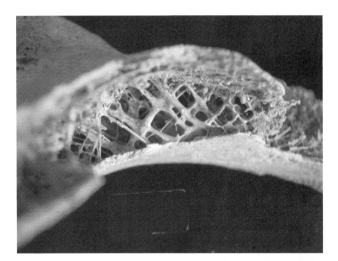

Figure 19.6   Sparse, thickened trabeculae in the pelvic bone of burial 30, indicative of osteoporosis

and 223), sometimes with the ulna also showing evidence of fracture (94). An elderly woman (30) had such severe osteoporosis that one lumbar vertebra showed a compression fracture (Fig 19.5) and her pelvic bones were osteopenic with coarsened trabeculae (Fig 19.6).

In men, osteoporosis can be associated with conditions that affect the production of testosterone, although this is comparatively rare, occurring in conditions such as leprosy and certain forms of cancer. A total of 29 male skeletons had widespread osteopenia, of which 41% (12/29) had some form of leprous involvement. When the levels of males with osteopenia were compared between Area A and Area B, there was seen to be a considerably higher prevalence in the former, with 22% (25/114) involvement compared with 5.4% (4/74) in the latter. Elderly males may also suffer from osteoporosis in extreme old age and this condition may have been responsible for some of the cases seen at Chichester.

In the literature other causes of osteoporosis include resorption of the bone due to lack of use (disuse atrophy), which may occur during chronic diseases. Arnstein (1972) noted that osteoporosis of the appendicular skeleton begins as early as eight weeks after paralysis occurs. Pain, trauma and/or infection with chronic debilitating conditions such as tuberculosis would have predisposed the individual to osteopenia. Six individuals with evidence for tuberculosis had this condition, four with lesions to the spine, one a child with tuberculous dactylitis

and the other an adult with a possible tuberculous lesion of the hip. A further five have inflammatory lesions on the ribs (18, 142, 197, 31, 148) possibly resulting from pulmonary tuberculosis (see Chapter 15). Regional osteopenia was present in three individuals with osteomyelitis, 193, 325 and 343; these individuals would have been unwell with a fever and in considerable pain, very unlikely to have used the affected limb. Burial 217 had some evidence for disuse atrophy of the lower leg. Burial 137a has three of the above features and is severely osteoporotic. The individual is a mature female with evidence for tuberculosis of the spine. She has a Colles' fracture of the forearm and an amputation of the lower leg with removal of the right foot. Localised osteoporosis was seen in the two elderly males with ankylosing spondylitis. In addition to fusion of the vertebral bodies by inflammatory ligamentous ossification, the spine becomes very brittle and osteoporotic in individuals with this condition.

Non-specific indicators of stress in adults

These are minor metabolic disorders manifested by osseous change. They result from the stresses and strains placed on the body during development. They may be due to a variety of causes including nutritional deprivation, disease and parasitic infection. Not all of these indicators are of equal utility and, in general, their greatest interpretative constraint is

Table 19.2 Comparison of the prevalence of *cribra orbitalia* between Area A and B

	Area A			Area B		
	o	*n*	*%*	*o*	*n*	*%*
Male	12	78	15.4	13	66	19.7
Female	3	13	23	21	55	38.2

the generalised nature of the pathological response. Used singly, they mean little but where they occur in large samples they may be used to indicate or highlight the evidence for long-term stress within the community. Enamel hypoplasia has already been discussed in Chapter 13.

Cribra orbitalia

Cribra orbitalia is visible as pitting, or an early 'pepper pot' type lesion, in the roof of the orbit. In arctic and temperate Europe the most likely aetiology is iron deficiency anaemia acquired during childhood. Furthermore, the iron deficiency was probably due to nutritional deficiency and/or intestinal blood loss through chronic parasitic infection (Stuart-Macadam 1982). Macadam also suggests that infectious disease may be a major aetiological factor in the development of iron deficiency anaemia,

although some sources suggest that iron deficiency anaemia may have had the effect of protecting the individual from infectious disease (Larsen 1997b). The bone changes result from the body's attempt to produce red blood cells to counteract the lack of iron. The porotic lesions probably only occur in childhood (Stuart-Macadam 1987a) although they may remain visible on the bone into adulthood. Of the 33 medieval sites studied by Roberts and Cox (2003, 234), an overall prevalence rate was given as 10.82%, with hospital sites having a higher rate of 25.6%. This range is well below the prevalence for Chichester where 29% of skulls (86/298) have lesions on the orbital roofs. The prevalence of *cribra orbitalia* is highest among juveniles and females, suggesting not only that these are the groups most susceptible to developing iron deficiency anaemia, but also that individuals with *cribra orbitalia* were less likely to survive into adulthood. Likewise the increased prevalence in women suggests that anaemia placed women under greater stress, particularly during pregnancy. A higher frequency of *cribra orbitalia* in women has been reported elsewhere, occurring in seven of the nine sites listed by Stuart-Macadam (1985). Another possibility is that those who did survive had the *cribra* remodelled until it was no longer visible. In the children there is no discernible age at which *cribra orbitalia* begins to heal, with both healed and active lesions evident in children from all age groups.

Table 19.3 Ages of those with *cribra orbitalia*

	1.0–2.5	2.5–6.5	6.6–10.5	10.6–14.5	14.6–17.0	Young	Middle	Mature
Area A								
Male						7	4	1
Female						2		
Unknown			1					
Total (A)			1			**9**	**4**	**1**
Area B								
Male						7	4	2
Female						7	5	9
Unknown	7	13	7	7	1	1	0	1
Total (B)	**7**	**13**	**7**	**7**	**1**	**15**	**9**	**12**

Table 19.4 Individuals with both *cribra orbitalia* and enamel hypoplasia

	Young adult	Middle adult	Mature adult	Prevalence	%
Area A					
Male	6	4		10/78	12.8
Female	2		1	3/12	25.0
Total (Area A)	**8**	**4**	**1**	**13/90**	**14.4**
Area B					
Male	5	4	2	11/70	15.7
Female	7	5	6	18/54	33.3
Total (Area B)	**12**	**9**	**8**	**29/124**	**23.3**

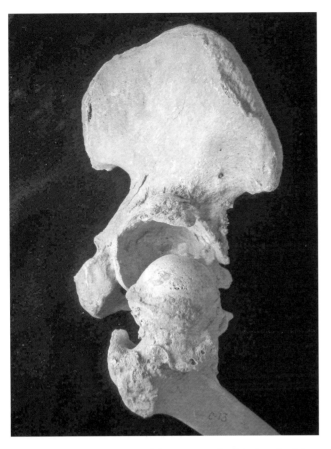

Figure 19.7 Hypertrophic osteoarthritis in the hips of burial 13, possibly secondary to a developmental condition such as Perthes' disease

When the prevalence of *cribra orbitalia* and enamel hypoplasia in the same individual is considered, Area B has almost twice that of Area A, arguing against the case for leprosy affecting the poorest and most nutritionally deprived members of society. Table 19.2 compares the number of individuals with *cribra orbitalia* in the two areas and Table 19.3 illustrates differences between age groups. Table 19.4 records the number of those with both enamel hypoplasia and *cribra orbitalia* present.

Vascular or circulatory disturbances

Perthes' disease

Three individuals exhibit changes to their femoral heads which are compatible with a diagnosis of Perthes' disease. This condition involves disruption of the blood supply to the femoral head epiphysis in childhood, often as a result of trauma. It occurs mainly in young boys between the ages of five and ten years and is often bilateral. The child walks with a characteristic limp. During adolescence the femoral head remodels into a mushroom shape and this leads to a lack of congruence with the acetabulum. Secondary osteoarthritis can occur as early as the age of 30 years. Burials 74 and 98 have enlarged femoral heads with a mushroom appearance, and the femoral neck also appears to be foreshortened. In burial 98 the condition is unilateral while 74 only has the right femur present. Burial 13 has bilateral changes with severe secondary osteoarthritis (Fig 19.7).

Osteochondritis dissecans

This is a localised disorder of the joint surface in which an area of subchondral bone becomes avascular and necrotic, separating to form a loose body in the joint (Adams 1981). It occurs in adolescents and young adults and is more common in males. The precise cause is unknown although impaired blood supply to the affected area has been suggested. There may be some inherent susceptibility to the disease and a familial occurrence has been observed (Stougaard 1964).

Thirty-two individuals, three of whom were adolescents (burials 90, 293 and 319), have some form of *osteochondritis dissecans*, representing 8.3% of the total assemblage. Fifty per cent (16/32) were male compared to 28.1% female and the rest were in the unsexed category. The majority, 40.6% (13/32), were in the mature age group.

Distribution of the lesions is shown in Table 19.5. The knee is a common site for *osteochondritis dissecans*, being affected in 80% of all cases (Roberts and Manchester 2005). Here eleven individuals were involved with seven lesions to the femoral condyles, four to the tibial condyles and one to the patella. The foot would also appear to be a common location with nine individuals affected, the first metatarsal being the most frequent site.

Activity-related injury and its treatment

Burial 18, a mature male, has evidence for a fracture to the spinous process of the first thoracic vertebra. This may be interpreted as the consequence of vertebral trauma at a very young age (Knüsel *et al* 1996, 428). It is associated with a crush fracture

Table 19.5 Location of *osteochondritis dissecans* lesions

Axis	Rib	Distal humerus	Proximal ulna	Distal femur	Proximal tibia	Distal tibia	Patella	Calcaneus	Talus	Other foot bones
1	1	5	1	7	4	4	1	1	1	7

of the fourth thoracic vertebra and severe osteo-arthritic changes throughout the vertebral column. Moreover, fusion of the spinal ligaments from the twelfth thoracic to the second lumbar vertebrae is suggestive of early DISH. Both elbows were affected by severe osteoarthritis due to stress placed on these joints over a prolonged period of time (Jurmain 1976).

The changes visible in the spine of this individual are thought to be activity-related lesions, the result of Schmitt's disease, the juvenile form of 'clay shov-eller's fracture'. This injury is induced by a single episode of overload on the spinous process. Continued movement prevents healing of the fracture. The individual would have had interscapular pain, and discomfort on repeating the movement. These injuries are most often recorded in rural labourers, particularly those shovelling in heavy clay soils, but root pulling, hay pitching, weight-lifting and also falls from a height can produce a similar lesion. Often the individual is tall and so predisposed to back strain. Burial 18 was 1.68m, about average for males from Chichester.

The appearance of the fracture in the first thoracic vertebra suggests that it was produced by an avulsion of the epiphysis of the spinous process and subsequent necrosis of the avulsed fragment. This suggests that the individual sustained the injury in adolescence or early adulthood when his spine was still developing. 'Shoveller's fracture' occurs in indi-viduals performing heavy work but is more common in those who are unaccustomed to the task in hand, as well as in those who are predisposed by an earlier injury. (The above descriptions and discussion are the work of Knüsel *et al* 1996.)

Treatment

It is possible that some form of treatment was practised on fractures in the medieval period, but there is no hard evidence for this. However, the good alignment of some of the fractures perhaps indicates intervention may have occurred. Knüsel and Göggel (1993) suggest some form of reduction and immobili-sation for fractures to the forearms of burial 115. This elderly male has changes resulting from abnormal posture and strenuous use of one lower limb to com-pensate for the other which was severely disabled due to fracture. This individual suffers from lepro-matous leprosy and is of relatively short stature at just over 5ft (158.5cm) tall. He had evidence for five major injuries. These include a Colles' fractures of the right radius with associated subluxation of the distal end of the ulna. The left arm is fractured in the midshaft of the radius and one of the carpal bones in the wrist has a compression fracture, resulting from a crush injury. Both elbows demonstrate soft tissue trauma which would have affected the arterial blood supply. The right femur has a malaligned fracture of the distal end, complicated by osteomyelitic infection (see Fig 17.8). The result is considerable shortening

of the limb illustrative of severe injury to a major weight-bearing bone. The right knee was affected by secondary osteoarthritis, with the body weight having shifted to the medial condyle where there is evidence for a plateau fracture.

Secondary degenerative changes to both hip sockets with polishing of the joint surface indicate that the individual continued to walk. Knüsel and Göggel (1993) suggest the disparity in size and shape of the bones of the lower extremities results from crutch-sustained locomotion. Normal movement of the right knee would have been difficult or impossible and the right limb was used solely as a support structure, the more robust left leg being the weight-bearing limb. The forearms show increased robusticity of the wrist and hand in response to crutch use, with the right side more developed in every respect than the left. The bones of the right wrist show marked osteoarthritic change but it is the pectoral girdle which shows the greatest degree of alteration. The osteoarthritic changes in the shoulder may relate to increased weight-bearing demands, perhaps made more extreme by an inappropriate crutch. The acromial process of the scapula has a humeral facet suggesting that the shoulder was often and repeat-edly under compression in lateral rotation. Such motions are required in crutch-aided locomotion when the person swings the crutch forward in front of him along the floor.

There was evidence for changes to the lumbar spine and sacrum, suggestive of an attempt to stabilise the lower back; less pronounced were changes to the thoracic vertebrae suggesting that his posture was permanently altered by these injuries.

Burial 117, a mature male, has an anterior dislo-cation of the right shoulder joint, associated with an impaction fracture of the right humeral head. The upper arm has become transfixed and it is likely that fusion of the joint could only have occurred in the absence of movement. In all probability, the arm was splinted and held slightly apart from the body.

Amputation

The only case for definite surgical intervention was in context 137, the fill of tomb 65 in Area A2. This contained the fragmentary remains of three indi-viduals; one, an adult female (burial 137a), had evidence of a healed amputation of the lower right leg with the removal of the foot and the distal end of the tibia and fibula (Roberts and Manchester 2005, 123). The limb was considerably shortened and the two bones have fused together during the healing process (Fig 19.8), with no evidence for a joint. The bone is very osteoporotic and atrophied. The individ-ual had clearly survived surgery and lived for some time after the amputation which, in the absence of antibiotics and sterile conditions, was itself an achievement.

The attendant problems of amputation include haemorrhage, shock and sepsis. In the mid-19th

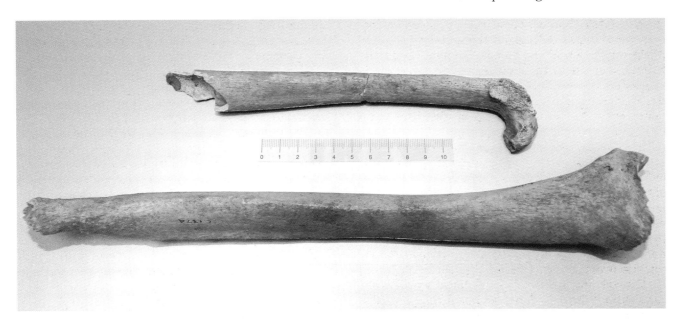

Figure 19.8 Amputation of the right foot of burial 137a just above the ankle (with a normal right tibia for comparison). Photo: Saul Crawshaw

century, mortality rates of up to 60% following amputation were recorded (Graham 1956). Speed in amputation was of the essence. Rogers and Waldron (1986) noted from 18th- to 19th-century Gloucester that there was some relationship between the amputation and the age of the individual. Conditions necessitating amputation in the elderly include gangrene, vascular disorders and tumours. In other age groups, compound fractures leading to osteomyelitis are more likely to have been the cause. In the context of a leprosarium, it might be speculated that this amputation resulted from infection of the foot due to secondary bacterial infection from nerve damage. However, despite being located in Area A2, burial 137a belongs to the latest phase of the site and appears to date from the 17th century, by which time leprosy had disappeared from all but the remotest corners of the British Isles.

Part 4

Discussion

20 Discussion *by Frances Lee and John Magilton*

Introduction

This is very much an interim account of the skeletal remains from St James' Hospital. Future students in Biological Anthropology at Bradford University, where the bones are lodged, will no doubt join those who have contributed, directly or indirectly, to this volume by discovering something new about the assemblage. If nothing else, it is hoped that publication will stimulate further research, not only on this group of skeletons but also on others of its type. It is twenty years since the analysis of the bones first began and, whilst it has been at times an onerous task to attempt to update some of the early work, it is a mark of the progress made within the discipline that such thorough revision has been necessary.

The burial archaeology

The key to section drawings of an excavation of the leper house at New Romney, Kent, carried out in 1959, has as one of its categories 'Graves or other Disturbances' (Rigold 1964, 55, fig 7). This is a reminder that human skeletal remains were until recently largely ignored, even by the more eminent archaeological practitioners of the day, unless the bones were accompanied by grave goods. Whilst the bones themselves are the central part of this report, the archaeological context is not without its interesting features, and it will become more significant as other cemeteries are excavated and broader comparisons become possible, for many of the conclusions from the archaeological study are in reality no more than possible avenues for future research.

The history of the hospital: a summary

The human remains from the hospital are by far the largest published sample to date from a documented English leprosarium and almshouse. Its cemetery is thought to have been in use from the time of the foundation of the hospital early in the 12th century to the mid-17th century or later, by which time the institution was in decline, but the earliest burials appear to lie outside the excavated area. As the hospital was originally founded for eight leper brethren, until late in the 15th century most of the burials were of male inmates, their carers and perhaps occasional benefactors. At some time before the start of the 16th century a change took place and women were formally admitted; in practice, a few women – servants, wives of inmates or benefactresses – were buried in the cemetery before then.

Even before the Reformation it was recognised that the hospital had outlived its original function and by 1594, when we have a list of inmates (Appendix 3 on CD), it had long been an almshouse providing care and sheltered accommodation for the deserving sick poor. By the end of the 17th century it was more or less moribund. The history is described and discussed in Chapter 5 in greater detail.

Leprosy, in the Middle Ages a spiritual contagion inflicted by God on sinners, manifested itself through symptoms caused by *M. leprae,* but not exclusively so. It would be anachronistic to ask whether those (not necessarily physicians) charged with diagnosing *lepra* in the Middle Ages were competent by looking at their success in identifying what is sometimes called Hansen's disease today. Symptoms **resembling** those caused by Hansen's disease were equally valid signs of the spiritual malaise *lepra* and the admission to a leper hospital of an individual with symptoms caused by something other than *M. leprae* would not have been deemed a 'mistake' by contemporaries.

The organisation of the cemetery

The distribution of men, women and children

The organisation of the cemetery is discussed at length in Chapter 7. Whilst some details remains speculative, the demographic and pathological profiles confirm a division into two distinct phases, the leprosarium and the almshouse, with a somewhat disorganised interface, confirming the picture derived from archaeology alone. In the earlier, south-western, part of the cemetery (Area A) 84% (106/126) of the adult burials were male, with almost half of them exhibiting some form of leprous change. Women numbered fourteen in all (11.1%); six of those were secondary (and potentially contemporary with burials in Area B) and only three of them (77, 339 and 365) had any evidence of leprosy. There were no obviously priestly burials in either part of the cemetery and the master may generally have sought and obtained burial at the cathedral.

Area B, the north-eastern part of the cemetery attributed to the almshouse phase, has a more normal population structure with a mortality rate of 40% before adulthood, slightly below average for the historic period. Males still outnumber females throughout, but the percentage of women appears to increase with time. This might be explicable if the changeover to admitting women had been gradual, and in the first instance admission may still have been restricted to those with leprosy but widened to include both sexes. Only 15% of adults buried in the almshouse were leprous, of whom two-thirds were male.

Juveniles could be buried in discrete areas of the cemetery, in particular in the ditches marking its north-eastern boundary, but others, generally the older children, might be buried in columns with the adults. They are not recorded in any of the documentation relating to the hospital and the reason for their presence must remain speculative.

The total cemetery population cannot be estimated with any confidence because we do not know how long inmates survived after admission, how many were accommodated, how many of those associated with the institution sought burial in the cemetery or how big the cemetery was. At a guess, assuming the cemetery to have been rectangular, the excavated sample may represent fewer than half of the original burials. It is possible too that there is another cemetery to be discovered if, for example, the staff were buried apart from the chronically ill.

Special burials

In death, as in life, some people were more equal than others and, as in life, attracted dependants. The two women buried in structure 237/256 were privileged not only to be allowed into what at the time was virtually an all-male cemetery but were honoured after death by those who sought to be buried as closely as possible to them. The same clustering may be observed at the other two 'special' graves and clustering alone points to a fourth focus not far beyond the excavation limits. The seeming lack of organisation in the middle of what was otherwise a fairly regular cemetery is attributable mostly to a period when those with influence were able to obtain burial in areas thought to have a special sanctity. Equally interesting are areas devoid of burials, some of which were access routes or even processional ways. Perhaps the only burial treated differently as a mark of disrespect was the syphilitic individual 277 whose grave was literally set apart from the rest. All the 'special' graves belong with the earlier cemetery, Area A. Hospital life was apparently much more egalitarian under the almshouse regime, perhaps because corrodians, who had obtained sheltered accommodation in return for a one-off payment, were rarely or no longer admitted or, if present, buried elsewhere.

Burial traditions and changes over time

By and large there was little to differentiate the earliest burials from the latest. Nails, interpreted as coffin nails, became commoner with time, but coffins may have been equally common in all periods; it was the method of holding the box together that changed. There was no real difference in laying out

practice between the earliest and latest burials, except that 'ear muffs', at other sites considered an early feature, were commoner in the later part of the cemetery. They may be a regional custom that, with future research, will be found to have spread from a discrete area. 'Grave goods' in the normal archaeological sense were absent apart from a chalk block incised with a cross, although they are occasionally found in contemporary graves elsewhere. Had there been a tradition of interring perishable goods with the deceased it would, of course, be undetectable except in rare circumstances.

The Black Death, a normally catastrophic event, must have impacted on the hospital community but we cannot see it in the burial record. The charnel pit has nothing to do with mass burial. It housed a collection of the larger and more recognisable human bones disturbed from elsewhere, not whole skeletons hurriedly interred. The Reformation, not an event but a process, is equally unrecognisable, and there is nothing physical to distinguish a 'Catholic' early burial from a 'Protestant' later one. The real division, between hospital and almshouse, seems from the historical record to have occurred at the end of the 15th century to reflect local realities.

Women, once they occur in the cemetery, seem to have been treated exactly as their male counterparts and can be distinguished only from their physical remains. Their distribution was random and they were more likely to be in a coffin. Children, especially young children and infants, were often given a separate place of burial, and in that sense discrimination existed, but it may have been no more than a matter of convenience to confine smaller grave pits to a discrete area. The unbaptised should not have found their way into the cemetery at all, but the children buried in the cemetery boundary ditch were by no means all neonates who may have died before baptism.

Most people were buried in winding sheets and coffins. The occasional buckle recovered from the excavation may indicate that a minority were interred with some item of ordinary clothing, although not necessarily worn in its accustomed way. A leather belt around a winding sheet would help to make an awkward parcel easier to handle, for example. Again, one of the exceptions is the woman in structure 237/256 with the pins around her skull. She may have been a religious.

Other uses for the cemetery

A single documentary reference supported by the nature of the pottery seems to indicate that the older part of the cemetery was in use as a garden whilst the rest was still open for burial. If true, it would be unsurprising as cemeteries could be used for a range of unconnected activities ranging from sporting to mercantile. What later became the earliest part of the excavated cemetery had initially contained a lime kiln, so the graveyard cannot have been reserved for interment from the time of the hospital's foundation.

The pathology

Metric and non-metric traits

The study of the metrical and non-metrical variants was largely inconclusive, unsurprisingly since it is becoming evident that these traits have a very complicated pattern of genetic inheritance (Saunders 1989). There is a cluster of burials in the vicinity of two stone-lined tombs and another possible concentration 10m to the north-east that was perhaps intended as a family plot, but the osteology cannot confirm this. The area immediately outside the hospital chapel may have been particularly sought for burial, but as the site of the chapel could not be established, clusters of burials cannot be attributed to a desire for this high-status location.

Dental disease

Dental disease becomes more prevalent with age, as would be expected. Calculus, periodontal disease, caries, abscesses and ante-mortem tooth loss are all commoner in the leprosarium (Area A) than in the almshouse (Area B), whilst women seem to have more teeth affected by caries, abscesses and ante-mortem loss in general. The evidence for dietary differences at the site is shown by the higher amounts of calculus in the leprosarium. Individuals with chronic illnesses were probably given a soft pulpy porridge high in soft carbohydrate, which would have encouraged the build up of plaque and in turn would have led to a rise in periodontal disease. Bony changes in the oronasal region associated with leprosy would have been a rich breeding ground for bacteria, encouraging the build-up of plaque, but a study by Woodward (1995) showed no significant difference in rates of dental disease between leprous and non-leprous groups.

Infectious diseases

Bacterial and viral infections would have accounted for most deaths in the pre-antibiotic era, with about half of the population dying during infancy or childhood (Ortner 2003). Although poor health and inadequate nutrition would have made individuals more susceptible to acute infection and debility, and osteomyelitis and other bone infections are also more common in the nutritionally compromised, acute infections would have resulted in rapid death long before the process had spread to bone, frustrating the medical historian as these diseases killed leaving little trace. Overworked and inadequately fed children living in squalor were more susceptible

to respiratory and gut infections than their earlier rural counterparts.

However, those in the cemetery of St James and St Mary Magdalene are not a representative cross-section of society. As individuals suffering from acute infectious conditions are unlikely to have survived long enough to be admitted, the chronic conditions are a more accurate reflection of the inmates' state of health. Inflammatory lesions present in bone are the result of chronic or sub-acute infections and are not the immediate cause of death. Nor are individuals with chronic disease necessarily those who were perceived as most unhealthy in life (Wood *et al* 1992). A total of 206 individuals show some infectious response in the skeleton and the true count was undoubtedly higher. Over half of those suffering from infectious conditions had specific infections caused by known bacteria, of which leprosy and tuberculosis are the most common. Treponemal disease was also present in at least one notable instance.

Leprosy

Diagnosis was often a religious and legal matter rather than a medical one, and even medieval physicians, who did not properly describe skin lesions, may not have been able to distinguish leprosy from psoriasis, scabies and eczema. Today the differential diagnoses include vitiligo, a skin condition; psoriasis; sarcoidosis; and acquired syphilis (Rubin 1974). There may have been some misdiagnosis and/or diagnostic overlap between leprosy and treponemal disease, with both correctly and misdiagnosed individuals being admitted to leprosaria. Leprosy was also thought to be a venereal disease because it was seen as unclean (Brody 1974, 54), and lepers were alleged to have abnormal sexual desires.

Despite the strict life, hospitals did provide food, shelter and clothing. As begging was acceptable, even lepers severely crippled through illness could contribute to the community's economy. The able-bodied looked after the others and did as much physical work (eg gardening) as their condition allowed, selling the produce for gain. Fear of disease was not sufficient to prevent the elderly and generally infirm from seeking admission, but they were doubtless isolated from the chronically ill and, in the early Middle Ages, the mechanisms of infection were misunderstood: leprosy was a visitation from God, not something to be caught.

Of the 384 or so skeletons excavated, at least 75 (19.5%) exhibited changes compatible with leprosy. Over 83% of all burials with evidence for leprosy were male, compared with 13.3% of women. The predominance of male lepers over female ones is explained by the original foundation being for men only.

The age of onset of leprosy is impossible to determine from those buried at St James' – we know only when they died. Nor is it possible to establish the effect of leprosy on longevity as specific selection

UNIVERSITY OF WINCHESTER
LIBRARY

Table 20.1   The number of men with leprosy as a percentage of the total for each age group, comparing the two areas of the cemetery (excluding the few whose age could be tied down no more closely than 'adult')

Area	Young men			Mid-adult men			Mature men			Total		
	n	*o*	*%*	*n*	*o*	*%*	*n*	*o*	*%*	*n*	*o*	*%*
A	21	26	81	18	30	60	10	39	26	49	95	52
B	3	22	14	2	30	7	4	24	17	9	76	12
Total	**24**	**48**	**50**	**20**	**60**	**33**	**14**	**63**	**22**	**58**	**171**	**32**

processes were in operation before admission to the hospital and cemetery could take place. Recent research suggests that the incubation period for the disease may not be as long as previously thought; indeed infants may have been able to contract the disease and intrauterine transmission may have been a possibility. Many references give the impression that children with leprosy were rare but this is far from the case, although it is rare in infants (Bryceson and Pfaltzgraff 1973, 30). No children from Chichester had skeletal changes resulting from leprosy. This is not only because of the long incubation period but also the result of an admissions policy that initially seems to have excluded children. Historical records suggest that generally children were admitted to leprosaria either alone or with parents. Many may not have had the infection upon admission, but were admitted with a leprous parent so as not to become orphans, only to become infected at a later date (Richards 1977).

Skeletal changes due to leprosy have already been discussed. There is an under-representation of individuals with leprosy in the skeletal record because osseous changes do not usually occur in the tuberculoid and early lepromatous stages. Anaesthesia and nerve damage occur early on in tuberculoid leprosy but the osseous changes are non-existent or at best minimal. It is therefore almost certain that most of those with tuberculoid leprosy and many with early lepromatous leprosy cannot be identified. Consequently, the potential through skeletal study to differentiate between those at different places on the immune spectrum is low. Hence questions about transmission of the disease and its impact on the community cannot be answered. The most mutilating and infectious form of leprosy (lepromatous) until recent years would have been the most common form (Pálfi 1991). Changes to the facial region occur only in lepromatous leprosy. Thirty-seven individuals had definite rhinomaxillary syndrome (RMS) with a further 20 having changes that are considered to be early RMS.

Lepers' ages at death

If we look at the ages at death of men in Area A, the cemetery when the hospital was to all intents male-only, there is an interesting contrast between the totals for all male burials and those for men afflicted with leprosy. By age alone, mature men of

46 years and over are the commonest (39/95; 41%), followed by males of 30–45 years (30/95; 31.6%), then young men of 18–30 years (26/95; 27.4%) and finally two subadults of 8–17 years. In other words, the older you were, the more likely you were to be in the hospital cemetery, but men of all ages were fairly evenly represented.

If only lepers from Area A are considered, the result is somewhat different (Table 20.1). Of the young men, 21 out of 26 (81%) were known or probable lepers and amongst the middle adults eighteen out of 30 (60%) had leprosy. Amongst the elderly only ten out of 39 (26%) had leprosy, even though a figure of at least 60% would be expected.[1] We may be seeing a conflation of two sets of figures, those for the leper hospital as originally founded and those for when it was *de facto* an almshouse for old men, although the latter are not totally disproportionately represented amongst the latest burials.

If we ignore the mature men, the prevalence of leprous skeletons works out at 69.6%, virtually identical to the 70% figure claimed for Naestved in Denmark (Møller-Christensen 1978). At Chichester the leper's prospects of surviving into the over-45 age group were less than those of dying before he reached thirty. Whilst we cannot assess the survival rate after diagnosis, it is a reasonable assumption that only those with the disease in an advanced and disfiguring form would normally have sought and gained hospital admission.

Of the men in Area B to whom an age could be assigned more closely than simply 'adult', only 12% (9/76) had leprosy, as opposed to seven women. The sample is too small for any firm conclusions to be drawn but, broadly speaking, the likelihood of suffering from leprosy seemed to be equally great for the oldest individuals whereas in Area A this was not the case.

The decline in leprosy by the later medieval period is well demonstrated by the hospital cemetery. In the earlier period, the leprosarium (Area A) has a significant clustering of leprous individuals with a total of 60 (49%) adults exhibiting some form of leprous change, while in the almshouse (Area B) there were only 24 (15%) (Table 7.1). Whilst it is difficult to argue that there is a significant change in the form of leprosy between the leper house and almshouse phases, it must be remembered that the lesions recorded are those present at the time of death rather than at the time of entry to the institution. The degree to which the inmate was affected, however, varies significantly between the two areas. Whereas in the leprosarium the majority of individuals have lesions compatible with a diagnosis of lepromatous leprosy, in the almshouse a higher proportion have possible or early rhinomaxillary changes and changes to the hands and feet.

The reasons for the decline in the prevalence of leprosy are not fully understood but attempted segregation, even if effective, is unlikely to have halted transmission. In the early stages of lepromatous leprosy there would be little nerve involvement and skin lesions are rarely noticed. Clinically, the disease would present itself as nasal congestion and oedema or swelling of the lower legs (Jopling and McDougall 1988). The most highly infectious individuals may have remained undetected in the community for some time and may well have hidden their symptoms as best they could for fear of being ostracised. Anaesthesia and nerve damage, on the other hand, occur early in tuberculoid leprosy. Detection through pigmentation change to the skin and lack of sensation to the extremities may have led to an early diagnosis.

The historical record confirms that segregation was neither effective nor important. During much of the Middle Ages leprosy was seen as a moral and spiritual contagion rather than a physically transmissible disease. The role of the leprosarium was to pray for founders and benefactors, not to contain infection. Segregation was not enforced; patients could receive visitors and were allowed home to their spouses. Wealthy lepers frequently retired to homes in the countryside, and the final sanction against hospital inmates for misbehaviour was expulsion. As alms gathering was an important source of income for hospitals, some contact with the general public was unavoidable unless the activity was restricted to proctors. Lepers not in hospitals had no alternative but to solicit alms personally.

The Black Death may have accelerated the decline in the disease as lepers were susceptible to plague because their immune systems were compromised. In addition, the reduction in total population may have reduced the potential for leprosy to spread. Richards (1977) suggests that lepers would also have been at risk financially, as they were dependent upon charity and were likely to suffer as a result of the economic recession following the plague. However, the same financial hardships would have applied to all hospital inmates. Those who survived the Black Death may have enjoyed a better standard of living as the resources of the countryside had a much smaller population to support.

The causes for the decline and eventual elimination of leprosy during the later medieval period in large parts of Britain were clearly multifactoral. Alterations may have occurred in the bacterium. However, social and environmental changes were also important (Roberts and Manchester 2005). Richards (1977) suggest that by the 16th century the disease was virtually non-existent and was probably rare in the 15th century. This decline coincides with a concurrent increase in tuberculosis, giving rise to the suggestion that tuberculosis may have afforded a degree of cross-immunity against leprosy as the two bacteria are closely related (Chaussinand 1948; Manchester 1991). Indeed today the BCG vaccine, used to prevent tubercular infection, is also found to give some protection against leprosy. Mathematical modelling by Leitman *et al* (1997) has also suggested that tuberculosis could have contributed to the decline of leprosy if the 'reproductive rate of leprosy was low'. Most tuberculous individuals in the cemetery occur in the later period, when there is a significant decline in the number of those with leprosy, apparently lending support to this theory. Other authors argue, however, that the fact that around 26% of those with leprosy in third world countries die as a result of their intercurrent tuberculous infection, mitigates against the argument for cross-immunity (Donahue *et al* 2005). Indeed, both leprous and tuberculous DNA were found by these authors during their analysis of skeletons from a variety of sources dating from the Roman period to the 15th century. It is evident that the debate about cross-immunity between leprosy and tuberculosis and its contribution to the decline in leprosy in late medieval Europe will continue for the foreseeable future.

TB and chronic diseases

Tuberculosis would have affected children and young adults in particular. Although only a handful of tuberculous individuals were recorded from the site, it is estimated that as few as 3–5% of sufferers would have presented with skeletal lesions (Resnick 1995). If these prevalence rates for skeletal involvement are accurate then, potentially, up to 180 individuals from Chichester could have been infected with TB. What is certain is that the disease would have had a tremendous impact socially and economically in the past. Unlike leprosy, it could be and often was fatal.

In Area A there were only two definite cases of tuberculosis, 53 and 331, both of them in the later part of the early cemetery (Area A2) and the former, 53, was a secondary burial within it; burial 137a, also found in this area, was associated with a 17th-century pottery sherd and is therefore also late in date. As modern clinical studies have shown that TB was the main cause of death in leper hospitals before the advent of antibiotics, an overlap between the two infections might have been expected in Area A. In all, seven skeletons from Area A were found to have rib lesions, five of which were in individuals also suffering from leprosy (8, 26, 31, 341, 365). Of the five, two (341, 365) were primary burials from the earliest cemetery (Area A1) and three were secondary burials from its later phase (Area A2). In Area B all the individuals with spinal lesions that could be caused by TB were from its later part, Area B2, reinforcing the suggestion that the disease became commoner in an era when, for whatever reason, leprosy was in retreat.

The study of the children showed that almost a quarter of the juvenile population had some evidence for chronic disease including tuberculosis, scurvy and rickets. Moreover the growth profiles also showed them to be disadvantaged, with stature lagging behind that of normal, healthy children. Poor health combined with inadequate or below-standard nutrition would all have been causative factors. It is likely that many children were admitted with sick parents, later succumbing to disease.

Stress indicators

Most serious metabolic disorders, and indeed the minor or non-specific stress indicators, were found mainly in the almshouse cemetery, Area B. These results again reflect the known history of the site rather than an increased susceptibility of the population to environmental stress. Area A has a lower rate of metabolic disease simply because its occupants were (mainly) the leper brethren, whereas the almshouse admitted both sexes and all ages with a wide variety of diseases, including vitamin deficiencies and severe anaemia. Moreover, many of these diseases predominantly affect the developing skeleton, and the leprosarium has very few subadults. *Cribra orbitalia,* often a consequence of malnourishment in childhood, may well be remodelled in later life. Interestingly the condition, frequently associated with anaemia, has a lower prevalence rate in the leprosarium. This is in direct contrast to Jopling's (1984) findings which suggest that lepromatous leprosy is frequently associated with mild anaemia.

Fractures

Many fractures were probably attributable to poor living conditions: low lighting and overcrowding would have increased the susceptibility to falls (Judd and Roberts 1998). Lepers were particularly at risk as a result of anaesthesia and sensory deficiencies. The claw hand would make the individuals less likely to break a fall successfully. The drop foot would have made the individual clumsier and therefore likely to trip (Judd and Roberts 1998), whilst eye infection impaired vision. Modern clinical data suggest that 30–35% of leprosy patients are susceptible to blindness, with an increase with age and length of time the disease is present. A third of long bone fractures were associated with lepromatous changes and these individuals would have been more susceptible to accidental injury.

Ante-mortem bone injury has also been used to suggest that the men of this community led physically active lives. Richards (1977) suggests that most leper hospitals in the earlier period owned land and farms that would have been tended by healthy members of the community and paid servants. Few of the lepers would have been fit enough to work and initially there would have been sufficient income to hire labour. However, by the 14th century, availability and cost of labour and the impecunious state of most hospitals resulted in healthy brothers and sisters being permitted to work for a living; many of these may have been relatives of the lepers (Richards 1977, 36).

Almost three-quarters of all fractures occurred in males and these were frequently more severe than those found in females. The less infirm inmates may have assisted in the maintenance of the hospital through agriculture and domestic labour, and a proportion of fractures would have resulted from these activities, mostly from accidental falls. As expected, the older the individuals the more likely they were to have fractured one or more bones, and the bedridden would have suffered disuse atrophy and osteoporosis. A comparison of fracture rates with other urban sites in Britain noted that not only did Chichester have a higher rate of long bone fracture but the prevalence of soft tissue trauma to areas such as the ankle joint was also higher. Osteoporosis was found to predispose the bones to injury, with 40% of all those with fractures having some degree of osteoporosis or osteopenia. This condition is not just found in post-menopausal women, but in other members of the group who would not normally be expected to be susceptible. Poor health and malnutrition may have been a factor. Nine individuals had evidence for multiple fractures and at least three must have been admitted as a result of these injuries and their inability to care for themselves. These include burial 137a with evidence for a lower leg amputation, 115 with a fractured femur and associated infection, and 98 with multiple fractures, particularly to the upper body.

Degenerative joint disease

Osteoarthritis and degenerative joint disease follow a similar pattern to other medieval sites in Britain, but have a noticeably higher prevalence rate. There is also a clear and expected increase in prevalence with age, with over half of the mature adults having at least one joint affected. Osteoarthritis was not uncommon in the past but compared to the present time there was considerably more involvement of the upper limb and hand. This is particularly marked in the male skeleton and suggests that these individuals were carrying out heavy labour, wrist fractures and osteoarthritis of the hip being more common in rural populations. Damage to the ankles and feet was most often seen in males and this is primarily due to secondary leprous involvement. Other joint diseases included DISH, which was present in three individuals, with early lesions in a further eight. This is considered to be a condition found in overweight mature males. In some reports (eg Rogers and Waldron 2001), it has been suggested that as these individuals were well nourished they were from higher social backgrounds. If true, it might be argued that the sufferers of DISH at Chichester were benefactors or other wealthy individuals paying for their place in the burial ground. The presence of gout in two individuals from Area A (25 and 128) and one from Area B (273) might also have a similar interpretation, gout having a close association with a high-protein diet and rich living. All three were mature males and two had leprosy.

Many of the individuals would have been seriously disabled and unable to care for themselves. These include the more mutilated leprous individuals. Skeleton 13 had severe secondary osteoarthritis to the hips resulting in the individual being forced into a sitting position, whilst skeleton 14, an adult male with the lower trunk and lower legs only present, had severe osteoarthritis of the left wrist and knee, suggesting the possible use of a crutch, or stick. Another, a mature male (115), had multiple fractures in addition to suffering from leprosy. There had been fractures of the left and right radii with secondary osteoarthritis of both wrists. The distal end of the right femur was badly distorted by osteoarthritis secondary to trauma, with associated osteomyelitis. The individual had continued to walk by using a crutch (Knüsel and Göggel 1993).

Evidence for treatment is rarely seen in archaeological populations. Skeleton 117 had a septic arthritis of the right shoulder with bony ankylosis and the joint had clearly been immobilised, suggesting the use of some form of splint. Burial 137a, a mature female, had been interred late in the life of the cemetery, although found at the western end. She had not only suffered from tuberculosis but had survived an amputation of the right foot. Osteoarthritis in her right elbow joint and wrist, and changes to the scapula, suggest that this elderly woman, despite losing her foot, had kept some degree of mobility by use of a crutch.

Conclusions

At least 384 skeletons were excavated from the hospital cemetery of St James and St Mary Magdalene, of which nearly 20% had some lesions associated with leprosy and a further 3–13% had non-specific infections whose distribution suggested early leprous changes. The site could clearly be divided into two areas. The first was the burial ground of the leper hospital with predominantly adult male burials of which 43% had some change resulting from leprosy. The almshouse phase had a more normal population structure with men, women and children present and only 20% of adult burials affected by leprosy. Whilst there appears to be a sig-

nificant change in the pattern of disease over the period in which the cemetery was in use, this is felt to reflect changes in the institution rather than the way in which diseases evolved. In the earlier period the admissions policy was confined to males afflicted with leprosy, many of whom may have suffered from the disease for many years. The diseases present in the leprosarium reflect this, representing many of the conditions that we normally associate with an aging population. Some of these are simply due to an active life and include degenerative and osteoarthritic conditions. However, there are also many individuals with fractures, dental disease, osteoporosis, neoplastic and metabolic conditions such as *hyperostosis frontalis interna* and DISH that are most common in the elderly.

In the later period, after refounding, a much broader range of conditions appears including tuberculosis (rare in the earlier period), the more severe congenital abnormalities, fractures and metabolic conditions such as scurvy and rickets. There is scant evidence for treatment apart from possible reduction and splinting of fractures. The function of the almshouse was to provide sheltered accommodation for the infirm rather than treatment for the infirmity.

The decline in leprosy is well illustrated at Chichester. Not only do sufferers decline in numbers in the later parts of the cemetery but the degree to which the skeleton was affected also lessens, with only a handful of skulls exhibiting definite rhinomaxillary syndrome in the almshouse phase. Although there is a significant increase in tuberculosis in the later phase, this most probably reflects the change in admissions policy rather than any connection between the two diseases. The idea that leprosy declined as a direct result of the rise in tuberculosis cannot be demonstrated at this site.

Perhaps the most disappointing and yet significant fact to emerge from this study was the inability conclusively to differentiate high-resistant leprosy (TL) from low-resistant leprosy (LL) in the absence of rhinomaxillary change, although there may be some indication from the presence or absence of symmetrical lesions in the upper and lower limbs. Without a precise differential diagnosis, we are unlikely fully to comprehend the decline in leprosy as an infectious disease.

Notes

1. We can look at the Area A burials of old men by period. They form a roughly a third of the earliest burials, around a quarter of intermediate ones and two-fifths of the latest.

Bibliography

Adams, J C, 1981 *Outline of Orthopaedics*. Edinburgh: Churchill Livingstone

Addy, S O, 1895 *Household Tales*. London: David Nutt

Agarwal, R P, 1980 Pattern of bone injuries in a hill area, Pauri-Garhwal, *J Indian Med Assoc,* **74**, 65–6

Andersen, J, 1969 *Studies in the Medieval Diagnosis of Leprosy in Denmark*. Copenhagen: Costers Bogtrykkeri

Andersen, J G, & Manchester, K, 1987 Grooving of the proximal phalanx in leprosy: a palaeopathological and radiological study, *J Archaeol Sci,* **14**, 77–82

Andersen, J G, & Manchester, K, 1988 Dorsal tarsal exostoses in leprosy: a palaeopathological and radiological study, *J Archaeol Sci,* **15**, 51–6

Andersen, J G, & Manchester, K, 1992 The rhino-maxillary syndrome in leprosy: a clinical, radiological and palaeopathological study, *Internat J Osteoarchaeol,* **2**, 121–9

Andersen, J G, Manchester, K & Ali, R S, 1992 Diaphyseal remodelling in leprosy: a radiological and palaeopathological study, *Internat J Osteoarchaeol,* **2**, 211–19

Andersen, J G, Manchester, K, & Roberts, C, 1994 Septic bone changes in leprosy: a clinical, radiological and palaeopathological review, *Internat J Osteoarchaeol,* **4**, 21–30

Anderson, S, 1996 Leprosy in a Medieval Churchyard in Norwich, *Proceedings from the First Annual Meeting of the Osteoarchaeology Research Group*. Oxford: Oxbow Books, 31–7

Anderson, S (ed), 1998 *Current and Recent Research in Osteoarchaeology*. Proceedings of the Third Annual Meeting of the Osteoarchaeology Research Group. Oxford: Oxbow

Arabaolaza, I, Ponce, P, & Boylston, A, 2007 Skeletal analysis, in J Adams and K Colls (eds), '*Out of darkness, cometh light': Life and Death in 19th Century Wolverhampton. Excavation of the Overflow Burial Ground of St Peter's Collegiate Church, Wolverhampton 2001–2002*. Birmingham Archaeology Monograph Series, **3**. BAR Brit Ser, **442**. Oxford: Archaeopress, 25–38

Arnstein, A R, 1972 Regional osteoporosis, *Orthop Clin North America*, **3**, 585

Atkins, P J, 1992 White poison? The social consequences of milk consumption, 1850–1930, *Soc Hist Med*, **15**, 207–26

Atkins, R, & Popescu, E, 2005 Archaeological Excavations along the A16/A158 Partney By-Pass, Lincolnshire. Cambridge: Cambridgeshire County Council

Atkins, R, & Popescu, E, in prep. The Hospital of St Mary Magdalen, Partney, Lincolnshire. *Medieval Archaeology*

Aufderheide, A, & Rodríguez-Martín, C, 1998 *Cambridge Encyclopedia of Human Paleopathology*. Cambridge: University Press

Aviv, R I, Rodger, E, & Hall, C M, 2002 Craniosynostosis, *Clin Radiol,* **57**, 93–102

Ayers, B, 1990 Norwich, *Current Archaeology,* **122**, 56–9

Baines, E, 1835 *History of Cotton Manufacture in Great Britain*

Barber, B, Chew, S, Dyson, T, & White, B, 2004 *The Cistercian Abbey of St Mary Stratford Langthorne, Essex: Archaeological Excavations for the London Underground Limited Jubilee Line Extension Project*. MoLAS Monograph, **18**, London: Museum of London Archaeological Service

Barber, L, & Sibun, L, 1998 The medieval hospital of St Nicholas, Lewes, East Sussex: excavations 1994. Archaeology South-East draft report 1994/148

Barker, E E, 1949 Sussex Anglo-Saxon Charters part III, *Sussex Archaeol Collect,* **88**, 51–113

Barnes, E, 1994 *Developmental Defects of the Axial Skeleton in Paleopathology*. Colorado: University Press of Colorado

Barton, R P E, 1979 Radiological changes of the paranasal sinuses in leprosy. *J Laryngol Otol,* **93**, 597–600

Bass, W M, 1981 *Human Osteology: a Laboratory and Field Manual of the Human Skeleton*. Missouri: Archaeological Society

Bassett, S (ed), 1992 *Death in Towns. Urban Responses to the Dying and the Dead, 100–1600*. Leicester: University Press

Batman, S, 1581 *The Doome Warning all the Men to Judgment*. London: Ralphe Nubery

Bayliss, A, Shepherd Popescu, E, Beavan-Athfield, N, Bronk Ramsey, C, & Cook, G T, 2004 The potential significance of dietary offsets for the interpretation of radiocarbon dates: an archaeologically significant example from medieval Norwich, *J Arch Sci,* **31**, 563–75

Bennett, K A, 1965 The aetiology and genetics of wormian bones, *Amer J Phys Anthropol*, **33**, 255–66

Bennike, P, Lewis, M, Schutkowski, H, & Valentin F, 2005 Comparisons of child morbidity in two contrasting medieval cemeteries from Denmark, *Amer J Phys Anthropol*, **128**, 734–46

Berry, A C, & Berry, R J, 1967 Epigenetic variation in the human cranium, *J Anat,* **101**, 361–79

Bhutani, L K, 1977 An ancient Briton adds to the story of leprosy, *Internat J Leprosy,* **45**, 66–7

Binford, C H, & Meyers W M, 1976 Diseases caused by mycobacteria, leprosy, in C H Binford & D H

Connor (eds), *Pathology of Tropical and Extraordinary Diseases*, vol 1. Washington, DC: Armed Forces Institute of Pathology, 205–25

Binski, P, 1996 *Medieval Death: Ritual and Interpretation*. London: British Museum Press

Bishop, M, 1970 *The Middle Ages*. New York: American Heritage Press

Bishop, M W, 1983 Burials from the cemetery of the Hospital of St Leonard, Newark, Nottinghamshire, *Trans Thoroton Soc Nottinghamshire*, **87**, 23–35

Bishop, N, & Fewtrell, M, 2003 Metabolic bone diseases of prematurity, in F Glorieux, J Pettifor & M Jüppner (eds), *Pediatric Bone: Biology and Diseases*. New York: Academic Press, 567–81

Blomefield, F, 1769 *An Essay towards a Topographical History of the County of Norfolk*. London: Fersfield

Boddington, A, 1980 A Christian Anglo-Saxon graveyard at Raunds, Northamptonshire, in P Rahtz, T Dickinson and L Watts (eds), *Anglo-Saxon Cemeteries 1979*. BAR Brit Ser **82**. Oxford: British Archaeological Reports, 373–82

Boddington, A, 1996 *Raunds Furnells: The Anglo-Saxon Church and Churchyard*, English Heritage Archaeological Report, **7**. London: English Heritage

Böni, A, & Kaganas, G, 1952 Ankylosing spondylitis: symptomatology and treatment, *Documenta Rheumatologica*, **3**

Boocock, P, Roberts, C, & Manchester, K, 1995a Maxillary sinusitis in medieval Chichester, England, *Amer J Phys Anthropol*, **98**, 483–95

Boocock, P, Roberts, C, & Manchester, K, 1995b Prevalence of maxillary sinusitis in leprous individuals from a medieval leprosy hospital, *Internat J Leprosy*, **63**, 265–8

Bown, J, & Stirland, A, forthcoming *Criminals and Paupers: Excavations at the Site of the Church and Graveyard of St Margaret in Combusto, Norwich, 1987*, East Anglian Archaeol

Boyle, D, Gerberich, S G, Gibson, R W, Maldonado, G, Robinson, R A, Martin, F, Renier, C, & Amandus, H, 1997 Injury from dairy cattle activities, *Epidemiology*, **8**, 37–41

Boylston, A, in prep Joint disease, in D Hurst (ed), *The excavations at Hereford Cathedral in 1993*

Brickley, M, 2000 The diagnosis of metabolic disease in archaeological bone, in Cox & Mays (eds) 2000, 183–98

Brickley, M, Berry, H, & Western, G, 2006 The people: physical anthropology, in M Brickley, S Buteux, J Adams & R Cherrington (eds), *St Martin's uncovered: investigations in the churchyard of St Martin's-in-the-Bull Ring, Birmingham, 2001*. Oxford: Oxbow, 90–151

Brickley, M, Mays, S, & Ives, R, 2005 Skeletal manifestations of vitamin D deficiency osteomalacia in documented historical collections, *Internat J Osteoarchaeol*, **15**, 389–403

Brickley, M, Miles, A, & Stainer, H, 1999 *The Cross Bones Burial Ground, Redcross Way, Southwark,* London. Archaeological excavations (1991–1998) for the London Underground Ltd Jubilee Line. MoLAS Monograph, **3**. London: Museum of London Archaeological Service

Bridges, P, 1991 Degenerative joint disease in hunter gatherers and agriculturalists from the South Eastern United States, *Amer J Phys Anthropol*, **85**, 379–91

Brody, S N, 1974 *The Disease of the Soul: Leprosy in Medieval Literature*. New York: Cornell

Brooks, S, & Suchey, J M, 1990 Skeletal age determination based on the os pubis: a comparison of the Acsádi-Nemeskéri and Suchey-Brooks methods, *Human Evol*, **5**, 227–38

Brothwell, D R, & Browne S, 1994 Pathology, in Lilley *et al* (eds) 1994, 457–94

Brothwell, D R, 1981 *Digging Up Bones*. 3rd edn. London: British Museum (Natural History)

Brothwell, D, & Powers, R, 1968 Congenital malformations of the skeleton in earlier man, in *The Skeletal Biology of Earlier Human Populations*, **8**. Symposium of the Society for the Study of Human Biology. Oxford: Pergamon Press, 173–203

Browne, S G, 1977 *Leprosy in England*. Kettering: Green

Brubaker M L, Meyers W M, & Bourland J, 1985 Leprosy in children one year of age and under, *Internat J Leprosy*, **53**, 517–23

Bruce-Mitford, R L S, 1976 The chapter house vestibule graves at Lincoln, in E Emmison & R Stephens (eds), *Tribute to an antiquary*. London: Leopard's Head Press

Bruintjes, T J D, 1990 The auditory ossicles in human skeletal remains from a leper cemetery in Chichester, England, *J Archaeol Sci*, **17**, 627–33

Bryceson, A, & Pfaltzgraff, R E, 1973 *Leprosy for Students of Medicine*. Edinburgh: Churchill Livingstone

Buckland, P C, Magilton, J R, & Hayfield, C, 1989 *The Archaeology of Doncaster*, **2**. BAR Brit Ser **202**, 1 and 2. Oxford: British Archaeological Reports

Busch, H M, Cogbill, T H, Landercasper, J, & Landercasper, B O, 1986 Blunt bovine and equine trauma, *J Trauma*, **26**, 559–60

Butler, L A S, 1987 Medieval urban religious houses, in J Schofield & R Leech (eds), *Urban Archaeology in Britain*. London: Council for British Archaeology Research Report, **61**, 167–76

Butler, L A S, 1993 The archaeology of urban monasteries in Britain, in Gilchrist & Mytum (eds) 1993, 79–86

Caffey, J, 1978 *Pediatric X-Ray Diagnosis*. Chicago: Tear Book Medical Publishers, Inc.

Cailliet, R, 1995 *Low Back Pain Syndrome* 5th edn. Philadelphia: FA Davis Co.

Cardy, A, 1997 The human bones, in Hill (ed) 1997, 519–62

Carlin, M, 1989 Medieval English hospitals, in Granshaw & Porter (eds) 1989, 21–39

Carter, C O, 1971 *Incidence and aetiology*, in A P Norman (ed), *Congenital Abnormalities in Infancy*, 2nd edn. London: Blackwell, 1–24

Caruth, I, & Anderson, S, 1997 *St Saviour's Hospital, Bury St Edmunds (BSE 013): a report on the archaeological excavations 1989–1994*. Suffolk County Council unpublished report 97/20

Carver, M O H (ed), 1980 *Medieval Worcester An Archaeological Framework. Trans Worcestershire Archaeol Soc* 3rd Ser, **7**

Casey, G M, Grant, A M, Roerig, D S, Boyd, J, Hill, M, London, M, Gelberg, K H, Hallman, E, & Pollock, J, 1997 Farm worker injuries associated with bulls, New York State 1991–1996, *American Association of Occupational Health News,* **45**, 393–6

Castellvi, A E, Goldstein, L A, & Chan, D P K, 1984 Lumbosacral transitional vertebrae and their relationship with lumbar extradural effects, *Spine,* **9**, 493–5

Cattaneo, C, Gelsthorpe, K, Phillips, P, & Sokol, R J, 1992 Reliable identification of human albumin in ancient bone using ELISA and monoclonal antibodies, *Amer J Phys Anthropol,* **87**, 365–72

Cavis-Brown, J, 1905 *An Old English Hospital: S. Mary's Chichester* (originally printed in *Newberry House Magazine* for May 1884)

Cawson, R A, 1968 *Essentials of Dental Surgery and Pathology*. Edinburgh: Churchill Livingstone

Centurion-Lara, A, Castro, C, Castillo, R, Shaffer, J M, Van Voorhis, W C, & Lukehart, S A, 1998 The flanking region sequences of the 15-kDa lipoprotein gene differentiate pathogenic treponemes, *J Infect Dis,* **177**, 1036–40

Cheng, J C, Metreweli, C, Mui-Kwan, Chen, T, & Tang, S, 2000 Correlation of ultrasonographic imaging of congenital muscular torticollis with clinical assessment in infants, *Ultrasound in Med Biol,* **26**, 1237–41

Chundun, Z, 1991 *The Significance of Rib Lesions in Individuals from Chichester Medieval Hospital*. Unpublished MSc thesis, University of Bradford

Clarke, D T-D, 1962 *Painted Glass from Leicester*. Leicester: Museums, Department of Antiquities

Clarke, N G, Carey, S E, Srikandi, W, Hirsch, R S, & Leppard, P I, 1986 Periodontal disease in ancient populations, *Amer J Phys Anthropol,* **71**, 173–83

Clay, R M, 1909 *The Mediæval Hospitals of England*, reprinted 1966. London: Frank Cass

Cohen, M M, 1986 *Craniosynostosis: Diagnosis, Evaluation, and Management*. New York: Raven Press

Connelly, J (ed), 1981 *DePalma's The Management of Fractures and Dislocations, an Atlas*. Philadelphia: W B Saunders

Corruccini, R S, 1974 An examination of the meaning of cranial discrete traits for human skeletal biological studies, *Amer J Phys Anthropol,* **40**, 425–46

Costa, R L, 1982 Periodontal disease in the prehistoric Ipiutak and Tigara skeletal remains from Point Hope, Alaska, *Amer J Phys Anthropol,* **59**, 97–110

Cotran, R S, Kumar, V, & Robbins, S L, 1994 *Robbins' Pathologic Basis of Disease*. Philadelphia: W B Saunders Co

Cox, J C, 1903 The chapel and guild of the Holy Ghost, in Doubleday and Page (eds) 1903, 214–15

Cox, M, 1996 *Life and death in Spitalfields*. York: Council for British Archaeology

Cox, M, 2000 Ageing adults from the skeleton, in Cox & Mays (eds) 2000, 61–81

Cox, M, & Mays, S (eds), 2000 *Human osteology in archaeology and forensic science*. London: Greenwich Medical Media

Crawford, S, 1993 Children, death and the afterlife in Anglo-Saxon England, in Filmer-Sankey (ed) 1993, 83–92

Criddle, L M, 2001 Livestock trauma in central Texas: cowboys, ranchers, and dudes, *J Emerg Nurs,* **27**, 132–40

Cullum, P H, 1991 Leperhouses and borough status in the thirteenth century, in P R Coss & S D Lloyd (eds), *Thirteenth Century England* **3**. Woodbridge: Boydell, 37–46

Cullum, P H, 1993 St Leonard's Hospital, York: the spatial and social analysis of an Augustinian hospital, in Gilchrist & Mytum (eds) 1993

Dabell, J A, 1999 *St. Wilfrid's Church Hickleton: The Building Development of a Parish Church*. Wombell: Thornsby Printers

Dahlberg, G, 1940 *Statistical Methods for Medical and Biological Students*. London: George Allen & Unwin

Dalby, G, 1993 *The Palaeopathology of Middle Ear and Mastoid Disease*. Unpublished PhD thesis, Bradford University

Dalby, G, Manchester, K, & Roberts, C A, 1993 Otosclerosis and stapedial footplate fixation in archaeological material, *Internat J Osteoarchaeol,* **3**, 207–12

Dangerfield, M E, Marshall, O, Stringer, E R, & Welch, V E 1938 Chichester Workhouse, *Sussex Archaeol Collect,* **79**, 131–67

Daniel, E, Koshy, S, Rao, G, & Rao, P, 2002 Ocular complications in newly diagnosed borderline lepromatous and lepromatous leprosy patients: baseline profile of the Indian cohort, *Brit J Ophthalmol,* **86**, 1336–40

Daniell, C, 1998 *Death and Burial in Medieval England 1066–1550*. London: Routledge

Daniell, C, 2001 Battle and trial: weapon injury burials of St Andrew's Church, Fishergate, York. *Medieval Archaeol* **45**, 220–6

Danielsen, K, 1970 Odontodysplasia leprosa in Danish mediaeval skeletons, *Tandlaegebladet,* **74**, 613–25

David, H, & Freedman, L S, 1990 Injuries caused by tripping over paving stones: an unappreciated problem, *Brit Med J,* **300**, 784–5

Davidson, P, & Horowitz, I, 1970 Skeletal tuberculosis: a review with patient presentations and discussion, *Amer J Med,* **48**, 77–84

Dawes, J, 1980 The skeletal material, in Dawes & Magilton 1980

Dawes, J D & Magilton, J R, 1980 *The Cemetery of St Helen-on-the-Walls, Aldwark.* The Archaeology of York **12/1**. London: Council for British Archaeology for York Archaeological Trust

De Beer Kaufman, P, 1977 The number of vertebrae in the Southern African negro, the American negro and the Bushman (San), *Amer J Phys Anthropol*, **47**, 409–14

De Maeseneer, M, DeMey, J, Debaere, C, Meysman, M, & Osteaux, M, 2000 Rib fractures induced by coughing: an unusual cause of acute chest pain, *Amer J Emerg Med*, **18**, 194–7

DePalma, A F, 1983 Biologic aging of the shoulder, in A F DePalma (ed), *Surgery of the shoulder.* Philadelphia: J B Lippincott Co, 211–41

Dias G, & Tayles, N, 1997 Abscess cavity: a misnomer, *Internat J Osteoarchaeol*, **7**, 548–54

Dick, W S, 1972 *An Introduction to Clinical Rheumatology.* Edinburgh: Churchill Livingstone

Dimich-Ward, H, Guernsey, J R, Pickett, W, Rennie, D, Hartling, L, & Brison, R J, 2004 Gender differences in the occurrence of farm related injuries, *Occup Environ Med*, **61**, 52–6

Dinn, R, 1992 Death and rebirth in late medieval Bury St Edmunds, in Bassett (ed) 1992, 151–69

Dols, M W, 1983 The leper in medieval Islamic society, *Speculum*, **58**, 891–916

Doub, H P, & Badgeley, C E, 1932 Roentgen signs of tuberculosis of the vertebral body, *Amer J Roentgenol*, **27**, 827–37

Doubleday, A, & Page, W (eds), 1903 *A History of the County of Hampshire and the Isle of Wight.* London: Victoria County Histories

Douglas, M T, 1991 Wryneck in the ancient Hawaiians, *Amer J Phys Anthropol*, **84**, 261–71

Du Toit, F P, & Gräbe, R P, 1979 Isolated fractures of the shaft of the ulna, *S Afr Med J*, **56**, 21–5

Duffy, E, 1992 *The Stripping of the Altars: Traditional Religion in England 1400–1580.* New Haven: Yale University Press

Ehrlich, I, & Kricun, M E, 1976 Radiographic findings in early acquired syphilis: case report and critical review, *Amer J Roentgenol*, **127**, 789–92

Eveleth, P B, & Tanner, J M, 1990 *Worldwide Variation in Human Growth.* Cambridge: University Press

Fagerlund, L W, 1886 *Finlands Leprosorier I.* Helsingfors: Finska Litteratur-sällskapets tryckeri

Farley, M, & Manchester, K, 1989 The Cemetery of the Leper Hospital of St Margaret, High Wycombe, Buckinghamshire, *Medieval Archaeol*, **33**, 82–9

Farrer, W, (ed) 1914–16 *Early Yorkshire Charters,* **1–3**. Yorks Archaeol Soc Record Ser, Extra Ser

Fenton, T W, De Jong, J L, & Haut, R C, 2003 Punched with a fist: the etiology of a fatal depressed cranial fracture, *J Forensic Sci*, **48**, 277–81

Fibiger, L, & Knüsel, C, 2005 Prevalence rates of spondylolysis in British skeletal populations, *Internat J Osteoarchaeol*, **15**, 164–74

Fields, S J, Spiers, M, Hershkovitz, I, & Livshits, G, 1995 Reliability of relation coefficients in the estimation of asymmetry, *Amer J Phys Anthropol*, **96**, 83–7

Filmer-Sankey, W, (ed) 1993 *Anglo-Saxon Studies in History and Archaeology* **6**

Finch, J, 2003 A reformation of meaning: commemoration and remembering the dead in the parish church, 1450–1640, in Gaimster & Gilchrist (eds) 2003, 437–49

Finnegan, M, 1973 Non metric variation of the infracranial skeleton, *J Anat*, **125**, 23–37

Fiorato, V, Boylston, A, & Knüsel, C, (eds), 2000 *Blood Red Roses. The Archaeology of a Mass Grave from the Battle of Towton AD 1461.* Oxford: Oxbow

Fleming, L, 1960 *Chartulary of the Priory of Boxgrove.* Sussex Record Society **59**

Foote, K, & Marriott, L, 2003 Weaning of infants, *Arch Dis Child*, **88**, 488–92

Forestier, J, & Lagier, R, 1971 Ankylosing hyperostosis of the spine, *Clinical Orthopaedics*, **74**, 65–83

Forrest, J, 1999 *The History of Morris Dancing 1458–1750.* Toronto: University Press

Foucault, M, 1965 *Madness and Civilization: A History of Insanity in the Age of Reason* (R Howard trans). London: Tavistock

Fraser, C M, Norris, S J, Weinstock, G M, White, O, Sutton, G G, Dodson, R, Gwinn, M, Hickey, E K, Clayton, R, Ketchum, K A, Sodergren, E, Hardham, J M, McLeod, M P, Salzberg, S, Peterson, J, Khalak, H, Richardson, D, Howell, J K, Chidambaram, M, Utterback, T, McDonald, L, Artiach, P, Bowman, C, Cotton, M D, Fujii, C, Garland, S, Hatch, B, Horst, K, Roberts, K, Sandusky, M, Weidman, J, Smith, H O & Venter, J C, 1998 Complete genome sequence of *Treponema pallidum*, the syphilis spirochete, *Science*, **281**, 375–88

Freed, S S, & Coulter-O'Berry, C, 2004 Identification and treatment of congenital muscular torticollis in infants, *J Prosthet and Orthot*, **16**, 18–23

Fry, S L, 1999 *Burial in Medieval Ireland, 900–1500: a Review of the Written Sources.* Dublin: Four Courts Press

Gaimster, D, & Gilchrist, R, 2003 *The Archaeology of the Reformation 1480–1580.* Society for Post-Medieval Archaeology, **1**. Leeds: Maney Publishing

Ganguli, P K, 1963 *Radiology of Bone and Joint Tuberculosis.* New York: Asia Publishing House

Gilchrist, R, 1992 Christian bodies and souls: the archaeology of life and death in later medieval hospitals, in Bassett (ed) 1992, 101–18

Gilchrist, R, 2003 Dust to dust: revealing the Reformation dead, in Gaimster & Gilchrist (eds) 2003, 399–414

Gilchrist, R, & Mytum, H, (eds), 1993 *Advances in Monastic Archaeology.* BAR Brit Ser **271**. Oxford: British Archaeological Reports

Gilchrist, R, & Sloane, B, 2005 *Requiem. The Medieval Monastic Cemetery in Britain*. London: Museum of London Archaeol Service

Gittings, C, 1984 *Death, Burial and the Individual in Early Modern England*. Beckenham: Croom Helm

Gittings, C, 1999 Sacred and secular: 1558–1660, in Jupp & Gittings (eds) 1999, 147–73

Godfrey, W H, 1928 Church of St Anne's Lewes: an anchorite's cell and other discoveries, *Sussex Archaeol Collect*, **69**, 159–69

Godfrey, W H (ed), 1935 Transcripts of Sussex Wills vol 1, *Sussex Record Society*, **41**

Godfrey, W H (ed), 1940–41 Transcripts of Sussex Wills vol 4, *Sussex Record Society* **45**

Godfrey, W H, 1955 *The English Almshouse with some Account of its Predecessor, the Medieval Hospital*. London: Faber & Faber

Godfrey, W H, 1959 Medieval Hospitals in Sussex. *Sussex Archaeol Collect*, **97**, 130–6

Goode, J L, 1993 *A Consideration of the Effects of Nerve Thickening on the Skeleton in Individuals Suffering from Leprosy*. Unpublished BSc dissertation, University of Bradford

Goodman, A H, & Rose, J C, 1990 Assessment of systemic physiological perturbates from dental enamel hypoplasias and associated histological structures, *Yearb Phys Anthropol*, **33**, 59–110

Gordon, H D, 1877 *The History of Harting*. London: W Davy & Son. (Reprinted 1975, Petersfield: Frank Westwood)

Gottfried, R S, 1983 *The Black Death*. London: Batsford

Graham, H, 1956 *Surgeons All*, 2nd edn. London: Rich & Cowan

Granshaw, L, & Porter, R, (eds) 1989 *The Hospital in History*. London: Routledge

Grauer, A, 1991 Life patterns of women from medieval York, in D Walde & N D Willows (eds), *The Archaeology of Gender. Proceedings of the 22nd Annual Chacmool Conference*. Calgary: The Archaeological Association of the University of Calgary, 407–13

Grauer, A L (ed) 1995 *Bodies of Evidence. Reconstructing History through Skeletal Analysis*. New York: Wiley-Liss

Grauer, A L, & Roberts, C A, 1996 Paleoepidemiology, healing, and possible treatment of trauma in the medieval cemetery population of St. Helen-on-the-Walls, York, England, *Amer J Phys Anthropol*, **100**, 531–44

Griffith, J P C, 1919 *The Diseases of Infants and Children*. London: W B Saunders Co.

Haas, C J, Zink, A, Pálfi, G, Szeimies, U, Nerlich, A G, 2000 Detection of leprosy in human remains by molecular identification of *Mycobacterium leprae*, *Amer J Clin Path*, **114**, 428–36

Hackett, C J, 1951 *Bone Lesions of Yaws in Uganda*. Oxford: Blackwell Scientific Publications

Hadler, N M, 1977 Industrial rheumatology: clinical investigation into the influence of the pattern of usage on the pattern of regional musculoskel-etal disease, *Arthritis and Rheumatism*, **20**, 1019–25

Hadley, D M, 2001 *Death in Medieval England: an Archaeology*. Stroud: Tempus

Hamilton, B, 2000 *The Leper King and his Heirs: Baldwin IV and the Crusader Kingdom of Jerusalem*. Cambridge: University Press

Harding, V, 2003 Choices and changes: death, burial and the English Reformation, in Gaimster & Gilchrist (eds) 2003, 386–98

Hardy J G, & Hartmann, J R, 1947 Tuberculosis dactylitis in childhood: prognosis, *J Pediat*, **30**, 146–56

Harland, J, & Wilkinson, T T (eds), 1867 *Lancashire Folk-lore Illustrative of the Superstitious Beliefs and Practices, Local Customs and Usages of the People of the County Palatine*. London: Warne (reissued in 2000)

Harley, E H, Sdralis, T, & Berkowitz, R G, 1997 Acute mastoiditis in children: a 12-year retrospective study, *Otolaryngol Head Neck Surg*, **166**, 26–30

Harman, M, 1985 The human remains in Lambrick (ed) 1985, 131–208

Harrison T R, Adams R D, Bennett, I L, Resnik, W H, Thorn, G W, & Wintrobe, M M, 1962 *Principle of Internal Medicine*. New York: McGraw-Hill

Harrison, A C, 1969 Excavations on the site of St Mary's Hospital, Strood, *Archaeologia Cantiana*, **84**, 139–69

Hatcher, J, 1986 Mortality in the 15th century: some new evidence, *Econ Hist Rev*, **39**, 19–38

Hawkes, S C & Wells, C, 1983 The inhumed skeletal material from an early Anglo-Saxon cemetery in Worthy Park, Kingsworthy, Hampshire, South England, *Paleobios*, **1**, 3–36

Hawkins, D, 1990 The Black Death and the new London cemeteries of 1348, *Antiquity*, **64**, 637–42

Hay, A, 1804 *The History of Chichester*. London

Hazlitt, W C, 1905 *Dictionary of Faiths and Folklore. Beliefs, Superstitions and Popular Customs*. London: Reeves & Turner, reprinted 1995

Heighway, C, & Bryant, R, 1999 *The Golden Minster: the Anglo-Saxon Minster and later Medieval Priory of St Oswald at Gloucester*. London: Council for British Archaeology Research Report, **117**

Henschen, F, 1949 *Morgagni's Syndrome*. Edinburgh: Oliver & Boyd

Herring, S W, 1994 Epigenetic and functional influences on skull growth, in J Hamken & B K Hall (eds), *The Skull Volume 1: Development*. Chicago: University of Chicago Press

Hershkovitz, I, Bedford, L, Jellema, L M, & Latimer B, 1996 Injuries to the skeleton due to prolonged activity in hand-to-hand combat, *Internat J Osteoarchaeol*, **6**, 167–78

Hershkovitz, I, Latimer, B, Dutour, O, Jellema, L M, Wish-Baratz, S, & Rothschild, C, 1997 Why do we fail in aging the skull from the sagittal suture?, *Amer J Phys Anthropol*, **103**, 393–9

Hershkovitz, I, Ring, B, & Kobyliansky, E, 1992

Craniofacial asymmetry in Bedouin adults, *Amer J Hum Biol*, **4**, 83–92

Hess, L, 1946 Ossicula wormiana, *Hum Biol*, **18**, 61–80

Hickish, A B, 1985 *Ear, Nose and Throat Disorders*. Edinburgh: Churchill Livingstone

Hill, P (ed), 1997 *Whithorn and St. Ninian: the Excavation of a Monastic Town 1984–91*. Stroud: Sutton Publishing

Hillson, S W, 1986 *Teeth*, 1st edn. Cambridge: University Press

Hillson S W, 2001 Recording dental caries in archaeological human remains, *Internat J Osteoarchaeol*, **11**, 249–89

Hillson, S W, 2005 *Teeth*, 2nd edn. Cambridge: University Press

Hillson S W, & Bond, S, 1997 Relationship of enamel hypoplasia to the pattern of tooth growth: a discussion, *Amer J Phys Anthropol*, **104**, 89–104

Holst, M, Isaac, L, Boylston, A, Roberts, C, 2001 *Hull Magistrates' Court (HMC94): Draft Report on the Human Skeletal Remains*. Unpublished report, University of Bradford

Holt, L E, 1906 *The Diseases of Infancy and Childhood*, 3rd edn. London: Sidney Appleton

Horrox, R, 1999 Purgatory, prayer and plague: 1150–1380, in Jupp & Gittings (eds) 1999, 90–118

Horsey, M, 1996 *A Study of Chichester Skeletal Collection using Radiographs to Investigate for Metastatic Carcinoma*. Unpublished BSc dissertation, University of Bradford

Houlbrooke, R, 1999 The age of decency: 1660–1760, in Jupp & Gittings (eds) 1999, 174–201

Hudson, T P (ed), 1997 *A History of the County of Sussex Volume V part 1. Arundel Rape (Southwestern part) including Arundel*. Oxford: Oxford University Press, for The Institute of Historical Research

Hurst, J G, Andrews, D D, & Milne, G (eds), 1979 *Wharram: a study of settlement on the Yorkshire Wolds*. **1**. Monograph Series, **8**. London: Society for Medieval Archaeology

Huskisson, E C, Dieppe, P A, Tucker, A K, & Cannell, L B, 1979 Another look at osteoarthritis, *Ann Rheum Dis*, **38**, 423–8

Hutchinson, R, 2003 Tombs of Brass are Spent: Reformation re-use of Monumental Brasses, in Gaimster & Gilchrist (eds) 2003, 450–68

Ihon, D, 1562 *A Description of a Monstrous Chylde, Borne at Chichester in Sussex*. London: Leonard Askel for Fraunces Godlyfi

Iscan, M Y, & Kennedy, K A R (eds), 1989 *Reconstruction of Life from the Skeleton*. New York: Alan R. Liss

Iscan, M Y, Loth, S R, and Wright, R K, 1984 Age estimation from the rib by phase analysis: white males, *J Forensic Sci*, **29**, 1094–104

Iscan, M Y, Loth, S R, and Wright, R K, 1985 Age estimation from the rib by phase analysis: white females, *J Forensic Sci*, **30**, 853–63

Iscan, M Y, & Loth, S, 1986 Estimation of age and determination of sex from the sternal rib, in Reichs (ed) 1986, 68–89

Jankauskas, R, 2003 The incidence of diffuse idiopathic skeletal hyperostosis and social status correlations in Lithuanian skeletal materials, *Internat J Osteoarchaeol*, **13**, 289–93

Jimenez, D F, Barone, C M, Argamaso, R V, Goodrich, J T, & Shprintzen, R J, 1994 Asterion region synostosis, *Cleft Palate Craniofac J*, **31**, 136–41

Johnston, F E, & Zimmer, L O, 1989 Assessment of growth and age in the immature skeleton, in Iscan & Kennedy (eds) 1989, 11–21

Johnston, T B, & Whillis, J, 1954 *Gray's Anatomy*. 31st edn. London: Longman, Green & Co.

Jones, M W, 1990 A study of trauma in an Amish community, *J Trauma*, **30**, 899–902

Jones, K L, 1997 *Smith's Recognizable Patterns of Human Malformation*. 5th edn. Philadelphia: Saunders

Jonsson, B, Stromquist, B, Egund, N, 1989 Anomalous lumbosacral articulations and low-back pain: evaluation and treatment, *Spine*, **14**, 831–4

Jopling, W H, 1971 *Handbook of Leprosy*, 2nd edn. London: Heinemann Medical

Jopling, W H, 1984 *Handbook of Leprosy*, 3rd edn. London: Heinemann Medical

Jopling, W H, & McDougall, A C, 1988 *Handbook of Leprosy*, 4th edn. London: Heinemann Professional

Jorde, L B, Fineman, R M, & Martin, R A, 1987 Epidemiology and genetics of neural tube defects: an application of the Utah Genealogical Database. *Amer J Phys Anthropol*, **62**, 23–32

Judd, M A, 2004 Trauma in the city of Kerma: ancient versus modern injury patterns, *Internat J Osteoarchaeol*, **14**, 34–51

Judd, M A, & Roberts, C A, 1998 Fracture patterns at the medieval leper hospital in Chichester, *Amer J Phys Anthropol*, **105**, 43–55

Judges, A V, 1930 *The Elizabethan Underworld*. London: Routledge (reprinted 1965)

Jupp, P C, & Gittings, C, (eds) 1999 *Death in England: an Illustrated History*. Manchester: University Press

Jurmain, R D, 1976 Stress and the etiology of osteoarthritis, *Amer J Phys Anthropol*, **46**, 353–66

Jurmain, R, 1999 *Stories from the skeleton. Behavioural reconstruction in human osteology*. Amsterdam: Gordon & Breach

Kabbani, H, & Raghuveer, T S, 2004 Craniosynostosis, *Amer Fam Physician*, **69**, 2863–70

Karlberg, J, 1998 The human growth curve, in S J Ulijaszek, F C Johnston & M A Preece (eds), *The Cambridge Encyclopedia of Human Growth and Development*. Cambridge: University Press, 108–15

Karmel-Ross, K, 1997 *Torticollis: Differential Diagnosis, Assessment and Treatment, Surgical Management and Bracing. Physical and Occupational Therapy in Pediatrics*. New York: Haworth Press

Katz, D, & Suchey, J M, 1986 Age determination of

the male os pubis, *Amer J Phys Anthropol,* **69**, 427–35

Kelley, M A, & Micozzi, M S, 1984 Rib lesions in chronic pulmonary tuberculosis, *Amer J Phys Anthropol,* **65**, 381–6

Kemmlert, K, & Lundholm, L, 2001 Slips, trips and falls in different work groups – with reference to age and from a preventative perspective, *Appl Ergon,* **32**, 149–53

Kenny, J, 1988 St Andrew's Church, East Street, *The Archaeology of Chichester and District 1988.* Chichester: Chichester District Council

Kerr, N W, & Ringrose, T, 1998 Factors affecting the lifespan of the human dentition in Britain prior to the seventeenth century, *Brit Dent J,* **184**, 242–6

Kerr, N W, 1998 The prevalence and natural history of periodontal disease in Britain from prehistoric to modern times, *Brit Dent J,* **185**, 527–35

Kershaw, I, 1973 The great famine and agrarian crisis in England, *Past and Present,* **59**, 3–50

King, J W, Brelsford, H J, & Tullos, H S, 1969 Analysis of the pitching arm of the professional baseball pitcher, *Clin Orthop Rel Res,* **67**, 116–23

Kipel, K, (ed), 2003 *The Cambridge Historical Dictionary of Disease.* Cambridge: University Press

Knapp, T R, 1992 Technical error of measurement: a methodological critique, *Amer J Phys Anthropol,* **87**(2), 235–6

Knowles, D, & Hadcock, R N, 1953 *Medieval Religious Houses: England and Wales,* 1st edn. London: Longman

Knowles, D, & Hadcock, R N, 1971 *Medieval Religious Houses: England and Wales,* 2nd edn. London: Longman

Knüsel, C J, 2002 More Circe than Cassandra: the Princes of Vix in ritualised social context, *Eur J Archaeol,* **5**(3), 275–308

Knüsel, C J & Göggel, S, 1993 A cripple from the medieval hospital of Sts James and Mary Magdalene, Chichester, *Internat J Osteoarchaeol,* **3**, 155–65

Knüsel, C, Roberts, C A, & Boylston, A, 1996 'When Adam Delved': an activity related lesion in three human skeletal populations, *Amer J Phys Anthropol,* **100**, 427–34

Kokich, V C, 1986 The biology of sutures, in Cohen (ed) 1986, 81–103

Krogman, W M, 1978 *The Human Skeleton in Forensic Medicine,* 3rd edn. Springfield: Charles C Thomas

Kulkarniu, V N, & Mehta, J M, 1983 Tarsal disintegration (TD) in leprosy, *Leprosy in India,* **55**, 338–69

Lambrick, G, (ed) 1985 Further excavations on the second site of the Dominican Priory, Oxford, *Oxoniensia,* **50**, 131–208

Lara, C B, & Nolesco, J O 1956 Self-healing or abortive, and residual forms of childhood leprosy and their probable significance, *Internat J Leprosy,* **24**, 245–63

Larsen, C S, 1997a *Bioarchaeology: Interpreting Behavior from the Human Skeleton.* Cambridge: Cambridge University Press

Larsen, C S, 1997b Anemia and the ancients, in K F Kiple (ed), *Plague, Pox and Pestilence.* London: Weidenfeld and Nicolson, 10–13

Laurence, K M, & Tew, B J, 1971 Natural history of spina bifida cystica and cranium bifidum cysticum, *Arch Disease Child,* **46**, 127

Laurence, K M, 1966 Survival of untreated spina bifida cystica, *Developmental Medicine and Child Neurology* Supplement **11**, 10–19

Laurence, K M, Bligh, A S, & Evans, K T, 1968 Vertebral and other abnormalities in parents and sibs of cases of spina bifida cystica and of anencephaly, *Developmental Childhood Neurology,* Suppl **16**, 107

Lavelle C L B, & Moore, W J, 1973 The incidence of agenesis and polygenesis in the primate dentition, *Amer J Phys Anthropol,* **38**, 671–80

Leach, R E, Baumgard, S, & Broom, J, 1973 Obesity: its relationship to osteoarthritis of the knee, *Ann Rheum Dis,* **25**, 271–3

Lechat, M F, 1961 Mutilations in leprosy, *Trop Geogr Med,* **13**, 99–103

Lee, F, & Magilton, J, 1989 The cemetery of the Hospital of St James and St Mary Magdalene, Chichester – a case study, *World Archaeol,* **21**, 273–82

Leighton, J, 2005 *Size Matters: A Craniometric Assessment of Congenital Conditions in Medieval Chichester.* Unpublished MSc dissertation, University of Bradford

Levene, M I, & Tudehope, D, 1993 *Essentials of Neonatal Medicine.* 2nd edn. Oxford: Blackwell Scientific

Lewis, G D, 1964 The Cemetery of St Mary Magdalene, Bidlington, *Sussex Archaeol Collect,* **102**, 1–8

Lewis, M E, 2002a Infant and childhood leprosy: clinical and palaeopathological implications, in Roberts *et al* (eds) 2002, 163–9

Lewis, M E, 2002b The impact of industrialisation: comparative study of child health in four sites from medieval and post-medieval England (850–1859 AD), *Amer J Phys Anth,* **119**, 211–23

Lewis, M E, 2004 Endocranial lesions in non-adult skeletons: understanding their aetiology, *Internat J Osteoarch,* **14**, 82–97

Lewis, M E, 2007 *The Bioarchaeology of Children: Perspectives from Biological and Forensic Anthropology.* Cambridge: University Press

Lewis, M, Roberts, C, & Manchester, K, 1995 Inflammatory bone changes in the leprous skeletons from the medieval hospital of St James and St Mary Magdalene, Chichester, England, *Internat J Leprosy,* **63**, 77–85

Lieverse, A R, 1999 Diet and the aetiology of dental calculus, *Internat J Osteoarchaeol,* **9**, 219–32

Lilley, J, Stroud, G, Brothwell, D R, & Williamson, M (eds), 1994 *The Jewish Burial Ground at Jewbury.* The Archaeology of York. The Medieval Cemeteries, **12**/3. York: Council for British Archaeology for York Archaeological Trust

Litten, J, 1991 *The English Way of Death*. London: R Hale

Livingstone, F B, 1991 On the origin of syphilis: an alternative hypothesis. *Curr Anthropol*, **32**, 587–90

Livshits, G, & Kobyliansky, E, 1991 Fluctuating asymmetry as a possible measure of developmental homeostasis in humans: a review, *Hum Biol*, **63**(4), 441–66

Loder, R, & Mayhew, H, 1988 Common fractures from a fall on an outstretched hand, *Amer Fam Physician*, **37**, 327–8

Lovell, N C, 1997 Trauma analysis in paleopathology, *Yearb Phys Anthropol*, **40**, 139–70

Lucy, S, & Reynolds, A, 2002 *Burial in Early Medieval England and Wales*. London: Society for Medieval Archaeology

Lukacs J, 1989 Dental palaeopathology: methods for reconstructing dietary patterns, in Iscan & Kennedy (eds) 1989, 261–86

Luongo, C W, 1997 *The Effects of Testicular Atrophy on Skeletons of Leprous Males: a Clinical and Palaeopathological Study*. Unpublished MSc thesis, University of Bradford

Lyne, M, 1997 *Lewes Priory. Excavations by Richard Lewis 1969–82*. Lewes: Priory Trust

MacPhee, T, & Cowley, G, 1975 *Essentials of Periodontology and Periodontics*, 2nd edn. Oxford: Blackwell

Magilton, J, 1979 Tickhill: the Topography of a Medieval Town, *Trans Hunter Archaeol Soc*, **10**, 344–9

Magilton, J R, 1980 *The Church of St Helen-on-the-Walls, Aldwark*. The Archaeology of York **10**/1. London: Council for British Archaeology for York Archaeological Trust

Magilton, J, 1986 Hospital of St James and St Mary Magdalene, Swanfield Drive, *The Archaeology of Chichester and District 1986*. Chichester: District Council, 12–15

Magilton, J, 1993 Further excavations at the leper hospital cemetery, Swanfield Drive, *The Archaeology of Chichester and District 1993*. Chichester: District Council, 37–41

Magilton, J, 1996 Chichester, the Burghal Hidage and the diversion of the River Lavant, *The Archaeology of Chichester and District 1993*. Chichester: District Council, 11–12

Magilton, J, & Lee, F, 1989 The leper hospital of St James and St Mary Magdalene, Chichester, in Roberts *et al* (eds) 1989, 249–65

Malim, T, & Hines, J, 1998 *The Anglo-Saxon Cemetery at Edix Hill (Barrington A), Cambridgeshire*. York: Council for British Archaeology Res Rep **112**

Malina, R M, & Buschang, P H, 1984 Anthropometric asymmetry in normal and mentally retarded males, *Ann Hum Biol*, **11**(6), 515–31

Manchester, K, 1981 A leprous skeleton of the 7th century from Eccles, Kent, and the present evidence of leprosy in early Britain, *J Archaeol Sci*, **8**, 205–9

Manchester, K, 1983 *The Archaeology of Disease*. Bradford: University Press

Manchester, K, 2002 Infective bone changes of leprosy, in Roberts *et al* (eds) 2002, 69–72

Manchester, K, & Roberts, C A, 1986 *Palaeopathological evidence of leprosy and tuberculosis in Britain*. SERC Report for grant no. 337.367

Manchester, K, & Roberts, C, 1989 The palaeopathology of leprosy in Britain: a review, *World Archaeol*, **21**, 265–72

Marcombe, D & Manchester, K, 1990 The Melton Mowbray 'leper head': an historical and medical investigation, *Medical History*, **34**, 86–91

Marcombe, D, 2003 *Leper Knights*. Woodbridge: Boydell

Martin, D L, & Frayer, D W (eds), 1997 *Troubled Times: Violence and Warfare in the Past*. Amsterdam: Gordon & Breach

Mawer, A, & Stenton, F M, 1929 *The Place-names of Sussex. Part 1*. English Place-Name Society **6**. Cambridge: University Press

Mays, S, 1991 The medieval burials from the Blackfriars friary, School Street, Ipswich, Suffolk (excavated 1986–88). English Heritage Ancient Monuments Lab rep **16**/19, part 1

Mays, S, 1998 *The Archaeology of Human Bones*. London: Routledge

Mays, S, 2006 The osteology of monasticism in medieval England, in R Gowland and C Knüsel (eds), *Social Archaeology of Funerary Remains*. Oxford: Oxbow, 179–89

McCann, A, 1978 *The History of the Church and Parish of St Andrew Oxmarket, Chichester (Chichester)*

McCann, A, 1987 Further notes on St James's Hospital, Chichester, *Sussex Archaeol Collect*, **125**, 252–4

McCann, T J, & Wilkinson, P M, 1972 The cricket match at Boxgrove in 1622, *Sussex Archaeol Collect*, **110**, 118–22

McDougall, A C, & Salter, D C, 1977 Thermography of the nose and ear in relation to the skin lesions of lepromatous leprosy, tuberculosis, leishmaniasis, and lupus pernio, *J Invest Dermatol*, **68**, 16–22

McKern, T W, 1970 Estimation of skeletal age: from puberty to about 30 years of age, in T D Stewart (ed), *Personal Identification in Mass Disasters*. Washington: Smithsonian Institution

McManus, I C, 1982 The distribution of skull asymmetry in man, *Ann Hum Biol*, **9**(2), 167–70

Meindl, R S, & Lovejoy, C O, 1985 Ectocranial suture closure: a revised method for the determination of skeletal age at death based on the lateral anterior sutures, *Amer J Phys Anthropol*, **68**, 57–66

Melikian, M, & Waldron, T, 2003 An examination of skulls from two British sites for possible evidence of scurvy, *Internat J Osteoarchaeol* **13**, 207–12

Melsom, R, Harboe, M, & Duncan, M E, 1982 IgA, IgM and IgA anti-*M-leprae* antibodies in babies of leprosy mothers during the first 2 years of life, *Clin Exper Immunol*, **49**, 532–42

Merbs, C, 2002 Spondylolysis in Inuit skeletons from Arctic Canada, *Internat J Osteoarchaeol*, **12**, 279–90

Mercier, E, 1915 *Leper Houses and Medieval Hospitals*. London: H K Lewis

Miles, A W, 2000 Two shoulder-joint dislocations in early 19th century Londoners, *Internat J Osteoarchaeol*, **10**, 125–34

Mitchell, P D, 2000 An evaluation of the leprosy of King Baldwin IV of Jerusalem in the context of the medieval world, in Hamilton (ed) 2000, 245–58

Møller, A P, & Pomiankowski, A, 1993 Fluctuating asymmetry and sexual selection, *Genetica*, **89**, 267–79

Møller, A P, & Swaddle, J P, 1998 *Asymmetry, Developmental Stability, and Evolution*. Oxford: University Press

Møller-Christensen, V, 1953 Ten Lepers from Naestved in Denmark, *Med Monograph*, **2**. Copenhagen: Danish Science Press

Møller-Christensen V, 1961 *Bone Changes in Leprosy*. Copenhagen: Munksgaard

Møller-Christensen V, 1974 Changes in the anterior nasal spine and the alveolar process of the maxillae in leprosy: a clinical examination, *Internat J Leprosy*, **42**, 431–5

Møller-Christensen V, 1978 *Leprosy Changes of the Skull*. Odense: University Press

Møller-Christensen V, 1982 *Aebelholt Kloster*. Copenhagen: Nationalmuseet

Møller-Christensen, V, & Hughes, D R, 1962 Two early cases of leprosy in Great Britain, *Man*, **62**, 177–9

Molleson, T I, & Cox, M J, 1993 *The Spitalfields Project 2 – the Anthropology: the middling sort*. CBA Research Report, **86**. London: Council for British Archaeology

Moore, K L, 1978 Malformations caused by environmental factors, in K L Moore (ed), *The Developing Human: Clinically Oriented Embryology*, 2nd edn. Philadelphia: W B Saunders Co, 133–44

Moorrees, C F A, Fanning, E A, & Hunt, E E, 1963a Formation and resorption of three deciduous teeth in children, *Amer J Phys Anthropol*, **21**, 205–13

Moorrees, C F A, Fanning, E A, & Hunt, E E, 1963b Age variation of formation stages for ten permanent teeth, *J Dent Res*, **42**, 1490–502

Mora, G, 1992 Stigma during the medieval and Renaissance periods, in P J Fink & A Tasman (eds), *Stigma and Mental Illness*. Washington, DC: American Psychiatric Press

Morgan, P, 1999 Of worms and war: 1380–1558, in Jupp & Gittings (eds) 1999, 119–46

Morgan, R R, 1992 *Chichester: a documentary history*. Chichester: Phillimore

Morris, J, 1976 *Domesday Book Sussex*. Chichester: Phillimore

Mossey, P, & Castilla, E (eds), 2003 *Global registry and database on craniofacial anomalies: report of a WHO registry meeting on craniofacial Anomalies Bauru, Brazil 4–6 December 2001*. Geneva, Switzerland: World Health Organization

Munby, J, 1984 Saxon Chichester and its predecessors, in J Haslam (ed), *Anglo-Saxon Towns in Southern England*. Chichester: Phillimore, 315–30

Munby, J, 1987 *St Mary's Hospital Chichester. A short history and guide*. Chichester: St Mary's Hospital Trustees

Murphy, T, 1959 Changing patterns of dentine exposure in human tooth attrition, *Amer J Phys Anthropol*, **17**, 167–78

Murray, J C, Daak-Hirsch, S, Buetwo, K H, Munger, R, Espina, L, Paglinawan, N, Villanueva, E, Rary, J, Magee, K, Magee, W, 1997 Clinical and epidemiologic studies of cleft lip and palate in the Philippines, *The Cleft Palate-Craniofacial Journal*, **34**(1), 7–10

Murray, K M E, 1935 Excavations on the site of the leper hospital, New Romney, *Archaeologia Cantiana*, **47**, 198–204

Neilson, C, & Coates, G, 2002 *Excavations in Advance of the Extension to the Harrison Learning Centre, University of Wolverhampton, West Midlands 2001: Post-Excavation Assessment and Updated Project Design*. Wolverhampton: Harrison Learning Centre

Newman, H N, 1999 Attrition, eruption and the periodontium, *J Dent Res*, **78**, 730–4

Nicholson, A, & Hill, P, 1997. The non-ferrous metals, in Hill (ed) 1997, 360–404

Nijhout, H F, & Davidowitz, G, 2003 Developmental perspectives on phenotypic variation, canalization, and fluctuating asymmetry, in M Polak (ed) *Developmental Instability: Causes and Consequences*. Oxford: University Press, 279–319

Nörlund, P, 1924 Buried Norsemen at Herjolfsnes. An archaeological and historical study, *Medd Om Grønland*, **67**, 1–271

Norris, M, 1992 Later medieval monumental brasses: an urban funerary industry and its representation of death, in Bassett (ed) 1992, 184–209

Norris, S J and the *Treponema Pallidum* Polypeptide Research Group, 1993 Polypeptides of *Treponema pallidum*: progress toward understanding their structural, function, and immunologic roles, *Microbiol Rev*, **57**, 750–79

Norwood, S, McAuley, C, Vallina, V L, Fernandez, L G, McLarty, J W, & Goodfried, G, 2000 Mechanisms and patterns of injuries related to large animals, *J Trauma*, **48**, 740–4

Noussitou, N J, Sansarricq, H, & Walter, J, 1978 *Leprosy in Children*. Geneva: World Health Organisation

O'Brien, E, 1999 *Post-Roman Britain to Anglo-Saxon England: Burial Practices Reviewed*. BAR Brit Ser **289**. Oxford: British Archaeological Reports

O'Loughlin, V D, 2004 Effects of different kinds of cranial deformation on the incidence of wormian bones, *Amer J Phys Anthropol*, **123**, 146–55

Ogata, S, & Uhthoff, H K, 1990 Acromial enthesopathy and rotator cuff tear, *Clin Orthop Rel Res*, **254**, 39–48

Ogden, A R, 2001 *Periodontal Disease in a Mediaeval Leper Hospital*. Unpublished MSc dissertation, University of Bradford

Ogden, A R, Boylston, A, & Vaughan, T, 2005 Tallow Hill Cemetery, Worcester, England: the importance of detailed study of post-mediaeval graveyards, in S Zakrzewski & M Clegg (eds), *Proceedings of the 5th Annual Conference of the British Association of Biological Anthropology and Osteoarchaeology, Southampton 2003*. BAR Internat Ser **1383**. Oxford: Tempus Reparatum, 51–8

Orme, N, 2001 *Medieval children*. New Haven: Yale University Press

Orme, N & Webster, M, 1995 *The English Medieval Hospital 1070–1570*. London & New Haven: Yale University Press

Ortner, D J, 2002 Observations on the pathogenesis of skeletal disease in leprosy, in Roberts *et al* (eds) 2002, 73–80

Ortner D, 2003 *Identification of Pathological Conditions in Human Skeletal Remains*, 2nd edn. Amsterdam: Academic Press

Ortner, D J, & Aufderheide, A C, 1991. *Human Paleopathology: Current Syntheses and Future Options*. Washington DC: Smithsonian Institution Press

Ortner, D, & Connell, B, 1996 Early inflammatory change in leprosy affecting the rhinomaxillary region, *Paleopathology Newsletter*, **96**, 8–11 (Case Report no. 19)

Ortner, D, Butler, W, Cafarella, J, & Milligan, L, 2001 Evidence of probable scurvy in subadults from archaeological sites in North America, *Amer J Phys Anthropol*, **114**, 343–51

Ortner, D, Kimmerle, E H, & Diez, M, 1999 Probable evidence of scurvy in subadults from archeological sites in Peru, *Amer J Phys Anthropol*, **108**, 321–31

Ortner, D J, Manchester, K, & Lee, F, 1991 Metastatic carcinoma in a leper skeleton from a medieval cemetery in Chichester, England, *Internat J Osteoarchaeol*, **1**, 91–8

Page, W (ed), 1907 *The Victoria History of the County of Sussex* **2**. London: Archibald Constable

Pálfi, G, 1991 The first osteoarchaeological evidence of leprosy in Hungary, *Internat J Osteoarchaeol*, **1**, 99–102

Pálfi, G, Zink, A, Hass, C, Marcsik, A, Dutour, O, & Nerlich, A, 2002 Historical and palaeopathological evidence of leprosy in Hungary, in Roberts *et al* (eds) 2002, 205–12

Palliser, D M, 1993 The topography of monastic houses in Yorkshire towns, in Gilchrist & Mytum (eds) 1993, 3–9

Palmer, A R, 1994 Fluctuating asymmetry analyses: a primer, in T A Markow (ed) *Developmental Instability: Its Origins and Evolutionary Implications*. Dordrecht, Netherlands: Kluwer, 335–64

Palmer, A R, & Strobeck, C, 1997 Fluctuating asymmetry and developmental instability: heritability or observable variation vs. heritability of inferred cause, *J Evol Biol*, **10**, 39–49

Palmer, A R, & Strobeck, C, 2003 Fluctuating asymmetry analyses revisited, in M Polak (ed), *Developmental Instability: Causes and Consequences*. Oxford: University Press, 279–319

Parry, E H, 1984 *Principles of Medicine in Africa*. Oxford: University Press

Peckham, W D, 1933 The Parishes of the City of Chichester, *Sussex Archaeol Collect*, **74**, 65–97

Peckham, W D (ed), 1942–43 The Chartulary of the High Church of Chichester, *Sussex Record Society*, **46**

Peckham, W D, 1948 Some Chichester Wills, 1483–1504, *Sussex Archaeol Collect*, **87**, 1–27

Peckham, W D, 1950 Chichester City Deeds, *Sussex Archaeol Collect*, **89**, 117–62

Peckham, W D, 1954 The valuation of Chichester Cathedral, 1535, *Sussex Archaeol Collect*, **92**, 157–77

Peckham, W D, 1959 *The Acts of the Dean and Chapter of the Cathedral Church of Chichester 1545–1642*. Sussex Record Society, extra volume

Pettifor, J, 2003 Nutritional rickets, in F Glorieux, J Pettifor & M Jüppner (eds), *Pediatric Bone: Biology and Diseases*. New York: Academic Press, 541–65

Pevsner, N, 1958 *Shropshire*. The Buildings of England. Harmondsworth: Penguin

Phenice, T W, 1969 A newly developed visual method of sexing the os pubis, *Amer J Phys Anthropol*, **30**, 297–302

Phillips, D, & Heywood, B, 1995 *Excavations at York Minster, Vol. I*. London: Royal Commission for Historical Monuments for England

Pitt, M J, 1988 Rickets and osteomalacia, in Resnick & Niwayama (eds) 1988, 2087–126

Platt, C, 1997 *King Death*. London: UCL Press

Popescu, E S, forthcoming *Norwich Castle: Excavations and Historical Survey 1987–98, part 1: Anglo-Saxon to c 1345* East Anglian Archaeology

Popescu, E S, & Mitchell, D, in prep A Leper Cemetery at Spittals Link, Huntingdon

Powell, A C, 1955 *The Hospital of the Blessed Mary, Chichester*. Chichester

Powell, F, 1996 The human remains, in Boddington (ed) 1996, 113–27

Prescott, E, 1992 *The English Medieval Hospital 1050–1640*. London: Seaby

Price, R, with Ponsford, M, 1998 *St Bartholomew's Hospital, Bristol. The Excavation of a Medieval Hospital: 1976–8*. CBA Research Report, **110**. York: Council for British Archaeology

Pugh, R B, 1981 The Knights Hospitallers of England as undertakers, *Speculum*, **56**, 566–74

Rafi, A, Spigelman, M, Stanford, J, Lemma, E, Donoghue, H, & Zias, J, 1994 DNA of *Mycobacterium leprae* detected in ancient bones, *Internat J Osteoarchaeol*, **4**, 287–90

Rahtz, P, Hirst, S, & Wright, S, 2000 *Cannington Cemetery*, Britannia Monograph **17**

Ralis, Z A, 1986 Epidemics of fractures during periods of snow and ice, *Brit Med J*, **293**, 484

Rawcliffe, C, 1995 *Medicine and Society in Later Medieval England*. Stroud: Sutton

Rawcliffe, C, 2000a *Medicine for the Soul: the Life, Death and Resurrection of an English Medieval Hospital*. Stroud: Sutton

Rawcliffe, C, 2000b Learning to love the leper: aspects of institutional charity in Anglo-Norman England, in J Gillingham (ed), *Anglo-Norman Studies*, **23**, 231–50

Ray, J E, 1931 *Sussex Chantry Records*. Sussex Record Society, **36**

Reader, R, 1974 New evidence for the antiquity of leprosy in early Britain, *J Archaeol Sci*, **1**, 205–7

Rees, R J W, & McDougall, A C, 1976 *Internat J Leprosy*, **44,** 99

Reichs, K (ed), 1986 *Forensic Osteology: Advances in the Identification of Human Remains*. Springfield, Illinois: Charles C Thomas

Rendall J R, McDougall A C, & Willis, L A, 1976 Lepromatous leprosy: intra-oral temperature studies with reference to involvement of the incisor teeth and pre-maxillary process, *Internat J Leprosy*, **44**, 462–86

Renier, D, Sainte-Rose, C, Marchae, D, & Hirsch, J F, 1982 Intracranial pressure in craniostenosis, *J Neurosurg*, **57**, 370–7

Resnick, D, 1995 *Diagnosis of Bone and Joint Disorders*, 3rd edn. Philadelphia: W B Saunders

Resnick, D, & Niwayama, G, 1983 Entheses and enthesopathy, *Radiology*, **146**, 1–9

Resnick, D, & Niwayama, G, 1988 *Diagnosis of Bone and Joint Disorders*, 2nd edn. Philadelphia: W B Saunders

Richards, J, 1991 *Sex, Dissidence and Damnation. Minority Groups in the Middle Ages*. London: Routledge

Richards, J D, Heighway, C, & Donaghey, S, 1989 *Union Terrace: Excavations in the Horsefair*. The Archaeology of York **11**/1. London: Council for British Archaeology for York Archaeological Trust

Richards, P, 1977 *The Medieval Leper and His Northern Heirs*. Woodbridge: D S Brewer

Richards, R R, & Corley, F G, 1996 Fractures of the shafts of the radius and ulna, in Rockwood *et al* (eds) 1996, 869–928

Richardson, R, 1988 *Death, Dissection and the Destitute*. Harmondsworth: Penguin

Richter, D, Hahn, M P, Ostermann, P A W, Ekkernkamp, A, & Muhr, G, 1996 Vertical deceleration injuries: a comparative study of the injury patterns of 101 patients after accidental and intentional high falls, *Injury,* **27**, 655–9

Ridley, D S, 1988 *Pathogenesis of Leprosy and Other Related Diseases*. Cambridge: University Press

Rigold, S E, 1964 Two Kentish hospitals re-examined: S. Mary, Ospringe and Ss Steven and Thomas, New Romney, *Archaeol Cantiana*, **79**, 31–69

Roberts, C A, 1986 Leprosy and Leprosaria in Medieval Britain, *Museum of Applied Science Center for Archaeology*, **4**, 15–21

Roberts, C, 1994 Treponematosis in Gloucester (England): theoretical and practical approach to the pre-Columbian theory, in O Dutour, G Pálfi, J Berato, & J-P Brun (eds), *The Origin of Syphilis in Europe: Before or After 1493?* Paris: Editions Errance, 101–8

Roberts, C A, 2002 The antiquity of leprosy in Britain: the skeletal evidence, in Roberts *et al* (eds) 2002, 213–21

Roberts, C A, & Buikstra, J E, 2003 *The Bioarchaeology of Tuberculosis: a Global View on a Re-emerging Disease*. Gainesville: University Press of Florida

Roberts, C A, & Cox, M, 2003 *Health and Disease in Britain: from Prehistory to the Present Day*. Stroud: Sutton Publishing

Roberts, C A, Lee, F, & Bintliff, J (eds), 1989 *Burial Archaeology. Current Research, Methods and Developments*. BAR Brit Ser **211**. Oxford: British Archaeological Reports

Roberts, C A, Lewis, M E, & Manchester, K (eds) 2002 *The Past and Present of Leprosy. Archaeological, Historical, Palaeopathological and Clinical Approaches*. BAR Internat Ser **1024**. Oxford: British Archaeological Reports

Roberts, C, & Manchester, K, 2005 *The Archaeology of Disease*. 3rd edn. Stroud: Sutton

Robinson, B, 2003 *St James and St Mary Magdalene Medieval Hospital – A GIS Based Study*. MSc thesis, University of Portsmouth

Rockwood, C A, Green, D P, Bucholz, R W, & Heckman, J D (eds), 1996 *Rockwood and Green's Fractures in Adults*. New York: Lippincott-Raven

Roffey, S, 2003 Deconstructing a symbolic world: the Reformation and the English Medieval parish chantry, in Gaimster & Gilchrist (eds) 2003, 341–55

Rogers, J, 2000 The palaeopathology of joint disease, in Cox & Mays (eds) 2000, 163–82

Rogers, J, Shepstone, L, & Dieppe, P, 1997 Bone formers: osteophyte and enthesophyte formation are positively associated, *Ann Rheum Dis*, **56**, 85–90

Rogers, J, & Waldron, T, 1986 Iatrogenic palaeopathology, *Proceedings of the 6th European meeting of the Palaeopathology Association*. Madrid, 31–5

Rogers, J, & Waldron, T, 1995 *A Field Guide to Joint Disease in Archaeology*. Chichester: John Wiley

Rogers, J, & Waldron, T, 2001 DISH and the monastic way of life, *Internat J Osteoarchaeol*, **11**, 357–65

Rogers, J, Waldron, T, Dieppe, P, & Watt, I, 1987 Arthropathies in palaeopathology: the basis of classification according to most probable cause, *J Archaeol Sci*, **14**, 179–93

Rogers, L, 1992 *Radiology of Skeletal Trauma*. New York: Churchill Livingstone

Rosser, G, 1989 *Medieval Westminster 1200–1540.* Oxford: University Press

Rothschild, B M, Calderon, F L, Coppa, A, & Rothschild, C, 2000 First European exposure to syphilis: the Dominican Republic at the time of Columbian contact, *Clin Infect Dis*, **31**, 936–41

Rothschild, B M, & Rothschild, C, 1995 Comparison of radiologic and gross examination for detection of cancer in defleshed skeletons, *Amer J Phys Anthropol*, **96**, 357–63

Rothschild, B M, & Woods, R J, 1991 Spondyloarthropathy: erosive arthritis in representative defleshed bones, *Amer J Phys Anthropol*, **85**, 125–34

Rouse, J, 1825 *The Beauties and Antiquities of the County of Sussex.* London: Fulham

Rowell, G 1977 *The liturgy of Christian burial: an introductory survey of the historical development of Christian burial.* London

Rubin, E, & Farber, J L, 1990 *Essential Pathology*, 3rd edn

Rubin, M, 1974 *Medieval English Medicine.* New York: Barnes & Noble

Rubin, M, 1987 *Charity and Community in Medieval Cambridge.* Cambridge: University Press

Rubin, M, 1989 Development and change in English hospitals, 1100–1500, in Granshaw & Porter (eds) 1989, 41–59

Salvin, A, 1857 (untitled note on Lindisfarne plaque) *Archaeol J*, **14**, 286

Salzman, L F, 1935 *Victoria History of the County of Sussex* **3**. Oxford: University Press

Salzman, L F, 1953 *Victoria History of the County of Sussex* **4**. Oxford: University Press

Santos, A L, & Roberts, C A, 2006 Anatomy of a serial killer: differential diagnosis of tuberculosis based on rib lesions of adult individuals from Coimbra identified skeletal collections, Portugal, *Amer J Phys Anthropol*, **130**, 38–49

Satchell, A E M, 1998 *The Emergence of Leper-houses in Medieval England.* Unpublished DPhil, University of Oxford

Saunders, S, 1989 Nonmetric skeletal variation, in Iscan & Kennedy (eds) 1989, 95–108

Saunders, S, & Hoppa, R D, 1993 Growth deficit in survivors and non-survivors: biological mortality bias in subadult skeletal samples, *Yearb Phys Anthropol*, **36**, 127–51

Sawyer, P H, 1968 *Anglo-Saxon Charters: an Annotated List and Bibliography.* London: Royal Historical Society

Scheepers, A, 1998 Correlation of oral surface temperatures and the lesions of leprosy, *Internat J Leprosy Mycobactl Dis*, **66**, 214–17

Scheepers, A, Lemmer, J, Lownie, J F, 1993 Oral manifestations of leprosy, *Leprosy Review*, **64**, 37–43

Scheuer, L, & Black, S, 2000 *Developmental Juvenile Osteology.* London: Academic Press

Schmorl, G, & Junghanns, H, 1971 *The Human Spine in Health and Disease*, 2nd American edn, trans E F Besemann. New York: Grune & Stratton

Schultz, M, 2001 Palaeohistopathology of bone: a new approach to the study of ancient diseases, *Yearb Phys Anthropol*, **44**, 106–47

Schultz, M, & Roberts, C, 2002 Diagnosis of leprosy in skeletons from an English later medieval hospital using histological analysis, in Roberts *et al* (eds) 2002, 89–105

Shepherd, J, Shapland, M, Pearce, N X, & Scully, C, 1990 Pattern, severity and aetiology of injuries in victims of assault, *J R Soc Med*, **83**, 75–8

Simpson, J Y, 1842 Leprosy and Leper Hospitals in Scotland and England, *Edinburgh Med Surg J*, **57**, 121–56

Sinha, A K, Kaeding, C C, & Wadley, G M, 1999 Upper extremity stress fractures in athletes: clinical features of 44 cases, *Clin J Sport Med*, **9**, 199–202

Skinner, M, Barkley, J, & Carlson, R L, 1989 Cranial asymmetry and muscular torticollis in prehistoric northwest coast natives from British Columbia (Canada), *J Paleopathol*, **3**(1), 18–34

Skinner, M, & Goodman, A H, 1992 Anthropological uses of developmental defects of enamel, in S R Saunders & M A Katzenberg (eds), *Skeletal Biology of Past Peoples: Research Methods.* New York: Wiley-Liss, 153–74

Smith, B H, 1991 Standards of human tooth formation and dental age assessment, in M A Kelley & C S Larsen (eds), *Advances in Dental Anthropology.* New York: Wiley-Liss, 143–68

Smith, G H, 1979 The Excavation of the Hospital of St Mary of Ospringe, commonly called Maison Dieu, *Archaeol Cantiana*, **115**, 81–184

Smith, M O, 1996 Parry fractures and female-directed interpersonal violence: implications from the Late Archaic Period of West Tennessee, *Internat J Osteoarch*, **6**, 84–91

Smith, T K, 1999 *An Investigation of the Pathogenesis of Absorption of the Alveolar Process of the Maxilla in Leprosy.* Unpublished MSc dissertation, Bradford University

Steer, F W, 1960 *The Royal West Sussex Hospital, the First Hundred Years, 1784–1884.* Chichester Papers, **15**. Chichester: Phillimore

Steer, F W, 1962a *Misericords in St Mary's Hospital, Chichester.* Chichester Papers, **28**. Chichester: Phillimore

Steer, F W, 1962b *The Memoirs of James Spershott.* Chichester Papers, **30**. Chichester: Phillimore

Steinbock, R T, 1976 *Palaeopathological Diagnosis and Interpretation.* Springfield, Illinois: Charles C Thomas

Stewart, T D, 1979 *Essentials of Forensic Anthropology: Especially as Developed in the United States.* Springfield, Illinois: Charles C Thomas

Stirland, A, 1994 Evidence for pre-Columbian treponematosis in medieval Europe, in O Dutour, G Pálfi, J Berato, & J-P Brun (eds), *The Origin of Syphilis in Europe: Before or After 1493?* Paris: Editions Errance, 109–15

Stirland, A, 2000 *Raising the Dead: the Skeleton*

Crew of Henry VIII's Great Ship, The Mary Rose. Chichester: John Wiley

Stone, R and Appleton-Fox, N, 1996 *A View from Hereford's Past: a Report on the Archaeological Excavation of Hereford Cathedral Close in 1993.* Hereford: Logaston Press

Storm, R A, 2006a Fluctuating asymmetry in the human cranium: differential diagnoses of taphonomical, pathological, and 'normal' population asymmetry, *Amer J Phys Anthropol,* **129**, Suppl 42, 172

Storm, R A, 2006b Medieval deviants: cranial fluctuating asymmetry population outliers, *Paleopathol Assoc Newsl,* **134**, 14–24

Storm, R A, forthcoming Human Skeletal Asymmetry: A Study of Biometrics and Fluctuating Asymmetry in Assessing Health and Social Status in Populations from the 7th to the 19th century in England. Unpublished PhD thesis, University of Bradford

Storm, R A, & Knüsel, C J, 2005 Fluctuating asymmetry: a potential osteological application, in S R Zakrzewski & M Clegg (eds), *Proceedings of the Fifth Annual Conference of the British Association for Biological Anthropology and Osteoarchaeology.* BAR International Ser **1383**. Oxford: Archaeopress, 113–18

Stougaard, J, 1964 Familial occurrence of osteochondritis dissecans, *J Bone Joint Surg,* **46**, 542–3

Stroud, G, & Kemp, R L, 1993 *Cemeteries of St Andrew, Fishergate.* The Archaeology of York **12**/2. York: Council for British Archaeology for York Archaeological Trust

Stuart-Macadam, P, 1982 *A correlative study of a palaeopathology of the skull.* Unpublished PhD thesis, University of Cambridge

Stuart-Macadam, P, 1985 Porotic hyperostosis: representative of a childhood condition, *Amer J Phys Anthropol,* **66**, 391–8

Stuart-Macadam P, 1987 Porotic hyperostosis: New evidence to support the anemia theory, *Amer J Phys Anthropol* **74**, 521–6

Stuart-Macadam, P L, 1988 Rickets as an interpretative tool, *J Paleopath,* **2**, 33–42

Stuart-Macadam, P 1991 Anemia in Roman Britain: Poundbury Camp, in H Bush and M Zvelebil (eds), *Health in Past Societies: Biocultural Interpretations of Human Skeletal Remains in Archaeological Contexts.* BAR Internat Ser, **567**. Oxford: Tempus Reparatum, 101–13

Sture, J F, 2001 *Biocultural Perspectives on Birth Defects in Medieval Urban and Rural English Populations.* Unpublished PhD thesis, University of Durham

Sture, J F, 2004 Vertebral arch clefts: Questioning the habitual diagnosis of spina bifida occulta, *Synergy,* July 2004, 17–20

Suchey, J M, Brooks, S T, & Katz, D, 1988 *Instructional materials accompanying female pubic symphyseal models of the Suchey-Brooks system.* Colorado

Sun, P P, & Persing, J A, 1999 Craniosynostosis, in

A L Albright, I F Pollack, & P D Adelson (eds), *Principles and Practice of Paediatric Neurosurgery.* New York: Thieme, 219–42

Swaddle, J P, Witter, M S, & Cuthill, I C, 1994 The analysis of fluctuating asymmetry, *Anim Behav,* **48**, 986–9

Sydes, B, 1984 *The Excavations of St Wilfrid's Church, Hickleton, Second Interim Report, September 1984.* Sheffield: The County Archaeological Service

Tatelman, M, & Drouillard, E J P, 1953 Tuberculosis of the ribs, *Amer J Roentgenol,* **70**, 923–35

Taunton, E L, 1897 *The English Black Monks of St Benedict* (2 vols). London

Taylor, A, 2001 *Burial Practice in Early England.* Stroud: Tempus

Ten Cate, A R, 1989 *Recent Advances in the Study of Dental Calculus.* Oxford: IRL Press at Oxford University Press

Tesorieri, M, 2006 Distinguishing specific lesions and patterning of treponemal disease in medieval and post-medieval Britain. Unpublished MSc dissertation, University of Bradford

Thomas, A C, 1985 *Exploration of a drowned landscape: archaeology and history of the Isles of Scilly.* London: Batsford

Thomas, C, Sloane, B, & Phillpotts, C, 1997 *Excavations at the Priory and Hospital of St Mary Spital, London,* MOLAS Monograph **1**. London: Museum of London Archaeology Service

Torgersen, J, 1951 The developmental genetics and evolutionary meaning of the metopic suture, *Amer J Phys Anthropol,* **9**(2), 193–207

Trotter, M, 1970 Estimation of stature from intact long limb bones, in T D Stewart (ed), *Personal identification in Mass Disasters.* Washington: Smithsonian Institution Press, 71–83

Turner, E, 1861 Hospitals in Sussex, *Sussex Archaeol Collect* **13**, 305–6

Urry, W, 1999 *Thomas Becket. His Last Days.* Stroud: Sutton

Van Valen, L, 1962 A study of fluctuating asymmetry, *Evolution,* **16**, 125–42

Vashishth, D, Verborgt, O, Divine, G, Shaffer, M B, & Fyhne, D P, 2000 Decline in osteocyte lacuna density in human cortical bone associated with accumulation of microcracks with age, *Bone,* **26**, 375–80

Wakely, J, 1996 Limits to interpretation of skeletal trauma: two case studies from Medieval Abingdon, England, *Internat J Osteoarchaeol,* **6**, 76–83

Waldron, T, 1991 The prevalence of, and the relationship between, some spinal diseases in a human skeletal population from London, *Internat J Osteoarchaeol,* **1**, 103–10

Waldron, T (H A), 1993 The health of the adults, in Molleson & Cox (eds) 1993

Waldron, T, 1994 *Counting the Dead: the Epidemiology of Skeletal Populations.* Chichester: John Wiley

Waldron, T, 1995 Changes in the distribution of

osteoarthritis over historical time, *Internat J Osteoarchaeol*, **5**, 385–9

Waldron, T, 2001 *Shadows in the Soil: Human Bones and Archaeology*. Stroud: Tempus

Walker, P L, 1997 Wife beating, boxing, and broken noses: skeletal evidence for the cultural patterning of violence, in Martin & Frayer (eds) 1997, 145–79

Walker, P L, Cook, D C, & Lambert, P M, 1997 Skeletal evidence for child abuse: a physical anthropological perspective, *J Forensic Sci*, **42**, 196–207

Walls, T, & Shingadia, D, 2004 Global epidemiology of pediatric tuberculosis, *J Infect*, **48**, 13–22

Ward, S, 1996 *A Consideration of Mental Retardation in Pre-Modern England: Historical and Anthropological Perspectives with a case study*. Unpublished MSc thesis, University of Bradford

Ward, S W, 1990 *Excavations at Chester: the Lesser Medieval Religious Houses, Sites Investigated 1964–1983*. Grosvenor Museum Archaeological Excavation and Survey Reports **6**. Chester: Grosvenor Museum

Warkany, J, 1971 *Congenital Malformations: Notes and Comments*. Chicago: Year Book Medical Publishers

Warwick, R, 1968 The skeletal remains, in L P Wenham (ed), *The Romano-British cemetery at Trentholme Drive, York*. Ministry of Public Buildings and Works: Archaeological Reports, **5**; 113–76

Webb, D, 2000 *Pilgrimage in Medieval England*. London: Hambledon

Webb, S, 1995 *Palaeopathology of Aboriginal Australians*. Cambridge: University Press

Weiss, K, 1973 Demographic models for anthropology, *Soc Am Arch, Memoir* **27**

Wells, C, 1962 A possible case of leprosy from a Saxon cemetery at Beckford. *Medical History*, **6**, 383–6

Wells, C, 1967 A leper cemetery at South Acre, Norfolk, *Medieval Archaeol*, **11**, 242–8

Westropp, T J, 2000 *Folklore of Clare. A Folklore Survey of County Clare* and *County Clare Folk-Tales and Myths*. Ennis: Clasp Press (originally published in *Folk-Lore: Transactions of the Folk-Lore Society* between June 1910 and December 1913)

White, W, 1988 *The Cemetery of St Nicholas Shambles*. London: Museum of London and the London and Middlesex Archaeological Society

WHO, 1997 *World Health Report*. Geneva: World Health Organisation

WHO, 2002 *Global Strategies to Reduce the Health-Care Burden of Craniofacial Anomalies: Report of WHO Meetings on International Collaborative Research on Craniofacial Anomalies, Geneva, Switzerland 5–8 November 2000; Park City, Utah, USA, 24–26 May 2001*. Geneva, Switzerland: World Health Organization

Wilczak, C, & Ortner D J, 2006 Unpublished report on a possible case of pre-Columbian leprosy from an archeological site in the Aleutian Islands. Alaska, USA, NMNH Catalog No. 366639

Wladis, A, Bostrom, L, & Nilsson, B, 1999 Unarmed violence-related injuries requiring hospitalization in Sweden from 1987 to 1994, *J Trauma*, **47**, 733–7

Woo, T L, 1931 On the asymmetry of the human skull, *Biometrika*, **22**, 324–52

Wood, J W, Milner, G R, Harpending, H C, & Weiss, K M, 1992 The osteological paradox: problems of inferring prehistoric health for skeletal samples, *Curr Anthropol*, **33**, 343–70

Woodward, A, 1995 *Analysis of Dental Calculus from Leprous and Non-leprous Individuals from the Medieval Cemetery of Chichester*. Unpublished BSc dissertation, University of Bradford

Workshop of European Anthropologists, 1980 Recommendations for age and sex diagnoses of skeleton, *J Hum Evol*, **9**, 517–49

Wright, H P, 1885 *The Story of the Domus Dei of Chichester*

Wyrsch, R B, Spindler, K P, & Stricker, P R, 1995 Scapular fracture in a professional boxer, *J Shoulder Elbow Surg*, **4**, 395–8

Yu, C C, Wong, F H, & Chen, Y R, 2004 Craniofacial deformity in patients with uncorrected congenital muscular torticollis: an assessment from three-dimensional compact tomography imaging, *Plast Reconstr Surg*, **113**, 24–33

Zadora-Rio, E, 2003 The making of churchyards and parish territories in the early-medieval landscape of France and England in the 7th–12th centuries: a reconsideration, *Medieval Archaeol*, **47**, 1–20

Zazryn, T R, Finch, C, & McCrory, P, 2003 A 16 year study of injuries to professional boxers in the state of Victoria, Australia, *Brit J Sports Med*, **37**, 321–4

Index

Illustrations are denoted by page numbers in *italics* or by *illus* where figures are scattered throughout the text. n – note.

UNIVERSITY OF WINCHESTER
LIBRARY